6-8-

Ariana,

Great meeting you.

God bless

Rick R.

God's Tiniest Angel and the Last Unicorn
By Rick R. Redalen, M.D.

God's Tiniest Angel and the Last Unicorn

One Christian's Incredible Life Adventure

———

By Rick R. Redalen, M.D.

Copyright © 2018 by Rick R. Redalen, M.D. All rights reserved.

Unless otherwise indicated, all material on these pages is copyrighted by Rick R. Redalen, M.D. All rights reserved. No part of these pages, either text or image may be used for any purpose other than personal use. Therefore, reproduction, modification or storage in a retrieval system or re transmission in any form or by any means, electronic, mechanical or otherwise, for reasons other than personal use, is strictly prohibited without prior written permission except in the case of brief quotations embodied in articles and reviews.

This work depicts actual events in the life of the author. Although it is written as truthfully as possible memory is flawed by nature. Some dialogue consistent with the character or nature of the person speaking has been created. All persons within are actual individuals; there are no composite characters. First names and/or initials of some individuals have been used to respect their privacy.

Cover Design: George Almasan

Interior Design: Gena Corcoran

Editor/Publisher: Shari Jo Sorchych

ISBN 978-1-7324252-0-0 (paper)

ISBN 978-1-7324252-1-7 (ebk)

ISBN 978-1-7324252-2-4 (ebk)

Published in the United States of America

"From everyone to whom much has been given, much will be required; and from the one to whom much has been entrusted, even more will be demanded."

The Holy Bible
Luke 12:48

Dedication

For my children Terra, Todd and Shari who were once the lights of my life

I have read a lot of great books in my life, but I have only read one that said,

"Come unto me, all ye that labour and are heavy laden, and I will give you rest."

*The Holy Bible, King James Version
Matthew 11:28*

Thank you!

All profits from the sale of God's Tiniest Angel and the Last Unicorn will be donated to charities, both in the United States and abroad, where the author has built schools and hospitals in areas of great need. The following alphabetical list is comprised of recipients of Dr. Redalen's support to date:

American Society for the Prevention of Cruelty to Animals
Angie's Friends
Arts for Animals Inc.
Biblica
Bisbee's Fish & Wildlife Conservation Fund Inc.
Center Point Church
Christian and Missionary Alliance
City Help, Inc of Phoenix DBA Phoenix Dream Center
Crown Financial Ministries - Fort Worth
CURE International
Diveheart Foundation
Families Fighting Flu
Feed My Starving Children
Food for the Soul (God's Company)
Fort Worth Crisis Pregnancy Center
Freedom to Read, Inc.
Glen Eyrie Christian Camps and Conferences
Here's Life Africa
Illinois Credo Recovery
Just One Orphan Care Corp.
Kidscapes Foundation
Lahuiokalani Ka'anapali Congregational Church
Liberty Elementary School
MedReach Inc.
Mesabi Range Youth for Christ
Milestone Church
National Mounted Warfare Foundation
Operation Mobilization
P.E.F. Israel Endowment Funds, Inc.
Patriot PAWS Service Dogs
R U 4 Children
Redalen Global Christian Ministries
Scriptel Ministries
Seattle Humane Society (Humane Society For Seattle/King County)
Texas Public Policy Foundation
The Central Fund of Israel
The Navigators
Trinity Vineyard Fellowship of Fort Worth
Trinity's Angels Ministries
Words of Life (Raymond Skaggs International Ministries)
World Challenge

Prologue

How do you relive a life on paper when you are nearing the end of life's final season?

It is no doubt that in my life, if shouldas, couldas, wouldas and ifs were fishes there would not be enough water on this planet for them all to swim at the same time.

Please do not think any of these words of mine are original. I am sure they have all been said before. I am just rearranging them to fit my life's story.

My story is about one of God's tiniest angels. Try hard to stick with me through some of this boring background so you understand where I am coming from. I'll try to make up for it in a bit. That will not be difficult as I have managed to squeeze in about four life times in this one I've lived and it has been anything except boring. I think those of us to which this has happened would probably try a little harder to ensure it did not happen if we realized in advance that if you live several lifetimes, you may also have to die in each one. Even the life of a fool is relived many times if not by the same person.

Mine is a life perhaps much like any other but in some regards perhaps a little different. I am a very ordinary man who has lived an extraordinary life.

I have had the good fortune of being able to take care of people and animals most of my life. I know of no greater love. I don't think anyone can understand the honor I felt as a physician when someone gave me the blessing of asking me to take care of a friend or loved one, their mom or dad, their child, their wife or husband. What greater compliment can there be. I am a physician with an unusually broad and unique educational experience and training in medicine. I am immensely blessed. God has endowed me with many exceptional abilities. I want you to always remember when I talk about doing things, it is really God doing them. It has nothing to do with me. I guess I am the messenger.

I am going to tell you how the life of an average Midwestern kid turns out when you are not the best at following God's directions. I guess He gave us all freedom of choice but I certainly used up more than my share of the bad ones.

Chapter One

Early Life

I spent most of the early days of my life growing up in the town of Williston in Northwestern North Dakota until the age of 18 when I graduated from Williston High School. Williston is located about 60 miles from Canada and 18 miles from Montana. Most of that schooling was uneventful. I believe the only distinction of the Redalen children in Williston High School was that my sister Cheryl and I were the only two students to get Cs in conduct. It was not a distinction you really wanted to have. Although it was not something my parents permitted or condoned, I grew up with the idea life should always be fun and my carefree attitude led to some problems. I think perhaps the Redalen children could have used a few more guidelines.

I am sure our parents, Ray and Gwen Redalen, wanted us to think completely for ourselves. We never heard at the kitchen table, "Finish your peas or you're not going to get dessert." They simply did not seem to care if we ate or not. We never heard a remark about report cards. After all they were our report cards and we would live with them for the rest of our lives. They did emphasize someday they would be important to us.

There was one thing I became known for in high school. I became interested in hypnosis in my junior year while listening to a psychology lecture by our teacher Mr. Leon Olson. He made the statement anyone can hypnotize someone. That intrigued me. Everything with respect to the mind was fascinating to me. My family was extremely high in extrasensory perception. An example, my grandma called my mom once years later and told her I was making wine in my basement. My mom asked me and of course I was. My entire life was filled with extrasensory events. As I became more educated, I realized these are really 'God' events. They have nothing to do with us or me other than God is using us as conveyors.

Following Mr. Olson's psychology lecture that day, I immediately headed for the public library. I checked out the few books they had on hypnosis and immediately committed them to memory. My first subject was Bette, my one and only girlfriend in high school who would eventually become my wife. Bette was an excellent subject; she entered deep stages of hypnosis the very first time I tried. The deepest stage of hypnosis is known as somnambulism. The patient or subject is known as the somnambulist. This word can be broken down into two parts meaning to sleep and to walk so this term is often seen in psychology texts as sleepwalking.

In hypnosis, good subjects are in a heightened state of receiving and believing suggestions offered to them. The hypnotist is simply a facilitator helping the subject get in touch with the cortical part of the brain which helps enable success. A very good subject may have complete amnesia of the event much the same as a sleepwalker does not remember walking in their sleep. Modern medicine has not been of much use in telling us what causes the dissociation between motor movement and cortical activity. This means we simply do not know how a sleepwalker can go out and drive a car around the neighborhood or perform other complex tasks without knowing they have done so. Good subjects also talk and are very susceptible to most suggestions offered by the hypnotist. It is generally thought people will not do anything while under hypnosis they would not do while awake. For a good subject this is basically not true. The hypnotist can make suggestions to the subject to do things they would not ordinarily do.

Bette and I had one problem in our initial foray into the world of hypnosis. I did not really know the correct way to wake someone and doing it abruptly with a clap of the hands as the stage hypnotists do for effect is not really the best way. Bette had a pretty bad headache on awakening. I did some more studying and learned that bringing someone out of hypnosis the right way made them think it was one of the most pleasurable sleeps they had ever had. That approach worked more like this: You are going to wake up at the count of three and as I count you will become more and more awake. One, you are starting to wake up and you feel very good. Two, you are nearly awake and you feel very, very good. Three, you are wide awake and you feel the best you have ever felt in your life. You feel wonderful and will have a beautiful day.

I kept experimenting with hypnosis.

It was not long before my parents heard about this and initially they thought I was a witch or someone from another realm. They said if I ever tried something like that again, I was to leave their house forever. As usual, I went my own way a little more secretively with hypnosis.

One day by good fortune our family doctor Carroll Marian Lund called my parents. He asked them if they would allow me to teach him hypnosis. That sealed the deal for me. If it was okay for our doctor, it was okay for their son. Dr. Lund was the father of one of my classmates, Karen, so he knew me as a patient but also someone who spent time in their home as a friend of their daughter. It was not long before my reputation got around and soon our home was filled with high school students wanting to watch my hypnosis shows. I think my parents became proud of my abilities. I would later use hypnosis in the middle of the street one night hypnotizing a student in a convertible in front of the Teen Canteen, the local hangout for high school students. I would also use it on the center of a wrestling mat at a state wrestling tournament. When I graduated from high school the editors of our year book captioned my picture, "You are under my spell." I will tell you some entertaining stories about hypnosis a little later. Hopefully they will make you laugh, which they sometimes do.

I continued my education in hypnosis. Dr. Lund gave me a large pile of information from the American Medical Association located at that time in Dearborn, Illinois. The material provided me far more information than I had managed to gather at our local library. I found my venture into the world of age regression fascinating. Imagine being able to take a person back in time to a former place in their life so they could remember what things were like then and their personality and manner of speech. In age regression, as you go back in time, the speech patterns change until in Bette's case, she was a little girl again. I did one interesting thing in the initial age regression exercises. I took handwriting samples. I regressed Bette back to the time she could print only and then could not write at all. We then gathered handwriting samples and compared them. It was truly fascinating. The historical handwriting samples were exactly the same as the years Bette was age regressed to. What on earth had changed? Are we going back and reusing tracks in the brain that were used during that time in our life? Are we always laying new roads as we go? I have read a person with Parkinson's disease can be age regressed back to the time they did not have tremors. The tremors disappear. Personally, I have not seen this, nor have I worked with anyone on age regression who had a neurological problem.

I had only one problem with age regression. I once regressed Bette back to a time when she was only perhaps three or four years old. She woke up and started crying and wanted her mommy. I rapidly learned you cannot move someone forward in time. How would that be possible? After all, you are now in a child's mind and since they have never been older, to suggest going forward in time cannot be done. I finally realized my only solution was to wake the person up and hope they were back in the here and now. First I had to put the child back to sleep. Fortunately for me, that is how it worked out.

I don't know if report cards were unimportant to our parents. Maybe Mom and Dad never had to worry about grades. Mom was Valedictorian when she graduated from her high school class in Devils Lake, North Dakota where she grew up. Dad was a star graduate and first in his college class in electronics when he graduated from the Bottineau School of Science in the eastern part of North Dakota. Dad grew up in Wildrose, North Dakota. Dad's education was unusual in that he only attended school through ninth grade until later in his teens when he was approached by the Shriners Organization and asked if he wanted to go to college.

Dad was like most kids who grew up in the "Dirty Thirties" in North Dakota. It was called the Dirty Thirties because due to lack of knowledge about crop rotation and good farming practices, when the droughts hit the Dakotas in the Thirties the skies were black or dark with dust. Most of the farmers had their entire farm blow away. By that I mean the topsoil just disappeared. The fences were like windrows with dirt accumulations up to three feet high. I of course did not experience this first hand but could see the damage my dad talked about while riding my horse out on the prairie. Fence rows often had large piles of dirt running the length of the fence.

If the blackened skies were not from dirt in the air which was bad enough, the skies were also blackened from the swarms of grasshoppers and locusts. The drought that killed most of the crops in the entire Midwestern United States left little to nothing for the people of those areas to live on. During this dreadful time many people were driven away from their homes and livelihood. The massive plagues of grasshoppers and locusts were left to finish off what was left of the meager remaining plant growth. There were massive army worm infestations that for brief periods of time completely covered everything in sight. During one such infestation in the Thirties the worms ate the handles off all hand tools and ate the paint off the houses. The people of the Dakotas who stayed and survived these times were truly hardy souls.

After Dad quit school in eighth or ninth grade to work to help his family, he used to wander the prairies picking up buffalo and cattle bones he would sell to fertilizer companies. Dad made ten cents per day, considered a fair wage. I can't imagine what unfair would have looked like.

They were paid by the pound so they would soak the bones in a stock water tank for a couple days before they brought the bones in to be sold so they would weigh more. I imagine the fertilizer people had that all figured out and probably paid less than a fair rate if they counted pennies like companies of today.

Thank heavens for all those buffalo hunters, huh? After all, they whittled the buffalo down from about 60,000,000 in the early 1800s to about 100 in the late 1800s. This was the great plan by our government to get rid of a race, right? I am talking about the Native American Indians. Take away their food and put them on reservations leaving their fertile and sometimes oil rich land free for the taking. Just think. There were no land oil leases back then so the Rockefellers of the world could get oil for free. By my reading, John David Rockefeller was not the altruistic humanitarian the great family that descended from him became. And the Indians, well I guess we gave them enough of a living on the reservation to keep them from starving. They could just subsist. Providing subsistence living is still working well today on our poor. Well what the heck, those are cheaper votes than paying other electoral dues.

This seems to be the very same philosophy our government employs today. Control the people by giving them just enough welfare to allow them to subsist. Don't provide enough so someone can get ahead but provide enough so they will still vote for the provider. I bet that is one of our government's favorite words. If they give the people just enough they can control their vote even if the ACORN people of the world have to drive the voters to the polls several times to vote.

That is one fact I have never quite figured out. Why do black people vote for Democrats in spite of all the entitlement when it was and is the Democrats that made and make up the Ku Klux Klan? I think most black people are oblivious to the fact Republicans supported black people since the time prior to the Klan. They must also be unaware of the fact white Republicans were lynched from the very same trees as blacks and that Democrats have failed to sign over two hundred bills introduced that forbade the lynching of blacks. Lyndon B. Johnson was one of the more well-known Democrats who refused to sign a bill forbidding the lynching of blacks.

Anyway, back to Dad's education. Dad grew up with a disability. His left leg was completely paralyzed, smaller than his good leg and also shorter. He contracted polio when he was three years old. At that time they did not know much about polio. They bundled Dad up and put him on a train to Minneapolis where he was received by the Sister Kinney Foundation. At that time they were thought to do the most with children who had polio. I think "most" was simply manipulation. They probably tried to maintain range of motion of the paralyzed limb. It was during that time the Shriners Hospital became familiar with Dad, leading them to offer a college education to this young man who had only attained a ninth grade education. Fortunately for our family, Dad had never let "formal" get in the way of his education.

One time when I was in the later grades, my dad talked to me about what I now realize was race. My dad fixed radios, televisions and most anything electronic. One day as I was entering his shop a distinguished looking Indian man was leaving.

Dad said, "Rick, I would like you to meet a friend of mine, Carl Renfroe. Carl, this is my oldest son Rick." Mr. Renfroe had a pleasant smile and a warm firm handshake. A moment later when Mr. Renfroe had left, Dad explained Carl was a good friend of his. Dad added that Mr. Renfroe was an Indian and Indians all had the same needs, wants, and desires as all of the rest of us. Dad said, "We are all the same. We may look a little different or have a different color of skin, but we are all the same." These were the only comments I would ever hear from either one of my parents on race. And although I grew up in a town of all Protestants, mostly Lutheran, along with a very small band of Catholics, religious differences were never discussed in our home.

Gosh, I had a few Catholic friends but I think the only thing us Protestant boys ever knew in high school about Catholics was you should go out with Catholic girls. I never did quite get the thinking behind that. Perhaps because the Catholics had larger families we subconsciously must have thought Catholic girls probably liked sex more than Protestant girls. Well, as all of you will recall, our high school brains never did work very well. At least growing up in North Dakota, I would like to think it is because our brains were probably frozen a good part of the year.

It was not until I was fifteen years old in 1958 I met the first black person I had ever seen. That may seem very strange to all of you, but in North Dakota in 1958, we did not have television and there were not a lot of publications with pictures of black people. I met a fifteen year old black boy in Pasco, Washington while on vacation. Pasco was one of The Tri-Cities along with Kennewick and Richland in Washington. We got to run around and play together for about three days.

Dad was right. He was exactly like me, only a different color. That lesson would evidently carry me through my entire life. I was in Kampala, Uganda a few years back and after about a dozen days, I remarked to a couple of other white missionaries, "I just realized we're nearly the only Caucasians in Kampala." Kampala is the capital of Uganda and has a population of about four to five million people. The missionaries accompanying me laughed and said, "You just noticed that?"

It was one of the days that made me think of my dad, silently thank him and suddenly realize Dad made me color blind. Man, some of our parents' lessons really sink in. It is only today while putting this down on paper I am wondering if my dad's disability was a strength that made him understand we are all the same regardless of race, beliefs, color, ability or lack thereof.

I feel almost ashamed to say this is the first time I have looked at this issue from where my father stood, his perspective.

If I could design a childhood to grow up in, I would not change one bit of mine. The challenges I faced were really more growth opportunities and experiences.

The Redalens were a strong Norwegian blood line. My Redalen grandparents had come from Norway via Ellis Island and then settled in North Dakota after crossing by ox-cart through half of the United States. My younger sister Susan and I were dark-skinned. We did not have the typical coloring of the Scandinavian race. We would later find out somewhere along the way, some French Indian blood had crept into our DNA. Well, oh hell, ya, someone was messing around. Not my mom or grandma mind you, but a little further back. My great grandmother looked exactly like an Indian princess. Good for them. I liked the dark skin.

My first recollection of early life was sleeping on a kitchen table on a feather tic, a gigantic pillow used as a mattress. At least that was the case in our family when the apartment was too small to add even a child's cot. The table was very small and barely held my whole body. I really don't think I ever fell off of it. If I did, I must have hit my head so hard I do not remember it. My parents and little sister Cheryl slept in a tiny bedroom with a small single bed in it. My gosh, can you imagine what an ardent overly protective social services department would or could do with that today. Imagine parents having a child in bed with them. The small bathroom, kitchen and little bedroom were all that comprised our little apartment. I drove by in later years to see if it was really as small as I remembered it. It was smaller. You could not have fit today's king size bed in it.

We later moved to a basement apartment after a furnace nearly ended our family's lives one night.

When I was in fourth grade after living in three separate basement apartments (Sieb's, Bratten's and Ellingson's), my dad bought an old house which he moved out into the country outside of Williston. We would be living two miles north of town. I remember the house cost $3,000 which seemed like a fortune to a child like me at the time. Mom and Dad started remodeling that old plaster and lath home which was up on cement blocks. We all slept upstairs while that process was going on. It seemed we were always breathing dust from the plaster. The only heat for the house was an old oil burner downstairs so the upstairs was either too hot in the summer or too cold in the winter. My bed was in the southeast corner of the house and a lot of the plaster was down so I could look outside between the laths and cracks in the walls of the house.

I guess my most memorable times were when we had blizzards; I could hear the howling wind and would sometimes wake up with nearly an inch of snow on top of my blankets. I was still plenty warm but the greatest chill was to have to run through snow to use an outdoor toilet during the night. It wasn't so great in the summer either but at least in winter I did not have to worry about the spiders that seemed to congregate in the outhouse during the hot summer days. We had electricity and a couple bare bulb electric lights. What a blessing that was. The Fifties were a time when the Rural Electric Association (REA) came to rural America. The REA brought electricity to the country and to the small rural towns of America where farmers often milked their cows with the light from a kerosene lantern. Just think, this was all little more than one half century ago.

There were only a couple of kids my age within walking distance when I was growing up. About a mile northwest of us were some friends, the Nehrings, Billy, Donny and Deedee. About a mile southwest lived my friend Jerry Olson.

Fortunately, Dad and Mom did not care how many pets we had so I actually had friends galore. All my furry friends were my closest buddies and I never lacked for entertainment or chores taking care of them. We had two horses, Bay and later Big Jube. Big Jube was an Appaloosa stallion. I also had a dog named Rex who was my best friend alongside of Bay. Rex was a border collie who never left my side when I was growing up. I had gotten Rex as the last of a litter of puppies. No one selected him because I guess they thought he was homely. How can a puppy be homely?

Rex grew up to be the most beautiful dog in the litter. I also had a pet crow named Caw who landed on my shoulder every morning when I walked out of the house to take care of all of our furries. I cannot name the myriad of pets I loved and cared for but they included a couple pet fox, two pet raccoons, a porcupine, a couple dozen rabbits, about forty pigeons and a couple of cats. We also had a white fluffy little Alaskan Samoyed named Penny. I had a little black rabbit with two white front feet and two white tips on his ears I called Tippy. When I let Tippy run loose he would always come when I called his name. Tippy behaved more like a pet dog than a lot of dogs do. He was also a lot more responsive to me than our cats. You could call our cats all day and no one would ever show up. I did catch immense numbers of turtles, snakes and frogs but I never had any for pets. I always let them go. I caught all of those scaly little critters in a park called Twin Lakes. Twin Lakes was about one mile north of my home and was absolutely teeming with all manner of water dwellers. Years later at a fortieth-class reunion of Williston High School, class of 61, Doug Vedvick, one of my childhood friends and I walked around Twin Lakes. There was nothing in these lakes that had once been filled with frogs and turtles galore. It is likely nothing could live there. Oh wow, what progress our society has made.

Caw was one of my favorite pets. Pretty original name for a crow I know but it worked for me and Caw. I had taken Caw out of a nest up near Harmon's farm in Wildrose. Caw had only a couple of feathers when I got him and I hand fed him every day until he was full grown. I fixed up a place for him to roost at night where he was safe from our other animals but other than that he was free to fly the heavens. I always loved it when I would come out in the morning and Caw would be soaring through the air. When he would see me, he would make a beeline for me and land on my shoulder. One day our big black cat tried to jump on Caw. He failed. Caw flew high in the air and circled looking at that cat sneaking around our garage trying to find Caw again. Finally, when Caw saw the opportunity he dove at the cat and sunk his claws into the cat's back. That was the last time that cat ever bothered my pet crow. I had Caw for only about a half year and then when fall migration came, Caw disappeared with a flock of them. I never saw Caw again, at least that I knew. It is hard to tell one crow from another even when they are one of your friends. At least no crow ever landed on my shoulder again. I hope he found a mate and raised a family of his own.

One of the biggest challenges and heart breaks growing up was when my horse Bay got caught in some barbed wire. Bay had a huge laceration that extended from well above her left hind hock and wrapped down to her pastern. In kid terms that would be a laceration from well above the knee that wound down the leg to the level of the upper hoof. Dad had the veterinarian see her and he said we would have to put her down. I put up a big fuss, protested strongly and would not hear of this.

The doctor then told me what was going to be required of me to try to keep her alive. He said he did not think I could do it, but Dad let me make the decision. The veterinarian told me even with all the best care I could give Bay, she might not survive. He assured me it was going to be a monumental task.

After all I was 12 years old. The care Bay required was going to necessitate me getting up at least once or twice a night to put hot medicated water down a sleeve my mom had made for Bay. The sleeve was filled with oats to retain heat and keep the leg warm and continually medicated with the compress. The sleeve fit over Bay's entire left hind quarter and was held up with a sling rigged to a cinch around the back of Bay's waist. Bay did not mind and seemed to know I was trying to help her. She was easy to work with, not that there was much else she could do. We made a sling for Bay to take her body weight off her injured leg so she hung partially suspended from the rafters over her stall for several weeks with nearly all of the weight off her wounded leg. Bay gradually got well and she avoided an early death.

I didn't realize it at the time, but I imagine my parents put in as much worry and had just as difficult a time as I did trying to save my friend. They encouraged me, but let me have complete responsibility for Bay's care. I look back knowing it is great to have responsibility from a young age because taking responsibility will stand you in good stead for the rest of your life. You will never want to be part of an entitlement society. It is a huge responsibility to have dozens of pets. A North Dakota winter, often with steady temperatures down to -45° F is difficult to cope with. Your pets require warm water at least a couple of times a day. Feeding and watering pets normally seems like a full-time job but much more so in the winter. In spite of all of this, one thing I almost always include in my prayers to this day is, "God please let me take care of your animals when I get to heaven." Other more recent, ever-present daily requests are, "God please nourish the gifts You have given me and please grant me wisdom to use those gifts." God is really faithful and He has blessed me beyond reason throughout my entire life.

I am sure all of you with pets have noticed your pets will never let you down. You probably do not have enough fingers and toes to count the times your family or friends have let you down as you have gone through life. Think hard. When has that happened with one of your pets?

Not that often, huh?

I think one of the earliest things I can recall wanting from my parents was a 22 caliber rifle or a .22. When I was in fourth grade I told my dad I found a guy who would sell me his .22 for ten bucks. Dad said okay. I was thrilled when Dad gave me the ten dollars to buy it. It was old, old, old with a hexagonal barrel. I brought it home and showed it to Dad. He asked me to hand it to him. He then promptly took the lead from a couple of cartridges and pounded them sideways down into the loading end of the barrel. I asked him, "What good is a rifle I cannot shoot?" He said, "When I see you handling this one properly, we'll get you one you can shoot." Dad taught me all the basics including how to handle your rifle when you are riding your horse. I rode with saddle and bareback. Dad had grown up riding a pony named Sparky. He rode side saddle his entire young life as was necessary with his one paralyzed leg. It simply did not allow him to ride with a leg on each side of the horse. He taught me never to carry my rifle when crossing a fence. Always set the rifle down, cross the fence and then grab the rifle. Never lift your rifle by the barrel pulling the dangerous end toward yourself. Never pull a rifle out of a case or from behind a seat the same way. Never have your rifle or any gun pointed toward anyone. Assume every gun or rifle you ever handle is loaded. It seems like only unloaded guns accidentally kill somebody. About a year later, Dad got me a single shot .22 I could actually shoot.

From about the time I was twelve years old I jumped on Bay with my rifle in the morning and took off across the fields with Rex following us every step of the way. I always left in early morning and came home when it started to get dark, likely because I was getting hungry.

It would be years later when he was in the early stages of lung cancer Dad would confide he and Mom worried about me every day when I took off with my horse and dog and rifle. They always wondered if I was coming back. I said to Dad, "If you were that worried, why did you let me go?" He said, "You do not teach independence to a young person without letting them be independent. You have grown up to be very independent and part of that is from making almost all your own decisions in your early years. We just stayed out of the way and gave guidance when it was needed." Did you ever notice the older you get the wiser your parents become?

When I was fourteen years old, Dad and Mom bought a new home on the Northwest side of Williston. We were going to be living at 1008 Ninth Avenue North. The house was a nice rambler and quite a step up from our little home in the country. My bedroom was downstairs next to an entertainment room and shared with Ron.

It was about the same time I met Bette Elaine Nelson while playing baseball on a small neighborhood lot near her house. The Nelson family lived on Seventh Avenue North and was about a mile south and two blocks east of our house. Bette was one of the original tomboys. She grew up with a bunch of brothers; her two older ones were great athletes. Her oldest brother Binks was the State Wrestling Champion in North Dakota from the first time Williston had a wrestling team. Binks was asked to wrestle for the U.S. Olympic team while still in high school. That was pretty much an unheard-of honor at the time. But when it came to wrestling, Binks Nelson was a pretty amazing person. No one ever tired of watching him wrestle because he was definitely entertaining to watch. Binks never lost a wrestling match while in high school. When Binks went on to college wrestling, he called up his dad Adrian crying one day because he had lost a match. In the NCAA national finals that year, Binks met the wrestler who beat him again and ran up the score to, as I recall, 15 to nothing before he pinned him for the national title. Bette's second oldest brother Dick was All State guard in football. No one received the accolades Binks did but Dick was just as great an athlete in his sport. Bette was also a fine athlete. She could hit a baseball or softball and run with the best of them.

Our entire high school of several hundred students had to run an obstacle course as part of our physical education program. I think the fact Bette set the school record was bothersome to most of the male jocks.

Bette and I became a steady item while in high school. We were pretty much inseparable and often met on the stairwell between classes to catch a quick hug and kiss. I guess it was common knowledge because one day Mrs. Ertresvag, my senior high school English teacher, handed me a poem she had written for us.

Give me a little leeway on this as I am trying to remember from 55 years ago. It went something like this:

I'll meet you for school
I'll walk you in the hallway
I'll meet you on the stairs.

I'll praise your looks
I'll call you fair
But must I tote those gosh darn books.

Anyway, don't think I missed that by much. God also blessed me with a decent memory. It made school easy but surely gave me a lot more time for goofing around and learning things I was interested in rather than required courses. Instead of study during most of my study halls I checked out novels from the library and read. I should have studied a little. I did not graduate with anywhere near the best grades in our school. I guess at the time, to me, the only thing that really counted was graduating.

By the time I was a freshman in high school, I had pretty much been kicked out of every class I ever attended at least once. I was not always kicked out gently. One day when I was in the eighth grade, an art teacher became exasperated enough with me that he hauled off and hit me in the face with a bunch of his muscle and a closed fist. I landed flat on my back prior to that dismissal. It didn't really dent my behavior but I did get better at ducking.

My behavioral misadventures ended dramatically when all of us entered Williston Senior High School.

Chapter Two

Williston High School

For the first time in my education, I was in the youngest class. We were sophomores. We met our principal Mr. Leon B. Olson for the first time in a large school study hall. Mr. Olson was a tall blonde Scandinavian with broad shoulders and not an ounce of fat on him. He spelled things out for us with crystal clarity. Mr. Olson said, "You are now in Senior High School and will be treated as young ladies and gentlemen. Misbehavior will not be tolerated. If you do not follow our rules there will be consequences. You young ladies may take a leave of absence or quit school if you are not in line. You young men may also quit school. The alternative is to come down to the locker room and get a spanking or put up your fists against me." Mr. Olson's reputation had preceded our meeting him. He was a Golden Gloves boxer. I don't recall anyone ever taking Mr. Olson up on his suggestions to test the validity or sincerity of what he said.

I guess one day a student thought he was beyond the grasp of Mr. Olson. Mr. Bob Peterson, our world history teacher, and Mr. Olson were walking out of the front door of the school. One of the senior students who would be graduating in a few days by the name of Lanny Caulkins was sitting in a car smoking in front of the school. Smoking was definitely not allowed near Williston High School. Mr. Olson said, "Hey Lanny, put out your cigarette." Then he said to Mr. Peterson, "He didn't hear me." He again said quite loudly, "Hey Lanny, put out your cigarette." Lanny just looked at Mr. Olson and took a long drag off his cigarette. Since he was graduating in a few days he thought he no longer had to take orders from Mr. Olson. That was probably not the best decision to make. In a few long strides Mr. Olson covered the distance to the car, reached through the window, grabbed Lanny by his shoulder and quickly jerked him through the window of his car. Lanny was a large young man who played tackle for the high school football team. I do not know how Mr. Olson could accomplish what he did but he dragged Lanny to the front steps of the high school and spanked him. I don't think Lanny ever smoked around school again, even after graduation.

Mr. Olson probably commanded more respect than any other teacher up to that point in my life. He was strict in many areas. If he ever saw a student not standing with their hand over their heart when the American flag was presented during sporting events, they were promptly told to leave the field or the building. Every year I can remember, Williston got the state award for the best conduct in state tournaments. Thanks, Mr. Olson. What ever happened to teachers like that? As far as that goes, what ever happened to students who respected their elders?

My relationship with Bette grew and matured while in high school. We felt as though we were really in love and when I was a junior and Bette was a sophomore, we decided to ask our parents if we could get married. We had one high school couple that married for the usual reason, pregnancy out of wedlock. They seemed to do very well and maintained a seemingly great relationship through their last couple years of high school in spite of having a child, a household and taking their classes. I do not know what happened to them after high school.

The answer from both sets of our parents was the same. And the nice thing about both sets of our parents is they handled our request with respect and thoughtfulness. Their feelings were, if we really loved each other that much it would keep until we both graduated from high school and had a year or two of college behind us. Bette and I agreed to abide by their wishes and wait to see how we felt about marriage.

I think our greatest worry was I would be heading off to college in another year and we were concerned about what the distance would do to us. I believe now this was the insecurity of youth. We just did not have a large enough ledger of life's experience built up to enable us to know how we would handle a little adversity. We were both happy and comfortable with our decision but it did not take long for us to find out how we would handle adversity. I was anxious to get out of high school and get on with life.

Bette and I had some long heart to heart conversations when I was ready to start applying to colleges. We finally decided we wanted to continue our relationship but that it was in our best interest to be able to date other people. It made sense as Bette was very popular and bound to be the next Homecoming Queen at Williston Senior High School. It did not make sense for her to be unable to attend prom and other functions just because I was gone. Although neither Bette nor I had ever dated another person or even kissed another person, we believed our relationship would survive.

When I first went off to look at colleges, I had decided on attending either Minot State College in Minot, North Dakota or North Dakota State University in Fargo. I chose those schools because I had friends in both areas. Three of my cousins went to college or were going to college in Minot. In those days we did not have the myriad of choices youngsters have today. Travel was not as easy or as prevalent. Back then we looked at a couple of hundred miles about like we look at a couple of thousand miles today. One of my lifelong friends Doug Vedvick and I went on the journey to look at schools.

The first college I looked at was North Dakota State University. The person I knew who could possibly be there was Joan Moore. We had been kids who seemed to like each other a lot growing up. We both went to Rickard Grade School and were in the same class. I had a crush on Joan while in the grades but she moved to Fargo with her parents when we were both sixth graders. Despite not having been in contact since then, I managed to find Joan. I remembered her mom worked at Daveaux Music Company in Fargo, the same store where my dad worked when we lived in a tiny trailer house in Moorhead, Minnesota, just across the Red River from Fargo. I was only four years old at that time.

Joan and I got together for a couple of nights and it felt as though we were back in grade school. We laughed a lot and had a great time. Joan lined Doug up with one of her friends and they also hit it off. Joan and I committed to stay in touch. I did not know for sure I would end up in Fargo. I leaned more toward Minot as it was closer to Williston and Bette. Unfortunately, Joan and I did not stay in touch and I never saw her again.

Doug and I went to Minot where we stayed with a distant cousin of mine. Dianne Hanson was a tall, brown skinned beauty who was the National Baton Twirling Champion and the head majorette for the Minot State Marching Band. She was a couple inches shy of six feet and strikingly beautiful. She absolutely stood out in a crowd.

Dianne and I were already friends since she visited Williston on our band day and later when she performed with her baton for Oil Discovery Days. When the lights were out in our field house and Dianne's batons were on fire, she could get a crowd of thousands standing and cheering. On one of those days I was in chemistry class and was supposed to pick up Dianne. I asked Mr. Rabinovitch if I could bring my cousin to class. When I returned with Dianne, dressed in her uniform with its dozens of gleaming medals, Mr. Rabinovitch said smiling, "I can see why you were so anxious to bring your cousin back to class Rick. Welcome to our class." I introduced Dianne to our class.

Dianne had stayed with us during those visits and we had become close. Bette also knew Dianne from her visits. I ended up inviting Dianne to Williston for a couple of weeks prior to starting school. Our plans were to have some fun on the water with a little swimming and skiing. Dianne was also enrolling in Minot. Being gone from Williston was now a little more appealing to me and I was starting not to dread the time Bette and I would be separated. It seemed Bette and I had both adapted well and moved on until we could see what the future held. Dianne and I already knew our plans for the next year. They were immediately obvious.

Doug and I got home on a warm afternoon. I had called Bette from a pay phone in Minot to let her know what time I would be home and that I would come straight to her house. When I arrived, she was standing on the corner crying. I knew immediately something was drastically wrong. Bette said, "Rick, I'm pregnant. I saw Dr. Joe Craven and he confirmed I am about three months pregnant." I told Bette not to worry and we would handle everything but I was distraught. It was obvious I was not as bright as I thought I was. I had studied the Encyclopedia Britannica carefully to calculate when a girl can get pregnant. Wrong. The tables are not always right when there are variables such as irregular periods.

I told Bette I would go home, talk to my parents and let them know. I drove home slowly. We lived less than a mile from each other. I decided I would tell Mom as she was the first parent I saw. When I told Mom, she became hysterical. She was screaming at me at the top of her lungs telling me I ruined my life. How could I go to college now? What would happen to me? I guess she was too distraught to bring Bette into the equation now that her son had knocked up his girlfriend.

I took off running out the front door and ran and ran and ran. Back in those days I handled all my problems by running. I don't know if subconsciously I thought I could run away from them. It was hot out and I had run seven or eight miles when I crossed the railroad tracks south of Williston and came to the Missouri River. I was contemplating swimming the river. I had been on the swimming team for years but where we lived the Missouri was known to be a treacherous river with many whirlpools and currents. It was thought no one could safely make it across. In the days I was growing up the Missouri made the Mississippi look like a small creek. It was backed up from the Garrison Dam which was at the time the largest Earth rolled dam in the world. It was larger than the Aswan Dam in Egypt.

The tracks I had crossed were supposedly the barrier marking where the less desirable of Williston society lived. One disparaging remark I can remember to this day is "They live on the wrong side of the tracks." I think they were probably just poor and certainly not undesirable at all. I guess we were probably the undesirables for thinking less of our fellow man.

For some reason, I became very tired and thought I would take a nap before swimming the river. It was as though someone had suddenly drugged me. I do not to this day think I was suicidal but if I was willing to take the chance to swim the 'Mighty Missouri' perhaps it was somewhere in my thoughts. Looking back, I don't think I felt that way.

I could see a small haystack about a quarter mile away from the river toward the direction from which I had come. I walked back to the haystack and laid down. The sun was beating down hard on me and I immediately fell asleep lying in the hay. Sometime later I awoke and felt as though I had things crawling all over me. There were crickets by the hundreds covering me completely. I jumped up and wildly brushed them off my face and hair and the rest of my body. I am not afraid of crickets but I did not want to be buried in them either.

I turned back toward the river. I thought I was rested enough to make it across. I noticed a little dilapidated shack with peeling remnants of white paint I had not seen while lying down in the haystack. That seemed a little strange since it was only a few hundred feet away. How could I not have noticed? I do not know why but I walked up and standing in the doorway of the shack was a disheveled man in coveralls and an old shirt with rather unkempt white hair and a beard. The dang doorway didn't even have a door in it.

I asked him if I could have a glass of water. He said to come in and sit down. I sat down on a little old wooden folding chair. The only other piece of furniture in the room was a little square table about four feet or so on the side. The inside of the shack was just bare old gray 2 X 4s and the same was true of the bare rafters overhead. The shack was tiny but he disappeared through a door and promptly came back with a glass of ice water. I was completely surprised as it did not look as if there was electricity in that little shack. Just plain water would have been fine.

The old man started talking to me. He said, "You know I thought about suicide one time." I was completely taken aback. I did not mention anything about swimming the river and I certainly did not mention suicide. What on earth was he talking about? He went on to say, "Do you see that rafter up there above this little table?" I nodded yes. He said, "I took the chair you are sitting on right now and got up on that table. I then tied a rope around my neck and tied the other end to that rafter. You know I thought for a little bit and then decided it was not a very good answer."

I was now completely bewildered. Who on earth was this little old bedraggled man? A mind reader? I really did not know what to say. I was speechless. I thanked him for the glass of water and left. Unfortunately, I was so taken aback by his thoughts, I did not even have the presence of mind to ask him why he felt suicidal and if he got better.

When I walked back down to the river I did not think swimming the river was probably a very good answer either. I walked rather slowly all the way home. It gave me some time to think and compose my thoughts. When I got home my brother Ronnie came out the door crying, saying, "I love you, Rick." He wrapped his arms around my waist and gave me a big hug. Ron was thirteen years old at the time.

Dad was the next person through the door. His words to me were, "Why on earth would you tell your mom Bette is pregnant? You know how excitable she can get. You bring those kinds of problems to me first.

So Bette is pregnant. What is the big deal? It happens every day. You are not the first couple to end up with a pregnancy. So what. We'll figure it out. What do you want to do?"

I replied, "Get married, I guess." He said, "Is that what you really want to do?" I said, "It was not that long ago Bette and I talked to you about getting married and we still love each other. I am going over to the Nelson's house to talk with Adrian and Doris (Bette's parents). Adrian was not quite as reasonable as Dad was. He did not get out a shotgun but I don't know what he would have done if he'd had one. Adrian told me in no uncertain terms we would get married immediately. It didn't sound as though I had much of a choice. They were understandably upset. I had helped change their second oldest daughter's life forever.

When I got home Dad and I had another discussion. I told him what Adrian had said. Now it was Dad's turn to be angry. He said, "No one gets married because they have to. They get married because they want to. Is this what you want?"

I said, "It is definitely the right and correct thing to do and I think Bette and I will make this work, although my plans have changed rather abruptly. Bette and I will have to talk this over as I am not the only one making this decision. It must be something we both want." Bette and I talked again and decided we would sleep on everything and talk again the next day to decide what we would do. I think sleeping on everything had already caused the problem we were again going to sleep on.

The next day, I only had one thing on my mind. I wanted to drive back to the river and talk to the little old man again. I needed to know what he knew about me that I didn't know. I drove the route I had run and when I came to the haystack beside the road, the little shack and little old man were gone. I was sure I must have made a mistake but I retraced my tracks several times and went right to the spot where a little old man in a little old shack had given me a glass of ice water. It definitely was not there.

That day I realized an angel had entered my life and intervened with my foolish thoughts. There was no other answer. An angel also intervened when I had similar but much more serious thoughts later in my life. I have no idea for certain whether or not it is the same angel presented differently.

Bette and I talked over the next couple of days. Neither set of parents tried to give us any input. My parents already knew I would go the direction I wanted to go and thought was right regardless of suggestions from elsewhere. Bette and I decided we were going to get married.

A few days later Dianne came and stayed with us at our home and we had some long talks. I do not think Bette was comfortable with this but Dianne and I had become very close in an extremely short period of time. I am certain that had Bette and I not messed things up, Dianne and I would have probably been together for the rest of our lives. It was hard on both of us and Bette too. We managed to get in a couple of weeks of swimming and skiing, but things were naturally awkward and strained.

All of us had had our hearts wounded. It makes me think of a verse I often tell people to think about: *Drink carefully from the cup of life filled graciously by our Lord, lest from a seeming tiny slip an ocean be outpoured.* I don't know the original author but know I am not clever enough to have thought of it.

Well, I could hardly call this a little slip but we certainly did pour out an ocean. Dianne and I probably had the hardest time of all over the next couple of years. We crossed paths at various times at Minot State Teachers College as it was then called and we knew instinctively we could not touch or hold each other again or even talk. We would be like two magnets.

Too bad love is not something you can stick a dagger through and kill. It remains with you in some form for the rest of your life. I think the best thing you can do with love is to cherish it and thank God for giving it to you, no matter how briefly and carry it warmly in your heart for the rest of your life.

Getting Married

A couple of weeks later, in July, Bette and I were married in the Lutheran Church on the end of Main Street in Williston by Pastor Casper P. Nervig. I was eighteen years old and Bette had just turned seventeen the month before. The wedding was small with friends of Bette's and mine and our immediate families attending. Dianne had returned to Minot in anticipation of starting college. I really missed her.

Following the wedding, we had a small cake at my parents' home. The wedding marked the time for us to make plans for the real world and the rest of our lives. What a joke that is. Every time I want to give God a good laugh, I tell him I have plans. Back then I did not talk to God nearly often enough. I guess I thought saying The Lord's Prayer every night was sufficient.

A couple of days later my dad asked me what our plans were. I told Dad I thought I was going to enroll in military service. He said, "What about college?" I said, "I don't know how I am going to swing college, being married and having a baby." Dad's reply was, "How do you know? Have you ever tried it?" It was a foolish question to drive the point home. He said, "If college does not work out for you, the service can always be a backup plan." I guess I thought that was good advice and I wanted to go to college. He added, "I know you will do well and make college work."

Minot State Teachers College – later Minot State University

Now the pressure was off. A decision had been made. Decisions are always good. It doesn't matter if the decision is right or wrong. Indecision is what kills you. You can do nothing with indecision. You can't work toward indecision. It has no direction. You can work toward a solution if you have a decision regardless of whether it is good or bad.

Bette and I decided we would like to attend school in Minot. My dad and Adrian decided we needed a car if we were going to go away to college. We certainly couldn't walk. We searched around and found a little ugly green Nash Rambler convertible. It had one of those little black rag tops that slid back on rails over the tops of the windows. You had to push the top down by hand but that was not even considered an inconvenience in the Sixties. Everyone thought it needed a paint job so we painted it this gorgeous turquoise color Bette and I loved.

One of the first days we had the chance we drove to Minot. The first place I stopped was at one of the local swimming pools on the west side of Minot where I knew a friend of mine was lifeguarding. Dick Zorn and I had met at a Western Division Track Meet javelin event in high school. I qualified for state on my last throw and then walked illegally across the line. Dick asked, "Why did you do that?" I said, "I really don't want to go to state. My dad and some friends are going fishing up on Lac La Ronge in Saskatchewan next week and I will not be able to go if I am at the state meet throwing the javelin." Lac La Ronge is one of the largest lakes in that province.

That was the last event for Dick and me so we decided to run around for the day. Later we met a sweet, beautiful little gal from Bismarck by the name of Dolly Igoe whose dad owned a construction company. She ran around with us for the day and we had a good time. I never saw Dolly again.

Let's get back to the swimming pool. When we arrived, Dick was busy in the lifeguard stand. When he took a break, I told him I had gotten married; of course neither he nor any of his friends believed me until they met Bette.

Our first night in Minot was a learning experience for Bette and me. We did not know how to go about renting a motel room. We had very little money and I think it was more a question of whether or not we would sleep in the car. People really don't sleep in a car the first night of their honeymoon, do they? That night was kind of embarrassing for both of us. We did not know if a motel would give us a room in view of our ages. I brought our wedding license in with me but they couldn't have cared less who rented a room. Oh well, it was a learning experience. Man-a-live, were kids inexperienced back in those days or what?

Dick offered his parents' basement to us after that first night so we could save some money. Since we were broke we were immensely grateful to Walter and Vie Zorn who took us in. The next morning Dick embarrassed the heck out of us in front of his parents when we were all sitting at breakfast. He said, "I know what you two were doing last night. We could hear that bed squeaking all night." My God, he was right. You couldn't breathe in that bed without it squeaking. We actually tried to sleep all night long without moving. Bette and I were too embarrassed to reply. Walt and Vie just laughed.

Bette and I picked up college application papers for me. I don't think we even considered we might not be accepted. I say we because everything Bette and I did was a team effort. Everything was we. It was never I, me or mine. I, or we, must have been extremely naive in those days. I thought if I signed up for college, I would automatically be accepted.

It was never even in the far reaches of my mind that college was not an automatic. I equated it with high school. You signed up, progressed and automatically graduated. Oh sure, you took a couple of classes along the way to satisfy requirements but they were automatic too, weren't they?

Shortly after applying for school, we were accepted. Of course! Why would we not be?

It was on my first day of applying for classes I met the supervisor assigned to me. His name was Dr. Harry Robinson, a tanned middle aged man of normal weight with a fairly well shaved balding head, a friendly face and a kindly smile. When I say balding, he had receding graying hair cut or shaved like many of our athletes today. I guess he was ahead (a head) of his time. Over the course of the next three years we would become friends.

Dr. Robinson asked me what I wanted to major in. I probably did not take much of this as seriously as I should have. It just really never entered my mind that here on day one at Minot State College, I would choose a course to enter a profession that would fulfill and hopefully satisfy us for the rest of our lives.

I told Dr. Robinson my desire was to study the para-psychological sciences at Duke University. I told him I was a hypnotist and came from a family with extremely developed powers of extrasensory perception. I wanted to learn more. It was then I found out I would first need to become a medical doctor and then specialize in psychiatry. I had always wanted to be a veterinarian too and since humans were only a small step down from animals that also appealed to me. I enrolled for all premed courses which I hoped would eventually land me in medical school.

I went home after registration that day and told Bette I was going to medical school to become a doctor. Bette automatically knew when I told her that was exactly what would happen. She said it sounded great. I knew from that day on nothing could possibly get in my way of becoming a physician. From what I heard from Dad my entire life, I knew I would become a physician in the near future. I never had a backup plan. That would never be in the cards.

We spent the next two days looking for an apartment. Back in the early Sixties people could discriminate as much as they wanted when it came to leasing an apartment. A lot of apartments specified no children. We were turned away from almost everywhere we sought housing because I imagine they figured two kids our age needing an apartment were soon going to have a baby.

We finally got a basement apartment that defies description. Bette and I were just happy we had a place to live. The apartment was filled with literally thousands of boxelder bugs. They didn't hurt anything. You just had to keep sweeping them up. We were too poor to have a vacuum of any kind. It is really too bad they were not good eating. We would have never starved. My aunt and uncle, Hazel and Marvin Harmon from Wildrose, North Dakota, visited us after we moved into our apartment. They were bringing my closest cousins Darrell and Sheila to school in Minot. Darrell was in his second year and Sheila and I were in our first. Hazel later would tell us she cried for days after seeing where we were living.

The married student housing on campus consisted of the wooden barracks left over from the internment camps from the Second World War where we had so kindly deposited those dangerous Japanese American Citizens. It is hard to believe what we used to do to our country's citizens. Within the first month we received a call from the college with an opening for us in their married student housing. For the next three years we lived at number 12, Wooden Barracks.

The price was unbelievable. We paid $32 per month for the next three years. Even that amount was difficult to pay some months. Most of the married students around us were veterans returning from being stationed in Korea which made Bette and me the kids on the block. The older students took us under their wings and helped us as much as they could. They would bring us over little carpet remnants or 9' by 12' carpets you could buy reasonably at a K-Mart to put on our gray painted cement floors or drapes to cover our windows.

The $32 rent was maybe reasonable for couples on veteran's wages, but nothing was ever reasonable for us. A huge treat in those days was for us to be able to go to Henry's Hamburgers and buy a couple of 9 cent hamburgers. By that I do not mean a couple hamburgers for each of us. We each got one hamburger and if we were feeling pretty flush, we would get a small order of fries.

I really enjoyed college. It was almost like Bette and I were celebrities among the kids our age. There were just no students our age back in the early Sixties attending college. I think the very few of us young people who had fallen into the marriage trap Bette and I had, automatically went out into life and started working. They progressed into life as a young family subsisting as best they could. I felt fortunate having the parents we had. Our parents did not give us money but they gave us encouragement.

In Williston High School, Bette and I were the only two young married students to attend college, at least as to the best of my knowledge. Bette was not the only girl in Williston High School who got pregnant. One of my friends got married at age 16; he and his wife finished high school even while taking care of their child.

Bette and I would eventually produce three beautiful children. There is certainly nothing unlucky about that, just inconvenient timing brought about by immature childish minds seeking fulfillment of desires. Isn't that a nice way of saying you didn't control your hormones?

There was always talk floating around of a chiropractor who performed abortions on the side in Williston. Quite the sideline to supplement your income, huh? Abortion was never a consideration for Bette and me. I think some well-meaning person volunteered the information for us right after we found out "we" were pregnant.

I do not think at that point in my life I had ever thought out the theological processes which were firmly ingrained in my mind later in life. Abortion was something I knew happened but not something I really considered as murder. In the late Fifties and early Sixties abortion was not in the news all the time and I do not remember ever hearing the issue being brought up. Well, at least until Bette and I got pregnant. I know for a fact it was not something ever talked about in my family. At age 18 I really did not have a clue about what abortion was or what it entailed.

Yes, and if us guys "knock a girl up" we are pregnant too. It is every bit as much our problem or blessing as it is that of our girlfriends. Looking back, I am almost 100% certain I did not consider this a blessing at the time. Probably far from it. I am sure it also put me on the top of the "A" (for asshole) list. How self-centered must I have been.

Chapter Three

Minot State College

In our early days of school, especially our first year in Minot, I think to many of the students our home represented a home away from home. There was seldom a weekend we did not have several fellow classmates congregate in our home including Sandy Listevit, a classmate from Williston and a cheerleader along with my cousin Sheila Harmon. Frequently all five Minot State cheerleaders would be at our home on the weekends. My cousin Sheila brought along a couple of other cheerleaders by the names of Delrae Underdall and Sugar Saunders. They were all well-known college cuties. This of course drew a number of the guys. We usually played cards because it was the only entertainment most of us could afford. Popcorn was our standby snack for the same reason.

Being a college student in those days was a lot different than it is now. Most of my classmates were working their way through school. I was a janitor in the science building along with Janus Guttarts. John (Janus) had escaped from Latvia on a bicycle in the middle of the night when they found out the Russians were coming through Latvia, rounding up all of the people, putting them on box cars and shipping them by rail to Siberia and other Russian destinations.

The Guttarts never saw the rest of their family and friends again. But it probably saved their lives along with that of their little girl. Mrs. Guttarts was pregnant at the time of the escape but lost that pregnancy. Janus ended up escaping with his family to a neighboring country. Over one year's time Janus went from 190 pounds down to 90 pounds. He worked for a slice of bread per day for his family and if he really produced well he received a small "dollop" of butter.

John taught me many valuable lessons and some lesser ones like learning what a dollop was. I quickly learned that even though someone is doing janitor work to support their family, it is not necessarily their field of expertise. And please do not think when I mention janitor work in this way I think it is any less a noble profession than perhaps a pastor, professor or physician.

Dad taught me valuable lessons about life. One of these lessons I recall exactly is that any profession, be it a ditch digger or President of the United States is honorable if it supports you and your family. That is not a very good example because I am sure many United States citizens do not feel some of our presidents have been honorable. Do your very best for whomever you work. Always give your best. It is only when you are an elected official of the people you can worry only about yourself and re-election.

I learned early in my association with John he was a veritable fountain of information. One day as we were waxing a hallway in the science building, a question was asked on a popular local radio station. The question was who was the first Nobel Prize winner in literature in India? I do not remember what the prize was. John said, "That is surely an easy question. The first Nobel Prize winner in literature from India was Rabindranath Tagore." He added, "The second winner from India was Rudyard Kipling." I was dumbfounded. I, in all my brilliance, was an idiot. I did not know either answer. Thus started my true and first education in college from one of my first professors, a janitor by the name of Janus Guttarts.

That early education served me well for the rest of my life. I would forever remember that we are always working and walking alongside of people in different professions and walks of life. Every one of them has a different story and every one of them knows more about some or many things in life we know nothing about. We are all experts in our own little ways learned from our walks along this path of life. We can all learn from each other so must always keep an open mind.

Bette's parents Adrian and Doris were good friends of ours as were my parents and we enjoyed spending time with both families. Adrian was a sportswriter for the Williston Herald and an assistant coach for our sophomore football coach Norm Furseth. Adrian was fun to be around and by being around the Nelson family I learned how to become a relatively good bridge player. Adrian would often be my partner. He always said, "Rick, pull up a chair and don't worry, I can win a game of bridge if I only have an apple crate for a partner." Our opponents were often Bette's grandpa, Harvey Larson and one other member of the Nelson family.

My parents gave us excellent advice one night when we asked them about how to have a good marriage. We also asked them to share the main problems in their marriage and what caused the most fights or disagreements between them. Dad answered that question as soon as it was out of my mouth. "You dang kids caused the most trouble for both of us."

Mom and Dad said there were three rules they lived by. The number one rule to avoid kid problems is to never have a disagreement about your children in front of them. Always appear united in front of them even if you are polar opposites in what you are thinking. If you do not do this, your child will come to you and say Mom said this or Dad said this. They will present what they want you to hear.

Children seem to be born with little psychology degrees. And as I would later find out they are honor students. They will try to get their parents to disagree about their point so it is imperative to discuss it together later and reach an agreement.

Number two, never fight about money. You are doing the best you can and you have to get along on the amount you have. You are probably both doing your best to survive on that amount. It is never worth fighting over.

Third and lastly, never go to bed mad at each other or fighting. Kiss each other good night even if you have to bite your tongue until it bleeds. Fall asleep in each other's arms. We were told if we firmly believed in these things our parents learned the hard way, we would have a happy marriage that would withstand any trials and tribulations we might face.

Bette and I wrote down those three rules and agreed we would abide by them. We signed them and lived by them. Mom and Dad were right. We formed a marriage we thought and knew no one could separate. Over the years it appeared as though our marriage was superglued.

Sidebar: I spent most of last night crying. The five o'clock news showed a number of dogs that were going to be put to sleep because the humane society cannot get them adopted. The tethers God put between my heart and that of animals is stronger than the ties he put between most mothers and their sons. To me this is not any different than humans walking into nurseries and orphanages and putting the babies and children to sleep because they have no one to take care of them. The pets we bring into this world are our children. We must treat them as such. One day our humanity must surpass technology or we are indeed a failed race.

I settled into the routine of working and studying. I worked every night at the science building trying to keep it spic and span and looking like new. I really did take pride in my work. I liked looking down those long tan tile hallways after they were cleaned and waxed. I couldn't see my face in them like a mirror but it was darn close.

One thing I learned cleaning the science building was that the women's bathrooms looked like pigs lived there. John had warned me about this in advance but I really thought he was greatly exaggerating. How wrong I was. Sanitary napkins were thrown around and not disposed of properly. Kleenexes from blown noses or wiped off lipstick or whatever were just thrown on the floor wherever they landed. All in all, it was a mess that did not change from day to day the entire time I cleaned the science building. There was a day and night difference between the ladies' and men's bathrooms. The men kept their bathroom facilities super clean.

After working, I would run home and start studying. Initially twenty hours of my classes were science courses. Five hours of math, five hours of biology, five hours of chemistry, five hours of anatomy and an English class. I found school to be easy for the most part. It was all memorization. For me that meant basically reading the material once or twice. Some of the reading like anatomy required a little more determination. You had to memorize the origins and insertions of the muscles of the body. So, for about 640 muscles that meant retaining over twelve hundred facts about origins and insertions. Once you knew where a muscle took off from, the origin, and where it landed, the insertion, you had no problem knowing the function of the muscle. There are only the three different types of muscles in the body. The skeletal muscles move the bones, the smooth muscles control involuntary movements such as the contractions of the bowels and lastly and most importantly, the cardiac muscle is remarkable in that it faithfully beats and keeps us alive for our entire life. I bet a lot of manufacturing plants in the U.S. are trying to figure how to make their workers out of cardiac muscle.

One thing I did not care for my first year of college is all of the freshmen were supposed to wear the school red and green beanie. Not only that, we were all supposed to grow beards and mustaches. I thought the tradition was demeaning and a little embarrassing. I would not have minded growing a beard but it would be quite a few years yet before I needed to shave. In fact, I would not need to shave until my first year of practice. One day Ed Huseman, one of the Minot State College wrestlers, and another couple upper class wrestlers tried attacking me and putting a beanie on my head. I took the beanie off, threw it on the ground and told one of them to step forward to try putting it on my head again. That did not happen. They suggested I wear it and I said, "If you think those beanies look so great, you wear it." I was never again harassed about not wearing a beanie. I guess they thought it was not worth getting bruised and bloodied over. Yeah, foolish, I know, but as a married student and the youngest one in married student housing I did not want to be running around with a beanie on. Sure wished I could have grown a beard. Heck, back then I always wondered when I would be able to grow hair on my legs.

My most difficult class was advanced algebra. I absolutely did not know how I got into an advanced math class in which I had no background. I obviously did not belong. I did not have the slightest idea what was going on. Even when I later finished the class, I did not know what we were doing. To this day I do not know the purpose of the class. Maybe someone would later use that information to put a man on the moon.

My first week of school, I was called over to "Old Main," I guess so named for being one of the oldest buildings on campus. The teacher requesting my presence was Mrs. Dixon, a pleasant, slightly plump woman with short cropped gray hair. She asked if I knew why I had been called to see her, which I did not. She informed me I had scored the highest reading and comprehension abilities score ever in the English department admissions screening. I read at over 600 words per minute with greater than 95 percent retention and comprehension. She went on to explain I should never receive less than an "A" in any of my entire educational curriculum. I am so glad I did not give her one of my usual flippant remarks such as, "I won't." One thing Mrs. Dixon likely did not know is taking at least 20 hours of sciences per quarter along with another class is not exactly a walk in the park. It is especially hard when you are trying to work full time to support a family and preparing to take care of a baby in your spare time.

I promptly proved Mrs. Dixon wrong. At the end of my first quarter and not quite the end of my algebra education, I went to see my instructor and asked her where I ranked in the class. She said, "Mr. Redalen, you rank 32nd in the class." I asked how many students were in the class. She replied, "Thirty three." I said, "I will see you next quarter to take the final test. I am not going to take the final test tomorrow and next quarter I am not coming to any of your classes when I retake your course. I will come to take the final test." I did as I said I would and scored a C on her final. Who knows? I think she probably felt sorry for me and upgraded me from an F to a C. Oh well, I was not too proud to accept pity. Even today I sometimes think I would like to go back and retake that class and uncover the big mystery. The only thing stopping me is the fact I would probably get an F again and everything would remain a mystery. I could no longer rationalize, could I?

The rest of my courses that first quarter were just plain old science courses and not that difficult. I got good grades. Anatomy and physiology were required so there were hundreds of students taking those classes. They were considered the weeding out classes for Physical Education (P.E.) majors. I realized I suddenly had a lot of friends in the jock department. They seemed to congregate around me during tests. I realized they were trying to see my test papers. I really did not care as it was their problem, not mine.

One night it became my problem. The night prior to a humanities test I heard a loud knock at our door. When I went to the door there were several of my jock classmates outside. They said, "Rick, we stole the final tests from Dr. Agamemnon's office. Will you fill them out for us?" Dr. A's tests were always four hundred to five hundred questions in length.

Humanities supposedly gave you a rounded education in many things but it required no thinking. It was just memorization of important facts you would use for the rest of your life. We had a pleasant slightly built elderly humanities professor we all called Dr. Agamemnon. His real name was Dr. Sheffield. Agamemnon was the mythological Greek king in the Trojan War. Humanities tests contained questions like how many columns are across the front of the Parthenon and how many columns make up the sides. The Parthenon is sitting on how may steps and what type of frieze does it have around the top. You can of course see how you will use this important information for the rest of your life.

My friends had about eight tests with them, each with five hundred questions. They had stolen a copy of each test they found. I answered all the questions I could on each test with my classmates sitting in our living room looking up the answers I did not know. I was getting a strong A in the class so did not feel it was going to change my grade in any way. Most of the questions were about the same with small variations.

When I finished all of the tests it was now only a few hours until we would have to take the exam. I told my buddies to read each test so they would know the answers. I also reassured them there was little variation among the tests and not that much to remember. However, they chose to do it their way. Each student made a crib sheet and then they mimeographed several crib sheets to bring to the exam.

Unfortunately for all of them the final test was again a variation and none of them could match up a crib sheet for their exam. They had all parked themselves rather close to me in the exam. They all had quizzical looks on their faces, but there was nothing I could do to help them.

When I finished the test I knew I had written a perfect test and had all five hundred questions right. Well why shouldn't I? I had just finished reading all of them. I picked out about thirty-five questions I thought might be difficult to answer and changed the answers into incorrect ones and turned my exam in.

The following day when I was walking down the old main hallway, Dr. A. yelled after me. All I could feel was fear. I had helped students cheat on their final exam and I feared I was getting kicked out of college. Dr. A. said, "Mr. Redalen, have you seen the final exam scores?" I replied I had not. Dr. A. put his arm around my shoulder and led me to the door of his office several feet away where the final exam test scores were posted. My score was about one hundred points above the next closest score. Dr. A. told me it was the finest test ever written for him in all of his years of teaching. I felt a little badly about ruining the curve but did not give a reason why my score was so good. It didn't change the 'A' I was getting anyway.

In biology and anatomy classes I always managed to have the highest or second highest grade in the college. It used to kind of bother me that an older student probably in his mid-thirties would occasionally beat me for the number one spot. He was probably smarter as he eventually became a professor in the sciences at Minot State. The 'F' I received in the algebra class would be the only 'F' I would receive during my entire educational career. It was a valuable lesson. I learned not to take classes I would fail. The trouble is when you are taking classes you do not have a clue about, you are not even smart enough to cheat. Just kidding! That was never a consideration.

School at Minot was fun but hard work. Any time you take mostly science overloads with labs for your entire time in school it is extremely difficult. There just were not enough hours in the day. I had to really get innovative sometimes to get in my lab work. In chemistry I always had several experiments going at the same time. I just did not have the time to wait while something was cooking if I could be doing another experiment that also required watching. Sometimes I would have an entire lab desk covered with beakers, distillation units and Erlenmeyer flasks. It was challenging, but a lot of fun.

One day in chemistry class everyone was gone except Jerry Pratt, a great friend of mine, and me. We decided to play a trick on Gerald Peterson whom we called Gerry. Gerry had a large two-to-three-day experiment set up and "cooking." We moved his entire experiment to another room and replaced all his equipment with broken lab glass we took out of the trash from the equipment check out room.

Then we began working on our experiments and waited to see Gerry's reaction when he returned. When he looked at his desk and saw all the broken glass and realized two days of his experiment had gone down the drain, we thought he was going to start crying. Jerry and I could hardly contain ourselves but did not let Gerry see.

He went down to Chairman and Dept. of Chemistry Mr. Moore's office to report what had happened. Mr. Moore's office was down at the other end of the science building. Pratt and I hurriedly swept all the broken glass into a large waste basket and hastily returned his experiment to the exact way we had found it. By the time Gerry returned with Mr. Moore, Pratt and I were back working nonchalantly on our own experiments. Gerry was speechless as he tried to explain to Mr. Moore that only minutes ago everything was broken. Mr. Moore left the lab with a rather puzzled look on his face, about as perplexed as Gerry.

Pratt and I were always trying to make the educational process more exciting and we often came up with ways to stave off boredom. Sometimes we cooked up unstable explosive mixtures we would put under the windows so when the windows went down, it sounded as if a large firecracker exploded. The concoction was easy to work with. When it was wet and in solution it was stable. When it dried, even a feather lightly brushed across the surface would make the residue explode. We also put the materials in the walkways so when students stepped on the material it would explode under their feet. It was not like nitroglycerin. It did not hurt anyone, not even their shoes. It just helped sustain their attention levels.

Chemistry labs all have different safety stations. There is always a fountain much like a water fountain to bend over and wash out your eyes with a steady stream of water should you get chemicals in your eyes. We also had a huge shower head in our lab in case you accidentally got your body doused with chemicals or you caught on fire. I never saw anything that exciting happen.

One day Pratt and I started wondering if the shower really worked. It was like an old-time toilet with a chain pull to start the shower. The shower was nearly a foot across so our thinking was if it worked it would be able to put a fire out in about a second. What we didn't know was if the shower turned off when you quit pulling the chain.

Curiosity is not always a good thing. We decided to hold a large garbage can under the faucet and pull the chain. Unfortunately when we let go of the chain, the water did not turn off. Pratt and I started laughing. Pretty soon the garbage can was full and overflowing. We both spied the sink at the same time and tried to empty 30 to 40 gallons from a very rapidly filling garbage can. The sink was only about one foot by one foot. Needless to say a river ran down the lab length desk. The few beakers and flasks sitting on the lab desk were whisked away and on to the floor landing in thousands of pieces. Pratt and I couldn't stop laughing as we put the garbage can back under the shower. Seconds later the water stopped. It was times like this it was handy to be the janitor in the science building. I got out mops and pails and we cleaned up for the next hour. It would have been nice if the misadventures in the chemistry lab had ended there.

School was not all work, study and no play. Minot had a lot of good athletics and Bette and I managed to go to our share of football, wrestling and basketball games. We were the perennial winners of the Division III NCAA tournament in wrestling. We were the mighty Minot State College Beavers. I don't think any of our cheerleaders liked to hear the crude remarks from their fellow collegians, "Save a tree, eat a beaver." It always sounded kind of laughable to our juvenile minds.

The first year of college was pretty unremarkable other than flunking my math class. Bette and I tried to drive back and forth between Williston and Minot as much as we could early on. I think we really inconvenienced our friends who used our little apartment as a home away from home. Back in those days you did not give away the keys to your apartment for your friends to use. That was probably good or we might have had more company!

After a couple months went by my dad sat me down one day. He said "Rick, you now have your own family. Your mom and I love having you kids come home to visit us, but it is time for you and Bette to start spending more time together developing your family into a strong unit similar to the one in which you were brought up. If you and Bette continue to spend as much time as possible here with your families, it will slow the development of your family.

"The strength of your family will be very important with your baby on the way. You will soon become parents and undertake the greatest challenges of your lives."

Dad was "just a radio and television repairman," but he was one of the greatest scholars I was ever exposed to in my life. I wish I could have recognized it during that time of my life. And isn't it amazing we know everything when we are young and we seem to get dumber as we grow older. What am I missing? Something just doesn't seem to mesh quite right here. Are all of you on the same page with me or am I the only one lost in the rabbit hole and singing on the wrong music verse? See what I mean? You can already tell how much less intelligent I'm becoming.

Bette and I started spending more time in our little apartment in Minot. It was really enjoyable and we loved being a family. It was great to be in love. What can be better than two children growing up in love and growing together into early adulthood? Everything we did in life we did together. We studied together. Bette would ask me the origins and insertions of the muscles when we prepared for our anatomy tests.

I always kidded Bette and told her she should take the tests as she was always better prepared than I was. I am pretty sure that was spot on. Bette was a great student as she had been in Williston High School. I often felt badly Bette was not enrolled in college classes. I had helped to cheat her out of her college years. And it was not just college years. It was also her final year of high school. Everyone in Williston knew Bette would have been the next Homecoming Queen. It was a burden I carried and tried not to let her see. I did not want my burden to weigh her down.

Even though Bette and I were a team and we would both 'graduate' together, you all know it is not the same. You do not get two caps and two gowns. Bette, my supporting cast who always cheered "You can do it" was not going to receive the same achievement award on graduation day. How is that fair? It was not.

Bette and I both knew, although unspoken, it would have been impossible for us to both be in school and successfully raise a baby. When I thought too deeply about that I kept my tears to myself. I am almost certain to this day Bette does not know where my thoughts were hidden or what soaked up my tears. She was such an important foundation for my entire life and I can never thank her enough for constantly being there for me. She was and is an integral part of what and who I am today.

Bette's pregnancy was pretty uneventful. We traveled back and forth to Williston for Bette to see her lifelong doctor for occasional prenatal care. Doctor Joe Craven always reassured us that everything was going along fine and to keep doing what we were doing. We had an obstetrician in Minot who we knew would be delivering our baby and he was always reassuring us, too. I guess young kids just need a lot of affirmation they are doing the right things. In 1961 we did not have all the worries about drugs, sexually transmitted diseases and the whole encyclopedia of things that can go wrong in a pregnancy today. I really do not think ignorance is bliss but I do know for certain the boundless amounts of information we have today in our healthcare system have simply not helped us reach a healthier place in life. How on earth does that work? You know more, but you actually know less?

Not too long after we settled in to a fairly "normal" life in school, we realized we were not going to make it financially on just the salary I was making as a janitor in school. I was working four hours per night doing my janitor work but at $1.26 per hour I only earned $25 per week. It was out of the question we would ask anyone for help. Even though our rent was only $32 per month, food, books, tuition and transportation used up more money than we made.

Bette applied for a job as a nursing aide in Trinity Hospital in Minot. She really liked the work and I am sure had circumstances been different, Bette would have made a great nurse. She was a kind and caring person. Trinity Hospital was where we had planned on having our baby. Shortly after Bette got a job as an aide, a job came open for the night bookstore manager for the college. Someone passed the information on to me and I interviewed with the student union manager. The daytime manager of the bookstore was a fellow by the name of Nate Owens. Nate and I seemed to hit it off and I became the night manager of the bookstore. They placed a lot of trust in me. Book sales were really strong at night at the start of each quarter. Sometimes I would have up to $12,000 in my cash register. I was given the combination to the safe in the office and every night I would 'deposit' a large wad of bills.

It seemed kind of strange sometimes to be handling so much money at a time when we did not know if we were going to make it from one day to the next. Oh well, it is nice to find out early in life that honor and integrity will help you avoid temptations as they are going to follow you around for the rest of your life. These are principles on which you can never compromise. If you ever let black fade to gray you will become lost.

We were doing a little better financially with both of us working. The biggest problem was the only time we would see each other was when we went to bed at night. We hardly got to talk and the amount of time we spent studying together became really limited.

Our pregnancy continued on uneventfully. Bette took great care of herself, me and our little baby growing inside. She seemed to be getting larger by the day and I was simply amazed that a little baby could be growing inside someone you love and you were an integral part of that.

It made me more innovative in trying to save money. When I look back I realize now that what I did was not exactly honest. Not exactly is a pleasant way of saying I was stealing and cheating. We never had enough money to call home. But calling was also the best way (we thought the only way) for Bette and me to let our parents know how we were doing and how the pregnancy was progressing.

We just could not afford the long distance phone charges. One day I saw two pay phones on the wall of the men's dormitory which were about two feet apart and I had an idea I thought might work. I called home and when the operator came on the line to ask me to deposit $1.25 I took my hand full of quarters and deposited them in the phone that was not being used while holding my receiver up to record the bells or tones of the unused phone. During those times the operator knew how much money you deposited by listening to the tones as the coins dropped through. The great thing was that the coins dropping through on the unused phone went right on through to the coin return. I would just take them all out and when the operator would come on and tell me to deposit another amount, I would simply use the same coins over and over until I was done with my call.

My phone plan worked really well for several months until some of the other students wised up to what I was doing. They started calling friends all over the world. I was disappointed when I showed up one day to make a call and the second phone on the wall had been removed. The only signs left were the holes in the wall where it had been attached.

One other thing helped us with the phone company. All the cords on the phone were covered with just a plastic or rubber type of insulation and if you managed to stick a needle through them and get lucky you could get a short-circuited call connection without the benefit of the operator. Of course after the phone company had enough problems with this the phone cords eventually became encased in a type of metal cable that was impervious to needle sticks. I think at the time I thought Ma Bell could afford to give us broke college students a little free time on the phone wires.

A couple of months went by. Bette and I were really missing our time together so one day we hit on the idea that if we bought one of the little $18 tape recorders, we could tape our little love notes to each other to share what our day had been like. It really stretched our finances but we made it work.

And we solved another problem. I decided I could record the bell tones on the phone and when the operator asked me to deposit money I would just play the tape recorder and deposit as much money as I needed. I always deposited more than was needed so I could talk longer but it was no problem. Now we were back to no expense, almost free long distance calling. The only inconvenience was I always had to go to a pay phone to make this work. It worked all the way through our time in college at Minot. I really do not know what to say now except, thanks Ma Bell.

It was not long before the cold weather began rolling in. Usually it did not snow prior to Thanksgiving but we always kind of hoped for a white Thanksgiving. Snow ushered in the winter season in North Dakota. And when you grow up in Williston which is about 18 miles East of Montana and less than a hundred miles south of Canada, you have a pretty good idea of what a hard winter is like.

Chapter Four

Becoming Parents

One weekend when we were nearing the end of the pregnancy we traveled to visit our families in Williston. We thought we might not have a lot of time to visit them once we had the baby. We also did not think it would be wise to travel a lot with a baby during the winter. We had a great time visiting that weekend but unexpectedly Bette started to have abdominal pain. Mom had five children and Bette's mom had eight children. Our parents recognized immediately that the abdominal pain was the early onset of labor.

We took Bette to Mercy Hospital where Dr. Joe Craven confirmed our moms' conclusion Bette was in early labor. I wanted to jump in the car and bring Bette back to Minot to have our baby. Dr. Joe said he did not think that was the best decision. I thought he was really just supporting both of our moms who thought we should stay in Williston and have the baby where we would have ready parental and family support should we need it.

I was pretty obstinate, but our families won out and I guess I was just outvoted. Of course in retrospect, I was wrong to want to bring my 17 year old wife on a 120 mile drive all the while betting on something I knew nothing about. It was certainly good the wisdom of our parents won that battle. How long does it take to have a baby and what was I going to do when or if it happened on the highway between Williston and Minot?

Obviously, reasoning was not one of my strong points at that age. Terra was born several hours later on November 4, 1961. When I look back now and see what foolish decisions you are willing to make when you are young, it is such a blessing if you have parents around to steer you in the right direction. I shudder to think what it would have been like to grow up without parental guidance as many children do today. What a disadvantage and world of difficulty for these children.

It really seemed strange to me to see Terra in the nursery and realize I was now a father, time for me to grow up and put aside my childish ways. It was at this time I remembered a verse in The Holy Bible. It went something like this: *When I was a child, I spoke as a child, I understood as a child, I thought as a child; but when I became a man, I put away my childish ways.* Those were good words from 1 Corinthians 13:11. And no, I did not remember where that verse was from. I had to look it up.

It was beyond the shadow of a doubt my life was now forever changed. I would have to learn new responsibilities. This little carbon copy made by God would be in my life forever and it was up to me to teach her the same amount of love and respect for fellow man and self my parents had taught me.

Bette stayed in the hospital for five days and during that time there were no problems for her or our baby. We finally got to bundle Terra Lynn Redalen and make our way home to number 12 Wooden Barracks at Minot State College. We were back in school but Bette was taking a break from being a nurse's aide to be a mom. It was a learning experience for us. I think both Bette and I thought we were more skilled at being a nurse aide and lawn care person than parents. It is kind of amazing you go through your high school years and you really have no idea how to take care of a baby. Why on earth is she crying? Does she have a messy diaper? Is she hungry? Is she warm or too warm? Does she have pain? My gosh, if she could only talk a little bit it would be a lot easier. How warm does her bottle have to be? Oh yea, that's right. Our moms said it should not be so warm as to feel hot when you sprinkle a little of the warm milk on your forearm.

Why on earth for something this important do they not teach you a little bit in school about what you do with a brand new husband-wife relationship and a new baby? Williston High School, do you think you may have been failing some of your students? Surely it is important to learn something about the world we live in. I know it is also important to learn some math and science and perhaps how to communicate properly. After all, the brightest thoughts in the world are worth nothing if you cannot convey them to someone else.

What on earth does the hospital do for you at the time of your baby's birth? You would think they would at least pass out a motor manual for you. You get one when buying a car. Surely a baby is more important than that. Couldn't you get something like a handler's book? You get more information when you buy a puppy.

Having a baby caused us to enter an entirely new world of responsibility. Nothing in life will change you more than when you become a parent. It is no longer a me, me, me or I, I, I, world. There is now a little person in your life who is entirely reliant on you.

And let me tell you, having a baby does not gain you any accolades from your friends and classmates. As Jerry Pratt said one day to me in our little barracks apartment, "What is she good for? She's just a little blob of squirming protoplasm with a mess at one end and a squawk at the other. Why on earth would people want to have them?" I would have told him to ask his mom, but I am sure after a statement like that, she might have had second thoughts.

During my three years of school in Minot I tried to get some better paying jobs but most of them did not pan out. I applied for a job as a night clerk in a motel on the east side of Minot out near the fair grounds. The manager said it just would not work hiring me. He said I looked like I was just beginning high school. My youthful looks turned out to be a problem when I applied for jobs a number of times in life. I did not know it at this early stage but my youthful appearance would later cause credibility problems when I was practicing medicine and caring for people.

After my first year in Minot I was glad to see summer coming. I got a job working on the college grounds crew, which consisted mostly of what the name implies. We worked on the grounds keeping the grass mowed and the weeds pulled, etc. I really enjoyed it. It was almost like a vacation because I worked a forty hour work week and had a three month break from school. Mowing was a lot of fun. Often the girls who had stayed over for summer classes were laying out on the lawns tanning in their swimsuits. We just kept mowing smaller and smaller circles around them until they would finally get the message and move to a freshly mowed spot. We mowers did not mind how long the little flirts stayed.

As we neared the end of the second summer Bette and I managed to scrimp and save enough money to go to Glacier National Park. The three of us would visit my grandparents. Grandpa and Grandma Redalen, my dad's mom and dad lived just outside of Whitefish, Montana south of town toward Kalispell.

Glacier National Park was so named because the park was formed during the little ice age thousands of years before. In the current day many glaciers have been left behind to continue to do the work God planned for them to do.

We were broke but our thinking was we had to eat anyway so it did not change finances. We had a little pup tent to sleep in and the national parks at that time did not charge for camping. We could stay with my grandpa and grandma Redalen in Whitefish which is a beautiful little mountain town just west of Glacier Park. It is also at the base of what is now Big Mountain Ski Resort just north of town. The only expense was gasoline which was less than 40 cents a gallon at the time. Our ten day vacation was a really welcome respite for both of us.

We drove to Glacier on Highway 2, a two lane paved highway that was one of the most traveled highways passing through the northern part of Montana. Eastern Montana scenery is pretty monotonous. It consists mostly of flat land covered in either prairie sod and sage brush or green wheat and closer to harvest, golden wheat. There are some rolling hills but for the most part the land is flat and in many places where crops are not grown, grazing cattle and a few sheep can be seen. Most of the cattle raised in the Dakotas and Montana are brown and white Herefords. Those cattle seemed to be a hardier strain which could survive the bitter cold winter of those states. Montana was an open range state; ranchers and farmers were allowed to let their cattle roam. The cattle were branded so the ranchers would be able to separate their herds. This was done without the benefit of fences to avoid limiting them to one space. It was the responsibility of the drivers on the Montana roads to watch out for the cattle. If you hit someone's cow, you were the one at fault. Because of the dangers of killing someone's cattle at night the speed limits in Montana were strictly enforced at night. You drove 55 mph or you were ticketed. In the daytime you drove as fast as conditions would bear.

It always fascinated me that when you were driving toward the mountains in Western Montana you could see the Rocky Mountains from so far away. The first time you saw the mountains you would think you would be driving in them within an hour or so. But it was always several hours as the range is so massive, you could actually see it from hundreds of miles away.

When we got to Glacier we camped out at the Fish Creek and Apgar Campgrounds just west of Lake McDonald, a crystal clear icy cold mountain lake fed by the melting snow and glaciers that cap the peaks surrounding the lake. The lakes in Glacier Park are not lakes where you usually see people swimming. It was painful on the feet just to wade in them. The water is kept very cold by the constant thawing of the ice and snow off the mountain throughout the summer depending on snowfall the previous winter. The icy cold temperature of the lakes was only surpassed by the beauty of the water nestled between the bases of the towering mountains.

The mountain lakes are generally as smooth as glass as the mountains shield them from any winds or breezes. The lustrous shimmering colors of the mountains reflect back from the mirror of water in front of you. The water of many mountain lakes at a certain time of day is iridescent in color because as the glaciers move down the side of the mountain, they grind and pulverize the rock beneath to a fine powder form. This extremely fine ground rock ends up in the water and because the particles are so fine they remain floating in the water by the mechanism of Brownian movement. Here is your science lesson for the day. Brownian movement is what happens when microscopic particles of rock stay suspended in the water because they are constantly bumping into other rock particles along with bumping into the particles or molecules of water. When the sun shines on this magical shimmering suspension it gives the water its beautiful iridescent hues. When we see the beautiful changing opalescent and luminous colors of a mountain lake it is as though we are looking into the heart of the most beautiful gem stone. It is a sight never forgotten.

Although I have seen the glaciers gradually receding and becoming smaller over just the sixty years since I started watching the ice flows in Glacier National Park it is hard for me to imagine that much of this beauty may disappear when there are no longer glaciers. And without a doubt our glaciers are definitely disappearing. Are we even now with our present knowledge going to continue to diminish these places of beauty so our grandchildren will never see or experience them except to view a picture on the Internet or in an ancient picture album? Just how are we going to explain this to our grandchildren and our elders? Yes, we thought it was just a small fire in the garage. We did not think it would spread to our whole house with our family inside. Yes, I guess it is okay to kill your children, grandchildren and future generations as long as you do it with the intent to save the economy. I have never tried to quench my thirst with a glass of oil or gasoline but cannot imagine it tasting as good.

Our vacation was not long enough, but it was still nice to be home. We missed our little apartment. We had managed to survive on our meager savings. We were even able to afford two small carvings made with cottonwood bark. The wood carver was a somewhat grizzled man by the name of Kenyan Kaiser. He said the one carving was of a mountain man and the other carving was how he pictured himself if he were a fur trader from yesteryear. The one head had a Viking helmet with horns and the self-portrait so to speak looked like the fur trader he had imagined himself to be with a fur hat carved on his head. Those carvings hang in my living room today. I still think of those times and wonder how we managed to afford a couple of dollars for some art.

Now it was back to the grind of working and studying. Our time was almost entirely occupied with Bette and me working and me going to school full time. Bette continued to work as a nurse's aide at Mercy Hospital and together we managed to raise our family and continue on toward our goal.

Our biggest problems were our finances and we constantly had to charge meager amounts of food to a little family grocery store about half a block west of the married student housing. One day in the cold of winter we ran out of all food we could provide to Terra. We were both pretty scared because we thought we had charged all we possibly could and did not know what we were going to do. Finally, I took it upon myself to become a thief. I went to a laundromat where we always washed our clothes and stole enough pop bottles to sell to get a quart of milk. We thought this would keep us going until we were paid in a couple of days. It did keep Terra fed and it really did not matter if Bette and I had food.

Well it mattered, it was just not as critical as our baby going hungry.

My most enjoyable classes in college were anatomy, physiology and biology. Dr. Hoffman, who taught biology, had a lot of idiosyncrasies that made him very interesting and fun to listen to. You never knew quite what he was going to do. He might interrupt an entire class to catch a cricket he saw jumping among the seats. He would usually just put them in his pocket and go on lecturing to us. His tests were great. If you could explain how his questions could be interpreted in a way that meant our wrong answer was now correct, he would give you credit for the question. One cold windy day I met Dr. Hoffman walking with his top coat on backwards. I asked him why he was wearing his coat backwards. He said because the wind was coming from the front, he was warmer with the buttons in back. It kept the wind out.

Another day there was a knock at our door and Dr. Hoffman was standing there. I asked him how he was doing and he asked me if I would mind reading an article in a magazine and then come and talk to him to share my comments. The article was about young marriage. I guess we met the requirements. The author did not seem to have much of a grip or understanding about young marriage. And why would he? The author was an older person commenting on something he seemed to know very little about. I reported to Dr. Hoffman the following day and said I thought the author seemed to know very little about young marriage. Dr. Hoffman said he agreed and asked if I would write an article about young marriage from my perspective. I did this but never sent it in to see if I could publish it. Writing was not easy back in those days. If you did not have a typewriter, everything was done in longhand. The world has really sped up.

Biology under Dr. Hoffman continued to be one of my best subjects. Out of a class of a couple of hundred students I always managed to rank number one or two in the class. Sometimes an older married student would slide in front of me and it irked me quite a bit when that happened. Fortunately it did not happen often.

Although school continued to be pretty uneventful, I managed to make a foolish mistake in chemistry class one night. Because many of us could not get our experiments done during regular class hours we often worked in the lab at night. One night I began to wonder if it would be possible to melt salt or NaCl. I looked up the melting point and it was about 1500 degrees Fahrenheit. The softening point of PYREX, the glassware I would use to heat the salt in was just over 1500 degrees Fahrenheit. I thought with a couple Fisher Bunsen burners with their flames aimed to meet at one point, maybe enough heat could be generated to melt table salt. I started out with a small test tube about half full of salt and after heating it for several minutes it began to glow a molten red color and the volume kept getting smaller and smaller until the salt melted completely down to a volume of probably a couple of peas. I foolishly wanted to see what salt would look like when recrystallized rapidly in water. It seemed that perhaps it would not come out as little cubes again. One of my classmates got me a huge open PYREX beaker filled with tap water. I told everyone to look away when I poured the molten salt into the water. I got much more than I expected. The explosion was so loud people on the other end of the science building came running to see what had happened. I called out to several students scattered around the room asking if they could see. Everybody rapidly affirmed they were okay and then they came running to me. It appeared I had the most damage from the blast; my hands and arms were covered with dozens of cuts. I had blood streaming down both arms but no damage to my face. The other students had some welts on their chests from small pieces of glass flying through the air. A small hole was blasted through the plate glass window across the lab. My friends took me over to Roger Beyer's home and his wife Luanne, a nurse, cleaned and bandaged me up and I was as good as new.

I was good until the next day in chemistry class. Mr. Moore, our chemistry instructor, called me into his office. He simply asked me if it was safe to have students working unsupervised in the chemistry lab at night. I informed him it was completely safe and I had done something very foolish with completely unforeseen and unintended consequences. I reassured him it would never happen again. Then seeing my bandaged hands and arms, he asked me if I was all right and I assured him I was. Who would ever have thought a tiny pea sized piece of molten salt would completely disintegrate a large beaker full of water. We did not find any pieces of glass much larger than a sliver. We also could find no recrystallized salt so I never learned if salt recrystallized back into little cuboids the same as they presented prior to melting. I was just eternally thankful my stupidity had not blinded someone.

Mr. Moore was a great teacher. He drilled into his students never to trust our memories when it came to doses on important medications or making up critical solutions. He said, "Look it up every time. Do not trust your memory." I later found out Mr. Moore had identical twin sons who were now young boys.

When his twins were born, silver nitrate was still used to put in the eyes of newborns. This was to ward off opthalmia neonatorum, conjunctivitis of the newborn which is often caused by the bacteria that cause gonorrhea. Babies who had gonococcal conjunctivitis needed to be treated along with their mother and any sexual partners. When Mr. Moore's boys were born, the nurse who mixed the silver nitrate solution made an error and mixed the solution too strong. Mr. Moore's identical twin sons were blinded by that error. It was no wonder he was such a stickler on things. An error that affects two people's lives forever is far too grave an error to chance repeating. Mr. Moore was certainly attempting to instill the knowledge in us that would ensure none of his students would ever replicate that mistake. Mr. Moore was not the person who made his students aware of what had happened to his children. It was another professor in the chemistry department. It seemed to me, more credos to Mr. Moore. He did not lay his problems on the backs of his students. He did not use his life experiences to make us more aware of the importance of the world of chemistry some of us would be entering. I would later in life see what effect memory errors can play in the life of a child. A pediatric oncologist in Dubuque, Iowa wrongfully overdosed a young child one day resulting in the death of the child.

College chemistry set the stage for a remarkable set of events. We had a great and seemingly intelligent inorganic chemistry teacher by the name of Dr. M. who was really admired by most of us I believe. He had a swarthy look about him, was of average height and I imagine Middle Eastern in origin. One day in class, Dr. M. yelled at me and told me to come and sit down in the front of the class. All of the students including me were quite taken aback. I asked Dr. M. what was wrong; he said I was talking about him. I reassured him I was not but he was rather adamant and obviously not going to take no for an answer. Everything seemed to even out after that and there were no more incidents until one day a month or two later.

Dr. M. dove behind a sofa in the student union, shouting that people were shooting at him. Some medics came to take Dr. M. away and we never saw him again. It is amazing to me when I look back that Dr. M. was obviously a paranoid schizophrenic. When you are in college and a teenager, all you think or know is that something is wrong. You just don't know what.

In 1974 I would meet Dr. M. again in Bethesda Hospital in St. Paul, Minnesota. At this time I was teaching at the University of Minnesota. I was walking into the doctor's lounge on the first floor of Bethesda and I ran into Dr. M. in the hallway. I was surprised and exclaimed, "Dr. M., what are you doing here?" He replied he was applying for an orderly job available in the hospital. Although I asked if there was any way I could help him, I never saw Dr. M. again. It made me feel very badly and I realized this brilliant man had somehow fallen through any safety nets we may have had for our differently disabled people. I say differently disabled because the term mentally ill seems to place these people in a class of substandard stigmatized societal strata. I guess if this was today and I was politically correct, the correct term is differently abled although I personally do not care for this reference. Maybe this goes back to my dad with polio. I just never pictured him as anything but totally able.

As we approached the end of our junior year, Dick Zorn asked me one day if I cared to ride with him to the University of North Dakota in Grand Forks. Dick was making arrangements to continue his studies in chemical engineering. I thought, why not. I can check out the medical school while we are there and I can see what I need to do to gain admittance.

I really liked the campus of the University of North Dakota (UND). This is not to be confused with North Dakota State University which is located in Fargo. They were bitter sports rivalries. Imagine that! Dick did what he needed to do to continue with engineering and in a couple of years he would graduate from UND with his chemical engineering degree.

Later we walked down the halls of the School of Medicine. The doors on many of the rooms were open so we wandered inside to see what was going on. Classes were not in session. The most remarkable and memorable to me were the many jars filled with pathology specimens, especially a baby in formaldehyde. The specimens were in what looked like fluid filled jugs a gallon in size or perhaps larger. The baby in formaldehyde had a misshapen face and did not seem to have a brain. I would later learn this was an anencephalic monster. I thought it appropriately named. Some blackened lungs in another jar seemed to suggest many reasons not to smoke.

As Dick and I wandered down the halls we came to the Office of the Dean. The Dean of the Medical School, Dr. Theodore Harwood, was not in but the assistant dean, Dean Arneson was and the secretary said we could see him in a couple of minutes. As we waited we could hear a mechanical voice on the other side of Dean Arneson's door. In a few minutes a kindly gray haired elderly gentleman who spoke to us through a mechanical voice box he held against his neck came out to visit us. We later found out he had cancer of the larynx and this was now his way of communicating. We could understand him very well but the voice sounded as if it was from a machine which indeed it was.

Dr. Arneson asked what he could do for us. I said I wanted to apply to medical school the following year. Dr. Arneson said I was far behind and should have applied by now. Dr. Arneson had misunderstood and thought I wanted to get in for the coming class. He scurried around getting me the necessary application papers and said for me to get them filled out immediately and back the following week if I was to have any chance of entrance into the next class.

I asked Dr. Arneson about his assisted speech and he asked us if we wanted to try it out. He said you just hold it against the side of your mid neck on either side and then just talk but without saying anything. He said the device would pick up the muscle movement and change it into sound. It was amazing. Now Dick and I sounded just like Dean Arneson. Best imitation of someone I ever did.

A grocery store on the way out of Grand Forks had bananas for 10 cents a pound. Recognizing a great deal, I think we bought about twenty pounds. I am surprised we were not growing tails by the time we got back to Minot; we were pretty sick of bananas.

On arriving that evening, I let Bette know we were going to be applying to medical school the following year instead of the year after. Bette was excited about it and things were turning out the way we knew would be best. It would mean forgoing my Bachelor of Science Degree as I could not complete the science courses needed for major and minor. Chemistry was a minimum of four years with no way to shorten it.

Summer school was not available for chemistry or biology. If the worst happened and I was not accepted, it would not be so bad as we had not planned on applying to medical school until the following year.

I filled out my application forms and sent them in immediately. I thought this was a long shot as the University of North Dakota only accepted students with degrees and I had none, nor could I get one by the time I would be admitted to medical school. Again, I thought we had nothing to lose as it would cut down on a year of school if by some long shot I was admitted.

After one to two months passed I was asked to return to the University of North Dakota for an interview with the Board of Medical Examiners of the School of Medicine. It was an exciting letter to receive. I still thought it unlikely for me to get an admission slot. After all there were 44 positions available and over 2200 applications. With the application requirements, I thought it very likely if I were admitted I would probably be the youngest most in-experienced student in the class. Admission to the University of North Dakota School of Medicine was definitely competitive.

On the day of my interview in Grand Forks, I was called into a large board room where nine or ten distinguished gentlemen in suits were seated around a board table. I think I was too young and inexperienced to be apprehensive. Most of the questions were pretty much as you would expect and then there were some unexpected ones. Why do you want to become a doctor? Why did you get married so young? No surprise answer there. How are you working your way through college? Does your wife want you to be a physician? What are your reading materials? Do you subscribe to any magazines you read regularly? The answer to most of these questions requiring a yes or no was no. All of our money was spent trying to survive. The only regular reading was the study of college courses. They asked with some incredulity how someone taking as many hours as I was taking in the sciences was making adequate grades. I explained that with taking care of a baby, going to school full time and working full time I was in a hurry to finish school. They thanked me for my time and I returned to Minot State College. I told Bette about how the interview had gone and that I was content in the way I answered the board's questions. I guess when you are young and dumb, nothing gets in the way of your vision.

Evidently the board was pleased with my answers as I received a letter about one month later saying my admission to the medical school class starting in the fall of 1964 had been granted. It was exciting and it made us happy. Our first step along the path of life had been finished in the shortest time and manner for which we could have hoped. We were going to be leaving Minot State Teacher's College and heading to the University of North Dakota School of Medicine.

Chapter Five
University of North Dakota

Our next chore would be to find an apartment in Grand Forks, hopefully in the married student housing. As it turned out the University of North Dakota had housing available near the medical school, which made the task easy. They were barracks which had been used for internment of the Japanese during the war, just like the ones in Minot. I believe we were very fortunate in this regard. How wonderful can it be to live in barracks where fellow Americans had once been confined simply because they looked different than other Americans? If we still lived by this premise or principle today, we would not know which Somali or Arab we should lock up next. Excuse me, confine next. After all, they all look pretty much alike. Pardon my sarcasm.

Mom and Dad came in Dad's pickup one weekend and we loaded all of our life's worldly goods. Kind of hard to imagine having everything you own fit into the back of a rather small pickup. As you go along further in life you wish that was still the case. It was not long before we were unloading everything at our new home. It was great! Like having another new beginning. Heck, it actually was a new beginning.

The barracks were more than adequate for us. The heat came from an oil burning pot belly stove in the corner of the living room, right next to the kitchen. We were going to be living in number 10, Tennis Village, as it was called. It was not much different than number 12, Wooden Barracks at Minot State Teacher's College.

One difference was a Russian Thistle grew out of a crack in the floor at the south end of our couch. We watered it and took care of it as it was the only plant we had in our apartment. What a blessing. And no, in no way do I mean that facetiously about our apartment or our plant. It was definitely a blessing. Just think, another roof over our head. The price was going to be $36 per month. Seems like nothing, doesn't it. But when you fight to survive on a day to day basis no amount of payment or debt is inconsequential.

Going to school was only a burden when it came to finances. But, being able to go to school was another blessing. Since we had started college we found that a number of classmates had gotten married and many of them had progressed in life by getting whatever job they could find to support a young family.

The plant growing in the crack of our floor was not the only thing that made our apartment a bit different. Our refrigerator had a broken latch and we had to tie the refrigerator door shut with a rope wrapped around the refrigerator. At least you had to really want something to eat to take the rope off, so in one way it was a good dietary aid.

When school started after the end of the summer it was really exciting to be finally studying medicine. It seemed medical school came fairly easily for me after taking the enormous overloads in sciences at Minot. I think I was blessed that school was not difficult. I was the youngest guy in our class and the only student without a degree. We had one younger female. Some of my classmates had their masters and doctorates. One classmate, a Phi Beta Kappa in pharmacy, would later flunk out of school along with a friend who was a doctorate in microbiology. A number of really bright students would flunk out of the freshman class. I believe the thinking was the students who transferred from the University of North Dakota School of Medicine had to be better than anyone else in the country. There were only two, two year medical schools in the country. One was ours, the University of North Dakota School of Medicine and the other was Dartmouth.

Our students had to be good if the school was going to be able to continue transferring its students to other reputable medical schools. And good we would be. But one thought always crossed my mind; shouldn't a school with over two thousand applicants be able to pick a class that would not have a failure?

Even though school was not difficult, I realized I had to work a lot harder than some of my classmates. Many of them had already had embryology, microbiology and biochemistry, not to mention other classes to which I had yet to be exposed. I was definitely at a disadvantage. The only student in our class who was younger than me was a beautiful girl by the name of Gypsy Carpenter. Gypsy's real name was Herschel. Strange name for a girl but I am sure no one thought about it after meeting Gypsy.

I did not always get the best grades because I was often reading about what I thought was interesting and necessary for me to someday take care of patients. My thoughts did not always coincide with those of my instructors. After all, who cares how many capsomeres there are in the coat of an RNA virus, etc. A capsomere is the outer covering of protein that protects the genetic material of a virus. Who cares? One day when we were taking a test in microbiology, one of my classmates Ted Coonrod must have become exasperated because there was so much baloney in the test that he got up and began writing on the black board. The definition of microbiology is: biology dealing with minutia. With that written, Ted simply walked out. He didn't quit school, he simply quit the test.

Medical students are not bright. One day our classmate Bob Rude said he could not go up the stairs in the library because he became too short of breath. Bright as we were, we volunteered he was simply out of shape. A day or two later when Bob became acutely short of breath and was taken to the hospital we all found out he had a bleeding ulcer and had nearly bled out. Good thing he did not have us for his doctors.

One great thing that happened in our first year of medical school was our son Todd Jon was born. Todd was huge, weighing in at 9 lb. 10 oz. Dr. Nelson who delivered Todd joked with me he thought Todd might be able to walk out of the nursery. I was really proud.

Within a couple of days the joking came to an end. Todd became critically ill and developed Staphylococcal and Streptococcal septicemia, an infection in his blood. Todd was baptized while he was in the nursery while Bette and I looked through the glass. The pediatricians taking care of him said his condition was critical. We shed immense amounts of tears and prayed a lot. Every waking moment at least one of us was at the hospital. Todd survived and later left the hospital, seemingly with no residual problems.

Todd rapidly put on weight and became a chubby baby. He weighed thirty pounds when he was six months old. Our friends told us he would never be able to walk because of his weight, but at seven months Todd was walking around our small barracks apartment like a little Sumo wrestler.

Our problems and concerns with Todd were not over. One day when I got home from school, Bette informed me one side of Todd's body was growing faster than the other side. I said, "Don't be foolish." Bette said, "No, I am serious." We got Todd undressed and surely his leg on the right side was larger than the other. It was very subtle. When I looked closely it seemed as if both of his arms were the same size. On even closer examination it became obvious the right side of his face was barely perceptively larger. Bette took Todd to his pediatrician Dr. Schaefer the following day, who said Todd had a very rare disease called hemi-hypertrophy or hemi-atrophy depending on how you wanted to look at it. Either one side was growing faster, hemi-hypertrophy, or one side was growing slower, hemi-atrophy. It did not matter to us how you looked at it or what you called it, it was not good. Our pediatrician, knowing I was a medical student, got me the only journal article he could find. Upon reading the article, Bette and I cried many more tears. At that point in time there were only 23 known cases in the world and almost all of them were mentally retarded, had renal carcinomas and grew up badly deformed. There were innumerable other problems and nothing to give us a glimmer of hope. Dr. Schaefer said all we could do was wait and see what would happen. Gradually we got back to the regular life of school. Todd seemed to be doing fine and we realized continual worry would serve no good purpose.

In our sophomore year of medical school, we all got to take a trip to the Mayo Clinic. Located in the small town of Rochester in southern Minnesota, it is probably the most famous medical setting in the world. It was great to be shown around; what an amazing place it was. Computers consumed the space of an entire floor of a building back then. There are so many physicians and nurses in Rochester I think the children grow up thinking the garbage men are physicians. Children never realize garbage men have far better jobs than physicians.

I think the most memorable part of the trip was when we went to a bar and had drinks that night and mixed with the go-go dancers. Dr. Taylor, our usually staid neuroanatomy teacher, was actually dancing on top of one of the tables. He was dancing to "These Boots Are Made for Walking" by Nancy Sinatra. It was a great song and he made it even greater. Who on earth prior to that night ever realized Dr. Taylor had a personality. He was so serious in our neuro class the brains were treated as if they were still alive and thinking. He let everyone know exactly how serious he was about the treatment of someone's brain that had been graciously donated for us to study. The class following us had evidently not realized quite how serious Dr. Taylor was. They disposed of apple cores in the containers brains were kept in. Dr. Taylor flunked the entire class. In medical school at the University of North Dakota, if you flunked a class, you were automatically out of medical school for good. Dr. Taylor could not be convinced to change his mind and so the entire class had to find a neuroanatomy class they could take in the summer. It was a disaster for many of those students. Dr. Taylor would later take a neuro job in another school. I do not know if political consequences led to taking another job because he was a great professor, well respected.

After leaving the go-go bar that night we all went over to someone's apartment and continued to enjoy ourselves. Someone asked if I would put on a hypnosis show. Of course, I foolishly said yes. It seemed back then, I was always anxious to demonstrate my skills. I found an excellent subject and was doing the usual tricks to demonstrate hypnosis, simple things like having someone eat an onion or lemon like an apple.

During my act, someone jumped me from behind and started pummeling me. It was a classmate of mine, L. M. Paul Lundstrom, another classmate of mine pulled L. off me and asked him what on earth was wrong. L. started shouting at me and said I was messing with people's brains and had no idea what I was doing. That ended the hypnosis show for the evening. We returned to Grand Forks the following day and it was back to the books again. There was no rest for the wicked and none for us good guys either. The altercation with my classmate was forgotten and the incident never came up again.

Medical school was not all work. One day just before Christmas as we were studying for final exams, one of my friends Paul Habighorst asked me if I would hypnotize him so he could prepare better for his final exam. Most of my classmates knew I was a hypnotist. We always called Paul 'Hobby Horse' because of his last name. I was getting bored with studying and so I thought, why not. Max M., another classmate, had just told me he would love to have my study schedule. I guess he thought I never studied. I said "Sure Hobby, I can hypnotize you." Paul wanted me to give him a post-hypnotic suggestion that he would not be so tired, could study all night and remember most of what he read and studied. I am not entirely sure hypnosis works like that but everything is in our head anyway, right?

Hobby was an excellent subject. He entered the deepest stages of hypnosis very quickly. I suggested to him he would have the greatest night of studying he had ever had, he would be bright and alert and be able to study all night right up until test time. Then I got the idea that perhaps I should have a little fun at Hobby's expense. I suggested to Hobby before going up into the carrels to start studying he had to sell a whole truckload of red headed monkeys. He was to sell the red headed monkeys two for a nickel, shouting at the top of his lungs. I also suggested he would not leave until he had sold all the monkeys which would all be sold by the time he finished his second trip around the library. I told him when he completed his second trip he would wake up, remember nothing, go up into the library to study and have the best night of studying he had ever had.

The greatest things about the deepest stages of hypnosis are the person hypnotized absolutely sees and hears everything you have suggested. Hobby was great. He was grabbing little monkeys off his shoulders and out of his truck. He would absolutely not give up until someone handed him a nickel and relieved him of a couple of his monkeys. Since everyone was studying for finals, the library was filled with medical students and student nurses. They did not know what was going on but many of them took the cue, gave Hobby a nickel and pretended to take the monkeys. Who on earth would not want to buy two cute little red headed monkeys at bargain prices like that.

The following day Paul came up to me and thanked me profusely for my help. He said he was sure he aced our test, he had studied all night and was completely alert for the entire test. I said, "You're welcome. I am happy for you." I was actually happier for myself. I was thankful no one had asked him about the red headed monkeys.

It was great to go home for Christmas with our families. My problem was not with being home. It would come when I got back to school. As I was walking down the main hallway at school one day I realized Hobby had spotted me from the other end of the building. He came running at me like a freight train only he had more steam coming out of his ears than a steam engine. He pulled up when he reached me, grabbed me by the neck of my shirt and shouted, "What did you do to me?" I said, "What do you mean, Hobby?" He said, "You know what I mean." I suggested he should be happy he did so well on his test. I also suggested he now had a little more change in his pocket and it was really newly found money. That did not seem to assuage Paul's feelings and he walked away mad. However I think he eventually got over it, just not enough to ask me to help him with any more studies.

I managed to keep having fun while in school. One night I got the optimistic idea to wake everyone up a bit. I dropped an M-80 down the elevator shaft of the library. M-80s are large firecrackers sometimes called salutes. My heavens, was that a bad idea. It sounded as if a good portion of the school had blown up. Law students came pouring out by the dozens from the law school across the street to see what was wrong. They all thought there had been a huge explosion in the medical school. I had been up on the top floor of the library when I dropped the M-80 and feigned innocence. What stupidity on my part. It was especially not funny when I found out that a few years previously someone had put an Erlenmeyer Flask of ether in the refrigerator and forgot to cork it. Needless to say, when the fridge filled up with ether fumes and a spark happened or the refrigerator began running, it blew the front door off the fridge and through a brick wall in the lab. No one in the school ever found out what caused the big explosion that night and I certainly never told anyone.

As spring rolled around again I was, as usual, looking for some diversion from studies. I went out and bought a bunch of balloons and talked a couple of my classmates into going out on top of the medical school and chucking water balloons at convertibles that drove by the College of Law. We filled a basket with water filled balloons and proceeded to the roof. One of the problems of getting out on the roof was we had to walk through the dog lab. There was just no quiet way to walk through a dog kennel. Although we thought everyone in the building could probably hear the commotion we proceeded with the plan. Once on the roof we began to target people on the sidewalk three stories below. We were having fun watching students dance; then I suddenly yelled, "Stop!" Dr. Erickson from the science building next door was walking below but it was too late to pull the balloons back. We ran back through the commotion of the dog lab and walked back to our studies trying to look sincere and studious.

Summer in Tennis Village was fun. We got a croquet league going and played croquet every night. We had a little straw hat we passed around that said Tennis Village Croquet Champion on the front. The winner wore that home every night. On the weekends we sometimes would organize a Tennis Village barbecue and beer weekend. One of our neighbors worked in the rehab center right behind Tennis Village. When I mentioned Tennis Village was behind the medical school, it would have been more accurate to say Tennis Village was right behind the rehab center and the school was the next building to the east.

One night our rehab nurse neighbor thought it would be a good idea to bring some of the kids over from the rehab center so they could party with us and get a break from their everyday lives. We brought five kids over in their wheel chairs. All of these kids were in their early twenties or late teens, about the same ages as most of us. All of them were paraplegics with their catheters in and the collection bags hanging on the side of their wheelchairs. We spent a lot of time emptying out those catheter bags and when we did not catch them soon enough we had some overflows. That was a minor problem.

We were all dancing and having a great time. One of the little gals was an eighteen year old who had been paralyzed a year earlier when caught in a tornado while working at the Minot Drive-In Theater. Her name was Joan. A couple hours into our party Joan told me the one thing she would miss from her paralysis was that she would never dance again. Joan was a slightly built beautiful young lady. I told her that was not true and then asked her to dance.

I checked with our neighbor first to make sure I could not do any damage. I was reassured that there was no damage I could do by holding Joan next to me and dancing. Then I bent down and grabbed Joan around the waist, grabbed her catheter bag and we danced and twirled around the yard for several dances. She was laughing and giggling like a typical high school girl and said this was the most fun she'd had since her accident. This was not a young lady who was ever going to allow a disability to get in her way. She had a vivacious, bubbly, sparkling personality. She was someone who, had I met her at any time in my single life and hers, after her accident, I would have been proud to call my girlfriend or my wife. She was going to be a good catch for some lucky young man one day.

I am sure our dancing put a bigger smile on my face than on Joan's. What a pleasure for me. It was a magnificent evening and the young people had a wonderful time. All of them seemed to be completely lost and caught up in our festivities. It got them temporarily away from their hospital setting and made them feel as though they were human and they still had a wonderful life ahead of them. It helped show them they were not going to miss out on a beat of life or one measure of happiness simply because of a disability. I thought of Dad.

Don't take that wrong. It is very discouraging to work and work toward goals in rehab and not really see anything is being accomplished. It often took months of preparation and hard work to accomplish small everyday tasks that had always been taken for granted before their injury. That is sometimes difficult to remember when your entire life has been changed by an accident. Your spirit and essence has been changed. It is always necessary to find our purpose for being, maintain it and recall that nothing has changed regarding our main purpose.

Later that night a little further into the party, Bette was becoming nauseated. Then she started throwing up. She said the world was starting to spin around and it was making her sick. I guess that was understandable as neither of us were really drinkers. One of the older married students told me to take Bette home. He told her to lie down on the bed, hang one leg out of the bed and keep it touching the floor so the world would quit spinning. That didn't make much sense to me as the world was not really spinning and your foot touching the floor wasn't likely to stop anything from spinning. However, I had no better ideas so that is what she did. It seemed to help. Bette quit vomiting and fell asleep none the worse for wear.

The parties at Tennis Village were a lot of fun. Most of them weren't drinking parties and more of them were croquet. I think our next door neighbors wished all of them were croquet. Every once in a while someone would get the urge to have a party at night and it simply was not safe to stay home. Almost invariably something would happen to the 'sticks in the mud'. One night when our village had tried getting the neighbors up who lived just next door to us, we just couldn't get them to come out regardless of all the noise we made. They were a Korean war veteran and his wife much the same as our neighbors in Minot had been. Then I had a bright idea how to wake them up. I would get up on top of the roof and drop one of my M-80 salutes down into their oil burner. We had already been partying for a little bit and as usual, drinking and good ideas usually do not come in tandem. I dropped the salute down into their potbellied oil burner. It sounded much like the explosion I created in the chemistry lab with my little salt experiment. We all found out the following day the explosive had blown the front door off their oil burner and all of the soot from inside the stove was now deposited every place it was not supposed to be. I felt badly but wanting to stay anonymous, did not volunteer to clean up.

Often after the end of the school day, my buddy Phil Johnson and I would get in a game of handball. Phil was quite a bit bigger than me but we had some really competitive games and were quite evenly matched. During a game one night I followed through with a strong forehand shot and as my right arm followed though, Phil was coming forward on my left and I hit him squarely and solidly on the nose. The crunch of breaking bone was audible. Phil's nose began gushing blood and shortly the front of his tee-shirt was covered. It stopped gushing almost as soon as it had started. Phil walked over to the corner of the court to get his keys and balls. I asked, "What are you doing?" Phil replied, "You broke my nose." I said, "You big pussy, it's just a broken nose. Get back here and finish the game." When we finished the game I took Phil to the hospital emergency room where one of the ENT men came in and saw him. His surgery the following morning took over an hour so I guess it was a little more broken than I thought it was. It was crooked and swollen but the surgeon got the kinks straightened out.

School continued rather uneventfully until I ran into a little bit of a snag. Three of my pathology professors, Dr. Wasdahl, Dr. Iverson and Dr. Pilot were always playing chess. I became interested in the game, shortly thereafter more fascinated and finally quite obsessed. It soon seemed I was playing a game of chess every chance I had. It is probably not good to take up games like that when you have an obsessive-compulsive personality as I think I did. It really became a compulsion of mine. Unfortunately when I went to bed at night, I would begin replaying games in my head and changing moves; it seemed as if I were continually watching a movie of the games played that day. Now if I had just made this move instead of that move, I would have ended up here, etc. etc. Dr. Wasdahl started keeping more of an eye on me and asking me if I had my pathology down. I always replied I had it cold. Then the night before a big pathology test a couple of friends asked me to go to East Grand Forks with them. We went into a bar and for the first time in my life, I had a couple drinks at my buddy's insistence. I believe it was only two drinks. I just was not used to drinking and got sick and felt the same the next day when it was time to take our final pathology test. I got there about one hour late for a four hour test and left after another hour. I went home and threw up. I felt miserable.

The following day, Dr. Wasdahl knew how to make me feel worse. He saw me the length of the hall and yelled at me. Then he unloaded on me and said if I ever pulled a shenanigan like that again, I could forget about ever becoming a doctor. He blamed it on playing chess all the time. He did not realize I was sick from drinking the night before. I did not think it had anything to do with playing chess all the time. I did not give him that excuse however because Dr. Wasdahl would have probably given me a 'D' on my test rather than the 'C' grade I got (down from the 'A' grade I had planned on). At least the 'C' grade allowed me to stay in school and I had dodged another mishap, be it somewhat miraculously and ungraciously.

Many of our classes offered a little humor. One day our internal medicine class was having a question and answer session. The class was taught by the former President of the American Diabetes Association, Dr. Ed Haunz, kind of a stern elderly, no-nonsense kind of guy. Classmate Jim Creighton was a mountain man kind of guy from western Montana. Jim looked a little bit like Bluto in the Popeye comics. By that I mean it looked as if Jim hadn't shaved for days about a second after he was done shaving. Dr. Haunz said, "Mr. Creighton, how many unknown diabetics are there in the United States?" Jim said, "If they are unknown, I guess you really wouldn't know, would you?" Wrong answer. Everyone in the classroom burst out laughing except Dr. Haunz who became quite angry. He said, "Mr. Creighton, I expect a serious answer when I ask a serious question." Dr. Haunz then went on with his lecture.

One day during a urology lecture, the professor was trying to get across how much dripping following urination was normal. He said, "No matter how many times you shake it the last three drops are always going to go into your pants." There was a little nervous laughter. It didn't take much to make young medical students squirm a little.

An internist once impressed on us to be objective and not to let personal opinions get in the way of good care. He said at one time early in his training he had this angelic, little blonde girl come in with abdominal pain. Because he could imagine her being the daughter of a preacher, he decided to defer a pelvic exam because of her angelic, youthful nature. Later that evening he was making rounds and through the cracked door of his patient's room he could see two young men in sailor uniforms sitting on her bed comfortably, visiting with her. The following morning he immediately scheduled his angelic young patient for a pelvic exam. On getting her up in the stirrups, the very first thing he saw standing out in big bold letters were the words Baby Doll, tattooed in bright big letters across her bottom. Angelic little baby doll had gonorrhea. That was the last time he did not perform a pelvic exam on a patient with abdominal pain.

Teaching with anecdotes by some of our professors made more of an impression than reading textbooks. For me it did.

Life continued. Todd seemed to be losing a little of the physical disparity in his face and legs as he began to stretch out and grow taller while maintaining his weight. Body symmetry seemed to be returning. Todd actually maintained his weight over the next three years so he was growing up to be a tall slender little boy rather than the short fat porker he had been. Nobody ever seemed to notice anything wrong with Todd and we soon forgot about the mental retardation part of the equation. Todd was bright as a whip. It seemed as though everything we had worried about was for naught. Isn't that about the way most worries go?

Among all of the other things going on Terra started having trouble focusing both of her eyes on one point. Terra Lynn had developed amblyopia and strabismus. The ophthalmologist we took her to said she needed a bilateral lateral rectus recession. In other words, she needed surgery to correct crossed eyes. One of the most common causes of this is a weakness in one eye. The brain does not get used to perceiving the signals appropriately. When Terra was going to have surgery, one of our friends asked her what was wrong with her eye and why she was having surgery. Terra calmly replied, "I have amblyopia. That means lazy eye." We had no idea Terra knew what the term amblyopia meant. When we asked her how she knew, she said, "I saw it on TV and knew that is what I had." Out of the mouths of babes. I do not recall how we paid for healthcare back in those days. I do know we could not afford insurance so I think the doctors always took care of the medical students gratuitously. What a change these days are!

Chapter Six

Summer then School

As my freshman summer rolled around I seriously needed a good job so we could maintain. The first job was with Allied Van Lines, moving furniture from homes into trucks. It was always a bunch of older guys yelling, "Hey kid, bring that couch out and put it in the front of the truck." It was astonishing to me the loads they thought you could move all by yourself while they sat and yelled instructions. It was no wonder they needed young strong backs on these crews. After a week, I realized this was not going to be a satisfying summer job. Actually, I knew after the first couple hours of work.

One thing I learned was whenever they went into a home for the first time, the first thing they did was make a beeline for the furniture likely to collect change when people were sitting. They treated this as finders, keepers. It didn't matter how much money they found in the movee's furniture; they stuffed it in their pockets and started yelling again. "Hey kid, get a move on. We ain't got all day."

I then applied for a job as a sign painter. After all, I could paint and how hard could it be to paint a sign. The owner of the sign painting company said to lay out a sign he needed to paint and if he liked my work when he came back a couple of hours later, I was hired. I laid the drawing of the sign out just fine and was quite satisfied with the lettering I laid out and my work. The problem was that when I was painting, some of the lettering was not straight enough. Try as I might, they just kept looking worse. In embarrassment, I left the sign painting premises and did not stick around for the criticism. The gentlemanly thing to do would have been to stick around and apologize for messing up his sign board.

The next job I applied for was at a civil engineering firm which was asking for a draftsman. I got a job doing drafting at the Richmond Engineering Firm. I told them a lie and said I had two years of college drafting. I had some drafting in high school and had done very well and I thought I could do it for a civil engineering firm. Richmond Engineering said they would give me a try.

As it turned out there was a school of engineering right out the front door of Tennis Village and every night there were engineering students working late. I went over to the College of Engineering as soon as I got the job, talked to some of the engineering students, told them what I had done and that I had fabricated my credentials. The engineering students laughed and said, "No problem. Anything you think you are going to have a problem with, bring it to us and we'll talk you through it and give you the information you need to remain on the job." I breathed a sigh of relief.

At the end of each work day, I always asked Mr. Richmond and his son Boots what I was going to be doing the next day. They would tell me and I would run over after work to the engineering school and run it by the students. They got a kick out of what I was doing and were always eager to help me. A couple of times I thought for sure I was in way over my head but they always reassured me it was a piece of cake. They always sat me down at a drafting table so it was like going to drafting school every night. They were an immense help. It was a gigantic, free engineering education from young dedicated student instructors eager to show off their skills.

One night as I was finding out my assignments for the next day Mr. Richmond asked me, "Rick, why do you always ask what you are going to be doing tomorrow?" I replied, "Well I haven't done any drafting for a couple years so I always want to brush up at night so I don't disappoint you." He smiled and seemed satisfied with my answer and even pleased I would think that much of my job. Heck, the job meant the world to me and I was just trying to keep it. After my furniture moving job, this was a job from heaven.

One night when I asked about my job for tomorrow, I became pretty worried. They asked me to lay out a parking lot, help with a little surveying and from all the elevations figure out the amount of land that needed to be removed from one area and filled into another. My God! Since when did draftsmen do that? What I thought to be a prodigious problem, the engineering students got a laugh from. Another piece of cake for them. They rapidly set my mind at ease. I learned how to run a transit, a small tripod mounted telescope for measuring horizontal and vertical angles, and they taught me the math needed to figure out the earth removal. After the engineering students explained this to me it really seemed relatively simple compared to what I had conjured up in my mind. Everything went by without a hitch or problem again. I was finally starting to feel very secure in this job. I realized with the school of engineering behind me, there was probably not going to be a problem they could not help me solve.

I went from doing parking lots and regular drafting to begin drafting plans for homes. I started asking the Richmonds if I could take these plans home at night to show my wife. I was really proud of my work. I knew had I really been in a college drafting course or taking drafting in engineering I would be getting 'A's. Bette reinforced my pride by giving me compliments on my drafting. A lot of the home plans were done for an addition in a newer part of town in the southeast part of Grand Forks called the Olson Addition. One of the weekend exercises we could afford was to drive around and look at some of the homes that were being built. We always kept our dreams alive by saying, "Someday we are going to live in a home like that." For sure, we couldn't walk into our own home yet, but we could open the doors to our dream and walk around there. Dreams are the sustenance of our minds. As long as we can dream we can be wherever we choose to be regardless of our circumstances.

During that summer Bette and I became friends with Boots and Bianca Richmond. Boots was a civil engineer like his father. Bianca, his wife, was from South America. We did some outdoor grilling and got an education from Bianca about what it was like growing up in Brazil. It was at this time in my life I began to be a little skeptical of our American newspapers.

In about March of 1965 American troops were sent to South Vietnam. It seemed to be another one of those "good" wars the United States would become involved in because the South Vietnamese were no longer able to maintain their positions in their fight against the North Vietnamese. The North Vietnamese were supported by the communist countries of China and Russia whereas the South Vietnamese were supported by the United States. We, the United States, had provided aid and advice to the South since the Fifties so we were not about to let the South be overrun by the North. Our cold war proxy fight was now going to escalate to soldiers on the ground.

When I say I began to distrust American newspapers, the reason was because of enemy deaths recorded in our newspapers. Boots and Bianca had maintained South American newspaper subscriptions and it seemed as if the South American newspaper accounts of battles never coincided with American newspapers. An exaggerated example might be another battle in Vietnam and another one sided victory, with one hundred enemy casualties and no American casualties. This never seemed to make much sense. How do Americans go into jungles they are not familiar with and fight enemies on their enemies' home turf and we do well and the enemy does poorly? I began to ask Boots to compare newspapers with me regarding the same battles. It seemed more parity was reported between battles when newspapers from South America were doing the reporting. The South American papers read more like I would have thought true accounts would read. Either our papers were wrong, biased, inadequate or just reporting what the American government wanted us to know.

After all the war in Vietnam was not exactly a popular war with the American people. As time went on the American government would soon find out just how angry the American people were against this seemingly ill thought out war. Imagine that! America having an ill thought out war. It is probably good for us to have all these wars to develop this valuable history to learn from so we will not repeat the same mistakes.

The valuable thing we learn from history is … we learn nothing from history. And after mapping out what all of the unintended consequences will be, we find out the unintended consequences are much more massive than we could possibly have imagined or conceived. Imagine that will you, something our government hasn't thought of. How could that be?

Boots, Bianca and Bette and I continued to associate with each other during that summer and I began to play a little handball against Boots. Boots was shorter than me and a little portly. I thought it unlikely he would be a huge challenge. Wrong. Boots pretty much destroyed me in handball. I decided wrongly that perhaps I could get even on the tennis court. Before playing tennis against Boots, I asked Mr. Richmond if Boots was any good in tennis. He informed me Boots had been the NCAA singles champion for two years. I still tried to get some games scheduled against Boots but we never managed to play. I'm sure I did not try hard enough. After all, the human mind can stand just so much humiliation. When I ask God to teach me humility, I always add, please do this without making me humble.

Soon summer was over and it was time to go back to school. Summer had been fun doing a job I really liked with people who were anxious to teach and seemed to like me. Some of the engineering students said they would miss our tutoring sessions. I thanked them profusely. At the end of the summer, the Richmonds asked me if I would consider quitting school and becoming a full-time draftsman for them. They offered me what I considered a huge salary at the time but I declined and said I was going to be a physician. Art, one of the draftsmen I had worked with through the summer, reaffirmed I had made the right decision. He had been in a similar situation and said in retrospect, he should have completed his education. It would have opened more doors and avenues in business and life to him. I asked Art why he didn't just go back to school. He replied, "Being married with children, it just would not be easy." Art stayed where he was.

The sophomore year of medical school was a lot more fun than the first. We were studying courses that seemed as if they might actually lead to taking care of patients. Pathology, the study of human diseases, was especially enjoyable. It was in this class we would begin to examine a lot of the pathology specimens Dick Zorn and I had observed while wandering through some of the rooms of the mostly empty medical school when we visited. We spent a lot of time looking at slides of pathology specimens. It was during this time we learned what normal tissue looked like. After all, if you do not know what normal is how on earth you will ever spot abnormal?

I learned one really astonishing fact during the study of pathology slides. When I mentioned it to one of our instructors, he said he had never heard of my observation. What I discovered was that while looking through my monocular microscope, I could memorize the slides much more rapidly if I looked through my left eye rather than my right eye. My instructors did not know why this would be but I surmised the myelin highway I had built up on one side must be more developed than the other.

When I would think of this many years later, I remembered I had been hit in the right eye with a thrown dirtball when I was about five years old. That eye had filled with blood; I spent more than a week in bed and had to sit up all the time. I could not see out of that eye at the time and there was no treatment so we had to let nature take its course. My ophthalmologist was Dr. Earl Korsmo. I do not remember if he reassured me that worst case scenario, I would only be blind in one eye. I regained my vision and there were seemingly no further complications. The blood resolved completely.

With several months of school left it was time to begin deciding where we wanted to go for our final two years of medical school. One of my classmates John Wahl and I decided we wanted to be in family medicine and we decided the best school was the University of Nebraska. Our reasoning was a Midwestern medical school would probably expose us to the education needed to obtain our goals. We heard back from the Dean's Office relatively soon that we had both been accepted and would enter the junior year of the medical school class that would graduate in 1968. Class of 68, just imagine, doesn't that sound good? Bette and I were elated. Two more years of our lives were mostly mapped out and the path to completion was within sight.

A preceptorship was required toward the end of our second year. We all got to go to a rural hospital to work with one of the local practitioners for exposure to medicine outside of a university setting. My classmate Phil Johnson and I decided we would go to Williston, North Dakota. I thought how great is this, getting to spend three months in my home town while satisfying my elective for school. I am not sure how it worked but Phil and I were assigned to work with Dr. Robert Koch, a family practitioner in his mid-thirties. Dr. Koch had started medical school a little later in life and had not been out of school that long. He was kind of gruff but really well liked and a great instructor for Phil and me.

I remember very well one of the first patients I was asked to work up was a woman in her mid-forties who was having some shortness of breath. It was from her I learned of my great gifts in medicine and to examine your entire patient. When I turned in my handwritten history and physical exam on my patient, Dr. Koch immediately noticed I had not done a breast exam. That was embarrassing. The only breast exam I had ever done had been on Bette and I guess you could not really call fondling an exam. I said, "I do not know how to do that," but subconsciously thought I was probably pretty good at it. Dr. Koch lectured me, "If you do not know how to do something you ask. You do not neglect your patient because of your lack of knowledge." The lesson was learned and never forgotten. As we neared the end of our question and answer session, he finally asked me why my patient was short of breath. I explained she had a previously undetected atrial septal defect and was developing a right to left shunt, no longer adequately supplying her cardiac needs. Dr. Koch looked at me somewhat incredulously and said, "Rick, do you really think a sophomore medical student is going to diagnose something like an atrial septal defect when she has been seen by multiple doctors and they have not found it?"

I admitted it seemed unlikely. In actuality, I knew nothing about atrial septal defects but I definitely knew my patient had one. At the time I did not know myself or the Lord well enough to give credit where it was due. He then said, "Now what would you think the correct diagnosis might be." I replied, "She as an atrial septal defect."

Dr. Koch said, "Rick if you hear hoof beats outside the hospital right now and you run out to look, what do you think you are going to see?" I replied, "Horses." Dr. Koch said, "Exactly! You are not going to see zebras." I understood what he was telling me. Dr. Koch then said, "Follow me." He led me down to radiologist Dr. Bob Olson's office and said, "Bob, will you pull the chest x-ray on Mrs. Johnson and tell this young student what you see? This young man thinks this patient has an atrial septal defect." Dr. Olson pointed out all the findings on the chest x-ray and said this patient has no signs of an atrial septal defect and no signs of right to left shunt.

Once again, Dr. Koch said, "Now, follow me." We found Dr. Joe Craven. He said, "Dr. Joe, this young man thinks your patient whom you have seen for years has an atrial septal defect causing her problems. Will you explain to him why she does not?" Dr. Joe, as everyone including his patients called him, listed a raft of reasons why I was wrong. Finally, as we walked away Dr. Koch asked me again what was wrong. I replied, "She has an atrial septal defect." A day later I even attached a stethoscope to an NG tube and tried listening to her heart through the esophagus and stomach so I would be listening closer to the defect. I had never heard of anyone doing this but it seemed reasonable to me. All I heard were normal heart sounds.

Over the next couple of days my patient continued to become more short of breath and was decompensating. She was going into mild failure and we still did not know what was wrong. Dr. Koch told me they were transferring her to the University of Minnesota School of Medicine.

About three days later I was studying in the doctor's lounge. Dr. Koch told me my patient had expired at the U of M. She died on the operating room table with an uncorrected and previously undiagnosed atrial septal defect. That is all Dr. Koch said. He walked out without saying another word. I never heard another word about Mrs. Johnson.

I am sure the physicians involved had conferred and wondered why I had been so adamant about the diagnosis and why I had been right about it. Had they asked me, I would not have been able to give a reason why I knew. I just knew with unwavering faith I was correct.

I couldn't quite figure things out at that point in my life. I attributed everything to being smart. I hadn't figured out that being gifted and being smart were on opposite sides of the world. I would find out later in life I would never fully understand the unimaginable gifts I was given. I finally accepted the gifts and would gradually learn to give credit to Him, as was due.

Another day I was sitting in the radiology office of Dr. Bob Olson while he was going over x-rays, providing educational points as he went. He put up a chest x-ray and said this is an elderly patient on the floor and you can see the subtle enlargement of the mediastinum right here. This patient almost certainly has a bronchogenic carcinoma. I thought I saw the name on the x-ray and it appeared to be Harvey Larson. I asked Dr. Olson and he confirmed it was. Dr. Joe Craven was also in the room and taking care of Harvey. I asked him if Mr. Larson knew what he had yet and Dr. Craven said, "No because we needed to do a bronchoscopy yet to get a definitive cytological exam for confirmation." Then he asked, "Why, Rick?" I replied that Harvey Larson was my wife's grandpa and everyone was worrying about what was going on with him. Dr. Craven reassured me he would let everyone know as soon as he was positive. Franky McCoy, our pathologist, let me know but I kept the information to myself and a couple of days later Harvey Larson and the rest of the family knew Harvey had cancer of the lung. The five year survival rate for cancer of the lung was about five percent so it was very unlikely Harvey would overcome this problem. Harvey was in his late seventies and had lived a long satisfying life. We would soon need to find one more bridge partner.

I had a few physicians who would occasionally look at my work and offer criticism. One of those physicians was an elderly family practitioner by the name of Dr. Wright. He sternly tore apart a history and physical I had turned out on one of his patients. Granted it was long and descriptive but was written in longhand and was like what was expected from us at the University of Nebraska. Dr. Wright asked me, "What on earth do you need all these five and ten dollar words for? Use plain English. Who knows what dyspnea is? Just say the patient is short of breath. Why say orthopnea? Just say your patient is short of breath when lying down. And so forth and so on."

I told this story to my dad who explained Dr. Wright is one of those old time doctors who is still very much respected. He also informed me Dr. Wright had been the president of the American Medical Association a few years back. Dad also told me Dr. Wright had taken out his tonsils years ago right in the office. That would be unheard of now. Dad sat in a chair and Dr. Wright sat in his lap facing Dad. He injected a local anesthetic and promptly removed the tonsils. Dad said he did fine and left the office a little later none the worse for wear. I couldn't imagine such a thing but old time doctors made do with the facilities and equipment they had.

Dr. Koch asked me to follow him out to a sunlit atrium on the second or third floor one day. The atrium faced the south and east and sunlight was streaming into the room. Dr. Koch introduced me to a patient half sitting and half lying in a chair. He was reading the newspaper and turning it with a stick about two to three feet long using only his right thumb and index finger. I suddenly realized the person appeared to be frozen in one spot. The only other movement were his eyes. Not even his chest cage moved for breathing.

Dr. Koch said, "Rick, take a good look at this man as this is probably the last person you will see in your life with this rare condition. He has the disease called osteogenesis imperfecta progressiva universalis." The condition had left this man's body one entire piece of bone. He let me knock on his chest and it was like knocking on a piece of wood. His arms and legs were hard like a piece of bone with skin over it. I said goodbye.

Dr. Koch then took me down to radiology; we pulled the x-rays and looked at them. It was as though you were looking at a body made of bone with occasional places that had retained some muscle. The only thing keeping this patient alive was the fact his diaphragm still worked. The retention of this lifesaving muscle allowed him to breathe. I couldn't imagine a lot of things worse than to have your mind trapped in this boney cage. Following our introduction, I would periodically stop in to say hi to help him pass the time of day. He seemed to enjoy my company.

My preceptorship in Williston continued to be a learning experience for me and Dr. Koch was an excellent instructor. Dr. Bob and his wife Mary Ann had our family over to their home several times. We got to be good friends. I was going to miss this great tutor when we left Williston. Phil and I had managed to squeeze in some tennis over the summer too, so it had not been all work.

As we neared the end of our second year of medical school in Grand Forks, I became aware of a scholarship available from the American College of Anesthesiology. The scholarship would fill up the entire summer between the University of North Dakota and the University of Nebraska. It was exactly what we were looking for. I applied for and was awarded a scholarship. I was thrilled to find out I would be working under Dr. Ed Huestad, an anesthesiologist who worked out of Lutheran Deaconess on the south side of Minneapolis.

What the scholarship did was provide a meager living for Bette, our children and me and additional instruction that would later become invaluable. Bette and I asked my mom and dad if we could stay with them for the summer. They said they would be happy to have us.

Dad and Mom had bought a farm just north of Princeton, Minnesota. And once more Dad and Mom loaded up their pickup with our meager belongings and moved us into a nice basement bedroom they had for us in rural Minnesota. The countryside was green and beautiful. Dad and Mom had bought 160 acres of tiled farm land. Tiled farm land has drainage pipes under it so it is constantly green although not submersed in water. What the tiling does is remove the subsurface water from the land so it is usable. Too much subsurface water prevents root development and in general is not good for growing crops.

Dad and Mom had sacrificed all they owned to buy this land. Dad sold a very lucrative radio and television repair shop in Williston to raise the money. The entire purpose of uprooting their family and removing my little sisters from their friends was to provide a means to keep Ron from going to Vietnam. In those days of the draft, one remaining son on the family farm would be exempted from the draft. That was a bad plan as my brother thought mainly about himself in those days and the immense numbers of problems he had in high school followed him right along. In 1966 he enlisted in the army to go to Vietnam. Dad and Mom's sacrifice had been for naught for an ungrateful son.

The first summer there Dad decided they would plant all of the land into cucumbers. It was a back breaking job but all the cucumbers got planted with everyone in the family pitching in.

I showed up at Lutheran Deaconess Hospital the first Monday after Bette, our children and I had arrived. Dr. Ed Huestad was a great guy and I realized immediately he was going to be fun to work with. The staff at the hospital was wonderful and I was going to be exposed to immense amounts of surgery.

After I had worked a couple of days I received a call from the Dean's Office at the University of Nebraska to submit my national board scores as soon as I received them. I was dumbstruck. I told them I had not even applied to take the national boards as they had said they were not necessary for my admission to Nebraska. They apologized and said now they had decided all students had to take them. They did say they would pull whatever strings necessary for me to take the boards as now the timeline had passed to even be able to sign up to take the exams. I explained my class had already been studying for the boards for the last six months and I did not know how I could possibly pass the boards with no preparation. They said I should not worry as they would still accept me if I did not receive passing scores. That didn't sound quite right to me. Why take a test if you do not have to pass it? I received this bombshell on a Friday. When I explained to Dr. Huestad what had happened, he said to return to Grand Forks to take my exam and what we had going on would keep until I got back. Bette and the kids and I spent Saturday together. Sunday morning I decided I had better take off for Grand Forks.

It was a cold, dreary, rainy Sunday when I left. I was also leaving with a hole in my heart. I had never been separated from Bette to speak of since about age fourteen. Dad and Mom were in Minneapolis doing something and we did not know what time they would be home so I left without saying goodbye. I had only thirty some dollars in my pocket and that was going to have to suffice until I was done taking the boards. It seemed like a long drive back to Grand Forks. I did not have enough money to get a room any place. I decided I would sleep on the couch in the medical school lounge every night. There was also a shower I could use in the lounge. I would just have to make sure I took my showers at a time of night when no one was there as the lounge was for both men and women. My classmates were amazed when they came in the first morning to begin studies and found me asleep on the couch. The couch was a brown Naugahyde type of material and was not that comfortable to sleep on. Naugahyde was an old American version of artificial leather produced by making a kind of plastic mixed with fabric. I guess it was a reasonable facsimile of leather for the time and probably a little more durable. The couch was long enough so I did not have to sleep rolled up in a ball. I had brought along a blanket and pillow so I was good to go.

Most of my classmates had been studying for several months preparing for the boards and now I would have to cram as much as I could into a couple of weeks. I really don't know why that should have bothered me. I hardly ever studied for final tests. I always had the idea that you either knew it by test time or did not. Without Bette and the kids, I studied from morning until night. I knew I would not be as well prepared as my classmates but thought I could probably do reasonably well or at least pass.

We all knew the hardest part of the national boards would be biochemistry. Dr. Cornatzer, our biochemistry professor, was from Georgia. He was a balding wise little man with a deep southern drawl and was fun to be around. He could usually make the medical students laugh. The only thing I can remember well from Dr. Cornatzer is to eat plenty of peanut butter. He said in his southern drawl that it was 27% protein and it was gooood for you. He drew that good out as long as he could make it. Imagine a professor from Georgia saying that even before the days of our Georgia peanut growing president, Jimmy Carter.

Dr. Cornatzer was one of the professors on the national board committee who helped prepare the board exam. He offered to give us special sessions so we would be well prepared for the biochemistry part of the test.

Many of us showed up for his first session but we soon realized this was a test for people who were getting their degree in biochemistry. Not a test likely to be of use to up and coming young physicians. It also did not seem to be a test easily passed even with Dr. Cornatzer's special tutoring. We did learn the passing grade on the national boards in biochemistry was 29 percent. Holy cow. It is a multiple choice test with only four answers to choose from. Even guessing on every question, you should be able to score 25 percent. As luck would have it, the biochemistry test was one of our last tests. I was sick and tired of testing by that time and anxious to get home to my family. I had never been separated from Bette, Terra or Todd this long.

I decided to wing it. I didn't bother to read the questions and just flew through the test putting the same answer down for every question. I was not really that committed. Not that committed! Really! I wasn't committed at all. If I was going to be transferring to the University of Nebraska regardless of my score, I really did not care that much. It was bad reasoning and laziness on my part. Biochemistry became the downfall of my board scores and kept me from passing the first part of the national boards. Oh well, if the medical school did not care if I passed, why should I?

Chapter Seven

Minneapolis-Lutheran Deaconess Hospital

I was in a hurry to get back to Princeton and get on with our lives. After driving back and forth from Princeton to Minneapolis for about one week it became apparent the drive was going to be really difficult in order to get to the hospital in time for the early surgeries. Driving meant rush hour traffic in the early morning and the same mess going home at night.

Dr. Huestad saw the dilemma and talked to the hospital administrator to see if they had an apartment they could put us up in. We would be living in a small upstairs apartment located only a block south of the hospital. It was great to be so close. The hours were great for a summer job. I would start in the hospital about 6 a.m. and generally be done about one or two in the afternoon. Our apartment was really hot and because we could not afford to buy a small window air conditioner, the temperature upstairs was probably well over 100° F every day and about half way through the night. With all the hot city pavement and sidewalks, it just seemed we could not get cooled down.

The most popular song in Minneapolis was by Lovin' Spoonful:
Hot town, summer in the city
Back of my neck getting dirty and gritty
Been down, isn't it a pity

Doesn't seem to be a shadow in the city
All around people looking half dead
Walking on the sidewalk, hotter than a match head
But at night it's a different world
Go out and find a girl
Come-on, come-on and dance all night
Despite the heat it'll be alright
And babe, don't you know it's a pity. Etc.

The average temperature for that July was in the high 80s and that dang song seemed to play about every hour. We soon learned how to handle the heat. We got a cooler, filled it with ice and went out to Lake Nokomis which was located in South Minneapolis, only about five or six miles from our apartment. We would lie around the lake until it got dark and then we would go to a drive-in theater to watch movies until the temperature went down to the point of just bearable. Although the area where we lived seemed to be safe enough, there definitely seemed to be some racial tension. It was nothing that ever affected us, but there seemed to be some unease. At that point in my life, I was not sure what that was all about. North Dakota kids didn't know much about racial tensions. All of us North Dakotan Swedes and Norwegians look pretty much alike. Maybe that is why black people say they all look alike, or was that us?

Perhaps it was more perceived than real. We had never lived in an area where we were in the minority. When you grow up in a small town in North Dakota, your exposure to other races is very limited. The only racial jokes we knew were about Swedes and Norwegians. We always said a Swedish monogrammed hanky was an index finger with a tattoo on it. Or you can always break a Swede's finger by hitting him in the nose. I always told Swedes about the 10,000 Swedes who ran through the weeds chased by one Norwegian at the battle of Copenhagen. Of course the Swedes always told the same jokes about the Norwegians except for the battle of Copenhagen of course. They just changed the nationality around to fit the circumstances. I remember the time the two Swedes mixed up their luggage at the airport. One grabbed the wrong brown paper bag.

My job at the hospital was great. It could hardly be called a job.

I don't think you could have better summer employment and it also allowed me a brief respite from the heat. Unfortunately Bette and the children did not get that same break from the hot days. It was a learning experience to be sure. What always seemed amazing to me was as I was learning to put people to sleep Dr. Huestad and the other anesthesiologists were always having me work on the young healthy people. At that point in time it seemed if I were to hurt someone by accident, it might be better if it were an old person rather than someone with their whole life in front of them. What idiotic thinking from someone who obviously wasn't thinking. What you do not understand at that young age is the very elderly walk on banana peels so to speak. They have to be kept in such delicate balance it takes someone with years of experience to handle their anesthetics. The young strong and healthy athletes were not much of a challenge to put to sleep and wake up. They recovered from their anesthetic quickly and were not subject to the whims of their body not handling medications well enough as would be the case when they got older.

One day when I was giving an anesthetic to a young athlete for an orthopedic procedure, the orthopedic surgeon asked me to hang up a unit of blood. There was a young student nurse named Jody Roe working with me. Jody was a cute little gal with big brown eyes who had almost as little experience as I did. I asked Jody to have the lab send up a unit of blood for us. I had never done this previously but had watched it done many times by now and it did not look that difficult. Jody and I were conferring behind the anesthesia screen (drapes) and trying to speak softly enough so the surgeon would not be bothered. We both decided we could handle the task so did not ask for an anesthetist or nurse with more experience to help. The blood arrived from the lab and hospital blood bank. We both knew at least enough to compare the chart identification with the blood so we were giving the correct unit of blood to the correct patient. There are much more sophisticated means of checking all of this out today to avoid errors. I am not sure what we did wrong but as I was hanging up the blood on the IV stand I had a small stream of blood running down my arm from the unit of blood. Jody and I both looked at each other with surprised looks and we could not help it, we started laughing. We tried to do it as quietly as possible of course. The elderly surgeon looked over the top of the anesthesia screen at us and said somewhat gruffly, "Is there a problem?" "No doctor," I replied. I did not want to confess that an inadequate sophomore medical student and a student nurse were trying to do a simple exercise in hanging blood they were not qualified or experienced enough to do.

I think it is the large numbers of early jobs in medicine that teach you to be humble. I would later teach young physicians it is best to learn humility early the easy way, or you will surely be taught it the hard way.

I had many fun experiences in Lutheran Deaconess Hospital. One night as Jody, an orderly and another student nurse and I were finishing up sterilizing surgical packs to be ready for the next day Jody took a syringe full of water and squirted me. Of course I retaliated. The next thing to happen was an ongoing and running water fight that carried us through all the surgical suites and supply rooms. I finally ended the squabble by putting Jody over my shoulder and bringing her into the doctors' changing room. Showers were available and I turned one on and held her under the shower until she was completely soaked. I was also completely soaked. We were laughing and having a good time until we realized the damage we had done. We all changed into dry scrub suits in our appropriate dressing rooms.

As we started to retrace the paths of our water fight we realized we had very probably contaminated many surgical packs with our foolishness. When surgical packs are sterilized they are taped shut. The tape develops sort of hash lines when it has reached the required temperature to tell you the process is done. This is to insure no bacteria are left on the instruments.

Every surgical pack that had so much as a drop of water on it had to be re-packed and re-sterilized. It ended up being one of the longest nights I put in while working on that job. Our thoughtlessness was never repeated.

One day when I was in an exploring mood, I wondered what was kept in the basement of the hospital. It was an eerie scene. I wandered into a huge room filled with dozens of iron lungs. Iron lungs were from days gone by when they were used to treat people with bulbar polio. When polio affected a person's brain stem it affected their ability to swallow, speak or even breathe. There was no treatment for the disease and we could only provide supportive care. Most people died when they got to this stage of the disease.

An iron lung breathed for the person by sucking the air out of what was called a tank respirator. The tank respirator completely enveloped the patient. Only their head stuck out of the tank and there was an airtight seal around the neck. When the air was sucked out of the tube or tank respirator the patient lived in, the patient's lungs expanded and when the suction was turned off the lungs inside of the bony thorax or chest would contract again. This was the mechanism to get air in and out of the lungs, allowing the person to breathe without having a tube in their trachea.

I could only imagine the horror of walking into a ward and seeing all of these tank respirators with patients' heads sticking out of them. I could not imagine what it was like to go to sleep at night while listening to the whoosh, whoosh, whoosh of a machine keeping me alive and the feelings of helplessness of the person stuck in the respirator. Can you conceive of laying there a couple of weeks wondering if you were ever going to breathe on your own again? I do not know if hospitals had auxiliary electrical supplies in those days, but I can't imagine myself wondering when a storm was going to come around and the electricity might go out.

Medicine was not inexpensive in those days either. The cost of an iron lung was about $1500, the price of a home at the time.

One other thing amazes me; neither Jonas Salk who developed the first successful polio vaccine nor Albert Sabin who developed the oral polio vaccine would ever become as famous as a person who could cross the goal line of a football field or stuff the basketball through a hoop better than anyone else.

Well I guess we Americans know what is most important in our society. Dang it. We have to keep our priorities straight. It amazes me how quickly we forget what these cures for disease mean to us. When we go long enough without the tragedies of death caused by polio, measles, whooping cough and Typhoid fever we become complacent and think we can go without the immunizations that made those diseases all but disappear.

Complacency is great. Our children who cannot think for themselves are allowed to die from diseases all but nearly wiped out because their parents were complacent. Can you picture the little tombstone epitaph, "I died of complacency. My parents were smart, just complacent."

Again, we learn nothing from history. Do you ever wonder why we bother to write down our history if we learn nothing from it? It always seems to repeat itself.

I learned a lot from all of the physicians giving anesthesia. One day we were running to a code and the doctor who arrived in front of me had just done the anesthetic for a thyroidectomy on the person lying in the bed who suddenly could not breathe. The anesthesiologist rapidly grabbed a scissor and scalpel and cut all the sutures out in the neck, jammed his fingers down into the wound and rapidly pulled out a large clot about the size of a baseball. The patient could suddenly take in a great big breath and seemed to get immediate relief. The surgeon was still in the hospital and the person was taken immediately back into surgery to find the artery that had broken loose. I asked the anesthesiologist how he knew to open the neck up immediately without even trying to put in an endotracheal tube. He said the trachea would have been compressed and the intubation probably would have been unsuccessful and wasted valuable time we did not have. He said the most likely thing compressing the trachea would be bleeding so that was the action to take.

It is fascinating when you see some of these dramatically good endings to great decisions; you rapidly want to follow in those physicians' shoes.

Not all endings are good. One day a female athlete about 34 years old was having a cervical fusion and there began to be problems in the post anesthesia recovery (PAR). They could not seem to maintain her blood pressure and she did not seem to be recovering from the anesthetic. As it turned out the patient had an injury to the spinal cord and it had resulted in quadriplegia. This would be how she would spend the rest of her life. There had been no problems with the surgery. However, sometimes the best possible procedure done by the best physician still leads to a bad outcome. There just doesn't seem to be a reason sometimes.

One day there was going to be a complicated surgery by Dr. Stu Arhelger and Dr. Arnie Kremin. Dr. Kremin had been the Chief of Surgery at Columbia University and President of the American College of Neck Surgeons. They were both great surgeons with great reputations. Sometimes along with great credentials come personalities that are a little challenging to work with. The surgery was to be a porta-caval shunt.

This is a difficult surgery that connects the portal vein which supplies most of the blood to the liver, to the vena cava which drains blood from most of the lower body. This is a surgery done to treat high blood pressure in the liver which is often caused by cirrhosis.

The patient was a smallish skinny guy. The distance between his xyphoid and pubic bone was only about two inches. The procedure would really have to be done through his sides. The surgery went on for hours and tempers were getting a little short. At the end of the procedure we were short a sponge and there were at least thirty piles of sponges on the floor. Each pile had ten sponges in it. A surgical sponge is a four by four piece of gauze with a radio-opaque string through it. This means you can pick it up on an x-ray. Dr. Arhelger asked for a recount and another and another and so on. Both surgeons went into the abdomen again looking for the lost sponge and said there was not one in there. After several more sponge counts and shorter tempers, I made the mistake of asking Dr. Arhelger if he wanted me to call x-ray. If looking daggers could have been bullets, I would probably not have made it out of that room. Dr. Arhelger asked for more sponge counts. The nurses were also getting frustrated, saying they were short a sponge and it was not on the floor.

Dr. Arhelger then asked for x-ray which could have been standing by, ready. Instead we had to wait for x-ray to get down to surgery and set up. They took a flat plate of the abdomen. One of the techs returned with the x-ray and when it was held up to the light, I pointed out the sponge in the right upper quadrant of the abdomen to Dr. Arhelger and suffered another stare. One thing you can do while you are young is see better than an elderly surgeon who is first looking over the top of his little reading glasses and then through them trying to decide which gave the best vision. The sponge was removed from above the liver and a long procedure could finally be closed. I decided after a long day, I never wanted to be a vascular surgeon.

The rest of the summer was enjoyable in spite of the heat. We were brown as berries by the end of the summer as we were in the sun almost every hour I was not in the hospital working and learning. I don't know where the saying 'brown as a berry' came from. Aren't most of them any other color except brown? I can't think of any brown berries.

The Huestads took us to the Chanhassen Dinner Theater one night to see the play *Carousel*. It was the first play Bette and I had ever seen that was professionally done. Chanhassen was a pretty well-known dinner theater and you could have a cocktail or two before dinner and then watch the play, which was great. We had a good time with the Huestads.

Chapter Eight
University of Nebraska

When the summer was over and my training period in anesthesia ended we were ready to see what the next season in our life would bring. It was just short of a four hundred mile drive from Minneapolis to Omaha. The University of Nebraska was in Lincoln which was about an hour southwest of Omaha but the medical school was in Omaha which was the largest city in Nebraska. Omaha was a large central United States location for cattle processing and meat packing. Bette and I really did not know much about Omaha other than where it was on the map. We had not visited the city and were pretty much arriving cold without even knowing where we were going to be staying. We had our clothes on our backs and the few dollars we had saved from work that summer. As we got closer to Omaha we began to run into miles and miles of National Guard vehicles lined up and either parked on the shoulder off the road or moving slowly on down the highway. Bette and I thought perhaps there were some type of National Guard field exercises going on and they all must be congregating in Omaha. As we got closer to the outskirts of Omaha we realized there must be something a lot bigger going on than just war game practice. We found out we were not arriving at the best of times in Omaha.

Racial riots had just broken out and the National Guard was called in to quell the unrest. There had been a heat wave in Omaha that probably did not help much with the social conflict. It was explained to us that most of the unrest was happening because of large job losses and industrial restructuring in the area. In August a 19 year old had been shot by an off-duty policeman which again raised tensions; riot police had to be called in to settle the crowds. A number of stores on the Near North Side of Omaha where the majority of the black population was living had been firebombed. The riots were basically confined to that main section of Omaha so we were not personally exposed to much of the violence.

Bette and I stayed in a small inexpensive motel for a couple of days while we looked for an apartment. We ran into many of the same problems we found in Minot as most apartments did not want children. I really think children were less welcome than pets even though the kids did not pee on or rip up the carpet. We eventually found a small two bedroom apartment on two floors between 42nd and Farnam Street. We fell in love with our little apartment; it was the nicest place we had lived since we got married. It was actually located across the street from the medical school so it was an ideal situation. I would be able to walk to school most days when my service was at the main medical school. It did not take long for us to realize Omaha was a meat packing and feed lot town. When the wind blew the right direction, which was from the south, you had a very good idea where the stockyards were without asking anybody. Because of all the cattle shipped in and out, Omaha also had a large railway station.

After moving into our little apartment we managed to pick up a few pieces of inexpensive furniture and pretty soon we felt content in our new home. I enrolled for my first classes and the first service I would have would be in psych service at the Nebraska Psychiatric Institute (NPI). That was great for me as everything was within walking distance. Our psych clinics were held in the main building of the medical school. NPI was about one block south of the main hospital which contained most of the services offered with the psych building as the only exception. The book library for the medical school was located east of the main building. Within a day I had most of my books and was excited about being able to study and read about medicine. I finally had the home stretch in sight and could hardly wait to prove my value taking care of patients.

After working at NPI at the University of Nebraska it was not long before I realized it was going to be extremely unlikely I would ever be a psychiatrist. All my thoughts about studying the parapsychological sciences at Duke University were rapidly going to pass by the wayside if not go down the drain completely. It just seemed as if many of the psych problems were of a nature not likely to be solved with counseling or medications. Many of these people were the victims of poor circumstances and unfortunate birth into an unhealthy social realm from which they would never be likely to escape.

I remember reading a disheartening chart of Dr. Tunaken's one day. His first comments on the early pages of the chart stated he thought this elderly black male would be a long time or lifelong patient with very little that could be done, that he would most likely have continuing mental disabilities and would have a difficult time ever fitting meaningfully into society. His observation had been made over twenty years prior and Dr. Tunaken had been a staff psychiatrist at Nebraska Psychiatric Institute since graduation from his residency program many years earlier. Goodness sakes. I only had part of the chart and it was nearly a foot thick. Dr. Tunaken had indeed nailed the diagnosis and this paranoid schizophrenic was probably functioning at the highest level he could ever hope to attain. He would never be able to care for himself adequately and would have to depend on those around him to render care.

I took care of a young black female who seemed as if she had the typical problems you would associate with having two children by the age of seventeen years. She lived on welfare at home with her mother and siblings. I asked her if it was the same father for both children and she did not know. When asked if she had an idea of who the father of her children was, she replied it could have been one of her brothers.

My pleasant little patient lived in a single bedroom and slept with seven other children in the same bed or on the floor. She did not know which of her brothers may have fathered her children. She said it was probably one of her three oldest brothers. As if that situation was not bad enough, she now was doing the best she could to take care of her own children in an already strained home.

She also did not know the identity of her own father. To the best of her knowledge, all of her brothers and sisters had different fathers. As time went on I would learn there were many families in similar living situations. It was not only but predominantly black families born into these straits in the mid-Sixties in Omaha, Nebraska. The only notable exceptions to this rule were the young athletes who ended up playing on the Cornhusker football team.

What can society possibly do to help people born into these unfortunate circumstances? Where do we start? It seemed to me, even as a young medical student, problems of this sort would overwhelm me if thrust upon me. These young people did not have a safety net. They did not have a means to get an education to break out of this mold. They did not even have a mother and father to encourage them and let them know their self-worth.

How is it possible for a young black teenager to get an education when you have taken it upon yourself to be responsible for your children, born into an even more depressing situation in life? It was obvious that no matter how industrious someone could be, life could hand you circumstances that were just far beyond your courage or ability to ever hope to overcome them. I cannot imagine feeling that helpless.

It was during my psych service I got my first education in the homosexual life style. I began taking care of a young white male who was, and I recall exactly, five foot five and weighed 125 pounds. I recall this accurately because he stated to me his body stats in our first meeting and in a very emphatic manner. Back then the word gay was not used and gay and lesbian were probably not in the vocabulary of many or perhaps any people I knew. I never knew what my young patient was in the psych ward for and I don't think he knew either. Also as a junior medical student, you are not smart enough to figure out why people are on the psych ward unless the patient is pulling little pink elephants out of the air.

At that point in time most professionals had gradually come to accept the fact you could not counsel patients out of being gay. I think everyone also accepted that gay people were born into this life style and it was not one of their own choosing. Later on I would find out most gays were totally against this thinking. They would say they had chosen their lifestyle and it had nothing to do with birth, heredity, DNA etc. After a couple days of talking to this young man I realized I was never going to be able to communicate well with him unless I learned his vocabulary. I finally said, "About half the time I really have no idea what you are talking about. Could you do me a favor and write up a vocabulary of the terms I need to know and hopefully I can be better informed when I am taking care of a 'gay' person again." Boy, did he ever create a new vocabulary for me. I was pretty well uninformed to put the case mildly. I do not know why I would have suspected otherwise but I must have gone through life with blinders on. However, as I would learn while my education was growing stronger, you cannot see what you do not know. Evidently kids growing up in North Dakota know about wheat fields and cows. They had never been exposed to the homosexual lifestyle and if they had and were like me, they did not recognize it.

One day I got another curve ball from my little patient. He was sitting and visiting with a priest when I arrived. He wanted to introduce me and he said, "This is my father." I said, "Nice to meet you, father." And then my patient said to me again, "This is my father." Again I said, "I can see it's your father." Then my patient said to me with slight exasperation, "I mean this is my dad." Both the priest and I were slightly embarrassed but it did not help me sort out my patient's mental psyche. I thought it would be a little harder in life if you were a gay male and your father was a father, or priest; you know what I mean.

One of my next patients at NPI was a pretty young girl by the name of Linda J. I could not seem to sort out why she was receiving treatment or what treatment she was receiving. She was not on medications and seemed to be like any other 18 year old female. Her only obvious treatment seemed to be talking to me on a daily basis.

One day the adolescent psychiatrist, Dr. Kenny, called me aside and asked me if I thought my patient needed psychiatric care. I replied, "I guess so otherwise she wouldn't be here if she didn't, would she?" Dr. Kenny informed me that what she needed was a friend. He said you don't need to look for problems in these young people you see. Most of them just need someone to talk to. It made my life in psychiatry a lot easier because it seemed as if the young people I tried to take care of were little different than I had been a couple of years earlier.

Linda and I got to be good friends. It is no wonder you become good friends with an attractive female when you are only separated by a couple years of age and talk the same talk. One day Linda brought in some pictures for me to look at after a concert she had attended. She was standing fully dressed in the doorway of a motel and standing beside her was a skinny guy in his skivvies. It was Mic Jagger. The Stones had just toured Omaha and evidently Linda was what would later be called a groupie. Linda and I kept track of each other for about the next year. We would call to talk to each other on a regular basis but with time we gradually lost touch. Linda was a great young lady. I hope she has had a good and fulfilling life.

Part of our psychiatric training took place at the Veterans Hospital on south 42nd Street. It was there we dealt with some of the more severely incapacitated people. The one instruction I could remember receiving clearly was you should wear a tie but not one that tied around your neck to ensure no one used your tie to dispatch you.

In that part of our training we entered into what were called lockdowns. You could only be buzzed in and out through doors that were locked at all times. After a few days in the lockdown, you rapidly understood why this was necessary. Some of the patients were rather threatening. I think they were this way because they also felt threatened. Someone had taken away their freedom and they reacted much the same as I imagine you and I would in similar circumstances.

I remember my first patient was a young black male who insisted no one could look into his eyes. When I asked him why, he replied, "Because I am Jesus Christ and no one can look into my eyes." I replied, "I can look directly into your eyes because I am God. I am your father." Forgive me God for the impersonation. I just could not think of anything else on the spur of the moment.

My patient seemed to accept my stated role and even though from that time on we could converse, I still could not get a grip on what we could do for some of our psychiatric patients. My patient was fine physically but his mind did not work correctly. The only medications we had at that time for profoundly mentally ill psychotics were the Phenothiazines, a class of medications which had been around since the Fifties. They were a dopamine antagonist and used as anti-psychotics, the most popular Thorazine. This class of medications at the time was considered one of the great triumphs in medicine for treating psychotics or people no longer in touch with reality. Even though we could help these people, we really did not know what was going on in that bony confine we call the skull. What on earth makes that marvelous brain tick? And what makes that marvelous brain sometimes tick out of tune with the rest of the population we considered normal? And what is normal anyway? Don't we all like to think of ourselves as normal? That means anyone not like us must be abnormal. Is something wrong with this logic? Since this is my logic, I guess not, as I am normal.

One of the problems I observed with my training in psychiatry was it seemed we really could not do much for our profoundly mentally ill patients. You don't have much to talk about with your instructor when you are talking about a paranoid schizophrenic. I mean they either are or they are not. You can't counsel a person not in touch with reality. They are just not in the same room as you and there doesn't seem to be a train or bus to take to get to the planet they are on. How frustrating can something be?

All of this probably made me look away from the profession of psychiatry. I wanted to be able to fix people. Not just tease them along through life without ever making them completely well. When you looked at some of the history of hospitals for the mentally ill it was discouraging. Some of the hospital names included the words 'for the incurably insane'. In days gone by there did not seem to be good guidelines for who needed hospitalization and who did not. Of the cases of genuine serious mental illness among the patients, many would not be considered mentally ill or in need of hospitalization today.

In the past patients were admitted for such reasons as domestic trouble, disappointment in love, financial trouble, heredity, masturbation, overwork, religious excitement, sun stroke and others. One young girl had been admitted to the asylum because of homesickness. This was old history from some of my research. Fortunately mental illness was not considered a problem in the aforementioned instances. Rather amazing though when you come to think that homes like this could be used for a family's convenience if they just wanted to get rid of someone for a while, or sometimes permanently. It did not appear to me that once a person was admitted to a state hospital there was a clear path to freedom. Of course, looking at it from the sight of the caregiver, why discharge anyone. They are the reason you have a job and normal people are easier to care for than psychotics.

If young people just need a friend as Dr. Kenny had suggested, can't they find a friend among their classmates in school? I guess for many the answer was probably no. Many of them chose a group to hang out with who were never going to contribute to their well-being and good mental health.

One day I rode with Dr. Kenny to the state hospital in Norfolk, Nebraska which was about a two hour ride from Omaha. It gave us a lot of time to talk and Dr. Kenny was a robust friendly physician who was fun to listen to. One story he told meant a lot to me. He said always make sure your own family was taken care of. In other words, make sure the shoemaker's children have shoes.

He started telling me about his family. His wife was a homemaker and stay at home mom for their two children, an older boy and a younger girl. He and his wife had always thought their boy was a genius, just like all parents think their children are, I am sure. They thought their girl was a little slow and that she was an average student. One day as Dr. Kenny was walking into a room in the clinic to see a patient, he noticed the patient had the same name as his daughter. He was surprised to see his wife and daughter sitting in the room waiting for him. Dr. Kenny asked his wife what on earth she was doing here. She replied, "I can never seem to get the time at home I need to talk to you about our daughter, so here we are. Let's talk."

Dr. Kenny and his wife had just received a call from the school. They thought they were going to have to hold his daughter back this year in school. She just was not keeping up with the rest of her class. This did not seem surprising to the Kennys as they had always thought their daughter might be a little slow.

The school thought that in view of the fact Dr. Kenny was the head of the Department of Adolescent Psychology of the prestigious University of Nebraska perhaps Dr. Kenny would like to run his daughter through a few psychological exams to see if any other problems were interfering with her learning abilities. Dr. Kenny agreed. After several days of testing they found out Dr. Kenny's daughter was a genius. She was simply bored stiff by the classes she was taking in school. Instead of holding her back, they would instead advance her two grades ahead of her class. From that time on Dr. Kenny told me his daughter was the model straight A student. His son ended up being an average student. Dr. Kenny reaffirmed his initial statement. "Take care of your own family."

One day at Norfolk several students from our class were listening to a talk given by Dr. Hepperlen, a physician who was the father of one of my classmates. Someone asked Dr. Hepperlen if they did any surgery in the state hospital. Dr. Hepperlen said occasionally when baby boys were born to girls that were hospitalized they made Jews out of them. Roger Friedman, a Jewish friend sitting beside me slid down in his seat and said, "That dumb bastard." Enough said about the state hospital's surgery not to mention the adeptness of Dr. Hepperlen at explaining the one procedure in what was then a tolerable socially acceptable manner.

It was interesting; at the University of Nebraska two of my good friends were Jewish. I was blessed by meeting both of them early in my studies. Stephen Gould helped me a good bit in my understanding of the Jewish faith. I hung out with Steve and he was a good friend of ours.

Steve was going with a Gentile girl and he was always concerned that if his parents found out they would be disappointed in him. He also explained it was expected Jews should marry within their faith. Bette and I were Norwegian Lutherans raised in North Dakota. We did not see much of a problem with this, meaning, why did it matter? It would be some years later I would learn what a big deal this really was to many Jewish people. I also found it strange when Steve told me one day he and Roger Friedman, another friend of mine, were the first Jewish students to ever be allowed into one of the medical school's fraternities.

No blacks were allowed in the fraternity to which they belonged. The one black student I was aware of joined another fraternity. Something or everything about this seemed completely wrong to me. If we were to become physicians and treat our fellow man, should we not all accept all our fellow men as one? How are we all to be one if a medical school actually allows discrimination? To be honest, it was not the medical school that was allowing discrimination. The fraternity organizations were allowing this to happen. It seemed to bother me a lot more than Stephen at the time. Stephen would later marry a Gentile girl, just not the one he was in love with while he was in school. I never found out what his parents said about that. He became a psychiatrist so I imagine he was able to figure out the problems completely. Roger Friedman became a super-specialized ophthalmologist.

Later that day we were making rounds in one of the large wards. It was filled with cribs and children with Down Syndrome, some hydrocephalics and 'perhaps' youngsters with other disabilities. The next observation lets you know why I used the word 'perhaps'.

As we passed the crib of one bright eyed, red haired, little boy he asked me what we were doing. I said we were just visiting. I asked him what he was doing there and he said he didn't know. He said his parents had just dropped him off and left him. His name was Davey. I never forgot the face or name of that little boy. I immediately cornered a nurse on the ward and asked her what that little boy was doing in the hospital. I said, "There is nothing wrong with him and he does not belong here." She was in complete agreement. I gave her my phone number and asked her to call me if for any reason that little red head was not gone from this place within the next week. She reassured me she would. That word 'perhaps' was used because if this bright-eyed little red head was here and did not belong, perhaps there were other children dumped here by unwanting parents. What is wrong with people? How do parents manage to live with themselves after dumping a precious child off at a state hospital as if they are unloading a bag of garbage? It is unconscionable.

One day a psych resident told us he had thought he was past the point of ever getting sick to his stomach from anything he saw in medicine. Then while he was eating in the cafeteria alongside one of the patients, the patient started vomiting. He said the patient vomited all the food he had just eaten back onto his plate. After filling his plate with vomitus, the patient took his soup spoon and ate it all again. The psych resident said he suddenly got sick. I guess some people just do not have the stomach for such things. Imagine that.

Yes, in psych we learned a lot about the wide diversions and walks of life among people of the world. What was normal to one person was definitely not normal to another. One of our assignments in psych service was for all of us to go to a theater to see X-rated movies. Omaha had a lot of lovely old theaters, many of which seemed to hold the luxury and beauty of days gone by. Unfortunately none of the X-rated theaters were in this category. So the edge of going to an X-rated film was not going to be taken off for us simply by sitting in a beautiful theater. It seemed strange, but about four of us decided to go together one night and get this assignment out of the way. I guess we thought there was safety in numbers. I do not know what we wanted to be safe from, but perhaps it was to share the embarrassment of being seen at an X-rated movie theater. I do not recall what we saw. However, I do remember we were all pretty embarrassed to buy tickets and walk in to see the movie.

Actually, from outward appearances the people already in the movie hall did not look much different from us. Well, why should they? I am not sure what lesson we were supposed to take away from the movie hall. Perhaps 'You can't necessarily spot a pervert as they look like you. And now you are one'. No one would ever guess the smut then seen on the movie screens would later be shown in the middle of the night on family television channels.

Regarding people in the movie theater looking the same as us medical students, I think that goes to reason. Someone once said, "One out of every three people in the world is crazy. Does the person on your right seem all right to you? Does the person on the left of you look okay? Well, then you are it!"

Oh well, we all survived our fun in the slum and could hardly wait until our next movie. Just kidding. I think we were all happy to have that assignment out of the way.

It was not that I did not like going to movies. "The Sound of Music" starring Julie Andrews and Christopher Plummer started playing in the summer of 1966 in a theater just down the street from us on Farnam. It was quite the eloquent production and the front door was manned by young men in white gloves and dressed in what looked like bellboy uniforms although I don't know how I would have known that. I don't think I had ever seen a bellboy. Fortunately, at this point in our lives Bette and I could afford to go to a movie, but unfortunately that was about all the time or money we had for entertainment. A few other notable movies during our time in Omaha were "American Graffiti" and "Bonnie and Clyde" for which we scrimped up enough money to go.

Most of our time was spent with me in school. I was on call almost every other day and would stay at the hospital most of the time, sleeping at the hospital during the night. Bette dutifully stayed home and took care of Terra and Todd. I was blessed to have such a good wife and family. I had little time for my family while I was in school. Our upstairs bedroom had one small closet and I would go in my closet and commit textbooks to memory for hours every night when I was home. I had papered the walls of the closet with scenes from a Geigy AG Drug Company calendar. They provided calendars to the medical students every year and the calendars were filled with great scenery. The walls of my closet were literally wall-papered with beautiful mountain and seashore scenes. It allowed me to transport myself free of the little closet sometimes and dream of days, spaces and places to come. I think it is really helpful to have dreams so you have a star you are reaching for. You are always keeping it in sight so as not to fall short. Dad used to say, "If you shoot for the stars but only hit the moon that is still pretty darn good."

One night when I went up to study, Terra had evidently decided she also wanted to study. As safe as all my study materials were in my little study hall, she had taken one of my pens and started scribbling on pages of my text books. It was amazing how long it must have taken that little student to get tired of studying. She had scribbled on hundreds of pages. I couldn't help but laugh. And why on earth would she keep changing pages? I guess she just needed fresh paper.

Friday nights were our relaxing nights. On Fridays I allowed myself two hours of watching TV. It was really the only break which was completely away from my studies. Two new television shows had come on which were "Star Trek" and the "Wild Wild West". "Star Trek" was about the futuristic Starship Enterprise whose mission was to seek out new life and new civilizations and to boldly go where no man has gone before. Those opening words of every show seemed to stick with a person. I think it is the goal of all of us in life even if not on a starship. And the "Wild Wild West" was just that. Both were escapes from the grind of studying all the time and a mind break for me. It was something the whole family could watch, enjoy some light entertainment together in our little apartment and it allowed me to spend some time with Bette and the kids. Usually our diet during the television breaks consisted of something nourishing like popcorn with lots of butter.

We enjoyed living in Omaha. Just across the river was the smaller city of Council Bluffs. Bette and I only went over to Council Bluffs when we were going to buy clothes for a special occasion. There was a Jewish clothing store in Council Bluffs where the owner, Stan, would sell clothes to the medical students for cost. I thought it was really good business sense because I knew if I stayed in Omaha, I would definitely give him my business when I was one day making a salary. There was one other smart business man when it came to working with medical students, a life insurance salesman by the name of George Deras. George would put on a supper every year for the junior and senior students. It was usually a chicken supper done nicely and there was never a charge for the meal. For medical students this was a big deal because most of us were not well enough funded to go out for a meal. In turn when Mr. Deras asked us if he could meet with us about our life insurance needs, most of us were agreeable. George set up insurance funds for us that he funded himself until a time when we were out in practice and able to pay for insurance on our own.

Omaha was a well laid out city with streets that actually went north and south and east and west without being cut up by a bunch of rivers or cliffs. The center of the city was at the intersection of the Missouri River and Dodge Street, one of the main thoroughfares through the city. It was a very clean city with wide streets and we gradually got used to the smell of the stockyards. Farnam Street took a little getting used to. With rush hour traffic in the morning it was a one way street heading east into downtown Omaha. With rush hour traffic in the evening it became a one way street headed west out of the city. In between those times it was a two way street. You wanted to have your watch or know the time if you were going to drive on Farnam. Since the medical school was located on 42nd and Farnam streets it seemed as though there was seldom a night without sirens going off as ambulances passed by on the way to the hospitals. For the first couple of months we lived there we would jump up in the night when we heard one car crashing into another. We always worried our car had been hit as we often parked on the street when the parking lot next to our apartment was full. Forty-Second Street was also the main path from Dodge Street to Douglas County Hospital and the Omaha Veterans Hospital.

My next service was at Douglas County Hospital, a nice place to work. There was quite a bit of latitude in treating patients at Douglas County since there was generally not enough staff supervision. Often times as a medical student you might be the only healthcare the patient received. Knowing you were that patient's lifeline gave you a huge incentive to do your very best. Douglas County Hospital was a real proving ground. Many of the patients were indigent and we did not have enough staff to care for the patients. We had wards full of patients and usually we would make rounds in groups but it was always the medical student giving the history and physical findings on his or her patient. If we did not get it right we would not get the necessary help from our residents and classmates and the patient might not receive proper care.

It was at Douglas County I would see my first case of Guillain Barre Syndrome in a young black 18 year old male. The only precipitating event we could determine was it followed an oral polio vaccine he had received a couple of weeks earlier. We did not know the cause of this disease at the time but it was deadly in that it could leave a person completely paralyzed. This young man was in the correct place as he could not get rid of secretions by himself without help and his breathing was becoming labored and compromised. I talked to one of our nurses but as a junior medical student I did not have the necessary credentials to demand additional care. The nurses informed me they did not have the personnel to have one on one nursing with the patient through the night. I let the nurse and resident know I was very concerned. They reassured me the patient would be well taken care of through the night and I should not worry. I stayed as late as I could that night and left concerned. I let the nurse know the patient had to be suctioned every hour, to check to ensure respirations were adequate and to call in help if they were not.

When I returned to Douglas County the following morning, I rushed to my patient's bed to find it empty. He had died during the night. This was a very disconcerting time for me. What was wrong with me that I did not take it upon myself to stay and make sure that young man was all right. I tried to rationalize this many times. The only saving grace was that eventually I would have had to leave the hospital and leave this young man in the care of those around me. The end result was going to be the same, or would it?

There is no treatment for this illness except supportive help. Most of these patients will gradually recover if they do not die of the respiratory failure when their diaphragm quits working and they can no longer breathe. This young man needed to be on a respirator and I could not order one to help him in a county hospital with limited resources. In spite of the seasoned nurses' explanation to this junior medical student that he would be fine, I was not reassured and did not believe them.

How can a county hospital be so limited in their staffing and help they could not go the extra mile to save a young life? Did the nursing staff really believe this young man needed no additional care? Does the medical staff of a hospital constantly filled with indigent patients gradually become jaded? Have the rose colored glasses they left school with grown smoky and clouded over? And what was so important in my own life that I did not stay and make sure that young man did not die? The answer is nothing. A dagger had been thrown and it went through my heart.

Being in a county hospital gave instructors quite a bit of leeway in their teaching. They could probably get by with a lot of instruction that would not have been allowed in a private hospital, at least without some repercussions from the front office administration.

One day in surgery an anesthesiologist was giving a couple of us a talk on estimating blood loss. He said physicians always underestimate blood loss when it happens slowly over a relatively long period of time. He also said blood loss was almost always overestimated when it was acute and happened rapidly. Then he said, "Let me give you an example." He was giving an anesthetic at the time. His patient was asleep on the operating room table. He took a 10cc syringe from his table and attached a needle. He then proceeded to stick the needle into a large vein on the neck of his patient and drew out 10ccs of blood. Today this would be viewed as assault and battery. He then proceeded to squirt the 10cc of blood all over the operating room. We were somewhat shocked but he got his point across. It literally looked as if someone had bled to death in the room. It was amazing what a scene you could make with such a small amount of blood. I guess he got his point across because I remember that demonstration now as clearly as if on the day. It left a lasting impression.

If you were truly interested in learning you could learn a lot from every patient you were blessed to work with. Always remember, everyone you ever meet knows more about something than you do. When you eventually become a doctor you will hopefully still be an expert in the small part of life you were privileged to study.

I remember an old black man by the name of Mr. Robinson who worked in the stockyards. Many of the stockyard workers did heavy manual work and because of their work environment they wore heavy knee high rubber boots. Mr. Robinson had developed a severe fungal infection covering both of his entire lower legs and feet. His legs were so severely infected it seemed to be taking forever for him to get better.

One of the treatments used at that time was gentian violet, an antiseptic dye. It also turned the patient's parts that soaked in it a lovely shade of violet as the name implied. Mr. Robinson's feet and lower legs were a beautiful dark purple color. It is not quite as remarkable on a black person as it is on a white person.

After a few weeks of making no noticeable progress on the fungal infection, Mr. Robinson told me one day it was time for him to return to work and make a living for his family. He could not afford to be in the hospital anymore. I asked Mr. Robinson to let me talk to a social worker and see if we could get him on disability. This he adamantly refused and said he had to work. He said, "I gots to feed my family."

I argued that if he returned to the stockyards in his condition he would probably continue to get worse. I literally begged him to just take a break from his job. I said we could probably get him on permanent disability as severe as his infection was. Mr. Robinson said, "I have my pride. I am not going to accept handouts from anybody." I learned another great lesson about honor and integrity. Some people just had too much pride to accept help from anybody. I admired Mr. Robinson for the rest of my life. Mr. Robinson, you taught me a lot.

One night when I was working late in the hospital a young black woman was brought in by a couple of young black men. I mention the color of these patients because this was still during the time of high racial tensions in Omaha. It influenced how people were behaving. The young lady was seen by me initially and I thought she had an acute abdomen and also severe PID (pelvic inflammatory disease). Her abdomen was rigid and the surgical resident I called thought she needed immediate surgery but was not really sure what he was going to find. She was running a high temperature and looked pretty toxic. Remember this was before the days of our present potent high priced antibiotics. It was also in the days when medicine was practiced with diagnostic acumen that carried us far beyond what the testing of today does. This young lady needed surgical intervention.

When I talked to the young men who had brought her in and explained her condition, they said they were going to go into surgery with her. I told them no one was allowed into surgery except the medical staff taking care of her. They would not accept this. They said I was not letting them go with her because they were black. I was getting a little irritated and exasperated by this time. I said, "I do not give a shit if you are red, white, or blue. You are not going into surgery." They left angrily and said they would be back. I just shrugged off their comment and went about my work.

Inside of about one hour the young men returned to the emergency department with an additional five young men. Now they all wanted to go into the surgical suite. Luckily when we took a call at Douglas County we always had officers of the law on call with us. As a couple of white officers were watching the drama unfold, they stepped between me and the angry young men. They pulled out their night sticks and were beating their night sticks in their hands and asking the small crowd, "Do you want him?" meaning me. They kept beating their night sticks in their hands and said, "Go ahead and get him. Just go through us." Then they gave the men an ultimatum. They could either leave quietly or go forcibly in squad cars down to the jail for a visit. The young men retreated and hung around the hospital emergency entrance for a while. I thanked the cops for putting me in jeopardy when I would have to leave in the morning. They reassured me I would be fine. They were right. There was no sign of the crowd in the morning.

On another evening a couple of white patrolmen brought in a surly, unruly young black man who was combative and threatening. It became obvious the situation was dangerous to the staff. The patrolmen kept trying to subdue him and then said they thought they better take him to jail without being checked. We acquiesced but really had no idea what was wrong with the combative young man. He was ushered back into the patrol car. After about twenty minutes the officers came back with the young man and said he had decided he wanted to be seen. In that brief period of absence, the man was now completely subdued and barely responsive. It was not obvious he had been beaten but I suspect something wrong had happened in that twenty minutes. We checked him out and admitted him for observation. I did not know what had happened between my patient and the officers but did not think it was probably anything that was going to improve race relations.

The racial problems were something I really could not comprehend. I understood there was tension that revolved around the fact there was a difference in skin color. It just did not make a lot of sense to a Caucasian Norwegian from North Dakota. I had grown up sheltered in a life that did not know racial dissension.

Why is it a bunch of Midwestern white people would cheer on their Cornhusker Football Team on the weekend knowing a good portion of their football team is black? I think the entire state of Nebraska was enamored by Johnny Rogers, one of the greatest running backs in the Big Eight at that time. Gale Sayers predated Johnny Rogers but was also from the Near North Side of Omaha. Sayers was one of the greatest and gifted running backs the NFL had ever seen. He had kind of snubbed Omaha when he graduated from high school and enrolled in school at Kansas, much to the chagrin of the people of Nebraska. When Kansas played their first game at the University of Nebraska, the Nebraskans being a little miffed, booed Sayers when he came out to take the opening kickoff. He ran it the length of the field for a touchdown. I guess it settled the crowd according to my Nebraska classmates who seemed to enjoy telling the story.

Some learning experiences become sharply etched in your mind. The head of the Department of Internal Medicine was a physician by the name of Dr. Virgil Grissom. John Wahl and I, being transfer students, did not know the background on the various professors so we really looked at them all about the same. However the stories surrounding Dr. Grissom were legendary and the students had a seemingly irrational fear, far out of proportion to the person I saw when I met him for the first time on the medical ward of Douglas County.

Dr. Grissom would make rounds with us some days and ask questions about all of our patients. Usually the group of students making rounds would consist of several medical students in addition to a resident and the chief of staff. Our patients were normally seen by a senior medical student in addition to us juniors. As we were making rounds one day, we came to the bed of one of my elderly patients who had some heart problems. Dr. Grissom began asking questions about the patient to the senior student who was also assigned to this patient. It appeared to me as though the glare from his squinting eyes would make the hearts of the medical students receiving the questions beat faster. The senior student did not begin sweating but perhaps he should have. It became immediately obvious to me Dr. Grissom knew more about my patient than I thought he would have had he never before seen the patient or the chart.

Dr. Grissom asked the senior student for the auscultory findings on the chest and heart and the senior student gave the findings of most people in this patient's age range. He then asked the senior student what the findings on the funduscopic exam (exam of the retina) were. The senior student said the patient had signs of hypertension with AV (arterio-venous) nicking with some arteriolar narrowing and with a normal appearing optic nerve.

Dr. Grissom then asked me, "Mr. Redalen, what were your findings on your funduscopic exam?" I said, "Dr. Grissom, I do not have all the skills of a senior student but I could not visualize the retina or optic nerve as the person has severe cataracts on both sides and is nearly blind." I had to honestly tell what the findings were. I realized Dr. Grissom, unbeknownst to us, had already examined this patient. I tried my best to provide a little cushion for the senior student, but he realized he had already put a bullet through his own heart when it came to Dr. Grissom. I was more than sure Dr. Grissom knew the senior student had not examined the patient. This is one more valuable lesson in life. If you do not know something, admit it. Do not try to bullshit your way through life. Many people's bullshit detectors are highly sophisticated.

When we came to the next patient, Dr. Grissom was asking the caregiver students what the problems were. The patient was a middle aged white male who appeared in generally good health. They explained the patient had some near fainting spells and he was developing intermittent but rather severe bradycardia (a slow heart rate). They explained he didn't have any conduction defects. His EKG was essentially normal and his slow heart rate had no ready explanation. The rest of the physical exam including his chest, heart and abdomen were essentially within normal limits, although he did have a large right inguinal hernia. The students demonstrated the massive hernia that hung almost all the way down to his knee and obviously held a good portion of the intestines outside the abdomen.

Dr. Grissom then began asking questions of all of us to explore the possible problems. He received multiple rather nondescript answers. When he came to me he said, "What do you think could be wrong, Mr. Redalen?" I replied that since everything else seemed to be normal, I wondered if he thought it possible the large hernia with so much small bowel in it could possibly receive enough squeezing and stimulation that it was causing a parasympathetic effect which in turn could cause a reflex slowing of the heart. Dr. Grissom smiled slightly and said, "That is a fascinating thought. I imagine that could be a possibility."

I suggested putting some stress on the hernia while the patient was being monitored to see if we could possibly reproduce the slow heart rate. Dr. Grissom seemed to think it was an excellent idea. I do not know if that was ever done. Often when making rounds on all of the patients on a floor, you got to see a variety of very interesting problems. You wished you could have follow-up and learn more from all of them. It was just that you often had your hands full with your own patients so you were not able to take advantage of all those opportunities. Sometimes you would inadvertently follow up when you ran into one of your friends who was taking care of the patient you were interested in and you could discuss what had happened.

It seemed I had found some favor in Dr. Grissom's eyes. Only a couple of weeks later Dr. Grissom was again making rounds when a code was called on an elderly white male with a cardiac arrest. I was first on the scene and took one of the leads on the code. Surprisingly the patient survived and did well. I say surprisingly because a lot of codes involving a cardiac arrest do not have satisfactory outcomes. Dr. Grissom was standing there watching and taking everything in. Sometime later Dr. Grissom approached me on the floor and said, "That was a very nice save, Mr. Redalen." One of his rare compliments felt good. I really appreciated Dr. Grissom and never felt the discomfort or fear of him my fellow students felt. To me he was a very kind and excellent professor.

One day a couple of weeks later I received a call from one of our nurses who said Dr. Grissom had requested a meeting with me that day when I was done with rounds; I was to come to his office in University Hospital. I was a little surprised but did not feel uneasy because all of my encounters with Dr. Grissom had been pleasant. When I arrived at his office, he asked me to have a chair. He told me he had been pleased by my performance and said other professors in the department also spoke favorably.

Dr. Grissom said, "We have an honors program in the medical school here at the University and I would like to see you enter that program." It sounded great but I asked what the advantages of being in that program would be. He said it permitted me to choose my own elective rather than going outstate and working with a rural physician.

I explained that being a transfer student, I had already had taken an elective in rural medicine in North Dakota working with a family practitioner by the name of Dr. Robert Koch. Since I had already fulfilled the University's requirements of the rural practice elective I would be able to choose my elective. Dr. Grissom said he hoped I would take an elective in Internal Medicine. I assured him I had already decided I would. He seemed pleased. When I told of my experience to my fellow classmates, they said, "You, dog. You just as good as already graduated with your M.D. Internal Medicine is the weed out course for all of us and if Dr. Grissom is treating you specially, you already have it made."

I think one of my favorite services was obstetrics. I realized if I was going to be a family practitioner, I better be good at delivering babies. Even though at that time I was not sure what I wanted to be, general medicine sounded good. I really liked all my services and I thought family medicine would be the most satisfying to me.

We had some great residents in obstetrics that were more than ready to share their knowledge. The three I worked with most were Dr. Gil Jones, Dr. Gill O'Rourke and Dr. Dietz. I got along well with all of them. I let them know what my future plans were and that I wanted to deliver as many babies as possible. They were more than willing to oblige. It was not long and I had delivered more babies than anyone in my class. I had let the residents know they could call me on holidays when I was off and I would come in and deliver babies. They showed me how to use forceps when the mother just could not seem to deliver the head of her baby. Sometimes the moms were tired. Sometimes their contractions had just run out of steam. The forceps provided some additional help for the mom from the delivering student or physician.

People often look at forceps as being hard on the baby. Forceps actually protect the baby. The forceps have a fixed distance between the blades and do not allow compression of the fetal head as it is being extruded from the birth canal. Therefore the metal cage of the forceps is protective. The greater danger is to the mother. Since the forceps cannot be compressed by the mother's pelvis there is sometimes a little bit more danger of lacerations to the mother's birth canal or outlet.

It was not long before the residents were letting me deliver all the babies I thought I could handle at night without waking them. They were grateful because the residency program offered you very little sleep. I think I was kind of like a sleep medication to them. They reciprocated by giving me more and more responsibility. Soon they were calling me on all holidays including Christmas when I sometimes would be the only medical student on the service. I gained a lot of valuable experience.

One of the fun things I did in obstetrics was to continue my practice of hypnosis. I did not want our staff or residents to worry about things they knew nothing about. I don't think I was dishonest. I just never told them what I was doing. Whenever we had patients who were unruly or just couldn't seem to relax, almost invariably the residents would come and get me whether or not it was my patient. They would say, "Rick could you sit with this girl for a while." Normally I could have the patient sound asleep within five to ten minutes. The residents would always come back in total amazement. They would say, "I do not know what you do to these girls but why is it they always fall asleep when you are around? What do you do anyway?" I always replied, "I just talk to them." I never confided to our patients or to the staff that I constantly used hypnosis. To all of you disbelievers out there, hypnosis is an extremely valuable tool. It is not just a stage show were people run around barking like a dog.

Hypnosis is not used much in medicine today. It is time consuming but very effective when you are a medical student with time on your hands. Not only would my hypnotized patients have an easier time in labor but they did better following the delivery. Posthypnotic suggestions are great.

Not to segue now, but on a side note, word later got out I was a hypnotist. One day I was called to the surgical department. The department head said they had a young girl who was badly burned over a large percentage of her body. They said they had heard I was a hypnotist and could I see her and determine if I could help her with her pain. The patient was a pleasant young lady but burned over 70% of her body with first, second and third degree burns. The physical therapy department was having difficulty putting her through range of motion exercises because of pain and if they did not accomplish something this young lady would be stuck in position with contractures, probably for the rest of her life.

Hypnosis was definitely helpful. The trouble was it became too helpful. The patient was starting to request me constantly, not just for PT (physical therapy), but also for dressing changes. These patients are full time jobs for many people on staff and it soon became apparent this patient was gradually going to take every spare minute I had to take care of her and some minutes I didn't have. It was sad but I gradually had to wean her off me and it was a difficult chore. I was not happy with my decision but it had become a necessity.

Sorry, let me get back to my obstetrics service. I got to the point that I was very comfortable with forceps. I found out one time it was sometimes difficult to see which way a head was coming if the girl came from home and had been in labor for a fairly long time. Most deliveries are vertex. That means they are head first. Most of them are OA or occiput anterior. That means the baby comes out facing the floor. This is the position most babies are delivered in. Head first with their face looking at the floor. The doctor determines the position of the fetal head in the vagina by feeling the sutures (these are the suture lines you can feel where the bones of the baby's head are growing together) and the fontanelles (the soft spots). Sometimes these land marks are difficult to feel.

One night when it was obvious I was going to have to do a forceps delivery, I was not sure of the position of the baby's head. When a woman has been in labor a long time the baby often develops a caput succedaneum. A caput is the swelling of a baby's head caused by pressure from the mother's pelvis for an extended time. The swelling is what makes it difficult to feel the fontanelles and determine accurately the position of the fetal head. Another way is to reach up alongside the baby's head and see if you can feel an ear and use that to help you determine which way the baby's head is facing. Of course you are betting it is a normal baby with the ears pointing forward.

Dr. Dietz, the youngest resident, came in to help me. I told him I thought it was OA but wasn't sure. Dr. Dietz thought I might be right, but then decided the baby was OP or occiput posterior. This meant the back of the baby's head was at the back of the mother's pelvis. He suggested I rotate the baby.

One of the forceps I had been taught to do rotations with were the Kielland forceps. This allowed you to apply the forceps to the baby's head and simply turn the shanks or handles leaving them in a straight line with the blades. The forceps I preferred were the Tucker-McLean Forceps with the Luikart modification. But using these forceps required a little more practice as you had to do a Scanzoni Maneuver; the handles of the forceps made a large arc as the baby's head was being turned. Dr.

Dietz however preferred the Kiellands so we went with his choice.

I applied the blades and on putting traction on the forceps it seemed as if the baby's head would just not budge. Being unsure, we checked our landmarks again and Dr. Dietz decided I had been right at first. We had rotated the head to an occiput posterior so we rotated the baby again. Now it was time to deliver the little critter. I pulled pretty hard and as Dr. Dietz watched, he offered to help. I gladly turned the forceps handles over to him. Dr. Dietz pulled very hard on the handles and finally the baby's head started to move. Darned if we hadn't rotated the baby the final time into the wrong position and we delivered the baby as an occiput posterior. So we both were wrong. The baby was out and none the worse for wear. When it is hard to feel fontanelles and sutures it is just hard to feel fontanelles and sutures.

One night although I had a baby to deliver most of the residents were going to get some errands done in the hospital. They were not concerned nor was I. The reasons for their lack of concern about the delivery were that the woman was having her 18th baby and had no prenatal problems although she had not been overly active in her prenatal care. The mother was large and we thought the baby was large also, but generally after that many deliveries all that is needed to deliver the baby is a catcher's mitt. Seriously, these babies usually come out so fast with one big contraction sometimes you have a hard time being ready. I did not think this would be an exception.

It seemed strange to me, but Dr. Dietz came in the room and said he decided to stay. He said for some reason he felt uneasy about this delivery. I told him I was happy to have him and hoped his feelings were wrong. The patient was already crowning but after a couple of big pushes against strong contractions, the baby was staying put. I told Dr. Dietz I was going to put on the forceps and give her some help as she was getting tired after a few more contractions; she was not the youngest OB patient on the floor. Dr. Dietz agreed.

It was an easy forceps application to an occiput anterior presentation. I began to put traction on and for what I thought would be a very easy delivery I found myself pulling with nearly all my might. The baby would not budge. I asked Dr. Dietz to take over. Dr. Dietz took the forceps handles and try as he could the baby did not budge. Meanwhile Dr. Dietz was calling for one of the senior residents.

Dr. Gil O'Rourke was on the floor and in the room immediately. It added some humor and levity to the situation. Our patient was yelling, "Oh Lordy, Lordy, help me, help me." Dr. O'Rourke came bouncing in the room not realizing the gravity of our situation and doing a dance saying, "I's here, I's here," meaning the Lord was here to save the day. Dr. O'Rourke had not seen all of what had happened before he got here. I think he thought he could give a couple of tugs and out would come the baby. Wrong. Dr. O'Rourke could not budge the baby.

The problem with a troublesome delivery like this is that you are now past the point of doing a C-section. A baby of this probable size will have its head so molded in the pelvis it would be a monumental if not impossible task to get that baby's head out of the mother's pelvis once the abdomen is open. The immensity of the situation is you would probably lose the baby and possibly have an unfortunate outcome with the mother.

All three of us realized the danger we were now facing. We had a mother pregnant many times and now with a baby so large we could not pull it out. Dr. O'Rourke asked our nurse to see if a staff obstetrician was available. Luckily, late though it was, Dr. Pearson who was the Chief of Staff of Obstetrics was still in house. We immediately informed him what was going on. He rapidly accessed the situation and asked the nurse for the axis traction handle for the forceps.

The axis traction handle can be applied to any set of forceps. It helps keep the traction on the fetal head in the exact correct direction and allows you to apply massive traction. Dr. Pearson had been doing studies with these forceps and would actually measure the amount of traction used. At first it appeared Dr. Pearson would be no more successful than the three attempting before him, but then he put his right foot upon and against the foot of the table and pulled with all of his strength. Finally the baby's head began to progress. Suddenly the baby's head was out. The head is the largest part that has to go through the pelvic outlet so now things looked more favorable. Dr. Pearson had extracted the baby's head with more than 150 pounds of force.

We thought the battle had been won, but we could not be thankful too quickly because now Dr. Pearson was trying to deliver the shoulder. It seemed too large to come out. We had the baby suctioned but the baby was still in danger with the body stuck in the uterus. It appeared Dr.

Pearson was not going to be able to deliver the body so both the fetus and the mother were again in serious danger.

Dr. Pearson tried numerous maneuvers as our feelings of helplessness and anxieties grew. Two of us pushed down on the abdomen so hard we felt as though we were crushing the baby while it was still in the womb. Dr. Pearson pushed his fingers in past the baby's neck trying to get his finger under the arm. Hopefully he could bring one of the arms out and then get the shoulder.

He could not seem to accomplish this either so he started pushing on the clavicle, which is often a last resort. Dr. Pearson was trying as hard as he could to break the baby's clavicle or collar bone. This maneuver if it can be accomplished allows you to narrow the baby's shoulder and gain just a little bit of room. This is also difficult to do with a large baby and Dr. Pearson trying as hard as he could was unable to fracture the clavicle. The only thing that could be done now was to pull on the baby's head and get the body delivered. If that baby did not come out we would probably have to open the mom and take it out in pieces. Finally a shoulder budged and slowly we had a limp unresponsive baby but showing signs of life. After much work, the baby lived. It had been an ordeal that taught me never ever to take a delivery for granted no matter how easy you think it will be. The baby weighed nearly 16 pounds. No wonder the problems.

The next couple of days would be just as worrisome. The severe shoulder dystocia this baby had can have severe consequences. We would have to worry about whether the baby had brain damage or whatever else a traumatic birth like this could do to the little one. The baby seemed to eat fairly well but we noticed immediately the baby could not move his right arm. The final diagnosis was Erb's palsy, a paralysis of the arm caused by injury to the main nerves to the arm. It is brachial plexus damage. The brachial plexus is the plexus of nerves that go to the arm and let it do the miraculous actions it performs in life. The damage may be bruised nerves at the minor spectrum of scale to completely torn and damaged nerves that will result in permanent paralysis. There is nothing to do. The baby will either get better over a period of months or it will remain permanent. Severe cases may require surgery or get better with rehabilitative treatment. The baby did as well as could be expected and mom did well also. They both went home in several days. I never learned the final outcome of that disturbing experience. Dr. Pearson was balding and when I next saw him the remaining hair was intact so I guess he handled everything all right. I have never been so thankful Dr. Dietz stayed behind to help me. I let him know how appreciative I was. We were both thankful more seasoned and experienced people were in the house.

Chapter Nine
Booth Memorial Hospital

One of the other racially charged atmospheres I worked in was Booth Memorial Hospital on the Near North Side of Omaha. The Near North Side was always talked about as though all of the black families in Omaha lived there. I am not sure if there was any truth in that but as a medical student with no time for anything but school, my family and I never spent much time sightseeing and driving around to figure out the demographics of Omaha.

Booth had its share of excitement. When we drove out to our service in Booth we didn't bother to stop for stop signs or red lights on the way to the hospital. It was just not considered prudent or safe. When we arrived at the hospital parking lot, we would jump out, run up to the hospital, unlock the plate glass and metal door with our key, hurry inside and lock the door behind us. I guess when I stop to think about it that is the only key to a hospital I have had in my entire medical career. I always thought it amazing that with all the vandalism in the neighborhood, the medical students' cars were never vandalized. I think it was a rough neighborhood's way of saying "We appreciate you."

Most of the medical students carried pistols in their cars for protection. I could not afford a pistol but carried the switchblade I had always carried in high school. Fortunately I never had to defend myself as I am sure that may not have ended well. If you don't grow up on the streets, you probably cannot take care of yourself like a toughened street person. If anything happened I would have probably ended up looking like Bad, Bad, Leroy Brown, the guy from the later Jim Croce song.

Well the two men took to fighting
And when they pulled them off the floor,
Leroy looked like a jigsaw puzzle
With a couple of pieces gone....

The young girls in Booth came into the hospital for a good portion of the end of their pregnancy. Most of the girls were white and I think they were sent away for the end of their pregnancies so as not to embarrass their proper white families.

Golly isn't it amazing how times change? Don't you think the neighbors of these young ladies would wonder why they would disappear for several months of the school year and then reappear looking all slim and refreshed? The young ladies were fun to work with. They were just young kids who had gotten pregnant a little earlier in life than they had planned.

Many of them gave their babies up for adoption. I speculate after you disappear from home for several months and come back with a baby, it would have not made much sense to have left in the first place. I believe the monumental decision of giving away her baby had already been made by the young lady and her family prior to coming to Booth. Or at least if it had not been made by the young lady it certainly had been made by her family.

The delivery room had a large plate glass window facing the north side of the neighborhood. The window had a couple of bullet or pellet gun holes in it and it always made me feel a little uneasy to have my back to the window while waiting for a baby to be delivered. There were no drapes covering the window. You were in the spotlight on center stage with your back to the neighborhood audience. When we delivered babies in Booth we never had residents working with us so the only care these young ladies received was from the medical students. We always stayed there nights and left in the morning.

One night, one of the medical students on the way to the hospital (I think it was Gary Biesecker), had a car pull in front of his and block him while another car blocked him from behind. The assailant held a gun to his head and demanded his wallet and wedding ring. Gary was frightened but unharmed and now missing a ring and billfold. Hope my recall is right on that Gary. It is kind of amazing how foggy your mind can get after only 48 years.

Another night, the night staff at Booth got a call and the person on the other end of the phone asked if we handled emergencies. The reply was, "We do not." I was not on call that evening. Only moments later there was a crash of breaking glass downstairs. The staff rushed downstairs to find an already dead body had been thrown through the plate glass window. This was just one more incident at Booth. And actually the dead-on-arrivals (DOAs) are a lot easier to care for, just unnerving when delivered through your window.

The only other unsettling event I can remember from Booth was the night when someone broke into the hospital, went up to the delivery floor, held a student at gun point and demanded narcotics. We did not carry narcotics in that hospital and probably for just that reason. The person left without injuring anyone other than battering a few psyches. Yes, we were getting a lot of training at the University of Nebraska and a lot of it was not on the medicine floors. But it did teach you about some of the events you would probably encounter again during your years of practicing medicine, assuming you survived your training.

One thing great about the state of Nebraska was they had a program for children with birth defects. Our son Todd Jon qualified for this program so we put him through all their testing. The other great thing about the program was the state paid all the costs of medical testing. The program was set up in such a way that any child with congenital problems would be cared for by the state regardless of the financial condition of the family. One caveat was the state was going to pay the expenses only for anyone that would have their standard of living compromised by taking care of the child with the birth problems. As students we certainly qualified for the program.

The physical differences on one side of Todd's body that had been more evident when Todd was just a baby were pretty much gone. He continued to have a discrepancy in leg lengths and these were taken care of by a built up shoe on the side with the shorter leg. All of Todd's testing came out normal. We knew we did not have to worry about his intellect as he was smart as a whip. His kidneys checked out fine and there was no sign of renal malignancy. Even though Todd seemed to be growing up just fine, we were pleased to hear he had been given a clean bill of health.

Later in my junior year I would be on the medicine service and come to know an outstanding professor by the name of LeeRoy Meyer. Dr. Meyer had been educated at the University of Nebraska and had become one of the outstanding teachers in the school. I don't really know how or why it happened but Dr. Meyer kind of adopted several of his students, took them under his wings and devoted a lot of time to them. One of my friends Bob Anderson and I were two of those students.

When groups of medical students were taught by Dr. Meyer, he would begin asking questions. Often he would ask questions he was relatively sure most of the group could not answer. When the entire group had their chance, he would then refer his question to Bob or me. We would invariably know the answer he was looking for. I spent a lot of time with Dr. Meyer. Even when I was not on the medicine service he would have me read electrocardiograms by the hundreds to the point that it became almost like reading a first grade primer about Dick and Jane. I began to think there was little about a heart tracing I could not decipher. My time with Dr. Meyer was spent between University Hospital, Douglas County and the Omaha Veterans Hospital.

It was a definite benefit to have the best instructor at the University of Nebraska on your side and pushing you to your limits. At times when he thought I would not have an answer to his question, he would ask Bob Anderson for the answer and Bob would often know. Dr. Meyer was a master psychologist at pitting us against each other. The competition between Bob and me began to extend into everything we did. Sometimes it was a pool game. Good luck to you on winning that, Bob. Sometimes it was tennis, but most often it was academics. When it came to testing, Bob was difficult to beat, but on the floor, I was usually the better student. Bob said to me one day he really did not care as much about treating patients as he did about the academics of medicine and for me it was the exact opposite. I wanted to care for patients.

Being friends with Dr. Meyer extended beyond the hospitals and occasionally he would invite several students out to have lunch or cocktails with him. Always though the best part of our relationships with him were constant learning opportunities and being pushed to do our best. Our best often made us excel far beyond where we would have been in our training.

One night at the veterans hospital I was seeing a patient with one of the interns doing his medicine service there. We had a patient with a cardiac arrhythmia. The patient was throwing wild PVCs, premature ventricular contractions or extra beats. The cardiogram showed them to be multifocal, coming from multiple areas of the heart. The patient was on digitalis and not a very large dose. The intern ordered more digoxin, a medication that makes the heart contract more effectively. But if your patient is toxic, it can also cause arrhythmias.

I suggested to the intern I thought it would be dangerous to give more digoxin. He said the patient was not toxic on that low dose. I argued that if I was right and he was wrong he would probably kill the patient. We could not get a stat digoxin blood level. It had to be a clinical decision. In 1967 there were no medications to treat digitalis intoxication. Digitalis toxicity was dangerous. The intern deferred to my judgment which was probably hard for him to do as I was a junior medical student. The patient's heart remained irritable but stable through the night and in the morning a serum lanoxin (digoxin) came back high and in the toxic range. The senior student came and talked to me and thanked me for arguing against his treatment. He said he would have killed that patient were it not for me. He added, "I would give anything to know all the medicine you know. Thanks again." I silently thanked Dr. Meyer.

There were other lessons I learned at the veterans hospital. One day one of the directors or supervisors from the business office came on to the floor and asked the staff if there was a need for equipment or furniture. He said they had a large surplus of money that had to be spent this fiscal year. He said to spend it on anything you need now or things you need in the future. Evidently if the surplus money was not spent that year it would not be available the following year. It could not be saved. It had to be spent. It was one of my first lessons on how the government did business.

The veterans hospital ran clinics on the bottom floor during the day and these were often manned by medical students and one of the Internist professors. It was always a good learning experience. One day when

Bob Anderson and I were in the clinic with Dr. Meyer he asked us to see a patient, an elderly black man who was being seen for large patches of white skin that were developing all over his body. Neither Bob nor I had seen this condition before. When we came out of the room, Dr. Meyer asked us, "Well what do you think?" We both looked at each other, and then I said, "I did not think it was all bad." Dr. Meyer said, "Why do you think that?" I said, "Well, he is turning white." Dr. Meyer, try as he might, could not help but burst out laughing. He knew I did not mean anything unkind by my comment. It just seemed funny at the time. I always seemed to open my mouth without first engaging my brain. When the laughing stopped, Dr. Meyer explained the condition was called Vitiligo, the development of patches of skin that were losing their pigment. At that time the cause was unknown. We would later come to learn it was an auto-immune disease; the body was making antibodies against the melanocytes in the body. Melanocytes are cells that produce the brown pigment in our skin. There was no treatment for the disease and it really produced no problems other than cosmetic.

We had many interesting professors all of whom taught us a great deal about medicine. One of our professors was a man by the name of Dr. Bartone, a urologist. In the first clinic we had at University Hospital with Dr. Bartone he lectured on the renal causes of hypertension.

A urologist in the Sixties was more in tune to their entire specialty. They actually knew what the kidneys were for as contrasted with the urologists of today that are more procedure doctors. If you actually want to know a little more about your kidneys today you go to a nephrologist. How sad the times have changed and our specialists' knowledge has been whittled down to the point they know nothing. That is not entirely true I guess. They know a whole lot about nothing.

One day Dr. Bartone asked me if I could explain all I know about how ACE inhibitors worked and their method of treating hypertension. I looked at my watch and said, "Dr. Bartone, we only have one half hour left of our class and that is much too short a time to explain all I know." Dr. Bartone asked me to indulge them and go ahead with the time we had remaining. I spoke for the full half hour on ACE inhibitors and had lot more to teach when our class ended. Dr. Bartone said, "Very good, Redalen. Very good." We hit it off great and I got along well with Dr. Bartone from that time on.

One day when Dr. Bartone was scheduled to lecture at the veterans hospital, I asked one of my friends who was going to be running the slide projector if he would let me run the projector for that day. He told me he needed the money, so I said he could have it. I just wanted to run the projector. He finally agreed. When Dr. Bartone was about to give his lecture, the lights went off and Dr. Bartone said, "First slide please." I put up my first slide which said Dr. Finkelstein and His Magic Jack-o-lantern Show. Dr. Bartone kind of harrumphed and said, "Next slide please." I then showed a slide of Dr. Bartone's. He proceeded with his lecture. After a couple more of his slides when he said, "Next slide," I put up a picture of one of Playboy's Playmates of the Month. Dr. Bartone harrumphed again and said, "Next slide please." Meanwhile about fifty medical students and physicians in the room began to laugh and after one more unwanted slide, Dr. Bartone yelled at the top of his voice, "Redalen, where are you? I know you are in here." I rapidly started crawling down the row in front of the line of chairs and students behind the projector and sneaked out the door. I left uproarious laughter behind me. School should not be all work and no play. In a profession as serious as medicine, we should take advantage of levity when the moment arises.

One of the most amazing professors at the University of Nebraska was a beautiful blonde pediatric cardiologist by the name of Dr. Carol Angle. I think all the male medical students who worked with Dr. Angle fell in love with her and secretly would rather have had her for a girlfriend than a professor. What was beyond amazing about Dr. Angle was she was deaf. She was not totally deaf but she would not hear you if you were talking behind her. What none of us could understand was the fact that when she had her stethoscope on the chest of a baby and was listening to their heart, she would point out the mostly inaudible heart sounds and murmurs and comment on the smallest nuances of them.

We students talked about this often and never understood. Did she pick up vibrations through her stethoscope? What allowed her to hear that little heart better than any of us? She had a God given ability far beyond anything we could hope to comprehend. Much to the chagrin of us all, Dr. Angle was married to a cardiologist. We always thought he was rather unkempt and not much of a catch for someone so great and gorgeous. But one thing he could do was read EKGs as fast as you could turn pages in a book. He was an amazing cardiologist.

My first service in neurology and neurosurgery was at the veterans hospital. My very first patient was a pleasant quadriplegic man in his mid-thirties whose name was Jack. Jack's entire life had changed when he and his wife were at a party one night where people were drinking and playing. Jack dove into a swimming pool and when he did not surface for air a couple of his friends dived in and pulled him out of the water. From then on his life would be forever changed. He had broken his neck and damaged his spinal cord.

It didn't seem like a good first neuro patient for me to have, because after all, what is there to figure out when your patient has a high cervical fracture that has severed or damaged his spinal cord rendering him completely paralyzed from the neck down. What I later figured out was it was not so much what I would learn about Jack's neurological condition but what he would teach me about life, survival and relationships. Isn't it strange for a young medical student to think that when you are seeing patients it is only their problems you are learning about? Nope, you are constantly learning about life. It lets me know how naive I was.

Jack's cervical fracture had been high enough it knocked out his ability to breath on his own. This meant the damage had to be above C-4, the level of innervation for the diaphragm. If you have damage at that level you no longer have muscles needed for respiration. The diaphragm is the sheet of muscle necessary to breath that separates your lungs from your abdomen. This meant Jack had to be on the respirator for breathing and he had a tracheostomy tube in his neck. He could get enough air past his vocal cords to talk to me.

As we got to know each other, I realized just how hard a life lying on a Stryker frame could be. A Stryker frame bed is one in which the patient is lying on their back or stomach all day long. The patient is flipped to one side or the other by the orderly or nurse every two hours twenty-four hours a day so the patient does not get bed sores. The person has a catheter in place which is connected to drainage to take care of urine disposal. Bowel movements presented another challenge. I used to enjoy seeing Jack and his two young children lying under his bed on the floor looking up at this face to talk to him. Sometimes they would be lying on their stomachs using pencils and crayons to entertain him by drawing pictures. Jack really enjoyed his little girl and boy. They were close together and about a little less than midway on the way to their teen years. The new life of physical confinement for their dad did not seem to affect their loving relationship. Even though Jack could no longer hug his children, it was obvious he could still love and hug them with his eyes. You people with furry children know what I am talking about. Don't you see sometimes how your pets and especially dogs are hugging you with those puppy dog eyes?

One day I asked Jack what it was like when he first found out he was going to be paralyzed for the rest of his life. He said all he ever thought about was dying. It occupied his every waking moment. One day when the electricity went out during a storm, all he had was enough air to get out one large, long whistle. An orderly came running in and breathed for him until they had electricity again. Jack said from that day on he did not want to die. He wanted to see his children grow up. He wanted to learn how to live life again as he was now. I marveled at his courage. I do not know if I would have forced out that whistle or tried to tough it out and die.

One day at the veterans hospital a couple of Russian neurosurgeons came through to see two of our patients with hemi-spherectomies; half of their brain had been removed. I cannot for the life of me imagine coming halfway around the world to see such medical tragedies.

Our neurosurgeon was one of those people who walked around the hospital with his shirt half unbuttoned exposing his hairy chest to the world. It was more like he strutted than walked, a strong indicator he was quite stuck on himself. It certainly could not have been from those two half brains he had removed. I would have been more impressed if he had taken those two half brains and put them together to make a whole one.

The only thought I had about our neurosurgeon was that someone had already removed half of his brain. Why else would you suggest to a family, "Well yes, I can save your loved one's life," without telling them, "I will just be keeping your loved one alive, not really saving their life. You will never know them as they were or have a meaningful conversation with them again."

I just couldn't rationalize why a family would allow their loved one to have half of their brain removed to treat cancer. Wouldn't it be better to die? From my observations it seemed obvious to me the families were done no favors by having their loved ones left like this. It had to have been an unbearable burden that left you with a heavy heart.

These two patients were evidently the only two adults in the world at that time to have half their brain removed to survive cancer. What a great accomplishment. They were wheel chair bound. They could not talk, so to speak. One of them would only occasionally swear. He seemed angry when he swore so perhaps there was some emotional aspect of his personality left. The other patient would burst into song at odd times. He often did not know all the words but you could discern what he was trying to sing and he could not carry a tune. I can't see a reason to live just to occasionally sing a song, even if you are a great singer, which he was not.

I am sorry I think this way but being alive just to be living is not really life. And if we survive this way, when God takes us home, do we go home like this or are we restored to the point where we thought we were the best in life? And is our best in life what we think it is or as God thinks it is? When we have glorified bodies, do we also have glorified minds? If we no longer remember the questions we had for God when we were young, will He remember them and answer them anyway? And if He provides us answers and we no longer remember the questions, will that help? Jeepers, just more and more questions. I hope I remember them so I can get God's answers.

One day Dr. Garcia was in radiology reading x-rays. He was pointing out various findings to the medical students. He came to a halt over a puzzling x-ray. He was looking at two kind of semicircular shadows in the middle of each lung. He had worked in veterans hospitals so long he had forgotten that maybe one day he would see the chest x-ray of a female. There were almost no veteran females back in the late Sixties. I had never seen a female as a patient in the veterans hospital. When one of the residents told him they were breast shadows, he became embarrassed. From that time on breast shadows were called ellipsoids of Garcia.

One time an intern asked me to go down and take care of a drunk for him. He said he was tired of seeing drunken veterans. It was true. We did seem to have our fair share, but I went to see the patient immediately. He had already been admitted and was in his room. He was alert and oriented. He knew where he was but was a little unsteady. I used one test on him I think was more to amuse medical students than to really accomplish anything. I held my hands about a foot apart with my thumb and index fingers together and pointing towards each other. I moved them up and down and asked the patient if he could see the string. He got a puzzled look on his face and cocked his head at different angles. He then said to me, "I just can't see that danged string."

I asked the nurse to get some D50 W, a 50% dextrose solution. I inserted a butterfly and gave him the dextrose solution. He suddenly became as clear and lucid as I was. He had been having a hypoglycemic reaction. As he was coming around he also knew what was wrong and could tell us he was a diabetic.

I called the intern and asked him to come down to the patient's room. When he arrived I asked him to talk to the patient and see what he thought was wrong. After a couple questions he asked, "What on earth did you do to him?" I said, "He is a diabetic and was having a hypoglycemic reaction." I hoped the intern would learn a lesson that would serve him in later years. Undiagnosed hypoglycemic reactions are dangerous.

When cold winter weather rolled around all the beds in the veterans hospital filled up. It seemed many of the veterans needed a place to stay for the winter. The somewhat derogatory term used by the medical students to describe them was 'snow birds'. It made me realize just how many veterans must be out wandering the streets, homeless. It was a very disquieting thought. The older veterans were fun to talk to and you could learn a lot from them. Many of them were survivors of WWI and WWII.

It was interesting to hear the stories of some of the men on ships during WWI. That was the time of one of the greatest flu epidemics and killers of more people than had ever been known in the history of the Earth. It had killed more people than the bubonic plague or Black Death of the mid-1300s. Estimates were that 50 to 100 million people were infected and between 20 and 30 million people died from the plague. It was truly a global disaster. Some of our navy men said so many sailors were deathly ill during the flu there were not enough healthy men to throw the bodies overboard so the bodies lay where they died. The ships floated aimlessly without a crew to steer them. That flu epidemic was unusual in that it killed young healthy people in the prime of their lives.

Strangely, the elderly and young were not hit as hard and were more likely to be spared. This was because they did not have great immune systems. The immune system of 1918 was what was attacked and consequently killed those infected. Young healthy people had stronger immune systems and the H1N1 virus caused their immune systems to work against them. The strong immune response their bodies could launch was killing them.

1967 was a difficult year for me. It was difficult not so much from the school perspective but was worrisome to me as my brother was in Vietnam. I do not think it was an overwhelming thought on my mind all the time but Vietnam was not something you could avoid hearing about. My brother was in the 101st Division of the Cavalry. It seemed from the news his division was on many fronts seeing a lot of action. One day I would hear about the Battle of Dak To. Another day I would hear about some atrocity perpetrated by American soldiers such as the My Lai Massacre lead by Lt. William Calley. We heard about horrors American soldiers were committing against the local women and children, families of the enemy but not our enemy. When you carry this thought out a bit further do we really have enemies in war? Are we not all just people sent in by governments that disagree with each other?

The brutality of the Vietnam War was not winning the hearts of the American people. Through it all I wrote letters to my brother Ron giving him encouragement and letting him know we loved him and were anxious to have him home again. We would send him gifts like beef jerky, pepperoni, cookies, warm woolen socks. It seemed strange to receive requests for warm clothes but in spite of being in a tropical climate the soldiers said they froze at night. Ron said the last thing the soldiers did at night prior to retiring was to scrape leeches off their bodies.

One day when I was on the obstetric service I was summoned by Mrs. Nims, a very pretty black woman, to take a phone call. I did not know why, but I became very uneasy and made up an excuse as to why I could not come to the phone. This sense of unease I felt seemed to grow rapidly by the day. I would do everything possible not to talk on a phone and I began to cut a wide swath to stay away from anything near a phone. I could not explain this sudden overwhelming anxiety. Finally, one night when the phone rang Bette said it was for me. I told her to tell them I was sick and could not take the phone and then I went in the bathroom and vomited. Bette came in and asked me what was wrong and it was then I confided to her something was happening to me that suddenly made me extremely scared to pick up a phone. I told her I was becoming physically ill. I was really scared and reasoned that if this continued I would not even be able to stay in medical school. My fear became overwhelming. No amount of reasoning seemed to get me out of what was happening to me.

A couple of days later, having avoided answering the phone again when I was paged in the hospital, everything was becoming more and more unsettling and unbearable. That evening I started searching for what had changed in my life. What had suddenly happened that left me in this state of paralysis? It suddenly stuck me. I was scared to answer the phone because I was afraid I was going to be told my brother had been killed in Vietnam. At that point of realization, all of the fears I had about the phone left me immediately. Anxiety is an apprehension or fear which comes from the anticipation of a threatening event or situation. I now realized the cause. Since I had something I could deal with, the fear was gone. I could handle this. With this realization came complete relief to me. It was if someone had pulled a gun away from my head. My heart was light again and the relief was enormous.

I guess if I had been the best son, I would have called Mom and Dad every day to help ease them through their journey of agony. Perhaps if I had been thinking about them constantly and their pain, I would not have developed my own anxiety problems. How selfish I must have been.

In retrospect, I realized the veterans hospital had not helped with my problem. When I would take care of young war casualties from Vietnam, most of the problems were surgical in nature. I could not help but wondering when seeing these young casualties if one of these could be my brother in a faraway land. If so, who was taking care of him? Were they taking care of him as they would their own brother?

One day a young man familiar with the 101st Airborne Division told me to stay in close touch with my brother. I believe it was his way of telling me to do my best so if I never saw my brother again, I would have known I did my best and would have no regrets that it was not good enough. He said the 101st Airborne Division was airlifted by helicopter from one front to another after another. They had a high mortality rate. Our conversation had not been comforting.

Veterans hospital had helped me in many ways however. I was doing a research project on diabetes. At the time there was a new medication on the market called DBI-TD. This medication was an extended release form of a phenethyl-biguanide. The beauty of this relatively new medication was it lowered the blood sugar of diabetics but did not lower the blood sugar of non-diabetics. It also had a low side effect profile. My thinking at the time was this could be used to test for diabetes. Dr. Meyer agreed to oversee my research and he agreed my thinking was sound. Everything seemed to line up. The hospital had a surplus of funds and I could use as much as needed to do my research. With all this in place we got one of our lab techs to do blood sugars and immune-reactive insulin assays exclusively for my project. With all the blood testing going on he was on a full time schedule getting lab work done.

First I had to get my controls so I talked twenty medical students into taking a glucose tolerance test. Dr. Meyer and I were among the controls. Unfortunately, when we were doing controls, Dr. Meyer and I were the only two that turned out to be abnormal. It was not a result we were happy with but the lab was rechecked on another day and there was no question we were both diabetic. Dr. Meyer was thought to be an adult onset diabetic. I was only twenty-three at the time so I was almost in the juvenile diabetic category or type 1.

When I looked back at my history, I realized I had probably been diabetic since my first days in medical school in North Dakota. I used to have periods of sweating and weakness and one of my friends told me I was having hypoglycemic episodes. Benny Barberio and his wife Sandy were friends of Bette's and mine. Benny was an early diabetic and said he had the same problems I had. At that time I did not know what hypoglycemia was. He said when I got this way to try taking a little orange juice with sugar in it or eating a candy bar. I followed his advice and it worked. My blood sugar was getting too low. On reflection I realized my problems had probably started late in my teenage years.

Dr. Meyer and I ended up being my first test subjects using DBI-TD. My theory seemed to hold up. Our blood sugars were dramatically lowered by the medication. My classmates whose blood sugars had been normal were not affected by the medication.

Now my thesis project could begin in earnest. I had a captive audience and I began doing glucose tolerance tests (GTT) on dozens of veterans. I let them know it was a research project I was doing but they would benefit by having a test for diabetes that was better than a blood sugar test. The test would better tell them how they handled a glucose load. After getting a regular glucose tolerance test (GTT) they would then get my DBI-TD tolerance test. It seemed as if all my ideas of using this as a test for diabetes were proving to be accurate. I was hopeful that after all the analytics were run we would find the DBI-TD tolerance test would end up being better than the GTT. It would be much easier to take a medication and see if it lowered your blood sugar than taking a glucose load and doing a bunch of blood sugar tests. My test would save time and money and not be such an onerous test to take.

When we had more than one hundred people in our study we were ready to run the statistics. It seemed to prove we had come up with a new test for diabetes. Both Dr. Meyer and I were excited about what we seemed to have proven. The paper was written up and reviewed by a couple of professors and everything was progressing nicely. I was going to submit the paper to the New England Journal of Medicine (NEJM) for publication. My work seemed to be fairly important and met all of the necessary requirements. I was excited and anxious. If I got my work published by NEJM it would be a big feather in my hat. It was one of the most prestigious medical journals of the time.

Then it was like a bombshell hit us. Cases of lactic acidosis were being reported with DBI. Not only that, but there were deaths reported from taking phenformin and alcohol together. Evidently the cases of lactic acidosis were accompanied by a 50% mortality rate. The medication was not immediately removed from the market but our thinking was we could not push a test for diabetes using a medication that appeared was headed for problems. That put an end to my research project. We decided the paper could not be submitted to the NEJM. I guess we could have continued trying to get our paper published as the medication had not been taken off the market, but I did not feel I could continue with a good conscience about doing so.

I started one more research project. I had discovered all or most of my diabetic patients had diabetic leg lesions. This was thought to be injury due to lack of insulin and or vascular damage to the small vessels supplying the skin. I found a salve the pharmacist thought might be a vehicle to carry insulin. I had patients putting this on the little leg lesions thinking that perhaps insulin delivered directly to the lesion could either stop the progression of the lesions or reverse them. I never got the response I hoped to see so that project came to an end and just as well. I was having progressively less time to work on diabetes although it was definitely an area of interest.

As we neared the end of our senior year and it appeared we were going to be RDs, it was time to start searching for internships. RDs stood for real doctors. As we neared graduation, we would often hear a lot of strange pages on the hospital paging system. The television show "The Fugitive" had gone off the air in 1967. I don't know why the switchboard operators didn't catch on, but you frequently heard, "Paging Dr. Richard Kimble, paging Dr. Richard Kimble." "The Fugitive" was a television show about a physician wrongly convicted of killing his wife and continually on the run from the law. He was the fugitive. I guess our hospital operators either didn't watch television or perhaps they thought we had a physician on staff named Richard Kimble. Another page we heard was, "Paging Dr. Deladumone." That was a medication used to treat menopause. I imagine you could not expect a hospital operator to know that. It did point out the fact the medical students were getting a little squirrely from the final pressures of school, or more likely some of them were squirrely before they started school.

One night a hospital was putting on a small event with hors d'oeuvres and drinks at the Dodge House, up on Dodge Street of course. The purpose of the event was to entice medical students to take a look at their hospital for a possible internship. Steve Gould and I decided we would take a look although it was still a couple of months until graduation. We probably wanted free eats and a couple of drinks more than anything else. I guess we assumed we were going to graduate, which was not a given because one of the requirements for graduation was to take and pass the national boards. I don't think either one of us was very concerned about that however. It was a nice get together and Steve and I dutifully talked to the hospital representatives to gather information. I do not even recall what hospital it was any more.

As Steve and I were driving away from the Dodge House we were no more than a couple hundred feet down the street heading north when a patrol car slammed on its brakes fifty to one hundred feet in front of us and slid to a stop. Suddenly an officer jumped out of his car and aimed his weapon right at us. A voice came from the speaker on the squad car. "Get out of the car with your hands up." Both Steve and I looked at each other and slid down in the seat so the officer could not see us to shoot us. The voice came on loudly again. "Get out of the car with your hands up." I said, "What do we do?" Steve said, "I guess we better get out of the car." We did so with our hands in the air. The officer then said, "Put your legs apart and away from the car and lean on the car with your hands on top." We did so. As I was the driver the officer seemed to me to have his gun mostly on me. We asked him what the problem was and he told us to be quiet. He kept his gun on us as he reached into the car to talk on his phone. Several long minutes went by. In the meantime another squad car had pulled up behind us, blocking any movement by us. Finally the officer on the radio said we were free to go. We asked the officer what this was all about. He said the Dodge House had just been robbed and we were the first people out. It took maybe a day for my nerves to quiet down.

You know, it was a great story to tell our friends and classmates though, and the more Steve told the story the bigger the gun got and the more threatening the officer became, if that was possible. Or maybe it was my exaggeration. Who remembers? It was fun to tell a story that kept our classmates somewhat interested and intrigued.

Damn, that whole incident was so scary and I think the thoughts going through Steve's mind and mine were, 'Holy cow, we put all this time in school and now someone is going to shoot us before we even get our diploma'.

Now, it would not say in the newspaper that Dr. Rick Redalen and Dr. Steven Gould were killed by an overly aggressive rookie cop as they were leaving the Dodge House last evening following their attendance at a hospital event. How fair would that be? But when is life ever fair. More likely the following day the newspaper would report the rookie who erroneously killed two medical students would be given a disciplinary suspension of one week off without pay.

Toward the end of our senior year, I applied for a couple of electives offered through the Mayo Clinic. They were kind of like scholarship applications although I don't believe they had any real academic significance other than receiving training in the most prestigious medical institution in the world. I was given permission to attend the Mayo Clinic for two additional months of training. I chose orthopedic surgery for one elective and I do not know why but I chose hematology for the other. Around about this time the talk became more serious about national boards. It was now definite the second part of the national boards were being taken more seriously than the first part. The administration let us know that in order to graduate, we were going to have to take and pass the national boards.

Since my electives at the Mayo Clinic were coming at an inopportune time when I really needed to be studying for my boards, I decided to pass on the electives. It was not going to do any good to have the electives on my resume if I failed to pass the boards.

Bette and I also began the process of deciding where we wanted to live for the next year during our internship which was an additional year of training following the senior year of medical school.

One of the first hospitals we visited was Bethesda Hospital in Minnesota when we were home visiting my parents during Christmas vacation. I was shown around by a very distinguished, tall, dark physician by the name of Dr. Richard Yadeau, the head of the department of surgery at that time. If my entire determination for an internship hinged on one person, this would have been the internship for me. Dr. Yadeau was truly an impressive individual and seemed even more so with his Eastern sophistication and accent which was a product of New York Medical College and University.

The next hospital we visited was Weld County Hospital in Greeley, Colorado. We had decided we wanted to move someplace out West. We had friends from high school who lived in Greeley, Julie and Buddy Hastings who had gotten married shortly after high school. Julie had been one of Bette's good friends. Weld County Hospital was very nice. The people who showed me around encouraged me to intern with their hospital and said they would make my internship a rewarding one. The administrator showed me the whole hospital and also took me out on the roof of the hospital. To the north were these huge dark patches that looked like fields. He asked me if I knew what the big dark fields were. I said no as I could not think of any crops that would be that large and dark. He informed me those were Monfort feeder lots filled with cattle. It seemed a little strange to me that with that many cattle you did not smell them.

The following morning when Bette and I got up and went outside, it smelled as if the entire town of Greeley was a feeder lot. The smell was so thick it was hard to breathe. Buddy and Julie said we would get used to it. Our thinking was that was not a smell we ever wanted to get used to, so we scratched Greeley off our list as we left town. Don't know for certain why we were so opposed to that bad smell, but it was probably partly because we had the stockyard smell in Omaha. It was just more severe in Greeley.

Chapter Ten

St. Benedict's Hospital

The last hospital we visited was St. Benedict's Hospital in Ogden, Utah. In 1968 Ogden was a town of about 90,000 people and was one of the cities located in what thousands of years earlier had been the bed of Lake Bountiful. Twenty-eight miles south of Ogden was Salt Lake City, home of the Mormon Tabernacle Choir. St. Benedict's Hospital was beautiful, quiet and peaceful, sitting at the base of the Wasatch Range of Mountains. The hospital was run by Benedictine Nuns. I met Sister Luke, the hospital administrator, who was from St. Cloud, Minnesota. The hospital was fresh and the people were friendly and it soon became apparent to me the only thing I could really tell about a hospital and what the internship would probably be like was that the floors were shiny and the hospital was clean. They all seemed to meet those specs.

Bette and I had to decide where we wanted to live for the coming year. We were not too hot on Minnesota as we visited Bethesda in the middle of winter and they had a lot of snow. In spite of how much fun we had only two years earlier during our tenure at Lutheran Deaconess and lying along Lake Nokomis all summer long we decided we did not want to put up with another Minnesota winter. We also did not like the thought of living in a large city and putting up with the crowds and driving congestion.

We found out two other students and their families were thinking of going to St. Benedict's, Carroll and Jean Cedarburg and Dick and Marley Holmes. Dick and Carroll were classmates of mine and although I did not know them well they seemed like class acts. Their wives also seemed to be great people. Dick and Marley were not parents yet as were Carroll and I. Marley was in graduate school with a year left to complete so Dick would be living most of the year as a bachelor, so to speak. After we did some talking, we finally all decided to go to Ogden. Our salary was going to be $530 per month. That was certainly more than we had been making as students, but it did not leave us with much money to do anything.

Dick and Carroll and I kicked around the salary quite a bit and I do not know why but we did not try to negotiate a higher salary and in actuality the money was better than some of the internships that paid only about three hundred dollars a month. We had decided we could supplement our income by moonlighting, working for pay in other hospitals on nights you were not scheduled. We had discussed this with Sister Luke and she seemed fine with us doing additional work to make ends meet.

One thing that enticed us to go to St. Benedict's was the fact Dr. Ross, one of the family practitioners, owned the Snowbasin Resort. He also owned the lodge and ski rentals. The hospital let us know this was one of the benefits of interning in Ogden. Dr. Ross gave out rental equipment and lift tickets to the medical students free of charge. We would really not know how great that perk was until the ski season started.

My other thought regarding an internship was I would probably learn as much in an internship as I put into it, but this was probably the only internship where I was going to learn how to fly down the mountainside on a pair of skis. That final thought sealed the deal for me. St. Benedict's it was going to be.

June rolled around and most of the students were getting pretty excited to move on in life. Some of my classmates were continuing on with their study at the University of Nebraska but many were fanning out to other locations to further their studies. One of the real problems facing Bette and me was the fact I had aimed everything and all my training toward becoming a family practitioner and following in the footsteps of the physicians I had observed throughout my entire life. I really wanted to be a doctor like our family doctor who seemed to me to take care of everything. The problem we were going to encounter was the Vietnam War was still going strong. In spite of its immense unpopularity, there seemed to be no end in sight.

All physicians had been funneled into the service on completion of medical training for a period of two years. The only way to side step going to Vietnam was to sign up for something called the "Berry Plan." The Berry Plan had been established during the Korean War by Frank Berry, the Assistant Secretary of Defense for Health Affairs. One of the options of this plan allowed a doctor to complete residency training in a specialty of his choice before fulfilling his military obligation. Everyone hoped the Vietnam War would be over by the time everyone completed their residency program. It was entirely conceivable this could happen as the war was becoming more and more unpopular with the American people. One of the derogatory terms used for physicians avoiding the draft in this manner was "Yellow Berets."

The lottery system was in place at the time and although I had received a lottery number higher than 350 the problem was my draft board was in North Dakota, a state that could never meet their quota for physicians. I was obviously going to get drafted regardless of my high number. I had talked to my draft board soon after receiving my lottery number. I was elated but that jubilant feeling quickly came to an end. The Williston draft board said it would not matter what my lottery number was.

Just about every student in my class signed up for the Berry Plan. It was the only way to get out of the draft. The decision Bette and I had to make was whether or not I should sign up. At the time there were no well-established residency programs in family medicine, the direction I wanted to go.

Ron was still in Vietnam and I thought I may as well go and take my chances. The decision may have been about life and death. We were all familiar with what was happening with physicians in Vietnam who did not have a residency behind them. Going into Vietnam without any special skills meant the young physicians were being used as medics on the front lines. The mortality rate was nearly 100%. When groups of medics went in, often in groups of twenty or more who had trained together, it was not uncommon for none of them to return.

I would later in my career have an acquaintance in Dubuque, Iowa by the name of Ferd Nessler, the owner of Nessler's Jewelry Store. Ferd related his Vietnam experience to me.

Ferd was still traumatized by Vietnam. He had gone to Nam with a group of twenty young medics and during his time there he had tagged over seven hundred GIs. Tagging them meant when you came to a casualty you could not save, you shot them up with enough morphine to allow them to die comfortably, pulled the tags off their neck and put them in their mouth and slammed their jaw shut. That was so later the body could be identified. When it came time for Ferd's discharge evidently a general came into their bunker and said, "Ferd, I think we are going to have to extend you. We don't have enough medics." I guess Ferd was probably a little crazy by this time. He pulled out his pistol and put it to the general's head and asked him if he would reconsider. The general said he had changed his mind and Ferd was leaving the front lines. Of the twenty young medics Ferd had gone to Vietnam with, only he was going home. It was entirely understandable to me why someone would not want their tour of duty extended.

I maintained contact with Dr. Meyer after he left for Vietnam. Since Dr. Meyer was an internist, he was put in charge of a 500 bed R & R hospital in Hong Kong. R & R stood for rest and recuperation. Ron had gone to one of these hospitals and he said all they did was sleep, eat and enjoy the air conditioning. Dr. Meyer said in his letters he really did not take care of any medical problems in his hospital; his wards were filled with surgical casualties. Above all, Dr. Meyer told me "Avoid the draft. Get into a residency program and put this war off as long as you can." He wrote constantly, "Rick, you will not survive this." It was too late. Bette and I had made our decision. I was going to take the internship in Ogden and then worry about the war and the draft later on in the year.

June and graduation came and went rapidly. One of the greatest things about my graduation day was Ron had returned from Vietnam. Bette, Mom and Dad had gotten both Ron and me a cake with some tiny American flags flying on it. The writing across the top of the cake said 'Congratulations Rick' and on the bottom it read 'Welcome Home Ron'. It was a wonderful celebration and couldn't have been timed more perfectly. Ron had flown into Omaha early enough to attend my graduation and Mom and Dad had driven down from Princeton.

Graduation is almost anticlimactic after you have been waiting for four years to get your diploma. Actually I guess we had been waiting for seven years. My degree let the world know the Degree of Doctorate in Medicine had been conferred upon Rick R. Redalen. It felt truly good and I was so happy. I felt as though it was a good accomplishment. At ages seventeen and eighteen, Bette and I had picked out our direction in life, kept our eye on the goal and by our own means and encouragement from our families and God had achieved earning a Doctorate in Medicine. We had accomplished a lot. Even though Bette did not have her diploma, she had indeed earned one every bit as much as I had. It was a team effort all the way and a goal I would not have accomplished without her.

One memorable day prior to graduation my classmate John Wahl came to our apartment. We had decided to attend some of the parties going on prior to our graduation. John had received a case of Ballantine's Scotch from one of his aunts. He brought two bottles to our apartment and thought we should have a couple of drinks prior to running over to one of the fraternity houses.

I had never tasted Scotch. Even though I did not like the taste, we had a couple of drinks mixed with water. Immediately on arriving at the fraternity house we were handed a couple of large plastic cups of beer. I was not a beer drinker either and the two did not mix very well.

Everyone was in a festive mood. Steve Gould and Roger Friedman were there along with Dick Foresman and a number of my other friends. It was not long, a couple of hours later, I was standing out on the front lawn of the fraternity and ended up with my arms around Assistant Dean Mary Jo Hen, giving her a big kiss. She looked at me and said, "I knew there was a reason I liked you transfer students so much." I would later get ribbed about that a lot. Everyone said I was the only one to ever kiss our assistant dean.

After more partying, we all decided to go out to eat at Ross's Steak House on the west side of Omaha. I was getting sicker and sicker from the drinking we had done and said I had to go home first. John took me home and a family was in our apartment looking at some of the furniture we were leaving behind. I went running past them into the bathroom and promptly vomited up our night of drinking. John was going to leave me but after getting rid of the liquids I felt better and went along to finish out the evening with a big steak. Later Bette informed me somewhat unhappily I had not helped with the sale by vomiting nearly in front of and certainly within earshot of a bunch of strangers.

As we were trying to sell some of our bulkier furniture and get ready to move, Todd seemed to be coming down with a stiff neck. He was running around and playing but just did not move his head. He was eating well and not running a temperature. Bette took him in to the children's pediatrician who gave Todd a clean bill of health.

The Cedarburgs and Holmeses had smaller cars than our great big Pontiac Grand Prix, so we decided we would pull a U-Haul loaded with their furniture and they would pull one loaded with our furniture. Pulling a 6 X 14 foot U-Haul was probably too much of a load as it almost seemed to be controlling the car.

Bette and I were leaving a little earlier than the other two couples and would be leading the way to Ogden.

As we drove down the highway it seemed to me Todd's neck was getting stiffer and stiffer. He would turn his whole body just to turn his head. The evening of that first day of driving, I asked Bette if she could drive for a while. I said, "Bette, the load we are pulling is almost as heavy as a car. You cannot swerve or you will lose control and the load will be pulling you." Bette understood. I lay down in the front seat and was sleeping with my head in Bette's lap. I do not think I had been asleep for more than an hour or so when I heard a scream. I sat straight up in the seat. What I saw was terrifying. We were going down the highway backwards being pulled by the trailer. There was nothing that could be done. What probably transpired in seconds seemed as though it dragged on forever. We finally hit the ditch and then everything went into slow motion. The car started to roll up on its side and as the trailer rolled the hitch broke loose. We landed upright on all four wheels and the trailer was nearly upside down in the ditch. A trucker who was directly behind us came running up to us to see if we were all right. He said he was really scared as all he could see were sparks and what looked like fire as we were being pulled down the highway. What we later thought he had been seeing was the U-Haul sliding down the highway on its side. Pretty soon we were surrounded by people offering to help. We also found out what had caused the accident. Bette had come upon a large piece of insulation laying across the highway and thought it was a log. One little swerve was all it took for the driving to be taken out of her hands.

The trucker said we should at least try to get the trailer back on its wheels and upright. With all of the help we were able to upright the trailer. Our back bumper was a little banged up but the hitch was still on it. The car looked as if we could still drive it and when we were done filling out reports with the highway patrol we went back into the little town we had just gone through and got a motel for the night. We didn't have much luck sleeping and in the morning we got help to get the U-Haul hooked back up to our car. A garage owner was really sympathetic to us and got the electrical all hooked up and did enough work on the hitch so we could pull the trailer again. Miraculously, the U-Haul looked like hell but could still be pulled and the padlock was still on the back door. We did not dare look inside and were really frightened by what we were going to find. We knew we carried Dick and Marley's wedding presents including all her wedding china.

The next day, Todd's neck seemed to get worse. He was still eating okay. I did not have any instruments with me so I could not examine him. We stopped in North Platte, Nebraska where a pediatrician examined Todd again and reassured us he could find nothing wrong. I was still very concerned and yet we went on down the road moving a mile at a time closer to Ogden. The next day when we arrived in Ogden the hospital staff showed us our apartment. We were going to be in an upstairs apartment close to the hospital. The housing was great and surpassed anything Bette and the children and I had ever lived in. It was wonderful. The back hospital entrance was only about a block away.

Todd's neck seemed to be getting worse so we took him into the Ogden Medical Clinic to their Department of Pediatrics. Again, the verdict was the same. Todd was okay. The pediatrician examining him could find nothing wrong. He gave Todd a clean bill of health and said the stiff neck was possibly muscular and would probably resolve in a couple days.

I was not satisfied and more than a little concerned. Todd had now been seen by three physicians in little more than four or five days and all of them said he was just fine. That night the Holmes and Cedarburgs arrived with the trailer containing our furniture. They were horrified when they saw the U-Haul Bette and I had been pulling. It looked like something out of a salvage yard. Marley started crying and was understandably worried about her china. Dick and Marley had only been married within the past couple of months and all of their worldly belongings were in the trailer. Her reaction was entirely understandable. It did not look like a lot could have survived in that trailer.

What I wanted out of our trailer and did not waste any time getting was my medical equipment. I wanted to check my son myself and not depend on the three previous physicians who said there was nothing wrong. There was definitely something wrong. They just were not astute or perceptive enough to find it. I examined Todd while he was sitting at our little kitchen table. He still said he did not hurt and felt okay but he could not move his head without turning his body.

Todd had a few swollen lymph nodes in his neck which was not too remarkable for the summer time when children's little immune systems would react magically to even minor bug bites. What I found next horrified me. I told Bette I thought Todd had a retropharyngeal abscess. I had never seen one before and did not have the vaguest idea of what one looked like, but I was still sure that is what it was. I was really frightened and in retrospect should have taken Todd directly to the hospital emergency department and demanded an ENT physician see him again, immediately. Instead I took Todd to bed with me and slept alongside him, checking him continually through the night.

I ran over to the hospital the first thing in the morning and said I wanted to see the best ENT doctor in town. Sue Baden, one of the first people I met in in the hospital, said that would be their uncle, Dr. DeMars. They said he was gruff and did not have much of a personality but he was the best Ogden had to offer.

Bette took Todd in to see Dr. DeMars, who gave her a good talking to and evidently at first thought we had neglected our son. He said this should not be happening to a physician's child. Todd was immediately admitted to St. Benedict's for emergency surgery. Dr. DeMars concurred with my diagnosis of retropharyngeal abscess.

Once in surgery, Dr. DeMars opened a large pocket of puss in the back of Todd's throat in the retropharyngeal space. The reason this was of such great concern, Dr. DeMars explained following surgery, was the abscess was near the point of rupture and had it ruptured down into the mediastinum or space around the heart in the center of the chest it could have caused a fatal infection with secondary mediastinitis. Dr. DeMars said we were extremely lucky to still have our son. He said the very large abscess was close to the point of rupture, which could have blocked the airway. There were many other possible complications that would have to be guarded against but we were truly blessed.

I want this to be a lesson to all of you. Just because a physician tells you your loved one is well and not to worry, if you feel the doctor is wrong, bring your loved one back and give the physician a second chance to examine them again. I say give the original doctor a second chance because on your return they will hopefully realize your concern and go the extra mile to find out what you are worried about.

All physicians can miss something. We are not perfect and if I have made a mistake on a little one or anyone, I want the chance to right my mistake. Obviously, our son had been examined by three probably excellent physicians and all of them had missed the fact Todd was heading toward a fatal outcome had we not acted in time. I still feel chagrined to think something like this could have happened right in my own household and right in front of me. I cannot begin to imagine the grief a parent, myself in this case, must or would feel to lose a child due to neglect, especially when they are not even responsible for the lack of care. We all are the first in line for caring for our children and they depend on us.

Todd was on intravenous antibiotics for several days but seemed to tolerate his hospitalization just as well as he had tolerated his abscess. He just did very well. One exciting thing happened while Todd was on the pediatric ward. One day Lassie was in town visiting children in the hospital pediatric wards. Lassie walked up and down the hallways and would stop so the little patients could pet him and then Lassie would give them his autograph so to speak. He could not write of course, but he would put his front paw down on an ink pad and then put it back down on a piece of paper giving each of the children a paw print to remember him by. The children enjoyed it as "Lassie" was a big hit show during that time about a Collie that was always in the right place at the right time saving or helping someone.

While visiting Todd my first time in the pediatric department, on the right hand side on the wall as I walked in was a pretty, serene picture of children playing in a field filled with flowers. It saddened you immediately when you saw the little plaque on the bottom that said: Dedicated to the memory of Bonnie Ross, Shawna Southwick and Mark Way.

I also met Evelyn Normington, an RN on the pediatric ward. She was a beautiful and pleasant girl with a big smile and a sparkling personality. Evelyn explained to me the children in the picture were the children of the three pediatricians who practiced at St. Benedict's. Their children had been playing and running together holding hands on the mountain behind St. Benedict's. She said somehow the three children all fell off the mountain together and had all died.

Dr. Ross was the first one on the scene after the accident and the only child alive was the son of Dr. Way. Dr. Ross left the bodies of his daughter Bonnie and Shawna to run down the mountain with Dr. Way's son Mark who died a short while later. Well, that was my first introduction to St. Benedict's Hospital. Evelyn said everyone in the hospital was grief stricken for weeks after the accident and a lot of tears had fallen. The three pediatricians were well loved in the community and the hospital staff acutely felt the families' pain. All of Ogden had fallen silent.

Evelyn and I became close friends throughout my internship year. I would stop in to talk with her often, even when I was no longer on my pediatric elective. Evelyn was a tall girl and throughout the year I kiddingly called her Big Lurch. Big Lurch was the gigantic character from the television show "The Adam's Family."

I did not know very much about Ogden, Utah until we got there. It was a beautiful city with a population of about 90,000. I had been told most of the people in Ogden were Mormon. I was looking at the telephone book for a number one day and noticed most of the churches were Latter-day Saints churches. I asked a nurse why this was so if everyone was a Mormon. The nurse laughed and told me The Churches of Jesus Christ of the Latter-day Saints are Mormon churches.

After looking through all of those listings I began to wonder if there were any other denominations in town. I was informed that between 90 and 95% of the population of Ogden was Mormon and about 85% of the people of Salt Lake City were Mormon. Bette and I were gradually meeting a lot of people through the hospital and we were forming wonderful new Mormon friendships.

Bette and I had a lot to learn about the Mormon faith. I learned practicing Mormons did not drink coke, coffee or alcohol. Fortunately, or unfortunately, as the case may be, for Bette and me, all of our friends were 'Jack' Mormons as they called themselves, Mormons who did not strictly follow some of the church guidelines.

Steve Johnson and I became close friends. Steve's dad was a well-known obstetrician in the Ogden area. Another friend of ours was John Howarth. John was in dental school in Michigan.

Two of our new friends were Frank and Sue Baden. Sue worked at the switchboard in the hospital and Frank worked around the hospital doing various jobs. I realized I was going to have to get a Book of Mormon and start studying their faith if I was going to learn more about the people of the area.

We had only been in Ogden a couple of days when two Mormon missionaries stopped by our apartment to educate us about their religion. They were nice and we were anxious to meet more people and make more friends.

My first welcome to the hospital was from the Department of Internal Medicine. A young Eastern trained internist gave us our welcome talk. I guess he was supposed to be a mentor for us during our training. Whit Bird was the name of the handsome young internist with brown hair in a Beatle cut. Dr. Bird seemed to have a bit of a haughty air about him that smacked of Eastern sophistication or maybe a little arrogance.

Dr. Bird asked us questions about what we intended to do with our lives and our medical careers. Dick Holmes said eventually he wanted to be an orthopedic surgeon. Carroll Cedarburg wanted to be an internist. I told Dr. Bird I wanted to be a family practitioner. Dr. Bird looked at me somewhat incredulously and said, "So you think you can learn about all of medicine." I said, "That is my goal." Dr. Bird said, "I may as well warn you right now you are going to have to work at least three to four times as hard as your fellow interns. It is very difficult to know all there is to know about all of medicine." I explained I was capable of doing that and learning the internal medicine portion from him and his colleagues. I was not entirely sure Dr. Bird was satisfied with my answer. I truly believed he had been indoctrinated out East to study a small part of medicine, because learning more would have been unfathomable to him or his instructors.

My first service to work on was the surgical service. One of my first patients was a middle aged lady with right upper quadrant abdominal pain. She had a number of interesting findings and I did not agree with the initial diagnosis of gallbladder problems. On taking a careful history and doing a complete physical exam the patient had a number of abnormalities. She had never menstruated. She was of small stature and presented with cubitus valgus. When standing facing forward with her arms facing forward at her side, her forearms deviated out from her side more than normal. She also had webbing of the neck. It was my thought my patient had Turner syndrome, a chromosomal abnormality that causes some of the traits my patient had. The chromosomal abnormality is the absence of one X chromosome.

I also found by history my patient had fallen on her butt about the time the abdominal pain started. I took this reasoning a step further and on exam found she had a very tender back at about the level of the gallbladder. From my physical exam it was my feeling that my patient probably had a compression fracture and the pain was going around her dermatome at that level and into the abdominal area. I also thought my diagnosis of Turner syndrome was correct and due to that syndrome my patient would have had an estrogen deficiency her entire life and she most likely had osteoporosis.

Without further studies or x-rays, I dictated my history and physical exam and put down my impression of compression fracture or fractures at about the level of T4 or T5. I wrote that the abdominal pain was caused by the back fractures which were secondary to her fall and osteoporosis and a lifelong lack of estrogen which was secondary to her Turner syndrome. I dictated what I thought her lab work and x-rays would show and that her oral cholecystogram which was an x-ray of her gallbladder would be normal.

About an hour or two later the surgeon assigned to the patient came walking down the hall and said, "Dr. Redalen, I want to talk to you. Would you please do me the favor of coming with me to see the patient you just saw and tell me what you see that I cannot see. Her lab and x-rays are back now. The problem I have is you dictated what the lab and x-rays would show and they were not available when you dictated your history and physical. How can you possibly know this?" I tried to explain to the surgeon as we were walking down the hall I am not sure why I know what someone has, but I do. You see my problem was I was not yet giving credit to God for what he was doing. I knew I was gifted. I just was not yet at a point in my life where I could let everyone know about those gifts.

This happened at the beginning of my internship and for the rest of the year, whenever that surgeon met me in the hall, regardless of how many nurses or physicians were around him, he would stop in his tracks and without fail bow to me, and with his bow he would always say, "Diagnostician, par Excellence." His bow and the title he conferred on me followed me for the rest of my internship.

Many of the Ogden physicians had unique personalities and abilities. One such physician was Dr. Moesinger, a slender, tall graying family practitioner who did just a little of everything. He was a great instructor for us young physicians but was probably best known as the State Horseshoe Champion. It was fun to watch him pitch horseshoes at hospital get-togethers. I really had no idea a person was capable of pitching one ringer after another almost endlessly.

One of the funny stories we heard from Dr. Moesinger was about delivering five babies of one of the couples he cared for. One day toward the end of her sixth pregnancy the patient came to Dr. Moesinger and told him she had been having an affair with a Chinese man and she was worried that the baby could be his rather than her husband's. Dr. Moesinger told her there was nothing to be done about it and to wait to see what would happen. Dr. Moesinger said, "Sure as heck when that baby was born it had Asian features and it was pretty obvious the baby was fathered by the Chinese guy. A couple of days later the husband of the woman came in and wanted to talk to Dr. Moesinger. He said, "Dr. Moesinger, that new baby we have doesn't look at all like the rest of our kids when they were born." Dr. Moesinger replied, "Don't worry, that child has a touch of Mongolism (a genetic disorder now referred to as Down Syndrome) but will be just fine." The husband seemed satisfied with the reply and left happily. He confided in us that the issue of the child never came up again. Dr. Moesinger was quite the character.

After we had been in our internships for about a month, it became evident all of the moonlighting shifts were being taken up by interns and residents from Salt Lake City. I mentioned this to Sister Luke who stated rather emphatically that our time should be spent taking care of patients in the hospital and studying and not spent trying to make additional money moonlighting. It seemed a little hard for me to imagine negotiating with a nun in a black habit with white trim about the business of our internship. I guess Sister Luke was an appropriate name as she was running a hospital and had taken the one disciple's name who was a physician.

I brought the issue to Carroll and Dick and they were angry as was I. We had been assured we would be able to augment our salaries by moonlighting. Carroll and Dick asked if I would be the spokesperson for us and talk to Sister Luke. I agreed.

I approached Sister Luke one afternoon in her office and said I wanted to talk to her as a representative of all of the interns. Sister Luke I guessed to be in her later forties and I should have known the CEO of St. Ben's was going to be a business person with a business demeanor.

I informed Sister Luke that Dr. Cedarburg, Dr. Holmes and myself had come to intern in St. Benedict's Hospital with the idea we could supplement our meager income moonlighting with night shifts in the emergency department. Sister Luke again emphatically replied that our time should be spent taking care of patients in Saint Benedict's and studying and not spent trying to make additional money moonlighting. I replied, "It is no more right that you help interns and residents from Salt Lake City and the University Hospital to circumvent the rules of their hospitals. You do not seem to care that you break other hospitals' rules with what you do here. You do not mind cutting off their nose as long as it butters your bread, do you Sister Luke?"

Sister Luke became infuriated. I guess I had gotten to her with my insults. Good! That was what I had intended. They were not really insults. They were the facts, plain and simple and Sister Luke realized that. She said, "Dr. Redalen, you should leave here immediately and come back when you can act like a gentleman." I said, "Sister Luke, this is as good as I get and you had better take me the way I am. I am not going to become more complacent as I simmer. You had also better pay attention to the demands of your interns and keep your word."

I told her I would not hesitate to let the hospitals in Salt Lake City know which of their doctors were moonlighting in St. Benedict's and make their lives rough. I was not interested in preserving jobs at the emergency department of Saint Benedict's at the expense of our own interns. Sister Luke, after hearing these threatening words, capitulated and said she would revisit the moonlighting issue.

Within the month Carroll, Dick and I were on the schedule to begin covering the St. Ben's emergency department. The meager salary we were now supplementing with moonlighting made life for us interns and our families much more bearable and attractive. I am not really sure in retrospect why the additional funds were important to us although they did allow us to make car payments. Bette and I went into a Woods Automobile Dealership one day and fell in love with an Oldsmobile Toronado. It was our first new car. I think Bette and I were optimistic we would be able to make payments on it when we got our next job. We arranged for payments that were about half of our meager internship salary which ballooned when we left Ogden and started life for real. It was a beautiful yellow car with a fawn colored leather interior.

Working in our St. Benedict's emergency department was good for us and became an integral part of our training. We were continually exposed to our physicians and their continual teaching as we got to know them. One of our full-time emergency room physicians was Dr. Jess Wallace. He had a great demeanor and was in full-time teaching mode. We interns got to do almost everything we were exposed to in the emergency department. Often when things were slow we might be the only physician in the emergency department if our head physician was catching some rest.

One night a bad motorcycle accident came in and only Paula, one of the young nurses, and I were present in the department. We moved as fast as we could but the two young men who appeared to be in their early twenties were in rough shape. One of the young men's entire right femur was out of his thigh and as he was struggling the bone kept coming up and slapping his abdomen. I asked Paula to pull on his leg while I tried to fasten it down and as she was pulling, she started screaming at the top of her lungs. I grabbed Paula by both of her shoulders and looking directly into her face, sternly and loudly said, "Paula, shut up and do your job." It was as though a switch had been pulled and Paula became the calm cool nurse I always worked with.

Paula and I were both covered in blood from young man whose femur had kept beating the abdomen as it automatically and continually flexed up and down. The orderly and the aid present with us were busy calling in orthopedics, neurosurgery and general surgery. The young men were not neurologically intact and we could not get a history on them. We did find out from the highway patrol they were both riding on one cycle which had been hit by a car and they had not been wearing helmets.

Eventually our entire team got the two young men stabilized after hours of work. They became a full time job in the intensive care unit until later in the evening when both of the young men died. All our work had been for naught. Many of these sad cases would prepare us for what was to come in later life. Many times the very best care you can offer is not going to save the life of your patient. And you must always do the very best you can so you never have to lie awake at night wondering if you could have done more.

The following day both Paula and I were working in the emergency department again. I asked, "Paula, what on earth happened the other night?" She replied that only the day before one of the doctors had asked her to put traction on a leg and suddenly she was sitting on the emergency department floor with the leg in her lap. The leg had come off. She thought it was going to happen again.

The emergency department taught you a lot about thinking out of the box. One day we had a middle aged man come in who was a cherry picker from one of the orchards. He was comatose and in falling out of a tree, had broken his neck. He was presenting with paralysis from the neck down. I had sandbagged his head in place and was doing some lab work on the patient. I was busy with an EKG when the orthopedic surgeon who came in to take care of the patient got upset with me. He said, "Redalen, why the hell are you wasting time with an EKG on this patient when it is obvious what is wrong with him? He has a head injury and broken neck. What on earth are you thinking?" I said, "Doctor, I want to know why he fell out of the cherry tree." My surgeon became momentarily pensive and said to go ahead. In medicine you always have to remember, what you see is the obvious, what is unseen may be the cause of your problems and your undoing, if you do not look beyond the obvious.

The EKG showed the man had sustained a massive MI, commonly referred to as a heart attack. I felt that was the reason he had fallen out of the tree. The patient most likely had a momentary arrhythmia that led to unconsciousness. The surgeon did not say anything more but was probably glad the EKG had been done. The patient went to an ICU instead of an orthopedic floor. Over the next twenty-four to forty-eight hours the patient would develop multiple cardiac arrhythmias that we could not seem to get under control and the patient died two days later. His head injury and broken neck would not play into the reason for his demise. They were incidental to the heart.

I don't think the orthopedic surgeon ever thanked me for that EKG. However, in the big picture, the orthopedic problems never had to be managed. It had really made no difference unless the next time one of his patients fell out of a cherry tree it made the surgeon think about why it may have happened. In medicine, if you do not think outside of the box, you are never going to see what is there. You are locked into your self-made box.

Our internship was filled with fun in addition to working on the floor all the time. I was really lucky. Working on the floor never seemed to be a job because I had chosen a profession in which I would never have to work. I would always be having fun except during the tragic times of course and there were bound to be some of those.

When we were fully settled into life at St. Benedict's it became readily apparent the hospital was a closely knit group and all of us that hung around together were pretty close to the same age.

Early in my internship the hospital lab got a new SMA-1260 auto-analyzer. You could put a sample of blood into the machine and it would turn out a relatively large battery of tests.

None of us had ever seen anything like this as it was new in the field of medicine. One great thing we soon found out, the machine used pure grain alcohol for running the tests. When Dave Young who ran the lab mentioned this to us one day we all came up with the idea that since no one in the hospital knew how much alcohol the machine consumed we could begin to requisition two liter bottles of alcohol for hospital parties. It was not long before we had several liters of alcohol stored in our closet in the intern's quarters.

We began to have pretty well attended parties in the intern's quarters. One thing became apparent. There was always an abundance of single females from the lab. What would you expect from a hospital? One day I had the idea that perhaps if we called the flight surgeon's office at Hill Air Force Base they would have a lot of single guys. I called and introduced myself and asked if they would care to attend a party at the intern's quarters in St. Benedict's Hospital. The reply was, "How many of us do you want?" When I replied five, the reply was, "We'll be there." And five pleasant young flyboys showed up.

I warned the young men they had to be careful of our punch because the bubbling punch bowl filled with dry ice tasted more like a benign carbonated drink than a potent alcoholic beverage. The warning was not sufficient. At the end of the night five young airmen were lying on the floor spread around our living room and Bette had placed newspapers around each one of them. One survivor out of the five said to me, "If you can get them out to the car, I can drive them home." I nixed that idea and they stayed with us through the morning until they recovered. All in all it was one of several well attended parties during the year.

St. Benedict's Hospital maintained an old jeep the interns and their families could check out for a run around the country side. It didn't have a top on it and I think for most of us it was the first convertible experience we had. Often we would run up to Snowbasin Resort owned by Dr. Ross. It was pretty as a postcard in the summertime just as it was in the winter when all the snow was in place. Another place Bette and I would take the kids was the Great Salt Lake Desert, pure white salt areas around Great Salt Lake. And they were just as the name described, flat as a pancake and nearly as white as the salt in your shaker. The salt flats of Great Salt Lake were similar to the Bonneville Salt Flats where many of the land speed records were set. It had its own beauty, not so much as the surrounding mountains but another testimonial to the great diversity God put on this Earth we share.

Often we would run up to Huntsville, Utah, nestled between the mountains on the highways just north of Ogden. Huntsville was most well-known to us because it was the location of one of the Trappist Monasteries. The Trappist monks all kept vows of silence so were not allowed to talk to each other. It was hard for me to imagine what it was like to be surrounded by fellow monks and yet never talk to each other. I am not sure what vows like that accomplish and of course couldn't ask them because they could not talk to visitors either. We could observe them walking around and going about their chores. The dress code if you could call it that was the same for all the monks. They all wore light brown robes tied about their waists with a length of white rope. The robes all had hoods on them which pretty much hid their faces.

We never saw one of the monks with their hood down. I guess their manner of dress would make choosing what outfits to wear every day pretty simplistic. One day as a small procession of monks were walking past us, Bette and I could see one of the young monks trying to look out from inside his hood at the pretty blonde standing beside me. He became obviously embarrassed when we saw him trying to hide his look and he ducked his head back inside his hood like a turtle hiding theirs inside their shell. It was another observation that made me realize the monastic life was not for me.

One of the main reasons Bette and I liked to visit the monks was they made bread out of the wheat they had grown themselves and then hand ground it between stone wheels. The bread was very heavy and felt more like a sack of potatoes than a loaf of bread. The monks were truly self-sufficient and all their daily activities translated into something that would maintain their livelihood. Bette and I also bought some of the many flavored honeys from the store maintained by the monks which spread on top of their homemade bread made a meal for us.

About once per year the monks were allowed to come into Ogden to be examined by us interns and we would see to their healthcare needs. Every once in a while we would find problems that needed attention. It was during the times of caring for the monks I would realize what vows of silence must have meant in turning away from the life the rest of us lived.

They were allowed to talk to their doctors and talk they did. Goodness sakes, when you made rounds during the day they could literally talk your ears off. I always tried to make rounds with my monk patients when I had plenty of time to sit and talk with them. You came to realize they were not much different than any of the rest of us on our life's journey. Just by examining them you learned they did one thing probably much more than the rest of us. The spent a lot of knee time. All the monks' knees were covered by large callouses which I attributed to the time they spent on their knees praying.

Some of the younger men I got the chance to talk with had joined the monastery to escape some of life's problems. Some wanted time for introspection to examine themselves and discover what life was all about. I thought good luck with that; it will probably change daily due to circumstances.

I tried to design my internship much the same as I had done with training in medical school. I let the obstetricians know I would be willing to come and work with their patients any time they needed someone at night if intern coverage would help. Most of the doctors were pleased to have the help. It allowed them more time at home with their families. It also allowed me to deliver a lot of babies I would never have otherwise had the opportunity to deliver.

One night we got in a patient from outstate Utah. The woman was sent to us in an ambulance by a family practitioner who must have suspected something was wrong. The patient came in accompanied by a flat plate x-ray of the abdomen and the fetal head looked abnormal. On examination our patient was pretty far along in her labor and it did not appear that it would be very long before she would deliver. Our obstetrician was not sure what we were going to see at delivery but allowed me to care for the patient through the period of labor. The couple was in their early fifties and was really excited to be having a baby. This was to be their first child.

By history, they had waited with eager anticipation throughout the pregnancy. The prenatal period had been mostly uneventful except the prospective mother's abdomen was a little larger than it should have been. The condition of the mother was called polyhydramnios. Polyhydramnios is a condition in which more than the normal amount of amniotic fluid is present. It can be the harbinger of an abnormal pregnancy with fetal problems. The doctor outstate must have had a suspicion of this but he had not confided any of his doubts to his prospective parents. I do not think the outstate physician was trying to get rid of a bad situation, but was likely making sure that if the baby had problems at least a tertiary care facility with advanced obstetric and pediatric care would be better equipped to handle both the mother and baby.

While I was caring for that patient, a young, apparently healthy but hostile white girl arrived in active labor. She was already pretty far along in labor and it would not be long before she would deliver. She spoke emphatically to my young nurse and me, "I do not want to know if this baby is born dead or alive. I want the baby removed from the delivery room as soon as it is born. I do not want to know if it is black or white and I do not want to know if it is male or female."

We let the staff physicians know they were getting close but already knew from the rapid progression my two nurses and I were probably going to be doing both of these deliveries by ourselves without other staff present.

St. Benedict's hospital only had two delivery rooms which were connected by a working station where the physician or nurse could lay the baby down or work on the baby doing resuscitation if that was required.

As it turned out the young healthy mother delivered first. I removed the baby immediately from the delivery room. It was a beautiful healthy baby boy. He breathed spontaneously and had an Apgar score of about nine. I left him lying on the table between the rooms.

No sooner had I laid the young mother's baby down than the nurse from the next room informed me my other elderly patient was crowning and ready to deliver. I only had time to change gowns and re-glove. The baby delivered precipitously and I rapidly went into the center room with this baby too, but for different reasons. This baby boy was an anencephalic monster. These babies are hideous looking little creatures born without a brain with their large open eyes staring out above their absent cranium. I laid this baby down alongside the healthy little boy that had just been delivered. My young nurse was still suctioning and caring for the healthy baby. We both looked at each other and thought what a cruel world this was. We have one baby without a brain, a monster in any sense of the word whose parents desperately want him. Lying alongside him is another baby, but this one a healthy baby boy whose mother does not even want to know if he is dead or alive, male or female, black or white. How cruel is that.

My young nurse looked at me and said, "Should we?" I felt absolutely helpless. Both babies were born white. The elderly couple so desperately wanted their baby. I said to my nurse, "If we do this, we may get by with this for a long time, maybe even years, but someday some circumstance may allow this elderly couple to find out this is not their baby and when that realization happens and the birth is traced back to you and me, everyone will know who was responsible. You and I will never be allowed to take care of patients again." Three people know what happened that night.

Chapter Eleven

Life Lessons

Not all my training was heavy on my heart. Some was light and cheery. On the obstetrical service I also met Tom Feeney. Tom was an elderly obstetrician who was lighthearted and fun to work with. I think Tom liked skiing more than delivering babies because we would soon find out that after the first snow fell if Tom was not in the delivery room, he was probably on the ski slopes.

Tom's brother Shelton Feeney worked in the hospital as an internist. Tom was talking about his brother one day who was an outdoorsman. What an understatement that was. Shelton was a great internist, but he probably taught us almost as much about firearms and firepower as most gun lobbyists could. I think the reason he was so into firearms was his grandmother was Mrs. Browning of Browning Firearm fame. Shelton could tell you the muzzle velocity of nearly every type of rifle shell there was. Not only that, he could tell you about the elevation of the trajectories of each of the bullets. He was a fountain of information on firearms and liked talking about them.

Tom shared a story with us one day about how his brother always went out picking mushrooms in the season and would always be the good dutiful brother and bring a large bag of them to him. He said he felt uneasy eating mushrooms his brother picked so he would always just thank Shelton for them and then a while later throw them out. He said, "Darned if I'm going to take a chance with my life based on my brother's mushroom judgment."

One day when Shelton was talking with us about some problems in internal medicine, he shared with us his stories about mushroom picking. He said in the spring he always went out looking for morels. Among mushroom hunters evidently morels were the gold standard when it came to picking. Evidently mushroom pickers all had their own SWATS about how to pick and find mushrooms. That acronym stood for scientific, wild-assed theories about finding mushrooms. Shelton said every spring he would find a good cache of mushrooms and always share them with his brother Tom. He also confided he was not sure but thought perhaps his brother would tell him how good they were but suspected he probably threw them out. Carroll, Dick and I laughed pretty heartily at that story but we never told Dr. Shelton he was right on.

One day when I was on the medicine service Shelton came to me and asked if I would take care of his grandma Browning. He said, "Grandma is getting to the age in life where she is failing, but she really wants to get to be 100 years old." I asked Dr. Feeney what was so magical about getting to be 100 if you had already made it to 99. He said she wanted that letter from the president congratulating her on getting to be 100 years old. He told me it would be a big favor to him and his family. I asked, "How far away is she from getting to be 100?" When he said, "Only a couple of months," inwardly I groaned. After seeing her I realized it was going to be a rather long job, not full time but certainly time consuming caring for grandma if she was going to see the sunny side of 100 years. Or for gosh sakes, would that be the dark side?

Mrs. Browning was housed in a bright sunny private room on the south side of the hospital on the internal medicine floor. I would go in and take care of her every day. She was not very responsive and could not talk to you. She was in the final stage of life and the poor dear should have been allowed to die. For all of Shelton's caring about Grandma, he rarely came in to see her in her final couple months of life. I guess that was okay. I certainly made up for his absence. I couldn't really fault him either. He was just following Grandma's wishes and he had seen her through most of the seventy some years he had been alive. Now it was my turn.

One day someone from the very expensive nursing home where Mrs. Browning was staying came into the hospital and asked to talk to Dr. Feeney. They said, "Dr. Feeney, is it okay if we give Mrs. Browning's room away? We could use her bed if she is not going to be returning to the home." At this point in time she had been gone for nearly a month. Dr. Feeney said, "Why don't you keep it reserved for her just in case." Then he added, "Mrs. Browning is not exactly a pauper you know and the family is paying for her room in the home every month. We'd like you to have it ready for her just in case."

My nurse and I thought we were probably committing a crime by not allowing our patient to die. Mrs. Browning gradually passed through those couple months of life. I am sure it seemed a lot longer to me than to her although the only thing keeping her alive must have been that dang letter in waiting. With only about a week to go it appeared the only humane thing to do was to let her pass gracefully. We even thought that it would be good to make her a cake, bring it in and congratulate her on getting to be 100. But with all our scheming and calculating on how to help her die happily even if we did not know she was happily dying, she died the day before she was 100 years old. I don't know what difference it made. She could not have read and appreciated the letter anyway. I don't think Shelton even told me thanks for my efforts, not that I needed any.

Whit Bird and I continued to bump heads intermittently during my training. I think he thought it arrogant of me to think I could learn everything I would need to know about practicing medicine across all specialties. He was obviously not enamored with the idea of family practitioners. I thought to myself it is good he knows his own limitations. Fortunately for the field I had chosen, his limitations were not mine.

It also seemed my initial visit to Sister Luke's office had not put me in her good graces. We would end up butting heads when I took care of the woman who had been the head of St. Benedict's nursing program in earlier years, the mother of one of the nurses on staff. Mrs. Boyle was evidently one of the matriarchs of the hospital who commanded a lot of respect and Sister Luke evidently thought I was an impertinent young physician who did not give her that respect.

The incident triggering another run in with Sister Luke was precipitated by my care of the mother of Mrs. Boyle. Mrs. Boyle senior came into the hospital complaining of abdominal pain and she was obviously critically ill. She was an advanced age white female presenting with an acute abdomen. Her abdomen was exquisitely tender all over but there was a complete absence of bowel sounds. It was my impression she had an intra-abdominal catastrophe that was going to end her life. I thought she had a superior mesenteric artery thrombosis, a clot in the large artery that supplies most of the small intestine, which causes a complete death of most of the small bowel. She would not survive. Their family doctor was a general practitioner who agreed with me but he called in one of the general surgeons who also agreed.

The Boyle's family doctor asked me to give her palliative care and keep her comfortable. Not long after the family's physician left Mrs. Boyle, the daughter, asked for the chart and began writing orders. I told her she did not have the right to begin writing orders for the care of her mother.

I did not know what position I was playing in this struggle but knew it was not proper for a nurse to begin writing orders that could not legally be carried out by our nurses, who were also being put in a bad position. There was clearly not going to be a satisfactory outcome for the situation or for Mrs. Boyle senior. After several hours of supportive care Mrs. Boyle senior passed away.

Several hours later I was called into Sister Luke's office and read the riot act. I had not given one of the major hospital supporters the respect she deserved. I informed Sister Luke I did not think it proper for a family member without the proper credentials to be writing orders and treating a family member's medical problems. Sister Luke, I am sure, knew I was right even if she did not support me. The issue never came up again.

I would find out the following day Kathy Boyle, the little gal we sometimes hired to babysit Terra and Todd, was the granddaughter of Mrs. Boyle senior. At least no harm was done to that relationship and Kathy continued on with her babysitting duties for us when needed.

One other specialty I tried to get extra training in during my time at St. Ben's was with one of the local plastic surgeons. I told Dr. Jerry Bergera I wanted to be a family practitioner but thought additional training in plastic surgery would be very beneficial to me and he was in agreement. From that time on whenever Dr. Bergera had cases come in during the night or any other time when I was not busy on my assigned service he would call me and I would serve as his assistant in surgery. I would learn immense amounts of surgery from Dr. Bergera in the field of cosmetics. By cosmetic I do not mean doing procedures to make people look better or give them a better figure. Dr. Bergera taught me how to do facial reconstructions following accidents and how to get the best possible results with very little to work with. I began to gain a lot of confidence in handling some severe trauma and found that just slowly piecing some of the puzzles back together again would produce amazing results. Another amazing thing is the wonderful way our bodies are made and the fantastic abilities to repair ourselves after a little help from a surgeon. Dr. Bergera also taught me to do some pretty fantastic Z-plasties. An example would be taking a lesion off the face and with the proper type of Z-cutting and moving some tissue around, you could barely see that a procedure had been done a few months later. There would seem to be no remnants of the problem left behind.

We had one surgeon, Dr. Grua, who was small in stature but that did not stop his ego from being a bit larger. Dr. Sterner, one of the family practitioners said to Dr. Grua, "Ernie, I have a patient who is having some severe external hemorrhoid problems. I think you should take a look at him and see what you can offer him surgically." Dr. Grua followed Dr. Sterner up to the floor and walked down to the patient's room. The patient, Mr. Willy Dee, was a large black man who was sitting in a tub in his room taking a sitz bath trying to ease the pain from his hemorrhoids. He was a cement worker but looked more like a professional wrestler or football player. Both Dr. Sterner and Dr. Grua walked into the room and without a word of introduction, Dr. Grua said to Mr. Dee, "Stand up." Dr. Grua, without any small talk, then told Mr. Dee to bend over so he could examine him. Then, without any pleasantries Dr. Grua rammed his gloved finger up Mr. Dee's rectum. With that came a groan of pain. Mr. Dee lunged forward, at which time Dr. Grua mistakenly said, "Hold still black boy." Mr. Dee turned around, put both of his hands around Dr. Grua's upper arms, lifted him into the air and turned back toward the front of the tub of water. He set Dr. Grua down on the floor of the tub with his shoes and socks now covered in bath water. Although Mr. Dee bent over he still had to look down at Dr. Grua to say to his face, "Don't you ever say that again." Dr. Grua, who looked as if he were having an other-worldly experience, said, "No sir." Mr. Willy Dee then picked up Dr. Grua and set him down again outside the tub of water from whence he came. Dr. Grua walked silently down the hall except for the unavoidable squish, squish, squish you could hear coming from his shoes.

It was days like this I learned to be humble in medicine, to treat people the way you want to be treated and learn humility the easy way or be taught it the hard way.

Part of what had happened in that patient's room I did not really understand. When I questioned some of my Mormon friends about the incident I was informed the black race was considered inferior by the Mormons at that time. I was also informed blacks were not permitted to be Elders in the Mormon Church. They could be members but were not allowed to serve. I was unable to corroborate this information. Later Brigham University would suffer athletic boycotts because the church did not offer priesthood to blacks. I did not lose respect for Dr. Grua and other than the one time with Willy Dee, he seemed to treat everyone the same. He certainly did not seem like a racist but I guess it would be hard to know as blacks were a rarity in Ogden, Utah.

Another day a pompous and arrogant obstetrician from the other side of town graced us with his presence. He rarely if ever came to St. Benedict's and was wearing a dapper suit, ready to go to a party. It was Friday night and almost time to relax after a long week of seeing patients. It is hard to imagine today but he always walked around with a cigar hanging out of his mouth. After a brief examination of a patient, he was doing a pelvic exam and kneading around on her abdomen. The patient was found to have a fecal impaction which he thought was part of the problem but decided he wanted her to have a couple of enemas and examine her again. He barked out his orders to one of our nurses and was griping about how slow everything was in our emergency room, making our staff uncomfortable.

None of us were happy with the ravings of this "foreign" physician invading our space. It was not long before he was barking orders again to our nurses to get his patient up in the stirrups again for another pelvic exam. The nurse who had administered the enema said the patient had not yet had the expected relief from the enemas. She informed him that the complete enema had probably not been expelled. Dr. X said, "Get her ready anyway. I am in hurry and not going to spend my entire evening in St. Benedict's emergency department."

Our nurse did as instructed. With his patient up in the stirrups he sat down on the stool at the end of the table and at the very moment he was going to insert a speculum the patient had a large involuntary contraction of the colon. Dr. X suddenly had his entire suit covered with the expected results of the enema and the cigar still hanging from his lips was now dripping in brown shit colored water. If that doesn't teach you humility, nothing will.

I don't know if that physician ever showed his face again at St. Benedict's but no one seemed to miss him.

Later on in my training I would again hear of the consequences of someone calling a black person "boy." At the time I realized at some point or another during their formative years these Mormon kids must have learned that.

One night a couple of belligerent, drunk teenagers came into the emergency department. They had evidently given the highway patrol plenty of reasons to be unhappy with them. I was informed they had demolished an exotic car worth about a quarter of a million dollars. They were unruly and the officers were more than unhappy with them. One of the nurses informed me these were children of two of the most prominent families in Ogden and their fathers were prominent physicians in the medical community. They suggested it would probably be good if we could find a reason to keep them in the hospital. Anything I did was not going to make their parents happy.

The kids were indeed misbehaving in our department and I was finding it less and less likely I was going to be doing them any favors on anybody's behalf by admitting them to the hospital. After examining them, other than ethanol intoxication, I could see no reason to use the hospital beds to dry them out. When I informed the officers I was returning the two young men to their custody they were pleased. The two young men left in handcuffs and my staff and I went back to taking care of an overly busy department. Protecting youth from having a police record when it is deserved at the time does no societal favors. Actions always have consequences.

A couple of hours later the officers who'd had the youths in custody ended up back in our department for another matter. I got the chance to talk to one of them and asked, "How are our two young behavior problems doing?" He smiled at me and said, "They are learning some manners." I smiled back and said, "What did they learn?" One officer said, "They learned right away you do not call a black jailer "boy." I just said, "Good for them." They were the last two people I heard of getting in trouble for calling somebody "boy" while I was in Utah.

I was on the emergency department shift a day later when one of the boys' fathers came down to our department asking for me. The physician introduced himself and said, "I understand my son gave you a hard time when he saw you the other night. I simply wanted to come down here and meet you and apologize for his behavior." I said, "I am sorry I did not keep him in the hospital but thought jail overnight might be a good learning experience." The doctor replied, "I think jail is the very best thing that could have happened to him and his buddy the other night and I just wanted to thank you for taking care of him." A couple of hours later the other father came in and also apologized for his child.

The fathers were stand-up acts even if their children hadn't been the previous night. One thing to take away from this, children usually emulate their parents in life and even though these kids had a night in their life they would later regret, a few years down the line they were probably going to end up the same as their fathers. Hopefully they would not have repeat performances later in life as fathers apologizing for their children.

If summer was a great time to be interning in the mountains, I think it was even better in the winter, mainly because Dr. Ross encouraged the interns to ski at Snowbasin and encouraged us to take advantage of his generosity. The interns and their families could use the rental equipment and lifts free of charge. This was a wonderful benefit for all of us as we would not have been able to afford to use the facilities much otherwise.

One of the great things about interning in a community where everybody has "Think Snow" bumper stickers is most of the doctors were skiers and when the first snow came, if we said we were going skiing for the afternoon after our work was done, none of them seemed to mind even a little bit. This was ski heaven and it felt like we were ski angels.

Both Steve Johnson and John Howarth attempted the task of teaching me to ski. John was the first one to take me out on the slopes. After I had been fitted for ski equipment John thought I should go down the bunny slope a few times to get the hang of it. The bunny slope was such a slight slope that you almost had to walk down it.

After a couple runs on the bunny slope John said I was ready for more of a challenge. He said I was ready for Wildcat. I should have known from the name I was not ready for that, but from the bottom, it didn't look too bad. Only when you got to the top of Wildcat could you see the steep mountain rising behind it and the top where the lift ride ended. I said, "John, you asshole." I could see this was nothing but trouble. Getting off the ski lift revealed there was going to be no easy way down and this was going to be a long difficult run. The only encouragement I got from John was when I fell once and slid a couple hundred yards down the mountain on my back. He yelled, "Keep going, that is the farthest you have made it in one run so far." It was a long day but eventually I ended up back at the lodge.

As time went on I got more comfortable on skis and Steve told me I did not have much form but was probably the fastest on the slopes. I really loved the speed.

One day when it had just snowed, Carroll Cedarburg and I decided we wanted to go out and ski powder. I guess we were overly ambitious in our thinking as neither one of us had ever skied powder.

When we got to the lodge early that morning it was a bright sunny beautiful day. Everything was stunning with its new layer of fresh snow. We talked to one of the ski lift operators on Wildcat and asked him if Porky was running. That was the top lift you could go to but it was not visible from the lodge because it was far up and behind Wildcat. When you got to the top of Wildcat, you would have to ski across and down to the bottom of Porky to get lifted to the top. The lift operator informed us a lift operator was at the bottom of Porky and someone would run us up to the top. It had not been groomed yet and no one had gone up to ski because the powder was too deep.

When you are in a community where everyone is always waiting for fresh powder and the lift operator tells you no one is going up, it should have been the clue for Carroll and me to take the day off. Foolishness prevailed and we were soon at the bottom of Porky. The Porky lift operator also told us the snow was too deep. Our problem was we could not get down the mountain without going to the top of Porky to ski down. When we got off the lift on the top of Porky the powder was up to our chins. We had to walk to a steep slope to begin to move. The snow was a huge impediment. Our first falls were frightening. Once down you would be covered with several feet of snow and your ski poles were of no use to get up as you could not touch bottom anyplace. Even being young and in excellent shape we were rapidly tiring from falling and trying to get back on our skis.

As the day moved on we both began to worry we would be spending the night on the mountain trying to stay warm. Our early morning fun had lasted into late afternoon and we were both worn out, tired and cold. When we finally got back to the lodge the dark parking lot was mostly empty. We had spent the entire day on the side of a mountain learning a valuable lesson. We had left in early morning daylight and comeback in darkness. It was a mistake we would not repeat.

About midway through my internship the physicians in Ogden, and I believe in all of Utah, set up the first Physicians Standard Review Organization (PSRO). The acronym was pronounced PEESROW and was the name always used. The physicians of Ogden felt they needed to police themselves so the federal government wouldn't step in to do it from afar, much less efficiently. They were absolutely correct in their thinking and ahead of their time. They had absolutely no idea how right they were. The knowledge I acquired from my experience with PSRO would serve me very well when I would later begin practice.

My internship progressed rather uneventfully and all of the services provided great opportunities. When Dr. Bird said I would have to work at least three to four times as hard as the other interns, he was spot on. Obstetrics and Dr. Bergera almost never failed to call me regardless of time of night or service I was on to help deliver babies or learn some new plastic surgery. I had immense learning experiences only because everyone appreciated my help.

We got to pick one elective and I thought orthopedic surgery would be of immense help in my practice. When I asked who the best orthopedic surgeon was, the surgical nursing staff unanimously agreed it was Dr. Charles Swindler. They warned me he was very stern and gruff. The next day I approached Dr. Swindler and introduced myself. Dr. Swindler looked up from the chart he was writing on and peered at me over the top of his glasses. "Hrumph," was all he said. I said I wanted to do an orthopedic surgery elective with him as my advisor. "Hrumph," was all he said again. I then asked him when and where I should show up. He said, "Show up to assist me in surgery tomorrow morning."

My relationship with Dr. Swindler was wonderful. He was a kind, gentle, benevolent spirit who managed to somehow pass himself off as a stern taskmaster. He was anything but that.

Later I would find out how much time he donated to the Shriners Hospital in Salt Lake City. He was magnificent with the children and had a heart of gold. This supposedly stern, rough physician would absolutely melt around those children.

One day I saw a little boy in a basket filled with pillows. Dr. Swindler explained to me this little boy had severe osteogenesis imperfecta, called at that time brittle bones and blue sclera. Blue sclera means the white parts of the eyes are bluish in color. This little boy was several years old and had suffered dozens of fractures. His disease was so severe even the gentlest handling produced fractures. Sometimes they occurred from the little boy simply moving in bed. I really couldn't imagine anything much worse. This little boy looked like a skinny little baby. At that time there was no treatment available for this dreaded disease and no matter how gentle the handling, fractures were going to occur.

Some other things I learned from working at Shriners were how to cast children caught early with club feet. This diagnosis could usually be made at the time of delivery although sometimes the feet of a baby are a little misshapen because of intrauterine crowding. If that is not the case it usually becomes apparent within a day or so.

It seems as if I would get to see Dr. Swindler nearly every day during ski season. It was amazing how many tibial fractures would come in off the ski slopes. Years before one of the radiologists had gotten all new ski equipment and was going to take up skiing until he came in one Monday to find over a dozen tibial fractures had come in over the weekend. He sold all his ski equipment without ever going skiing.

One thing you learned well while interning in a skiing community is to put on a long leg cast in a hurry. You had no choice. One Minnesota nurse said to me years later while I was putting on a long leg cast, "Wow, I have never seen a cast put on that fast in my life." I told her it was the benefit of ski country training.

When Christmas rolled around Bette and our children and I were more than ready to go home to see our family. We drove in one of the worst snowstorms of the season and when we stopped in a large truck stop about one hundred miles outside of Rapid City, South Dakota the roads were considered impassable. We talked to the highway patrol and they said the road plows would be out in the morning.

We had our new Oldsmobile Toronado and the front wheel drive seemed to be almost unstoppable in snow. We decided to proceed as we knew we probably could not get stuck. What we didn't foresee was getting lost while driving down a wide four lane highway. The road seemed to be getting narrower and narrower and then we came to a sign that told us we were on the scenic route through Black Hills National Forest.

We now had one half tank of gas, probably could not find our way back and were sitting on the side of a mountain with the snow getting deeper and deeper. When it quit snowing we could see a beautiful full moon and a ski lodge miles off in the distance. The only way to get there was to walk. Bette and I, having grown up in North Dakota, know what happens when people get out of their cars in a blizzard. It wasn't snowing right then but a wind could create a blinding blizzard in minutes. There are hundreds of North Dakota grave sites reinforcing this thinking.

Finally, the road was covered with more and more snow and I had to walk in front of the car to see where the road was and if I thought we could make it through. The car did just fine in the light powdery snow even when it was over the top of the hood. Bette and the children realized our dilemma and for a while were all crying. We were on a road that would not be traveled again until spring or summer. At one point it took us four hours to go fifteen miles.

We had to keep going. When our gas gauge read empty we pulled out onto a major four lane highway near a sign that said it was twenty miles to Rapid City. We had by God's grace, made it all the way through Black Hills National Forest scenic route in the middle of winter.

I had corresponded with a young surgeon Paul Hedenstrom in the town of Princeton who was looking for a family practitioner to join him. Paul and his wife Betty and their two children, Mary and Bobby were fun to be around. Mary and Bobby were tall slender kids close to six feet tall and were twelve and thirteen years of age respectively. It was understandable as their dad was about 6' 3", dark and handsome. Their mom Betty was also tall and slender. One of the early discussions we had about how to differentiate which Betty or Bette we were talking about was kind of funny. Betty Hedenstrom did not want to be called 'old Betty' and we laughed when she suggested she did not want to be called 'big Betty' either.

The four of us gradually ironed out an agreement. I agreed to come to Princeton and practice medicine with Paul for a starting salary of $40,000 which was the smallest salary I had been offered. But, since salary was last on the list of the ten most important things to us, it did not dissuade us.

As the internship was winding down we realized there were a lot of friends we were going to dearly miss when we left Ogden. One day during the last months in our internship Steve Johnson asked me if I wanted to go water skiing later in the day. I decided I would go snow skiing in the morning and waterski in the afternoon so I could later say I had done both in one day.

About one month prior to the end of our internship, I received a letter from the draft board. The letter stated I had been inducted into the draft. My physical was to take place in Salt Lake City and a bus would be coming to pick up the inductees from the City of Ogden. The day of the trip to Salt Lake arrived and I was among an entire bus load of young men. After the first letter from LeeRoy Meyer, I had received several more and all of them said to run to Canada. I just could not. It was morally reprehensible to me.

After taking my physical, about one or two weeks prior to my leaving for the service I received a letter from my draft department saying that I was being deferred from the draft. Princeton had suddenly lost all their physicians except for Paul Hedenstrom. It was declared a medical disaster area, therefore the deferment.

I was somewhat bewildered. I didn't think anything would get me out of the draft. I called my draft board and they were upset with me and said I obviously knew some very important people. I told them I knew nothing and nobody. They said all the senators and representatives from Minnesota had written letters for me, along with Hubert Humphrey, General Hershey and a number of congressional leaders. I was completely at a loss to explain it.

I called up Paul and Betty and told them what had happened. I had let them know I was being drafted. I did not know it at the time, but Betty Hedenstrom worked for Congressman Zwach. She had told them of my draft and did not want to share anything with me as she thought it might get my hopes up, possibly for nothing if they could not get me deferred. That deferment in all probability saved my life. As an intern without additional training, I would have been a medic on the front line and very likely would have ended up the way Ferd Nessler's friends did. God works in wonderful ways and man is He farsighted.

On a lighter note Betty, Paul's Betty, shared with me she had forgotten to put her car in park earlier in the week and it rolled down the street until it came to rest when it hit my mom and dad's car. She said, "Of all the cars I could have hit in all of Princeton, it had to be your mom and dad's." Oh well. Cars can be fixed.

Chapter Twelve

Princeton, Minnesota

A few days later Paul called me and was somewhat elated. He said you are going to be happy to know I hired one of your classmates from Nebraska to join us. I said great. Who is it? My heart dropped when he told me the classmate was L. M. I tried to feign happiness but my heart said something far different. I got on the phone right away and called Paul Lundstrom, nicknamed Lumpy, a good friend and the student who pulled L. off my back while we were at Rochester visiting the Mayo Clinic. Lumpy gave me his condolences.

We had a long talk; I was trying hard to determine whether or not I should go to Princeton. We bantered back and forth and then we both kind of gave L. the benefit of the doubt. Maybe he had changed. Perhaps he was on medication. We both knew in our hearts people really did not change. Psychiatric conditions could be treated but more than likely would not disappear. At that time I was not thinking of what would happen to my Vietnam status and the draft if I pulled out of practicing in Princeton. After the way my draft board had talked to me when they found out I was deferred, I was sure it was information they would relish having.

Bette and the children and I packed our bags and traveled to Princeton, Minnesota. It was exciting to be entering another season of our lives. Bette and I had picked out our first new home in the northern part of Princeton. Terra and Todd were excited about having their own bedrooms. They did lay the upstairs carpeting downstairs and vice versa but it looked pretty good so we really did not care. When you have the nicest roof over your head you have ever had, how could you fuss about something like that.

Another nice thing was my parents were our next door neighbors. I know for a lot of people that would spell trouble but both sets of our parents were among our very best friends. Bette and I never used my mom and dad for handy next door babysitters but years later they confided they wished we had. I guess guarding against abusing our parents with too much babysitting, we went the other way and abused them in a different way. The secret is to talk to the people around you. You do not have to try to guess what everyone is thinking. Ask them! If God had wanted us to read minds he would have put Braille on our heads instead of bumps. I guess the phrenologists did not figure this out. They read the bumps.

We lived in a young neighborhood and in no time the kids had made lots of friends with children their own age. The Nelsons lived just down south on the corner of our block and the Kreie's lived across the street. Both families were teachers in the local schools. A highway patrolman lived across the street from us and teachers lived on the other side of our house. We loved our community and attended a local Lutheran church. As it turned out the pastor of our church was the father of Blair Lomborg, my sister Susan's boyfriend. Blair and Susie were inseparable for years and remained close friends after going their separate ways following high school and early college.

Settling into practice at Princeton Medical Clinic seemed completely natural. I felt comfortable. I had done a good job of designing my training to fit the practice of family medicine.

When Bette and I arrived in Princeton Paul Hedenstrom had not taken a day off covering the city for a long time. My first day of work was the Fourth of July, 1969, a memorable day for me. Paul and Betty had taken their kids out to their cabin on Green Lake to celebrate. Since their cabin was only a few miles east of Princeton, Paul said he would come into town if I needed him. I was the only physician in town so covering the hospital for the day seemed a good way to get initiated.

One of my first patients was a farmer whose tractor had rolled over on him and he came in with a flail chest. It was not something we had the capability of handling in Princeton and a call to Paul confirmed my thinking. With some stabilization of his chest I sent him off to the North Memorial Hospital to the care of surgeons I would later come to know.

My second patient of the day I remember as well to this day as if it happened last week. I was at our home which was only about a mile north of Princeton when I received a frantic telephone call. A woman said her little girl just got hit in the side of the head by a rock thrown out by her grandfather's mower. She was unconscious and not moving. I said, "Come immediately to the hospital emergency room and I will be waiting for you."

I arrived at the hospital and waited on the curb until a car came flying up and ground to a stop. I ran to the car, threw open the door, lifted a lifeless beautiful little blonde child out of her mother's arms and ran into the emergency room. I laid her on the examining table and could at a glance tell we were in dire straits. The angelic little face looked as if she were sleeping but when I looked at her pupils they were already dilated. I did not even take the time to see if they responded to light. I grabbed the endoscope from my nurse and looked into her larynx, which was filled with vomitus. As I was trying to suction her, Dick Propson, one of our anesthetists, came in and asked if he could help. I told Dick I was trying to get an airway and her passages were filled with vomitus. Dick, who was more proficient than I was, also tried suctioning and while he was doing that I assessed the little angel more completely. Her pupils were fixed and dilated and did not react to light. She was completely unresponsive to stimuli. Dick said, "It is no use Rick." Both her right and left main stem bronchi were filled with vomitus and she could not be ventilated. Even though this little girl's heart was still beating, she was going to die and there was nothing we could do about it. Dick by now had suctioned as much vomitus out as he possibly could and then intubated her but no air could be forced into the lungs. A couple of minutes later I pronounced this beautiful little girl dead.

It seemed unimaginable to me. All this little girl was doing was watching her grandpa mow the lawn and now a little stone thrown by the mower had caused her death.

I went out and talked to the young mom who was sobbing frantically. She said, "She is my only little girl and I will never be able to have another." The mom looked terribly young and I tried to console her. I wrapped my arms around her and said, "You are a young woman. Why do you say you will not be able to have another child?" She said, "I have advanced cancer of the cervix and I am having a complete hysterectomy on Monday." The mom was nineteen years old, little more than a child herself. Now my heart was crying. She said, "My doctor lives on Green Lake. Would you please call him for me?"

I left briefly and called her doctor whom I reached with my first call. I explained what had happened, told him his patient had requested him and that it would be a favor to me if he came to the hospital to help console this young mom.

Her doctor showed up about twenty minutes later while I was still talking to the mom and her parents. He was rather brusque in his manner and certainly did not present the empathetic front I thought would be appropriate for the circumstances. He said to the young mom, "Just calm down. This is not the end of the world." What the hell was he talking about anyway? It was the end of the world for this darling little blonde child. I am sure the young mom thought at that time it was the end of the world for her.

I realized I wished I had not called this physician. A moment later he said to me, "She always was an excitable child and gets upset by almost nothing or anything." I said, "Doctor, this young lady just lost her only child." He reaffirmed what he had just said.

That day had a profound effect on me for the rest of my life. That night when finally home, I went into my bedroom alone and knelt alongside my bed. I talked to God. I cried and cried and called out to Him. I remembered clearly an iteration of a verse from a poem called *The Toys*, by Coventry Patmore which I had read years earlier:

So when that night I pray'd
To God, I wept, and said:
Ah, when at last we lie with tranced breath,
Not vexing Thee in death,
And Thou rememberest of what toys
We made our joys,
How weakly understood
Thy great commanded good,

Then, fatherly not less
Than I whom Thou hast moulded from the clay,
Thou'lt leave Thy wrath, and say,
"I will be sorry for their childishness."

I wept and wept and prayed and prayed. I managed to control my emotions while in the hospital but when I got home and was alone in the solitude of my bedroom, the rains of heaven were completely unleashed. I knelt alongside my bed and prayed, "Dear heavenly Father, please look down upon me today and hear my heart. Dear Father in heaven, if I ever talk to a patient like the physician I saw today, please strike me dead. Do this so I never have to take another breath. Do it immediately. I do not want to care for people in that manner if I ever become so calloused in life that I cannot feel their pain. Please do not let me live to care for your children if I become this way." God has guided me well and though my heart is often broken to the point of wearing it on my sleeve I would rather have my life this way.

I recalled a conversation I had years ago with one of our adult psychiatrists at the University of Nebraska, Dr. Tunaken. He thought a physician should not empathize with their patient to the point where the physician was also feeling grief. He thought if you did that you would become unable to carry on a good treatment relationship with your patient. I told Dr. Tunaken I felt exactly the opposite. How can you not feel grief if your patient has just lost a child or suffered some other tragedy? Dr. Tunaken thought it was necessary to guard against that. We never did come to agreement on that and today I still feel that only if you know how your patient is feeling are you able to offer empathy and compassion for what your patient is going through. Also, when you feel what they are feeling, your tears will flow.

Practicing medicine in a small town was something that became more enjoyable by the day. Paul was always really helpful. One thing amazed me. Even though you could take care of someone with severe congestive heart failure, renal problems or hepatic failure, there were many little things you just did not learn in medical school. An example would be simple things like taking care of plantar warts, head lice, etc.

Dr. Art Lundholm

Paul was not my only instructor in Princeton. His uncle Art Lundholm, Chief of Pathology and the Chief of Surgery in Bethesda Hospital in St. Paul for many years, also practiced in the clinic with Paul. Dr. Lundholm was a walking encyclopedia of medical information. It seemed as if there was never a problem he had not taken care of in the past. Not only that but he was an accomplished urologist. Art had been trained at the University of Sweden and went on to the University of Heidelberg to complete his training. His father had also taken the same path in medical education.

They were first or among the first urologists in the state. Paul told me Art and his dad had done the first TURPs in the state of Minnesota. A TURP is a transurethral resection of the prostate. As men get older their prostates often get bigger; this surgery removed the portion of the prostate from inside the bladder that was causing difficulty urinating. They brought this technology from Sweden and Germany. Art showed me the old resectoscopes they used long ago. A resectoscope allowed the surgeon to cut the prostate away by going in through the urethra. Art taught me all of these procedures. Dr. Art would have me look through the scope as he, then I, identified all the land marks. Then as he cut away pieces of the prostate, I would do the same on the other side and then again identify all the landmarks. After multiple procedures with me doing half, Art would have me do the procedure and then examine my work. I became experienced quickly and it was not long before I could do a TURP almost as rapidly as Art.

Art talked of the olden days in surgery when the only anesthetic they had was ether. Ether was given by dropping drops of liquid ether on to an ether mask, little more than some cloth held in the shape of a mask by a wire frame. He told of doing a Cesarean section one night in the country when using the kitchen table as an operating room table. There was no electricity in the country so they did the operation with four people holding kerosene lanterns over their heads around the four corners of the table. Their anesthetist was giving an ether anesthetic. It is hard to imagine ether in the presence of kerosene lanterns. Ether is extremely flammable and very explosive with even a tiny spark, but it is also much heavier than air. So as the drip anesthetic was being given the ether fumes would fall to the floor. The kerosene lanterns held overhead by the four lantern holders kept the flames away from the ether. Should one of those lantern holders have passed out, everyone in the home would have been killed instantly.

Surgery was also accomplished much faster in years gone by. Because anesthetics were not as effective or safe as modern anesthetics the surgery was done as fast as was safe and possible. Later on while teaching at the University of Minnesota in Bethesda Hospital, I would have a chance to talk to an elderly nurse who had worked for years with Dr. Lundholm. She said Art and one of his colleagues had performed an appendectomy in seven minutes. I could at least conceive of it. As time went on I would find with practice it would take me 45 to 50 seconds to remove a baby during a C-section.

Princeton Medical Clinic was located only several hundred feet away from the hospital so it was convenient to see a patient in the hospital if there were problems. In a small hospital and clinic it seems as if it is mostly one big happy family.

One of the incredible things to me in our small hospital was the breadth and depth of knowledge of our nurses. It seemed there were no medical problems they could not handle. I had never been in a hospital of less than a couple of hundred beds and now here I was in a thirty-five bed hospital that functioned as well or better than any of the large hospitals where I had practiced. The small community and hospital offered an intimacy that worked wondrously in the care of a patient. The understanding and familiarity the nurses had of most of the patients in our hospital were invaluable. All of our nurses were a pleasure to work with and we were blessed to have an especially valuable nurse by the name of Mary Newton. Mary and her husband Bob had been living in the Princeton area for a number of years.

It became apparent early on that when practicing in a small town you were continually tied to the hospital. This was in the day prior to portable phones or cell phones. Paul and I decided to try out some walkie talkies with fairly good range. Paul and Betty brought a couple over to our house one night for us to try out. Paul and I were running around the neighborhood to see how they would work. Paul was talking to me saying, "Batman to Robin, Batman to Robin." I would imagine that if anyone saw us or heard us they would think we were acting like overgrown kids. All four of us were laughing after our tryout. Betty and Bette said we were both crazy.

Every now and then when we were together Paul would say, "Let's go out and blow up the damn feather factory." There was a feather factory just a couple of miles southeast of town and when the wind was from the right direction, it smelled as though it was in the back yard. Paul always said this good-naturedly, always laughing when he said it, but in actuality, it did not sound like such a bad idea.

Paul had a lot of entertaining stories from his early years in medicine. I think one of the funniest ones was about a time when he was practicing in St. Cloud, Minnesota a few years earlier. He was in a clinic with multiple professionals practicing with shared offices. He said one of his friends, Ted Diedolf, a dentist from across the hall came running in one day saying excitedly, "Paul, I think one of my patients just died!"

Paul went running with him into the room of a patient sitting with his head hanging forward, still in the dentist's chair. Paul used his stethoscope to examine the patient and confirmed his friend's fears. Dr. Diedolf had a waiting room full of people. He did not want an ambulance to come and drag his dead patient through a room full of patients. They looked out the back window and wondered if they could lower the patient out the back window with a sheet to the alley below and take him from there. After all, it was only several feet to the ground as the clinic was on the first floor. What were these two grown men thinking anyway? It was just humorous to me. They ended up tying the patient up in a chair with rollers on it, putting a sheet over him and rolling him out through the waiting room where a patient waiting to be seen said, "Well there goes another one."

After a couple of years of practice in Princeton we would hire a couple of nurses from the University of Minnesota. After they had been in Princeton working for a couple of months they confided to me they could not even comprehend how a hospital the size of ours could function. They confessed that although they thought they would arrive and be able to teach our nurses a wealth of information, they were wrong. It was the other way around. They also thought medical care in Princeton was probably superior to the care they witnessed at the University of Minnesota where they had both spent the majority of their practice years.

Bette and the children and I would often visit Paul and Betty out at their cabin on Green Lake. One day Paul handed me a stethoscope and asked me to take a listen to Skipper's heart. He was concerned Skipper was having a little congestive heart failure. Skipper was the third child of Paul and Betty, a furry English Springer Spaniel child. Paul asked me what I could hear. I replied, "Just a lot of crackling hair." I was not much help. Paul had already started using a mild diuretic on Skipper and thought his breathing had improved over the past couple of weeks.

L. M., his wife M. and their children arrived in Princeton about two weeks after we did. L. and I reintroduced ourselves and acted as if there was nothing but friendship between us. I remained cautious and vigilant. L. seemed all right on the outside but I still wished I could see inside his head. After he had been there maybe one or two weeks a code was called on an elderly woman on the medical floor of the hospital. It was then I really began to have my doubts about L. again. While I was intubating the patient he began with chest compressions. With the very first compression he pushed that elderly woman's sternum almost to her backbone. You could hear the fracturing of all her ribs. It sounded like the crushing of a giant bag of popcorn. I told him to be careful. But I knew the damage was done and the woman promptly expired. He could not have done more harm to that elderly patient if he had tried.

I got L. alone in a room a little while later and asked him what the hell he was thinking. He said it was necessary to do chest compressions like that. I informed him that even had the patient lived she would not have survived after he broke all of her ribs. L. only acknowledged me without necessarily agreeing with me.

As the weeks went by I was becoming more and more uncomfortable working in the clinic with L. I was standing alongside him one day when he was putting something above his head into a closet. As he raised his arms up in the air I could see a shoulder holster with a pistol in it. I asked him if he was armed and he replied without hesitation he was. I then asked what in the hell he was doing with a firearm in the clinic. He explained you never can know what kind of people you are going to run into. You need to be prepared. L. was actually the only person I had run into in the clinic so far I thought I needed preparing for. It was a sobering thought with no consolation. It was apparent L. was definitely a paranoid schizophrenic and obviously not being treated for it.

As dangerous as L. appeared, I was growing more paranoid by the day. However, my paranoia was entirely rational from where I stood, based on what I had observed.

After about a month, L.'s wife M. came in to see me and said she had taken a fall down the stairs. She had a broken arm and a black eye and bruises over a good part of her body. I asked her how it happened and she said she just tripped. I felt very strongly M. had been beaten. I was quite sure she had not fallen down the stairs although I guess she could have been pushed down them after the beating. But, when I asked her if everything was going well at home, she said just fine but was not convincing. I felt M. was definitely hiding something. I took care of M. but started watching L. more closely. I never had the opportunity to see L.'s children in the clinic so did not know if they showed signs of abuse.

Another couple of weeks went by before L. literally blew up at me. He said, "What in the hell are you doing seeing one of my patients?" I said, "What on earth are you talking about?" He said, "I saw the patient who just came walking out of your examining room and she was my patient." I just replied, "L., she asked to see me. And these patients are not yours or mine they are patients of the clinic and we see whoever asks to see us. They are not our property." He then blew up at the office girls and asked them why they were scheduling his patients with Dr. Redalen. They gave him pretty much the same reply. Paranoia was again showing through. The fact that L. was still carrying the pistol every day bothered me. It was always a sobering thought.

L., M., Bette and I did not socialize. We never became what I would call friends. I just did not feel comfortable being around him. We both liked M. but it was just not in the cards to be only her friend though obviously she needed one. M. was always friendly but guarded. I honestly did not know if she was a battered woman but strongly suspected so.

As the time went by L. did more and more little things that made me realize the paranoia was always at the surface and a stone's throw away. Bette and I talked frequently and I shared with her my concerns. Finally one day after several more improper incidents, Bette and I decided we were going to leave Princeton.

A couple of days earlier I had been called to the hospital to see a patient. I walked by the hospital cafeteria and although the lights were off I could see someone lying on a cafeteria room dining table. I walked in and turned on the lights and L. was lying there handling a large hunting knife. When I asked him if he was okay he said he was just fine. I asked him what he was doing with the big knife. The sum total of his explanation was it was a hunting knife. I did not push the issue to see what he was doing with a large knife in the hospital. Perhaps it was benign and nothing to worry about, but it was definitely strange and only reinforced my thinking about L.

We really had no idea what was going to happen with L. and his family when we moved out of Princeton, but neither Bette nor I wanted to stick around to find out. We both remained concerned about M. and the children. We no longer considered it safe for our family. I am sure all of you know there are times when you have strong feelings about a person or circumstance but cannot really put a finger on what is wrong. I could have passed off an instance here or there about L., but collectively I could not ignore them. L. was definitely dangerous and I was the one most likely to be the recipient of his paranoia. I did not worry about myself, but I was not going to take those chances with my family.

I went in to talk with Paul the following day and asked if Bette and I could meet with him and Betty that evening. I shared all my concerns with them and said we loved knowing them as our friends but could not stay in Princeton even though we had established a lot of good relationships. I told Paul I liked everything about practicing with him and the office could not have made me happier.

As I suspected, Paul was oblivious to most of what was going on. He had some doubts and misgivings about L. but nothing he could really put his finger on. I told him about the shoulder holster and the pistol and the bouts of paranoia. Paul did not realize L. was carrying a gun every day in the clinic. I shared also what had happened in medical school on our trip to the Rochester Mayo Clinic. I also let him know L. came to our class from a class that had been one year ahead of my class in North Dakota. I told them L. had been dismissed from the North Dakota School of Medicine for a year. Rumors were it was over a car accident L. had been in. The girl in the car with L. had been killed. I let Paul and Betty know I only knew these as rumors, not facts and perhaps it had nothing to do with what was going on. I also informed him that L. had never shared with any of his classmates why he was dismissed for one year. The only thing I knew about the supposed incident was all based on rumors. I told them Max, L.'s younger brother, was also in my medical school class and that he was a nice guy who had never shared anything about his brother. In fact, watching them during our second year of school, if one did not know they were brothers, you would never have figured it out from their relationship. In retrospect I never knew if they were friends. I also knew L. and Max had two older brothers who had attended the school and were now practicing physicians.

It was obvious in our working relationship Paul and I were good friends who cared a lot about each other. The same could be said to be true of Bette and Betty. L. and Paul were associates. They were nothing more.

When we shared our decision with Paul and Betty, they were visibly upset. They asked us to please stay and try to work things out. We both said we had thought about all of this at length and had numerous discussions. It was my opinion things could not get better and that L. needed professional help. We said we were also concerned about the safety of M. and their children. I simply did not have enough information to forcibly have L. hospitalized and the state was not going to simply hospitalize one of their doctors on my suspicions. Even if I had enough information, I was not going to force the issue against a gun carrying paranoid schizophrenic.

Paul and Betty made a quick decision. They asked if we would stay if L. was gone. I said I did not want Paul to fire L. just so Bette and I could stay in Princeton. I also said I did not think that might be a safe decision. I told Paul the added pressure could make L. decompensate completely. After several hours of talking Paul and Betty said they were going to fire L. They had a number of reasons of their own. They said L. was just not popular with the office personnel and really had no friends in the office. We had thirteen girls working in our office and twelve of them had become patients of mine. Not only that, they and their families had all become friends of ours.

Paul called Bob Nord, our business manager and accountant, and asked him to come up for a meeting the next day. He informed Bob what he was going to do. They also consulted an attorney.

When Bette and I left the Hedenstrom home that evening I am sure neither Bette nor I felt relieved. The heavy weight on our shoulders seemed to have remained. I was not looking forward to going to work the next day. I also felt I would not be any less uncomfortable than I had been the past couple of weeks. It was now mid-November and I had made it nearly four months in what I considered an uncomfortable and nearly impossible practice situation.

The following day was not as bad as I thought it would be. Paul had taken his Cessna 182 out flying for morning flight lessons at Minneapolis International Airport with his instruments instructor. Paul loved flying. He had his pilot's license at age fifteen. At that time you could not get a license to drive a car until you were sixteen. Paul's dad had always had a plane so it made sense for Paul to start flying. Guess it was safer to fly than drive. What seemed most interesting was that with all his years of flying he was only now getting his instruments rating. Paul said, "I always use the instruments when I fly but now I want to make it legal and get my instruments license."

Paul told everyone he would be back at noon and that we were having a business meeting late in the afternoon and evening. When noon rolled around I went out for my usual run to use up some of my nervous energy. I was not looking forward to this meeting even though it seemed everything had been decided. I was most uncomfortable thinking how L. might react.

When I got back to the clinic at 1 p.m. it was a bright warm sunny day for November but something was wrong. Joyce, Becky, Cheryl Spande and Jackie Ryan were all out in the parking lot. As I got closer I could see all of them were crying. When I got out of the car, Joyce Thompson said, "We just got a call and were told that Dr. Hedenstrom was killed a short while ago in a plane crash. They evidently had engine failure on takeoff and could not land the plane." I was shell shocked. I asked if Betty or the kids knew. They said no and asked if I would tell them.

I walked up to the door at the Hedenstrom home and rang the doorbell. When Betty opened the door and saw the look on my face she became horrified and said, "Oh no, Rick." I just nodded my head and said, "Paul was killed in his plane at the airport a short while ago along with his flight instructor."

It was unimaginable. The two of them had over sixty years of flying experience between them. When you are taking off in an airplane and have engine failure on takeoff and are too low to recover there is just nothing that can be done. You are going to go nose first into the ground.

Betty asked if I would go and collect the children from their schools. I asked Betty how she wanted me to handle that. She said, "If you are getting the children from their schools they are going to know something bad has happened and I would really appreciate if you would tell them, Rick. Also, I am not sure I can give them news like that." I agreed to handle it. First, I picked up Bobby at his school. I told him his dad had just been killed in a plane accident. Bobby just nodded his head and remained solemn. I was the one with tears running down my face. I could not imagine the pain he was feeling but keeping it all inside. The same was true with Mary when I got her from her school. Both Bobby and Mary handled the news of their father's death the same. They remained calm and collected while I felt like I was falling apart on the inside.

We returned to their home; Betty was making calls to family and friends, letting them know the bad news. Betty had also called Bob Nord and asked him to come. Everything was being set into motion earlier than planned. Betty wanted to know how I wanted to handle the meeting we were going to have. I really did not want to handle the meeting. I did not feel it was my place to fire L. I really did not know how I could take care of everything by myself but Betty Hedenstrom asked if I would. She also asked me if I would take over the clinic and although I really did not want to own a clinic, Betty insisted the town needed me. I could understand her thinking and did not want to suddenly abandon my patients and if we left town, that is exactly what would happen.

The meeting took place as planned that evening. Bob Nord, Hedenstrom's attorney, Betty, L., M. and I were all there. We had mutually decided what had to happen at that meeting. I was asked to be the spokesperson for Betty. I told L. the purpose of the meeting. I also said the meeting had been planned prior to Paul's death which had happened only a couple hours earlier. I told L. he was being terminated from the Hedenstrom's practice. L. said, "You can't fire me, Rick." At this time Betty informed L. I was taking over the clinic with the blessing of Paul and her and everyone had decided the best thing for the clinic was to let him go.

L. did not show any signs of shock but it was apparent he was upset, angry and irritated. L. had a sport jacket on as he always did and I did not know if he was carrying a gun. The thought of him angry and perhaps carrying a pistol was uncomfortable for me. We all left the meeting a short while after L. had departed without incident. I agreed to stay and continue practicing and would run the clinic to the best of my ability.

The following evening, I saw a young boy named Bobby Bunger in the office. Bobby had appendicitis and I told his parents his appendix had to be removed. I also informed them I would be calling in Dr. Lundholm to do the surgery. They were agreeable and Dr. Lundholm arrived from Cambridge where he lived about an hour later. When my patient was prepped and draped and Art and I had scrubbed in, we went into the operating room and I went to the left side of the table. Dr. Lundholm asked me if I always did surgery from that side of the table. I said, "No, not if I am the surgeon." Dr. Lundholm said, "Then get over to the right side of the table and I will assist you." That was the beginning of my surgical residency under Dr. Arthur Lundholm.

After a couple of days, Paul's military funeral was held. It was hard to control the tears when the 21-gun salute went off and *Taps* was played. The color guard went through the ceremony of folding the flag and presenting it to Betty. I was sitting alongside Betty, Bobby and Mary. I do not know how they held back the tears but they remained calm and reserved the same as when they had received the news their father had died. The same was not true of me.

The funeral was large and I met a number of the Hedenstrom's friends. It seemed as if Paul and Betty must have known half of the countryside. The most notable couple I met was Dr. Richard Lillehei and his wife Bijou. Dr. Lillehei was a professor of surgery at the University of Minnesota, a world renowned transplant surgeon and a member of one of the state's most well-known medical families. He had done the first successful pancreas transplant in the world and the first human transplant of the large and small bowel. He was also of world renown in the treatment of shock, organ preservation, open heart surgery and kidney transplants. It is likely that everyone in Minnesota had heard of the Lilleheis. Dr. Lillehei's older brother Walt was a world renowned open heart surgeon and his brother Jim was a well-known cardiologist and internist.

After meeting Rich Lillehei we had time to talk and he told me a little about his longtime friendship with Paul. They had come to know each other and become friends while they were both in training at the University of Minnesota. Dr. Lillehei told me if I ever had need of help in surgery, he would gladly come up to Princeton and assist me. It was hard to imagine one of the world's greatest transplant surgeons offering to assist me in surgery. I told Dr. Lillehei I was truly honored by his offer.

A little later Dr. Lillehei dropped a piece of cake off his plate and Terri Kapsner, the wife of Chuck Kapsner, one of the local Princeton pharmacists, asked him if he had ever dropped a liver while he was in surgery. Dr. Lillehei laughed and said, "No, thank heavens." We all had a good laugh.

Within a few days we were back working in the clinic again. I was having trouble seeing how I would be able to take care of an entire town by myself. L. had not presented any more problems. He did not show up at Paul's funeral service either which was a blessing in itself. Life in the clinic seemed to return gradually to normal.

Then late one night I got a call from L. who said he was going to kill me. It seemed to reinforce what I had said about L. Not only that but we found out L. was going to stay in Princeton. It seems one of the local businessmen had decided to build him a clinic. I guess he thought it would be a good investment. I found out that he thought the reason L. was dismissed from the clinic was because I did not want the competition in medicine.

I could not imagine how anyone would think I would not want another physician in town because I did not want competition. That made no sense. How was one physician going to care for an entire small city population? The person who had decided to fund the clinic for Dr. L. was Cliff Sanderson, a person with considerable resources. He was also the uncle of Mary Ellen Erickson who was married to a friend of mine, Mitch, who worked in the hospital lab. Evidently they had tried to talk Cliff out of building the clinic but could not seem to change his mind. I don't think they dared share too much about L. without worrying about libel and slander consequences. None of what we thought about L. was provable.

Bette and I were worried about the threat L. had made to me. I was also concerned about the safety of my family as I did not think L. would hesitate to hurt them. We shared the information with our next door neighbor, Lee Holbrook, a Minnesota State Highway Patrolman. He was concerned and involved the local Princeton police. The consensus of authorities was there was nothing anyone could do about a threat. L. had to actually try to kill me before they could do anything. We started receiving more threatening telephone calls from L.

Lee Holbrook parked his marked state cruiser in front of our house all the time when he was home. He thought that might dissuade anyone from entering our home if they thought law enforcement was there. L. started showing up at the hospital at bizarre times in the middle of the night to make rounds and did not hesitate to wake his patients up during these odd times of day or night. The nurses talked to me and asked what they could do. We decided there was very little they could do just because a physician wanted to come around in the middle of the night and make rounds. L.'s odd behavior continued and the hospital personnel were becoming more concerned. Mary Ellen said her uncle was also beginning to have misgivings about L. who at times was talking inappropriately in the hospital. I began to wonder if he was on medications that were causing the odd behavior. Could the answer be as simple as that?

After several weeks everything culminated with L. being arrested and taken to a hospital for treatment. I never found out more than that. Should this have happened later in my medical career I think I would have tried to be more of a help to L. He was intelligent and knew medicine. Once he had gotten past the bumps in the road he would probably have been a good physician.

Chapter Thirteen

After Paul's Funeral

Life gradually returned to a little more normal around the clinic. However, it was still lonely in the office without Paul's big hearty laugh ringing through the halls. One day soon after Paul's funeral Dr. Lundholm came and put his arm around my shoulders and said, "Rick, I don't know how long I will be around but I will try to teach you as much as I can before I leave." The additional fifty years of life Dr. Lundholm had on me was invaluable. We were exactly fifty years apart in age and our birthday was coincidentally on the same day, March 14. I was twenty-six years old and Dr. Lundholm was seventy-six years old.

Art was a great teacher. It was like being in a daily residency program with one of the best mentors you could ever hope to have. I was again exposed to wonderful opportunities. Art began teaching me general surgery, urology and pathology. I was working on three residencies in one. When I reflect back on those times, I cannot think of a better way for a young physician to learn than having one great mentor beside them day after day teaching and guiding them. Even though it was like cutting on the dotted line where your mentor told you to cut, I was getting good at cutting on those lines.

One day when we were doing a suprapubic prostatectomy Art said, "Would you like me to show you how old man Plummer did it at the Mayo Clinic?" Dr. Plummer, the first urologist at the Mayo Clinic, had married one of the Mayo daughters and become well known in his own right. When you are doing a suprapubic prostatectomy you enter the bladder through an incision on the lower abdominal wall. Once in the bladder, just jamming your finger down into and through the prostatic urethra would split the prostate open like an apple. Then by swiping your finger between the prostate and its capsule all the way around the prostate, the entire prostate can be shelled out in one piece. It is quick and easy. This is exactly what Art did that day and out came a prostate about the size of an orange. He then threw the huge prostate over his shoulder. I was amazed and asked; "Art what on earth are you doing?" He just replied, "Well, that was the way old man Plummer did it." What also amazed me was the prostate bounced around the room like a little super ball. I performed a number of suprapubic prostatectomies but never did one like "old man Plummer."

In the early days of my practice we did not have the great medications that are available today to treat peptic ulcer disease. Often if we had a massive G.I. bleed it resulted in rapidly opening the abdomen and getting inside to find out what was bleeding. We did not have endoscopes to look inside the stomach and small bowel to determine the site of bleeding or the means to stop it. The treatment of a G.I. bleed would often be a gastrectomy, removing the stomach that secreted the acid which caused the ulcer. The bleeding was usually from the first part of the small bowel or duodenum, almost always caused by ulceration in that part of the bowel, a duodenal ulcer. Duodenal ulcers were nearly always benign, meaning they were not cancerous. Under Dr. Lundholm's guidance I was able to perform very advanced surgeries such as a gastrectomy at a much earlier time in my training than I could have achieved in a surgical residency. A gastrectomy may otherwise have been a surgery I could only have performed in my last year of residency.

Art continued to teach me general surgery and it was a craft I really enjoyed. I not only wanted to be an accomplished surgeon but I wanted my surgery to be beautiful. I wanted it to look good like pictures in textbooks, and look good they usually did.

It became very trying at times to be the only physician in a small town. There were often just not enough hours in the day to get everything done. I was also a little OCD, (obsessive compulsive) which made things more difficult. I would never go home without having returned all of the calls I received during the day. I would never go home with a mess on my desk. Generally my days would start at 6 a.m. and end around 5:30 to 6 p.m. The week went from early Monday morning through Saturday at noon. One of the difficult things for a solo physician practicing in a small town was the never ending barrage of telephone calls after work. Sometimes I would answer the telephone 20-30 times between the time I got home and about one in the morning. It became tiring.

One night when I was very tired I received a call from someone at about 3 a.m. who told me they had severe back pain. I told them to go to the hospital and I would call in something for pain and to come in to see me in the morning. My nurse called after seeing the patient and told me it was routine back pain that did not require me to see the patient immediately. The patient did not show up in the clinic the following day. That evening I received a phone call from the same person with the same complaint. Again they went to the hospital for pain meds. Again they were a no show in the clinic. The third night it was the same story and I got mad and told the patient not to call me again. The trouble was I had now been awakened in the middle of the night for the third time when I was already running on empty. I was so irritated I could not go back to sleep.

I talked to Bette about my feelings and told her I had to come up with a better way to handle my anger about an event such as last night. It was almost like a light bulb went off in my head. I thought it could have been me on the phone calling that man for help. My solution forever after was this phrase that would go through my head thousands of times over years to come: *But for the grace of God, there go I.* Never, from that day on did I ever suffer anger from an unwanted or foolish call. Never again would I ever consider calls foolish or unwanted. They were simply ways of constantly reminding me of God's grace and the gifts he had given me.

The next night a patient called me at about the same time and said, "Dr. Redalen, I was supposed to see you today in the clinic but forgot my appointment. Is it okay if I come in tomorrow to see you?" Of course, it was already tomorrow and he had forgotten his appointment yesterday. This time I was able to laugh a little bit about the call because the patient was calling in the middle of the night to say he had forgotten his appointment during the day. *But for the grace of God, there go I.* I think it is necessary as we go through life to put ourselves in the other person's place before reacting hastily.

Bette was nearing the third trimester of our pregnancy. Our baby was due in February. We had decided we would limit our family to three children. The pregnancy was going normally and thus far was uneventful so we did not anticipate problems. Bette and I had discussed the end of pregnancy and delivery at length. Although Bette was fine with me delivering our baby, I told her I did not want to deliver my own child. I felt if on the outside chance something beyond my control happened I would be second guessing myself for the rest of my life. I did not want to take that chance.

I recalled that while at the University of Nebraska, a resident at the University had taken care of his little boy for a seemingly minor flu like problem. Unfortunately, the little boy died of meningitis and encephalitis. Even though he had done nothing wrong, the young physician had a hard time living with it. He would always be second guessing himself.

Bette and I learned a medical physician by the name of Norman Metcalf had retired a couple of years earlier from family practice in Princeton to pursue a residency in anesthesiology from the University of Minnesota. Dr. Metcalf and his family still lived in Princeton. He had evidently completed his residency and was now traveling back and forth between Princeton and the University where he was a practicing anesthesiologist. I managed to get in touch with Dr. Metcalf through Chuck Kapsner, our local druggist and owner of Kapsner Drugstore.

Dr. Metcalf and I arranged for him and his wife Lois to come over to our home one evening. It was on the first night we had ever met them that I asked Dr. Metcalf if he would consider coming back to Princeton and working in a family practice again.

Norm's old family practice partner Dr. Magnuson had passed away a short time before from cancer of the colon. Dr. Magnuson had evidently worked hard his entire life and thought he would retire young so he and his wife could travel the world. Instead he died at the age of 54 without ever having really traveled. Now his widow was traveling the world by herself. I guess in a way, the death of Dr. Magnuson was one event that helped me stay out of Vietnam. Perhaps his death saved the life of another.

Norm and Lois were unsure if they wanted to make that transition again. As I said, family practice in a small town is difficult mentally and physically. Norm, Lois, Bette and I were all sitting on couches in our living room. Norm and Lois were very affable and likable. Norm was

42 years old and felt he had a lot of practice years left in him. Lois was a housewife and stay at home mom. They had three children who were in high school; their oldest son Mike was in college. They decided they would go home and talk about it and discuss it with their family.

It made good sense to me. Norm would get a break from traveling in rush hour traffic twice a day and he would also be around to watch his son's basketball games when the season started. I pleaded with Norm to consider being our doctor and delivering our baby when the time came. He acquiesced, if he was around.

Norm and Lois said they would let us know their decision in a couple of days and I could tell before they left that night they were seriously considering the possibility. Norm called me a couple of days later and said he thought he would like to join me in the family practice clinic. He said he missed seeing the patients he had taken care of for so many years. That was easy to understand. In a small town your patients often become your friends and you are not only seeing them in your office but more often than not associating with them outside of your practice.

I had informed Norm I was beginning to do quite a bit of surgery and that Dr. Lundholm was a great mentor. Norm would be able to administer anesthesia as he wanted, although we had two great anesthetists, Dick Propson and Marie Bloomquist. Norm liked the idea.

Our arrangement worked out well. I would schedule difficult surgeries on days when I knew my mentor was available and on days when Dr. Lundholm was not available, Norm and I would do surgery and I would have Norm as my assistant. During these procedures Dick or Marie would handle the anesthesia. It was a nice working arrangement and gradually we all came to know each other well and identified and discerned each person's capabilities. We felt there was very little in the everyday realm of general surgery we could not do. Some of this was because it was forced on us when emergencies came into our hospital and my partner and I were the only ones standing between someone living or dying.

Even on days when I was doing minor surgery such as a breast biopsy it was a learning experience. Dr. Lundholm would make me scrub out of surgery and take the tissue sample down to the lab where he would instruct me in preparing frozen sections. I would use the microtome to cut the samples, put them on a slide and then stain and read them under the microscope. Dr. Lundholm would always be alongside me to point out the different cells. If there was a malignancy, the treatment at the time was a radical mastectomy. Art would always point out the subtle differences in the cells, why one was something that could kill you and another a normal cell which sustains us from day to day.

My pathology teaching did not end when I left the surgical suite for the day. Dr. Lundholm would provide me with boxes of slides to study at home at night in spare time I did not have. This was the pathology part of my residency. Later Norm and I began to question if our doing surgery and then doing our own pathology could ever cause problems. In other words, would anyone in our profession ever question our ethics? We knew of Dr. Lundholm's eminent qualifications and reputation. We did not distrust anything he did. It was just us questioning the way we were handling things.

One day we brought this concern to the attention of Dr. Lundholm. He said he did not have a problem with bringing in outside pathologists to examine our surgical specimens. I think he was proud of us questioning our ethics about how to handle this issue and then to do things a different way so there could never be an ethics question. It was perhaps a little overboard, but we followed through on the idea.

A couple of days later I contacted the pathologists at Bethesda Hospital where Dr. Lundholm had been the Chief of Pathology for so many years of his life. I talked to Dr. Anderson and asked them if they would start coming to Princeton once a month for our staff meetings to review our pathology specimens, make recommendations to us and do some teaching. I said, "Perhaps we can have our own CPC." A CPC is a clinical pathological conference where pathology is reviewed and a discussion is held to determine the correctness of the surgery according to current area standards.

Dr. Anderson, after about one trip to Princeton, confided to me one day he felt a little uncomfortable going over Dr. Lundholm's readings of slides. He said Dr. Lundholm had trained both him and the other pathologist at Bethesda hospital. Dr. Anderson also said Dr. Lundholm was one of the most respected pathologists in Minnesota and that his expertise far outweighed what they knew. Dr. Lundholm was in fact the expert they would use if they were having trouble determining when something was malignant. I assured him Dr. Lundholm did not have a problem with the review and he would probably like to continue to see Dr. Anderson and his partner and visit when they came up.

We explained to Dr. Anderson where we were coming from. We did not want anyone reviewing our records ever to think we were in any way deviating from a standard of protocol. I liken it to a person bringing in a car to a mechanic to be worked on. If the mechanic says you need a new motor, the mechanic is going to have secondary gain because he is replacing the motor. Is that mechanic as likely to tell you your car is good for another 10,000 miles or so and the replacement can wait? Shoot, that wasn't a very good analogy. It sounded better in my head. We did not want to be operating on people and then justifying the need for the procedure with our own pathology.

Every day in the surgery suite was a learning experience for me. I would spend hours each night studying prior to procedures. Even procedures I had done many times required me to study anatomical variations. I would try to define and determine ahead of time possible failures for a procedure. An example might be when doing a gallbladder (cholecystectomy) I would study the anatomy to determine what might be an aberrant course for a hepatic artery. What would be my immediate course of action should I cut that artery? Where was it necessary to put your fingers to stop the bleeding enough for you to see and handle the problem? Fortunately the studying that prepared me to handle these problems also allowed me to avoid them so as never to have to handle them. Preparation is golden no matter how many times you have done a procedure.

One thing I learned is some surgeons are just better than other surgeons. They are more gifted and able to use their expertise coupled with hand to eye coordination to dexterously work wonders in the procedures they do. There are also preparations outside of surgery that make you better. I would often spend hours when watching TV practicing tying knots. I used to take a can and punch a nail hole in the bottom of it so I could put a string or suture through and practice tying knots on the inside of the can. It simulated for me some of the tight places in the belly where it was necessary to be able to throw down several square knots on top of each other without ever really seeing them. This would be invaluable in later years working with vascular surgeons and being able to tie 10 square knots in a row while doing a vascular graft or similar surgery.

It was necessary because the continual pumping of a vessel could untie a couple of knots and later cause a catastrophe if a suture broke loose. I had to do this by touch as the sutures used in vascular work are almost too fine to see.

Our team really functioned well in the operating room and I was proud to work with my team. It seemed every day my mentor Dr. Arthur Lundholm would teach me something new.

When we first started doing TURPs (transurethral resection of the prostate) Art would show me how to insert the instruments through the urethra and into the bladder. TURPs were done to treat enlarged prostates, a condition called benign prostatic hyperplasia. The prostate gland is in the base of the bladder and as men age it tends to become enlarged. When it gets too large it causes trouble urinating. Art showed me how to insert a urethral sound and then insert the resectoscope into the bladder. He taught me all the landmarks to go by and also how to avoid cutting the urethral sphincter, which would render the patient incontinent, a very undesirable outcome. The resectoscope was an instrument that allowed you to look through the scope and resect away chips from the prostate. The cutting loop on the end of the resectoscope was a small wire loop that would burn through pieces of the prostate as you went along. As pieces were cut away little red geysers of blood would start shooting from the cut surface and these were rapidly cauterized as you proceeded. You can imagine that if this were not done, you would soon be trying to see through a sea of blood. While doing the procedure, continual irrigation through the resectoscope would keep your field of vision clear.

During my first TURPs Art would cut a piece of the prostate from one side and then have me look through the scope at what he had done and then he would say now you do the same thing on the other side and make it look like mine. So went my first training in urology. It is amazing to me now that some of this had ever been made into a specialty. A TURP was something you could teach the average high school student to do with a little training. It doesn't really take someone trained in urology to do a procedure like this. I think some physicians would like to have people think it takes a very special person to do what they do, but that probably is not true. It just takes an average person who has chosen to do that.

Is it really necessary to have someone go through four years of college, four years of medical school, one year of internship, general surgery residency training and then specialize in urology to do a procedure you could teach a high school student to do in a week? I understand. Really, I do. The people in these specialties in all probability would not like to hear this. They have all gone through extensive training and it would not seem right if someone could come along and start doing a simple procedure without putting in the years of time they had invested and paid for. Thinking like that might eventually put them out of a very lucrative job. And after all, they went to school because of the compassionate streak they had in them to save mankind. They didn't go to school for the big bucks.

My Lundholm Mentor Residency Program progressed rapidly. Art always stressed being fast but never to sacrifice being fast for being good. It was the little things he continually harped about that made me the excellent surgeon I became. If I was doing a Cholecystectomy (gallbladder) and sponged off a small amount of blood, Art would say, "Why did you do that?" I would reply, "Because I did not want that blood there." He would always say, "It added nothing to your procedure and it took time. Don't waste time needlessly. It may not seem important now but someday those seconds may be the seconds between life and death. In surgery, never make an unnecessary motion. Every little move with your hands should be done with purpose."

Every day was exciting in one form or another practicing medicine in a small town. Princeton only had a population of 3,500 people but at the time I started practicing there were 3,600 kids in the school system. Most of the people living in the lake country of Minnesota actually lived around the lakes. The population stated for towns was a little misleading.

Terra and Todd seemed to love school and we thought they seemed to be good students. Thinking someone is doing well and whether or not they are actually doing well is another story. I had met with the children's teachers prior to them starting school and told them to make sure they toed the line and not to withhold discipline when it was needed. I said, "I do not want you to beat my children but I do expect you to make them behave. You are with my children more than I am every day so I am depending on you as much as my wife and I to turn out valuable children and future citizens for our society." This was very much the same talk I always gave to my nurses. You are with my patients eight hours per day and spend far more time than I am able to spend. Please always feel free to make suggestions on how I may take better care of my patients. If there is something you suggest to me that I feel should not be done, I will explain why and it will be a learning experience for both of us.

Terra was a great reader and was almost always reading a book. When she was in third grade she was reading a book by Dr. Haim G. Ginott. The book was *Teacher & Child*, a book supposedly for parents and teachers. One day Terra came home and said her teacher Ms. Errabo had noticed her reading that book. Terra said a situation had come up in class between Ms. Errabo and another student. After handling the situation, Ms. Errabo approached Terra in front of her class and asked Terra if she had handled the situation correctly. Terra said, "Yes Ms. Errabo. You handled it just the way Dr. Ginott would have." Terra then confided in me, "Dad, I lied. Ms. Errabo completely mishandled the situation. I didn't think I could say that to her though in front of the entire class." I said, "Terra, sometimes we have to tell a small lie to protect people. I do not think you did anything wrong. That does not mean I condone lying but sometimes it is necessary to protect those around you even if it includes a small lie."

Life as the child of a physician in a small town was not always easy. I do not know why people seem to think the children of teachers, physicians and pastors etc. are any different from their children, but that is sometimes the thinking. Terra came home from school one day with a disgusted look on her face. She confronted me angrily and said, "Dad, I am tired of being Dr. Redalen's child. I am TERRA REDALEN. I am a person. I am myself. I am not just Dr. Redalen's child. I was introduced again today as your child. I am just tired of being introduced as Dr. Redalen's child. It is almost as if I do not have a name." I tried to soothe Terra's feelings and said I understood. I felt really badly for her. I did not like the fact my children were looked upon differently just because they were the town's physician's children.

It was not long before our last daughter Shari Laree was born. She was a little blonde haired bundle of joy. It was a better time in life for us to have a baby and we were suddenly having what we thought was our last child. Bette went into labor rapidly and I called the hospital to let them know we were coming. We lived in the city on the north side of town so getting to the hospital was only a five minute trip. When we arrived the nurses had not reached Norm and as I was scrubbing in, it looked as if I was going to have to deliver our baby after all. Just as Bette was crowning and the delivery was about to happen, Norm came scurrying in, put on a gown and gloves and delivered a beautiful little baby girl. Suddenly we had a beautiful new little addition to our family. The name Shari Laree had been picked out for a girl long before.

Bette had told our friends in Grand Forks Dick and Donna Zorn what name we had picked out. They liked the name Shari Laree and gave it to their daughter who was born first. This made Bette a little mad at the time but what the heck, there are a million Bobs out there in the world. Although we had not seen any girls named Shari Laree I still doubt it was original. We were not likely the first (or second) people to name their daughter Shari Laree.

What was nice about having a baby at this time in our life was we now had the means to support the little one. There would be no more stealing pop bottles. It is nice to have had the experience with two children and know a little more about what to do and how to do it. We no longer needed the motor manual on how to take care of a new baby. We felt perhaps we could even help write one. Knowing more is not necessarily going to keep you out of serious trouble, however, as we would later find out.

Only a couple of weeks went by and we were going to have Shari baptized in the Lutheran church where Pastor Lomborg preached. On the day of Shari's baptism she looked like a little angel after Bette dressed her in a lacy bright baptismal gown. As we were walking out the door the telephone rang and one of the nurses from the hospital was on the line, "Dr. Redalen, we need you at the hospital as soon as possible. We have a dire emergency." With a rapid explanation, I flew out the door and sped to the hospital.

I was met at the hospital door by one of our nurses. Dick Propson and Marie Bloomquist were already there. A normal saline IV had already been started and was running wide open. Dick and Marie always knew what to do and did not stand on formality to wait for an order from a physician to do the obvious.

Lying on a gurney in our emergency department was a little girl unconscious and in a state of shock. By history she and her little brother had been riding in the back of her dad's pickup when they had been struck from behind by a speeding car. The little boy was dead when the ambulance arrived on the scene and they rapidly loaded the little girl hoping to get help in time to save her.

Norm arrived at the hospital only seconds after I did and my rapid assessment of the little girl showed she was still breathing but very shallowly, she had a tachycardia (rapid heart rate) with a barely discernable thread pulse, but she was completely unresponsive to any painful stimuli. She had no markings on her head to explain her state of coma and perhaps it was just from the state of shock. We had to get her into the surgical suite immediately. Although her abdomen was soft, something was causing the shock and without any visible trauma to her chest or abdomen, I was guessing she was having a massive bleed in the belly. I had asked for a chest x-ray in the ED. It was normal and this strengthened my opinion our problem was in the abdomen.

With almost no prep we opened her abdomen in surgery and indeed her belly was filled with blood. After suctioning the blood out of the abdomen, it appeared the source of bleeding was from the liver and she had also had trauma to the mesentery that was bleeding rapidly. It seemed like a lot of damage considering there were no obvious signs of trauma.

Once the bleeding was stopped and we had replaced fluids with crystalloids and colloids, the little girl seemed to stabilize so we could safely arrange for transfer to St. Cloud, a larger city twenty-eight miles due west of Princeton. The little girl's head and abdominal injuries would be better cared for in the tertiary care hospital in St. Cloud.

I was sorry to have missed Shari's baptism but because of my absence a little girl was hopefully going to have a full life ahead of her. That was the blessing given to me. Once more my family suffered because of medicine. Bette had taken pictures and when they were developed, Shari looked like a little angel.

It was fun watching Shari grow up. She became a bright bubbly little girl and was gifted with an amazing capacity to learn. Shari could say her ABCs and count to 30 when she was eighteen months old. She quickly learned how to answer the phone appropriately. Well, maybe not always appropriately. One day when Shari was three or four years old she picked up the phone from an end table right beside the couch where I was sitting. She did not give me a chance to answer it. Shari said, "Dr. Redalen's residence, can I help you." She then said, "Dr. Redalen is not available right now." She then got a very disgusted look on her face and said, "I said he is not here," and she angrily slammed the phone down and walked away without giving me a glance. I could not help but laugh under my breath. She was already becoming a good little gate keeper for her father.

I did not know when Shari's remarkable memory started but she really startled me one day when one of my friends showed up at our front door unexpectedly. It was my high school friend Doug Vedvick. When he walked through the door, Shari said, "Hi Doug, how are you doing?" Doug's visit was unannounced and Shari had not seen Doug since she was a baby.

Todd was another story. He was also very bright but mischievous. He seemed to get into his share of minor scrapes in school. One day one of his teachers confided in me that it was difficult to discipline Todd. She said, "How do you discipline a child who is winking at you while you are talking to them?"

Todd had picked up on my habit of winking at people. I used winking as a friendly way to say hi or acknowledge someone with a wink and a smile. Todd had learned my habit well. I had learned the habit at almost the same age as Todd. My doctor's nurse in the clinic in Williston always greeted me with a wink and a smile. She was beautiful and I loved it so I copied her ways.

One day Todd brought home a note from his teacher which stated: Todd is not very attentive in school and is usually not interested in doing his class assignments. He is mostly interested in playing.

I don't know where he got that from. Bette and I knew Todd was intelligent and we were not concerned that he could not do the work. We talked to Todd and told him he had better start paying attention and getting his school work done. I said, "If you don't watch out Todd, you are going to flunk and be left behind the friends in your class when they pass and you don't." Todd's reply was, "Gee, Dad, you mean you can even flunk first grade?" He figured if you were in first grade you would automatically pass into the next one. I think he had that wrong.

When winter rolled around the Metcalfs would flood their back yard and turn it into a hockey arena. The boards for our hockey rink were the snow banks that were shoveled up around the sides of the rink. The locals in the neighborhood, the Metcalfs and I would suit up and play hockey. We had many great games through the winter and we always looked forward to suiting up. We wore the same equipment as the real hockey players minus the shoulder pads but our goalies did not wear full pads. We did not check and we did not shoot slap shots so it made our games safe. In all the years we played no one was ever badly hurt, nothing requiring more than a couple stitches one time for one of the players. That solitary time was when an opposing player from out of town got caught in the head with a skate and we were playing a lot rougher on a city rink with boards.

Each of us had one day off a week and my day off from the clinic was Thursday. Every Thursday Bette and I would head off down to Minneapolis and park in the city parking garage across the street from the Nankin, a well-known Chinese restaurant in Minneapolis located on Hennepin Avenue. For over 80 years the downtown Minneapolis landmark was a destination restaurant and probably the most famous Chinese restaurant in the Midwest. Bette and I would get a bite to eat and I would always have a rusty nail. A rusty nail was a drink made with a shot of scotch and a shot of Drambuie, a Scottish liqueur. It became our tradition.

Following our meal at the Nankin we would go to the movie hall just down the street on Hennepin Avenue and pick out a movie to see. We did not much really care what movie we saw. It was just good to get out of town. When you are a physician in a small town there is almost no place you can go where people do not know you. It was absolutely impossible to go out to eat without many well-meaning and kindly people walking by and stopping to talk to you. They were always very kindly but Bette and I really enjoyed the anonymity of Minneapolis.

After the movie, we would almost invariably walk around Dayton's Department Store and do some window shopping, then walk across to the shops on the bottom of the IDS Tower and do the same. The IDS Tower was then the tallest building in the Minneapolis-St. Paul metroplex. The population of Minneapolis proper at that time was between 400,000 and 500,000 people. It was a nice sized city. Not too big and not too small and probably one of the most cultural cities in the Midwest. Bette and I would always make sure we were back in Princeton by the time our children got out of school.

During the winter months our entire family spent every evening downstairs with a big fire going in our fireplace. It was great sitting around the fire with our children listening to the fire snap and crackle as big logs of maple, hickory and oak were constantly burning. The fire gave off warmth that could be felt on your face and bare skin from any place in the room. We always had a big stack of full size oak logs that needed splitting outside in the garage that adjoined our family room downstairs. Whenever we started to get a little low on wood I would go out to the garage and in no time split another big pile. It was good exercise and it was fun. Todd wanted to help me but I convinced him it would be better for him to wait until he got a little older and bigger so he would not hurt himself. That seemed to satisfy him.

I began reading a book called *Great Religions of the World*. I read to my children about Buddhism, Islam, the Jewish Faith, Baha'i, Christianity and many other minor faiths. One night after reading about several of the faiths to my children, Terra asked, "What are we Dad?" I said, "We are Christians." She said, "If we are Christians, why do we study other faiths?" I told my children I wanted them to be informed about other religions. I said, "We were born into Christian homes but I want you to be aware of other religions so when you choose Christianity you are an informed Christian and know why you have chosen it. I want you to choose it because you know and believe in Christ and know it is right. This will give you a firm foundation to stand on for the rest of your life."

Bette would sometimes get a little irritated with me for talking to our children as if they were grownups. She would say, "Rick, they are just children." I would always reply, "That does not mean they cannot act and talk like grown-ups. When you talk baby talk to a baby that is what they are going to grow up talking like." Bette and I always received compliments on the manners of our children and it always put smiles on our faces.

My surgical foundation continued to grow under the watchful eyes of Dr. Lundholm. He was a real Library of Congress in medicine when it came to surgical skills and information. He also could think way outside of the box. One time a person came into Bethesda Hospital in St. Paul with a bloody nose the physician in the emergency department could not stop.

The protocol is to pack the back and the front of the nose with a nasal pack. When this had failed after the patient had already been forced to sit with ice packs on for twenty to thirty minutes, he called for an ENT doctor.

The ENT physician felt he could pack the nose better but he also failed. By now the patient had IVs going and was receiving blood. A general surgeon was called in and was going to one of the last extremes to treat a nosebleed. He was going into the neck to tie off the external carotid artery. He was not going to continue trying what had already failed. The patient was taken to surgery and the external carotid artery was tied off. In spite of this extreme measure when the procedure was done an unmistakable gusher of blood was still evident from the posterior nose. One of the problems is the nose receives vascular supply from the carotid artery and it cannot be tied off because it also supplies the brain.

The doctors were now becoming desperate. It is extremely unusual to have someone bleed out from a nose bleed but it has happened. Dr. Lundholm was called in to lend his expertise. He was rapidly informed of what had not worked and then Art did what no one else had thought of. With the patient still asleep from tying off of the external carotid, Art split the person's nose right down the middle and into the side that was bleeding. He put sutures right into and surrounding the uncontrollable artery and immediately brought the bleeding to a stop. That is what I mean about thinking outside of the box. Had someone such as Dr. Lundholm not thought of the almost unthinkable, it is likely that patient would have bled to death.

Treating a nose bleed sounds so easy and simple. Most nose bleeds are in the anterior (front) part of the nose. This is usually from dry mucous membranes coming from the anterior ethmoidal artery which supplies that part of the nose although the nose is extremely vascular and has many vessels and collateral circulation. Usually just pinching the nose gently for about ten minutes will stop the bleed and after that a little Vaseline in the nose every morning will prevent the problems that come from dry mucous membranes. When the nose bleed is in the posterior (back) part of the nose like the problem described above it may not be easy to treat and may require another level of expertise.

It may sound strange but many ED physicians would rather treat a cardiac arrest than a difficult bloody nose (epistaxis).

Chapter Fourteen
Our first time on Maui

One day we received a flyer in the mail about a refresher course for family practitioners offered by the Minnesota State Medical Association that was to take place on the Island of Maui. Bette and I talked it over and decided to go. We had never been to Hawaii and it seemed like a pleasant recourse to get away from it all for a bit.

It was not long before Bette and I were excited at the prospect of seeing Hawaii. It was something we had often heard about but now we were going to be experiencing it firsthand. On the day of our departure we said goodbye to our children who had been placed in good hands. One of my favorite lab techs in the hospital was going to be staying in our home with the children. Debbie Grunke was a cute, vivacious, little brunette with long hair and big blue eyes. Debbie had a laughing personality and the children loved her at first sight. Having Debbie in our home made being away easy since we did not have to worry about the children while we were gone.

Bette and I went down to Wold International which was the name of the Minneapolis Airport at that time and we were soon headed to our dream destination. We landed first in Honolulu and from there jumped a shuttle for the short flight to Kahului, Maui. There we rented a car and proceeded to the town of Lahaina. We stayed just a little north of

Lahaina in a grand old hotel called the Royal Hawaiian. We were on the seventh floor and our balcony looked out over the Royal Ka'anapali Golf Course.

One of the first pictures I took of Bette was of her standing on our balcony, a beautiful blonde in a purple bikini, smiling at me in our room. Bette was slender and perfect in every way. We could not have been happier. After putting our clothes away in our room, we went down to the first floor. When we got off the elevator there was a nice jewelry store in the lobby of the hotel. We went in and looked around momentarily but were anxious to see the grounds.

We went into a coffee shop right next door that said 'Welcome' on the front door. There was a sign going out that said 'Mahalo'. When we asked what that meant, the hostess told us it simply means thank you.

The first day had been a long one and we retired early. The bed was soft and comfortable and we slept well through the night. We both woke up at about the same time. I did not look at the clock but went out on the balcony and it was pitch dark. I looked at my watch and it was 4 a.m. Holy cow, we were five hours behind and had awakened at 9 a.m. our time at home.

The lectures every day were great. One of my favorite lecturers was a pediatric surgeon by the name of Tague Chisholm. I recall being fascinated by his lecture on gastroschisis, a birth defect that occurs when the abdomen of a baby has not closed properly and the intestines are lying outside of the baby's belly when it is born. The intestines are covered with the normal peritoneum which is the lining of the abdominal or belly cavity. The peritoneum is a thin layer of tissue much like a slippery, see through layer of saran wrap that looks more like wet toilet paper but is much tougher. Dr. Chisholm had treated over five hundred of these cases. That in itself was unimaginable but Dr. Chisholm's worldwide reputation drew patients from all over the planet. The method he used was simple and ingenious to my way of thinking. He kept the babies in a very clean if not sterile environment and then painted the peritoneum every day in Povidone Iodine or Betadine which is the trade name. The peritoneum would gradually shrink and pull the sides of the abdominal wall together at which time when the defect was small enough, the abdominal wall could be surgically repaired.

The only other point I can remember right now about the lectures was at the end of a slide show a physician brought up a slide of a pretty Hawaiian wahini standing in water, looking coyly over her shoulder. Her only cover was the smile on her face. The slide was captioned Pau, which means 'the end'. Wahini is the Hawaiian term for a beautiful young girl and indeed she was.

We had a great time in Hawaii and loved the lush verdant environment. There was invariably a small burst of rain in the early afternoon shortly after lunch and from our room, we could always see beautiful rainbows over the Ka'anapali Golf Course and against the mountains to the East. God is really quite the painter. The beautiful palm trees swaying in the breeze were a picture of heaven on Earth.

On a day off, we headed for the leeward side of the island which is more tropical and gets more rain so is even lusher. Bette and I cautiously drove through Kahului on the way to Hana. We were told in advance about the 'Hana Highway', about a fifty mile stretch of road between Kahului and Hana. It was renowned for the several hundred turns and switchbacks in the road which was not much wider than a huge kitchen table. Two cars could meet and pass but you had to be careful. The many bridges you crossed dated back to the middle of the century. Many of them, if not almost all, had been built by the Work Projects Administration or WPA as it was better known. The WPA had been put in place by Franklin D. Roosevelt as one of the many Great Depression relief programs and had helped put millions of American workers, many unskilled, back to work. Bette and I visited a beautiful little four bed brick hospital. We met a nurse by the name of Mrs. Wilhelm whose husband Sam was a handyman around the Hana Hospital. They were the usual charming Hawaiian couple, although at that time we had only met one couple. When they found out I was a physician, they regaled us with many stories about the hospital and the people living in town.

It was during this time we got the chance to meet Dr. Milton Howell. Dr. Howell and his wife lived just a few hundred yards away from his little four bed hospital. Dr. Howell told us what life was like being the only physician in the area for the small town of Hana. We learned from the entirely Hawaiian population that they are extremely hard working and industrious. Almost all married couples work two jobs just to satisfy the lavish cost of living in Hawaii.

Before our departure from the hospital, Dr. Howell asked me if I would consider doing a locum tenans for him some time while he and his wife traveled back to the mainland. I was honored and said I would be happy to. I honestly did not expect to hear from Dr. Howell. I thought his request was probably a nice thing to say to a visiting physician.

Bette and I were anxious to get back to our children and it was not many days before we were back on Northwest Orient, heading out of Kahului back to Minneapolis. When we were taking off, it seemed as if the runway was too short for our plane and a physician in the back of the plane shouted "Throw the damn pineapples off the plane!" It got a laugh from everyone, but it also sounded like a great idea. Prior to boarding our plane it seemed as if everyone in our group except for us had a big box of pineapples.

Life in Princeton progressed in a rather mundane way. We were back to the same old grind. Bette and the children and I were happy and we seemed to have no real problems other than the everyday problems everyone faces. The children were doing well in school and the teachers were satisfied with their work.

I was still studying constantly into the wee hours of the morning every night. Doctor Lundholm loaded me down with work, but it was work I asked for. I would sit for at least an hour every night studying pathology slides from Dr. Lundholm's collection. Whenever I had questions, Dr. Lundholm would sit down and go over the slides with me and point out the pathology and how to recognize mitotic or malignant cells.

One day I told Bette it seemed strange to me not to have a goal. We always had goals. It was our goal to finish college, then to finish medical school, then to finish internship and then start practicing. Although I was in a continual learning mode, I felt unsettled about not having further goals in life. Just getting better in the practice of medicine everyday wasn't a specific goal. It was more like that was going to happen automatically as you progressed in life.

One thing I did regardless of weather or other conflicts was to run every day. I would usually log 10-15 miles per day. I would run to the entire extent of speed I was able. I thought the proper way to train was to run every run as though it was the last run of your life. That was the way I had read Kip Keino, a great African runner from Kenya, trained. He would not put in many miles but would run them in world class times. This was considerably different than American runners who trained by running much greater distances. I was in great shape and told Bette I had decided to win the gold medal in the mile run in the in the 1972 Summer Olympic Games. The last Olympics had been held in 1968 in Mexico City, Mexico. Bette replied, "I think that is great Rick. I do not have a single solitary doubt you will accomplish it."

In my early practice years in Princeton one problem was that my little sisters Susie and Sallie's friends called me Ricky because that is what my little sisters called me. Dozens of young teenagers who were friends of my sisters crowded into our office for their school physicals. My office girls laughed and thought all of the giggling young girls were funny but I absolutely looked like one of their classmates which is how they reacted to me. I guess you can expect nothing more from young teenagers being examined by a young doctor they call Ricky. My office girls started teasing me good-naturedly that a lot of little high school girls had a crush on me. It was flattering and I think sometimes perhaps, true.

One day in those early times I walked into one of my examining rooms to find this gorgeous, curvaceous girl sitting on my examining table wearing only a smile. I did not show one bit of surprise and simply said, "My goodness, you are going to catch a cold sitting there like that. I will get you something to cover up with." I grabbed a gown and held it out for her to step into. My exam proceeded as if nothing had happened.

It can be challenging when you are a young physician seeing patients of the opposite sex who often are in a close relationship with you for various reasons. It was always necessary to be vigilant. In a short time I became much better at handling both subtle and overt advances by young women. When a young beautiful female came in and told me they were in love with me, I usually said, "That is very flattering and I consider it a huge compliment, but I am happily married and I would never consider doing anything to compromise my relationship with my family." Most of the time I could handle it well enough not to lose my patient but sometimes that was not the case.

One day about four or five months after we'd been in Maui I got a surprise in the mail, a letter from Dr. Milton Howell. Dr. Howell reminded me I had expressed an interest in covering his practice while he and Mrs. Howell visited their family on the mainland. He asked if I was still interested. I assured him I was, but he said he would give me a call in a couple of days after I talked it over with Bette.

Bette and I were definitely interested. We had loved our time in Maui and now we would have a chance to go back there with our children. What could be more ideal? Bette and I discussed it first and then we presented it to Terra, Todd and Shari. It probably took Bette and the children and me all of about one minute to make up our collective minds. Hot dog, we were headed back to Maui.

It was only a couple of days later Dr. Howell and I conferred about covering his practice. I told him we would be happy to. I informed him our three children would be with us and he assured us that would be fine. They offered us their home to use for the entire time we were there. We were excited and anxious to get on the road, so to speak.

I more than met the needs required to fill the practice of 'Dr. Milton Howell'. I delivered babies, did general surgery and could handle nearly any emergency that would come into the hospital. Well golly, that is certainly being a little big on yourself thinking you can handle anything. Of course you can't, but God surely can.

The next couple of weeks were filled with excitement and getting ready to go to Hawaii. Soon we were all packed and heading for the airport. We flew the non-stop Northwest Orient flight to Honolulu in an almost empty Boeing 747, the largest plane we had ever seen, let alone be on. What was strangest about the flight was that it was nearly empty. Terra, Todd and Shari ran up and down the aisles for the entire flight until they finally wore out and went to sleep all stretched out in whatever space they chose. How on earth does an airline fly a jumbo jet to Hawaii with only a dozen or so people on board?

When we got to Honolulu I had to meet with a representative of the Hawaiian State Board of Medical Examiners (HSBME). I had taken the test they required on Hale Mohalu, which in Hawaiian means house of leprosy. I took the test on Hansen's disease or leprosy because it was still endemic in the Hawaiian Islands and there was a leper colony on Molokai. I would later learn of the immense political battles that would occur over the treatment of this disease and those who suffered from it. The battles of course always centered around money. Why keep a leper colony open for only a handful of lepers? However, when the lepers marched in the parades, they always made sure they portrayed themselves with their worst cases. People with missing parts and misshapen bodies often did not portray a picture of loveliness, even as one of God's lovely people.

After meeting with the HSBME representative, Bette and the kids and I made a beeline for the airport. We knew we were on a tight time line as were the Howells. We jumped on Hawaiian Air for the short jaunt to Maui where it was also necessary for me to meet with a medical representative. We had a hard time locating the office for our meeting, but luckily it was in Kahului where we landed.

We would stop to ask the locals directions to our destination and they were the same from everyone. 'Just go a little ways that way brudda' and then they would point a different direction and say 'when you get to that corner just go a little ways that way brudda'. I would keep on asking what distance a little ways was. The answer was always the same. 'It's just a little ways brudda'. After what seemed like a myriad of wrong turns this brudda finally got to the right spot. It was not long before we were on our way to the other side of the island, once again traveling along the 'Road to Hana'.

I drove the road to Hana as fast as I thought I could safely go. It did not seem that long ago Bette and I had navigated this serpentine tropical path. When we got into the little town of Hana we stopped to ask directions to Dr. Howell's house. The elderly Hawaiian we asked just jumped into the back seat with our kids and said, "I will show you. My name Witchi Tanaka." It turned out Witchi was one of the town characters. He kind of showed us all over the little town in about five minutes regardless of the fact we told him we were in an immense hurry.

As we pulled into the driveway of the Howell's home they were waiting, ready to go. They said, with a huge smile on their faces, "I see you met our town greeter, Witchi." They rushed out the door and were in a major hurry to make their plane. They had just five minutes to tell us which days their maid came in and that they always fed the little scruffy tannish colored terrier standing on the steps with them. They said his name was Alii. That meant God in Hawaiian. Little scruffy Alii looked anything but deified but you couldn't help being taken in by his big black, smiling eyes.

All of the windows in the Howell's home were wide open with screens as our only protection from the outside world. They said they just left everything open all the time. There were two bedrooms and one bathroom. There was a large beautiful wooden table in the kitchen dining room area we later found out was made of Koa wood.

There was a small TV sitting in the living room but we were soon to find out we didn't know what for. The little set only picked up one channel which you could barely see. We later found that when the locals wanted to watch TV they would drive up on the side of a small mountain just west of the city, plug a portable TV into their car lighter, set the TV on the hood of the car and take in the programs they could pick up from the big island of Hawaii which you could barely see in the distance on a very clear day.

I can honestly say our first night sleeping in the Howell house was an experience to remember. It seemed strange to go to bed with only the door and window screens between you and the world outdoors. At first it seemed a little unnerving. I got up to go to the bathroom and on top of a small window ledge at eye level were two small green geckos sitting with their little front feet on top of my toothbrush. They looked at me quizzically as if to ask, "What are you doing here?" I turned out the bathroom light leaving the little geckos alone to finish brushing their teeth.

When we woke up the next morning it was Sunday and try as hard as I could with the little TV, I was not going to be able to pick up a football game. I already knew I was going to badly miss games on the weekends. How on earth does someone get into such habit patterns in life that you miss them even when you are in a tropical paradise? It took about one weekend for that concern to absolutely and completely dissipate.

The first week day we woke up in the Howell home, the maid the Howells had told us about showed up with a smile on her face and a big stalk of bananas in one hand. Helen was a great little Hawaiian gal who arrived bright and cheery every other day to clean and fix our noon meal. She taught us how to break off a hand of bananas. She made papaya for us every day and taught us that it was especially good if you squeezed a little fresh lime juice on it. Her meals were great and we ate every day on that gorgeous beautiful shiny Koa wood table.

There was a huge avocado tree behind the house. Dr. Howell had a type of basket on a long pole that was used to pick avocados. The avocados were huge and made up at least three or four of the size avocados I had ever seen for sale in our markets on the mainland. I loved eating them and seldom a day went by that I was not chowing down on one of them sprinkled with a lot of salt and pepper.

One of the first things we had to do when we were settled in was to get Terra and Todd enrolled in the local school. There was only one school in Hana and they had only one small friendly young blonde teacher. I no longer recall her name. Shame on me. She was also a Haole which means a non-native Hawaiian, usually white, so she truly stood out from the rest of the employees and children in school who were all brown skinned Hawaiians.

Terra and Todd were a curiosity in the school. They were the only Caucasian children so they, like their teacher, truly stood out from the other children. I thought it would be a great learning experience for our children. Not only would they be exposed to a completely different culture but they would also learn what it felt to be a minority for the first time in their lives. What could possibly be better than that?

What I thought would be ideal turned out was not the same as what Terra and Todd thought was ideal. They both came home from school the first day crying and upset. When we asked them what was wrong, they both sobbed that they could not understand the other children. I laughed a little and said that was not so bad. They would learn what the other children were saying and the other children would also learn from them.

Behind closed doors, I had to laugh. I thought of myself trying to get directions when we were in Kahului to simply get to the office of one of the board of medical examiners. It was exasperating to me with all my experience in medicine and hearing all manner of speech. I could only imagine the exasperation of my children when I thought back to the directions 'only a little way brudda'.

I was anxious to begin my first day of work. My introduction to the people in the hospital had been on the previous trip we had made to Hana. Mrs. Wilhelm greeted me and showed me around. The hospital was immaculate and seemed as if it was brand new. It was hard for me to imagine practicing in a four bed hospital but I was looking forward to it.

I would start seeing patients at 10 a.m., take a noon lunch of one hour and then walk back to the hospital and see patients from 1 to 4 p.m. I wore a white dressy Hawaiian shirt with bright trim around the bottom and light brown dress pants my first day of work. I thought I looked pretty Hawaiian.

When I walked through the front door of the hospital that day, I was greeted warmly by everyone working in the hospital. Each person put a Hawaiian Lei around my neck and gave me a hug and a kiss on the cheek. I could not believe it but every patient who came into the hospital clinic that day repeated the same ceremony. By the day's end I had at least ten pounds of beautiful Plumeria and orchid lei's hanging around my neck. It was a beautiful day in paradise and one I would never forget. Each patient beamed with smiles when they greeted me again in the examining room. I am sure I smelled like a flower garden.

I had a lot to learn. The very first pelvic exam I was going to do, Mrs. Wilhelm was saying to the patient, "Okoli down, Okoli down, Okoli down." I said, "What are you saying?" Mrs. Wilhelm replied, "I am telling her to slide her butt down to the end of the table." Okoli means bottom. Made better sense to me when Bette and I were at a luau one night and somebody raised their glass in a toast saying, "Okoli Maluna" meaning bottoms up.

Every day was a learning experience for me and my family. As I was about to walk through the front door of the hospital one day I could see a guy in shorts and tee-shirt bending over someone in a dental chair. I could hear him saying, "Big Puka." I stuck my head inside the door to say hi. A pleasant smiling guy with short blonde hair wearing little round wire-framed glasses turned around and greeted me. We introduced ourselves and that was the beginning of my friendship with Bruno West. Bruno was the itinerant dentist who came in once a week from his Honolulu office on the island of Oahu to take care of the locals. I asked Bruno what he was saying and he smiled and said, "Big puka means big hole. This little guy has a big cavity."

Bruno and I were about the same age and we had the same interests in life. When we were not working we were jogging or throwing a football around. I was still running all the time and was probably in the best shape I had been in my life. I could not possibly imagine how things could have been better. It was if God had sprinkled pixie dust on us freeing us from the cares of the world. Actually we were living in another world and it was called paradise. Hana actually was known by a lot of the islanders as "Heavenly Hana."

The Howells had a huge Plumeria tree in their front yard and the sweet fragrance of these flowers which were the main flowers used to make Hawaiian Leis was amazing. I got to enjoy that fragrance the first thing when I went out walking to work in the morning, when I returned for lunch and came home in the evening. The children and Alii had become good friends and Alii followed them around as if he had known them for their entire lives.

One day a beautiful blonde patient named Anna Marie Richards was waiting in an examining room. Anna Marie was in her ninth month of pregnancy and breathtakingly gorgeous. As I was examining Anna Marie for her prenatal check, I noticed they had her age wrong on her chart. They had down age 44 years and it appeared to me she was about 18 years to 20 years old. I went out and told Mrs. Wilhelm, who said to me, "No, that is the correct age. Anna Marie is a bit older than she looks. Pretty amazing, isn't she?"

I went back into the room and Anna Marie and I became almost great friends at our first meeting. She was an international model from Germany. Her husband was a surveyor and was on the island trying to survey the Island of Maui. I would later have a chance to talk to him and the challenges he faced were nothing short of incredible. In the time of King Kamehameha, Hawaiian land was given to families in pie shaped pieces (The word for family is houlies). Some of the land and the descriptions go back as far in time to when Captain Cook first discovered the islands. The description may read: this land belongs to the Mauna Lani Family and runs from this point on the top of Haleakala down to the lava flow here and the giant eucalyptus tree by the harbor there. It seemed almost inconceivable to me they could ever come up with the actual owners of the land, but they and the state of Hawaii were surely trying.

As Anna Marie was in her last month of pregnancy I would see her every week. She told me about her world travels as an international model and it seemed to me to be a story out of a fairy tale. Anna Marie lived in Paris and one day out of the blue she asked me if I would like to come to Paris and visit for a while. She wanted to introduce me to one of her 'beautiful girlfriends' who owned ten banks in Paris. Evidently her friend was from a very wealthy family and Anna Marie said I would really enjoy meeting her.

Anna Marie was making the trip sound more and more enjoyable. She said I could stay in a friend's house that was vacant most of the time and I would have full run of the house and the use of his car. The name of their friend was James Mason, the English actor who along with Kirk Douglas had made the movie "Twenty Thousand Leagues Under the Sea" so enjoyable. It all sounded wonderful and then I had to return to reality. That reality was a family I loved and we were having the time of our lives in the very first paradise we had ever visited.

One day I had a new patient come to the hospital in active labor during a tropical rainstorm and when I say tropical rainstorm it means you feel as though you are walking through a sheet of water. I was already at the hospital. She was one of the little hippy girls who lived out in the forest some place. I had taken care of a few of these young nature people who seemed to live off the land but also lived off society. The little gal was in her sixth month of pregnancy and was almost fully dilated when she arrived.

This little one was obviously going to be leaving his maternal incubator a little too soon. I delivered a tiny two pound baby boy. I rapidly put in an umbilical catheter, checked the blood sugar and got that under control with a little dextrose. I found a little bottle of albumin and gave what I thought was the appropriate amount of that as a plasma expander. I really could have used a neonatal intensivist but what could be done in a four bed hospital would have been severely limited. We had a plastic covered baby bassinet and we rigged up some heating lamps over it trying to keep the little one warm. The infant was breathing well on his own thus far.

It was readily apparent we did not have the means to keep the little one in Hana Hospital. They simply did not have the means to care for a premature infant. Mrs. Howell said we would have to call air transport from Kahului. I probably had an incredulous look on my face. "It is a tropical thunderstorm out there Mrs. Wilhelm. A plane cannot fly in this weather." She said it would not be a problem. Even though I was a young pilot, I knew I would be grounded forever if I ever had the audacity to take off in a plane in weather like this. It was inconceivable.

I continued working on the baby and the next thing I knew, Mrs. Wilhelm was saying, "Dr. Redalen, the plane is here to take the baby." I said, "I am not sure the baby can go on a plane alone. This baby may need someone to assist with breathing." To this Mrs. Wilhelm replied, "You will be on the plane with the baby." I was dumbfounded. I could not imagine flying in a thunderstorm in which you could not see across the road from the hospital. Mrs. Wilhelm added, "Dr. Howell would." I guess that sealed the deal for me. If Dr. Howell could do it so could I. Not only that, I had this beautiful tiny two pound baby boy who needed more help than we could give the little one in Hana.

We got down to the little Hana airport a couple miles up the highway towards Kahului. I was so busy ambuing the baby and paying attention to aerating my little patient that I no longer thought about the weather. Now it was just me and the infant. I leaned over the passenger seat doing most of the breathing for the little one swaddled in a baby blanket in the back seat of the plane. Conditions were far from ideal and I was beginning to wonder if I would arrive with a live baby. One of the next things I felt were the wheels touching the ground. There was an ambulance waiting for us and within minutes we were in the neonatal unit at Kahului Memorial Hospital. A pediatrician was waiting there to take over for me. It was a gigantic relief. The pediatrician looked at the little one and my notes and read about the fluids, dextrose and albumin given. He got a rather surprised look on his face and said "You did a great job. Thanks to you, I think this little one has a good chance."

I walked out of the nursery and standing there was my pilot who I now could do a better job of meeting and he said, "Well, are you ready to take off?" I replied, "It is still a tropical thunderstorm out there and there is no longer an emergency. Don't you think we should take off when we can see?" The pilot replied he had flown in far worse weather than this. I thought how the hell was that possible? Truly, if you were flying in worse weather than this you would have to be in a submarine. We took off for the airport and it was not long before we were airborne again. The problem was this time the only person I had to worry about was myself. The flight with the baby was a different story. I had a little person more important than myself to worry about and care for.

I literally could not see much of anything outside the windows of the plane. I only saw sheets of water hitting the windshields. I then started looking at the plane's instrument panel. I think I did a double take. I asked the pilot, "Is your altimeter correct?" He looked at me a little quizzically and said, "Yes, it is."

I couldn't believe we were flying only fifty feet above the surface. I asked, "How do you know you do not have an obstacle over fifty feet tall in front of you?" He then turned and smiled at me again and replied,

"Because we are over water, not land." He then told me to look out the side window and asked me if I saw the faint white line only about a couple hundred feet away and off to our side. The line was slightly below us as we were only fifty feet above the water. I replied that I did. He said the line is caused by waves hitting against the cliffs. That was his guideline.

Well what a comforting feeling it is to know you are flying blind with only sheer rock cliffs one hundred feet away, using the waves crashing against those cliffs as your guide. What an unimaginable sense of relief that was.

Well now that was comforting. I now knew I was flying with a certifiable nut. I did not know how we would be able to land in this mush and suddenly my pilot says, "Well we're here." To which I replied, "Where?" He said "Right there." We were already descending from fifty feet. I could not make out anything I was truly sure of and suddenly our wheels were touching down on firm ground.

I was surprised. We had made it. I truly hoped I would never take another trip like that for as long as I lived. This long day had come to an end. As soon as I got back to the hospital we got Kahului on the line and I talked to the pediatrician taking care of the baby. He said everything was going well and he thought the little one was going to survive. He again praised me for getting the infant to him and having done so with extremely limited resources. I was thankful for the baby. I was also thankful the pilot and I had survived.

Bette and I were fortunate to have the children with us on this trip and it was a great time to be in Hawaii. They were celebrating Aloha Days in Hana and on the weekend parades and bands were going to come from the other islands to celebrate. We attended all the festivities. There were horses from all the other islands and they were decorated with flower wreaths around their necks and their riders were dressed in bright Hawaiian outfits. There were all manners of paniolos, Hawaiian for cowboys, with their horses decorated almost as brightly as the cowboys were.

One interesting thing was that wherever we went Shari was a huge hit. All of the dark skinned Hawaiians wanted to come up and rub little Shari's head and feel her skin. Most of them had probably never been exposed to a little person this blonde and fair. They were truly enchanted by the look and feel of Shari and Bette. We got quite the kick out of having this little celebrity with us.

Bette and the children and I were sitting on the side of a hill and a long haired hippy type guy sat down alongside of us playing a recorder. You know, one of those kind of piccolo-like instruments you play by pumping your fingers up and down. Man could he move those fingers and make some beautiful music. I asked him his name and he said, "Fingers, everybody calls me Fingers." Fingers entertained all of us for quite a while. We took loads of pictures and recorded a lot of beautiful memories.

Several evenings later Mrs. Wilhelm called to tell me Anna Marie was in the hospital in active labor. I ran down to the hospital and by the time I arrived Anna Marie was already pushing. I examined her to find she was completely dilated and had gone through her entire labor at home until it was time to have the baby. The baby was crowning but I did not know if Anna Marie would have the steam to push the baby out. I asked Mrs. Wilhelm to have some forceps ready in case they were needed. I was more than a little surprised and concerned when she said they did not have them. She said Dr. Howell had never had to use them. I hoped that record would hold true. What I guess concerned me the most was my patient was 44 years old and a primigravida. Even though you look like you are a teenager a 44 year old body does not have the pelvic elasticity of a teenager.

Anna Marie asked if she could get up on her hands and knees and push and said that is how they sometimes do it in Europe. I said, "That would be fine. You can push in any position that feels comfortable to you." Anna Marie was in extremely good shape and labor did not seem to faze her. I did not know where Mr. Richards was, but believe he had returned to Europe for something to do with business. It was not long before we had a beautiful baby boy.

Often I would go down to the bay and swim with the locals during my free time. One day one of the local Hawaiian men came up to me and said, "You first haole doctor ever be with us." I was surprised. What he was saying to me was that I was the first white doctor who had ever associated with them. It felt good to me they acknowledged me and liked having me among them. I kept the practice of almost daily swims with the locals for as long as we were in Hana.

All of this seemed to play into how Bette and I were accepted among the people. One night we were invited to a native luau in the home of one of the locals. Mrs. Wilhelm told us we should feel honored because she did not ever recall a time in all the years of visiting doctors and their families that a doctor and his wife had been invited into the home of a local for a special luau. I cannot even begin to describe the beauty of the Hawaiian people. Their simplistic lifestyle was elegant far beyond that of the most sophisticated aristocrat.

The evening was beautiful. We were served food and drinks and felt we were welcomed into the realm of family. It was warm and relaxing and then suddenly all the lights were turned off. A beautiful brown skinned Hawaiian girl came out with candles sitting in the palms of her hands. She was moving and swaying to a soft Hawaiian love song. She moved with grace and agility, how I think an angel would move. It was a soft slow sensuous hula and one more night to remember.

During our stay in Hana, Bette had become friends with the wife of the manager of the Hana Ranch. They spent a lot of time together. The Hana Ranch was well known for their celebrity guests. One constant was Sidney Portier. Another was Richard Prior and there were a host of other well knowns on that side of the island. One night Bette and I were invited to a luau at the Ranch. It was quite the affair. We were all given leis and there was the usual entertainment. I was sitting by someone who was talking about orchids. I asked him if he had seen all the orchids Dr. Howell had. He kind of frowned and said you can hardly call that an orchid collection. He said to come to his address the next day and he would show me what orchids should look like.

The following day we went to the address provided. It was a couple of miles up the Gold Coast. The home was owned by the Governor of Samoa, one he kept as a summer home he used only about a month out of the year. The home was a gigantic most elegant mansion with grounds that looked as if they were cared for by a crew using a scissors and fingernail clippers they were so pristine.

The gentleman we had met the night before explained he was a PhD in horticulture and was the sole person in charge of twelve garden boys whose entire job was to keep the grounds looking perfect and exact, as though they were something out of a painting.

Our host led us to a large room full of orchids collected from all over

God's Tiniest Angel and the Last Unicorn

the world. The room containing the orchids was stunning. Its temperature, humidity and light were controlled exactly with timers running twenty-four hours a day. The orchids were every color of the rainbow and ranged in size from that of a basketball to the size of a tiny thimble. They were exquisite to say the least.

I could see now why he minimized the yard full of orchids Dr. Howell had. Even though Bette and I were still young and not widely traveled I never in my lifetime expected to see a collection of orchids this magnificent. To this point in life it is true. We thanked our host and left.

Even though Bette and I spent the good portion of our time right in Hana, we did have the chance to drive the Hana Highway to Lahaina about once a week. The reason is I had two leper patients in the clinic and I would have to make the drive weekly to get their medications from the hospital in Kahului. I don't recall for sure why it was necessary. I do recall that leprosy at that point in time could be controlled with some medications called repository napthones. Leprosy is a disease caused by a bacterium called Mycobacterium Leprae, the same genus of bacteria that causes tuberculosis with the bacterium Mycobacterium Tuberculosis. There are a number of similarities between these two diseases. If you would like a little trivia thrown in, leprosy is also carried by the armadillo.

We all enjoyed going into Lahaina and we would get to run around and do some of the touristy things. It was always fun meandering among the shops and looking at trinkets and clothes for sale that were not like anything we had ever seen in our travels.

On the south side of Lahaina was a large Banyan tree that was supposedly the largest Banyan tree in the world. It was immense and the branches stuck out so far from the tree that wooden supports had been put up under the branches to help hold them up. All of the branches had dozens of aerial prop roots growing down from the branches and into the ground which helped support the branches. Some of these roots were almost the size of small trees themselves. I really doubted the branches needed the man made wooden support anymore.

It was fun also to walk along the harbor and look at the fishing boats going out and coming back with their catch of the day. It looked like a fun way to make a living but I imagine if you were doing so on a daily basis it would soon turn in to work. You could tell from the faces of the fishermen the sun had definitely taken its toll over the years. Their faces were bronzed and craggy from the years of sun exposure. It did not look as though most of them had ever heard of sun screen.

Each day toward the end of day as the sun was going down, we would begin our trip back to Hana. Often on the way we would stop at a fruit stand or small shop outside of Kahului and pick up some snacks or fruit to munch on for the trek home.

We had found the best time to drive back to Hana was at night. Night made it nice because when driving through the switchbacks and hairpin turns, you could see lights if someone was coming around a curve in the darkness. I guess it never dawned on me that someone could be driving with their lights off, in which case we would have had trouble. Both Bette and I felt safer doing the drive at night. One problem was if a tree had fallen over the road at night you were going to be stuck until morning.

When the occasional tree fell across the road during the day, you would simply wait until enough muscle arrived to move it off the road. Sometimes the trees were so massive you would have to wait until you had over fifty people on both sides of the tree lifting. In the three months we spent in Hana and all the trips we made over the 'Hana Highway,' we never ran into a tree so large that the small army gathered on both sides of the tree could not move it and some of the trees were truly massive.

Whenever Bruno and I had spare time we would invariably go out running or throw a football around. We spent some time looking for a parcel of land to buy and eventually found eighteen acres of land just north of Hana about a mile from the small Hana airport. It was reasonably priced for land on the island and Bruno and I seriously contemplated buying it but decided to hold off for a while.

After we had been in Hana for a couple of weeks the children's teacher asked us out for an evening of visiting. She lived on the south side of town and her small home appeared to sit precariously on the edge of a cliff. At first when I looked out the window toward the ocean I was semi-afraid my standing weight might send the home tumbling over the cliff. The house stayed put on the edge of the cliff however and Bette and I looked out on a beautiful unobstructed view of the ocean.

She told us what it was like to be teaching in Hana. The school in Hana was the only unaccredited school in the entire state of Hawaii and

I believe until we came she was the only Caucasian in town besides the Howells and the Lindberghs. As we were eating dinner, I spotted a huge spider moving up the wall. I said, "Oh my God will you look at that!" She replied, "It is just a spider." Goodness it was about the size of a child's catcher's mitt. I said, "Are you going to kill it?" "Oh no," she replied. "They eat bugs." I said, "It looks big enough to eat people too." She just laughed. Bette and I ended the pleasant evening late and finally drove home in the moonlight.

All of us went to church on Sundays. We attended the same church as Anne Morrow and Charles Lindbergh in hopes of seeing the famous aviator. We never saw him or his wife and we later found out he had been ill. Charles Lindbergh was not just famous for flying solo across the Atlantic from New York to Paris in 1927, but the couple became even more world renowned when the Lindbergh's twenty month old son was kidnapped in 1932 in what was termed the crime of the century. Their little boy was later found dead.

The Lindberghs were very good friends of the Howells and Anne Morrow had written a note in one of the Howell's scrapbooks when she had presented them with her book, *Hour of Gold, Hour of Lead: Diaries and Letters of Anne Morrow Lindbergh*. She said in her note she hoped they would forgive her childlike prattlings. The book was about the early years of the Lindbergh marriage, flying adventures and the kidnapping of their first child. Mrs. Lindbergh became a very well-known author in all of her compassion, sensitivity and soulfulness.

The Howells had two gigantic scrapbooks in their living room they invited us to look through in our spare time. The books were a treasure trove of Who's Who in the world. It was hard to conceive of who in the world had not visited the Howells and taken advantage of their magnanimous hospitality. One book held writings from many kings and queens around the world. Ruth and Norman Vincent Peal had also written in their scrapbook. I could have spent literally months going through those scrapbooks. I am sorry now I did not photograph some of those pages. Although it would have seemed an undeserved intrusion on someone's privacy, the Howells left them out for the world to see.

One day as Mrs. Wilhelm and I were standing in the doorway of the hospital conversing, a person came up to get a drink at the outdoor fountain directly to the left of the front entrance. She asked me if I would like to hear a cute story and of course I said yes.

She said one day a family had a flat tire right in front of the hospital. An old man came by and asked if he could help them change it. The old man changed the tire by himself at which time the father of the family gave him a dollar. The old man said thank you and went walking down the road. Mrs. Wilhelm had been watching all of this and then the family came up to the front of the hospital to get a drink from the fountain. Mrs. Wilhelm asked them if they knew the man who had changed their tire, but they did not. They had not introduced themselves. Mrs. Wilhelm then said, "That kindly old man who changed your tire was Charles Lindbergh."

One delicacy we ran into in Hana was Maui Potato Chips. I never ate potato chips of any kind, but the Maui Potato Chips were the best chips I had ever tasted. One day I hit on an idea. I said to Bruno, "Why don't we find out who makes Maui Potato Chips and see if they want to start a potato chip factory on the mainland. We could start it in Minneapolis and I could oversee it." Bruno thought the idea was fantastic. We knew Maui Potato Chips were produced on Maui so now we had to find out who owned the company.

Bette and the children and I were going to be returning to the mainland very shortly so Bruno said he would do the leg work and explore building a potato chip factory in Minneapolis. We were both excited about the possibilities. Whenever Maui Potato Chips arrived in Hana they were sold out within the day. The same was true when the stores in Lahaina received their shipments.

A couple of weeks went by following our return to Princeton before I got a call from Bruno. He said he had talked to Dewey Kobayashi the owner of the factory that made Maui Potato Chips. He said Mr. Kobayashi had spent time in Minneapolis during the war and had always wanted to go back. He told me he loved Minneapolis. He said the thought of building a potato chip factory there was exciting to him.

Bruno said the little family run business grossed about $300,000 a year and they only netted about eight to ten percent. They only made thirty-some thousand dollars a year so Bruno said it would dramatically change their financial life. I said, "Golly Bruno, I am a little worn out from traveling back and forth to Hawaii. Surely this can wait for a couple of months until I can come back so we can get the paperwork signed."

Bruno called me back about one month later. Mr. Kobayashi had called him and said he received an offer from a large U.S. potato chip maker. He had been offered $5,000,000 for his potato chip recipe. Bruno said Mr. Kobayashi had thought much more about building a factory in Minneapolis, reconsidered and now did not want to proceed with those plans. It was understandable as later there was a picture of Mr. Kobayashi on the front of a financial journal with him holding his hands up in the air, elbows bent. The caption under the picture said "No more offers please." At that time it was rumored he had been offered one hundred million dollars.

As I wrote this, I decided to see what had ever happened and I found the following:

> **KAHULUI, Hawaii, March 14**—Dewey Kobayashi, whose Kitch'n Cook'd brand potato chips won worldwide popularity, has died at his home on the island of Maui.
>
> He was 56 years old. Because he wanted to continue his quiet life in Hawaii, Mr. Kobayashi had turned down large sums of money to franchise or expand his potato chip operation. He ran his family business using mainland potatoes and a recipe his parents learned while they were interned on the mainland in World War II.

After reading Mr. Kobayashi's obituary, I could now understand what had happened to this young man when he was only fifteen years old. He and his family had been uprooted and placed in an internment camp in Minneapolis during the war. It is hard to conceive of American citizens being locked up in an internment camp simply because they were Japanese.

I could only imagine what that exposure had done to him. Whatever it had done, it obviously had not damaged him to the point where it affected his love of Minneapolis. Who knows, perhaps he fell in love with a girl. Isn't that what makes all of us eager to return to a place we once loved? I am glad Mr. Kobayashi had not seen Minneapolis again. He would have been disappointed that nothing was as it had been in his youth. I knew this from personal experience.

I was happy for Mr. Kobayashi and the decision he had made. He had decided to keep his family recipe and his small factory as it was. He wanted to maintain his simplistic lovely family life. Not many people are able to make immense decisions with such integrity. I often thought, what if? But you know what I said about if ifs were fishes.

In all honesty I knew in my heart right after Bruno's call that had Bruno and I been partners with Mr. Kobayashi, we would have honored his wishes regardless of any words on a piece of worthless paper. You do that because that is the right thing to do. I always wished I had invited Mr. Kobayashi and his family to my home in Princeton so he could see what Minneapolis had become in spite of the fact that things are never the same many years later.

Chapter Fifteen
Return to my Practice

It was nice to be home after being away for three months. The first thing I did when we got back to Princeton was to go to the office. My desk was literally stacked with mail about four feet deep. It was that day I made a life changing decision. I could not stand it if everything was not always in order. For one thing, that meant having a clean desk. Bette took my picture as I stood behind my desk holding up two huge hands full of mail. I made the statement that from this day going forward, I was going to try to overcome my compulsiveness to have everything perfect. Sometimes I still have a difficult time with that.

Life returned to normal. I was doing a lot of surgery and a lot of counseling. The surgery was a continual learning curve and every day Dr. Lundholm was teaching me something new. How great to have a mentor who is an elder statesman.

It was always fun to watch Art take care of patients in the office too. The elderly Swedes, Norwegians and Germans loved Dr. Lundholm. One of the reasons was because no matter which language they spoke, Art always conversed with them in their native tongue. Once in a while when they were standing in the doorway talking in their native tongue, Art would look over at me listening intently and he would wink with a big smile on his face. This was going to be one thing Uncle Art, as we sometimes lovingly called him, was not going to be able to teach me.

By the third year of practice in the Princeton Medical Clinic, Norm and I had brought in three more family practice physicians. They were Ray Wood, Dave Bue and Myron Doebler. In spite of having four partners, I was the only physician in our clinic who offered counseling.

One day Norm approached me and asked, "Rick, do you think it is strange that so many young women are coming to you for counseling?" I said, "I really have not given it any thought." I then tried to explain it away. I said, "I am the only one in our office that does not mind providing counseling and I am good at it and comfortable with it." I also said, "I think young females are the ones to need counseling more than older women and also men this age just do not go to a physician to talk about their problems. It is more of a societal norm and not really an issue to my way of thinking."

I decided to call a psychiatrist friend in a neighboring town and talk about my partner's concern. I explained that I counseled an inordinate number of young females and asked if that should be a concern to me. My friend said, "No, Rick. That is what I would expect you to be seeing in your patient population. Young women are exactly the demographic group you will be seeing and that is exactly the same as in my population of patients. They are predominantly young women. The other point I want to make with you is that if you are good in this area, women tend to spread the word to their friends and often young women looking for counseling or even just someone to talk to who have heard about you, will search you out."

That took the concern off my shoulders. I told Norm what I had done to address the problem and told him of my conversation with my psychiatrist friend. That seemed to take any worries off Norm's plate and the issue never came up again. I imagine one of the reasons it never came up was Norm wanted no part of it.

It did come up with Bette though. Bette was my barometer when it came to counseling. Some days she would say to me, "Rick, I think you should tell the office girls to back off on counseling patients for a while." I would reply, "Is it showing that much again?" Bette would say, "Yes, you are getting down a little more lately. Take a little break." It seemed whenever I started doing too much counseling some of it would begin to weigh on me and Bette would always spot it before I did. If any young physicians or counselors are reading this book, keep in mind this one premise: If you are ever having marital problems or are even in the middle of some difficult relationship issues, that is definitely not the time for you to be counseling. You simply will not and cannot be objective.

Not all of the counseling I did was pleasant. Some of it seemed to place a very heavy burden on my shoulders. I had one depressed patient who came to me on a regular basis. When we explored what was happening in her home it was obvious she had plenty of reasons to be depressed. Her husband would bring his friends home at night after work and charge his buddies a six pack of beer for the right to have sex with his wife. How degrading that your husband thinks your body is only worth a six pack of beer. What kind of rock do these people live under?

I asked her to get out of her house. She said she had tried that. She went to the home of an aunt and uncle and told them her story. She said they locked her in a room and would only give her a can of spam to eat every day along with water. She said several weeks went by before she got the opportunity to run from them and run she did. Sometimes you just wonder how people can possibly live and behave in this inhumane manner. There was little I could do to console my patient. Societal problems such as this seem to defy society's solutions. Do anguishing problems such as this just propagate incessantly?

One day I got a call from a hospital psychiatrist some distance away from Princeton. He said he had just admitted a patient of mine to his psychiatric service. Evidently my patient had just caused a big accident when she threw herself in front of a semi trying to kill herself. The accident was caused by the semi driver trying to miss her. She was fine but was now in the hospital. I told him I wished it was her son of a bitch husband who had jumped in front of the semi. The psychiatrist said I did not have to worry about her husband. He had just put a shotgun to his head and blown it off an hour or two earlier. I never saw that patient again.

I realized early in my career that with young children and the elderly, I had to introduce myself as Dr. Redalen. Most of the time I introduced myself as Rick. I was not much of one to get hung up on formalities. After all, patients were in the office to see me for medical problems and they knew I was a physician. The elderly had grown up in times when familiarity with their doctor was pretty much unheard of. They never called me by my first name and I honored them by introducing myself as Dr. Redalen, exactly what they expected. To do otherwise would have been awkward for them.

Mitch Erickson and Steph Altfillish called me from the floor one day; they could not get blood from a patient of mine. They asked if I would come and talk to him. The patient was an obese twelve year old who was being obstinate and combative but we needed to take blood. I unprofessionally sat on top of him and told them to take the blood. Today I would probably be charged with assault and battery.

There were sometimes humorous incidents in the lab. A patient showed up at the lab one morning when Steph and a couple of other female lab techs were on duty. The person asked them if this was where he gave a semen specimen. Steph said it was. The patient then said with some incredulity, "You mean right here?" Steph again said yes. The person looked around nervously, went into the lab and stood behind a refrigerator. Our female techs looked at each other nervously and ran out the door. Their suspicions about what was happening behind the refrigerator were correct. When they came back to the lab about ten minutes later a freshly used condom filled with semen was lying on their desk beside a microscope.

I guess with that patient neither Norm nor I gave a good enough explanation of how to give a semen sample. Norm and I usually did three or four vasectomies every Friday afternoon. At the time I was running Planned Parenthood in St. Cloud two nights per week and many of the vasectomies we did were referrals from the clinic for families looking for more permanent birth control methods. The vasectomies were quick and easy and Norm and I worked together well to get them done as expediently as possible.

It was remarkable that no matter how much instruction you gave your patients some of them were just poor at following them. I gave all of them good post-op instructions. I would tell them to go home and take it easy and get two cold beers out of the refrigerator. Use one to put on your operative site and another to drink. It was always disconcerting to me when one of our vasectomy patients would show up on a Monday or over the weekend to tell me they were having problems.

The problems were almost always from lack of care by the patient. When you have a vasectomy, it is important you do not go out on your farm and put in a mile of fence posts. It is important you do not go horseback riding for hours following your procedure. As you can imagine these patients came in with testicles the size of grapefruits, usually a color from royal purple to nearly black like a bowling ball. I would usually give them my mild version of hell and tell them they were going to be fine but their foolishness was going to cause them a much slower recovery than the two day weekend recovery period for patients who had bothered to follow instructions.

Another vasectomy story came at a later point in life from Rayville, Louisiana. One patient came in to the hospital to give a fresh semen sample so it could be examined for sperm motility and morphology, which essentially means how well they swim and if they look okay. The lab techs told him if he went back into a private lounge area and filled a condom with a fresh sample they would examine the specimen immediately to check on the motility. They said they would be waiting in the lab for him and to bring the specimen right back. The patient disappeared into the private room and the lab techs waited and waited. After about an hour went by, they were wondering what on earth had happened to their patient. It was about this time the patient came back to the lab looking quite disgruntled and asked, "Can you at least turn off that damn Christmas music?"

As my surgical education continued I was always asking Norm if I was as good as the best surgeons at the university where he trained and he always reassured me I was. Of course, since I was his partner I don't know if he would have told me otherwise. He said one day when I was doing a gastrectomy he really didn't think I needed Dr. Lundholm around for surgery any more but I said, "Dr. Lundholm increases my comfort level. When he is here I always know we will never run into anything he has not previously seen." In all honesty, Dr. Art was my security blanket and I was not ready to be weaned.

Some problems I encountered I really wished had fallen into another surgeon's lap. I had scheduled one patient for what I thought was going to be a routine gastrectomy because his upper GI series showed an abnormal stomach. We were not sure what the abnormality was and the gastric mucosa was hypertrophic (enlarged) and did not look right. My patient was a tough old farmer by the name of Gerald Sager. By this time I had done a number of gastrectomies and I felt comfortable doing them. On this particular day however, what I found when I got into the abdomen was a huge sarcoma that had destroyed much of the stomach. Dr. Lundholm confirmed this grossly and with a frozen section.

A small portion of the fundus (top) of the stomach had been spared and the most distal antrum also appeared tumor free on gross exam. I proceeded to remove the entire stomach except for the very top and I removed almost the entire antrum almost down to the duodenum. I then swung a loop of small bowel up and opened it to anastomose with the top of the stomach to provide a very small gastric pouch so he could hopefully still eat. When we were all finished the surgery looked good but I was more than concerned I would not have a good outcome.

The following day I had a long talk with Gerald and told him I wanted him to either go down to the Mayo Clinic or the University of Minnesota and start on chemotherapy or radiation or doing whatever they thought could provide a better outcome. Gerald went to the university and after about a month he came into the office and said, "To hell with the university." He was not going back. I told Gerald I was concerned that I may not have removed the entire tumor but my patient was not convinced and went his own way.

About a year later Mr. Sager came in to say, "Hi, Doc. I'm still here and eating normally and feeling great." He came in every year at least once to reassure me I had done a great job.

Years later I was working in the Cambridge Emergency Room. A young man by the name of Gerald Sager came in. I told him I used to have a patient in Princeton by that name and he said that was his father. I explained what a heck of a surgical problem we had and he said his dad was alive and well and as healthy as both of us. I told him to say hi for me. I was thankful all my worries had been for naught. It was evident Gerald Sager senior had chosen the right course of action by foregoing all other follow up treatment. So it was as usual. The patient knows more than his doctor, at least a good share of the time.

In years gone by there was a lot more latitude in taking care of a patient. One night I was called into the ED to take care of a little boy who had fallen off his bicycle. The little boy had sustained a superficial laceration to his leg. I asked the mother of the little boy if it was okay if my little daughter Shari watched me sew up his leg. She said it was fine so I asked the little boy and he also gave me the okay with a little grimace on his face.

I explained in detail to Shari how we washed the cut with Betadine to kill all the germs that could cause an infection and how we sew it up so the skin can more easily grow back together. I showed her how we dressed the wound after so it would stay clean. I told Shari that in about 7 to 10 days we will take the stitches out and it will be as good as new. When we were driving home in the car I asked, "Well Shari, did you learn anything tonight?" Shari replied, "Yes, I did daddy." I asked, "What did you learn?" Shari very sweetly and innocently replied, "Don't fall off your bicycle." Today Shari's presence would be considered an invasion of privacy or a HIPPA violation.

As time went along we needed a new surgical tech in the OR. I asked Mary Newton one day who was their very best nurse's aid in the hospital; Mary responded it was a girl by the name of Cindy Rohr. I asked if they minded if we took Cindy down to surgery and trained her to be a surgical tech. It would be a great education for Cindy and open a new career for her.

Mary said that would be fine and she thought Cindy would do well working with us. Our surgical team worked with Cindy and soon she was a great tech. It did not take long before she was able to anticipate what instrument I was going to need and always had it ready to slap in my hand before I asked.

Cindy, her husband Jack and Bette and I became good friends and we would occasionally go out for dinner or go to a movie and get a bite to eat at the Nankin. Cindy and Jack lived only about a half mile east of where we lived. I went running every day through the woods down by the Rum River that ran through Princeton and I would often see Cindy as I ran by their house.

Small towns have their share of gossip but one day Terra came home and confronted me. She said the kids in school were talking about me, saying I was going out with one of their teachers' wives. The teacher in question was Doug Schumacher, a friend of mine I played basketball with and hung out with. His wife Paula was a beautiful raven haired woman who was an aide in the hospital. She also worked up on the medical floor. Doug and Paula both came to the occasional parties or get-togethers at our home.

I had not heard this rumor but reassured Terra I was not seeing Mr.

Schumacher's wife. This was the wife of one of their favorite teachers. Lately an anesthetist from St. Cloud had been coming to the hospital who was about my size with dark curly hair like me and like me he drove a red Volkswagen that looked like the twin of my car. His name was also Rick.

I began to put two and two together and confronted Paula one day when she was alone. I asked her if she was seeing the anesthetist from St. Cloud. Paula became a little embarrassed but denied seeing him. I told her my daughter Terra came home from school upset because the children in school told Terra her dad, meaning me, was going out with Mr. Schumacher's wife.

I said, "Paula, the only thing I can think of is that you are going out behind Doug's back with Rick the anesthetist from St. Cloud. It is none of my business but you and Doug are our friends. You surely realize you cannot run around with someone in a town the size of Princeton and think you are going to go undetected. I am surprised Doug has not found out by now if all the kids in the school system know about it. Unfortunately, they think it is me you are running around with. It is not up to me what you do, Paula, but you have Doug and your children to think about and I do not want my reputation soiled by your activities." I became a little angry with Paula as I could see everything I was saying to her was hitting home. I said, "If you are bound and determined to screw around with someone other than your husband, please have the courtesy to keep it over in St. Cloud, and if I hear otherwise I will come and talk to you and Doug personally."

I think the majority of damage had already been done and I do not think I convinced Terra I was faithful to their mother. It made me think of a wooden plaque that hung on the living room wall of our friends Ken and Carol Carling. Carol was one of my nurses in the clinic. The plaque said: *The greatest thing you can do for your children is to love their mother.* The plaque probably should have said: The greatest thing you can do for your children is leave their mother if you are messing around in someone else's nest. Of course the opposite was also true.

When summers rolled around Norm, the two Metcalf boys, Mike and Pete and I were out on the tennis courts almost every chance we had. All the Metcalfs were good tennis players and it seemed like most of the time Pete and I were teamed up against Norm and Mike. One day when we were playing a high ball came just over the net at the right height for a great slam. Norm was across from me at the net and when he saw what was going to happen he dropped like rock on his back. Pete walked up to the net, bent over looking at his dad and simply said, "Darn, you missed him."

I had tried golf for one summer, but it just took too much time for what I got out of it. My partner in the league was Chuck Kapsner, our local pharmacist from Kapsner Drug. Kapsner Drug had been around Princeton forever. Chuck's father, Alex, had started the store when he was a young man. Chuck and Alex were well loved in town and it was great for the people to have a family druggist who knew not only the patient but also their family. What a change was going to come in the near future when corporate America would enter the picture and do away with family drug stores. What a loss for the people.

Chuck and I were not the worst golfers in our league but we were far from the best. One thing that always drove me nuts when playing with Chuck was how many cotton picking times he would address the ball. He would address the ball several times, back away, take one more practice swing and then go through the same routine. One day when my exasperation level was nearing a high, I said, "Chuck, if you do not hit that ball pretty soon you are going to be in the rough." I was implying that the grass was going to grow up around his ball.

Al Bornholt, one of the local dentists, and his wife Jo were two of the best golfers in the town of Princeton. Al was the club champion almost every year as was Jo for the women. I played my very first golf game with Al at his invitation. On the first tee-off which was right below the clubhouse window so everyone could watch, I whiffed three times. I then picked up the ball and threw it as far as I could toward the green. I said, "That's better." Al just laughed.

Chuck always told a story about his father Alex when he worked in Starbuck, Minnesota in earlier years. An old Norwegian came in to the pharmacy one day and wanted a "urnal." Chuck's dad asked him what kind of "urinal" he wanted and the old man replied with his thick Norwegian accent, "Just a "urnal."" Alex then asked him if he wanted a female or male urinal. The old Norwegian was now exasperated and said angrily, "I want the "Starbuck Urnal."

What he was saying was he wanted the local newspaper, The Starbuck Journal. Communication is important. Quite a few years later I would end up helping out in their Starbuck, Minnesota clinic. The city was indeed made up of mostly Norwegians. I got along with them just great and being Norwegian sealed the deal. And of course, to me they didn't have accents. They all talked just like my grandpa and grandma and all my other older relatives. Heck, I still have a cousin Sheila my age who has talked that way her entire life. I guess you can take a Scandinavian girl out of North Dakota as her husband Mike Kohl did, but you can't take the Scandinavian out of the girl. I probably would even have known what a "urnal" was.

A young physician practicing in a small town faces a lot of challenges and one day while I was working in the ER, a mother and father came in carrying their comatose young daughter. The nine year old girl by the name of Julie F. had started getting a little sick earlier in the day but suddenly in a matter of only an hour or so, had become unresponsive. By history Julie had a younger sister who developed juvenile diabetes at a very young age.

On examination I could find nothing outwardly wrong with Julie other than she was breathing very rapidly and had a rapid pulse. She had no pathological reflexes, no signs of trauma and she had a strong smell of acetone on her breath. My immediate diagnosis was diabetic coma and I promptly gave her 100 units of regular insulin in the IV we already had going. A couple of minutes later Julie's blood sugar came back and was in the nine hundred range. Julie was definitely in a diabetic coma and her lab revealed she was also very acidotic.

After all the research and studying I had done at the University of Nebraska, I did not think a case of diabetic coma would be difficult or worrisome for me to treat. At that point in time we were using boluses (large single doses) of insulin in people whose blood sugar was out of control and I gave Julie another bolus of 100 units of insulin. After two hundred units of insulin, I was still not seeing a response and Julie remained comatose. We continued with her hydration and I began to give more boluses of insulin and slowly we were making some headway with the blood sugar. The needle was moving very slowly and I was continuing to give more and more insulin. Was still comatose but stable. I gradually got her acid base levels under what I thought was satisfactory control. It was not long before Julie had received several thousand units of insulin.

It was now early evening and we had exhausted all of the regular insulin supplies in the city of Princeton. We obtained as much regular insulin as we could from all the cities surrounding Princeton. This was back in the day when you did not have U100 insulin so not only was Julie getting massive doses of insulin but she was also getting a lot of additional fluids just with the insulin boluses. Julie's blood sugar was gradually coming down a little and she was starting to show a little movement, but the minute we stopped giving insulin everything went rapidly backward. To make a long story shorter, over a twenty four hour time period, little Julie F. had received over 180,000 units of insulin which at that time was more than insulin than anyone had previously received in the world. She had more than a quart of insulin in her. During this time period Julie was sitting up in bed and talking to us.

While all of this was going on I had tried to reach Ed Haunz who was one of my former professors and also the past President of the American Diabetes Association. Dr. Haunz was in Canada fishing and could not be reached. I had also called and reached my mentor at the University of Nebraska, Dr. LeeRoy Meyer. I let Dr. Meyer know what I had been doing for Julie. I explained her severe insulin resistance and that every time I tried to back off on the insulin she lapsed back into coma. I said backing off on the insulin was not a possibility at this point.

I told Dr. Meyer I had also given her large doses of steroids in an attempt to break the severe insulin resistance. None of my tests gave me a hint about what was causing the severe resistance. There was also a possibility Julie may have had antibodies to insulin. I had read that sometimes the siblings of a diabetic patient will occasionally try insulin on themselves unbeknownst to the rest of the family. Her family did not think that was a possibility but on the outside chance, the steroids would help if she were having an antigen-antibody response.

Dr. Meyer reassured me I was already doing everything he could possibly think of. He said to keep doing what I was doing. He had nothing more to offer. All the while we were using up most of the insulin stores in the surrounding area, so a special private flight was coming up from Kansas City with a new U500 insulin to be delivered to us. I slept in Julie's room that night in the empty patient bed. Her problems required constant monitoring until it finally looked as if she was going to be stable enough for me to transfer her to Minneapolis.

I was able to reach Dr. Donnel Etzweiler, a pediatric endocrinologist and known expert in the field of diabetes, about Julie. I accompanied her in the ambulance down to see Dr. Etzweiler. There I passed off the care of one of the most difficult diabetics I would ever have the opportunity to care for. It had been a satisfying experience and Julie was alert and talking and thanking me for taking care of her. Her parents were equally grateful.

When I told Dr. Etzweiler what had been going on, he appeared to be concerned if not horrified at the amount of insulin Julie had been given. He said he had never heard of such a thing. I replied that I had not either but a little girl was alive because I had been willing to do so. Dr. Etzweiler said, "But, she is going to become hypoglycemic." I replied, "Hopefully. I would rather treat hypoglycemia than a diabetic coma someone may not wake up from."

My ambulance crew and I left Dr. Etzweiler with all his concerns and misgivings. I had not been back in Princeton for an hour when Dr. Etzweiler was on the phone saying Julie was back in a coma. I became a little upset and said she would only be back in a coma if he was withholding insulin. He said he was and he did not want to give her more insulin in view of all she had already been given. I said, "Listen Dr. Etzweiler, that little girl is alive because of all the insulin she received. If you continue to withhold insulin you will as good as kill your patient. If you do not feel you can handle it let me know and I will come down and handle it for you."

Dr. Etzweiler responded by giving Julie twenty units of insulin IV. He then called me back because she had not responded. I asked, "How do you expect her to respond to the miniscule dose you are giving her? She has been receiving a couple thousand units of insulin at a time. PUSH the insulin or lose your patient." Dr. Etzweiler spent more time on the phone with me than he did with Julie. He was truly uncomfortable and in a territory where he had no experience.

I told him how many thousands of units of insulin should be given and he reluctantly followed my advice. Over a little time, Julie again became responsive. Finally, after more than twenty-four hours of intensive insulin therapy Julie became hypoglycemic for the first time. Now her blood sugar was too low. Dr. Etzweiler said he could handle it.

About an hour later Dr. Etzweiler again called and he was somewhat exasperated and angry. He said, "There is a lot more wrong with this patient than you saw. She now has a spleen that is down to her iliac crest and a liver extending halfway down her belly. She has other things drastically wrong."

I replied, "Let me guess. I am betting you are treating her hypoglycemia with D50-W. That is a fifty percent glucose solution. Dr. Etzweiler said he was. I said, "Congratulations! You have just filled up her little liver and spleen with glycogen and her body is doing the very best it can to handle the hypertonic glucose you are pouring into her."

I told Dr. Etzweiler to replace the D50-W immediately with a 5 or 10% glucose solution and give her a shot of Susphrine. I explained the Susphrine would mobilize the glycogen so her liver and spleen would rapidly return to normal size. Expert Dr. Etzweiler was very reluctant to take advice from a lowly family practitioner from Princeton, Minnesota, but take my advice he did.

Several hours later Julie was alert, lively and sitting up and eating. Her liver and spleen were no longer palpable and her abdominal findings were normal. Little Julie F. had set new records in the annals of medicine.

Chapter Sixteen

Error in Judgment

Shortly after this incident, Bette and the children and I were informed by the Nelson family that Adrian had been sick and was still not feeling well. They were not sure what was wrong and worried for a while that he would become critical. Bette and I flew down the highway out of Princeton as soon as we found out. When we arrived in Williston, we were met by a worried family and as soon as we got settled in, I went to the hospital to talk with Adrian's doctors. It turned out that initial testing had shown some elevated amylases and lipases, enzymes that were sometimes elevated with an inflammation of the pancreas.

There had not been a definitive diagnosis made but the concern was pancreatic cancer. Adrian had also had an unexplainable bout of thrombophlebitis, a clotting in the veins. He had no pathology present that would predispose him to this which was also sometimes a sign of cancer of the pancreas. Adrian had one major risk factor and that was he had been a smoker for his entire life. He did not drink at all so alcoholic cirrhosis was not a consideration in his case. We were waiting for more definitive testing. All there was to do was wait. Adrian had developed some ascites which is an accumulation of fluid in the abdomen. This was not a good sign. There was really nothing more any of us could do so we decided to go home and take care of business. I thought it very likely we would be leaving for Williston again sooner than we cared to. We arrived back in Princeton without problems and went about our daily tasks knowing we would be leaving again but not knowing when.

In the meantime, I was scheduled to go to a meeting of the American

Diabetes Association (ADA) in Omaha. I did not think this was a good time to go but Bette thought I should keep my plans. I already had my airline tickets, a reservation for a stay in the Dodge House in Omaha and had paid for the conference. The added benefit was I would get to present Julie F. and talk about her treatment. It would be a learning experience for me to see if I could have done something better in her treatment. I was excited about that.

I decided to go to the ADA meeting, which could not have been better for me as I was allowed to present Julie F. It was completely fresh in my mind. What was really great was Dr. Ed Haunz, my former internal medicine professor from the University of North Dakota and the past president of the ADA was present as was my other former professor and outstanding diabetologist, Dr. LeeRoy Meyer. Leo Krall, the head of the Department of Diabetology at Harvard Medical School and the head of the Department of Diabetology at the Joslin Clinic was also present. The Joslin Clinic was the largest outpatient treatment center for diabetes in the world. I did not hear from Dr. Etzweiler again following the Julie episode. A few months later however, he appeared with me at the University of Nebraska on a panel when little Julie was presented as a very interesting case. Donnel Etzweiler and I rounded out the field.

Following my presentation of Julie F. and after much discussion, the consensus was unanimous. All three experts in the field of diabetes congratulated me on my care of Julie F. They said she was one lucky little girl. She ended up with a physician who would push the limits of care and do something that had never been done before. She was alive because of me and my excellent care and daring to push the limits. Dr. Etzweiler continued to get more of an education and he remained fairly quiet. He was not active in the exchange about this interesting little girl. Julie's history and case was presented around the country in numerous conferences as a very unusual case and a learning experience for everyone who heard about it. I was never asked to come and present and think I had probably left a bad taste in Dr. Etzweiler's mouth. I would certainly have liked to hear how he presented the case.

I had some fun during the ADA conference with three young nurses from Iowa. I believe they were from Cedar Rapids or Waterloo. One of the nurses was Annie Grau. Her husband owned a Chevrolet dealership in the town where they lived. We all ran together for the three days we were there and of course took in a few happy hours.

One night the subject of hypnosis came up and the young nurses asked if I would come to one of their rooms and put on a demonstration. It turned out Annie was a great subject and I showed the other two girls a little of the mystery of hypnosis. I showed them a few of the minor things we could do with hypnosis and they were fascinated by it. Following that conference at Omaha, I would never have the opportunity to see those three young ladies again. I truly wish them well and I hope they have had a good life.

Alone in my room one night, I was having a lot of anxiety and was worried about Adrian. I was also worried about Bette and concerned with how she was going to take his illness if the outcome was not satisfactory as Bette was extremely close to her father. I already knew the outcome was not going to be pleasant.

During my stay in Omaha, I had my first if not last nearly fatal error in judgment. In my early days of practice I carried my black 'doctor's bag' with me wherever I went. It was just a habit and of course when you are prepared you never have to use it. One night I looked through my bag to see if I had something to help me sleep. Wanting sleep and relief from anxiety so badly, I injected myself intravenously with 50mg of Demerol. Demerol was a narcotic we often used at that time for pain relief following surgery or for any other pain. To this day I do not know how I could have been so careless in my thinking.

What happened next was the complete disintegration of any care I had in the world. My cares, apprehension and concerns floated out of my being as if they were on a magic carpet. I felt as though I was the one on the magic carpet ride far away from the angst, worries and anxieties of the world. I could not possibly envision ever feeling this good. When they talk about euphoria, no one can possibly conceive of what it is until they have experienced IV Demerol. The sudden calm rush of peaceful tranquility through your body is inconceivable. I realized after taking one dose that this medication was trouble. Any medication that could make a person feel this unimaginably good was definitely a drug of possible abuse.

A couple of days after I was back in Minneapolis we were going about life when we found out Adrian was back in the hospital. He was having difficulty breathing and was on oxygen. The family was really concerned and wanted us in Williston. I think having a physician in the family kind of spearheading the care gives everyone a little relief. It was as though it would be all right if Rick was there. I knew that was not true.

When we got to Mercy Hospital and saw Adrian I realized he was nearing the end. His ascites had increased rather significantly since our visit but he was still in good spirits with a smile on his face. The next day I sat down with his doctors and went over his x-rays. On an upper GI he had a widened C loop of the duodenum which is the first part of the small bowel as it leaves the stomach. This is where the head of the pancreas lies and it was further evidence and probable confirmation of cancer of the head of the pancreas. There was no chance of survival without a miracle.

The next day Binks asked me what he had to get geared up for. He said he could handle anything coming but it would help him if he knew ahead of time how much he had to prepare. I said, "Binks, prepare for the worst. A death from pancreatic cancer is not good. The person will have their breathing compromised by all the fluid in the belly and almost anything can happen to end life suddenly. It is best if we pray for a rapid and somewhat comfortable death." Binks nodded his head and said thanks.

Adrian still got to spend some quality time with his family. He knew he did not have much time left. When I came in one day he was typing away on his old typewriter where I had seen him sit for hours while he was preparing the sports page for the Williston Herald, our hometown newspaper. I asked him what he was writing. He said he was writing his obituary. He said, "Those damn papers never get anything right and I want them to at least get my obituary right."

I had never thought about it before but there probably are not a lot of people who write their own obituary. It is probably not a bad idea. I guess if I ever write my obituary I will write nothing but good things about myself and then when I die, I'll get to wear that 'dead man's halo'. You know how it is when a person dies. Suddenly they have been nothing but a saint their entire life even if the exact opposite is true.

Adrian had a final request from his family before he departed. He wanted to set aside one day with each of his children to spend with him individually, so he could talk to each one of them. I had no idea what he wanted to talk about but when Bette's turn came she left their conversation later in the day with many questions that were troubling her. She brought those troubles to me.

Bette said, "Rick, I had a really nice talk with my dad, but he said something that was very troubling to me." He said, "Rick is really a great and wonderful human being. Make sure you are never a hardship on Rick."

Bette asked, "Why would my daddy say to me to never be a hardship on you? What does he see?" I said, "Bette, I do not know why he would say that. Why don't you ask him?" Adrian was a very close friend of mine and I could not imagine him saying something like that to Bette. I did not know what he knew or saw that I could not. It was as perplexing to me as it was to Bette. We had never had any problems in our marriage and certainly nothing ever that someone could latch on to in observation that would suggest later problems.

It was not long after each of the Nelson children had their time with their father Adrian became more ill. The ascites was becoming marked and breathing was becoming more and more difficult. The family was spending as much time with him as was possible. Dr. Joe Craven, his personal physician, was keeping him comfortable with shots of morphine, a potent narcotic painkiller. Bette never had the chance to be alone with her father to ask him what he meant when he told her never to be a hardship on me.

I could tell each day was bringing us all very close to the end. One night when I was pretty sure the ordeal would not go on for another day, I suggested to the family to get a little more rest the next morning. I would be there early and would call them if they should come. I was at the hospital very early the next morning and Adrian was not doing well. He was also in a lot of pain.

Dr. Ruffalo was a young surgeon making rounds for the weekend. When he came into Adrian's room, I asked him if he would give Adrian more morphine as he was in a lot of pain. He said, "I can't do that, Rick. More morphine in the shape he is in could kill him." I said, "By withholding the morphine do you think he is going to live?" Dr. Ruffalo just walked away. I was pretty disgusted with this young surgeon who did not have a clue. Sometimes you wonder where a person's head is. I knew in Dr. Ruffalo's case it was up his ass.

A minute later Dr. Joe came walking down the hall. I said, "Dr. Joe, Dr. Ruffalo was just here and he refused my request for more morphine for Adrian's pain. Would you please give him some?" Dr. Joe, being the warm compassionate human being he was, answered, "Yes, of course Rick. I am going to take care of him the exact same way that you and I want to be taken care of at the end of our lives. That is only right."

The nurse came down and immediately administered some morphine through Adrian's IV. Adrian was cranked up high in his bed but was still having difficulty breathing. I did not want to call the family and have them remember their dad dying while gasping for air. Adrian reached out his hand to me asking me to help. At the same time blood came gushing out of his mouth and obviously a huge artery in the GI tract had just been eroded into by the cancer and now the artery was spewing blood into the small bowel and stomach. I could not help my friend. I cranked the head of Adrian's bed down and he immediately drowned in his own blood. I was holding him in my arms and crying. Sometimes the things we do in life to help another are almost unthinkable and entirely unbearable. I had spared Bette's family the grief I could not spare myself.

After Adrian died, I went down to the nurses' station and asked them if they could clean up the room immediately, clean up Adrian and get him into a fresh gown so it looked as if he had just fallen asleep. I asked the nurses not to contact the family and that I would do it after I showered the blood off and got cleaned up. The nurses were immensely helpful to me and the family. We had all gotten to know each other well while I was in Williston on my preceptorship under Dr. Koch.

I went out to the car for a fresh change of clothes, went in the doctor's lounge, showered and changed. I threw my blood soaked clothes away. After I was cleaned up and looked relatively fresh I went down to Adrian's room. He looked like he was peacefully sleeping and the blood soaked gown and bedding were gone. I called up Doris, Adrian's wife and then Bette. I told them they should all come to the hospital as Adrian had just passed away in his sleep.

When the family arrived in Adrian's room in the hospital, Adrian looked finally peaceful. The family wanted to know what had happened and if he suffered. I said, "Your dad and I were talking and he had just received some medication to help with comfort. He had just fallen asleep and while he was sleeping he just slipped away. There was no discomfort or pain. He died in his sleep." I could see no reason why the family should know otherwise. Nothing was to be gained. I would carry that burden with me for the rest of my life always praying I had done the right thing.

Following Adrian's funeral, Bette and I returned home. I would soon find out what the most painful part of Adrian's death would become for me and my children. I started finding small notes around the house of conversations Bette was having with her father. The notes would have all kinds of questions on them to her father. She would ask, "Daddy, why did you ask me not to be a hardship on Rick?" There were many notes and they all seemed to center around that theme. Bette went into a deep depression and spent a lot of time crying. Nothing I could do seemed to comfort or console her.

By this time of course, I was practicing medicine and doing surgery and seeing patients every day. I was slowly thinking about the loss of my friend less. I had to go about caring for the living. I could not do that well if I went to work every day living in the past. Bette did not have this same escape and relief from her broken heart. She seemed to keep dwelling on her father's death and the problems seemed to center on her last day spent alone with her father. It all revolved around what Adrian had said about her treatment of me. Nothing I said would console her. The children were back in school and they had bounced back to normality as young and resilient children usually do.

During this time I would often get telephone calls from a patient of mine by the name of Helen K. The phone calls were always long and involved and they frequently came in the middle of the night. The calls were long enough and frequent enough they were beginning to upset and irritate Bette. She could hear the entire conversation as our phone was on the nightstand beside our bed. The phone calls were often not about anything specific. Helen just wanted to talk.

One day I got a call from the telephone company asking who had called and talked to me for over two hours. I told them I did not know. The person on the other end of the line was a little irritated. She asked, "How on earth can you talk to someone for two hours and not know who it was?" I said, "I was probably sleeping on my end of the phone call. That's how."

I think it was almost like my adolescent psychiatry teacher had taught me. These young people do not need a psychiatrist, they need a friend. I had met Helen in the clinic one day when she came to see me as a patient. She was a young very attractive blonde who talked a little rough but was fun to talk to. She was always making suggestive remarks and constantly told me we should 'get it on' some day.

Helen had some back problems so one day I decided to hospitalize her. At that time we were still using bucks traction for treatment of severe back pain. The main reason she was hospitalized though was to provide regular and frequent physical therapy to her back with alternating hot and cold packs. It also gave me the opportunity to talk to her face to face and try to discern what real issues she was having trouble with. I really did not know and could not get it out of her during our lengthy telephone calls.

One of the first days when I was making rounds with Imogene Summers, one of our RN's, Helen was obviously a little intoxicated. I asked her where she had gotten alcohol while in the hospital. She refused to answer but suggested to Imogene she get lost for a while. I could stay and have some fun between the sheets with her. Imogene got a little red in the face and laughed nervously. I told Helen to settle down and behave herself. She just laughed and said we could have a good time. I really did not doubt that at all. I really liked Helen's fun, somewhat raucous and unruly personality. I just took all of what she said good-naturedly, laughed and was not in the least bit offended by it. I don't think Imogene was offended either, just horrified.

Later that evening I received one of my usual calls from Helen at about 2 a.m. This time Bette knew Helen was calling from the hospital as I had told her my patient caller was in the hospital. After the call had gone on for about twenty minutes Bette nudged me in the side and said "For God's sake, Rick. Your patient is in the hospital and nothing is going to happen to her there."

I covered the mouthpiece and told Bette I should talk to her because she needed someone to talk to. I think Bette perhaps thought I was the one who needed to talk and not my patient. Bette was becoming angrier so I somewhat reluctantly told Helen I had to go. I said good night and told her to try to get some sleep. That was not true. I did not have to go. I told Bette I should have kept talking. She said I was being foolish and

I could talk to my patient in the morning.

An hour or two later one of our night nurses called me from the hospital and said I had to come immediately. My patient Helen K. had slashed her wrists and there was blood everywhere. I rushed to the hospital and ran up the stairs. It was true, there was blood everywhere. It looked as if Helen had purposely tried to paint the room in blood. Rather than handling that phone call as I knew I should have I now had to call out a surgical crew in the middle of the night and handle severed tendons and vessels.

Helen did fine. I kept her in the hospital and we spent quite a few hours talking. After that night, Bette never again suggested I not talk to a patient. I am sure she felt very badly about what had happened and I think she felt she was partly to blame. The extra half hour I could have spent longer on the phone had turned into lengthy surgery.

I discharged Helen a few days later and when she returned to the clinic to get her stitches out her wounds had healed nicely. The day when she came to the clinic, she had a beautiful little red Persian kitten with her. She said she wanted me to have it as a present. Helen said she raised Persians and this one was special. I guess that was Helen's way of saying goodbye because I never saw her again. It is always a wonder to me how someone can enter your life and you develop close bonds with them and keep them in your mind for the rest of your life and wonder what happened to them. It always leaves me with an emptiness and questions.

I also began taking care of a patient by the name of Hazel M. Her husband Andrew had been a patient of mine for a couple of years although I had never seen Hazel. They were Jehovah's Witnesses. The importance of that will soon become apparent. We had all been through some difficult times with Andrew, who previously had come in and presented with an acute abdomen. He had been having abdominal pain for several days and when he showed up at our clinic he was gravely ill. Andrew was in his seventies and was like a lot of people of that era. They only came to the doctor when they realized they may only have a day or two to live without medical care. It was my opinion at the time that since most of his pain was in the left lower quadrant of the abdomen he most likely had ruptured a diverticulum. Norm and I did an exploratory laparotomy.

In surgery we found the entire left lower quadrant of the abdomen was filled with pus and it appeared he had indeed ruptured a "tic." It was necessary for me to do a left colectomy on him and construct a colostomy in his right upper quadrant. This means I removed his left colon and made an artificial opening through the abdominal wall so the contents of the colon could be removed since the rectum could no longer eliminate the intestinal contents. During Andrew's hospitalization he became progressively more anemic but because of his faith he would not allow us to give him blood.

Jehovah's Witnesses refuse to take blood based on their belief that blood represents life and only God is the giver of life.

Not too many years earlier I was exposed for the first time to these beliefs while I was at the University of Nebraska. The patient I became familiar with and am going to describe was not a patient under my care. A young lady who had come into the university to have a baby did not progress on to a normal vaginal delivery. She ended up requiring a C-section and delivered a beautiful little baby boy. During the C-section the patient lost a lot of blood and required a transfusion. The patient was not married and accompanied only by her family who refused to allow blood to be given. The obstetricians wished to honor the family's religious convictions but their daughter continued to go downhill and become shocky. In spite of pleading with the parents and letting them know their daughter was in danger of dying they would not relent in their beliefs. Their daughter expired a short while later. I would later learn that no blood products can be received in this faith including all components of blood.

Following a several week recovery period, Andrew did well with his colostomy care but was anxious to return to a more normal life. I worried that Andrew's re-anastomotic surgery might be beyond my skill set and expertise. I was going to have to mobilize his transverse colon enough to swing it down into the pelvis and reconnect it with the remnant of the recto-sigmoid colon I had to sew shut after removing the left colon. I sent him down to Mayo Clinic. They sent him back to me and said I had staged my procedures excellently and they saw no reason for them to do the definitive procedure. I accomplished Andrew's re-anastomoses without problems and my stature as a surgeon had increased in both Andrew and Hazel's eyes. They now trusted me completely with their health issues. I think the fact Mayo Clinic had sent him back to me and complimented me on the job I was doing reinforced their opinion of me.

I had come to know Hazel quite well during the time when her husband was so sick and this was probably the reason she was now coming to me with difficult problems.

Hazel said she'd had a weepy lesion on her chest for several months and now it was soiling her clothes enough so it was becoming much more of a problem. When I examined Hazel, she had a large carcinoma of her right breast that had eaten through the skin and was now presenting as an oozing, weeping mass of pink tissue that in some areas was bleeding although very slowly. I chided Hazel for waiting so long to seek help. She said, "Dr. Redalen, you know Andrew and I do not like to go to doctors. That is why Andrew waited so long to get help."

I said, "Hazel, there is no way I can remove this large mass in your breast without taking the entire breast off with a simple mastectomy. The tumor which has spread throughout your breast will not heal if we take off just the draining mass. Hazel said, "That is fine with me as long as I quit soiling all my clothes." Hazel was informed that we had to do a complete workup prior to the mastectomy to determine the extent of her problems.

The workup revealed Hazel's problems were much more extensive than I had thought and it was not just the lesion on her breast. She had cancer which had metastasized (spread) involving or surrounding and growing into the stomach, small bowel, kidneys, ureters, bladder and with multiple lesions in her lungs. If there is any kind of dim light in a problem like this it is that with so much of her body riddled with cancer, it must be very slowly growing. It was still hard to imagine that her only complaint was the drainage from her breast.

I tried to explain that her cancer was so far advanced it did not seem to make a lot of sense to do the mastectomy. I said, "Hazel I do not think I can help you by removing your breast," but Hazel wanted to get rid of the drainage from her chest. She requested I perform the procedure regardless of the outcome.

I performed a simple mastectomy on Hazel, who was extremely anemic. I said, "Hazel you would do so much better if we could give you blood." She said, "Then why are you not giving me blood?" I replied, "Because you and Andrew had refused it when Andrew needed it so I just did not ask you and was doing the best I could without it." She said, "Don't pay any attention to Andrew's foolish beliefs. I do not have any misgivings about receiving blood." Well, with one less problem to deal with we transfused Helen up to a level where she said she felt as good as she had in a long time. Hazel went home as requested after only a couple of days. I did not think it would be long before Hazel was back in the hospital again.

I had finally taken up flying lessons after having put it off indefinitely. I was taking lessons at the little local Princeton airport, which was nothing more than a little single grass strip airport. The first time I had signed up for flying lessons my partner Paul Hedenstrom had been killed in his accident. That scared Bette enough she simply did not want me to fly. The second time I signed up for flying lessons I was called out to an empty field across from the little flight service station we had in Princeton to be coroner for a small plane that had crashed in the field across the highway. There were supposedly four people in the plane. Veico Harala, the person who would later become my flight instructor, had witnessed the crash. He said a man and his wife and two children had taken off in heavy fog and by the time they disappeared into the fog, Veico could hear the engine at full throttle. By the time the plane was over him again it was upside down and the pilot was gunning it at full throttle until they hit the ground. While he thought he was at full throttle climbing he had in fact become disoriented and did not know which way was up. Again, Bette did not want me to fly.

Now I finally had many opportunities to fly and took as much time as possible away from my practice. Paul always told me flying gave him a diversion that allowed him to leave all his worries behind on the ground. I learned how to fly in a Cessna 152. Veico was my instructor and after only a very short time he said I was ready to solo. I guess he wanted to save me money. I said, "Do I know as much as you do now so I can handle everything you can handle?" He said, "Of course not. I have been flying all my life." I said, "As long as that is the case I would like to continue my lessons." It was quite a long time before I soloed and by then my instructor had given me enough instrument training I had enough hours to take my instruments exam. I was not preparing for that written exam however.

Finally I went down to an airport near Anoka to a flight instructor there and scheduled my flight exam. The instructor walked with me out to the plane and said, "Take a good look at me." He walked all bent over and with some difficulty. He said this, "This is how you can end up looking if you are not always paying attention to what you are doing. In the little bit of time I was not paying attention to my flying I crashed and this was my result. I am crippled for the rest of my life for a brief moment of inattention."

When we got out to the plane I did the pre-flight exam of the plane. My instructor asked me why I had waited so long to take my exam. I told him the same thing I had told Veico. The instructor told me I had enough hours to take an instruments exam so that is what he was going to give me. When we got in the plane he said to put on the hood, which is like a cap you put on that doesn't allow you to see outside of your plane. You can only fly by using the instruments directly in front of you.

The start of my flight exam went exactly the way no student pilot wants to start out their exam. I took off with the hood covering my eyes so I could only see the instrument panel. No problem. I was heading easily down the runway but no sooner did we get into the air we could hear this loud clanging. I looked at my instructor and asked, "What on earth is that?" He looked at me and asked, "Do you have your seat belt on?" For gosh sakes, I had missed one of the most basic rules. Put your seat belt on. It was my seat belt clanging outside the plane against the fuselage.

Following that faux pas, my exam went smoothly. When we were back on land, my instructor said, "Very good job, today you passed a full instruments exam and did it very well. Now take your written instruments exam so I can certify you for real." I was now a bona fide pilot and soon I had my pilot's license. I was proud of the license but it was easier to fly a plane than drive a car and flying a plane did not really do anything for me. For me, flying was a way to get from point A to point B more expediently than driving. Man was that wrong thinking. The way I drove it was a lot faster to get from point A to point B in a car than in a slow little Cessna 152.

It was not long before the kids were saying, "Dad, take us for a ride in the airplane." I would always say, "No, I do not want you riding with me. You can ride with professional pilots in the big planes when the time comes." Bette thought I was foolish but I said, "I will never trust my children being in a plane I am flying." My children never flew with me.

I tried as hard as I could to get our life back on the right track. One night I lit a fire in the fireplace and Bette and I slept downstairs on our pull out couch in front of the fireplace. You know how everything gets better in front of a snapping crackling campfire. We usually felt the same in our home. Sitting in front of the fireplace was always a happy time for our family. That night it did not seem to quell Bette's anxiety. She was crying and I was not able to console her. She pleaded for me to give her something to help her sleep. The only medications I kept around our home were in the black bag I used for house calls. I finally relented and looked in my bag for some Valium. Usually I had some minor tranquilizer in my bag since it was rarely used. Because it had been so long since I had looked in my bag I did not realize I had no minor injectable tranquilizer or any anxiolytic agent to take by mouth.

What I did have in my bag was the bottle of Demerol I had used in Omaha. Here was a second fatal flaw in my thinking. I remembered how that one injection had taken away the cares of the world. Would it be so bad to give Bette one night of rest from her tormented mind? With almost no foresight as to the possible outcome of a single shot of relief, I drew up 50mg of Demerol in a syringe and gave Bette her first shot of this narcotic. As we lay in front of the fireplace, Bette had the same reaction to the medication as I did. It took away the cares of her world. She said, "Rick, I have never felt this good in my life. What did you give me?" I said, "I had a vial of Valium in my little black bag." Bette drifted off to sleep. We had an otherwise relaxing night in front of the fireplace.

The following day, I went into work as I always did without giving thought to the previous night. When I came home at noon, Bette asked me what I had given her last night. When I told her I had given her an injection of Valium, Bette replied, "That is not true Rick. You do not have any Valium in your bag. I checked and the only injectable I could find in your bag was a bottle of Demerol." I became a little angry and asked Bette what she thought she was doing going through my medical supplies in my bag. Bette had the same response I'd had from the single solitary injection of pain relief. She had felt as though the problems of the world had disappeared. The problem was the medication was not designed to take away mental pain and anguish. It was to be used only for physical pain.

I suddenly realized what a terrible error in judgment I had made. I had let the person closest to me in my life realize she could get rid of all her pain and the cares of the world simply by taking a simple injection of medication. The trouble was this medication was not meant to be used in the way I had just misused it.

I recalled that while at the University of North Dakota School of Medicine my class had discussed a movie our psychiatry professor had us watch one afternoon. It was about a physician in practice who, as his problems were building, decided to self-administer a shot of medication. The medication he used was Demerol. The movie showed the increasing use of the medication from day to day and the relatively constant and unrelenting downhill spiral his life was taking. We all pretty much agreed that what we had watched was not the way to handle problems. Our professor showed us this movie to warn us to be on guard against abuses of medications we would always have around us in our life of medicine. He also emphasized that the practice of medicine had this one, what he called, occupational hazard. He also stressed that nearly 50% of physicians at one time or another abuse drugs and almost 50% of physicians have ongoing drug abuse in their family in some way or another, be it alcohol or prescription medications.

In spite of watching the movie about a good physician's decline into oblivion, I did not think at this time any medication could or should get away from your control. It certainly could never get out of my control. As a doctor seeing patients all of the time how on earth did I rationalize what I was now trying to rationalize? And how do you keep practicing medicine if this gets out of control? I realized if that happened, my life would drift into oblivion the same as the physician in the movie we had watched as sophomore medical students.

Several weeks later Hazel M. came into the clinic and said she was rapidly losing weight. Hazel looked as though she had lost twenty to thirty pounds since I last saw her. She was looking gaunt and as if she did not have much time left in this world. She was now having trouble eating and would not keep down much of what she ate. I admitted her to the hospital and started her on IVs and a soft bland diet. With the dietary changes and intravenous therapy the vomiting abated and she was doing better but had become too weak to return home.

Hazel's downward trend was unrelenting and I told both her and Andrew they should perhaps call the family and let them know I did not feel Hazel could stay with us much longer. This was at a point in my life when I thought I could actually guess when someone would pass away. I did not realize God had not put a bar code expiration date on her. Only He knew exactly when someone was going to pass away.

Hazel by this time had dropped to 60 pounds having lost nearly 100 pounds by history (what she weighed prior to my taking care of her). Their family members arrived from all over the United States and were at her side daily. Other than the intravenous therapy we were giving her and medications for pain control there was little else to be done.

One of Hazel's sons, grasping at straws, wanted to know if Laetrile might work for her. I had heard of Laetrile as a medication used elsewhere in the world for treatment of cancer but it was not approved by the U.S. Food and Drug Administration. The other name for the drug was amygdalin. I knew some people were going to Mexico to buy this drug illegally. It could be given by mouth or intravenously. Why on earth should any medication someone wants to take when they are facing a life threatening or life ending illness be considered illegal? Isn't our government overstepping their bounds a little bit?

After talking with the family, I said I would do some research and see what I could find out about Laetrile. I later reported back to them Laetrile was the extract from the pits of some fruits and it was believed the anticancer property of the drug was cyanide. Since cyanide is the drug used in the gas chamber to end someone's life, it did not seem reasonable to me to take it to prolong life. Cyanide inhaled in the gas chamber prevents your body from absorbing oxygen so your body rapidly dies from lack of oxygen. I guess our FDA must have used the same line of reasoning since it was illegal in the U.S. I explained to the family that most of the research done on Laetrile did not seem to support the treatment of cancer. I said it was used around the world for the treatment of cancer but our own country had found no convincing studies supporting that use. I did not recommend it, but on the other hand it appeared Hazel was going to die so if they wanted to obtain it and she wanted to take it, I would not stand in their way.

Hazel continued to maintain status quo and after a couple of weeks her family came to talk to me at the office. They wondered the same things I wondered about. How on earth long can their mother go on this way? We all thought she would die a couple of weeks ago. After all, I was the one who asked them to come to bid their mother good bye. I told the family I had no idea what was keeping Hazel alive. Had I been a little closer to God during those times I would have known who was keeping her alive and it was not due to my simple support. The other thing that should have given me a clue was Hazel's mantra during that time, "As long as you are taking care of me I will be all right." I did not tumble to the fact that through me, God was keeping her all right.

A couple more weeks went by and gradually the entire family had to get back to their lives. Suddenly one day Hazel announced she was ready to go home. I said, "Hazel that is simply not possible." She said the only thing keeping her in the hospital was the IV and she could have that at home. She then asked me if I could stop out in the country where they lived to check on her IVs once in a while. I had showed them how to hang up another IV when it ran out and they seemed adept at doing so. Hazel and Andrew lived east of Princeton, just a half mile or so from land Bette and I had purchased to build a home on. I agreed I would periodically stop by. Another couple of weeks went by and Hazel had started eating again so the IVs were discontinued. She reaffirmed to me every time I saw her that as long as I was taking care of her she would be all right.

Shortly after Hazel returned home I consulted with an oncologist who thought it might be worthwhile to have Hazel try what was called a Cooper Regimen. The regimen consisted of rather intense chemotherapy consisting of cyclophosphamide, methotrexate, 5-fluorouracil, vincristine and prednisone. Hazel was agreeable to trying this regimen, but it meant I would have to travel regularly to their home to administer medications. Hazel tolerated the medications fairly well but had some ongoing problems with pain, nausea and vomiting. Since I thought she was in a continual fight for her life, I felt justified in continuing her treatment despite possible toxicities or forming a habit. Hazel's pain medication dosage was escalating because the initial small doses of Demerol no longer seemed to work. One night when she asked if she could have an injection for her pain, she did not seem to get the same level of relief she usually attained. She asked for another injection which I gave her. Again, she had no relief and it was not making sense to me. I withdrew a small amount of Demerol away from Hazel's sight and squirted it into my hand. It did not smell like the medication was supposed to and when I then put my tongue into the small pool of medication in my palm it tasted like saline. It was then I realized the medication in my bag had been removed and replaced with normal saline.

When I arrived home that night Bette and I got into a contentious discussion. I asked her what had happened to the medication in my bag but it was obvious what had happened. I was angry and asked her how she could allow me to compromise the care of my patient, but I was as responsible as Bette was. I was the one who had done the unthinkable. I had started an avalanche. It was not a slippery slope you slid down, it was a cliff and we had both fallen off.

Hazel began to look much healthier. Pretty soon it was difficult to discern she had ever been sick. I didn't think everything that was happening was due to her medications. All of the little age spots people get as they grow older were disappearing along with spots of actinic keratosis and what lay people call liver spots. Her skin appeared to be returning to how it had probably looked thirty years earlier. After Hazel completed her Cooper's Regimen I began to only see her about once a week. I provided her with medications for pain control but I did not really know if she needed them anymore. She was taking Demerol and evidently responded to the medication the same as Bette and I had. Her requests were more frequent.

By this time both Bette and I were abusing Demerol. I rapidly found out why it is called the doctor's cocktail. I also found out it was the drug of choice of abuse by physicians across the country. It was understandable. A medication that could be taken by almost anyone that not only takes the cares of the world away but makes you feel the best you have ever felt in your life. The euphoria produced was overwhelming. The other positive for this medication was there was no hangover and there were no residuals. After the effects of the medication had worn off over a couple of hours you could not tell you had taken anything.

The unbreakable bonds between Bette and me began to unravel and the undying relationship we had which could never be threatened was now vulnerable. One night we were invited to a party in St. Cloud to the home of Rick, the anesthetist I thought was messing around with Paula S. Both Doug and Paula were at the party along with Cindy and Jack. As I walked into the living room by myself while everyone was talking in the kitchen, Cindy walked up to me and planted a long slow sensuous kiss on my lips. It was the first time in my life I had kissed someone other than Bette. It was exciting and felt good but I was physically sick at the time. I do not know why but shortly after that kiss I told Bette we had to go home as I was not feeling well. I thought about that kiss all the way home and once again I had done the unthinkable. I was not happy with myself but this was only the beginning of our problems.

Bette had become infatuated with a musician by the name of Bill Worster who played lead vocal in a band we used to watch in one of the St. Cloud taverns. We would always go to that bar for a couple of drinks after I was done working in the family practice clinic. We would always laugh and have a good time while we were there. Our relationship continued to unravel. It seemed okay on the surface but underneath we both knew we had problems. Problems in a physician's family in a small town are also problematic from the standpoint of getting help. Bette's drug use had escalated as had mine, so I would find various ways to order narcotics. Demerol was the drug of choice.

Chapter Seventeen

Drug Abuse

One night when I came home from work there was no sign of Bette in the house and our children had not seen her when they came home from school. I fixed our children's supper. We all watched some television. I was worried deep inside about her whereabouts. There was no word from her, so late that night I went to bed after tucking in the children. At about 3 a.m. there was a knock at the door and the doorbell was also ringing. I went downstairs in my pajamas and answered the door to find two Princeton Police Department officers at my door.

I said, "Good evening officers. What seems to be the problem that brings you to my door at this time of night? I have a phone so you could have called me." They said. "Dr. Redalen, your clinic has just been broken into. The plate glass window in the door on the south side of the clinic has been smashed out completely. A nurse outside the hospital while this was happening saw who did this and went into the hospital to call us. We just came from the clinic. The nurse who saw the person said she could not be completely sure in the dark, but she thought the person looked like your wife. The description she gave us matches the description of your wife." I said to the officers, "She must have been mistaken. My wife is upstairs in bed sleeping. Would you like me to wake her to talk to you?" I hoped against all hopes they would believe me and not ask me to wake up a person who was not home. The officers said, "We are sorry to have troubled you, Dr. Redalen. We are going to have someone come in and board up the window in the door right now so you do not have to come down to the clinic." Now I was really worried. I had no idea where Bette was and she had probably taken all of the narcotics from the office.

The following day my suspicions were confirmed. All the injectable narcotics in the office had been stolen. I still had no idea where Bette was and now was worried about whether she was still alive. About noon I received a call from the Cambridge Police Department. They said, "Dr Redalen, we have your wife here in custody in the Cambridge Police Department. She is impaired and was just taken into custody following an accident in which she sideswiped a truck going at tremendous rates of speed putting people and property around her in jeopardy."

When I arrived at the Cambridge Police Department, Bette was crying and distraught but she was unharmed physically which was my main concern at the time. I was just thankful to see her alive. The police had issued a citation for reckless driving. They had followed Bette for some distance and said she was going at speeds approaching 90 to 100 miles per hour and would not stop for them. She was driving our yellow Oldsmobile Toronado.

I read the citation for reckless driving and it said the occupant of the vehicle was driving with wanton disregard for all persons and property. The police department said they were not going to press charges but wanted me to get Bette into immediate psychiatric care. No blood had been drawn so there was not going to be a record of narcotics in her blood. I arranged for Bette to go to a psychiatric ward in Golden Valley, Minnesota. She was very much against it but I said it was necessary if she was going to avoid criminal charges and possibly more. More of what, I did not know. This was new territory for me and not ground I wanted to become familiar with.

Bette's time in Golden Valley went by slowly for both of us. After several days it seemed as if she was her old self. The final diagnosis by the psychiatrist she was seeing was severe depression. We had both avoided talking about our issues of drug abuse. We both inwardly knew this would not only threaten our way of life but would also be a threat to our medical practice. I remained really angry at Bette for what had happened but the anger probably should have been directed at me for starting the landslide we seemed to be on. Life seemed to be returning to normal after Bette got home.

Unfortunately, Bette's hospitalization had started another family tumbling down a slippery slope. While Bette was in the hospital, my partner Norm had talked to the hospital personnel and had Cindy Rohr fired from her job as our surgical tech. Cindy depended on her job to help support herself and her family. I talked to Ellen Green who was not only an RN in the hospital but was also Cindy's aunt. Ellen said Cindy had left Princeton and returned to Babbitt, Minnesota, the small town in northern Minnesota where she grew up. Her family still lived in Babbitt, which was a mining town on the eastern part of the Mesabi Iron Range.

When I found out I was extremely angry and I asked Norm what on earth was happening. He explained to me that since Bette was in the hospital with depression, he thought Cindy was partly responsible. I asked him if he was crazy and told him to immediately take whatever steps were necessary for him to have her re-instated. I explained that Jack, Cindy, Bette and I were friends but that is where the relationship ended. Norm said it was too late for Cindy's reinstatement and return to Princeton Community Hospital. I asked Bette why she had told Norm Cindy was responsible. Bette apologized but it was past the time for apologies. I told Bette I was going up to Babbitt to bring Cindy back.

In a couple of days I returned from Babbitt with Cindy and Chad and Kelly, her two young children. I brought them to my parents' home who lived next door to us. My parents were furious with me and asked me what I thought I was doing bringing another woman into their house. I tried my best to explain to them what had happened. They simply refused to believe me. They thought the same as my partner Norm thought, that another woman was responsible for Bette being in a psych ward and I was responsible for what had happened. When I told them of Bette's drug use which was now out of control, they did not believe me. They said they did not believe Bette was heavily involved in drug use and they would hear none of it. Only a day or two after Bette came home from the hospital she was badly impaired when I came home from the office. She could not walk by herself or talk coherently. My parents were out in the back yard and I asked Bette to come out to talk to them. Bette was crying and asked me not to do this. I literally carried her out of the house and into our back yard and dropped her on the lawn. I yelled at my parents, "This is what I am talking about!" Bette lay in the grass where I had dropped her, was crying and could not walk without my help. She could barely talk and her speech was unintelligible. My parents were speechless but I had gotten my point across. They now perhaps believed a little of what I had told them.

My idea that life was getting nearly back to normal was so far from the truth it had no basis in reality. Wishful thinking about normality does not make it so. Our life was in shambles. As time went by and it was close to Christmas, Bette asked if I would mind if she visited her sister Deanne and her husband Jeff in Boston. Deanne's husband was a student in nuclear medicine at Massachusetts Institute of Technology (MIT) which was located in Cambridge, Massachusetts. It made sense as to who Deanne would marry. She was a brain child who had graduated Summa Cum Laude from North Dakota State University College of Pharmacy and had married another of the same intellectual prowess who was studying how to build nuclear reactors at MIT.

Bette said Veico, my flight instructor, was driving out east over Christmas and she could ride with him to Boston. I did not even think to ask how she knew Veico was traveling to the East Coast and simply said I didn't mind if it was okay with Veico. They left a couple of days later for the East Coast. The day after they left Bette called to say she and Veico were snowed in. They had stopped in Niagara Falls, New York and would probably be there for at least a day or two until the roads were cleared. Bette did not want to worry me when I could not reach her at Deanne and Jeff's home after her anticipated arrival time.

That evening I had my first revelation about what was actually going on in our home and with our relationship. When the news came on television that evening, the broadcaster said that an unusually warm weather front had gone through New York and that Niagara Falls had set new records for high temperatures. What a complete fool I had been. Bette was not going out to see her sister. She was going out to Massachusetts to get away with my flight instructor. I was clueless.

When Bette got home, I did not mention anything about what I knew. Bette was still not herself and her father's death had completely changed her. I thought in my mind, I can forgive her. She has been my most faithful companion and friend for my entire life. Surely she will become that person again.

Even though my parents lived next door, I did not confide in them what was happening between us. I was still the goat in their eyes. During that time, Cindy and I had become closer friends and we became intimate. Bette and I were becoming more distant and Cindy and I were becoming closer. It seemed like a fair trade off.

While all of this was going on, Cindy had gotten a job as a surgical tech in the St. Cloud Hospital Department of Surgery. It truly surprised me that Bette was now requesting on a regular basis that we should go to St. Cloud to bring Cindy and her children some groceries. It did not make good sense to me that she wanted to befriend a girl she thought I was close to and had gotten fired from her job. Her story was always the same. She said. "Why don't you just go in and visit Cindy by yourself. I will go shopping and come back to pick you up in a couple of hours." I did not mind and Cindy and I enjoyed our time alone. Our intimacy was growing and I was becoming progressively distant from my wife.

Again, I was clueless about what was going on. After dropping me off and supposedly going shopping for a couple of hours she was going to visit another paramour. I did not find this out immediately and really had no thoughts about why Bette was suggesting I visit Cindy. The person involved this time was Bill Worster, the lead singer in the band we had gotten to know. I do not know how Bette had worked out all these liaisons but she had kept her secrets well. Obviously I had no idea what was going on during my days at work. Then one day a dozen roses from Bill arrived at our front door. I asked Bette why Bill Worster would be sending her roses and she sloughed it off saying he was just a good friend of ours. I said, "Good friends do not send roses to the wife of their supposed other friend." During this same time span, Bette began making strange sexual requests, different things we had not experimented with in our physical relationship. It was from those requests I knew Bette was involved with another person. Since Bette always wanted to drop me off with Cindy in St. Cloud I knew the person she was involved with was Bill Worster. No wonder he had sent her a dozen roses.

As I was walking down the street in Princeton one day I ran into Peter Wojciechowsky, a friend of mine who owned the only furniture store in Princeton. Pete's last name was too hard for everyone to pronounce, let alone spell, so everyone called him Pete Woody. Pete said to me, "Rick, would you mind starting to pay on the furniture you bought from us several months ago?" Bette and I had bought some furniture on installment from Pete's furniture store. I said, "What are you talking about, Pete?" He explained they had not received a payment in several months.

I told him I had no idea. Pete said he did not think I knew because Bette always handled our check book and was the one usually making payments. I said, "I will find out immediately what is going on and get you caught up in payments."

When I started going through our finances I could not account for $30,000 to $35,000. I confronted Bette but she just said she had no idea. I was never able to find where the money went. When I asked her why she had stopped making payments on our furniture, she said it had slipped her mind.

When summer rolled around we started chumming around more with Rich and Betty B. Rich was a person I had bought a couple cars from. Rich worked for his father-in-law at Odegard's garage and car dealership. One day as we were leaving to see the Cornhuskers game in Lincoln, Nebraska, Rich showed up at our doorstep with a brand new Cougar automobile he had brought from the car lot at Odegard's. He said he thought we might enjoy driving a new car down to Lincoln. I told Rich that was a lot of miles to put on a brand new car but he said it didn't matter and he would enjoy letting us use it. Again, I wondered what was going on. It now appeared Bette had yet another person involved in her life. It was not too hard to tell by the way they looked at each other. Cheryl and Harlan Spande were going to the game with us and we were looking forward to a good time, but a cloud hung over my head.

We arrived in Omaha to stay the following evening. I had called my friend LeeRoy Meyer ahead of time and we went to his home which was located several miles west of Omaha for supper with him. LeeRoy had a beautiful home and we watched the sun go down through his panoramic back window. It was a beautiful sight but all of this was outweighed by the thoughts going through my head. I knew something was wrong. I just did not know how wrong everything was. The only things I knew for certain about our relationship were my own indiscretions and infidelities. After eating dinner with LeeRoy that evening, we returned to our motel on the west side of Omaha to get a good night's rest before driving the 50 some miles to Lincoln for the game the next day.

That night I could not get to sleep so I went out on the top balcony of the motel where we were staying. I was deeply troubled and seriously considered jumping off the balcony to the concrete several floors below. I was crying and distraught. After standing on the balcony and contemplating for about half an hour I went back to my room and instead wrote down my thoughts.

To this day I can still remember the feelings of anguish and thoughts ringing through my head. The thoughts were the following and I put them down in poetry:

As I lay awake waiting rest for the day
I can hear the clock pass time away
Unable to sleep as thoughts unwind
Are images and past and times gone by
God how I ache with pain deep inside
My mind wants to scream
My body to cry
God how can you watch your child so torn
With a heart that is broken
And a mind oh so forlorn
Is this the life God you give to this sinner
Then take it back God and I'll be the giver

After writing those few lines of poetry, I went back on the balcony to contemplate some more. I finally decided nothing I was thinking was even definite and perhaps nothing was as I thought it was. We would go to the game tomorrow with Cheryl and Harley and when we got back to Princeton, everything would be back to normal. How wrong I was. It was not long after getting back to Princeton Bette disappeared again. I took care of my children and fixed their meals and got them off to school as best I could. I just told them their mother had gone off to visit some friends of hers. They asked me when she was coming back and I told them she'd be back in a couple of days. I sheltered my children the best I could and we tried to live life normally. I still read to them in the evenings.

One night I was called early in the evening to come to the hospital to take care of a patient in active labor. The delivery had taken a couple of hours and when I got home it was a warm moon lit night and I could see Bette sitting out on the lawn as I was driving into our driveway. When I got out of the car I could see she was crying softly and had tears running down her face. She said, "Rick, I do not want to be married to a doctor anymore."

After she had been gone for a couple of days she called me and said she and Rich were in South Dakota and were getting married. I asked, "What on earth are you two space cadets thinking? You are already married. Are you both taking up bigamy now? Where on earth are your heads? Are you both stark raving mad? Does Betty B. know you and her husband have run off together and are in another state planning to get married?" Bette replied, "No we have not called Betty B. yet." I said, "Get your asses back here immediately. Do not call Betty and put her through this anguish."

Betty B. had been through some psychological problems of her own and I knew from what Rich said she was sometimes on precarious footing. A day after Bette called me with her nutty news Betty B. called me crying and asked, "Rick, do you know your Bette and my husband have run away together?" I said, "Yes I do, Betty. I found out yesterday where they were. I avoided calling you because I thought they were not thinking clearly and I did not want to worry you with news neither you nor I could do anything about. I am so sorry for you Betty. Don't worry and I am sure they will be home soon."

Evidently the two space cadets had called Betty B. regardless of what I had said. It was a couple more days before Bette and Rich returned from their honeymoon, vacation from their spouses or whatever they called it. Our children did not find out. Evidently the trip did more damage than Rich B. thought it would. A very short time later Rich was fired or let go from the large dealership his father-in-law owned and he was soon working at another car dealership in Cambridge.

To this day our children do not know of all their mother's indiscretions. I guess when this book is finally published, they will. I called Rich B. a couple of years ago and asked him if he would please send an e-mail to my children and tell them what had happened. I said, "Rich, my children still blame me for all of what happened in our marriage." Rich apologized again for his and Bette's behavior and said his wife Betty still had some mental problems. He asked me not to talk to her or call her.

Following Rich's agreement to email my children and some deep contemplation I finally decided I had nothing to gain by letting my children know what had really gone on in our marriage that ultimately destroyed and ripped apart our family. I thought perhaps it would destroy the only remaining relationship they had with one genetic parent. That would have served no one well. Perhaps not even me.

Around about this same time I received a call from Don Asp who had been a physician in family practice in Mille Lacs, a city also on the Rum River but about eighteen miles north of Princeton. He had left Mille Lacs to become a professor in the Department of Family Practice at the University of Minnesota. There were twenty-four young physicians under his teaching at Bethesda Hospital in St. Paul. At that time family practice residencies had three year requirements so Don had eight residents under him in each year of their residency.

Bethesda Hospital was where Dr. Lundholm had been Chief of Pathology, General Surgery and Urology for many years. Don asked, "Rick, are you doing as much surgery as you always did?" I replied I was. He asked me if I would consider teaching in the University of Minnesota (UofM) Department of Family Practice. He said he thought my skills in surgery would be valuable to their family practice residents. Don believed basic surgery skills were necessary to the residents if they were to go out and practice in a small town. I told Don I would go home, discuss it with my wife and get back to him. I went home that day and shared the offer with Bette. I think we both thought the change would do us some good. I think I really thought perhaps it would take us away from the relationships we had formed that were threatening to destroy our family and marriage. Perhaps a geographical cure would be better than nothing.

Bette and I decided I should take the job at Bethesda and I would be joining Don Asp as Assistant Professor in the Department of Family Practice. I still harbored ill will toward my partner Norman Metcalf. I had asked him repeatedly to get Cindy's job back in surgery but he declined. Perhaps it was my fault, since I had not let anyone in my office know what was going on with Bette and me.

I hired a Realtor from a company in St. Paul and told him I was looking for a home. One day as we were riding around I saw a beautiful almost castle like home on a hill several miles outside of White Bear Lake. White Bear was an exclusive suburb on the northeast side of St. Paul. I pointed at the castle and jokingly said, "That is the home we want." I said it jokingly as I knew it would be way out of any price range we could afford. The following day my Realtor called and said the castle home was for sale. As it turned out the woman who owned the home was in an unfortunate situation due to bad luck and the home was now for sale. Her husband had just been killed in a hang glider accident and she could not afford to keep the home. The home had been built for Georgiana A. M. Clotilde Mott Mohls by her parents who allegedly lived in a $40 million home on the shores of White Bear Lake.

The home was located on a seven acre lot at 101st and Joliet, very close to some riding stables called Victoria Station in what was mostly countryside. I looked at the home the following day and it was a castle, only quite a bit nicer. The home was a 12,000 square foot mansion exquisitely done by marvelous craftsmen. The kitchen was papered with individually hand painted 4 by 4 inch squares from Europe. The dining room was carpeted in luxuriously laid very plush pure white carpeting and had a huge wood burning fireplace. The upstairs master bedroom was carpeted in the same white carpeting and also had a huge wood burning fireplace. The master bedroom closet had individually placed thermostats to control the temperature of the closet separately from the rest of the house. Some of the bathrooms had cut crystal and gold fixtures and the walls of the bathroom downstairs had been papered with nudes imported from Europe. The family room adjoining the kitchen also had a large wood burning fireplace. And so forth and so on. The house was huge and immaculate with a four car garage. The upstairs even had a built in phone booth.

We bought the home. It was a distress sale or we could not have possibly afforded it. The Realtor had given me the bank appraisal at a $5 million replacement cost on the property. It was truly a dream home. Unfortunately, a dream home does not necessarily reconstruct a nearly broken relationship as I hoped it could. Bette and I still owned our home in Princeton.

I told Bette after we moved in I had only two requirements of her. I wanted her to stay off the damn phone and to stay off alcohol and all medications. That warning went unheeded and the first night I returned home from work Bette was on the phone with Veico Harala, my former flight instructor who was now living in Reykjavik, the capital city of Iceland. Bette was lying on the floor with the phone hanging out of the upstairs phone booth and not only was she on a long distance call, but she was also inebriated or stoned from a combination of alcohol and or drugs.

That month our phone bill was for over $900. This was at a time when a customary phone bill might be $30 to $40. Those had been quite the phone calls. I carried that phone bill with me for years to always remind me what had destroyed our relationship. That is not to say the phone calls had anything to do with the destruction but it was a good reminder of what had happened.

It seemed the geographical cure had not helped our situation and it was not long before Bette was showing signs of severe depression again. She often said I had isolated her from her friends and she did not like living where we now were. In reality I had removed Bette from the proximity of her boyfriends and removed myself from the proximity of Cindy.

None of the geographical cures worked and soon Cindy had taken a job in Stillwater, Minnesota to be closer to me. Stillwater was only about a 20 minute drive east of our new home. She had not consulted me about moving and I was surprised when she left her great job in St. Cloud to take a new job at the Stillwater hospital. There is always a need for great surgical techs and Cindy was welcome at Stillwater.

One winter night rolled around when it was snowing and storming very hard so I called Bette and told her I was going to stay in my apartment in the resident's quarters. The roads were bad and the visibility was poor. The hospital had provided me with a very nice apartment located just across the street from the hospital. About three o'clock in the morning the wind had stopped blowing, the snow was gently falling and it was a beautiful full moon lit morning. I walked outside and the bright moonlight shone on a now sparkling landscape with a fresh snowy blanket.

I had too many thoughts churning through my mind and I decided on the spur of the moment to go home and surprise Bette. I thought she would be happy to see me and want to snuggle up to me. I did not think at the time I would be the one surprised. When I got to our home another car was in our driveway and the person I found with Bette was Rich B. I suggested to Rich he should leave immediately.

Rich tried to make excuses and said they were only talking. I said, "Rich, I do not appreciate another man coming into my home to talk to my wife at three o'clock in the morning and that goes especially for someone my wife has obviously called to let them know I would not be home." Then Rich said, "We just wanted to talk a little." I suggested he leave our home immediately before he got hurt.

I did not think that after my wife had run off for several days with Rich B. (just the latest one) and called to tell me they were getting married they were getting together simply to talk. The only saving grace for them and perhaps me was I did not catch them in bed together.

It was not long after Bette decided she wanted to live in Fargo, North Dakota. I asked, "What is in Fargo?" Bette told me she had friends there. I did not know how that could be and Bette did not care to explain it. Evidently, now there was a fourth guy in Bette's life. I would soon learn Bette was living with a guy by the name of Duane J., the person Bette would later marry. This would eventually take place a couple of days after our divorce was final. Bette certainly did not let any grass grow under her feet. I did not know about the rest of her racetrack. I guess after Bette tried out the other three guys the fourth one was a charm.

It is strange but after all of the different guys my wife was involved with I still thought I could forgive her. Our marriage had been perfect and indestructible right up until the time Bette's father Adrian had died. I had considered it completely impervious to harm. I still felt that whatever was going on with Bette was the result of some mental illness or whatever had occurred the day she spent with her father before he died to completely change her behavior. I had always told Bette through our entire marriage if she could ever find someone who treats her better than I did to go for it. I guess she had finally found someone. It took her enough tries to find that special someone. Soon after Bette moved to Fargo she gathered up our children and removed them from my life forever. My children were 14, 9, and 5 years of age.

I had thought right up until that time there was still a chance for our relationship to recover. It now appeared Bette was never going to give that recovery a chance. I think her father's warning to her never to be a hardship on me had fallen on deaf ears or perhaps she was causing all this heartache now so she wouldn't be a hardship on me later.

It is interesting that it may take several years to build a huge building but when the building has lost its usefulness or because of age it is destroyed by a gigantic implosion, and gone in less than a minute. The same is true of relationships. You can build the very best relationship over perhaps twenty years or more and then with one moment of indiscretion or thoughtlessness the relationship and trust built up over all those years can be destroyed in a moment. There are so many instances in life where you just do not get "do overs." You need to get it right the first time. A second chance may never come around.

I did not find out where Bette had taken our children for some time. It seemed through some of our mutual friends as though they were still in the area but the children were kept away from me. It was heartbreaking for me. During the time span when I did not know where my children were or what had happened to them I became very ill. It got to the point where I could keep virtually no food in my stomach and I lost thirty pounds of weight over a couple of months. My training and hopes to win the gold medal in the coming Olympics were dashed.

There had never really been a goal I set for myself in life I did not accomplish, but evidently now I had a couple of them. I had failed in the sacred union Bette and I had kept for years and now it was very unlikely I was ever going to win a gold medal in the Olympics. I don't really know why the second goal was so important to me as athletic achievement had never been important during my school years. I just realized I could achieve that goal.

During the years prior to our breakup Todd had often been my faithful running companion. I would make sure I ran at a pace where he could keep up but he was always bound and determined to keep up. When we would get home Todd would always say, if I did not get it out first, "I'm a pretty good runner, aren't I, Dad?" I would always reply, "Yes Todd, you are a great runner." Yes, he was a great runner but now my faithful little companion was not there. My children were perhaps my greatest incentives to win a gold medal. I always told them the same as my dad had told me: "You can do anything in this world you put your mind to if you keep your eye on your goal and do not waver in your beliefs." I believed that with all my heart and drove it home to my children every day.

After Bette had obviously left for good, Cindy moved from Stillwater and she, Chad and Kelly came to live with me. Although they kept me somewhat occupied, I was just not the father figure to them I should have been. Anything I did with Cindy and Jack's children made me feel guilty that I was not doing these things with my own children. I did not allow them to move into my children's bedrooms and I kept them the same as my children had left them. That was simply wrong. I am sure in the back of my mind I must have known my children were never going to be back. Bette was going to make sure of it. Another thing that constantly bothered me was Jack Rohr was probably going through the same pain I was since his children were living with Cindy and me. I was a good share of the reason for Jack's pain. I do not know how you go back and ask forgiveness from someone for something so unforgivable.

During these very difficult first several months it was drug use that seemed to keep me going. I had been quite good at getting Demerol from the hospital pharmacy. I was friends with all the people in and around the pharmacy. I never got my drugs from them though. I thought I was pretty normal most of the time if not all the time. I did not take drugs and then see patients or take drugs while at work. Going that far was still taboo to me.

The only thing that seemed to keep me alive in those days was to work nearly twenty-four hours per day. I worked at Bethesda every day and then worked at St. Cloud in the family planning clinic two evenings per week. When weekends rolled around I would do surgery at Moose Lake Community Hospital. Dr. Ray Christensen had contacted me at Bethesda a week earlier and asked me if I would do the elective general surgery that accumulated at their hospital during the week.

Cindy would come with me on those weekends and we would work together in surgery. I basically did all of the general surgery that came into the hospital except for emergency procedures that came in during the week when I was not available.

During the summer Cindy and I lived in a little cabin on the lake and often we would take a canoe out and paddle around. It was fun and was a nice way to relax on the weekends. It also gave me the chance to follow up on my patients after surgery and make sure there were no post-op complications. Usually we would drive up from the Twin Cities on Thursday night and then do surgery on Fridays and Saturdays. One night Dr. Christensen had a young man come in who was presenting with an acute abdomen and Chris diagnosed him with appendicitis. He did not usually do surgery but thought he could easily take out an appendix. He was not worried because he knew I would be coming in shortly and could take care of any possible problems he might run into that he could not handle. Unfortunately, on this rare night, Cindy and I had decided to get up early in the morning and drive up to Moose Lake.

When we walked in the hospital that morning I saw Chris the first thing. He was still in anguish from what he described as his lengthy appendectomy the night before. He asked, "Where on earth were you last night? I needed you." He then recounted the sweating he did when he got into the abdomen and couldn't find his patient's appendix. He said he searched and he searched and he just could not find the appendix. He had to scrub out of surgery and get on the phone and call one of his general surgery friends from Duluth.

I said, "Chris, your patient most likely had a retrocecal appendix." I could guess that was the case as a complete congenital absence of the appendix is extremely rare. The majority of life-long surgeons have never seen a congenital absence of an appendix. Chris said those were the first words out of the mouth of his friend in Duluth. He said his friend had to guide him over the phone as to what to do.

I said, "It is really easy after you have done a few. You just take down or mobilize the cecum and the right ascending colon but only after you have searched the ileocecal area completely. Generally the appendix will be lying somewhere directly behind these structures. You then remove the appendix and fix the colon back down where you had taken it from."

Chris said, "That is exactly what I did but I was so scared and worried I was going to cut the wrong thing someplace." I told him not to worry, it would more than likely be fine and if there were any problems or complications over the weekend I would take care of them. He exclaimed, "Great! I just won the record for completing the world's longest appendectomy." I just laughed. Sometimes an easy surgery ends up being very difficult. I reassured Chris his appy would heal up the same as an easy appendectomy.

I was reminded of what Doctor Lundholm had said to me one day when I was removing a girl's appendix through a very small incision. She still wanted to wear a bikini and did not want to have a noticeable scar. Art said, "I'm going to start calling you Key Hole Kelly." Art said there was a surgeon at Bethesda who would go to these great lengths to do procedures through a very small incision. His nickname was Key Hole Kelly. Art added, "Rick, the incision heals from side to side not end to end."

When I first started going to Moose Lake I started seeing an inordinate number of inmates coming in with an officer from the Sandstone Correctional Facility. One of our nurses explained to me it was one of the ways the prisoners could get out of the prison for a mini day vacation in the hospital. I would work these prisoners up knowing I was not going to find anything. These were generally healthy young males and after wasting a couple hours of my time and that of other hospital personnel not to mention the prison guard who had to bring them in, wait and take them back, I would send them back to prison. I could tell they thought it was cute. They thought they were putting one over on us with their feigned bellyaches.

One day when a healthy young prisoner came in with the usual stomach ache, I decided I would put an end to this right now. I had blood drawn for some routine tests and when the results came back I would have blood drawn again for some more tests. I would then have my nurse give them a couple of enemas to clean them out so I could do a sigmoidoscopic exam. I then told them they were not sufficiently cleaned out so they had to go through the whole enema thing again. I said they were still not ready so we repeated the whole regimen again and by this time they had a pretty sore rectum.

After more testing I told them everything looks pretty good so we'll send you back to the dorm. I told them I was still not entirely satisfied with my exam so I would have the prison bring them back in four hours and we would repeat the sigmoidoscopy. After doing that for a couple more prisoners the people from the Sandstone prison quit showing up in the emergency room. The problem was solved and prisoners decided the day away from the prison was not worth getting their rectum cleaned out a half dozen times and getting a tube shoved up their bottom three or four times. God bless those poor prisoners and their sore bottoms.

One thing us physicians have to always remember is that even when you see a hypochondriac on a nearly daily basis you must always keep in mind that even a hypochondriac who thinks they are sick all the time will most likely die of a bona fide genuine organic illness one day. I always thought the epitaph on their tombstone would read, "See, I told you I was sick."

Summers were fun for Cindy and me and they seemed to be a real break after putting in so many hours during the week seeing patients. It seemed as if we were always in a hurry though and during the week

I kept the little Cessna 152 I had learned to fly in on a grass strip near my home in White Bear. When we went to St. Cloud to run the family planning clinic on Tuesday and Thursday nights we would jump in the plane and fly to St. Cloud. Someone from the clinic would be waiting to pick us up and take us to the clinic.

One day we were late and in a big hurry as we arrived at the grass strip to take off for St. Cloud. I had topped off the tanks the day before. The temperature was in the 90s and it was very humid. I took off toward the east and it was going to be close as to whether or not I would clear the corn stalks at the end of the field. I did not. I jumped out of the plane, grabbed the tail of the plane and swung it around so we could try to take off going the other direction. First I had to clean a few corn stalks off the plane's struts. The field was longer going the other direction in that we did not have corn growing at the other end.

A few hundred feet beyond the field was a little farm house and a barn we were going to have to clear. There was no wind and the wind sock hung straight down from the pole. I made one of the most stupid and hurried decisions of my life. I should have had Cindy drive to an alternate airport and pick her up there. I had to deal not only with the added weight of full tanks, but the additional weight of having a passenger on board.

Instead of me being smart, we took off and I really thought I could clear the structures at the end of the field. We were easily airborne but we just did not have the power to climb. It appeared we were not going to clear the house by only a couple feet but now it was too late to abort the takeoff. I waited until the very last seconds, tilted the wings and flew between the house and the barn thinking all the way through my bank that we would surely stall. We had just enough power to avoid stalling and once through I immediately leveled the plane. We had avoided a disaster by the narrowest of margins.

I had done the unforgivable and put another person's life in danger for the sake of getting to work on time. That experience really shook me and it was then I decided to leave flying up to the professionals. After a month or so and reliving that experience in my mind over and over, I hung up my pilot's license for good. What I had done was not only unforgivable it was reprehensible and deplorable. Had God not been in the cockpit that day, I would not be writing this now.

There is a saying among pilots: *There are old pilots and there are bold pilots but there are no old, bold pilots.* Just how true is that. You do not get to make bold decisions on an everyday basis in aeronautics and expect to live long.

Chapter Eighteen
Working like Mad

At the family planning clinic we would see young girls all night either with an STD (sexually transmitted disease) or for birth control pills. The family planning clinic could get the pills from one of the drug companies for only about ten cents a pack which lasted for a month. So giving them away for almost nothing made us a great place for young broke females to come for birth control. The girls with the STDs were happy to be able to see a doctor they did not know because they were too embarrassed to see their own family doctor. We did not charge for our services so that also was life saving for them.

It was interesting to me that I was called in to be part of a city council discussion on dealing with the STDs in St. Cloud and the surrounding area. What really dumbfounded me one night was when one of the town's physicians said the meeting was just a waste of time. He blatantly said, "We do not have sexually transmitted diseases in St. Cloud, Minnesota." What was even more remarkable to me was that he actually believed it. It was not really his fault. He was only located a couple of miles from the family planning clinic and I guess we were taking care of any patients who may have gone to him as their family physician.

I explained to him what the situation really was in St. Cloud. I said, "Many weeks we will take care of at least a half dozen girls with gonorrhea and pelvic inflammatory disease (PID) is really rampant. Chlamydia is another serious problem in that many men who carry it simply do not know they have it." The doctor hearing these numbers from right down the road was shell shocked. Information like that wakes up some of these physicians so they can start screening these young girls earlier, identify their problems in a more timely way and possibly prevent some of the spread. Many of the venereal diseases are very silent and girls do not get help unless they know something is wrong.

During my time working at the family planning clinic, St. Cloud State College approached me and asked if I would consider being a preceptor for a couple of their students who were in their physician's assistant program. I told them I would be honored. The two people I would be tutoring would be Barry Radin whom I already worked with regularly at the family planning clinic and a young woman by the name of Michelle Mears. They were good students and I basically reinforced what they had already learned while working at the clinic. They learned how to do pelvic exams and examine an abdomen if we had a young lady come in with PID symptoms. Almost all of the evening patients could be treated by us with antibiotics. We used amazingly small doses of penicillin when I had first started treating PID. We were giving Bicillin CR in doses of about 1.2 million units. Within a very short time we were giving doses of 2.4 million units then to 4.8, 9.6 and so on. Obviously, the gonorrhea organism was becoming very resistant to penicillin.

When doses of penicillin went high, it was inconceivable to give someone that much penicillin in their buttock, so we gave an oral alternative that was just as effective if the patient took their medication as ordered. I would always explain how important it was and to refrain from any type of sexual activity until they were re-cultured and we knew our treatment was effective.

I occasionally ran into patients who had been receiving the intra-muscular injections. Often they had just run out of money so that was the reason they were now being seen in the family planning clinic. When they found out they could have been treated with oral medications instead of the huge painful shots of penicillin, they were displeased to say the least. I often thought the physicians who gave these shots were probably giving them as a form of punishment for contracting a sexually transmitted disease. I bet they wouldn't have given that shot in the ass to themselves if they were treating their own gonorrhea.

Usually the nights after working in the family planning clinic, we would all go to one of the local clubs, listen to the bands and dance. My crew was all one happy bunch when we finished at the clinic every night. We were even happier when we left the pub. I know it must sound as if we just worked and partied but that is not the case. Emergency Department medicine is a high stress environment at times and often the most important thing people in medicine can do is to go out and relieve their stress. We are not drinking to forget but to perhaps to unwind a little bit at the end of our day. Please do not think this is behavior we ever exhibit prior to going into work. That would not be acceptable.

I continued to push myself with work so some nights I would cover the Apple Valley Emergency Department, the only certified emergency department run by a clinic. It was a relatively new, well run clinic with a great staff that was fun to work in. I kept trying to push myself as hard as I possibly could to keep my mind off my children. Whenever I started seeing patients, it was as if a light switch came on and suddenly my patients would take front and center stage. It allowed me moments of sanity when everything else would disappear in my life. It was just my patients and me.

It was some months before I found out where Bette and the kids were. The guy she was going with was a hospital administrator and now they lived with my children in Watford City, North Dakota located about forty-five to fifty miles southeast of Williston. It was a town we always drove through on our way home to Williston when we were going to school in Grand Forks.

The nights when I was working I thought I was doing okay and I mean only okay. I was not doing well. My drug use had escalated and it seemed like I ran entirely on nervous energy. I just could not seem to get rest. The Demerol gave me a sweet reprieve of a few hours free of pain. Every night when I laid down to rest I would have a picture of my children by me so I would go to sleep crying and in the morning wake up crying. It was difficult to keep food down and I had a terrible time trying to maintain my weight and stay alive. I had quit working out which had always kept me alive and functioning. Working out was just no longer possible.

The girls would sometimes wonder what was wrong with me the mornings after I had not taken Demerol the previous night. They often thought I was on speed because of my weight loss and nervous energy. I just explained it away by telling them I did not need much sleep. In actuality I was living on almost no sleep. Going without sleep began to be the norm. The more I stayed awake the more nervous energy I had. Once I went without going to bed for seventeen days.

My depression seemed to get deeper and deeper and I was really getting into a dark place. It seemed to be a hole that had no bottom and I could not seem to claw my way out of it. When I thought I could no longer go on, I would take another shot to try to survive for one more hour. The problem now was becoming my body's swiftly growing tolerance of Demerol. At one time I would take two to three hundred milligrams slowly by IV. Later on the doses to take away the anguish would have killed me when I first began abusing narcotics.

One night as I was waiting for Cindy to get home, I began having a seizure. I was conscious and alert and knew I was seizing but could not stop the seizure. I tried biting the shag carpet in the family room where I had collapsed on the floor. I wanted to stop hitting my face and head on the floor. After what seemed like hours of seizing, but realistically only part of an hour, Cindy came walking through the door. I was still partially seizing and I told her to immediately get a shot of Valium out of my bag and give it to me intravenously if she could. My seizing did not allow that to happen so she gave me ten milligrams intra-muscular (IM) into my thigh. After about ten minutes or so, I finally stopped seizing.

What had happened was I had taken enough Demerol that metabolites of the meperidine were building up in my blood. That metabolite was nor-meperidine which caused irritability of the nervous system and when the metabolites got high enough they could cause seizures. When I took large doses of Demerol, I would sometimes self-medicate with Valium to try to prevent the seizures. Usually it would work. Don't doctors really have it nice? We had enough medical knowledge that when we experienced bad side effects we could add another medication to alleviate them. Hopefully we figured everything out well enough in our self-induced stupors to get it right and live for another day.

I was playing more and more with fire and it would not be long before I was going to get badly burned if I could not get off the medications. I now considered myself to be on an extremely thin tightrope and every day became more one of life and death. Death and dying started to constantly occupy my mind. I thought death would be a welcome reprieve from all of this.

The drug use was a continual problem. One night I woke up on the plush white carpeting of the master bedroom upstairs. As I gradually opened my eyes I could see my t-shirt was soaked in blood and as I looked around the bathroom it looked as if I had spray painted the floor, the cabinet and part of the mirrors with blood. There was a large syringe with a much larger needle than I ever used on the floor next to me.

It appeared that when I had tried to hit a large antecubital vein I must have passed out or not been coherent enough to know I had hit the brachial artery. The pressure in the artery had evidently blown the plunger out of the syringe and then kept spurting. Somehow or another the needle and syringe were now out of my arm and the bleeding had stopped. When my ability to function returned quite some time later, I spent the next several hours washing the dark red carpet back to snowy white. I was begging God, asking him for relief and the courage to stop the drugs. I knew I was simply lying to myself and to God. One more broken bargain with my Maker.

I finally went into the university, rounded up Dr. Kelly, our psychiatrist and Dr. Galen Nelson, our psychologist and met with both of them. I explained to them that my life was in shambles and I felt as though I was heading toward a disastrous ending. I explained my crazy working hours and that I did okay as long as I was working as I would escape into the world of medicine and my patients. They both reassured me my depression was to be expected and unavoidable considering my current circumstances. They both said it would be impossible to suddenly lose the family I had built my life around and expect for it to go smoothly and without problems.

They pointed out what a good job I was doing with our residents and that my department was running well. That part was true. It seemed all of the people I worked with thought I lived an idyllic life without problems. One great suggestion Dr. Kelly and Dr. Nelson made was for me to buy a dog so I would have someone to be accountable to every day and the dog would also make me keep a schedule. I loved animals and they always seemed to make me feel warm and fuzzy so I went to a pet store and bought two baby Old English Sheepdogs.

I named them Flower and Blossom. They were beautiful and I loved them and it seemed to help for a while. I would spend hours every day just brushing them. The sheepdogs managed to get around well and go jogging with me in spite of the big bangs of hair hanging over their eyes.

One day I screamed at Flower to watch out but I was not fast enough and she ran into a stop sign. It did not seem to bother her and off she went again. If I called my furry children from a distance they would run as fast as possible toward the sound of my voice, sometimes running a few feet past me, then sitting down to try to see where I was. By then I was behind them. They were always fun to watch.

I was still functioning okay while I was at work and I was scrubbing in almost daily with a number of the surgeons on the Bethesda staff. I sometimes scrubbed in with Sam Hunter, a thoracic surgeon who had implanted the first bipolar pacemaker in the United States. A bronze plaque still hung on a first floor wall in Bethesda commemorating the event. I also scrubbed in as frequently as possible with a great and gifted surgeon by the name of Richard Yadeau known by everyone as Dick. He subspecialized in oncological surgery and was always taking care of difficult surgical cases.

After working with Dr. Yadeau for several months, he asked me if I would cover all his surgical patients for him when he went out of town for a few days. I was more than happy to do so and happy he had expressed so much confidence in me by asking me to cover his postoperative patients rather than one of the more experienced surgeons who usually covered for him. When Dr. Yadeau returned and had been back in the hospital for a few days he stopped me in the hall to talk to me and thank me for covering for him while he was gone. He said, "I don't know if I can have you cover for me again, Rick. My patients gave you so many compliments it seems as if they may rather see you than me." He was kidding of course but I had gotten along well with them.

Not long after this Dr. Yadeau approached me one day and asked, "Rick, would you consider being my partner in my surgical practice?" He said, "You are really gifted in surgery and the way you get along with everyone, you would make a great partner." He added, "You do know of course, Rick, you would have to leave and take a general surgery residency." I said, "Yes of course, I do know that." I thanked him for his great confidence in me. He asked, "You also know of course, don't you, that you will never be as good a surgeon as I am?" I was a little surprised he would say that, but I asked him why. He said, "Rick, the reason for that is you will never find an assistant as gifted as you are." I just laughed.

I had additional reasons for wanting to take a surgical residency beyond the one Dr. Yadeau had provided. I thought that by getting us out of Minnesota perhaps there was still time to save our marriage. I shared this with Bette, who had returned home to the children and me after her trip with Rich B. I didn't share my thoughts with her about trying to save our marriage but only my thoughts about what Dr. Yadeau had said. I thought there was still a possibility to salvage our relationship, our family and our home. I really did not think Bette was inclined to leave Minnesota and I had no idea what ongoing relationships she was trying to preserve.

A week or two after Dr. Yadeau's offer I told him I was going out to the West Coast to look at surgical residencies. He was pleased and wished me good luck. I had called Dick Zorn and asked him what hospital or hospitals in Seattle offered a great surgical residency. Dick had taken his orthopedic surgery training at the University of Washington and was familiar with the area hospitals. He suggested Swedish Hospital and or Virginia Mason Hospital. I called them both and within a couple of days I was meeting with them. I brought hundreds of surgical cases with me that I had done. I included voluminous amounts of information including my workups, my surgical procedures, op notes and the notes on discharge.

Both Swedish and Virginia Mason offered me a surgical residency immediately after meeting with me and both said I could start immediately. Both hospitals were in the middle of the year for a residency but said they would be willing to forgive one and one-half years of the residency since I had so much experience. I would be starting in the middle of the second year of a general surgical residency. Both residency program offers were more than I could have hoped for.

Both hospitals told me I had already done more surgery than any of their graduating residents. The dialogue I had with both hospitals went something like this. "Why do you want to take a residency? We probably cannot add anything to what you already know except perhaps some thoracic surgery. What are you going to do when you complete your residency? Are you going to be doing any thoracic surgery?" I replied, "No. You do not know if I am any good." They replied, "We know you are very good. No family practitioner can do this volume of surgery with no surgical deaths or complications and not be good." I said, "The reason is, when I see a surgical case I know is going to do very poorly, I call one of you super specialists with all of the credentials to come to our hospital and get the outcome consequences I would be getting if I did the surgery. A family practitioner in a small town cannot afford to have surgical fatalities." The head of surgery said, "That also says you are very good and with good judgment."

Both hospitals must have gone through this in the past as both hospitals gave pretty much the same advice. Both surgical program directors asked me if I would have trouble taking directions from surgeons my age all the while knowing more than all of them. I said, "I do not have much going in the way of ego problems and that would present no problem for me. Even though I will enter a program with my surgical background, I am sure your residents will accept me and I know I can learn something from all of them. Perhaps I can even teach them a little. We all have our own tricks."

Bette and I stuck around for a couple days before leaving for Minnesota. We went back the way we had come and took our time going through Glacier National Park. It was middle to late summer and we enjoyed the park and the majesty of the mountains. The trip gave Bette and me a lot of time to talk. The hospitals had not really dissuaded me but they really did not think the surgical residency would add much to my skills. What it would have done though is allow me to be a partner with one of the greatest surgeons in the Twin Cities area. One other consideration I kept mulling around in the back of my mind was the fact Bette did not seem overly enamored with the Seattle area. I thought that was a little strange since we had been friends with Dick and Donna for several years. I truly felt there was something or someone Bette was missing back home and it did not seem to be our children. I was soon to find out it was Duane J.

Our thoracic and cardiovascular surgeon Dr. Ray Bonnabeau had come from the University of West Virginia. He was a tall, dark, good looking, personable surgeon and got along well with everybody. It did not take me long to get to know him well. Soon he asked me to scrub in with him and not long after I was asked to be first assistant in some of his open heart procedures. I did not do this more than a couple of times. I could see that if I scrubbed in as first assistant, I was taking up a valuable space at the table a young resident could take and learn to be a heart surgeon someday. I did not have that same inclination. I had no desire to be a cardiovascular surgeon. At a young age I realized surgery is just that. It is simply surgery. Some surgical specialties sound more glamorous, like open heart procedures. The last procedure I had scrubbed in on had been an aortic and mitral valve replacement. The patient was an elderly male and we had him on bypass by about 8:30 or 9 a.m. and I later had to scrub out at about 6 p.m. that evening to go back to Bethesda. A senior surgical resident took my place and the next day I would find out the procedure finally ended near midnight. Every time they had tried to get him off the heart-lung machine a portion of his aorta would burst through an atheromatous plaque. They would try multiple times to patch it but ultimately it could not be done and despite the very best efforts by this gifted surgeon, the patient ended up dying on the operating room table. The very best efforts in the world, even when performed by a very experienced and gifted team sometimes fail.

I think some of these different opportunities in the hospital convinced me I was still functioning at some level of competence. I didn't think I would be asked to scrub in as first assistant on open heart procedures unless I was maintaining competent surgical skills.

It seemed that in worrying only about myself and my me, me, me, world I was not paying enough attention to know what was going on around me. Suddenly one day my associate in our family practice program disappeared for a few days. I was then informed by someone in our department that Donald A. had been hospitalized for the treatment of alcoholism. I felt I had let my friend Don down by not knowing he was having problems. He was often absent from work but I attributed those to all the staff meetings held by the Department of Family Practice over at University Hospital. That is what happens when you are wrapped up in your own problems and are trying to survive. Survival mode is just that.

After a while, the dark thoughts started to race through my mind again when I was home alone at night. I prayed and prayed for relief. I was having some really deep belief problems. Many of my conversations with God were to try to rationalize my feelings and talk to Him about forgiving suicide. When you are lost in the depths of suicidal thoughts you have no one around you, not even God. At least I did not have Him around me in a meaningful way. Later in life I would tell patients that when they feel as though they are sinking in the dark ocean depths of despair to try to remember their Lifeguard walks on water. At that time, I had no lifeguard.

Not seeing my children bothered me immensely. Bette was going to make that part of life as difficult as possible. One of the most bothersome things was she did not want me to know where they were staying. One day I sat down with Dr. Nelson and Dr. Kelly again and let them know what I was going through with my children. I asked them what they thought about me going to court and fighting it out to see who would have custody. They said, "Rick, look at the impossible life you lead." It was true. I was working as many hours in a day as possible to stay sane.

They also told me the court often sided with the mother in battles such as this and asked if I thought I could win if this went to court. I replied affirmatively, informing them of all the things Bette had been involved with including all of the different men she had been involved with.

They asked me if Bette was a good parent and I admitted that prior to becoming sick, she was a great parent. They asked me who would be the best parent right now as much as I was working. I admitted Bette would be the best parent as far as time spent with the children. Drs. Nelson and Kelly had talked me around in a circle until I knew the best decision for my children. They were not going to be staying with me. I had to keep their welfare in mind and not my own.

Finally one night when I was again lying awake in my upstairs bedroom I decided I'd had enough of all of this. The only thing on my mind was to do away with my pain. The loss of my children was unbearable and I felt this was exactly what Bette wanted for me.

It was during one of these nights I finally rationalized that if I accidentally killed myself He would certainly not hold me responsible. I thought an accident was forgivable. I took out my rifle, put the barrel under my chin and taped it to my neck so it could not move. I pumped a shell into the chamber and took the safety off. I then put my left thumb through the trigger guard and then taped that hand to the finger guard and stock. I lay down on the hallway floor upstairs and prayed. I now had it well fixed so when I eventually went to sleep I would never see another morning. I then talked to God and said, "Lord, I really do not want to willfully take my life but surely when I fall asleep, You will not hold me responsible for not waking up." That night became one of the longest nights of my life but as daylight streamed through the windows in the morning, I was still alive. I had managed to stay awake all night no matter how tired I was. God had seen me through the night. I had survived to see one more day. I was often just taking life an hour at a time let alone a string of twenty-four.

I took all of the tape off my neck and hand, put the safety back on and went into the shower to prepare for another day. This bizarre, sick behavior continued for several weeks. I bought more tape as it was needed. It seemed the less I slept the more God kept me awake at night so I could not accidentally fall asleep and take my life. Despite this darkest time in my life, I had lived. I would think perhaps I would see my children again until the darkness of night would come around again and I would relive the nightmare.

Bette and I were also going through the legal nightmare of attorneys. When there is a lot of money involved attorneys are like sharks that taste blood in the water. In the state of Minnesota, the husband is responsible for all legal debts regardless of the amount. Bette of course knew this so she decided to start changing attorneys about as often as she changed her clothes. Sometimes the legal bills would hit several thousand dollars per week.

One day Bette asked me if I would accompany her to her attorney's office on Lake Street in St. Paul to talk with him about reconciliation. He looked like a little weasel but I listened to what he had to say. The little bastard certainly was not interested in helping put our marriage back together. He was there only to finish shredding what was left of it.

He wanted to know what our finances were like and if I was going to keep providing money for Bette. We were sitting in two chairs in front of his desk. Finally, when I had had enough I stood up, reached across his desk and grabbed him by his tie. I jerked him over his desk and pulled his face up to mine and said, "If you ever want me in your office for something like this again, I am going to beat the living shit out of you and if you have a wife and family I am also going to hurt them." He was visibly terrified. I think he thought I was going to commence with hurting him immediately. He stuttered and stammered a little bit and said it would not happen again. I got up and left. It did not happen again.

Bette changed attorneys. I think she wanted someone a little larger and more muscular who would not be so easily intimidated.

That miserable attorney of Bette's did not file assault and battery charges against me. The little prick was damn lucky he did not, as I would have beaten the tar out of him when and if I got out on bail while we were waiting for the court date.

Some of the things that happened were probably good for me. I was a lot better at handling anger than I was at handling depression. Who knows? Bette may have saved my life with her miserable behavior. I also realized during this time I was far from being a paragon of virtue.

I still visited the Molenars in Princeton about once a week or at least once every other week. I would visit my parents which felt good and seeing them made me feel half way normal and sane. They were always supportive, throwing buoys and life jackets out to me. They couldn't walk on water the same as my Savior but they surely helped me float.

Bette called me one day and said she and her brothers, Dick and Tom, were coming to the house that night with a U-Haul truck. Dick was her second oldest brother and Tom was the next one in line after him. They were going to load up everything Bette thought she had coming. She thought she owned everything that was formerly joint property. She did not have the children with her and she said they were safe. I imagine that meant they with her current friend whoever that might be this week.

That night when they showed up with the truck, Bette started telling them to haul things out. She arrived at our home angry but for what reason I did not know. Young Thomas was grabbing just about anything he could. Why not? They did not know of Bette's problems. She was their kind, loving, caring sister who did not do anything wrong. Tom then took the ax I used for splitting wood for the fireplace out of the garage and threw it as far as he could out in the field by our home into about one foot deep snow. I pulled out my rifle, chambered a shell, put the barrel to Tom's head and told him to retrieve the ax or he was going to have a piece of lead in his brain that probably would not need retrieval. Dick became scared and tried to appease my anger and calm the tension. Dick told Tom to go get the ax and keep his hands off my property. Tom did just that and I put my rifle down.

When Bette had taken everything she thought she had a right to, she had removed all of the dishes and silverware from our house. What do

I mean ours? I guess now this home was entirely mine. What Bette left me was one sheet for my bed that was also going to serve as my pillow. No other bedding was left. She left me one plate, one glass, one butter knife, one fork, and one spoon. I am guessing the reason I was left one of everything was that if I collected as many girlfriends as Bette had boyfriends, she wanted them to eat off the kitchen table with their fingers.

I had no idea what had made Bette hate me so badly but evidently it had grown. She had probably built up all this hatred against herself after Adrian had told her never to be a hardship on me. She was now channeling this hatred toward me and I could not really imagine how anyone could have been more of a hardship or more hateful. I never thought she would take it out on our children but it was obvious she was only thinking about what she perceived as her own wellbeing. She couldn't have cared less about our children.

She was mentally the same hurtful unkind person she had become since this disaster between us had started. Bette was certainly not behaving normally. I surmised she was probably on a mind-altering drug. I really did not care anymore. At that point in time I simply wished this person I no longer knew would slip up with her drug dosage someday and end her own life as I had contemplated doing with mine. How does a relationship with a person you formerly loved and was your lifelong friend come to such a bitter end? It was simply beyond me. It was hard to imagine the death of her father had produced this unimaginable end. I still did not know what warning signs Adrian had seen in his daughter but his warnings to her about me led to no happy ending.

It was really evident Bette cared only about herself. She had inserted herself into the relationship of two of our friends. She knew one of those friends was dealing with difficult psychiatric issues. Bette simply did not care if other lives were ruined.

Somewhere around about this time frame Bette wanted to meet. She brought her boyfriend Duane J. with her to meet me in our home in Princeton. Why would anyone want to introduce their boyfriend to the man she is still married to? It made no sense to me. After they had been there for a while Duane asked me if he could talk to me alone so we went downstairs into the family room. Duane said, "I just want to make sure you are planning on sending money to us to take care of your children." I grabbed him by the clothes on the front of his neck, lifted him about a foot off the floor and pinned him up against the wall with my forearm against his neck. I said, "You miserable little bastard, you have my family living with you at your home. Do not talk to me right now about what my responsibilities are to my children." It was a good thing during those times I was not homicidal or Bette would have certainly put a lot of men's lives in danger. I allowed Duane to slide down the wall to his feet. Bette and Duane left in a hurry.

I continued teaching the family practice residents and hoped some of the basics I was teaching were sinking in. I knew from the small number of deliveries we had at Bethesda that none of my residents were going to be able to go out to a small town alone and be proficient enough to handle all deliveries. Obstetrics is kind of like working in an emergency department. Ninety-nine percent of what you do is so routine a high school student could handle the deliveries most of the time. It is the one percentage of terror that comes around when you absolutely must possess the expertise and training to avoid an unfortunate outcome.

One foggy night, I received a call from Norm Metcalf. Norm asked, "Rick can you come up here in the morning to relocate an Austin-Moore prosthesis for us?" I asked, "What do you mean relocate it?" Usually this happened immediately post op or a few days after the procedure. An Austin-Moore is the artificial ball we put into a hip when a person has a high sub-capital fracture of the femur. The head (ball) of the femur has a very poor blood supply and it is necessary to put in a new ball to get a satisfactory result from a high fracture that has likely impeded its blood supply. Norm said Dr. Jim Andre had done the procedure and it had dislocated when the patient tried rolling over in bed. I said to have Dr. Andre put it back in but Norm said he had left on vacation and refused to come back. I cursed that surgeon under my breath. Norm then volunteered that the patient had the same prosthesis on the other side and just loved the way it turned out. I asked, "Why don't you call that surgeon since she thought the world of him." Norm said, "We are, Rick. You are that surgeon." I said, "I will see you at 8 a.m."

I left very early that morning as the fog that had been bad when I went to bed was still miserably heavy in the morning. I arrived right on time. The patient was prepped and draped and the view-finder had the x-ray up which indeed showed a dislocated prosthesis. Ordinarily

I do not operate on a patient whom I had not seen first. I was able to do this only because of my confidence in my partner. I knew he would not make the mistake of the wrong hip again. I operated on the patient to find her good doctor must have really been in a hurry. He had not bothered to adequately sew up the capsule. The tough fibrous covering was virtually the only protection from letting the prosthesis dislocate. It would have been possible to break up a good repair with inadequate care of the patient following the procedure, but this was not the case. This was a very poor surgical repair. My patient did well however and it was good to see her again. She was happy and it was fun to scrub in for surgery in Princeton again. My patient never dislocated again following my surgery. Of all the Austin-Moore prosthetics I had placed, the only dislocation I had ever had to take care of was that of Dr. Andre, his fault by being in a hurry. We always need to fix our own complications or mistakes. I had scrubbed in with Dr. Andre a number of times and had doubts about him from the first time. He did not handle tissues as gently as I thought he should. Sometimes we had a little active bleeding and I would suggest stopping it. He would say, "Anything that starts bleeding will stop bleeding." Yea, well eventually that will be true I guess.

His partner Jim Seay was an excellent surgeon but he always said, "Never let a little skin stand between you and your diagnosis." The other thing he always said was, "When in doubt, cut it out." Fortunately, he learned enough other things in his training to be a good surgeon. One thing I found peculiar was the fact you never saw anyone flunk out of a residency program. That statement should give you something to think about. The person who may be the greatest technician or surgeon in the world may be surpassed academically by a person who can't tie a knot on the technical side of things. Who do you think you want for your surgeon? Do you want the great technician, or the surgeon with the two left hands who cannot tie his shoes?

Our divorce proceedings progressed at glacial speeds. There was not much to argue about that was worth arguing about anymore. In the end the only people coming out ahead were going to be Bette's attorneys. I had talked to a few of my friends. I was sick and tired of everything so one day I went into the courthouse and signed over everything I owned to Bette and the children. I had decided I would give up the world if I owned it, not to deal with Bette any more. I got to keep a couple of cars and the home in White Bear Lake.

Regardless of all my work, life was disintegrating around me. Much of this was probably not even my fault. One day a deputy showed up to arrest me on my front steps because I supposedly owed money on flowers I had bought. They were flowers for my children which of course they never received. The bill was for $66. I was in the process of opening the door. He asked, "Who lives here?" I replied, "I do." As he looked inside our cavernous atrium with the beautiful walnut stair casing winding up the side of the wall to a large balcony overhead, he replied that a woman lived here. I said, "A woman did, but I bought the home from her some months ago." He then asked if he could use my phone. I heard some angry talk coming from the phone. He asked, "What the hell are you doing sending me out to arrest someone who lives in a multi-million dollar home for an insignificant bill?" He turned around to leave and said, "I am sorry sir."

Another day a deputy showed up to arrest me for a large phone bill. I just stood in the doorway and put out my wrists. I just said, "Go ahead, it's been a shitty day and you couldn't make it any worse." He also asked me who owned this home and he left without me when I told him I did.

I later got a call from the attorney from the phone company who said my phone was going to be shut off if I did not pay the phone bill. I informed him I was a physician and did not think he would want to be the person legally responsible for shutting off my phone. I explained the phone company owed me money and that the phone bill had been paid several times. He called back several minutes later and said the phone company owed me several hundred dollars and asked why I kept paying the bill. I told him I had more important things on my mind than arguing with a phone company. I received a check in the mail the next day for several hundred dollars and then they cut off my phone the same day. Incredible! Phone companies were the same back then as they are now. It is true that when life is going bad, everything goes bad.

Some of the things going on were indeed my fault. The Minnesota State Board of Medical Examiners called me one day. A pharmacist from Stillwater had called them and said I had attempted to pass off a script for Demerol to them stating I wanted it for a patient. I said that was true. The person on the phone asked why I wanted an injectable for a patient. I explained I stopped in periodically to see patients in their homes. The state board said they were going to have to look into this some more and I told them to go ahead. For all you drug users out there the thing to take away from this is to never deal with authorities when you are under the influence of drugs and not thinking clearly. Of course, if you are taking drugs while reading this you are not going to remember my sage advice.

Chapter Nineteen

Treatment

About this time I was contacted by a hospital in Kenmare, North Dakota to see if I would consider coming to their hospital, working in their clinic and covering the city of Kenmare. That sounded good as I was planning to leave my position at the University. I was sick of the politics there. The other thing was, I was still considered a fair haired boy there and I did not want that destroyed by a state investigation of possible drug abuse. I thought they were bound to find out about multiple scripts I had made out for Demerol. I also thought by having another good paying job I would not have to lose the home in White Bear. None of your thinking works well when you are clouded with so many mental issues. It would be some years later I would finally learn that none of the material things in life we think are important really are. The other thing to keep in mind is that money blows in the wind and with the next breath of air it is gone.

Going to Kenmare meant I would be getting away from all the memories in Minnesota. Unfortunately, as I already knew, geographical cures just do not work. Well on second thought, perhaps once in a while for hay fever and asthma. Cindy and I both looked forward to the move. A secondary benefit for me was I would be in the same place as my children. I had found out they had moved to Kenmare where Bette's husband Duane J. had evidently taken a job as hospital administrator. I had second hand knowledge that my children were in school there. I thought being married to someone who was working in a hospital was an appropriate place for Bette as I still thought she would have to be close to a drug supply. In all honesty, I did not know if this were true or not. I really hoped my children were going to be living in a Christian home and becoming grounded in Christian faith.

When we got to Kenmare, we were given a very nice home to live in which was owned by the hospital. Now Chad and Kelly had their own bedrooms, a place for their toys and their own private little play hideaway. Our home was only a block away from the hospital, an easy walk back and forth. The nurse administrator at the hospital was a person by the name of Alice Sands, a pleasant middle aged Registered Nurse with a great fund of knowledge. All the nurses I worked with in Kenmare were great. I know it is hard for the general population to know what great care they receive in a small hospital, but as for me, I would choose a small hospital any day. The staff knows their patients and if the least little thing goes wrong, they are always way ahead of the game.

I was really blessed to be back working in a small hospital again. The staff was supportive and it was not long before they became aware of my marital problems and the loss of my children. I tried to stay in contact with my children and sent Terra, Todd and Shari presents on their birthdays. I added cards and flowers for Shari and Terra. I never received replies from any of them. When I tried calling, Bette would always say they were not home or they were unavailable. I guess she learned that from Shari who as a small child told my patients I was not available when they called and then slammed the phone down.

Cindy and I maintained a relatively normal life in Kenmare. We bought some horses and saddles and stabled them in a small barn that had a small pasture which we rented just a couple of miles from our home. It was relaxing to go muck out stalls and feed the horses the same as I had done much of my early life. It was wonderful to put my arms around my horses' necks again and dream of happier days gone by. Our lives would have been idyllic if I could have just buried the memories of my entire former life and how it had become unraveled. Cindy and I had a close physical relationship and a really good home life. I was still not a good father to Jack and Cindy's children although they were great children. They were cute as bug's ears and would try to give me as much loving as I could receive. I just felt so very guilty returning love to children I could not give to mine.

We became great friends with Lew and Sue F. I really loved both of them and they had a young son and two beautiful daughters who hung around our house all the time. They became great friends to Cindy and me. I really missed my children so I would have adopted the F. children in a second. I am going to have to leave out names in much of this. I am so sorry to all of our friends from back then and to people I unintentionally hurt.

Cindy, Lew, Sue and I used to play cards a lot. In small towns in the country cards were often one of the main forms of entertainment. It was one of the great things about living in a small town in North Dakota during those times. You did not have your nose glued to a television set. You might have one or two channels if you were lucky in some areas of the country.

I was able to return to running again and it felt great. The F. children would then challenge me to a run and they would pick out a hill or other marker west of town. I guess they thought old people could not keep up with young people. They would sometimes bring other challengers with them, but mere high school students were not much of a challenge and it was often a testimonial to their running prowess if they could keep me in sight at the end of a long run. The next challenges were swimming races in the local pool, but those were even more lop-sided.

While we were in Kenmare a Swine Flu Outbreak had been predicted. A number of people were perturbed with me as I did not allow the H1N1 immunization to be given in our clinic or our hospital. One evening "The Beauty and the Beast" was playing on television in the hospital waiting room. A couple of our nurses were standing outside the registration window as George C. Scott who played the beast was coming on. I asked my nurses to look at him. He had the snout of a pig. I told them he had just received the swine flu vaccine. They just laughed but I hope I made a point. I explained there was no indication this vaccine would be necessary. I also explained this was an election year so people and parties were acting a little irrationally. The irrationality was the fact they were trying to produce a complicated vaccine overnight to prevent an unlikely H1N1 world pandemic. Neither of the presidential candidates, Jimmy Carter or Gerald Ford, wanted to be the president who refused to give the lifesaving immunization to meet the terrible forthcoming crisis that could kill the world.

The predicted swine flu outbreak was to be a strain of the H1N1 influenza virus, later to become known as the swine flu debacle. What happened is what often happens when you take shortcuts to save the world. The outbreak killed one person in Fort Dix. However, the side effects from the mass immunization and the vaccine itself caused five hundred cases of Guillain-Barre Syndrome resulting in 25 deaths. So our government acting hastily managed to kill at least 24 more people than the disease itself had killed and the solitary H1N1 was only ever found in Fort Dix. The cost of the vaccination program was $135,000,000. After about 40 million people were immunized over a couple of months, it was stopped when it was determined the vaccine was most likely causing the Guillain-Barre Syndrome. I always wondered if any of our elected officials took that damn immunization. It is astonishing what our government officials are willing to do to win an election.

During this time my addictions did a flip again. That is a strange thing about addiction interaction disorders. It does not matter what you are addicted to as long as it is something. What I took up this time was vanilla ice cream. I would eat about five quarts of vanilla ice cream per day. The problem was I really could not go without it. I ate my other meals but the ice cream cravings were always present. I would get up two to three times a night just to have a dish of ice cream. I did not gain a pound of weight in spite of the fact I was still eating my regular meals. I was not bothering to check my blood sugar levels regularly as I thought there was nothing I was going to change if they were out of whack. That addiction, as bizarre as it was, was incredibly strong and I had to have my ice cream every day to feel normal. One night I went to the fridge at about 1 a.m. and panicked when I realized we had run out of ice cream. I actually got in the car and drove 55 miles to Minot and drove around until I found a store where I could get ice cream. How strange is it to run into a convenience store and ask them for a plastic spoon so you can devour a pint of ice cream immediately in their parking lot to control your addiction until you got home. Who on earth gets up and drives over 100 miles during the night for ice cream. I was too embarrassed to tell anyone about it. I never contemplated taking ice cream IV but some of these weird cravings are so strange and it is even stranger to have the problem by mouth.

Cindy and I developed friendships with Pat and Marsha K. who were also from the Minneapolis-St. Paul area so we had a lot in common. Pat was a local attorney who would later be elected as the city judge. When a bunch of us got together we would often yell, "the Judge beats his wife, the Judge beats his wife" but it was all good-natured and not true of course. Marsha, Pat's wife, was a cute skinny little gal who taught school. Pat, in contrast to his wife, was a tall broad shouldered guy who had at one time played goalie on the Boston Bruin's Hockey Team. He had reflexes like a cat which served him well when we played tennis together. We developed a great friendship as did Marsha and Cindy.

One weekend I got someone from a nearby town to cover call for me and the four of us went to Minneapolis for a couple of days. We got rooms in the Thunderbird Hotel and did some eating and drinking. Even though Cindy and I were not much of drinkers, we probably overdid things a little. Just north of the Thunderbird in Bloomington and beyond Interstate 494 was Lake Nokomis where Bette and our children and I used to hang around in the summertime while we were waiting for our apartment to cool down. We decided to go hang out there around the waterfront for most of the evening. I somehow was separated from the others for a while and I just laid in the grass on a gentle hill on the southwest side of the lake thinking about my children. I became pretty maudlin and cried for a while. I guess I didn't become separated by accident. I just wanted to be alone.

Not far away from me I could hear people splashing around in the water, yelling for a friend for quite a while. I guess they got tired of looking and drove away. The following day I found out someone had drowned near where I had been lying that evening so I guess that must have been the friend they were yelling for. The next day I realized I should have gone and talked to them about what was wrong and then helped them look.

We returned to Kenmare and went back to our usual routine. It was fun to be doing surgery again in a small town. Drug company reps and equipment sales reps would come through the same as in the city. One day a rep came through and asked if we performed breast augmentations. I explained I was relatively new to the practice and we had not done any thus far. The rep showed my nurses and me a video on the procedure and dang if after the video it seemed like more than half of my nurses wanted to have an augmentation. The rep was letting all the nurses hold a silastic prosthesis in their hands while he was telling them it would feel just like their normal breasts. They asked me if I could do it. I said it was a relatively easy procedure and it would be no problem. I had done a number of them with Dr. Yadeau, although not the primary physician as they are an entirely cosmetic procedure and the patient was entrusting their new bust line to the primary surgeon, not his helper.

I let my nurses know as is true of many procedures in medicine everything is fine if there are no complications. It is when there are complications things do not go so well. I warned all of them about all of the different problems that can arise with augmentation. I mentioned just a few of the problems such as infection, sloughing off breast tissue if the prosthesis is too large, rupture of a prosthesis from trauma, etc. I jokingly said, "I think you can buy silicone augmentations that just stick to your breast." They were not interested and didn't have a sense of humor either.

I talked the nurses into waiting for a little while. I did not want them making spur of the moment decisions just because a model looked good in her new bra size. I told them after a couple of months if they still wanted the procedure we could talk about it again and then decide. If their decision was still positive and they wanted the procedure, I said I would do the procedure on one person. They could decide who was to be first and if they all liked it we could proceed as they desired. I like ladies the way God made them and I was not really enthusiastic about altering what God had made. I think it is a lot like the trees and shrubs you see on the countryside. If God had wanted them all pruned and round he probably would have made them that way.

I continued to try to see my children. I never heard anything when I sent them gifts or flowers. Bette was not very accommodating, but on one occasion she agreed to meet me at the Ramada Inn on the north side of Minot. I was so excited. One early evening we met Bette, her husband and the children in the atrium of the Ramada Inn. As soon as I came in Shari said, "Look Daddy, I brought you a present." Little Shari was holding a big round stone. I took the stone and said, "Thank you, honey." Bette immediately said, "I just came here to tell you I decided you can't see the children." I was holding the big round stone in my hands and my first inclination was to use it. They immediately left and I drove home to Kenmare crying and frustrated.

I started using Demerol again. I am sure when most people think of abusing drugs they picture the drug users you see on TV. You may picture someone completely out of it and unable to function. The truth of the matter is that often when a physician is abusing a medication like Demerol, it is usually in a controlled atmosphere. I always had Narcan, a narcotic reversing agent, with me so I could immediately reverse the effects of Demerol with a single shot. I could be sound asleep one minute and wide awake the next. I did not have to worry about someone thinking I was on drugs or drinking. I could go from a stupor to normality at light speed. The doctorate of medicine degree comes in handy for some things other than just fixing people.

It is difficult, even as the months roll by, to get used to being without your children. There is always an empty space in your heart. Christmas is the time of year when you usually take your children out shopping to buy presents for their mother, for one thing. It's the time when you go window shopping just to enjoy the season.

When the movie "It's A Wonderful Life" played on television every Christmas, it would always bring tears to my eyes and make my heart hurt thinking of my children. The movie is about an angel named Clarence who was trying help a compassionate but frustrated, suicidal person learn what life would have been like for everyone around him if he had never existed. The main actors were Jimmy Stewart, Donna Reed and Lionel Barrymore. It was a routine family favorite we had always watched around Christmas time. If you did not have your family around you, it was a tearjerker. Our tradition had been shattered.

Christmas that year became a little more memorable when on Christmas Eve Bette called me to say she was having her husband adopt my children. Not too shocking Bette would try to hurt me as deeply as possible on Christmas Eve. I said, "Bette, if you ever call me again, I will kill you." Bette asked, "Rick, are you trying to threaten me?" I said, "Bette in my entire life have you ever known me not to accomplish everything I said I would?" Bette became very quiet and answered no. I hung up and that was the last I ever heard from Bette.

Not too long after all of this transpired I was told I was going to be taken to Heartview Foundation in Mandan for treatment of drug abuse. I was told my brother Ron had been instrumental in this chain of events but he had not seen or talked to me for the past six months so it did not make sense. However, he later confirmed it. I told Alice Sands, my nurse, I had to get some things out of the doctor's lounge. I was allowed to do that unsupervised. Once in the doctor's lounge I stocked up on syringes full of Demerol and put them inside the tops of my socks. I knew they were not going to be frisking a doctor to see what he had on him.

I was then taken by an officer in uniform to Mercy Hospital in Minot where I was going to spend the night in the locked psych ward until I was transferred to Heartview. The psych ward was up on one of the top floors of the hospital. I was put in a locked room late that night and was by myself. That evening I used up my syringes full of Demerol and pushed out a wire screen made out of something like cyclone fence that was, I imagine, to keep inpatients from jumping out windows. After prying open the containment screen an inch or so, I dropped the empty syringes to the ground three to four stories below.

I was released from my room in the morning for breakfast and allowed to mingle among all of the other crazies. I met a young man outside of the nurse's station later in the morning. I asked him how he was doing and he said great. He had received electro-convulsive-therapy. (ECT) a few hours earlier. ECT used to be a last resort for the treatment of major depressive episodes.

It appeared from my observations over the years it was used more for a revenue generator. Obviously if your shrink can do a procedure and be paid handsomely for it, why not do that rather than write out a script, especially if you can do this week after week and perhaps even get paid daily if you keep them as an inpatient. All of that is well and good.

The young man I was talking to had eaten breakfast a couple hours earlier so I asked him what he had to eat. He gave me a puzzled look and said he did not know. I asked him what type of activities they were doing during the day. Again, he replied he did not know. This may sound cruel to you but I was simply reaffirming what I thought about ECT.

I guess ECT must be great if you cannot remember you were depressed. The other great thing about ECT is the patient cannot remember they had ETC so the doctor in charge can keep frying their brain and memories to oblivion. It is kind of nice to be able to give someone your name if they ask you. I did not embarrass the young man by asking him his name or where he lived. I do not know if he could have answered me. Remember Jack Nicholson in the movie "One Flew Over the Cuckoo's Nest?" Do you think he could have told you his name after ECT?

Case rested.

It was cold and windy outside when someone finally came to take me to Mandan. Heartview Foundation was a plain old light colored brick building. It did not look very warm and inviting sitting in the winter North Dakota snow. I was admitted to a room with three other inmates. By that I mean it was a large room with four beds. I don't really know what they called us. Maybe we were patients but that didn't sound quite right either. The age range was pretty much across the board. A lot of people there were of an age where I thought it would be a waste of time to start treatment for some addiction. I doubt the elderly were there for a brief vacation. Most of them I would learn had been coerced by their families. I really could not see the value of changing your life style if you were in your seventies.

When I was registered, I was informed I was there voluntarily. I asked, "Then why didn't you just call me up and ask me to come rather than wasting a deputy's time and having someone bring me?" They just gave me a blank look and said I was free to go if I did not want to stay. They told me Heartview was not a lockup facility and any one of our people can come or go as they please but must follow the rules if they stay. I volunteered to stay. I was here. I wanted to get the most out of this. I thought at this place in my life, if I did not get help soon, it was most likely going to terminate prematurely.

At Heartview everything ran on schedules, which is part of the side of rehabilitation. Learn how to keep schedules and stay out of trouble. That was no problem for me. I was always keeping schedules. This place was no different.

I was assigned to a group of about nine people but the number changed from time to time as people came and went. Every day everyone would introduce themselves and say, "I'm Howdy Doody and I'm a drug addict and an alcoholic." Everyone would reply, "Good morning Howdy Doody," etc. After the second or third day of introducing myself as an alcoholic and a drug addict, I asked, "Why does everyone say they are both a drug addict and an alcoholic?" Rachel, our very own bull dyke, blonde butch cut counselor said, "Because if you have one addiction, you probably have the other." I said, "That does not make much sense to me. I don't drink." From that day on, I introduced myself as, "I'm Rick Redalen and I'm a drug addict." Rachel didn't appear to like it very well but did not say anything. It would not be much later I would learn there is also a marked difference between a drug addict and a drug abuser.

One thing you learn very rapidly in a treatment center is not to inhale. It was a smoke filled environment, very tough for non-smokers. They should have passed out gas masks to all of us. If you could get cancer from second hand smoke inside a couple of months, we were all going to have it. A good share of the people seemed to be chain smokers, at least you never saw them without a cigarette. The rationale in a treatment center back then was never to try to give up two habits at the same time. What kind of rationale is that? If you really subscribed to that thought process, wouldn't you just give up drinking and keep taking drugs or vice versa. But I guess the counselors considered drinking and drugging as one habit and the inhalation of smoke as something completely different. It seemed to me as if it would be better to give up everything all together at the same time.

When the entire bunch of patients met for one large session in the mornings with everyone present, our head counselor Dick would put on his show by talking to us as he continually sipped on a glass of water and became drunker and drunker. That is at least how it appeared by his actions. But in all honesty, how would we poor patients know any different? It could have been just plain old gin or vodka. He did do a good drunk act and at one time appeared to trip over the edge of a rug as if it were an eight inch curb. Perhaps it wasn't an act at all.

Our group sessions with our counselors were okay. Rachel would sometimes grow uneasy when she was encroaching on my counseling territory. I imagine when you have another counselor in your midst with professional training it is probably a little intimidating, especially if they are a little uncertain in unfamiliar territory. After all, the only claim to fame and the only degree on the wall for most of these counselors would be a label soaked off the side of a Jack Daniels bottle. Yeah, the counselors were all a bunch of former drunks or addicts. I don't think they had any professional counselors at Heartview. If they actually earned degrees what would the degree say? Perhaps, "You have passed a field sobriety test." Or, "You are cleared to help someone else accomplish the same." Or "Falling on your face will be a sign of failure."

Another thing a treatment center teaches you is a new vocabulary. It is rather limited to a couple of words, but once you have learned to use fuck in an every other word fashion, you have pretty much graduated Fuck 101. What an accomplishment. What seemed strange to me is after the continual bombardment of your mind by that repulsive word for only a week or so, when people used it, it was kind of like using and hearing a, and or the.

We were allowed to have visitors and a number of friends would come down on weekends to spend time with me. The first couple to visit me was Sue and Lew F. When Lew came into the visiting room we went downstairs to get a cup of coffee. Lew said, "Rick, what on earth is going on? What are you doing in a damn treatment center? I'm with you every other day. We play tennis. We get together and play cards. I know for a fact you do not use drugs." I said, "Lew, I am sorry to disappoint you but I do abuse drugs." I explained I never used drugs at a time when he or any of my other friends could see me. I confided I was in the right place now, he should not worry and everything would be all right. I could tell Lew was disappointed. He still did not believe me and I don't think Sue did either. How could the guy who their daughters hung around with all the time be a drug user? They just did not see it or fathom it. It was difficult for them to comprehend and watching their reaction hurt my heart.

Once in a while during our group sessions a counselor other than Dick would get up and tell us their hard luck stories and what drinking had done to their families. Come to think of it, most of the people in the treatment center were abusing alcohol. I do not recall that one person was in for abusing drugs, discounting myself of course. Anyway, one day one of the counselors started regaling us with his story of drink and what it did to his family. It sounded more to me like it bothered other families more. He had come home one night and kicked in the door of his condominium. I guess you should remember the number of your condo if they all look alike. He told us how he frightened the people on the other side of the door when he kicked in the door of the wrong condominium. He told us of another day when multitudes of well-dressed people were walking past him and looking down at him. When he looked up he saw he had been sleeping near the front doors of one of the area churches.

In my early go-arounds, Rachel decided most of my problems had to do with girls. I really didn't agree. I got along with girls just fine. Quite well, in fact. I failed to see how having a number of girlfriends around most of the time could be causing me problems. They passed the same verdict on another younger guy by the name of Jeff. Both Jeff's and my counselors said we were not to associate with any of the girls at Heartview. They did not mention the girls outside I guess because Jeff and I were always inside. Jeff and I became friends and we used to get our exercise by putting on our winter coats and walking around the grounds.

After we had been in Heartview for a couple of weeks we were allowed to go out as a group to a movie if we could get a group together that wanted to go. I managed to sit by the cutest well-built girl in Heartview, Stacey Gilmore. I remember the first movie we went to was a horror flick about a female ax murderer by the name of Lizzie Borden and I think Lizzie was played by Diane Baker. The story was Lizzie Borden took an ax and gave her mother forty whacks and when the forty whacks were through, she gave her father forty-two. It was not much for entertainment but was considerably better than sitting around Heartview for the evening.

It seemed to me most of the young people in Heartview were just plain ordinary kids. None of them seemed much more messed up than the everyday youngsters I would see in my practice. A number of them had grown up in broken homes and it seemed they missed one of their parents. It did not seem to me that any of them were addicts. They were occasionally abusing drugs and that is entirely different than being an addict.

Some of the alcoholics were rather creative. I ran into a friend from Minot who was taking math curriculum to become a math teacher. Tom was always worried he would be picked up with an open container so he hit upon a very innovative and creative way to solve the problem. Tom would fill up his window washer reservoir with vodka. He took the hose that went to the windshield wipers and rerouted it so it squirted out just below the dash on the driver's side. When Tom was driving down the road, he could just push the window washer button and it distributed almost exactly a shot right below his dash. It appeared alcohol hadn't clouded his thinking as much as it could have.

Tom confided in me he had blackouts. I learned a lot about blackouts when staying at Heartview. They sounded awful to me. I guess the majority of people had all done things they were not pleased with when they were in a blackout. One of their major concerns was they did not know how they had treated someone while they had been in a blackout so that seemed to be a main concern of many of them.

Tom said he and his wife and little girl had been on a camping trip on the east coast a short while ago. He said evidently he had left the camp with his little girl in the back seat of the car. He did not recall drinking but said he suddenly came out of a blackout, looked at the speedometer and was going over 100 miles per hour. He said the road they were on was winding and treacherous. He rapidly brought the car to a stop. It was then he realized his baby daughter was sleeping in the back seat and he had no idea where they were. He did not even know what state he was in or what state they had been in. Tom said he drove around for hours before he started to get some recall and then finally remembered enough to get himself and his daughter back to the campsite where his wife was waiting for them. He said his wife did not realize he had been in a blackout and she believed him when he said he had just gotten lost for a little bit.

I got into it one day with a number of the counselors at Heartview when one of the elderly alcoholics started going into the delirium tremens (DTs). A counselor was simply observing the person drooling, vomiting, sweating profusely and finally having a grand mal seizure. I asked the counselors where their crash cart was. They said they did not have one. I asked them to give him an IM benzodiazepine. They said they did not have that medication in the center and no one was authorized to give it. I said, "Get some and I am authorized and licensed to give it." They told me the patient would be all right. The truth was none of them had any training in handling a severe withdrawal and there is probably nothing more dangerous than withdrawal from alcohol. Untreated DTs can carry nearly as high as a 15% mortality rate. I later got some of the counselors together and told them they had no right to simply watch someone go into severe withdrawal without the means to handle the emergency. They were not happy with my assessment and I suspect deep inside they knew I was right.

I did not think it my fault but in our smaller sessions run by Rachel it seemed a number of the people in my group looked to me to provide answers. I knew this was becoming frustrating for Rachel. I hardly ever opened my mouth, but my presence still caused problems.

However, I had some value in these groups as a counselor. One day a young boy in our group who was about 15 years old broke down crying. He suddenly blurted out that he was a 'fairy'. He sobbed uncontrollably. Rachel looked at me and I realized that on this occasion she wanted me to intervene and welcomed my input. I explained to the youngster that at his young age it was not unusual to have some gender uncertainties. I tried to lighten up the group. I said, "Heck at young ages, young people are still trying to figure out the differences between the sexes." I also told him as we get older it still creates problems in our thinking.

During this time a couple of his family members were present. The young boy started describing how he liked to watch boys while they were taking showers after physical education classes. I countered that the human body is quite beautiful and to just enjoy looking at someone taking a shower does not necessarily mean someone is homosexual. Our talk that day continued on for the better part of the hour and no one interrupted. At the end of the session, I think the youngster felt a little better and I think the family also felt relieved I had put a spin on everything that allowed them to leave not feeling so heavy in their hearts. I suggested if he continued to feel confused about his sexuality perhaps he should talk to a professional when he got home. I explained it is probably a little more urgent if he feels his chemical use was to cover the feelings he was having trouble dealing with. I felt the boy was probably on site at Heartview when he first thought he was gay. He was definitely most likely gay but had never in any way acted on it.

After everyone had been in Heartview for several weeks they would have a family week for our groups. Our families were supposed to show up and tell the group how difficult we had made it for them. I guess this was more of a magical jack-o-lantern show. Well sorry, but I just do not know how else you are supposed to label some of this bullshit. Why drag families halfway around the country simply to tell you how bad you have been. Obviously the younger people in our groups knew what their parents thought or they would not be there. They certainly did not come for a vacation away from school for a while.

When it came to people my age, how on earth would our families be able to tell how much we had destroyed the family when we were not even around home anymore? It was kind of a joke and the counselors expected you to break down and cry. They expected the same of your parents and siblings. Hell, I was surprised they did not want the neighbor's cat and dog involved in some manner. Their magical sign of progress was you letting it all out. You were entering the enchanted zone and lickity-split you would soon be well.

After being in Heartview for about a month, you were allowed to take a couple days off and leave the center. The center had told Cindy to return home and not just home to Kenmare but to her home in Minnesota. They decided since Cindy and I were abusing drugs together splitting us up was the entire solution to our problems. Heck, it is always great if you can blame someone else isn't it. What seemed supernatural to me was they could get Cindy to buy in on their thinking. Cindy returned to her home in Babbitt, Minnesota to be with her parents.

I was alone again and I could take off for the evening to do as I wanted. All I had to do was not drink or take drugs. That was no problem. I asked Stacey if she wanted to take off for the evening. She said, "Great. It is about time we got a "Fuck Pass." I was a little taken aback and asked her what she was talking about. She asked, "Haven't you heard? Everyone calls these 'fuck passes' because you get to go out and shack up for a night." I felt better already. After all, Cindy and I had only been separated for about a month and it appeared I already had a new person in my life. Stacey and I picked up some snacks, immediately got a room and shacked up for the night. Stacey was like the most beautiful dream right off the front page of Playboy. The truth of the matter was all Stacey and I did was snuggle and cuddle and talk all night long. It was great to feel normal again and close to someone. I was not going to ruin that beautiful evening by taking advantage of a 19 year old beauty by ravaging her body with my 32 years of experience. It would not be too long before I would come to realize the 19 year old would be the one taking advantage of the inexperienced 32 year old.

It was then Stacey confided in me she thought I was gay. I asked, "What on earth are you talking about?" She said all of the girls in the center talked about Jeff and me. They thought it was a pity the two best looking guys in the place were gay. Well, I thought it was great they liked our looks but I told her Jeff and I were far from gay. Stacey asked, "Why are you always together and never hitting on any of us girls?" I explained Jeff and I were warned to stay away from all the girls. Stacey thought that was hilarious and we both had a big laugh together. I guess Jeff and I had not thought that out very well.

It was great spending the night with Stacey and we vowed to do so again. We did every chance we got and there was no keeping us apart at the center anymore. It was obvious we were going to be having a long relationship. I was not allowed to have further contact with Cindy. I followed most of the rules of the center because not doing so would have put my North Dakota medical license in jeopardy. The stresses and strains of the counseling had pretty much destroyed the relationship Cindy and I had.

One thing became increasingly clear in this particular treatment center; they were masters at destroying relationships.

I became friends with a wonderful man by the name of Tony Downs. Tony's main problem was he was a very wealthy multimillionaire, which did not seem to fit well with Rachel during our counseling sessions. You were supposed to be a down and out bedraggled person in a ditch if you were an alcoholic. Rachel did not like to hear Tony's life story and how he lived it. Tony was happily married and about sixty-five years old. He had obtained his wealth by raising chickens and selling eggs, millions of chickens and millions of eggs. Tony prided himself on not drinking and driving so he rode in the back of a large chauffeur driven limousine. The chauffeur would drive him between his chicken ranches and Tony would sit in back drinking from the bar. Tony had a great sense of humor, was fun to be around and told great stories.

One of his stories still brings a smile to my face but it also points out the hazards of drinking. Tony said on one of his binges he went out and bought a new car and he could still remember buying the new Cadillac. He decided he wanted to tour around the country for a while so he picked up a beautiful girl and her brother. He didn't remember much about them other than he had fun with his young date for a number of weeks. Tony and the girl would sit in the back of the car making out and drinking while her brother drove. Tony picked up the tab but said he was probably in a blackout most of the time. He wished he could have remembered more completely just how much fun he'd had and where he had enjoyed it. He really wished he could have remembered the girl better. He did remember she was a knockout. When Tony ended up back home the new car had about twenty-eight thousand miles on it. When he was able to review his credit card bills to see where they had been he discovered they had literally been all over the United States.

Tony's time rolled around to take a day off. He had the same restrictions as the rest of us. No drinking. An additional restriction placed on Tony was he could not see his wife. I thought that was mean and uncalled for but I did not make the rules. Tony stayed with his wife over the weekend. When he returned, he confessed he had stayed with his wife who had come to Mandan. They promptly told Tony to leave and he would not be allowed to finish his treatment. I think it was a blow to Tony's pride. I talked with the counselors and said I did not think it was right to kick Tony out. They said he had disobeyed the rules. I told them they could fuck their rules. Yes, after a little time in the wards I could use that word as well as any of them. After all my arguing and pushing back, Tony left Heartview to drive back to Minneapolis. He stopped at a bar on the way out of Mandan and was killed in an automobile accident a few hours later. I read the counselors at Heartview Foundation the fucking riot act. It was no consolation. My good friend Tony was dead thanks to non-thinking counselors who wanted to be in control, especially if they could be in control of a wealthy man whose station in life they were never going to achieve. Yea, if you are a counselor who cannot control your own life, why not try to control somebody else's.

It would only be two days later a slender, attractive, irritable, uptight young girl would come in for treatment from Canada. It was obvious she was strung out and in a fairly bad way. She was petulant and having a hard time being there. I did not know how she had arrived but thought she had come in by car. I tried talking to her but that was difficult. Probably not more than about one day after arrival, she drank a bottle of finger nail polish. She was desperate. Again, the same as Tony, they decided she had to leave. I was privy by circumstances to the situation. I argued once more for this young lady to stay. I felt anyone so desperate that they would drink fingernail polish more than anything needed to stay. I was again overruled by that super bright set of counselors with their Jack Daniels Diplomas. That young lady whose name I no longer remember died in an automobile accident on her way back to Canada. These assholes in their high and mighty ivory cloud had seen to the death of two fine people who may have had a life before them were it not for these pricks and their short-sighted power trips.

I received a summons one day to present myself at the head counselor's office. I could tell it was going to be enjoyable when I arrived as every counselor in Heartview was there and appeared to have their guns loaded. They said, "Mr. Redalen we do not appreciate you questioning our authority all the time." I said, "That is Dr. Redalen to all of you here, and what seems to be your problem." Rachel was the first to speak. She said, "You control every session you are in." I said, "Most of the time I do not even open my mouth." She said, "You do not have to. Everyone looks to you for answers." I simply replied, "Do a better job of controlling your group sessions." Another young male counselor said I was intimidating to him. I told him that was his problem, not mine. A more senior male counselor said I was the most manipulative person they had ever had in the center. I thanked him. He became a little angry and said that was not meant as a compliment. I said, "If you don't mind, I'll still take it as one." That seemed to hurt his ego a little. Oh, well. I said, "It is also kind of a compliment to have all you counselors get together to handle one person. Do I require this much attention?" All in all, I thought our session went well for me, but I left thinking they did not feel the same. I guess I was wrong. They really didn't have their guns loaded. They were all firing blanks that day.

I could not seem to please my counselor most of the time. When we had question and answer periods about alcohol they just could not seem to understand that I only occasionally had a drink and I did not have a favorite drink or alcohol preference. They insinuated I was lying and simply believed very little of what I said.

The center decided to send me to Minot for a day or two of evaluation. Minot is about one hundred miles north of Bismarck. I asked, "What is so special about Minot?" They said, "There is a physician there we would like you to see. He is an MD with specialties in ortho-molecular biology and his specialty is the diagnosis and treatment of chemical dependency. He is considered the best in the state and the expert we use." I said, "Why are we doing this now? I only have a couple more weeks to complete the treatment you have designed for me." They simply said, "Nothing about you seems to ring true for us."

I was taken to Minot and spent a couple of days interviewing and testing. The physician doing the testing was a pleasant middle aged man who was fun to talk to. The tests were pretty long question and answer tests varying from multiple choice to whatever. After two solid days of testing, we had a long talk. He said, "Dr. Redalen, congratulations. You have no signs of chemical dependency." I said, "I abuse drugs." He said, "That may be. I believe you. Your testing shows that you are not chemically dependent." I said, "How do you know I didn't lie?" He smiled and said, "You know better than that. You know these tests are the same as the Minnesota Multiphasic Personality Inventory (MMPI)." MMPI was a well-known, much used test that had a built in lie scale which means you cannot lie in the test without the test picking it up. He said, "I think what happens is that when your diabetes gets out of control, you develop anxiety and then try to kill the anxiety with drugs. I think if you can get your diabetes under control you will not abuse drugs. Anyway, I consider you completely normal except for the control of your diabetes. Control that and you will not abuse drugs. It was nice meeting you." He said he would be sending a copy of my studies and his opinion back to Heartview Foundation.

He must have called ahead and I guess the foundation did not like his findings. On my return to Mandan, they promptly discharged me, a polite way of saying they kicked me out. It was one of the standard twelve step programs and thankfully the twelfth step was really one I did not have to do in a treatment center. The twelfth step was to have a spiritual awakening from learning the previous 11 steps and to practice the principles we had learned in the affairs of our daily lives.

I wandered around the center until I found Stacey and told her what had happened. Stacey said, "Give me a minute to collect my things and let's get the hell out of this hole." At the same time Stacey and I were going to leave, one of our friends, Pearl Steinberg, also decided to leave. She wanted to know if we could give her a ride to her home in Regina, Saskatchewan. We thought we could do that. Stacey and I were really on no schedule.

Chapter Twenty

Traveling with Stacey

Regina was about 350 miles northeast of Mandan in Saskatchewan, the Canadian province adjacent to the northern border of North Dakota. I was familiar with Regina because every year after the Williston High School Coyotes football team had finished our spring training, our treat was to travel to watch the Saskatchewan Roughriders play the Winnipeg, Manitoba Blue Bombers in a professional football matchup. It was a one day bus trip the whole team looked forward to.

Within a few minutes Stacey, Pearl and I were on our way to Kenmare to clear out the home the hospital had so graciously allowed Cindy, Chad, Kelly and me to use.

Stacey and I packed up the meager belongings I had left in Kenmare, stored them in a friend's shed and we were on our way. The only thing I didn't store was a large screen television set I sold to the local pharmacist, D.J. However, when I came around to get a check, he said he would pay me some other time, meaning he was not going to pay me at all.

I wonder sometimes about the moral fiber of man. He knew we were in trouble financially and he was going to take advantage of it. Quite the man or lack thereof. This is what he could tell his children when they were growing up: "Son, if you run into friends in trouble, take advantage of them. It is your chance to screw someone and make a couple of bucks while doing so. It makes you feel good." Goodbye, Kenmare. I had left there without anyone becoming silicone richer. It was just as well. All my nurses looked beautiful and perfect just the way God had made them.

Prior to leaving Kenmare I hooked up with a couple of our teacher friends, Ken and Collette Boyer. They told me they had been in touch with Cindy and confirmed she had gotten married and was now regretting getting married on the rebound from me. Her name was now Cindy Tuomela and she wanted to see me.

Stacey and Pearl and I headed up to Saskatchewan. Our trip was uneventful. When we got there we met Sorrel Steinberg. I guess I was never sure of the relationship between Pearl and Sorrel and did not want to ask. I did find out Sorrel was one of the wealthiest Jewish businessmen in Regina. At the time he was the head of a $200,000,000 hospital building program. He took us to the Legislative Assembly Building of Saskatchewan, quite the building. Sorrel introduced us to a number of the members of the Legislative Assembly. It was obvious Sorrel was very well known and we walked rather freely through many of the elaborate offices.

I took leave of the Steinbergs to return to Minnesota for a couple of days. I let them know I was going back to talk about a relationship that was now over and Stacey, Pearl and Sorrel all understood. I entered Minnesota from Canada at the International Falls Port of Entry. I linked up with Cindy and it was obvious we were still in love with each other but now it was complicated. Cindy was married. I asked her what on earth she was thinking to get married so soon after ending a relationship. I said, "Even if we never got together it was too soon to get married." I had little to talk about since I was now with Stacey, but at least I was not married. We had some nice talks over two days and we parted friends. I thought it very unlikely Cindy would remain married. I returned to Regina. In all honesty I was anxious to get back to Stacey, where my heart really was now.

Pearl and Sorrel showed us a lot more of Regina. Sorrel asked me to stay in Regina and go into practice. I said, "I do not have a Canadian Medical License or hospital privileges for that matter." Sorrel reassured me he could get everything done within a couple days. I had no doubt that was the case. We accepted their hospitality for several more days.

Stacey was fun to be around and it was easy to see why Pearl and Sorrel really took a liking to her. I had fallen in love with her almost overnight. There was nothing not to like. I told Sorrel I thought Stacey and I should be on our way.

One day I was going through some photo books lying on one of the coffee tables. I noticed their children sitting on the lap of a tall black man. I commented to Pearl, "This looks just like Bill Russell." She said, "It should look just like Bill Russell. That is him." I asked, "How do you know Bill Russell?" Pearl replied, "He is a personal friend and their coach." I still did not get it. I asked, "The coach of whom?" Pearl said, "He is the coach of our Seattle Supersonics. We own the Supersonics." Now I was more confused because I did not know how Pearl fit into Seattle or Regina. I did not want to ask and I just left well enough alone. Bill Russel was surely in a lot of their family albums and pictures.

After several days Stacey and I decided it was time to leave before we overstayed our welcome. Pearl and Sorrel expressed their regret and asked us to stay longer but we declined and went on our way. We had to go back through Kenmare to pick up one of our cars. I had purchased a burnt orange 1976 Cadillac Eldorado when they announced it was to be the last convertible produced. I bought it off the showroom floor at the Annual Twin Cities Auto Show. Cadillac reneged on its deal though and again produced a convertible in 1977 so still wanting to have the last Cadillac convertible produced I ordered a beautiful silver Cadillac convertible. I brought both of those cars to Kenmare so on occasion I took quite a ribbing. People would ask if I bought them for bookends. They looked exactly alike except for color.

Larry Johnson, a friend who lived just a few miles west of Kenmare had offered to store one of the convertibles in a barn of his. When I got to his place I think my jaw probably dropped open as the barn the car was stored in had burned to the ground. Sitting in the middle of the burned out space was a melted frame of something. I was standing there trying to figure out what a Cadillac Convertible looks like when it's melted. Just about that time Larry came out and said, "Your car is okay." He told me about the ordeal he had gone through trying to get my car out before it burned up. My car was sitting in another building with the driver's side window broken out from where he smashed it with a pipe because the keys were locked inside when the fire started. I thanked

Larry and said, "If you ever store a car for me again please let it burn before risking your life just to save a car."

Stacey and I were soon on the road. A physician friend Dick Foresman who was running a dialysis unit in a small town in Nebraska had contacted me about working with him but when we got there the position was not really something I would have cared to do so we got back on the road. We finally ended up renting a very inexpensive cabin just north of Lyons, Colorado, a little cow town located about sixteen miles north of Boulder on the way to Rocky Mountain National Park. Just up the road was Estes Park, a beautiful little mountain tourist town where it was fun to hang out.

Initially when Stacey and I moved into our little cabin we wondered what we would do to fill up our days, but it was not long before we could not find enough time in our day to get everything done. Almost every day I would climb the mountain behind our cabin. It was about a half mile climb and I was usually quite winded by the time I got to the top. I had found a large square flat rock up there which was a couple feet off the ground and by the time I arrived in mid-morning the rock was nice and warm and I would lie on it for about an hour and pray. It was relaxing and calmed my mind. It was my one-on-one time alone with God in which there were no interruptions. It was like a daily cleansing of my soul and it always prepared me for the day ahead.

Stacey and I joined the little Methodist Church on the north and east side of the main street in Lyons. Pastor Don Sanders was a large rotund man with a strong, hearty laugh. He greeted and welcomed Stacey and me into his church and we became regular members. Pastor Don always had a huge ready smile and we waited eagerly for his sermon every Sunday. We became fast friends over the next year.

Stacey and I did not have a wealth of resources so we often hitchhiked around the area. It was always kind of interesting as this area of Colorado was made up mostly of a lot of liberal, free hanging, pot smoking or white line snorting people. They were all pretty friendly and easy going. When Stacey and I got picked up by a van or a pickup, it usually was less than a minute or so before we were asked if we wanted a puff on a joint. Neither Stacey nor I were much into pot so most if not all of the time we politely declined. On a rare occasion, we would take a small puff to be friendly. Of course we didn't inhale. Occasionally if we got the inclination we would drive into Denver and go to a dollar movie downtown. The most expensive thing about going to the movie was the popcorn and a mutually shared drink. One of those Denver movies on a warm summer day saved my life.

I would almost always sit in front of the big window reading during the day when I had spare time. One day we decided to drive into Denver to see a movie. The movie we ended up seeing was "The Island of Dr. Moreau" starring Burt Lancaster and Michael York. It was a strange movie about a man rescued, Michael York, who was brought to an island by Doctor Moreau, Burt Lancaster. The rescued man soon finds out that experimental animals on the island are being turned into strange rather hideous looking humans by the mad Doctor Moreau.

When we arrived back at our cabin that day, it was all boarded up across the front. We went to the office which was really just a trailer house and asked what had happened. An eighteen wheeler had been driving down the highway at the usual rate of speed and as he was turning the gradual corner in front of our cabins one of the wheels had come off. The wheel had enough speed that when it hit a small bump in front of the swimming pool for our compound, it became airborne until it had cleared the pool and then it went right in through the front of our cabin where I was always sitting and reading. It continued through the wall and went out our cabin the same way it came in, through the back wall. Had Stacey and I not gone to a movie that day, I would have been lying in a morgue. Thank God for watching over me once again. How blessed am I?

The bar scene was pretty much out for us. We did not have money we could waste on drinks nor did we have the money to spend on a bottle of booze. It was easy for us to abide by Heartview Foundation's principles. You can't drink and drug if you have no money. It was easy to see how hard core drug addicts could get into trouble though if they could not go without their maintenance medications. I would imagine they just went out and stole or robbed someone of convenience for them. Of course, it was not a robbery of convenience if you were on the receiving end.

One great thing about two addicts living together is that when you don't have any money you just switch your addiction to sex and that became our main entertainment. Now I was the student. Stacey had really been around the block when it came to sex.

I am not sure I would want my daughter to grow up the way Stacey had grown up. At the age of 14, Stacey's parents had allowed her to take off with a 35 year old man and travel around the country. As sweet as Stacey was, she was tough as nails and was certainly able to take care of herself. She was not someone I would have wanted to tangle with. Beautiful innocent appearing little Stacey taught me more about sex than I had learned in my entire lifetime. It reminded me of this saying: Men always want their ladies to be good in bed but they should also be virgins. Those two things don't really go together, do they?

Even though we remained addicts, it was definitely not related to man-made chemicals anymore. It was pure unadulterated physical attraction that grew by the day. It soon was to the point that Stacey and I sometimes had a difficult time going more than a couple of hours without making love. It was wonderful, pure and beautiful. We never told anyone, but Stacey and I were now husband and wife by common law marriage in Colorado.

We really enjoyed the outdoors and spent a lot of time hiking through the mountains. One day we thought it would be fun to take a canoe down the fast running creek across the road from the little cabin we lived in. We of course did not have a canoe so we did the next best thing. We went to a department store and found a child's blow up wading pool. Stacey and I reasoned it would be big enough to hold us both and we could use it as a raft to keep us afloat. We bought the smallest most inexpensive pool we could find. We took it home, blew it up and were ready for business. We went across the road to launch our adventure, laughing like a couple of kids. We jumped into the cold water and were soon seated in our makeshift little life raft. We went floating rapidly down the cold mountain stream. Every little ways the raft was just not able to carry us over the jutting rocks and suddenly we would hit our bottoms on one of the boulders jutting up into the stream. It was uncomfortable. We had obviously not thought this out very well. Suddenly down the stream a little ways we could see a barbed wire fence strung across the stream. Who on earth would put a barb wire fence across this little stream? Obviously, it was someone who wanted to contain their cattle. We could not get out of our raft in time to avoid running into the fence. Not only were the cattle safe, it also kept our little raft out and sunk it with a barrage of puncture wounds. We had managed to make it a grand total of one half mile if we were generous in our estimates. Stacey and I could not keep from laughing. Even if the trip had been short it was memorable and well worth the couple of bucks we spent for our raft.

We found a softball team for Stacey to join in Lyons. I was quite amazed to see muscular, slender, little Stacey hit the ball. She was one of the best hitters on the team and I was her cheering section. Lyons was good for Stacey and me. Our relationship grew and we were able to teach each other a lot about what we thought about life. We continued on in our church life and Stacey and I became good friends with Pastor Don and his wife.

Our cabin was at the base of the Big Thompson Canyon. In 1976 there had been a huge flash flood that swept Thompson Canyon during freakish weather conditions and people had been unable to evacuate in time. The ranger trying to warn every one of the possible flash flood had been killed by the flood. The small stream that was usually about a couple feet deep had suddenly swelled to about twenty feet deep trapping and killing the people in the canyon that were unable to get to high ground. About 145 people had died. A number of bodies had never been found. The powers of the flood were so great that large truck axles were ripped from their frames and twisted like children twist their play dough. There was a small building just east of Estes Park which was dedicated as a memorial to the deaths and damage the flood had caused. It had been the deadliest natural disaster the state of Colorado had ever sustained.

There were a lot of summer storms that rapidly raised the depth of the stream across from our cabin. Stacey and I would listen almost continually to the news from the weather station. For about four or five nights in a row we would hear, "There is a possibility of flash floods tonight in Thompson River Canyon." Every night we would go up the highway toward Estes Park until we came to a small gravel road that took us far up the mountainside and sleep in the car until morning.

One night on a fully moonlit mountainside and on our fourth or fifth evacuation I asked, "What do you think?" It was evident the possible flash flood was not going to happen under a full moon. We were obviously thinking the same thing. It was a warm, quiet, beautiful and peaceful night on the mountain top but we were tired of sleeping in our little car. By this point in time we had sold both of the Cadillac Eldorados to provide cash to live on and were driving a little old Chevy coupe. I looked at Stacey and she said, "Let's get the heck out of here."

Very shortly we were packed up and on the road again. We decided to head for the Florida Keys. Stacey's parents lived in the Keys and she wanted me to meet them. The Keys are a group of small islands that run from Miami down to Key West. Stacey and I were in no hurry so we drove very leisurely and had fun sightseeing along the way. Stacey was fun to travel with. She had traveled a lot in her life.

Stacey always wore skin tight jeans on her perfect figure. She often drew looks of admiration from both men and women. One day we stopped at a large truck stop to get a bite to eat. Stacey said she was going to the restroom to wash up and go to the bathroom. I was facing the women's rest room and when Stacey walked past a big trucker I could see the look in his eyes. He immediately got up from his meal to follow Stacey. I could not help but smiling. I realized there was not going to be a good ending for that trucker following this gorgeous little gal to the women's rest room.

I knew Stacey to always be on heightened alert to her surroundings. She had not missed a beat and as she pushed the women's rest room door open she instantly whirled and hit the man full on in the chest with the heel of her hand. His breath left him in a gasp and he almost fell back on his ass, completely surprised when little Stacey said, "Where the fuck do you think you are going, asshole?" That man wished he could have died on the spot and he turned around and hurriedly walked out. He did not even return to his booth and the food he had left sitting there uneaten. I never really had to worry about Stacey taking care of herself. As I said, she had been around the block.

I later found out Stacey had grown up in a life of luxury. Stacey's parents were very wealthy and lived in a large mansion on Islamorada Key on one of the inland water ways. Islamorada was located on about mile marker 88 or 89. The Key locations could be found by simply knowing what mile marker they were on. Key zero was Key West and the Keys were numbered from Key West up to Miami. The string of tropical islands that stretches about 120 miles off the southern tip of Florida is a great vacation destination spot. The islands are unique in that they divide the Atlantic Ocean on the east from the Gulf of Mexico on the west. The gateway to the keys, Key Largo is the first Key you drive through as you leave the mainland of Florida.

Stacey's life of luxury had led her to be friends with a lot of unusual people or at least well known people. One of her friends was the rock singer Suzi Quarto. Another friend of hers was Jimmy Buffet. Wealth definitely has its privileges.

When I met Stacey's parents they were warm and welcoming people. They lived in a beautiful mansion up on stilts like all homes in The Keys. Homes were built on piling footings which were driven for months deep down into the coral reefs. The continual pounding of pile drivers when the footings were being ready to be poured was a little annoying if your domicile was located near one of the pounding sites. Floyd Gilmore, Stacey's dad, was a retired automobile dealership owner. He and his brother Lloyd had earned their millions by not only being dealership owners but also owning all General Motor Dealerships in the entire city of Detroit.

It was early evening when we got to the Gilmore's. Floyd and Donna asked us to have supper with them. Stacey and I were happy to oblige as we were tired from being on the road all day. Floyd and Donna suggested we go downstairs and clean up. They asked that we please make ourselves at home and to plan on staying with them until we decided where we were going to light for a while. Beneath the huge home on pilings was an entire other home set between the pilings. It was a beautiful apartment. After we cleaned up we went upstairs and joined Stacey's parents out on their beautiful back lanai. The Gilmores had a great view of the Atlantic Ocean and The Keys spread out for miles before them. We could see fish jumping in the inland waterway just below us. There was a 24 foot fishing boat tied up to the pier that stretched the width of their lot down below.

Floyd offered me a glass of scotch and I said, "I am not much of a scotch drinker." He replied, "You will be." So I had a couple of glasses of scotch with Floyd. I was soon to learn Floyd was a connoisseur of fine scotch. He had an entire bedroom completely filled with rows of scotch he had collected from all over the world. He proudly showed me his "Scotch Room." Impressive. He would tell me where he had gathered each collection. Drinking a couple of glasses of scotch straight up became a ritual Floyd and I would observe every night before supper. He would teach me about each scotch, what taste to look for and to learn the subtle differences of each one. Floyd was entirely right. It would not be long before I would become a much better educated scotch drinker and I would soon look forward to our glasses of scotch every evening. It would not be too many months before I actually thought I could describe and taste some of the tastes Floyd was teaching me about. I think he was trying to put a little sophistication into the person his daughter was living with. Floyd and I became good friends.

Our days were pretty routine. It was a laid back place to live. We got a lot of surf time if you could call it that. There is no surf board type surf, just Atlantic and Gulf water and a lot of it. It does not matter which direction you look when you live in The Keys, you see water. There were always a lot of nice brown bodies to look at and most of the girls seemed to show theirs off well. I really loved the culture and I could see us fitting in there for the rest of our lives. It was idyllic to say the least.

I was adept at skin diving and was in good enough shape to free dive down to a depth of 40 feet. I found that out by accident one day trying to retrieve a lost anchor for Floyd. Stacey and I would often take the boat out and run around doing nothing in particular. Some days Donna would slowly pull us behind their boat and either Stacey or I would hold up a hand when we would spot a conch. I always kidded Donna that she thought she was trolling for sharks and Stacey and I were the bait.

In all of the time we dove we never saw a shark. But when I was spearfishing, it would not be long before I would be surrounded by dozens of Barracuda. They always kept a respectable distance from me but the big eyes and rows of needle like teeth were unnerving. When those teeth hit their prey they could do all the damage of a row of razor blades. We tried to never spear in one spot too long because the Barracuda, much like sharks, could smell the blood of the speared fish from several hundred meters away. The Barracuda were lightning fast predators.

There were some simple rules to go by. Never have on any jewelry or anything bright, shiny or sparkly. Never remove a fish you have speared while you are under the water. Swim to your boat and with your spear and hands above the water, remove the fish from your spear and put it in the boat. A Barracuda can close the gap of one hundred feet to the fish on the end of your spear in literally the blink of an eye. If that Barracuda accidentally hits your hand or wrist, you are very likely to lose both.

When we were out catching our supper, or more accurately I should say spearing our supper, I would often bend over the boat with my mask on my face to look around and make sure I was not jumping into trouble. One day, I was relieved I took this precaution. As soon as my head entered the water I could see what appeared to be hundreds of Barracuda all in one school under our boat. I hated to think what could have happened to me had I jumped in unannounced and frightened them.

I had run into a couple of locals at the Tiki Bar and it seems everyone was anxious to tell their Barracuda and shark stories. One gentleman showed me his wrist one night. It looked as if he had slashed it. But no, he was simply leaning over to clean the side of his boat one day when suddenly he was hit by a Barracuda. The hit had instantly slashed all his flexor tendons. He had to be rushed to the hospital for a major surgery.

Another gentleman showed me his shoulder which was covered with a good number of healed linear scars. This person had been spearing fish and a Barracuda kept inching closer and closer to him. After keeping some distance the Barracuda passed about six feet in front of him. He thought it was the perfect time to get rid of this fish. He fired his spear but because of the lightening quickness of a Barracuda, it only got a glancing blow from the spear and within one fleeting part of a second the diver had become the prey. The Barracuda was gone but his shoulder was slashed open to the bone resulting in a major surgical repair.

Some of the stories were humorous. One fellow recounted a day when between him and a big lobster he was hunting was about a six foot long nurse shark. Nurse sharks are thought to be pretty harmless and certainly are not sharks that attack humans. He decided he had to have that lobster so he grabbed the nurse shark by the tail to pull it out of the way. The shark turned instantly and hit him on the shoulder. It didn't cut him but left a bruise like a big hickey.

I could tell Floyd probably wished Stacey would settle down and start a family. Both Floyd and Donna gave subtle hints to that end. Stacey and I did not mind at first as we were obviously both in love. We were getting to know The Keys pretty well and enjoyed the laid back atmosphere. We had gradually grown tired of doing not much of anything, so Floyd asked me if I would like a job working for one of the largest contractors in The Keys. Gene was a friend of Floyd's and after Floyd introduced the two of us Gene asked me if I would like a job in construction. I explained I knew nothing about it but would enjoy learning.

Gene first introduced me to a couple of his head people, Wayne Cushing and Ronnie Hehmeyer. Wayne had been a head chemist for Coca Cola and then when Disney World had opened he started an import business from Taiwan. He had retired from that and gone to work for Gene building homes in The Keys. Ronnie had grown up in Pennsylvania as an accomplished high school wrestler who had won the Pennsylvania State Wrestling Championship in one of the middle weight classes. Both Ronnie and Wayne worked for Gene's construction company in whichever way he needed them. They were kind of jacks of all trades. Wayne and Ronnie were virtually the only two about whom I knew a little of their background.

Gene's main building sites were in Islamorada and Lower Matecumbe Key. Since Floyd and Donna lived in Islamorada, it was convenient for me to work for Gene. I enjoyed learning the ins and outs of building a home out of solid reinforced concrete. After the piling footings had been set deep down into the coral reef, the pilings would be poured first along with the first floor of solid reinforced concrete. Then using forms, virtually the whole home including the roof was poured six inch thick solid reinforced concrete. It had to meet the housing codes and withstand 200 mph winds. I really do not know what the hell that was good for if the home was under twenty feet of water.

I enjoyed the manual labor and got along well with all the guys. Almost invariably after work we would go to the Tiki Bar or a place called Plantation Yacht Harbor for beers or cocktails, both on Islamorada Key. The Tiki Bar sat on the Atlantic side of The Key. One well known customer that you could count on to be there almost every day was Mickey Mantle. Mr. Mantle still appeared to like it when people asked him for autographs. He was affable and would always say hi.

Plantation Yacht Harbor was a little more upscale and you could occasionally spot Hollywood heavyweights wandering in and out. The Keys were a strange place. You were either wealthy or poor as a church mouse with the latter category fitting me. You literally needed a scorecard to keep everyone straight. One night a beautiful young lady sat down, wanted to buy me a drink and asked me if I would go to Europe with her for the weekend. I said I had a girlfriend. She said she didn't mind. A couple of minutes later a well-dressed distinguished looking man came in with a trophy girl hanging on his arm. The young lady sitting beside me whose name I still did not know said she wanted to introduce me to her husband. She said the trophy was his girlfriend. This was the typical evening in the Florida Keys. Stacey came in a little later and we had a bite to eat.

One night when I was leaving the Tiki Bar to meet some friends at Plantation Yacht Harbor I was picked up by one of the local patrol cars. I pulled over to the side of the road and the officer walked up to the car and asked me to get out. I was not concerned as I had only one drink at the Tiki Bar. The officer said to me, "Have you been drinking?" I replied, "Yes, officer I have." He asked me where I was going and I said I was meeting some friends for a cocktail at Plantation Yacht Harbor. He asked, "Can you walk a straight line from your car to me?" I said, "Officer, I'll do you one better. I'll walk a straight line on my hands from my car to you." The officer smiled at me, laughed and said, "Aw, get the heck out of here." Back in those days I could walk on my hands about as well as on my feet for quite a long distance. The officer told me to have a nice evening and to drive safely.

The temperature in the Florida Keys is relatively constant. We were always working in the heat and one of the workers warned me that I should start taking salt tablets and drinking more water. He offered me a couple of salt tablets but I declined as I did not bring drinking water with me. I thought I was accustomed to the heat. A little later in the morning I suddenly became very sick and started vomiting. A couple of workers came over to me and offered me salt tablets again and some of their water. It was too late because I did not see it coming. I couldn't keep anything down. They said I had to hurry to get to a cool place because I was having a heat stroke. They explained this is how it starts out.

I returned to the lower level of the Gilmore home and jumped in the coldest shower I could get from the cold water tap. Unfortunately, the cold water in the summer in the Florida Keys is lukewarm. I got out the largest fan we had, laid down on the floor of the shower all wet letting the fan blow on me, hoping I could cool down. I could not keep ice water down so I put a plastic bag full of ice on my neck. This ordeal went on for a couple of hours and the vomiting continued. Finally, a little later in the afternoon I was able to begin to keep ice water down and once my body temperature returned to normal I began to feel a little better.

I returned to my fellow workers toward the end of our shift and thanked them for taking care of me. They said this was not uncommon and the only way to guard against it was to take in plenty of salt and continually intake water all day long. I followed their advice and never had it happen again.

One day we started working remodeling the Green Turtle, one of the upscale eating establishments right off the highway. When we started tearing off the wall covering, between the walls were millions of cockroaches. Literally everyplace you looked the spaces between the walls were alive. We could not do anything until we were able to get rid of shovels full of cockroaches. It was filthy. Stacy and her parents and I used to eat there occasionally. That would never happen again. I did not care how much remodeling we did, it was always going to be The Cockroach Motel.

I was a quick study for Gene and initially when he would give me a day's work to do I would always finish it in half a day. When he gave me a week of unsupervised work to do I would finish in two to three days. And so forth and so on. After a couple of months working for Gene, he and his wife had Stacey and me over for supper one night. Gene asked me if I would like to take over his construction company in the next year or two.

He said, "Rick, I am getting close to retirement. You can actually take over this company in its entirety as soon as you say you are ready." I replied, "Gene, you have all kinds of people better qualified than me to run your construction company." Gene said, "That may be true today but it will not be true in one or two more months. You are the best worker I have ever had and the quickest study. You never have to be told something more than once. You are also the fastest most efficient worker I have ever had." I told Gene my enjoyment was not in getting the job done, but having fun implementing and then racing myself against my own time clock to see how fast I could get it done. I made it fun by using time as my challenge, not the job. I always know I can do anything. The time it takes is the challenge. It was much like being back in college chemistry. I was fast, efficient and organized. I told Gene I would keep it in the back of my mind and continue doing the job I was doing.

Stacey and I had an enjoyable evening. I thanked Gene for the challenge he had offered me, but I was again feeling the tug of medicine. I said, "Gene, I think I would really enjoy running your construction company and would promise to do a good job for you, but I think it is now time for me to return to medicine." I told him I would think about it for a while but asked if we could just forget about it until I made some decisions in my life. Stacey and I talked to Floyd and Donna and they both thought it was a wonderful opportunity for us, but only if I didn't want to practice medicine again. I told them I did not think this would be the case.

Floyd asked to talk to me alone one day. He said he would rather his daughter be married than to be living with someone. I don't think he watched her that closely when she was 14 and traveling around the country with someone twice her age. Floyd also said he would build us a house if we would stay in The Keys and he also volunteered he would build me a clinic. This was an enormous opportunity but I just could not see being tied to someone financially and that is what I thought would happen if Stacey and I stayed around. It had nothing to do with Floyd and Donna. They were great people and they certainly would have made good in-laws. It was just Stacey and I did not want to be pushed and we did not want anyone interfering with our relationship.

There were a few constants in The Keys Stacey and I loved. One of these constants was the incredibly beautiful sunsets we were privileged to watch every night. There are signs all over The Keys about the most beautiful sunsets in the world. If you live or stay there for a week or more you come to know what they are talking about. As the sun was going down every evening, Stacey and I would grab our camera and then run to get the best view. You quickly learn trying to capture sunsets that no matter how many sunsets you capture, you never get to reproduce them as well as the great Painter made them. He is simply something else. What a creation He has made.

One morning I came to work and everything had changed. No one said hi, boo, shit, how's your mother? I worked for a few minutes before I saw Ronnie Hehmeyer. I asked, "Ronnie, what is going on here today? Did somebody die?" He simply looked at me and then passed by without even a reply or nod of recognition. I went up to him and said, "Okay then jerk, what is wrong with you?" Ronnie looked me right in the eyes and said, "You are an asshole," then turned and walked away. I followed him and asked, "What on earth is wrong with you today? What did I do to you?" Ronnie replied, "You are a goddamned doctor." I am sorry God, but that is what he said. He added, "What are you doing? Are you just playing with us plain ordinary people to get your kicks? You have no business here. Why didn't you tell us you were a doctor?"

I said, "Ronnie, you and I are friends. We eat together, we drink together, we work together. Look at how you and the rest of the guys are treating me today. Just because you found out I am a physician, you now are treating me like a pariah. If I had told you up front what I am, you would have probably treated me exactly the way you are now. Had that been the case as I suspect it would have, you would have never come to know me.

"I anticipated this reaction from all of you so I did not say anything. I simply wanted to be accepted by everyone and knew that was probably not going to happen if I told you up front I am a doctor. Doing it my way enabled all of you to work alongside me day after day and see that I could work as hard as all of you and do as good a job as all of you and be a friend to all of you. I am the same as all of you, just a little different and you did not even know that until now.

"I am the same person today as I was yesterday. It is just that now you know a little bit more about me." Ronnie just looked at me without speaking and walked away. I worked alone for the most part of that day and everyone steered a fairly wide berth of me. This was one of the rare days when Gene had not given me a boatload of work to do by myself. I had to suffer alone amidst all my fellow workers. I wasn't a leper but could just as well have been.

That afternoon, Ronnie approached me and said, "Rick, I have been thinking over what you said. I now understand why you didn't tell us you were a doctor. You are probably right and we would have never given you the chance to try to fit in. You are also right in that you proved to all of us you could work alongside of us and do every job that came along as well as we could and many times better."

Ronnie added, "I have to offer you an apology." I just said, "Apology accepted. Are we good then?" Ronnie smiled and said, "We're good." That evening at quitting time Ronnie suggested we go for a beer at the Tiki Bar. Wayne met us there and it was happy hour for us the same as ever.

Nearly everything had returned to normal the following day when I returned to work. Some things had changed however. In some ways the workers seemed to give me a slightly added measure of respect.

Everyone was okay with me now and it was good to be just one of the workers again. The fact I was a physician no longer mattered. I was just a fellow worker.

Just when I thought the doctor business was behind me, Ronnie came up to me and said, "Rick, since I found out you're a doctor I am a little worried. You work in some jobs where you could lose a finger or a hand. You should not be using power tools." I said, "You guys need your fingers and hands just as much as me. We get dressed and hold our children the same way. I am careful." Ronnie added, "Be really careful." That was kind of great. I had gone from being ostracized a few days ago to being put in a position where my friends and fellow workers were now going to protect and watch out for me.

Working in construction also taught me the value of communication. The city of Miami was where we purchased many of our aluminum windows. Unfortunately, the main pick up location was run mainly by Cubans. When Wayne would go to pick up a load of windows for our sites, the sizes would often be wrong. We would have to point it out and they would redo the windows, requiring two trips to get one job done. During time sensitive projects of which we had few, it would definitely slow us down.

The Cuban revolution had taken place in the mid to later Fifties. In 1959 Fidel Castro had overthrown the Batista dictatorship and assumed the leadership role in Cuba. Following the revolution many Cubans fled to Miami, which became almost like a little Cuba. Every job in the Miami area required you to be bilingual. What that really meant without being overtly discriminatory was you had to be able to speak Spanish. The people hiring you couldn't have cared less if you spoke English.

The Cuban revolution also displaced many wealthy Americans. One such displaced family was that of Floyd and Lloyd Gilmore, who had owned a $5 million hunting lodge in Cuba prior to the revolution. It was there they entertained the Who's Who of people from the United States. Some of their neighbors were among the wealthy elite until Castro seized the property of several thousand American property owners. This was part of the reason for all the embargoes placed on Cuba. The amount of money Cuba owed American land owners in Cuba went into the hundreds of millions of dollars.

One day while working at the Green Turtle, I did something to create a little diversion to get the guys' minds off cockroaches. Under some loose boards lying around outside, there was a beautiful little yellow, black and red snake. I grabbed the little guy by the tail and brought him inside. Someone screamed coral snake and everybody abandoned their work stations for the outdoors. I let him go a few seconds after he tried to strike me a couple of times. There is a mnemonic which helps you remember whether or not a red, yellow and black snake is dangerous or venomous. What you have to remember is red on yellow kills a fellow, red on black is my friend Jack. I guess if you don't remember this or are color blind it is best to leave tri-colored snakes alone. Everybody returned to work as soon as I put the little guy outside. Growing up in North Dakota, I simply wasn't afraid of snakes of any kind.

I continued to learn about racial relations while I lived and worked in the Keys. One day I had an ungodly hard job. One of our cement trucks could not get into a small area and we had 18,000 pounds of cement that had to be hand lifted up to a roof. The only two people to handle the cement were a young black man named David and myself. David was a solid piece of well sculpted muscle, very pleasant and soft spoken. It was all I could do to lift the buckets up to my waist using both hands and arms then David would grab them with one hand from me, lift them above his head and dump them out on to the roof. David was doing a job I could never have done. I was just not strong enough. When we finished that impossible job late that afternoon I asked David about getting a beer after work. He said fine. A few minutes after we were finished, David disappeared.

Later I was talking with Wayne at the Tiki Bar. I told him I had worked side by side so to speak with a young pleasant black man for the entire day and when I offered to buy him a beer after work he suddenly disappeared. Wayne said, "That would not work down here in The Keys, Rick. The blacks in this area do not associate with the whites." How weird is that? The people living in The Keys come from all over. You would think all the racial tensions of the south would have been left behind. David and I never had the opportunity to work together again. I felt badly if I had not impressed on him well enough that day we were equals.

How does someone grow up feeling as though they are inferior to someone else? I did not know if I would ever figure it out. I definitely knew I was glad I had my parents growing up. My dad's words always rang steadily in my ears. "You can do anything in life you want to do. If you persevere and keep your focus you will always succeed." Because of hearing that my entire life I had developed and grown up knowing I could accomplish anything. In the back of my mind I knew that included taking over Gene's construction company should I ever want to fall back on that option.

Stacey and I started having discussions about trying something different, a change of pace. Stacey said she wanted to meet my parents so we decided to head up north. It was hard to leave The Keys but it was also easy to see how a person could settle in to this tropical paradise leaving the cares of the world and also your ambitions behind, wherever you had left them. It was time to go.

When Stacey and I arrived at my mom and dad's place, Stacey was welcomed with open arms. My parents loved little Stacey, but what was not to love. Stacey reciprocated and returned their love. I still did not know what direction I was going to go. Dad talked to me at length one day and asked when I was going to start practicing medicine again. I told him I had not made a decision. Dad said, "Rick, you are a doctor. You are supposed to be taking care of people. That is what God made you for. That is what your gifts are supposed to be used for." Later when Dad came to me and asked if I had made a decision, I replied, "Yes, I've made a decision." Dad asked, "What is your decision?" I replied, "My decision is I do not have to make a decision right now." Dad was obviously a little perturbed. He asked, "What the heck kind of a decision is that?" I just said, "It is not necessary to decide at this time what I want to do for the rest of my life or even a small part of my life going forward. When I make that decision, I hope it will be the right one." I could almost see the thoughts going through my dad's head, probably something like, "My son, the bum."

We had not been in Princeton for very long when Mom and Dad asked us if we wanted to go on a vacation. We headed south to meet Hazel and Marvin and the first place we camped out together was in Durango, Colorado. It was a great time for Stacey and me. Marvin and Hazel had always been like my second set of parents so it was fun for us all to be together. One night Stacey and I said we would treat our parents to chicken and dumpling soup. We cooked up a big pot of soup for the evening meal. The evenings were jacket and sweater weather so the hot soup tasted good. Not only that, we had done a good job and the soup really was delicious.

The following day we took off across the countryside and eventually the next stop was a large campground north of Salt Lake City called Cherry Peak Campground. The only memorable part of that night of camping was Marvin got lost when going out to find a bathroom and by the time we realized he was not coming back it was completely dark out and we could not find him. Quite some time later he wandered back into camp. It had been a one and one-half hour bathroom trip. There appeared to be a junk yard dog on a big chain in a tent not far from us. Anytime someone wandered close to that camp site it appeared as if the dog was going to break the chain and have that person for lunch. Stacey did not seem to mind. She walked up to the dog as if they had been friends forever, bent down, tickled him under his chin and said, "Oh poor baby, are you having a bad day?" Leave it to Stacey to change a mad dog into a face licking friend.

At this point, Mom and Dad turned their travels to head for home and we went with Hazel and Marvin to our next stop, Las Vegas. It was warm and we arrived late so we got rooms in one of the old casinos on the west side of the city for the night. We all went out and walked around for a bit and then hit the beds so we could get an early start in the morning. While Stacey and I were out exploring with Hazel and Marvin, I had put my billfold between the mattresses and took just a few dollars with us. After all, we did not even have enough money to bet in the casinos. That billfold held all the money Stacey and I had in the world. Short of the couple of hundred dollars in my pocket, the billfold contained about $8600, all of our remaining cash.

The following day we headed out for what was going to be our final destination, Hazel and Marvin's home in Phoenix, Arizona. We stopped to take a tour of Hoover Dam, formerly known as Boulder Dam. The damn backed up the Colorado River and was on the border between Nevada on the east and Arizona on the west. When you look at the bottom of the dam on the side opposite Lake Mead it seems impossible that work crews back in the Thirties would have had the wherewithal to construct something this massive to hold back this immense body of water. It was said Lake Mead held the second largest body of water by volume in the United States. The immense turbines we looked at under the damn supplied electrical power to three states.

After the great sight-seeing tour we headed on down the road and it was not long before we had to stop for gas. It was at that painful moment when I reached for my billfold and found my pocket empty I realized the billfold containing all of our money was still in our hotel room in Las Vegas between two mattresses. There was nothing we could do about it until we got to a phone. I called the hotel, asked for security and let them know our room number. Security said they would check for it immediately. They called me back and said they were sending my billfold to me in Phoenix today. Stacey and I were astounded when my billfold arrived a couple of days later and every dollar that had been in the billfold was still there. It arrived in a tattered nearly torn through envelope but arrived nonetheless. If the security guard I talked to had been there, I would have given him a big kiss and a tip. God bless that honest man.

Stacey and I stayed with Hazel and Marvin for a week or two. Stacey got to meet my cousins, Sheila Kohl who was married to Mike and Darrell and his wife Sandra. We stayed around for a few barbecues, spent some delightful evenings with everyone and then after seeing quite a bit of Phoenix decided it was time for me to go back to work.

We drove back to the Twin Cities to stay with my mom and dad again at the beginning of March.

Chapter Twenty-one

Dubuque

I received a call one day from someone in Dubuque, Iowa who identified himself as Dr. Carroll Sinnard. He asked if I could spare a little time to talk to him. He had gotten my name from someone at the University of Nebraska where I had been graduated. He told me he had graduated from the University of Nebraska School of Medicine a couple of years earlier than me. He explained he was in family practice in Dubuque and asked if I would consider coming down, looking at his practice and perhaps going into practice with him. He said it was a golden opportunity and Dubuque was "starving" for family practitioners.

I said to Dr. Sinnard, "I am not interested in going into practice in Dubuque, Iowa. In fact I have never even heard of Dubuque, Iowa and I have no desire to live in Iowa. I heard in Minnesota that Iowa had to put in artificial turf in their stadium just to keep the cheerleaders from grazing at halftime." I realized it was probably one of the standard slams from competing neighboring states. I was not rude but I was not about to consider going into practice in Iowa. That was the end of our conversation.

About twenty minutes later our phone rang again and it was Carroll Sinnard. He asked for a couple more minutes of my time. He began to expound on all the great attributes of Dubuque. Evidently Dubuque was a beautiful city adjacent to the Mississippi River named after an early settler by the name of Julien Dubuque. Dr. Sinnard went on to explain about all the great colleges there and said the opportunities in medicine were immense. In spite of how wonderful Dr. Sinnard made Dubuque sound, I was simply not interested in going to Dubuque, Iowa. I said, "Thanks, but no thanks."

About another hour passed before Dr. Sinnard was ringing me up again, asking for a little more of my time. Not wanting to be rude to a fellow classmate from the University of Nebraska, I listened to what he had to say. This was not the last call from Dr. Sinnard and finally after a couple more calls he said, "What do you have to lose by coming down to Dubuque for a weekend and just looking around? If you do not have plans to starting practicing again in any particular place, you should at least do yourself the favor of looking." I informed Dr. Sinnard that when I was able, I spent my birthdays celebrating with Dr. Art Lundholm. Our birthdays were fifty years apart on March 14 and I did not know how many more we would have to celebrate. Dr. Sinnard said we would still have plenty of time to celebrate when I got back after the weekend. Finally, I acquiesced and I got in the car the next day for a pretty drive down Highway 52 which led all the way from Minneapolis into Dubuque.

I met Dr. Carroll and his wife Linda Sinnard at Xavier Hospital, a Catholic hospital on the hilly north side of Dubuque. Dr. Carroll's wife Linda was a beautiful raven haired woman dressed in a suit. He wore a sport coat. I was dressed casually, as usual. I wasn't dressed like a bum mind you, but I was dressed such that no bums would be rolling me on the street trying to steal my clothes. They showed me around the hospital and introduced me to some of the nurses who were all friendly.

As we walked through the hospital we met an Indian physician in the hallway. Dr. Sinnard said to me, "Dr. Redalen, this is Dr. Mullapudi, a cardiovascular surgeon who does all of the bypass surgeries in this part of the country." Carroll explained I was a family practitioner and was here to look at practice opportunities in Dubuque. We shook hands and Carroll went on to explain that Dr. Mullapudi's wife was also a physician and anesthesiologist. They usually worked together. Dr. Mullapudi was a small man with a pleasant smile. As we walked away, Dr. Sinnard started telling me a story about when he had met Dr. Mullapudi, who introduced himself by his first name, Ratnam. Dr. Sinnard said pleased, "Pleased to meet you. What do they call you?" To which Dr. Mullapudi responded, "Ratnam." Dr. Sinnard started laughing. I guess it was a little funny.

Later Linda and Carroll showed me around the city. Dubuque was a beautiful picturesque river town made up of high bluffs and crags with an old time flavor of many river towns. The Sinnards took me up to Eagle Point Park located on what appeared to be the highest river bluffs in the area on the north end of the city. The park was as gorgeous and majestic as any city park I had ever been in. It was appropriately named because as we faced east, standing on a high bluff overlooking the Mississippi River, dozens of American Eagles soared over head. I believe if that had been the only part of Dubuque I ever saw, it probably would have sold me on the city. The park was heavily wooded and covered a large expanse of ground. There were hundreds of picnic tables. It was a great place to meditate and get closer to God. Unfortunately, in those days I was just not very bent on forming a closer relationship with my Maker.

Carroll and Linda told me a lot about the history of Dubuque. They also told me a lot about where they had met in Thermopolis, Wyoming. Linda had worked in a bank. I learned they also had a little boy by the name of Taylor who was nine or ten years old. One of the main things I learned was Dubuque was about as Roman Catholic as Ogden, Utah was Mormon, perhaps a little more Catholic than the Vatican. Carroll said Dubuque was about 90% Roman Catholic and there were almost as many nuns and priests as there were people in the community. Carroll's office was up in the Stonehill area a very short distance but down the hill from a large Catholic convent. Mount St. Francis was located on one of the highest hills just northeast of Xavier Hospital.

That evening the three of us went out to eat at a beautiful club called Timmerman's Supper Club on the east side of the Mississippi. It was one of the most well known in the area, located on a high bluff overlooking the Mississippi River to the south. We sat at a window table with a gorgeous view and to make things even better there were dozens of bunnies hopping around just outside our window. They looked more like a bunch of tame rabbits interspersed with cotton tails rather than all wild rabbits as one would expect to see. Evidently the club owners fed the rabbits in the vicinity to keep them around. It was added warm fuzzy entertainment.

Following a delightful supper, it was getting late and Carroll suggested we see what the night life was like around Dubuque. As it turned out this was going to be my first exposure to the Illinois side of Dubuque, East Dubuque. I found out when the bars closed down in Dubuque, many of the patrons would head over to East Dubuque on the opposite side of the river. The bars in East Dubuque closed an hour later than the bars in Dubuque. I was a little surprised when Carroll led Linda and me into a strip club named The Land of Milk and Honey. Looking down the main street of East Dubuque, it appeared to me as if the entire city was a single street of strip clubs. We sat down at a table and Carroll ordered us all a drink. I thought it to be a very odd place to take someone you wanted to recruit to practice medicine. After sipping our drinks and talking for a while Dr. Sinnard started talking about East Dubuque and said it could be a pretty rough place sometimes. Well imagine that, a line of strip joints offering more alcohol to late night drinkers that could get a little rough at times. Carroll said we didn't have to worry. He pulled a little snub nosed pistol out from his jacket pocket and said he was always prepared. I really considered this to be a little over the top and I began to wonder why on earth a physician would bring me to a place like this and then show me a loaded revolver he carried in his jacket pocket. It was just bizarre.

Following the time we spent in the strip joint, Carroll said another favorite place people went after a night of drinking was to Mulgrew's Tavern and Liquor store. The word another threw me a little bit. Did that mean the first place we went was also a favorite place? I found out Mulgrew's had been around forever and they were most famous for foot long hot dogs smothered in chopped onions and chili. After finishing that digestive tract challenge, I was ready to go home and hit the bed at the Dubuque Inn. We planned for breakfast in the morning before I headed out. I had enjoyed Dubuque and thought it would be a good place to resume practice. Carroll's persistence had paid off in spite of the absolutely crazy way he marketed Dubuque to me.

I had kind of sloughed off Carroll's little idiosyncrasies and looked beyond to what I thought were the possibilities in that quaint, charming little river town, probably not something I should have done. All of the little peculiarities and eccentricities you spot in a person should give you reason to take heed. I guess a person, meaning me, who is willing to overlook nuttiness like that is probably as nutty as the person putting on the demonstration. I think there might be something to the saying, 'First impressions are usually right'.

Thinking back, those little idiosyncrasies were far from little. I would enter practice on a salary and within six months become a partner if we were agreeable to everything and worked well together. A little later as I was getting ready to leave, Carroll insisted I drive home in his new Bill Blass special edition Lincoln Continental Mark IV. I did not want to take his car. He said he wanted to give me the car as part of my signing bonus. The car was beautiful, dark blue with tan leather accents. Carroll was insistent and as I drove out of town it felt good to be driving a new car. I thought perhaps Carroll had given me the car as one more assurance I would be returning to Iowa. After all, if I did not plan on signing a contract when I got back, I was at least going to see Carroll again to give him back his car.

I returned to Princeton that day after a leisurely sunny drive home. Upon arrival, I informed my parents I was going back into practice again with a family practitioner in Dubuque. I told Mom and Dad I had met a really nice couple, that Carroll was a handsome young physician in his very early forties with a nice wife and family. I told them about how pretty the City of Dubuque was and about Xavier Hospital where I would probably be spending most of my time while doing inpatient work.

I had shared with Carroll I did not want to be practicing out of all three hospitals in Dubuque. I saw what that type of practice did to the doctors in St. Paul. It seemed to me Dr. Richard Yadeau practicing in one hospital had the only type of life I would desire. The other physicians practicing in Bethesda seemed to spend the majority of their days running among several hospitals. It was just not a good way to practice medicine. What happens when you are a general surgeon with simultaneous emergencies in two different hospitals located forty-five minutes apart?

What I did not tell Mom and Dad was about our trip to East Dubuque. That evening still bothered me. I could not seem to put it out of my mind. I could never imagine entertaining a physician I was trying to hire as Carroll and Linda had seen fit to entertain me. The thoughts lingered. You know how they always say one out of three people is crazy? Well when I sat between Carroll and Linda, they both looked okay, so I was it.

Both Mom and Dad were happy I was returning to work and was going to be seeing patients again. They felt medicine was God's calling in life for me and the course I should be following. I ran around and said goodbye to my many friends. One tragedy had happened during my few days away from Princeton. My dear, dear friend and mentor Dr. Arthur Lundholm had passed away before we had a chance to celebrate our birthdays. I broke down and cried. My guru and guide who along with God had made me what I was, had passed away. I would never have the opportunity and blessing to celebrate another birthday with Art and Aggie Lundholm. Never again would I hear him ask, "Did you tie off that right gastric artery twice?"

The one thing I would have to do before starting practice with Carroll was to get an Iowa license to practice medicine. This was a formality but when it came to the section of questions a little more than sensitive for me about drug usage I reasoned if I answered them honestly, I would probably never get a license to practice medicine in Iowa. Remember, these were the days prior to the Internet where you can look up and find out when someone had their last bowel movement. Today with the high speed Internet, nothing is sacred. I talked to Dr. Sinnard about answering the questions. I had leveled with him about all of this when I met him and Linda. Dr. Sinnard simply said he did not care about it. Carroll said, "This is behind you now. That is your past and we are beyond that." I talked to Carroll when it came to filling out the application for the Iowa license and he asked, "Are you also going to tell them you jacked off in the closet when you were a little boy?" After talking at length with Carroll, I made the wrong choice. I lied on all those questions and I got a temporary Iowa license to practice medicine.

I enjoyed practicing medicine again and Carroll's office was a lot of fun. He had hired a fairly young staff of entirely females and they were all about dating age for me. A young gal by the name of Sharon VanDermeer, the office manager, was married to a middle aged man by the name of Bill VanDermeer. Bill was the vice president of the bank in East Dubuque. After a couple weeks of working for Carroll, I asked him if he minded if I dated anyone in the office. He said that was of no concern to him.

I guess I should have known better but I started dating our office nurse by the name of Janice. Jan was a great little gal with a wonderful personality. We had a lot of fun together. By little I do mean little. Everything about this little brunette was exquisitely tiny and finely built. Jan let me know in no uncertain terms however she was not going to be in an exclusive relationship with me. She said she did not limit herself to dating one person, which did not make a lot of sense to me. Jan volunteered upon my asking that she was not seeing anyone else and had not been dating anyone else steadily. So I thought, 'Why would you not just work on one relationship rather than dating around, continually looking?'

That was a new one on me. I always thought I was irresistible enough that someone would not want to lose me by letting me date other women. I am just kidding of course. I always felt sure of myself but that did not extend to the opposite sex. How can anybody ever feel sure of themselves when it comes to women? They are from Venus, right? I really didn't feel I had ever made that long trip to Mars yet.

One day Carroll came to me and said, "Sharon told me you were giving courtesy to all of the nuns and priests who are seeing you. That word will soon get around this city and pretty soon you will not have time to see paying patients. Rick, the nuns and priests of this area do not expect to be seen for free. There are just too many of them for us to afford giving that courtesy." I realized immediately Carroll was probably right as in a very short time I was seeing inordinate numbers of Catholic clergy. If I kept up my benevolence, laity would become the rarity. That very day, I gave up providing courtesy medical services. I felt a little uneasy about it but saw the necessity.

A very beautiful young nun came into the office one day. We hit it off really well and had a very long talk. I asked her what had convinced her to become a nun. She had grown up in a Roman Catholic family and they had always wanted to have a nun in their family. It sounded more to me like she was elected by her family to serve that role. It did not sound to me as if she had Catholicism as an inner driving force that had grown within her throughout her life. When I asked her what was the hardest thing about being a nun, she readily replied, "The hardest thing about being a Sister is abstinence. That is absolutely the very hardest part of living in a convent." I never saw that beautiful young spirit again. I always wondered where her path would lead.

Following that meeting I firmly believed a very beautiful young lady could not serve her faith as well within the constraints of living in a convent, locked away, in my eyes at least, worshiping God all day. I personally do not think God wants us to do that either. We can best worship God by serving our fellow man and being good stewards of the gifts he has given us. I really did not think her life as a nun was going to be long term. The world had much more to offer and she would better serve the Catholic Church working in a congregation than sheltered away in a convent.

It was not very long before someone in the competing medical arena decided to run a background check on me and they found out that I had been in a drug treatment center in Mandan. Within days my license to practice medicine was revoked by the State of Iowa. Soon the Dubuque newspaper The Telegraph Herald was abuzz about the doctor now practicing in Dubuque who was an ex-drug user who had been in a drug treatment center in North Dakota. Not only that but the doctor in question, Dr. Rick Redalen, had lied on his medical application to practice in Iowa.

I probably should have been pleased. After all, wasn't I having a big enough impact on Dubuque for someone to investigate me? Dubuque was a rather closed society. I don't know if outsiders ever felt like they were Dubuquers.

Letters to the editor started pouring in. By this time I had spent a couple of months practicing and working out of Xavier Hospital. I had already gained a lot of loyal friends among my patients and they were also loyal supporters. Even though I had cared for them for a brief time, they were willing to write letters and voice their support for me.

One such couple that wrote a very strong letter of support was the family of Jim and Char Muntz. They wrote they had seen me in the clinic and were very pleased with the care they received from me. They said had I been honest with the board of medical examiners to begin with, I probably would have had the same outcome. They said people deserve second chances and they backed me completely. Jim and Char remain very close friends of mine today. They still live in Dubuque and have a winter home in Arizona. I still love them as much today as I did back then when they went out on a limb to take a stand for me.

One of the most remarkable things to me during this entire time was the fact so many complete strangers would step forward to write letters of support. It seemed like it took forever to me, but eventually all of this passed and I was practicing full time again. As usual, all the publicity a person receives is like receiving free advertising. When I arrived in Dubuque I received a letter from the local medical society saying it would be appropriate for me to have three blurbs in the local papers saying I was entering the practice of medicine in the City of Dubuque.

How many other professions do you think have cutoffs for the number of advertisements you can have in the local papers? To that point, don't you wish attorneys could only advertise their practice three times? But what the heck, attorneys have to make a living too. How the hell could a poor unprincipled attorney make a living if he could not sue physicians who were trying their best to take care of the attorney's family and friends.

Certainly television networks would have to find many more advertisers if they did not have their ads on air constantly to sue physicians for using a drug that now twenty years later was causing problems. After all, these attorneys know this clairvoyant physician should surely have known that in another twenty years, science would find something wrong with the drug the physician was now prescribing.

I did not know at the time if it was a state law that physicians could only advertise their practice three times, but not wanting to piss anybody off, I did not mind. My daily appointment book was already filled every day. Not only that, the Telegraph Herald continued to provide free advertising almost daily. The ads were not exactly written in the manner I would have preferred, but I decided all publicity is good. It does not matter if it was meant to be that way, it just happens. I would guess the local physicians were tiring of seeing my name and picture in the news. They probably did not like me getting all my free publicity even if it was bad.

Practicing with Carroll was fun and often when Friday night would roll around, Carroll and Linda were not averse to taking the entire office out for happy hour. Our entire group would dance the whole night. By this time I had also started running all the time with Norma, our little office lab gal. By running, I do not mean running around. Norma was into the workout scene pretty much the same as I was. She was a beautiful little gal and easy to love. Jan was still of the mind she was not going to go steady with anybody and the office ran smoothly without any glitches in spite of me going out with a couple of the girls. Both Jan and

Norma were aware of each other and remained close friends.

Within a couple of weeks of being in Dubuque I started looking for a more permanent place to live. One day a Realtor showed me some three level condominiums near the office. I looked at one I really liked and decided to buy it. The entire condominium was finished in dark wood work and light brown carpeting, with everything done in soft earth tones. There was a free standing fireplace on the bottom level which opened up into a one car garage. A carpeted stairwell led up to the second level which also featured a freestanding fireplace. The front of the second floor was made up of a dining-living room combination and had a balcony which was entered through large sliding glass doors. The upstairs had two nice sized bedrooms and two bathrooms. It was the perfect place for a single guy with no baggage. By that I mean no boxes of junk carried over from multiple years of marriage and family.

Our group was probably not the best role model for physicians in the community. We had a great time when we were out on the town and when one of the fiddlers in one of the bands would take off on the Orange Blossom Special we were a little unruly on the dance floor. In spite of our familiarity on the weekends it did nothing to diminish our professional demeanor during the week when we were seeing patients.

I had become popular in the office in a rather short time and it seemed more patients were requesting to see me than Dr. Sinnard at times. That probably had nothing to do with me really. People just wanted to see this new doctor in town who was causing so much commotion. In all honesty, there was probably more in the local newspaper about me than all the other physicians put together. The talk and commotion did not go over well with the medical profession in Dubuque.

I found the physicians in Dubuque were a little cliquish and really had their own little boys' club. It was immediately obvious they did not like outsiders and especially outsiders who were family practitioners. After all this was a town of specialists. Specialists know everything, right? I rapidly found out Dubuque physicians would not only not welcome you, they would do anything they could to make you feel uncomfortable.

Fortunately for me, I was not the type of person who felt uncomfortable around anybody. That was especially true of physicians. They were no different than anyone else, in spite of what some of them thought about themselves. Over the next several years I would be dragged in front of one board after another in Dubuque. Invariably when I left those meetings they knew they had picked the wrong person to tangle with and it was not long before everyone in Dubuque knew the M.D. behind Rick Redalen's name stood for 'Maverick Doctor'.

I did most of my work at Xavier Hospital which welcomed me with open arms. Xavier Hospital was pretty much on life support. Most of the physicians in town practiced at Mercy Hospital and Finley Hospital. Mercy was the large Catholic hospital in town, much larger than Finley and Xavier. Xavier was on the north end of Dubuque and a little inconvenient and out of the way for most of the doctors. Mercy and Finley were a little more centralized. It was easy to understand why most of the doctors preferred not to go to Xavier. It was more time consuming in a world where time seemed to be shrinking.

I quickly learned one physician had faithfully gone the extra miles all the time to help keep the Xavier Hospital doors open, a kind of crusty lovable older physician by the name of Don Sharp. Dr. Sharp was called lovingly by the people of Xavier 'The Xavier Savior' and that is exactly what he was. He alone was admitting enough patients to keep the hospital on life support, the only physician in the community doing so.

The rest of the physicians were doing their best to send their patients to Finley or Mercy. They really only went to Xavier when they could not talk their patient into going elsewhere. Dr. Don Sharp who was in his later sixties had almost single-handedly delivered almost half of the people living in Dubuque. He spent his entire life in Dubuque as the one most well-known obstetrician in a city made up of Roman Catholics with large families. At one point in time he had been delivering over ten babies a day. He did this day in and day out. Dr. Sharp's manner of speaking was kind of rough around the edges but the people of Dubuque loved him in spite of his unsophisticated ways.

When I began applying for privileges in Xavier and the rest of the hospitals it became evident this was going to be a battle to the very end. Having done so many different surgeries, the surgical department was a little surprised at my privilege request. One arrogant smart ass asked if there was any surgery I didn't do. I replied I was not doing any neurosurgery. After all, one smart-ass remark deserves another doesn't it? I did not want to allow myself to be denigrated in such a way and confined to the small space they wanted me in.

Dr. Province, one of the family practitioners, said, "It is obvious from Dr. Redalen's records he has successfully performed surgery in a rather large number of specialties. Why don't we give Dr. Redalen the privileges he requests and he will rapidly show us his abilities." Another family practitioner seconded the motion. The physicians sitting around the conference table were rather aghast. It was obvious from their own diminutive, inadequate views on medicine they could not possibly understand that someone could have all these skills.

I personally thought after practicing and teaching at the University of Minnesota, specialists obviously knew their place in medicine. They were kind of like Whit Bird in my internship. They thought no one could know all of medicine. On the other hand, I thought they were so limited in the scope of medicine they practiced that they could not possibly do so in their narrow field of endeavor. How on earth could these people connect the dots?

It was obvious I was fighting an uphill battle against a gathering of physicians of limited wit whose only means of existence in life was to limit the boundaries of those around them so they could survive. I could understand that. A physician just decides everything they have learned in medical school is just too broad to put into practice.

So the specialist says, "How about I just study the one chapter devoted to liver. I bet I can make a living knowing just 'liver'. Won't that be much easier than knowing everything? And you know what? If I tell all my patients that I know more about 'liver' because I committed that chapter to memory, I can also charge more because the general population is uneducated in these areas. I am sure that is the case because they believe everything the politicians tell them and I am smarter than that because I only believe half of what the politicians tell me."

"Well wait a minute. Liver doctor doesn't sound too fancy. You can buy liver in the grocery store and people probably think: What is there to know about that little shiny red chunk of meat. I'll just look this up in the dictionary and find a better name. Well my dictionary says that 'hepato' in Greek means liver and 'logia' means study. How about I call myself a hepatologist. That should be worth a few extra bucks when the bills are sent out. Yup, a liver doctor is what I'm going to be."

They weren't worried about patients, they were worried about turf.

Imagine that will you. Doctors who are more concerned about themselves than their patients. Have you ever noticed how people who think they do one thing well will pass laws to make licenses necessary so someone who wants to do what they do will have to devote an inordinate amount of time to get the necessary licenses? Never mind the fact the person who already did what the specialist is now doing did so far better prior to the time the specialist finished his training, perhaps even did so better prior to the time the specialist was cutting his baby teeth.

Let me give you an example of what happens in the field of medicine. I am not going to give you a psychology course dealing with the minds of the elitists who practice their specialty to the exclusion of everything else. Suppose you have a family practitioner who has been doing surgery for many years who is the only one in the area offering surgery. Now comes along a young surgeon fresh out of his residency program who wants to make sure that anyone doing surgery has been trained in an accredited surgery program. Why wouldn't he or she? All of the patients requiring surgery have to come to the young surgeon who has to build a practice. He or she simply eliminates the person who was doing all of the surgery so those patients go to the specialist. Obviously, the person who has been doing all the surgery for the past thirty years cannot be doing it as well as the brand new university trained surgeon, can he? Of course not. And who will be the judge of that? Well, of course, it is the brand new surgeon, many of whom have a hard time not tying their rubber gloves in knots during surgery.

I have never heard of a surgical resident flunking out of their residency program. After all, the university makes money off their residents by charging big dollars for procedures and paying their residents in peanuts. They are even going to make money on a bad surgical resident with few or no skills. The surgeon also needs an assistant for most surgeries. Generally the assistant is paid by the surgeon in one way or another if the assistant is another practicing surgeon. A surgical resident assisting the head or lead surgeon on one of the surgeon's private patients is paid by the training program. The surgeon is fulfilling the duty of teaching the resident.

A glaring example of this is many hospital cardiologists feel they are the only ones who can read an EKG, an electrocardiogram or a tracing made of how the electrical currents are flowing through your heart. Now why does it take a specialist to do that? Because the cardiologists say it does. In many hospitals in days gone by and probably now, in the morning the cardiologist comes in and reads the cardiograms done in the emergency department the night before. It does not matter that the code run on a person the night before had come to the emergency department by ambulance with a heart that was not beating. Our excellently trained paramedics were doing the miraculous job they always do, keeping the patient alive with God's help and supporting the life of a technically dead person. They get the patient to the hospital emergency department which has enough resources to continue their lifesaving work. Now the live patient is transferred to the intensive care unit.

In walks the cardiologist in the morning. This is great. He has a stack of fifty cardiograms that were done in the emergency department the previous night. He may see dollar signs. He must. Why on earth would a cardiologist be reading a cardiogram after it had already been read the night before by the emergency department physician? Whatever he puts down on the cardiogram has no bearing on what was already done on the patient, does it! If the cardiologist writes on the cardiogram I'd like ham and eggs for my breakfast, it really makes no difference for the care of the patient. On the other hand, suppose the patient did not survive the code. In that case the cardiologist is simply reading a cardiogram to charge the deceased family for a service no longer needed. Does this make sense to any of you?

It reminds me of the conversation the emergency physician was having with his physician father who was doing pathology. The father was kidding his son, "You guys in the ED seldom get anything right the first time." His son said, "Well Dad, that may be true and you guys always get it right but it makes no difference." Unless you are in forensics, I guess it doesn't matter what you say about a dead body. It sometimes satisfies curiosity.

One day I was making rounds on the medical floor of Finley Hospital. I had been warned that none of the doctors were going to greet me. They wanted me to feel uncomfortable. I recognized Dr. Howell, one of the most well-known internists in Dubuque, standing at the nurses' station with about eight to ten nurses, a couple who were waiting on him. Dr. Howell was with Dodge Street Internists. The situation presented me with the opportune time to attack. I walked up to Dr. Howell and said,

"Good morning Dr. Howell." Dr. Howell turned his back to me and said nothing. I walked around to the front of him again and said a little more loudly, "Good morning Dr. Howell." Once more the obstinate Dr. Howell turned his back to me. I wondered who on earth wants to make a belittled spectacle of themselves in front of the nurses they work with every day. I walked around to the front of Dr. Howell again and said very loudly, "Good morning Dr. Howell." By this time all the nurses were watching Dr. Howell and wondering how he was going to handle this verbal assault on the old guard, from a new doctor who was at least thirty years his junior. Dr. Howell finally said, "Good morning Dr. Redalen."

That was the last time in Dubuque, Iowa a physician would not greet me in the morning with, "Good morning Dr. Redalen." None of them wanted to be taught the lesson Dr. Howell had been taught. It is better to learn your lessons the easy way than the hard way. If I ever had the opportunity to teach young physicians again, I was going to put this lesson right in there with my lessons about humility.

Surgical privileges became another matter. Not only were they not going to give me surgical privileges, they also refused to give me privileges to assist in surgery. I received this news at a very inopportune time. I had scheduled one of my patients for a colectomy the following day and now suddenly I could not even assist in her surgery. Dr. Luke Faber was doing the surgery. I did not care for Dr. Luke Faber, a pompous arrogant little ass. He was known in Dubuque to be a good surgeon but one whose laurels rested mainly on his father, now deceased, who had been a very much loved physician in the community. Dr. Luke was not held in the same esteem. I had met Dr. Luke's younger brother Denny who was a very cordial and likable urologist. It was hard not to like Denny.

The nurses were a huge help to me in my effort to get a ramped-up start in Dubuque. They liked me because I treated them like most physicians in Minnesota treated all nurses, as a valuable part of our team. In Dubuque the physicians thought they were demigods and whatever they said should go. One of the nurses overheard Dr. Luke Faber say Dr. Redalen was a schizophrenic who thought he could do any surgical procedure known to man. I filed that away along with a litany of other great compliments I heard about myself.

On the morning of surgery for my colectomy patient, I found Dr. Faber in the surgical lounge and asked him who was going to be assisting him. He introduced me to his son, a junior medical student, and said his son would be assisting him. This was pretty much Dubuque exhibiting her medical colors in all her glory. A surgeon who had done several hundred major surgeries, assisted in open heart procedures, assisted Dr. Dick Yadeau, one of the greatest surgeons in the Minneapolis-St. Paul area and taught surgery at the University of Minnesota was not even allowed to assist in surgery on his own patient. But at least a well-qualified medical student could assist.

Not wanting to make a scene in the surgical lounge, I asked Dr. Faber if he would step outside and talk to me. I said, "Dr. Faber, I hear from one of our nurses you think I might be a schizophrenic. I can assure you that is not the case and I will go you one better. I am probably a better surgeon than you think you are. I suggest you get together with your colleagues and give me appropriate privileges. I do not ever want to hear again you are taking your son into surgery to assist on one of my patients as a learning experience at the expense of the relationship I have with my patient." Dr. Faber, a diminutive man, was obviously intimidated and said he would take care of it. A little later they gave me privileges to assist in surgery. How magnanimous and benevolent of them, correct? Physicians are only good at confronting another physician when they have a group of physicians at their side to bolster their confidence even when they know they are wrong. Unfortunately for the doctors wishing to confront me, I always found out they came to the gunfight without bullets in their guns. Stupidity never trumps knowledge.

About this same time frame the assault from the medical establishment seemed never ending. I received a call from Lois Nyens one morning. She asked, "Dr. Redalen, were you ever in prison?" I replied, "No, of course not. Why?" She said, "Dr. William W. was just making rounds in the hospital and he said you had been in prison for a couple of years for selling drugs to children." I said, "Don't worry. I will have a talk with him and he will be talking to you shortly. After he does I want you to call me back." I reached Dr. Bill on the phone and told him what I had just been told by Lois Nyens. I said, "Dr. Bill, do you know me?" He said, "No." I asked, "Have you ever met me?" He again replied, "No." I told him he was to go immediately back to the hospital and tell the nurses he talked to that he does not know me nor would he even recognize me if he saw me and everything he said was a lie. I said, "You are to do this immediately and if you do not, I am going to drag you through so much mud, you and your family will never be clean again." I added, "I will immediately bring slander suits against you and you will never again practice with your head held high in this city. Once you have told the nurses and whoever else you talked to that you lied, I want you to ask them to call me to tell me you have apologized to them for the lies. Do you understand?" Dr. W. was tremulous, crying and apologizing. I was relentless and angry. I said, "Get it done."

I received a call from Lois Nyens about a half hour later. Dr. W. had shown up at the nurse's station and asked them to gather everyone he had talked to when he was at their station. She said, "Dr. W. was crying and upset and wringing his hands and told us he had never met you, Dr. Redalen. He said he would not even know you if you passed each other on the street. He said he lied to all of us and was just repeating some of the stories going around about you. He was a complete blubbering mess when he left us, Dr. Redalen. I am so sorry for you." I said, "You do not have to be sorry for me, Lois. There is very little life can hand me that I cannot handle."

A couple of days went by. I was notified by the pathology department that the sections had come back on my colectomy patient. The lymph nodes had all come back as positive for metastases. My patient was not going to have a good outcome from this surgery. I decided I had better run to the hospital and talk to her and try to give her some encouragement. When I arrived at the nurses' station and asked for the chart, one of the nurses asked to speak with me. She said Dr. Luke Faber had just been to see my patient. I had just missed him. She said, "Dr. Faber in his usually blunt manner told her she had a couple of months to live and to get her affairs in order." In the brief time I had been in Dubuque, I had heard Dr. Faber was not one to mince words and pretty much said things like they were but I could not imagine him saying that to one of his wealthy clients, the inherently superior people of Dubuque. Yup, one of those deals, every one of those superiors thought everyone else lived on "the other side of the tracks."

I immediately had Dr. Faber paged. When he answered the phone I said I wanted to talk to him. I met Dr. Faber on the surgical floor and asked him if he had really said the things to my patient as the nurse had related to me. He informed me he had. I asked him who the hell he thought he was saying something like that to my patient. I told him he had no business taking away the hope of a patient by saying she was going to die in a couple of months. I said, "You do not know that. God is the only one who knows that." He said, "The patient has a right to know." I was livid and enraged inside. I said, "You have deliberately and purposefully tried to hurt one of my patients. I do not know what type of pleasure you get from that but it is perverse." The gloves were definitely off between Dr. Faber and me. He may have been technically a good or even great surgeon but in my eyes he was a very poor physician. He was indeed a very poor example of humanity.

I went back to the nurse's station and we both went to see my patient who was still beside herself from Dr. Faber's poorly presented information. I tried to console her with my very best counseling, but Dr. Faber had definitely done his damage. I explained to my patient I would be taking care of her and she should try not to worry. I explained that I did not know what would happen. I said, "Dr. Faber, in spite of what he may have said, does not know what your outcome will be. Only God knows what is going to happen in your life. I know for a fact God has not put a bar code expiration date on your foot that we poor mortals can read. I will help you through this to the best of my ability and if there are things you are worried about, I will try to answer all of your questions. Regardless of when God wants to take you home, whatever happens will be for the best and you have to keep that in your mind as we go forward. And I do mean you and me. I will be at your side for all of this."

In my experience many patients seem to be predictors of their outcomes when it comes to cancer. Some patients just say, "So what. I am not going to let it get the best of me." Although this is the course some patients take, there are also patients who think a cancer diagnosis is an immediate death sentence. One patient who had lung cancer died within two weeks of finding out the diagnosis. Apparently the death was from lung cancer although it could not have possibly have killed him that rapidly. He simply made up his mind he was supposed to die. I likened these instances to the voodoo deaths you read about when a witch doctor puts a hex on someone and then they die. What on earth is that all about?

Only a couple of weeks went by before my patient with colon cancer had gone on a rather precipitous downhill course. I had visited her in her home in East Dubuque several times as it was difficult for her to make it to my office. Dr. Faber's death discourse to her had certainly not helped elevate her demeanor. I guess she was doing as well with everything as she could. One of her daughters lived in California and could not come to be with her mom during those last weeks. I had met her daughter, Lisa, who lived in Dubuque, a beautiful little gal in her early twenties.

I received a strange call from Lisa's sister one day while I was busy in the clinic. She said, "I have a strange request I hope you will help me with. Today is Lisa's birthday and she has been spending every day with Mom. She is depressed over what has been going on with Mom and I have not been able to be of any help to her. Would you please do me the favor of getting a bottle of champagne, bringing it to Mom's house and spending the night celebrating Lisa's birthday?" Having spent time with Lisa, I knew it was not going to be hard to spend an evening with her. I told her sister I did not know about spending the night, but Lisa and I did spend the night talking and sharing the bottle of champagne. I felt uneasy with her mom in the next room dying of cancer. Lisa and I remained very good friends for some time after her mom's death.

Chapter Twenty-two

Parting Company

At the clinic both Carroll and I always had a full day of appointments. Sharon brought it to my attention one day when we were alone and talking that Dr. Sinnard might be feeling a little jealous. I asked "Why would you say something like that?" Dr. Sinnard had said a couple of days ago he was tired of hearing how great Dr. Redalen is. He had asked, "Don't they know who brought him here?" I said, "Sharon, the people are just trying to support Dr. Sinnard because of all the pressure he has had to face from me being here." Sharon also voiced Dr. Sinnard said, "I'm surprised he isn't worn down to a nubbin now with all the running around he is doing." I was a little taken aback by that statement since Carroll was the one who said it was okay for me to date girls from the office.

It was fun to be seeing patients on a daily basis and delivering babies. Lois Nyens who had about thirty years in the labor and delivery department and her husband Joe became good friends of mine and we would go out to eat once in a while. Around about the time I started delivering babies again I met Kim Splinter who shared with me she had just started nursing school in Freeport, Illinois. Kim asked me one day if I played tennis. When I replied that I did, she suggested we play tennis someday. We agreed to meet at the tennis courts up near one of the small Bible colleges across from the apartments where I lived. The tennis courts were right next to one of the city's golf courses called Bunker Hill.

I showed up to meet Kim one afternoon with three of the best tennis racquets available at the time. Kim looked a little surprised when she saw me. She said, "I thought I saw your wooden tennis racquets in the back of your car yesterday." I replied, "Oh, those old antiques. I was going to throw them away but decided maybe I would run into some kids during office hours who wanted them for starter racquets." Kim didn't tell me that when she saw those racquets she thought I would be a good mark for her to beat at a few games of tennis. Unfortunately for Kim, she had guessed wrong and was no match for me. I let up on my game so we could have some volleys. At least now I had someone to play tennis with and it got so we played tennis about every chance we got. I really cared a lot for Kim. We got to be better friends and then we started seeing each other off the tennis courts. It was not long before Kim and I became intimate. We had grown to love each other.

I had gradually made a number of other friends in Dubuque. One was a guy by the name of Doug Zickuhr, a great athlete. He had been the Iowa State Racquetball Champion a number of times in unlimited competition and had also been a national water ski champion. Doug wanted me to teach him how to play tennis. He said by the end of the summer he would be the best tennis player in Dubuque. I said, "Doug by the end of the summer, you will never beat me in a game of tennis, and I am a mere shadow of my former self." That pretty much set the stage for the tennis Doug and I played. He was always extremely competitive but would never get to the point where he would be real competition for me. Most days we played singles at Eagle Point Park. He was big and powerful and no one could hit the tennis ball harder, but he was not always accurate. One hot afternoon when we were midway into a match I was winning, Doug picked up his balls and towel and walked off the court without saying a word. I was left standing there wondering what was wrong.

I saw Doug at the YMCA a couple of weeks later and I asked him why he had been such a jerk that day on the tennis court. I could tell he was still mad at me. He said, "Rick, I can take getting beat by someone but I do not expect you to simply play with me and not give me your best." I said, "Doug, if I played all out in tennis, we would simply not have a game. My game would be a hard serve and perhaps one volley and the point would be over. How is that any different from when we play racquetball together? If you played your best against me in racquetball, I would never get a point and you know that. The way it is now you always keep me in the game and we get to have fun playing. I learn a lot and you are a good teacher. The same is true of our tennis games. I can be a very good teacher for you if you let me. Make up your mind that you are good in many sports but are just never going to beat me in tennis." Doug and I seemed to come to a mutual understanding that worked for all of our times together. We remained good friends and played a lot of tennis.

Doug and I were playing tennis on the Loras College courts one day. Kim came down to the court crying and said her parents were not going to let me see her anymore. I had never even met Kim's parents but I could pretty much imagine what had happened. She had probably let them know I was a physician who worked at Xavier Hospital where Kim also worked. They put two and two together and came up with the fact I was too old to be seeing their daughter. They were right, of course. Kim was a teenager and I was thirty-four. I do not know why, but at that point in my life the thought of statuary rape never entered my mind. Kim was only seventeen at the time. I reassured Kim everything would be all right, but she left crying and distraught. Doug and I finished our tennis games and I told Doug I was going to go over to Kim's house.

I knew where Kim lived as I had dropped her off a number of times at her home. I drove over and knocked on Gene and Nell Splinter's door. Nell's real name I would come to know later was Genelda. I introduced myself and said I was the person who had been playing tennis with their daughter lately. I explained that Kim and I had been running around together outside of the tennis court and I would like to keep seeing her and growing our relationship with their blessing. It was not very long before I became good friends of all the Splinters, including Kim's two younger sisters Jill and Judy.

After being over at the Splinter's home a couple of times, Kim said, "I know there is one game you can't beat me at." I asked what that was. She said, "We have a ping-pong table in the basement and you can't beat me in ping-pong." I said, "Well let's have a match and I'll try." I did not let on to Kim I was seldom beaten at ping-pong. Kim realized after a couple of points this was not going to be a game she could hope to win against me. It turned out I would not have had to allow a single point had I really wanted to embarrass my opponent but I made the games competitive. It was like we were back on the tennis court competitively.

Kim would never ever win but we had fun.

During my first summer in Dubuque, Kim introduced me to her friend Susie Kunnert. The Kunnerts were a well-known family in Dubuque that owned not only the Shot Tower which was the best pizza place in Dubuque but also Kunnert's Sporting Goods.

Susie had two brothers with big names in basketball. They had been stars on the basketball court while attending Wahlert Catholic High School. Her brother Kevin was in the NBA and played as a center-forward for the Chicago Bulls. The Kunnert name was well respected in Dubuque. Wahlert was a well-known high school in Dubuque with strong academic and athletic programs.

Susie, Kim, Doug and I were on the tennis courts almost as much as we were off. We would play mixed doubles and were pretty evenly matched. We would play until we got tired and sometimes as a treat, Susie would call up the Shot Tower and have pizza and drinks delivered to us on the tennis courts up in Eagle Point Park where we usually played.

One day I asked Kim if she would like to go to Hawaii for about ten days. Kim was keen on the idea so we made our reservations at the Royal Hawaiian and off we went to Maui. I had spent a lot of time on Maui so it was not something new for me. We landed at the Kahului airport in Kahului and made our way from there by rental car to Lahaina.

The Royal Hawaiian was located on the ocean just north of Lahaina a few miles and sat on the Royal Ka'anapali Golf Course. Our room was on the south side of the hotel and looked out on the golf course. It was beautiful with the palm trees swaying in the wind and when you looked to the west you could see the ocean waves crashing in on the beach.

After checking in I took Kim downtown to see Lahaina, an old whaling village that had been an active port for whaling ships in former glory days and was at one time the center for the global whaling industry. In the early to mid-1800s, hundreds of whaling ships stopped in Hawaii and Lahaina was one of the main ports. Now Lahaina was probably the main tourist attraction on the island of Maui. We stopped and had a drink at the Organ Grinder, a bar and eatery sitting on the second story over a shop located ocean side on Front Street. It was the first building at the north end of the walkway along and overlooking the ocean with its waves crashing loudly on the rough lava beach below.

Kim and I brought our racquets and played tennis while we were on

Maui. It did not take long to meet another tennis playing couple and we became friends. We played doubles on the Royal Hawaiian courts and after long hours of tennis in the hot sun, we would go out for a meal and have some cocktails to wind down the evening. Kim and I had a great time on Maui and the time seemed to fly by. It was not long before we were saying goodbye to our friends and on our way back to the mainland. In Hawaii, you always have to say mainland. It is mildly offensive if you say you are heading back to the states. After all you are leaving a state. You are not heading back to them.

It did not take Kim and me long to get back to our tennis routine in Dubuque. We both looked a lot healthier as we had dark bronze tans. Kim, like me, was brown skinned so we both looked more like islanders when we got back than many of the real islanders. Many of the people on Maui were California transplants and the light skinned blondes looked a little out of place. Regardless, it was good to be home.

Now that I was back in Dubuque, Jan would come and watch me play tennis for hours and then we would often go home together. Early in my tennis days with Kim, Jan would not usually come to watch. She really had little interest in tennis. As time went on and Kim and I spent more and more time together, Jan seemed to become more interested. I think Jan wanted to make sure I was heading the correct direction following our tennis matches. Jan was always friendly to Kim and Kim reciprocated. I would not say they became friends but they were cordial.

After Kim and I had been gone for ten days to a tropical isle, it seemed Jan was starting to think more seriously about our relationship. She did not say anything, but I suspect she now realized that not being in a committed relationship may have its downfalls. She had not objected when we were leaving, but she was happy when I got back.

One day after our trip to Hawaii, Jan said she wanted to talk to me about something serious. I asked her what that was. Jan said, "Rick, I don't want you to be seeing other girls anymore. I am ready to settle down to a one on one relationship and I think we should just date each other exclusively." I said, "Jan that is not the way things work. You cannot tell me you do not want us to be exclusively together and then suddenly change your mind."

This was not a problem for Kim as Kim knew I was dating a couple of girls in my office. I was always honest with anyone I dated. I told Kim and Jan, "I am never getting married again and if I ever do I am never going to start a family again." I said, "The one family I thought I would have for the rest of my life, which I do not have any more, is enough. Had I known in advance what would happen to my family I loved so much, I would never in a thousand years have had them."

I had escaped with my life from the very worst pain a person can ever know and I would never take that chance again. Life is not a dice table of 'do overs'. It is a give it all you've got table where you try to land on Go. Unfortunately it takes more than one person to make that happen.

Eventually my ideas about never having another family would taint every relationship I entered into. I almost always dated younger girls and of course they wanted to have a family. Kim kept saying she wanted to have seven kids. That was hard for me to imagine but most of the Catholics in Dubuque had rather large families. I was reminded of what us high school boys thought about going out with Catholic girls which would not be difficult in Dubuque. Every girl I met was a Catholic, including Jan and Kim. Eventually, I stopped asking, "Are you Catholic?"

When I came in the office one day, Dr. Sinnard was lying on a table and the girls were doing an EKG on him. I asked him what the problem was and he replied he was having an insurance physical and he was just doing a cardiogram ahead of time to make sure everything was okay. I asked Carroll if he had any reasons to suspect it would not be okay and he said no. I had no reason to suspect otherwise. Carroll didn't ask me to read his EKG and I did not think it polite to look at it without being asked. Carroll and Linda were both the pictures of health. Our clinic practice was always a good time. Everyone seemed to get along and liked each other. Prior to this I never thought a group of girls would get along well.

I was a little uncertain what to expect sometimes with Carroll. He was an excellent physician and I had no doubts about his ability as a doctor. His patients really loved him or at the very least, liked him. One day he said he'd gotten into an altercation with someone in a traffic scrum. He had evidently pulled out his pistol and threatened the other driver. He assured me it was no big deal and nothing would come of it. I could not seem to get any more information than that from Carroll. He told me the police had come, but he expounded no further. All in all, it seemed a little strange and inexplicable to me. I didn't feel people should be pulling guns and pointing them at other people. It made me feel in some ways as though I was back in Princeton. What on earth is it with doctors and guns?

Jan and Kim and I continued our very good relationships. Jan had started living with me most of the time which worked out fine as Kim still lived with her parents. Prior to this Jan had always wanted to go home to her apartment at night. She had a great big beautiful apartment in one of the old Dubuque mansions a couple of blocks from Finley Hospital. I think one of the reasons Jan started staying with me all the time was to make sure I was not staying with anyone else.

During this time Carroll had gotten another physician from the University of Nebraska to join his practice. Bill Wignal was a young family man who had recently finished a family practice residency. Bill did not even stay long enough to form a following before he and his wife decided Dubuque was not the place for them. They moved to join a practice in a small town in Colorado. I really didn't blame him. If you were not a pretty strong character ready to fight for your rights the struggle was probably not worthwhile. I could have found a lot of places with welcoming arms for a new physician. Dubuque was just a bunch of old time physicians protecting their turf by keeping out other physicians who did not join their clique. Dubuque was a difficult place to feel welcome if you were an outsider moving in to practice medicine.

Cindy called wanting to know if she could come down to Dubuque. She had found out where I was living from mutual friends. She had divorced and changed her name from Tuomela back to Rohr. I said I would be happy to see her again. I told her I was dating, but did not mind if she wanted to come down. Cindy had saved a little money so Cindy, Chad and Kelly came down and rented an apartment in East Dubuque. Cindy and I started seeing each other again and our relationship took off from right where it had stopped. It was nice to see Chad and Kelly who had grown immensely in the little time we had been apart. They were cute well behaved children. Life was more complicated as now I was seeing Cindy, playing tennis with Kim and sleeping at night with Jan. Strangely enough, everybody knew everybody and we all seemed to get along well. I think we could have been a great family. Probably not like The Waltons but close.

Cindy and I began spending more time together and we also spent time together with Carroll and Linda. We'd often go out for supper at Timmerman's Supper Club. One night as we were waiting for a table, Carroll took a call over his portable phone. These were not the mobile portable phones we know today, but big old clunkers that could be loud. We were standing at the bar and it was noisy so Carroll turned his phone up as far as it would go so he could hear. Suddenly, like it was over a loud speaker that everyone in the bar could hear, the person on the other end of the line said very loudly, "Dr. Sinnard, this is Bertha (not her real name)." The bar quieted down so Dr. Sinnard could hear and as loudly as you can imagine she blurted out, "I think I have gonorrhea." Dr. Sinnard got a horrified look on his face as he was trying to turn down his phone, and he exclaimed, "Now all the people of Dubuque think you have gonorrhea!"

Sometimes I would begin to feel uncomfortable if we were out socializing. Linda would often drink a little more than was socially acceptable and then become friendlier than was acceptable. Usually, if not always, those advances were toward me. Carroll never said anything and as gentlemanly as possible I would try unsuccessfully to put distance between Linda and me. It was just not a good situation and I could not see it coming to a good end.

One night Carroll suggested Cindy and I come with them on their boat down to Bellevue, a little town on the Mississippi located by Lock and Dam No. 12. It was a straight shot about twenty-five miles down the river. There was a small restaurant on the water with docks for tying up your boat. Boaters would frequently motor down there from Dubuque to have an evening meal. It was a scenic route by river and relaxing for a night out. Cindy and I accepted their invitation. Carroll had brought a goodly supply of alcohol for our trip. We had a pleasant time floating down the river and imbibed some more over a great meal of fried catfish. On the way back, Linda became somewhat amorous and her affection was again directed at me. Carroll said nothing to dissuade her and Cindy who was watching all of this in her skimpy bikini decided to make advances on Carroll. I knew Cindy could see the difficult time I was having fending Linda off but rather than help, she threw herself at Carroll. I was heated inside and distraught with Cindy. I thought she could see I was disturbed but that did not stop her advances.

When we finally arrived in Dubuque, I took Cindy to her apartment.

I asked her what on earth she was doing. She said, "Well I was doing the same thing with Carroll as you were doing with Linda." I exclaimed loudly, "I was being attacked by Linda and you could see me trying to fight her off!" I told her it was very poor thinking on her part if she thought I would watch her force herself on another man after what I had just finished going through with Bette. I asked, "What on earth were you thinking?" I left angrily saying, "I will talk to you tomorrow," which was a Saturday.

I went over to Cindy's apartment the next morning. I told Cindy I had thought a lot about what had happened the night before. I said I did not want to be in another relationship with a woman who could wantonly throw herself at another man with a complete disregard for me. I asked, "How on earth could you have let this happen?" It was hurtful to me, but I knew that as close and as rapidly as Cindy and I had rekindled our past, we had also just destroyed any future we might have with drinking and poor choices. I said goodbye to Cindy, Chad and Kelly with a very heavy heart. That was the last time I ever saw them. They were standing on the back porch of their apartment as I drove away. I never knew where they had gone. I do wish them well.

Strange things continued happening with Carroll. He and Linda decided to take a little break now that I was in the office working every day. They said they went back to the small town of Thermopolis, Wyoming where they used to live. Carroll said they had gone to the bank where he and Linda met and he had gotten into an altercation with the bank president. That was about all Carroll told me about the incident other than he had armed himself with a roll of quarters in his right hand in case the engagement came to blows. Evidently Carroll must have had some inclination of what could happen. I did not know but read between the lines that perhaps the bank president was one of Linda's old paramours or maybe even an ex-husband. Carroll and Linda did not expound and it seemed when I asked questions about why they left Thermopolis after living there in the first place the only answer I got was it had gotten too small for them. That did not make much sense either. Had the town really shrunk or had they gotten too big for the town. Anyway, the topic was off limits.

It was not long after that incident Carroll and I decided to part company. I thought perhaps the reason was my practice had grown quickly with a large enough following that the appointment books were filled every day. I don't know if the Linda and Cindy debacle had anything to do with it but there were some tensions between us that were not going to allow our partnership to move forward. The day I left Carroll's office, it no longer felt as though it was our office. We did not part on good terms and I did not really know why. We had always gotten along well right up until this time.

I went home to contemplate what I was going to do. Shortly after arriving at home I heard some noise down outside the garage of my condominium. I looked outside on the porch and saw the Bill Blass Special Carroll had given me to seal our partnership deal disappearing up the hill. I had no problem with that and my little old Chevrolet still worked just fine for getting around.

Chapter Twenty-three
Mid-American Medical Services

After leaving the practice, I went back to running all of the time and playing some racquetball. One morning I received a call from a physician from Madison, Wisconsin, a guy by the name of John Kirkpatrick. He introduced himself and asked me if I was looking for a job. He said he had heard about me from some mutual friends from our past. John said he and another physician by the name of Griff Ferrell owned a company called Mid-American Medical Services that managed emergency department contracts. He said they had the contracts to run twenty-two emergency departments in Iowa, Illinois and Wisconsin. I let him know I did not have a Wisconsin license. John said that would be no problem and he asked if I would come and visit their office in Madison. I said, "Why not. I am not doing anything right now and am between jobs." I looked on a map and it appeared the distance from Dubuque to Madison was close to one hundred miles, or about an hour and one-half drive. The weather was beautiful, bright and sunny and I took off within the hour.

U.S. 151 was a two lane highway that ran all the way from Dubuque to Madison. The drive was made up of lush green hillsides and pastures, interspersed with small towns typical of rural Wisconsin. Within a couple of hours I was winding my way near the capitol building in the center of Madison, just east of the University of Wisconsin. The plush office was on the eighteenth floor of James Wilson Plaza on the north shores of Lake Monona. As I walked in the door, there was a large balcony facing south across Lake Monona. The lake was alive with people out enjoying the water and the beautiful weather. Mid-American Medical Services owned the office building with this breathtakingly gorgeous view.

I was introduced to John Kirkpatrick, a friendly guy soundly built and about 5'10" with premature thinning of the hair. John ushered me into his office and explained to me in a little more detail what Mid-American Medical Services was all about. John said Griff was not around for the day and was probably working in an ED someplace. John said they had started the company a couple of years earlier and that it was a relatively new service offered by only a couple of companies in the United States.

John said he and Griff would go around to hospitals that did not have emergency departments staffed by physicians. They would explain to the staff and administration what a valuable service it was to the physicians utilizing their hospitals to have full time emergency department physicians on call. As far as I was concerned that was almost a no sell. I would have loved to have that available to me when I was in private practice. Of course, once a medical staff heard about the benefits of coverage like this they were ready to lobby the administration to make it happen.

There were really no drawbacks other than the cost of the service. It took a minimum of three physicians to cover an emergency department if it was a department that required only one physician on the floor for one shift. Generally the shifts were twelve hours so if the ED staff consisted of three it meant there was very little time off. Physicians were not salaried and were paid on an hourly basis. In a slower emergency department the shifts were often twenty-four hours. That was not difficult in a slower department, but in a busy department a physician might be awake for twenty-four hours without much of a break.

John said they were opening a new contract and asked if I would care to be the director of the emergency department of Holy Family Hospital in Manitowoc, Wisconsin on the shores of Lake Michigan and against the mouth of the Manitowoc River. I thought it sounded great and all I wanted to know was when I would start. I did not really care what the hospital looked like and I knew I would get along well with any staff they had. John said the contract did not go into effect for a couple of months and he thought I would have my Wisconsin license by that time. I worked in the office of Mid-American for that little bit of time, helped with staffing of some of the EDs and took care of some last minute chores in Dubuque.

John asked me to stay the night in Madison at the Concourse Hotel, also owned by Mid-American. I stayed in the Presidents Club which was an exclusive set of rooms upstairs with a private elevator and a large welcoming lounge. A friend of John Kirkpatrick's by the name of Darrell Wilde had built the Concourse. Mid-American had also bought the Hilton in St. Petersburg and renamed it the Bayfront Concourse. Mid-American Medical Services was definitely a company with a lot of irons in the fire.

Within a couple of months I had my license and John and I took a trip to Manitowoc. Holy Family Hospital had been getting weekend coverage from itinerant residents who were hired to work on weekends from 6 p.m. Friday night through 9 p.m. Sunday night. When Mid-American took over the contract, it would now be 24/7 coverage every day of the year.

Manitowoc was a beautiful town and it was only a short jaunt to the shores of Lake Michigan which was very much like Lake Superior in northern Minnesota and every bit as cold. One difference was Lake Michigan was surrounded with sand dunes and sparsely scattered thatches of dune grass. There was an old WWII submarine anchored in one of the bays, the USS Cobia, a national historic landmark. I was later told by one of the pediatricians the most exciting thing to do in Manitowoc was to go down to the harbor and watch the submarine rust. I learned Manitowoc had been the building site of twenty-eight submarines used in WWII.

After being shown around the city for just a little bit we visited the hospital where we were greeted with a warm reception. First we met Gary Weeks the assistant director of the hospital, a warm and friendly red headed young man with a receding hairline. Gary introduced us to the hospital administrator, Don Orleans who was also warm and friendly. Gary asked us to follow him down to the emergency department. He began introductions and then said he would leave us in the care of the emergency department head nurse, a warm pretty blonde RN by the name of Kathy Eisenchenk. She introduced us around. I noticed John introduced himself as Dr. Kirkpatrick. I introduced myself as I always did, "I am Rick." After a couple of introductions John followed suit. We were introduced to Judy Paral, a tall, beautiful, brown eyed, brown skinned beauty. Not usually the way I would describe a nurse but JP and I hit it off the minute our eyes met. You all know how sometimes when you meet a person you know immediately you are going to have a relationship, don't you? That is how it went with JP and me. It was at first glance.

I started work a couple of days later and almost immediately a young internist named John Hodgson joined us. John was married to a girl by the name of Diana but she would not be joining John for some time. In the beginning the only two full time physicians in the emergency department were John and me. The rest of the shifts were filled in with John Kirkpatrick, Tom Burns, Griff Ferrell and a smattering of whomever else was free to help. In the beginning I would sometimes end up doing 48 hour shifts. I really didn't mind as usually a catnap here and there were more than enough sleep to tide me over. John did not like to work that many hours; however, I still sometimes used work to ward off deeper feelings about my family, so it worked just fine for me.

Neither John nor I were raving about where they put us up to sleep at night if we got the chance to sleep. More often than not we would fall asleep in a chair in the lounge where we congregated to write orders or take a brief break. Our temporary quarters were in the morgue across the hall. There were eight stainless steel tables on the south wall of our small room that slid in and out of their cooler to keep the bodies cold while they waited for transfer. When they slid out they didn't hit our bed on the opposite wall but almost. It never seemed to fail that once you were sound asleep someone would invariably come in with a body and you would hear the clanging of the refrigerator door opening and then the clunk of the body as it was shoved onto the stainless steel tray. You would then hear the clang of the refrigerator door slamming shut again. The nursing and ambulance crews tried to be mindful of us sleeping, but it was still difficult sometimes. Oh well, after the temporary commotion our new roommates were always quiet. When you think of it, why should you complain about the clunking of a few bodies being put away during the night when in between you heard the sirens of ambulances coming and going all night.

Everyone was happy to have new doctors in the emergency department. It saved the staff a lot of broken up days. It was nice patients could show up in the emergency department that could better handle emergencies than their offices. We would call the physician when we were done examining their patient. When admissions seemed necessary, we would call the staff physician for the patient, give them a brief history and our findings and why their patient needed hospitalization. We would often write the admission orders and the patient's doctor could then see them when their office hours ended for the day.

I gradually got to know most of the physicians on staff and they were a cordial bunch. At least most of the time. One day in the elevator I said to an elderly doctor I had not met, but knew was on staff, "Good morning, you must be one of the local docs." He gave me a rather unfriendly look and asked, "You didn't see anyone tie a boat up to me yet did you?" Oh well, I guess I knew my charming personality was not going to hit home runs all the time.

When the staff physicians came to know John Hodgson and me better and knew we lived in town, they treated us more like hospital staff rather than the itinerant medical residents they had grown used to showing up to work periodically to make ends meet. The best thing about having emergency physicians on staff was the local physicians got to know you and knew your capabilities. At that point in time there were no Emergency Medicine Residencies so all physicians did not come with the same degree of skills and abilities. There was very little I could not do in the emergency room. I could not think of anything that could come in I would feel uncomfortable with. One day as I was turning the ED over to John who was just coming on, a boating accident came in. The propeller had run down the length of a swimmer's body. The cuts were not deep but the patient had cuts approximately every inch down the entire leg beginning at the ankle and ending at the buttock. I had not had the opportunity to see how John would handle trauma so I decided to stick around and see for myself. I watched him begin to sew and it was almost painful to see how slowly and painstakingly he was repairing his patient. It was apparent to me this was going to be an all-day patient for this young internist. I walked up to where John was working and asked him if I could lend a hand. John looked relieved and readily agreed. I asked for a Keith Needle on my suture and went to work. I finished sewing that entire leg while John was still working on his second laceration. He thanked me profusely and said he had never seen someone work so fast. I just replied, "It comes with practice and experience John. It will not be long before you will have these skills."

JP and I got to work a lot together and our ED was a group of like-minded individuals. When a number of us were off together, we would often go out for happy hour or have a drink and dance together. JP and I started arranging our schedules so we were always working together and getting off at the same time. If we got off in the morning at 8 a.m., we would head over to Two Rivers to a place called Kurtz's Bar and Pub, famous for their ham sandwiches. It was a destination diner for people from all over the area. After we stocked up on up on ham sandwiches we would walk across the street to the liquor store and get and a couple of bottles of champagne. Then we would go up to one of the parks and spread out a blanket between some sand dunes and fall asleep. When we woke up we would have a couple of glasses of champagne, eat our sandwiches and fall back asleep. We spent our time there until it got either cold or dark or we got hungry and thirsty again. Sometimes we would go directly to a movie theater and watch a show. I can still remember the night we went to "Alien" which had the tag line, "In space, no one can hear you scream." Sigourney Weaver was in it but a good actress does not always make the movie good. Such was the case with "Alien."

JP told me she was in the process of going through an uncontested divorce. I heard many stories about how she was mistreated. She was forced to go out and shovel the driveway when she was in her ninth month of pregnancy. She said when she and her husband broke up he had taken her dog and had it put to sleep. I could not imagine what type of hideous monster would do something like that. Her husband sounded like a first class jerk. JP and I continued to grow closer and closer and we were trying to steal as many minutes away together as we could. There did not seem to be enough hours in the day for us. JP told me she had a little blonde haired boy by the name of Matt who was three years old. I had never met him because he was always home with his dad or his sitter.

Within a couple weeks of working in Manitowoc, I rented a great apartment up on the second floor of an old mansion about a mile or two from the hospital and only about a mile from the shores of the lake. JP would spend most of her time off with me and the times we were not working we were either in bed at my apartment or on a blanket soaking up sun on a sand dune. It was hard not to be happy. I really enjoyed working with our staff. We were one big happy family and even better was the fact we functioned as a well-oiled unit during life threatening emergency situations.

Shortly after getting the apartment, Michelle Mears, a Physician's Assistant from St. Cloud moved in with me. Michelle had traveled with me around Wisconsin a bit. We had looked at a practice in Tomahawk, Wisconsin and had a nice job offer from there. An older physician who worked there wanted to retire. His office was in an older brick building and the inside of the office was dated. The practice was fine but I would have been the only doctor caring for the community and I did not like the idea of being on call all of the time. It seemed for a while as if Michelle and I would end up working together.

That part would have been ideal, both of us working together day after day. No doubt Michelle would have made a great assistant, not to mention she was a gorgeous blonde with an uplifting personality. That was not all that was gorgeous about Michelle. She observed what went on in the emergency department while I was working and she also traveled back and forth to Dubuque with me. She was a fun companion and a quick study when it came to medicine. She was helpful in every way the same as she had been when we worked together in St. Cloud.

Michelle and I got along great while we were living together. It was a platonic relationship most of the time. We got into a bit of an argument one night when Michelle complained to me, "I don't know if I would have come to live with you if I knew you had a bedroom that was like Grand Central Station." I said, "Why on earth should that make any difference to you? It is not like our relationship is any more than friends." She replied, "I really do not like to see all the girls coming and going." I thought perhaps Michelle cared more for me than she let on. From my perspective, she would have been an easy person to fall in love with.

A great thing happened. Gary Weeks came in one day during the first couple weeks in the hospital and wanted to know if he could show me new sleep quarters. The new quarters were up on the fourth floor of the hospital in a room as far removed from the elevators as you could get on the north end of the hospital. The room was huge, all you could want for your private bedroom. The only trouble was now you were so far away from the emergency department you would be short of breath by the time you got there if you ran down the stairs during a true emergency. John Hodson, Michael Barton nor I complained. We were happy to have been moved away from the coolers and onto a floor that was no longer used, so we had complete privacy.

Our crews of ambulance paramedics were dynamite to work with. They could handle some of the absolutely worst trauma or cardiac arrests and always get the patient to our emergency department in the best shape we could hope for. One of the first days I worked with the director of our paramedics, I told him, "If you get the patient to me alive, I can almost with certainty guarantee you, if at all humanely possible from my side of the equation, that person is going to walk out of here alive a few days later." That same director came to me a couple of months later and said, "You weren't kidding were you. It seems everyone we bring to your emergency department walks out a few days later. You cannot imagine how good that makes our crews feel to know they are turning over their patient directly to a physician trained to take care of them and not arrive in an empty emergency department to wait up to half an hour for a staff physician to get there. And what is worse, if the patient has something their doctor is not trained to handle, we wait again for someone to be called."

I think ED crews become more closely knit because they always work very closely together and are trying to save the life of someone on the gurney who is very close to the people standing just outside your door. You are the one who has to go out there and tell them their little one is going to be just fine. In the other tragic times when the life saving split second is not offered, you are the bearer of unthinkable news to those people outside the door.

One night a young man come in who had put a rifle to his temple and shot himself in the head. His mother was first standing in the doorway screaming, "Save my son!" I performed a craniotomy on him and I could still hear her when the door was closed. Sometimes it is best not to save someone's son. That is a hard call to make when you have a teenager lying on your table with their pulse going down rapidly to where the heart rate is thirty and the blood pressure is well over two hundred systolic and the diastolic is over one hundred and fifty. This happens only when the brain is getting ready to herniate through the base of the skull and all life will cease in seconds. The mother is still screaming as the skull is broken away around the bullet hole and as you are hit in the face with brains and blood, you know your error. Let him die!

Unfortunately, as I said before, you do not get do overs. That eighteen year old young man lived. His mom would probably live many deaths over and over as she would watch him lying in a bed for years in a fetal position. I talked to the neurosurgeon that night in Green Bay where he was transferred. I asked, "I should have let him die, shouldn't I?" He said, "Of course I can say that now. Everything looks clear through our retro-spectro-scope." Yes, looking back we know the right thing to do. Sometimes.

I am going to fast forward a year in time when you will see that perhaps the young man described above, now a patient in a fetal position lying in a bed up on the third or fourth floor, serves a purpose in life. JP handed me a chart one night and said, "We have a young man in here who wants to end his life." I handled these cases in almost as many different ways as we have people wanting to do this. I talked with this young man at length and asked him what he was going to do. He said he was going to put a gun to his head and pull the trigger. I always have to read these people right because if I read them wrong I am going to have a death on my hands. On this evening I asked the young man to follow me. We took the elevator up to the third floor, walked down the hall together and into the room of the young man I had partially saved almost one year ago. I said, "This nineteen year old man had the same idea. Fortunately we managed to save him." He looked wide eyed at the young man wasted away in fetal position. I said, "See this empty bed beside him. I have saved that bed especially for you. You just let me know how long you want us to hold your reservation." He changed his mind and wanted to go home.

Of course, this would not end well for me. I was called down to administration the morning of my next shift. Both Don Orleans and Gary Weeks were in a bad mood. They asked me what on earth I thought I was doing bringing a suicidal patient up on the floor and violating the privacy of a patient. I said, "The patient didn't seem to mind. In fact he said nothing." This was not the reply they wanted to hear from me. They asked, "Don't you know we could be sued for you doing something like that?" I asked who was going to tell anyone since the young man lying upstairs was in a vegetative state. I wondered which of my nurses had squealed on me. I decided it was probably one of the nurses on the floor since they had no more allegiance to me than any other physician. I knew my emergency department nurses protected me to the max all the time.

I said to Don and Gary, "Look, I made a mistake taking a one in a million chance to save our patient up on the floor nearly one year ago. If that person can now save the life of another young man, I wanted to take it. That was within my discretion. I knew it was wrong. But, I was willing to take the chance and I think that chance worked. I think the young man I took up there will always see that young man lying there curled up in fetal position in a vegetative state, knowing it could have been him. He will not want to end up that way. My tragic save of one life may be a lifesaver for another. I'm sorry." I walked out. Nothing more ever came of that episode. It was never mentioned again.

Let me explain my statement of one in a million. One time during my training a person came in who had shot himself in the head much the same as my young patient had. In that particular instance the bullet had just ricocheted around in the skull for a distance but the patient survived and was neurologically intact. That is the chance I had taken when I performed the craniotomy on the patient who did not have that same end result. Lead poisoning usually does not have happy endings.

Not all the time spent in the emergency departments is serious and some serious things you handle also have a humorous side. One night I was working on a patient of Nate Owens', one of those grand old doctors who took care of everybody. I was running a code on one of Nate's patients who had a cardiac arrest. Nate came in the room while I was working and I said, "Nate, this doesn't look good." The code had been difficult and dicey all along. I had pulled out all stops.

Just about that time the patient's heart arrested and we just could not get it going again. Nate was watching and said, "I will go out and tell the family." I agreed that would be fine. About sixty seconds later the patient's heart started beating spontaneously with a strong regular rhythm. We started doing CPR again after another arrest. Then the patient grew stronger and stronger. Nate stopped back in the room to tell me he had let the family know their dad had passed away. I explained what had happened so Nate stood and watched his patient. By now this was at least one half hour after Nate had told the family of the patient's death. Everything kept moving along and the patient continued to maintain blood pressure and pulse. After about an hour had passed, Nate asked me, "Rick, what do I tell the family now? I can hardly go out and tell them we made a mistake and their dad is alive." I said, "Just wait a little bit Nate, he is not out of the woods." About that time the patient arrested again and we pulled out all stops but the patient died this time in spite of all of our heroics.

I think Nate probably breathed a small sigh of relief. But now he was worried about what the death certificate would say. He asked, "What if they look at the death certificate and see it says the time of death was an hour after I told them their dad was dead?" I said, "I do not think they are going to notice something like that Nate and if they do they will just think they looked at their watch wrong when you told them." Later that was a little funny but not at the time.

I got to know Nate a lot better over the next several months. He was probably in his mid-fifties to early sixties and practiced with a couple of young family practitioners in Manitowoc. Nate had been the president of the American Medical Association a few years earlier, had a great reputation as a physician and had a soft easy going demeanor. Nate had one trait that distinguished him from many other physicians and made him great. He was one of those guys who would never let a patient go untreated or cared for. He was indeed in a class almost all by himself. Whatever class ranks above 'class act' is definitely the class Nate was in.

One night I had called over one half dozen physicians to care for an inebriated individual in our emergency department. Each doctor had in turn refused. The person was someone who abused our department on a regular basis. Our doctors had literally had enough of this person. He would end up coming to the emergency department by ambulance for a minor injury or complaint and want to be cared for.

Emergency departments have one ongoing problem. When someone presents to your emergency department and is obviously intoxicated, you almost always have to keep them at least long enough to get them past their period of impairment. On this particular evening after refusals from several of our staff physicians to come in and care for this person, I finally called the one person who I knew would never refuse. I explained my problem to Nate and he replied as I knew he would, "Well Rick, just admit him under me, write a couple of orders for admission and I'll be in to see him in a little bit unless you are concerned he needs to be looked at sooner. Someone needs to take care of the poor guy." I breathed a sigh of relief. Dr. Nate Owen always came through. I thanked him profusely, apologized for calling him and told him he was my last chance. He reassured me and said, "It is not a problem, Rick." It was a problem for me though. Each one of those physicians who had turned me down had a duty to come and take care of that unwanted individual. They knew I would eventually have to find someone to admit him. I suspect a number of them, if not most, probably knew that someone would be Nate.

It is easy to understand where doctors come from. There are certain members of our community who will always be the first to request care when they are having medical problems but do very little to help themselves. Patients who come to the emergency department in an impaired condition also require care and they are covered by federal guidelines called the COBRA or EMTALA laws. Please bear with me a minute or two while I burden you with some federal laws and guidelines that affect all of us. These guidelines are contained in the Federal Emergency Medical Treatment and Labor Act, also known as the Anti-Dumping Laws. These laws require hospitals to provide an examination and the necessary stabilizing treatment without consideration of insurance or the ability to pay when a patient presents to an emergency room for care of an emergency medical condition.

In other words, a patient falls under the guidelines of the Consolidated Omnibus Budget Reconciliation Act of 1986. EMTALA is Section 1867 (a) of the Social Security Act which is within the section of the U.S. Code which governs Medicare. EMTALA was a law passed as a part of the COBRA laws and covers all participating hospitals. Unless a hospital participates they cannot accept payment from the Department of Health and Human Services or Centers for Medicare and Medicaid. It applies to all hospitals in the U.S. except the Shriners Hospital for Crippled Children and most military hospitals. These laws apply to all patients, not just Medicare patients. The purpose of the statute is to prevent hospitals from rejecting patients, refusing to treat them or transferring them to "charity hospitals" or "county hospitals" because they are unable to pay or are covered under Medicare or Medicaid. One very real problem with this law is that if you go into an urgent care center that does not have a contract with the federal government, the care center cannot see you. If you are having a heart attack it is your tough luck, thanks to your government at work for you.

The trouble with all these laws is that often the only people who know about them are the patients who abuse them all of the time and there is no easy way to put an end to it. Let me give you an example of a patient I will call Johnny. He likes to drink at a bar several miles from his apartment. Fortunately for Johnny the bar he frequents is located very near a hospital. He calls the ambulance service, says he is having chest pain and he goes to Hospital A. Johnny arrives at Hospital A, has his usual requisite tests done and then he goes over to the bar and drinks for the night with his friends and gets a ride home with one of them.

Sometimes patients use the ambulance to get to the local bingo game close to a hospital. They may use slightly different stories but they know which complaints will get them the fastest service from their 'yellow cab'. Shoot, I forgot, it is not the yellow cab it is the white "van" with the "red cross" and the word AMBULANCE in front. The great thing about these expensive rides is that society pays for it. There is no reason for these abusers to stop using an ambulance. Even though it costs society several hundred dollars, it saves them twenty dollars for the cab ride. Despite explaining this over and over to the abusers, their answer was usually, "I just did not have money for a taxi." Well, I asked, "How do you have money to drink?" The answer of course was they would not have money to drink or play bingo if they paid for a taxi and why do that when an ambulance is free.

One evening while I was on call a person who came into the emergency department was lying down on a gurney covered with a sheet from the waist down. I asked him what seemed to be the problem. He replied that a block of granite had fallen on his feet. I asked him, "How heavy was the block?" He said, "Oh, about 60 tons." I am sure my eyes got pretty wide and I exclaimed, "Sixty tons?" He said, "Yeah, about that much." I pulled off the sheet and sure enough, it looked like 60 tons had fallen on his feet. He had tall laced up work boots on. But from the front of the ankle on out to the tips of the toes he had feet shaped like Daffy Duck. Everything was squashed out completely flat. It just looked really funny. It took us the better part of an hour to get his work boots cut off. When we did, we saw pure white feet that had all of the blood squeezed out of them. The feet from the front of the ankles on were about half a centimeter thick. When you looked at the bottom of the feet, all of the metacarpals had been forced right through the skin. There was really nothing I could do for him and he denied any pain. I imagine those pain fibers were so squashed they could not carry an impulse.

I looked to see who was on ortho for the evening and it was a young orthopedic surgeon by the name of Barry Bast. He was about the same age as me and we got along great. I gave him a call and told him I had an interesting case he had probably never seen before. Barry said he'd be right there. When Barry walked into the room I introduced him to the patient who by now had a sheet covering him again. When Barry pulled off the sheet, his eyes grew wide and suddenly he started laughing. He apologized to the patient but continued to laugh a little. He said, "I have never seen anything like this in my life." Indeed, the feet looked like Daffy Duck's. By now it was seven or eight o'clock at night and Barry told the patient they were going to have to do a midfoot amputation but it could wait until morning. Barry admitted the patient and scheduled him for surgery. When Barry arrived in the morning, the patient's feet had re-vascularized during the night and were now the size of great big foot shaped clubs. A couple of months later that patient left the hospital in a wheel chair with both of his feet and they looked relatively normal.

John Hodgson's and my relationship with the hospital staff grew steadily. The staff gradually came to realize what a blessing we were for them to have around. One of the cardiologists said to me one day how happy he was to see I was working that night. I asked why and he said, "Rick, do you know how terrified I get if they call a code up in the unit? We are not used to handling codes; they come few and far between and our nurses can handle them better than most of the cardiologists." I reassured him he didn't have to worry. I also told him if he ever had a code he felt uncomfortable with and I was in the hospital to call me up to the unit. I would be glad to help him out if he needed me.

Soon we were invited to all of the staff gatherings and it was not long before we were going to barbecues and other get-togethers. We had become well ensconced in our space. In spite of how much I enjoyed emergency medicine, I really missed family practice and doing surgery and decided I was going to start doing family practice again in Dubuque. I was spending too much time working for Mid-American to enjoy life and JP and I enjoyed life to the max. Both John Kirkpatrick and Griff had come to know me and they had asked me to start bidding their contracts for them with other hospitals. They said I just did a far better job than they did. It seemed if I was not working in an ED I was in our Navajo with our full time pilot Randy Pilgreen, a pleasant guy a few years older than me who worked full time as a pilot for Mid-American. Griff and John made the Navajo and Randy available and at my disposal. Randy and I became close friends and he got me around the countryside in good style. Having your own plane and pilot was immensely valuable. When you did not have to run your schedule according to the airlines, you could often get three days of work crammed into one.

One of the first big multi-million dollar contracts I got to bid was with Rockford Memorial Hospital in Rockford, Illinois. Rockford was a very busy emergency department and they had several ED physicians. The contract for Rockford Memorial was owned by a physician by the name of Marty Sands.

Generally ED contracts would run for one year at a time and the hospitals would always be looking for someone who could provide the services a little less expensively while adding benefits. The reason we were bidding the Rockford contract was because it was up for bid again. Dallas, the administrator of Rockford, wanted the services of Mid-American but he also wanted to keep the physicians they presently had working. He felt they had a good staff who all did a good job and worked well with their staff physicians.

I found out the physicians in their emergency department were being grossly underpaid and I had a hard time imagining what hold Marty Sands had on them. Obviously I could not get this contract unless I could convince the physicians currently working in the hospital of the advantages of working for Mid-American. When I approached all of them, I really didn't have a lot more to offer other than an increase in salary of ten dollars per hour. Even though that was a significant increase pay, to the credit of those young physicians, they stuck with Dr.

Sands and continued working for him. That was one contract we did not get.

In the early years of emergency medicine there was often no allegiance by hospitals to their emergency department physicians. Emergency medicine had not yet become a specialty. For these very reasons there was often no social commitment from ED physicians working a contract. Most of the itinerant physicians lived elsewhere. They would come in and fill their shift and when the shift was done be out the door and on their way home.

Working in the emergency departments was a way to supplement their incomes while they were performing indentured servitude in their residencies and internships. This was not much different from someone working at McDonald's and the hospitals had about the same ties to their emergency department doctors as McDonald's has to their workers. It was all understandable. The young physicians we hired knew they were not going to be working in the emergency department for the rest of their lives. Most of them were in so much demand to fill emergency department slots they were very independent. In more direct terms this meant if they did not like something, they said to hell with you and went on to the next needy hospital.

We staffed the hospitals with the best physicians we could recruit but the talent varied widely. There was not a good way to determine what their particular skills and weaknesses were when hiring young doctors. I would always ask if there were any problems they might encounter they would not feel comfortable with but often young doctors had not yet identified their weaknesses. How can you know if you cannot handle something if you have never seen it? Many of them voiced a concern they would not be conformable handling an obstetrical delivery, routine or not.

When I recruited physicians for our emergency department contracts I would try to recruit the person best suited for the job at the time. I first wanted family practitioners because they could handle most everything that came into the department. My second choices were pediatricians and general surgeons. I would use internists if they were comfortable suturing up a laceration. Even though all of us in our training years are exposed to just about everything, there are still things we have not been exposed to.

My time with Mid-American became more demanding and if I was not on a plane between emergency departments, I was in one of the departments working. There came one point in time when I did not set foot in my home in Dubuque inside of six months. It was getting to be too much. Not only that, Kim was driving up to see me on my available weekends every other weekend she was free. Jan was driving up to see me on alternate weekends.

Sometimes Randy would pick me up very early in the morning and we could be in Minneapolis, Madison and Chicago all within the same day. It was a great way to pick up physicians and their spouses and show them the different hospitals where we had slots available. Doing all of this while flying commercially would have been a nightmare. Bringing hospital administrators to our office in Madison while we were trying to seal a deal for a new ED contract was also very beneficial. The administrators could immediately see Mid-American was successful. The ride back home in our plane with a full bar supplying cocktails during the flight was not unwelcome either.

During this time a new physician came to work with us by the name of Michael Barton, a 65 year old general surgeon of the Jewish faith. He was a little blunt and abrasive at times but we got along well and perhaps part of that was he never exhibited those traits to me. Michael had an interesting life history. He had been in WWII and had fought against Rommel in North Africa. He had also been on the Israeli Olympic Boxing and Swim teams and had driven the Grand Prix Circuit in Europe for two years. Mike was truly a man of many talents and interests. Through all this Mike wanted to come to the United States. Another of his goals in life was to become an American grandmaster in chess. When he arrived in the United States he joined the Manhattan Chess Club. Mike played chess at the club regularly and one day when no one was around and he was looking for a game, one of the other regulars at the club introduced him to a very young chess player he thought would give him a good game. Mike sat down to play this young kid who was chewing on a candy bar and whose hair was sticking out in all directions. Mike said he learned the youngster's name was Bobby Fisher who later became one of the greatest chess players in the world.

Mike and I got along well and nights we were both off we would occasionally go out and get a bite to eat and have a couple of drinks. One night I asked Mike if he would go to this one bar with me. There were about one hundred motorcycles around it. Both Mike and I had been warned to stay away from this bar but I thought I would like to see what it was all about. When we walked in the door the bar suddenly became eerily quiet. Everyone turned around to look at us. They were not overly friendly looks. Then suddenly this big deep base voice from down at the end of the bar yelled down to me, "Doc, welcome to our house." Walking toward us from the end of the bar was this gigantic biker I had stitched up a couple of times in the ED. His thumbs were as big as my wrists. The rest of the bar turned back to their drinks. Suddenly we were okay. My biker friend bought us a couple of drinks, we talked for a while and he told us to hurry back when we were preparing to leave.

Not long after Michael joined me I met another young physician in Madison at a party hosted by Mid-American. David Olp was a handsome young man with a smiling personality and pleasant demeanor whose companion was a beautiful blonde named Sherry. Dave had taken a couple of years of radiology and a little training in internal medicine. He said he had not yet decided what he wanted to do in the field of medicine. I asked Dave if he wanted to come and do family practice in Dubuque. Dave said he would like to give it a try. I told him I was just starting a practice in Dubuque and to stay in touch.

You see strange things in the emergency department. One night a patient came in and said his doctor was Dr. Schmeikel, a general surgeon, and he wanted his doctor called. The patient said he had sat on a flashlight and it slipped into his anus. JP was the nurse for the patient and so she called Dr. Schmeikel, who arrived shortly. JP had all the instruments ready to do a sigmoidoscopic exam. While he was looking through the scope, JP quietly asked him, "Do you really think there is a flashlight up there?" Dr. Schmeikel replied, "I'm not sure but if there isn't, he has a light from someplace else up there shining back at me." If you are an ED doctor stories such as this are voluminous.

One night I went into an examining room to see a young man sitting on the examining table. When I asked what was wrong, he told me he had an embarrassing problem. I reassured him. I said, "I am relatively sure anything you tell me will be something I have heard or seen a dozen times before." He looked a little relieved. I asked, "Okay, what seems to be your problem?" He said, "My girlfriend and I were having sex last night and she put a small wooden ice crusher up my ass." I asked him how big it was and he made a small circle with his thumb and index finger. I then asked how long it was and he held out his hands with about eight inches between his forefingers. I put on a glove and did a rectal exam on him and did not feel anything. I asked him if he was having any rectal or abdominal pain or if he'd had a bowel movement since they lost their toy. He replied, "No I'm not in any discomfort and I have not had a bowel movement since yesterday." I asked him if they had been drinking when they were messing around and if he was sure it was in there. He replied they were drinking a little and he was sure.

I said, "Look, something as small as you describe will come out the first time you have a bowel movement. Usually that is nothing to worry about. What I want you to do is just go home and eat normally. If this has not come out by tomorrow morning or you develop any abdominal or rectal pain of any kind I want you to see your personal physician or come directly back to the emergency department. At the very worst, it is still no problem; we will do a proctoscopic exam where we look through your anus and into the bottom of your large bowel and we will simply retrieve the ice crusher. Don't worry, it will more than likely come out with your first bowel movement."

JP and I were off the next morning so we went out by the lake and hung out in the sand dunes for the day. We really had an idyllic life and there wasn't much about it I would change. We both had a couple of days off together and ran around and had fun.

When I returned to work a few days later, as I was walking down the hall from the front of the hospital I could see the young man I had seen a couple of days earlier who complained of having a foreign object up his anus. Not only that, he was bent over and appeared to be in discomfort or pain. I saw him and exclaimed, "What on earth are you doing here?" I was immediately concerned and was afraid of what he was going to tell me.

He said, "That ice crusher hasn't come out yet." I said, "You were to see your doctor or get back into the emergency room immediately if it did not pass with a bowel movement the following day or if you started to have abdominal pain." My patient said, "For God's sake, do you think I was going to tell that embarrassing story to another doctor?" I, of course, could not remember the last time I had been embarrassed by a medical problem.

It was now three days since the incident, he had not had a bowel movement in that time and now he was complaining of abdominal pain. I did an exam of his belly and was relieved to find his abdomen was soft. At least I was relatively sure he had not gotten a hole in his colon. My nurse for this night was Valerie, one of our younger nurses who had not, I thought, been exposed to a lot in the world despite her nursing background. I asked her to set the patient up for a sigmoidoscopic exam and to get out a snare in case I needed it. A snare is kind of just like it sounds. It is a long slender hollow tube longer than the sigmoidoscope. A very thin wire fits through the tube and comes out the end. It is like a small wire lasso. When the distal end of the wire goes through the snare it automatically widens when it is pushed through the end. This allows you to put your lasso around any object you come in contact with and hopefully pull that object out the way it went in. A snare was usually put around a polyp we might see in the colon to remove it to be examined through the microscope after slides were made.

Valerie had put the patient in a comfortable kneeling position over the jack-knifed table. I inserted the sigmoidoscope and went in about seven or eight centimeters and at this point I could see the end of the ice crusher. But the end I was looking at was about double the size he had explained to me. I was not sure the snare was going to be large enough to retrieve this foreign body. After maneuvering the snare around a bit, I was mildly surprised and easily able to fit my snare over the round end of what I thought was more like a small bat. As I started removing my sigmoidoscope, fortunately the end of the foreign body came along with it and once I had my gloved fingers around the end, I removed my snare. I then began pulling out a long and then longer still, little league baseball bat with Louisville Slugger written neatly up the side. I could not help but noticing Valerie's eyes through all of this. Her large blue eyes were literally the size of saucers.

My patient groaned with relief. The blank look on Valerie's eyes remained. We lowered and flattened out the table and I asked my patient to roll over on his back. I examined his abdomen again and it was soft and unremarkable. I asked him to sit up and asked if he had any questions. He said none and was obviously anxious to leave our department. I asked him if he wanted his little slugger and he said no with an embarrassed look on his face. No one in the department wanted it for their boys either. I guess no one was interested in a bat with a story behind it or a 'behind' with a bat in it.

I relayed this story to a friend who worked at the emergency department in Hurst-Euless-Bedford (HEB) midway between Dallas and Fort Worth. Mary Jo just laughed when I told her the story. I told her the funniest part of the story was the look in my nurse's eyes when the bat was retrieved. She said that the prior week a rather large lady had come in because of a vaginal discharge and an itch. On the vaginal exam they found a dead canary in the vaginal canal. I guess they thought removing the canary would probably solve her problems. They didn't find any eggs. After you have practiced medicine long enough there is literally nothing that can surprise you.

Chapter Twenty-four

Double Duty

I started arranging my schedule in the emergency department so I would get off every Friday at noon. I would return Monday morning and start the shifts over again. I did this to arrange my time in Dubuque so I could get a family practice started. I rented an office on the eighth floor of the Dubuque Building, an older building located in downtown Dubuque that occupied about a quarter of one city block. There were numerous offices located in the building but the only medical office was that of Drs. Thomas and Carol Sonnito. Tom and Carol would later become good friends. They traveled all over the United States doing forensic psychology. Tom had written a great book on voir dire, the process of jury selection.

I was still helping Mid-American bid contracts and hire physicians for their emergency departments. Randy and I flew to Minneapolis early one morning and picked up a physician by the name of Barry S. and his wife Pam. We brought them down to our office in Madison and proceeded from there to Dubuque. I wanted to show Barry the emergency department we staffed at Xavier Hospital to see if he would be interested in working there. One thing to keep in mind when you are hiring physicians, if you did not sell the wife, it was often going to be a tough sell to get her husband. Luckily for me Pam liked the area. One of the other things she liked was Finley Hospital. Pam was an ICU nurse and planned on working when and if they got settled in Dubuque.

I offered to Barry, "If you and Pam decide to practice in Dubuque, I can let you live in my condominium on Stonehill until you get a home of your own." Barry and Pam decided Dubuque suited them well. They liked my condominium and decided it would be an ideal place for them to live. I showed them the office I had worked in when I first came to Dubuque and showed them around the area. I did not introduce them to Carroll or Carroll's practice. I also let him know my plans to return to Dubuque. I let him know I would soon be opening a family practice clinic in the Dubuque Building but was still working with Mid-American for a short while until I could get everything set up.

I suddenly got an unexpected call from Jan one Sunday while I was busy in the ED at Holy Family. Jan said, "Rick, Carroll Sinnard just passed away a few hours ago today. I just heard it on the news. He seemed fine when he came in to work on Friday. They said he was forty-two years old. He would have been forty-three next month." Jan was still working at Dr. Sinnard's clinic. Suddenly the beautiful clinic Carroll had set up was empty. I felt badly for Carroll's wife Linda, their little boy Taylor, his family and for his office girls who were now suddenly out of a job. I had never talked to Carroll or Linda again following our parting. It was not because I had not wanted to. I saw them out at the Dubuque Inn a couple of times and thought about it, but foolishly did not act on it. I knew Linda would be devastated because she was dependent on the care and loving Carroll lavished on her and I could not see her going on about life on her own. Also, Linda was twelve years younger than Carroll so she had a lot of life in front of her and a lot to learn.

Jan called me a day or two later and said they were having Carroll's wake in a couple of days. She told me the funeral would be the day following. She asked me if I wanted to go. I told Jan I would like to honor Carroll but I did not want to be a distraction or make Linda or Carroll's family uncomfortable although I really only knew Linda. I said to Jan, "If you see Linda you can give her my condolences and tell her I am very sorry for her loss. And please give her a hug from me."

About one week after the funeral Linda Sinnard called me and said she wanted to meet with me if I would be okay with that. I assured her I would. She wanted to talk to me about what to do with Carroll's practice and wanted to run some ideas by me. I said I would be more than happy to come down and talk to her.

I was still running back and forth between Manitowoc and Dubuque. One of my ongoing thoughts was I absolutely could not continue to work the hours I was maintaining. If I kept up the same pace I was working and continuing to drive I would likely come to the same end as Carroll. It is just not good to be working from nine p.m. on Fridays to 8 a.m. Monday mornings, trying to make the five and one-half hour drive to Dubuque to be in the office by noon on Mondays and then, leaving at 4 or 5 p.m. on Fridays to be back in the ED at 9 p.m. I was working about 100 hours per week with 10 hours of driving thrown in if I was not driving in my sleep. Sometimes my driving was reckless. One day I slammed on my brakes as I was coming over a hill in the Wisconsin countryside and my Fuzz-Buster went off showing 140 mph. I barely got down to the speed limit when I topped the hill and fortunately did not get a ticket.

I had a few calls with Linda and told her what I had in mind. I said I was coming back to Dubuque to resume family practice. I asked her what she was planning to do with Carroll's practice. That was what she wanted to talk to me about. She asked if I would come back and practice in Carroll's office again. I said that would be ideal for me. I knew all of the office girls and got along with all of them just great. Too great with a couple of them, I guess. I knew it would feel empty in that office without Carroll, but thought if it all would work well with Barry, this might be a great new start.

I took a few days off and got together with Linda's attorneys. Linda looked great as she always did dressed up in a pant suit. We hugged, I offered my condolences about Carroll and asked how little Taylor was doing. At seeing me, Linda shed a few tears again and after a brief moment we proceeded with business. Linda introduced me to her attorneys, we discussed everything and together we negotiated what we both felt was a fair deal.

Shortly after Linda and I had conferred for a couple days, I introduced Barry to Linda and said I would have Barry work with Linda's attorneys on the final paperwork. Linda was happy with the negotiations and was going to have her attorneys draw up the papers to consummate the deal. During this negotiating I had been running back and forth between Dubuque and Manitowoc and was getting tired and worn out. I told Linda I would return to Dubuque for the final paperwork and then sign off on everything.

Instead I gave Barry the go ahead to sign the paperwork for both of us. There would still be time required to get everything set up for us to start work. I had resumed talking to our office girls and they were all excited to have me coming back to the office. We had all gotten along really well and it was going to be like a family reunion.

What I did not know in these final pre-signing moments was Barry was negotiating a contract for himself and cutting me out. It never ceases to amaze me how some people can allow you to take them in and even give them your home to live in and then with the ethics and morality of a snake cut the person out who has fed and clothed them. It was hard for me to imagine his wife Pam may also have been behind this duplicitous behavior. The complete deception and dishonesty of this individual was beyond my scope of reasoning.

I did not find out any of this until the day the contract was signed. Jan tearfully called me and informed me of Barry's dishonesty. She and the rest of the girls said Barry was a snake. They had all been privy to the dealings that were going on between Linda and me. They were just as excited about me coming back as I was. They were all happy not to be losing their jobs and we would all be working together again. Barry obviously did not understand in the slightest all of the loyalties that had already been developed between Carroll's office girls and me. Jan said everyone wanted to be working with me again, but she said, "We all agreed Rick, you do not want to be practicing with someone with the ethics of Barry S." Jan said all the office girls had talked and they agreed the office was not going to be a fun place to work anymore. The person who was to be their new employer already had won complete disfavor in the hearts of the people he now had to work with every day. What a stellar way to start a new path in life. Barry immediately lost his office nurse. Jan quit the day she heard what Barry had done.

Jan and I had been discussing things all along right up until the occasion of Carroll's death. I knew she wanted to come along with me in my new practice when I eventually started it. Now she had her opportunity. In spite of this minor bump, we were both excited. I guess the major lesson for me to take away from this was to know the moral fiber of my practice partner which I would eventually have found out, probably sooner than later.

I look at people like this potential partner and always wonder in awe.

How is it that some people grow up with no moral turpitude? Absolute depravity this severe eventually leads to deviation from the norms of treatment. If you are willing to deviate from truthfulness and bend societal rules you can never be a good physician to my way of thinking. None of Barry's behavior slowed me down much. I had already begun making the arrangements for getting an office so now I would move on as planned.

I rented an office on the eighth floor of the Dubuque Building with Jan's help. Little Janice McDonnell and her cold little hands helped me pick it out. I say that jokingly and with a smile on my face even now. It seemed like about every time Jan came out of a patient's room, they would exclaim, "Boy that little nurse of yours sure has cold hands!" When I heard the comment I would always chuckle or laugh a little and say, "She surely does." I thought, "You should try going to bed with her at night if you really want to know what cold hands feel like."

The office was kind of a rundown shack of a place that needed a lot of fixing. By that, I mean our little space was not so pleasing to the eye. There was electricity and there was no plaster falling off the walls, but the floors were that old type of alternating dark brown and light brown tile squares. It was a step down for little Jan and me, but the funny thing was it brought excitement to both of us. We were now embarked on a new journey, starting a new practice. The big old Dubuque Building itself was fine. And I loved the fact little Jan was going to be working alongside of me on a daily basis again. What a blessing. It is absolutely amazing how even the dreariest of circumstances are enjoyable when you use them as a growth experience and move on from them. We were going to have fun.

I managed to hire a receptionist through Jan by the name of Sheila Sharkey. Jan knew Sheila and thought she would be a tremendous asset in the office. Jan gave me a little warning however, that the Sharkey name in Dubuque carries a little baggage with it. The boys could get into trouble sometimes. I assured Jan it was doubtful to me they could have ever gotten into more trouble than I had. I met Sheila one Monday when I came into work. Sheila was a medium sized pretty brunette who was tremulous and obviously was frightened at the thought of meeting me. I tried to put her at ease. I asked, "What on earth is wrong? I'm not going to bite you." I smiled and shook her cold, sweaty hand, gave her a hug and said, "Relax, we're going to have fun here." Sheila told me she didn't know anything about being an office girl. I told her I didn't either and we could learn together. At that reply she laughed and the tension was gone. Jan was laughing too. I knew inside of the first five minutes I had a great start on my new office and these girls would be my friends and with me to the end.

Little Jan was great at getting things organized and she set us up similarly to what we had going in Carroll's office. She had gotten in touch with Hawkeye Medical Supplies which I believe was out of Iowa City. Jan and their salesman had come up with a good starting office inventory and from the very beginning I had everything I needed to see patients and give care in our fledgling office. Initially, we had two examining rooms which were going to have to do until a larger space became available.

It was interesting to me that as much fun as I had in the emergency department, I was always in a hurry to get back to Dubuque for my family practice. Things were slow at first and everything we did was a learning experience for all of us. When I would come in the office for the first month or so, I would lean back in my chair and catch all the sleep I could. Sheila asked me one day, "Aren't you worried we'll never get any patients in here?" I said, "Not at all. Just enjoy these slow times because it will not be long before you are working late every night and won't have time for lunch." Later on, Sheila would remind me of that statement many times. Sheila said, "It was like you were a fortune teller." I said, "No Sheila, I just know how I practice medicine. I just treat people the way I want them to treat me. If you do that you will always have too much to do."

That we did. We always had too much to do.

I had my usual problems applying for privileges. The doctors in Dubuque just did not want you in town if you were a family practitioner. Their problems were obvious to me. How could they know what privileges to give a family practitioner when they did not know how to do family practice? After all, the only part of family practice they could do was the one tiny part of their specialty. A family practitioner could not be as smart as they were, could he?

Let me give you an example. This happened later in my time in Dubuque but the example fits in well here. While I was down scrubbing in for surgery one day I ran into one of our ENT doctors, Dr. Tom Benda. I had just referred one of my patients to Tom and he had done a very complete and thorough workup on a patient of mine with labyrinthitis. He had left no stone unturned. I asked, "Tom is it always necessary to do so many tests on a patient with labyrinthitis?" Tom replied, "Absolutely, Rick. Almost all patients referred to me with labyrinthitis are given the tests I just did on your patient. Why do you ask?" I replied, "I was just trying to get an idea what patient population you see and now from your answer, I can guess. The reason I say this is for about every one to two hundred patients I see with labyrinthitis, I refer about one to you. I am guessing all the other doctors must do the same. The other several hundred patients we see with labyrinthitis we don't refer to specialists all get well on their own. You are seeing all of our stubborn ones. The rare 'problem child' for us, so to speak. Actually, most of our patients are adults." Tom looked at me completely bewildered. I think it was the first time he ever realized what a skewed population of patients he saw. Now let's get back to the specialists.

How the hell are they supposed to know what a family practitioner can and cannot take care of? Obviously if Dr. Benda had gone through my charts he could have or would have incorrectly surmised I had not taken proper care of one hundred to two hundred patients. Wouldn't he? After all he knows all patients deserve a far more complete exam than what a family practitioner gives. On the other hand, suppose one hundred family practitioners went through Dr. Benda's charts. Could they rightly assume Dr. Benda had purposefully ordered boat loads of tests on his patients so he could afford a nicer car? Of course not! They are both wrong in their assumptions, aren't they? How do we meet in the middle on these battle grounds? We have to you know if we ever want to return to good medical care in the United States.

Because of the skewed patient populations specialists see, they cannot possibly be given the job of deciding what family practitioners can do in their clinics or hospitals. But this is often the case and the specialist greatly limits what the family doctor can do. Why not? Then the patient with the minor ear ache can go to the ENT doctor and get better care. Right? No, that is wrong. The patient will hopefully get the same care from both physicians. But here comes the problem, the specialist had to go to another five years of school to learn about all the other small infrequent or rare things in their specialty they do not get to see enough of every day to make a living. Therefore, they are delegated to seeing the minor mundane things day in and day out simply to make ends meet. Because there are so many specialists they have to protect their turf. They can only do this by limiting the privileges of all the physicians around them as much as they can or they will not achieve the level of comfort in life they thought their specialty would provide. Eventually the specialists even believe they offer better care; however quite the opposite is true. For the most part nothing works as well as knowing your whole patient. That is why our nation survived so well and for so long with only family practitioners.

Another thought to ponder, why is it the age of our population is not continually on the rise? Shouldn't our age be increasing a hell of a lot faster? If our age increased as rapidly as our healthcare costs have gone up, we should be living to about 500 years of age by now. It is probably going to take us that long to pay off our healthcare bills. After all now that we have a specialist for every possible imaginable body conflict, isn't it absolutely amazing we made it out of our teens without them? How did we get by without all of this technology and since we have all of this technology we should all live to be far older shouldn't we?

I would gradually get most of the privileges I wanted in Dubuque. Not all of them mind you. Especially not the privileges specialists thought they were the only ones smart enough to do. It made no difference to them I had done more surgery than the young surgeons entering the group practices in the city. The different boards would call me in to meet with them every time they had the chance in the beginning of my practice. I usually knew why I was going to be called in. Other times though I did not. The meetings in general dealt more with harassment that an actual treatment problem.

I was called in for an obstetrics board meeting one day. All our obstetricians were present in their entire imperial splendor. I sat down at one end of the table. They asked me if I knew why I was being called into their meeting. I said, "I would imagine you want me to answer a question or questions you specialists cannot answer. I will try to help you." Might as well start out with them pissed off at me because I knew that is how they were going to be when I left the meeting. They said, "Dr. Redalen, you showed up to do a delivery the other night and asked for some mouth wash." I replied, "I don't recall, but I guess so, if you say so. Am I here because I was impaired or am I here because I used mouth wash?" Their response, "No you are not here because you were impaired. Why did you ask for the mouthwash?" I said, "I had just finished an anchovy pizza at the Shot Tower. What should I have asked for? Another anchovy?" I stood up, turned abruptly, walked out and they all looked about as senseless as they had when I walked in. At least you can see why many doctors become specialists. Ordinary physician practice life is too onerous for them.

It is always interesting to me why meetings such as this are called. Who on earth brings it to the attention of someone when a physician asks one of his nurses for some mouthwash? Who has time for this kind of bullshit in their lives? On the other hand, perhaps the people concerned with insignificant things such as this do not really have a life. The other thing they would soon learn from me was that if you are going bear hunting, it would be wise to put bullets in your gun.

Jan and Sheila would always ask me after one of the staff meetings I had been called to attend to tell them what had happened. They knew the staff never called me in for the purpose of giving me a compliment. When I relayed what went on during the meeting they would tell me I should not keep saying things that made the other doctors mad at me. I always let them know it was not my intention to create controversy but it seemed to follow me. I also did nothing to make it go away. All the physicians in Dubuque wore suits to work every day. Even when a physician came in to see a patient in the emergency department during the night they had on a suit. I on the other hand almost always wore a pair of jeans and a casual shirt. Often on weekends I would be dressed in jeans and a t-shirt. No one ever commented on my manner of dress, but I did stand out from the rest of the physicians. And it was obvious no one appreciated the way I stood out from the physician crowd.

A new neurologist came on staff and we met walking down the halls of Finley Hospital one day. I introduced myself to Lynn Kramer, a pleasant, slender, dark haired gentleman with a friendly smile. Lynn was dressed in blue jeans and a casual shirt. He was a recent arrival in town and had joined one of the local groups. We talked a little bit and Lynn explained he and his wife were looking for a house and they thought they were going to enjoy living in Dubuque. I said, "I see you haven't been indoctrinated yet." Lynn replied, "What do you mean?" I said, "You're dressed the same as I am. That will change within the next week or two." Lynn got a funny look on his face and said, "Naw, that won't change, the way I dress will always be the same." A couple of days later I met Lynn again in the hallway of Finley Hospital wearing a fine-looking shirt and tie. Lynn obviously recalled our conversation and my indoctrination comment. We shook hands, looked at each other, smiled and then laughed a little. I said, "I see you're indoctrinated now. I believe what comes next is the country club circuit." I jokingly said, "See you on the links." He said, "You know Rick, I really didn't believe you, but you were right." As soon as Lynn said that, I realized I would never fit into one of those groups.

It seemed from my point of view most of the physicians in Dubuque belonged to the country club set. I'm not entirely sure why, but I never saw myself belonging to a group of people who separated themselves with artificial barriers from another group of people who could not probably afford to be there. I felt it was important for everyone to have equal opportunity and equal access. I am not sure what that access is. In Dubuque it seemed I fit in better with the pool shooting, beer drinking crowds in the small bars. I joined a pool league and always enjoyed my nights out. The games rotated through all the small establishments in the city and we were all really competitive but it was a good time. Our pool teams were made up of five players. One of our players would be paired off against one of their players. We would shoot games of eight ball and the winner would get a point and so forth on down the line. In eight ball one of the players breaks the rack of fifteen balls and depending on whether or not one is made on the break, that person shoots the ball made. So he or she will either shoot stripes or solids. If he makes both a stripe and a solid on the break he gets his choice. If a ball isn't made on the break then the other player gets to shoot and has their choice of stripes or solids. Once a player has made all of his balls he gets to shoot at the eight ball. The person who sinks the eight ball first wins the game and the point. I always did well in the league shooting because most of the pool players started drinking beer the minute they got there and continued until the minute they went home. I didn't drink beer so I always had an advantage. It was like I had a huge handicap because they were handicapped.

One day Sheila called me and said the pediatricians had called to request my presence at one of their noon staff meetings in a couple of hours. I asked her what they had requested. She said they wanted to talk to me about giving a steroid to a baby I had admitted with bronchiolitis. It seemed odd to me to be called to a pediatric staff meeting because of that, but I reluctantly went to the meeting. It was simply a nuisance as far as I was concerned. It was an inconvenience for the pediatricians to be there so they may as well inconvenience someone else. At least when you get called into a staff meeting they have the courtesy to act on whatever they want you to be there for, first. On this day one of the pediatricians said he didn't agree with me giving Depo-Medrol to a baby I had hospitalized a couple of weeks earlier in the pediatric unit. I handed out some journal articles that recommended giving steroids for bronchiolitis. I really did not think steroids helped much either but would not admit that to the doctor who disagreed with me. I said because of this baby's social situation I knew I could not completely depend on the parents to do everything that needed to be done. I thought a small long acting dose of steroids might possibly help and I certainly do not think it hurt. The pediatrician reiterated he would not have done it and he did not necessarily agree with the publications I had provided. I answered, "What you need to do then is write a book so the rest of us can have the benefit of your experience and I can get up to date with the best way to treat bronchiolitis." I asked if the other pediatricians had any more questions. They all smiled, not wanting to prolong the agony.

One privilege I did not have was to start an oxytocin drip on a patient to induce labor. I had admitted one of my OB patients to the obstetric floor at Finley and called Dr. Jim Hall in for a consultation. Can you imagine a group of obstetricians who are so hard up for work they are not even going to give me privileges to start an induction? Dr. Hall came into the room, I introduced him to my patient and he did a vaginal exam after which time we walked out. He said, "That woman's cervix is so hard she won't deliver in the next few weeks." I guess he disregarded the fact she was already overdue by a couple of weeks. I disagreed and asked him to write an order to start induction. He did so. The IV was started which pushed my patient into active labor so the drip could be immediately discontinued. My patient delivered a couple of hours later. I did not know where Dr. Hall went to school but he evidently skipped all his rotations. He certainly did not know when a cervix was 'ripe'.

I learned one thing in Dubuque while first there. If you want the doctor's lounge completely quiet all you had to do was to have me walk in. There would be instant unease and stillness. This did not last for long but it would continue as long as I was the topic of conversation.

During one of our noon meetings a doctor's staff privileges came up for review. The physician being discussed was a relatively new Indian physician from Dyersville. I had talked to him several times and he was a very pleasant gentleman. I really knew nothing about his professional credentials, although I have never met an Indian physician who was not superbly credentialed and knowledgeable. I had grown up in a state with many Indian physicians and it seemed all of them were very well trained. One Indian physician explained it to me this way. Most of the Indian physicians went to medical school in India, which had reciprocity with England so the physician went there for more training. England had reciprocity with Canada so this was one more step in their over-training curriculum. Canada had reciprocity with North Dakota and so in this circuitous route, they ended up being some of the best trained physicians in North Dakota and probably in our country. Nothing in my experience would lead me to think otherwise. What the doctors were discussing in this noon meeting was the doctor's treatment of a man he had hospitalized with hyperkalemia, high serum potassium. On the chart the patient had extremely high potassium and the doctor had initiated treatment. The staff physicians said the doctor should have known a person could not survive with potassium that high. He had stopped the treatment only a short while later when the repeat potassium came back as normal.

The hospital medical staff was voting to take away his privileges. At that time he was the only physician in Dyersville. Not only that, the physician in question was not present to defend himself. I could see the wheels turning. If Dyersville has no doctor those patients will have to come to Dubuque. That is a lot easier for me. Why should I, a well-trained physician living here, drive all the way to Dyersville every day just to see patients? After all, they only have to make the drive when they need to see a doctor or are sick. I'll have to go every day. Isn't my time more valuable than theirs?

It soon became obvious no one was going to support this man and allow him to keep his admitting privileges at the hospital. I decided to speak up for him and as usual was one against the masses. I asked, "What if the patient's potassium was really that high and what if it was very acute? What would you have done to this man's privileges if the potassium came back and was still elevated, not at a lethal level but still very high and he had not initiated treatment? You would surely have taken away his privileges and this time for doing nothing. Had the worst case scenario happened and the patient died, you would have surmised his lack of treatment was the cause of the patient's death. According to your thinking, he was going to be wrong no matter what direction he took." One physician said, "Dr. Redalen, you know a patient is not going to be alive with serum potassium that high." I replied, "Yes, I do, but to do nothing is taking that small chance for the repeat to come back at a nearly lethal range. What was hurt by the physician treating him? Absolutely nothing was lost." In spite of my using the best logic I could to defend this physician, they took away his privileges. They had their desired result, one less physician to compete with.

I want you to know that the majority of physicians and nurses are good people. Many if not most entered their professions for the correct reasons which I consider to be altruism and compassion. Indeed, almost all of them did if they entered our profession 30 to 40 years ago.

It was not long before our practice grew to a size that required a larger office if we were going to continue to adequately take care of everyone. We looked at a spacious area on the third floor and decided to relocate to that level. Our new office was going to be 3,000 square feet so it was going to provide all the room we would need. We had to look forward to the time we would be adding physicians to our group.

It was not long before Sheila, Jan and I were spending our spare time drawing up plans for how we thought the examining rooms should look and what size we thought they should be. When we thought we had a pretty good idea of how everything should fit in and look Shelia's husband Tom Sharkey, who had done a lot of construction, offered to help us lay everything out. Tom was in industrial construction and his expertise was invaluable. It did not take long for Tom to measure things out. I was working with him and soon under his guidance you could see a pretty good skeleton of chalk lines which gave us a clear idea where everything was going to go. I asked Tom if the people who came in to frame this would know what all the different arrows and lines meant. Tom smiled, laughed at me a little and reassured me they would know.

At this point in time all I had ever done was to simply meet Tom Sharkey when Sheila had introduced us shortly after she started working. I really hadn't gotten to know him very well other than as Sheila's husband. As I got to know him better, he had a great demeanor, ready smile and the good looks of someone who would have been a perfect fit on a movie set. He was about six feet tall, lean, muscular, strong, in good shape and fun to be around. Sheila had found a great husband and father for their children. As time went on I would come to know Tom a lot better and we would become good friends.

The office examining rooms were spacious but we managed to fit in six equal sized rooms facing the west side of our space. This gave all the examining rooms a bright feeling with a western exposure. Each room had its own windows looking out on the street below and brand new examining room tables also done in earth tones. And yet with the sunny exposure, people on the street below could not look into our rooms so it was ideal. We decided we had to have x-ray which was an enormous expense not to mention the leaded walls and door we had to provide. Everything was done in earth tones with beige carpeting. Our reception area was filled with modern furniture, orthopedically designed for ease of getting up and down. The furniture was bright orange and the fluorescent lighting made for a very cheery workplace. When it was all done, we were proud of the job we had done picking everything out.

My practice in Dubuque grew rapidly and I was soon booked to the very max number of patients I could see every day. One day when a county social worker was in my office, she said, "Dr. Redalen, you really amaze me." I asked, "Why is that?" She replied, "Two patients I just saw leaving your office are some of the very dregs of society." I did not tell her I had told the two people who had just left they had to have a shower before they could be seen. These two scruffy unkempt patients lived in a boxcar down by the river and probably bathed once a year if that. I had to do this for the protection of my other patients. They said they would get one and come back. And indeed they did. I don't know why they didn't think of this more than once a year. I told my patient social worker, "Everyone deserves healthcare and it is not up to me to sort out who receives it. I am here to provide it in equal measure."

A couple of days later one of my patients, William Blum, Sr., who was the patriarch of one of the wealthiest Jewish families in Dubuque and the father of our city attorney who was also the attorney for the Dubuque Human Rights Commission, asked me a question, "Do you know why I come to see you, Dr. Redalen?" I replied, "No, I do not." I knew he could certainly have his choice of any physician in the city. He said, "Because when I come here, you treat me just the same as you treat all of your patients and that is how I know I am getting good care." He added, "I do not want to receive special treatment because of who I am." I said, "I am pleased you have chosen me." The fact of the matter is, if a physician ever starts treating people differently because of their station in life, the person will be receiving poor treatment from that physician regardless of their station in life. All treatment must be equal and comparable. My Jewish patriarch's statement reaffirmed my thinking.

On this particular day, Mr. Blum was having a little shortness of breath. On examination, he was well oxygenated with pink mucous membranes, a clear chest and regular heart with no signs of failure, a soft abdomen with no enlargement of his liver or spleen and no pitting edema of his lower extremities. I could find no evidence of congestive heart failure which is what I suspected. His history really didn't go along with that and he was sleeping lying flat at night with only one pillow. I asked him to go up to Finley Hospital which is where I was doing most of my stress testing at the time. I say up because Finley Hospital is up on top of the hill due west from the office and on the same street.

I met Mr. Blum Sr. at Finley and the respiratory therapy department had him hooked up and ready to go when I arrived. We did a stress test with Modified Bruce Protocol. A stress test monitors a patient's electrical heart rhythm while they are exercising. It is performed by hooking up electrodes to a patient's chest much the same as when they have an electrocardiogram. We watch for changes in our patient, their electrical conduction and other parameters we think show they may be getting into trouble.

The stress test was negative but exercise capacity was diminished. I discharged Mr. Blum and asked him to see me in about one week. I asked him to gradually increase his daily walking regimen and to let me know if his breathing was getting better or to see me immediately if he got worse. About an hour after he left my office Dr. Blum called, "Dr.

Redalen, I have been walking around uptown and I got this really bad toothache. I was a little short of breath so I sat down and the toothache went away. I then started walking again and the toothache came back." I asked if he had anyone with him and he replied he did. I said, "Have them take you immediately to Mercy Hospital and I will have Dr. Mullapudi see you." I called Dr. Mullapudi and gave him the history on Mr. Blum and told him I suspected he was having angina and it was manifesting itself as a toothache. Mr. Blum had an immediate cardiac catheterization and ended up heading straight into surgery for a three or four vessel bypass. It was a prime example of not all heart attacks or angina necessarily producing chest pain.

Life in Dubuque became a lot more fun as time went along. I was still maintaining my travels between Madison and the various hospitals in Wisconsin with my time mostly spent in Holy Family Hospital in Manitowoc. I was doing almost no bidding for contracts and my time in Wisconsin was winding down. I had not yet talked to Griff and John about quitting work in the ED but in some ways they probably would have been thankful had I done so. Companies like Mid-American often lose contracts to their physicians. The main reason for this is obvious. The hospital administrator thinks if he can hire the physicians directly he can cut out the middle man, in this case Mid-American. The administrator asks their emergency room physicians if they would like to make a little more money and work directly for the hospital.

The physicians working for them may receive a little higher hourly wage. For instance, rather than $30 per hour they would be paid $35 or $40, the amount their employer is collecting for the contract. The physician forgets the huge value their employer provides by always being 'Johnny on the spot' when they have an emergency or family celebration they would like to attend and can do so because they are an employee. Their employer, such as Mid-American, takes up the slack and covers for them. Mid-American can do this with the hundreds of physicians on the payroll they can call for an unexpected favor. That part of being an employee is extremely valuable.

When a self-serving physician decides to undercut their employer just to make a few more dollars per hour the value of the employer is often realized the first time they suddenly have a vacancy and need to fill an ED shift or lose the contract. In that case, if they cannot find someone, they are the one to fill the shift.

Now they are the ones under the gun. Leaving a shift open in a large hospital is just not an option. These are multi-million dollar contracts and the hospital cannot suddenly let an entire staff of physicians who are covering their own practices risk an unattended emergency department. The staff physicians may have already planned on being out of town over night or for the weekend. That is a slight hospital administrators may lose their jobs for. If not their jobs, they certainly can lose their favor with the hospital staff.

I continued to have fun doing both types of practice. I loved emergency medicine but loved family practice more.

I managed to teach continually while I was in Manitowoc. I was called to the top floor one day with a code in progress. An elderly man was lying on the floor receiving CPR. I asked the nurse what was wrong. She said their patient was sitting in his chair eating and just started having a heart attack. I could see a plate of spaghetti and meatballs sitting on his tray. I grabbed away the mask from the person doing the ambu and said to get out of the way. I did a couple of large abdominal thrusts, reached down the man's throat and came out with a large meatball. This man would have surely died had I not come up for that code. I explained you have to play the percentages and if a person is eating something that can obstruct them, bet on an airway obstruction. They thanked me and I hoped they remembered.

On another day I was called into the radiology department for a code going on there. It was one of the family practitioners who practiced with Buzz. The ED team was running the code. I asked the physician on attendance what was going on. He said they were just doing an IVP and the patient had a heart attack. I said, "Give me the epinephrine. Your patient is having an anaphylactic reaction." He argued with me. I persisted, grabbed the epinephrine out of the crash cart and injected into the IV present to give the dye for the IVP. The patient promptly sat straight up and exclaimed, "What happened?" I said, "You just had an allergic reaction." The doctor just shook his head, realizing I had saved his patient. You can never get air through lungs in anaphylactic shock. What is worse, not recognizing it will invariably result in death.

I knew that once I had my practice built up enough I would be leaving emergency medicine. In Manitowoc, about the only practice I could see myself working in was family practice with Nate.

I just loved the way Nate took care of patients. They always came first. One morning, I got a call from Buzz, one of the family practitioners who worked in the office with Nate. Buzz asked, "Rick, have you seen Nate?" I replied, "No Buzz, why what's the problem?" Buzz said, "Nate didn't come in for work this morning. We called his wife who thought he was at the hospital working. We have had him paged and have called some ERs in the area and we cannot locate him. You and Nate were always such good friends; we just thought maybe he went to visit you." I apologized but said, "No, I have not seen him but will definitely keep my eyes open." I called later that afternoon and asked if they had seen Nate yet. Buzz replied "No, and there is no word from anyone. We also have the police department looking for him. His family is out looking for him too but has not seen him." I got a call from Buzz a couple of days later. Buzz, said, "Rick, I have some really bad news. The police department found Nate's car down by the lake parked under a tree in a hidden section of trees. Nate was sitting in the driver's seat with his feet up on the seat. He was looking out on the lake. He was dead. He had a bottle of empty pills and a bottle of booze that it looked as if he had finished." I said, "I am so sorry, Buzz. You know Nate was one of my closest friends in Manitowoc. I am so very sorry." I hung up the phone, went into my office, shut the door and cried. Some people are just so very special on this planet, it is no wonder God calls them home and wants their services up there.

I was back in Manitowoc a couple of days later and sought out Nate's partners to give them my condolences. They were still very traumatized and dazed. I think it is especially hard on physicians to lose a loved one or partner and to know you did not pick up on this and prevent it from happening. You are bound to shoulder a lot of the blame and responsibility yourself, although there is never anything you can do to prevent suicide. People who have made up their mind to take their life are going to succeed if not now, definitely later unless something changes drastically. The hospital was a very sad place too. They had all lost a loved one of their own. There were very few other physicians in Holy Family who were respected more than Nate. Some losses are absolutely irreplaceable.

I had now come to the place in time when I was ready to practice full time in Dubuque. I was anxious to get back. I guess it was just bad timing for all of us as John Kirkpatrick and Griff Ferrell called to meet with me. I had just finished my shift at the hospital and we met in the hospital corridor of Holy Family. By this time I had used almost every ounce of energy I had running back and forth between Manitowoc and Dubuque.

Griff and John approached me and said, "Rick, we have some great news for you. How would you like to take over all of Mid-American including our real estate assets and all our hospital contracts? We would set you up so that paying off the debt you would incur would be barely noticeable in your paychecks." It was a gigantic offer that would never come along again in my life. I would be immensely wealthy overnight. I said to Griff and John, "I have a better idea, how about if I quit and you find someone else to take over your enterprise."

Griff and John were shell-shocked. They exclaimed, "Rick, how can you pass up a chance like this? You may never have an opportunity like this again for the rest of your life!" I agreed with them. I said, "I have really enjoyed working with you guys and enjoyed all you have taught me about bidding hospital contracts. It has been a great learning experience for me, but I have grown tired. I do not think I can continue this pace much longer and hope to survive. I appreciate you both very much and know you will find someone to take my place." I left later that day and had not scheduled myself for any more shifts so it was the last time I would be driving this stretch of highway. It was a beautiful drive but I was not going to miss it.

It was nice to be practicing in our bright new office. We put an ad in the paper for an x-ray tech. We had a couple apply but it seemed to us as though no one was looking for a job. One person came in dressed in sloppy dirty blue jeans and an old paint stained shirt. To top that off she had her hair up in great big round curlers. I wondered what on earth was she thinking. We had a number of non-promising applicants like that. Finally Dianne applied, a pretty, curly haired blonde of medium build and height who seemed to be just the kind person we were looking for. After a couple of weeks on the job she showed us our judgment was sound.

The location of our office was a plus for us. It brought us in proximity to the largest population concentration of the city. After being in town full time for a couple of months, Monsignor Gannon from Loras

College came to talk to me one day. He said he had heard a lot of good things about me and asked if I would be on the board of the Jackson County Mental Health Center. He asked me to come to a picnic the board was having a couple days later, a barbecue at Eagle Point Park. I was allowed to bring a date as the other doctors on the board were all bringing their wives. Jan and I went to the picnic and mixed nicely with everyone. They all treated us nicely to our faces. Two of the doctors who were from Medical Associates also treated us kindly.

Two days later I would find out just the type of hypocrites Medical Associates had on their staff. Monsignor Gannon again came to my office. He looked a little chagrined and was wringing his hands. He said he felt very badly about coming to talk with me. Monsignor Gannon said after the picnic, he was approached by the physicians from Medical Associates, who told him if the Jackson County Mental Health Board brought Dr. Redalen on, they were all going to resign their positions on the board. Since the wives of the physicians also treated Jan and me kindly, I wondered what a husband says to his wife about his hypocritical ways. Can't gain them much of a measure of respect I wouldn't think. Hopefully they would not have to tell their children of their behavior. They would not like their children to grow up like them, I wouldn't think.

Not long after this, I was approached by the Tri-County Citizen's Committee on Drug Abuse and Alcoholism and asked if I would be their medical director. I gladly accepted. I soon started a Narcotics Anonymous Chapter. We had a good turnout for weekly meetings in one of the downtown office buildings that loaned us one of their conference rooms. It seemed everything that had previously caused me problems was now was presenting me with opportunities. I guess I was following the line, "If life gives you lemons, make lemonade."

Because of my activities in all of these drug related sidelines, I was becoming popular with a lot of other people who had drug problems in the community. I think they felt comfortable coming to me as they thought a doctor with recent problems similar to theirs may be a more understanding individual. I am pretty sure they were correct in their thinking. I did feel a closeness to all of these people. One thing you find out after having abused drugs for a couple of years, when a year has gone by you think 'I really have this whipped now and my thinking is pretty much back to normal'. Then year two rolls around and you think the same and so forth and so on. What I finally realized was it took me about five years before my thinking was truly what I thought was normal again. It was nothing you could really put your finger on, more of an indescribable feeling.

During my entire time in Dubuque, I was approached by people who abused drugs and wanted help. Most of the people did not want to be on drugs any longer. Often the drug scene had destroyed relationships that were precious to them. Drug use often left them broke and destitute. Many had lost their jobs and a good many had found themselves incarcerated. About the only benefit of being in jail is it gives the drug user a forced vacation from use. Incarceration in some cases saved the person's life.

One day I received a call from a surgeon's wife in Des Moines. She said she had read about me in the paper and thought I would have some understanding of what she and her husband were going through. She said they were having substance abuse problems. I definitely could sympathize with her and her husband although her husband did not know his wife was calling and he was the one abusing. She said he would probably have been furious if he knew she had called. I promised everything she said to me would remain between the two of us.

Her husband was a general surgeon and had been shooting up for the past two years. Like me, he was abusing Demerol, the doctor's cocktail. She said he wanted help but just did not dare go to a treatment center. She said he always took his medications with him and would go in the bathroom and shoot up immediately prior to surgery. I knew he was probably functioning well in surgery because no complaints had been brought against him and his wife said he got along with his nurses superbly. The above description of her husband is also what allows him to keep using. He is functioning well enough that none of his associates realize he is having a problem.

This is one of the big problems in medicine. Physicians who want to get help for an addiction face the consequences of discipline by their state medical board. Not only are they likely to be forced into treatment which often comes with a huge price tag but they also face the loss of their medical license followed by the burden of loss of income.

All of these burdens forced on a physician are mitigating factors against the professional seeking treatment. The doctor weighs all these aspects when trying to decide what to do. All of us who have been through these trials are well aware of how disastrous the penalties and consequences can be. The loss of your job may mean the loss of your position in a perhaps prestigious group; they may feel they cannot sacrifice their image and reputation in what they perceive as a threat to their otherwise reputable character. Few of us in medicine are really good at handling these problems. Larger groups sometimes have a professional from outside their group handle problems such as these to avoid the familiarity of their partner.

Chapter Twenty-five

Obstetric Insanity

Family practice was becoming more fun. I was beginning to have more challenges with the increase in my patient population. It seemed as if gradually the rest of the physicians in the community were beginning to accept me. Most of the different services such as peds, surgery, and OB had gradually gotten to the point where they knew I was going to be a permanent fixture and there was no reason to keep bringing me up before their little board meetings.

I took care of a large population of Medicaid patients in the community. It seemed that when the word got around there was a doctor in Dubuque who would see Medicaid patients, I became even more in demand. Dubuque was unusual in that regard. It seemed to me many of the community's physicians would not see underprivileged people, which included all Medicaid patients. I had no way of knowing, only anecdotal information I received from some of our welfare services. One day social services called and asked me if I would fit in one of their patients who was on Medicaid and had a number of problems. I said of course. When the patient got to my office his problems required much more of a workup than just being seen. When I informed social services he needed a lot of additional services, they informed me they could not cover him because of severe budgetary problems. I asked why they sent him to me and they said I was the only one on their list of physicians who would handle his problems. I really didn't understand all the reasons why, but I did know I was now placed in the class with Dr. Nate Owens. I decided I should consider that an honor and get on with taking care of my patient.

I realized if someone considers you special enough to take care of some special circumstance you had better try to act special.

After thinking I was finally past the point of getting called in front of the different special committees questioning my care of patients, Sheila called and said the Obstetrics Committee wanted to talk to me at their noon luncheon. She didn't know what they wanted to talk to me about. Upon arriving at our meeting, it was the usual bunch of obstetricians. I had no clue why they wanted to talk to me.

One of the young obstetricians asked me why I was delivering so many Medicaid patients. I replied, "I delivered them because they came to me for their care. I believe the main reason they come to me for their care is that none of you obstetricians accept Medicaid. I do accept Medicaid." Another young obstetrician said, "We do not think you should be delivering Medicaid patients."

When the young obstetrician said 'we', I realized he was speaking for the entire staff present that day. Obviously this was a reversed meeting. What a bunch of assholes. Not only that, they have a young, uninformed and probably dumb obstetrician whom they have chosen to take the lead. The more informed physicians in Dubuque had learned they did not want to be the brunt of the barrage of questions I would assault them with during these sessions. I had to at least give them credit for that.

I replied, "What is your reason for that?" They said the Medicaid patients are high risk and we do not think a family practitioner should be taking care of high risk patients. I asked, "What part about these patients is high risk? Also, please elaborate on what particular high risk problems these patients may have that any other obstetric patient of yours could not have?" They replied, "In our experience, these patients are not as good about prenatal care. They are poor at keeping their appointments. They sometimes do not take their vitamins."

I replied, "In your experience, is this the way all Medicaid patients are? Do you think perhaps some of them care about this little baby inside of them as much as your more affluent patients do? Let's just assume maybe a small percentage of them care about their pregnancy as much as we could possibly wish for. What questions will I use to pick those patients out?" The panel of obstetricians looked at each other perhaps waiting for just one of them to come up with an answer that would rescue all of them from their arrogance and self-serving ways. I realized this was a bunch of physicians I should take pity on. They were the very same physicians I prayed I would never become that one day in Princeton when I knelt praying beside my bed.

I saved them from their silence. I said, "Doctors, I take care of all these Medicaid patients because not one of you has the shred of decency to do so. If this Medicaid patient were your daughter, would you like to have her loaded up on a bus every day for the two hour ride to Iowa City?" Iowa City was where the University of Iowa was located. The university accepted all patients regardless of financial background, race, creed or color. "Just suppose this young lady is having a problem that needs to be tended to sooner. What good is it going to do her to be sitting on a bus and then hoping she gets around the University Hospital with enough time to receive the care she needs? A bus to my way of thinking is like an emergency department waiting room. Nothing good is going to happen there. This is what happens in a waiting room: the patient dies, gets well or gets tired of waiting and leaves."

"What happens when this patient who has been keeping all her appointments at the university goes into labor? Do we just hope the bus has an obstetrician driving it? Or do we hope she makes it in time? I already know what all of you are thinking, it is not my problem. Let me explain. It is your problem. You are the ones who did not want to see Medicaid patients. You are the ones who put this poor undeserving pregnant young lady on a bus for everything from prenatal care right up until delivery. We then hope she will make it back to the university two hours away in time for her delivery. And then she can jump back on the bus for her six week check and bring the little baby along with her. After all, I am sure you all think the little ones may as well get used to this care as it is likely what will happen to them growing up."

"This is what is going to happen today following this meeting. I am going to keep on taking care of Medicaid patients and give them the best prenatal care I can. I am going to be delivering their babies utilizing local Dubuque hospitals. The only thing I can glean from this meeting today is that you all feel Medicaid patients are high risk and yet you cannot tell me what the high risks are. I will tell you what I think you are feeling. Medicaid patients are high risk to your billfold. The Medicaid patients do not pay as well. Granted. But that is something I do not care about. Good day."

I thought following that meeting the Obstetrics Committee would be done with me. I did not think they wanted to be ridden roughshod over again by a physician from another state. It was probably especially true of a doctor from Minnesota, one of their rival states.

I was called to Finley Hospital one night to see a patient of mine who was a term pregnancy and in active labor. Gail had been operated on as an infant to correct a congenital heart defect, a Tetralogy of Fallot. Since the time of her correction and throughout all of her developmental years she had no further problems associated with her cardiac status. I had done some reading and studying about corrections and found out that a successful correction without further problems represented no significant risk to pregnancy.

Gail had an uneventful prenatal course and presented with no additional problems. On this particular evening, Gail arrived at the hospital presenting with a vertex occiput anterior presentation. This meant the baby is coming out the right way. The baby will come out looking at the ceiling. All of Gail's vitals were normal. Her heart was regular and she had no signs of failure. She had developed no edema. It appeared this was going to be an uneventful delivery. That is something all of us physicians hope when we are delivering a baby. We hope it is uneventful. The deliveries that are not uneventful are the ones that give us gray hair if we still have some.

I delivered Gail's baby, a normal baby boy who was pink and cried immediately and had a good Apgar. I massaged Gail's uterus and with a little fundal pressure, delivered an intact placenta and everything was normal. Blood loss was minimal.

Suddenly Gail became less responsive. She was still warm and smiling at her baby but suddenly my nurse said she could not get a blood pressure. I listened to her chest and she was still breathing with shallow respirations and it was clear. Her heart was regular but she was tachycardic. Gail sensed my concern and asked me what was wrong and if the baby was all right. I replied, "The baby is fine. Your blood pressure is lower than I like." I had asked for lab immediately and they were drawing blood to type and crossmatch and do the routine blood panel, electrolytes and blood gases.

Gail was becoming less responsive, we could still not get a blood pressure and she had a thready pulse. I called a full code in anticipation we might soon lose everything. We had a 21 gauge IV of normal saline going. We opened this wide open and we were already starting another large bore IV to pour the fluids into her. The ED physician came up to the room and started some vasopressors while I was trying to ascertain what was happening.

By this time Peter Schmidt had arrived. Peter was one of our seasoned obstetricians who had been talking of retiring. Peter asked me all the usual questions and exclaimed that there did not seem to be any unusual blood loss from looking at the floor and my sponges. I replied it had been a very normal delivery with minimal to less than normal blood loss, certainly less than one unit and suddenly my patient bottomed out. I explained she had a corrected Tetralogy of Fallot but had presented with no prenatal problems. I said her cardiac history otherwise was uneventful.

Within a couple minutes my patient's blood pressure had returned and she was acting normally. I simply said, "Gail, you gave us a little scare. Your blood pressure bottomed out for a couple minutes." Following that brief scare, I thanked Peter for coming in and also thanked the ED physician for getting there so rapidly. All was well. Gail and her baby did fine and were discharged a couple of days later.

I never came up with a reason as to why Gail had crashed that evening. I told her to abstain from having another pregnancy until she could have a thorough cardiac workup to make sure everything was all right. Gail asked me why she should have a cardiac workup if she had another pregnancy. I said, "I do not have a reason but I do not have a reason for why you crashed during delivery. I assume everything will be fine just as your prenatal cardiac history and prenatal care were fine."

I also explained that subsequent pregnancies should probably be delivered in a tertiary care center unless her future doctors said otherwise.

It was not more than a few weeks later I was called in front of the obstetrics committee again. Not only was I called to appear in front of them, I received a certified letter in the mail the day before that stated all of my privileges for labor and delivery had been rescinded. To put it succinctly, the letter said from this time forward, all obstetrical privileges of Dr. Rick Redalen are hereby terminated. Dr. Redalen can no longer deliver babies at any of the Dubuque hospitals.

Gail was a Medicaid patient so perhaps they wanted to blame her delivery crash on that fact. I thought the revocation of privileges was a bit of a drastic step to take to force someone to stop seeing Medicaid patients. It was nice getting the letter ahead of time. Forewarned is forearmed. I went to the meeting prepared. Once again one of the young obstetricians began asking me questions about my patient's delivery a few weeks earlier. The obstetric patient in question of course was Gail.

They said, "Dr. Redalen, once again you have chosen to take it upon yourself to deliver high risk pregnancies." I replied, "Yes, I know my patient was Medicaid but I told all of you all I was going to keep on delivering Medicaid patients." They were immediately somewhat angered. They said, "Dr. Redalen this is not about you delivering a Medicaid patient. It is about delivering a high risk cardiac patient. You had no business trying to deliver that patient." I asked, "What was high risk about my patient?"

Teresa Eckart, one of our younger female obstetricians decided somewhat foolishly to insert herself into the discussion. She said, "Dr. Redalen, your patient according to your own history and physical, had a history of a Tetralogy of Fallot." I said, "Yes she did. Why do you think that is a problem Dr. Eckart?" Teresa said, "You have no business delivering an obstetric patient with cardiac problems." I asked, "Theresa, do you even know what a Tetralogy of Fallot is?" Teresa became immediately irate and snapped back at me, "I do not need anatomy lessons from you, Dr. Redalen." I just smiled and said, "No you do not need to get anatomy lessons from me, but you do need to get them from somebody." I think I had just found the way to light her fire. I always feel a little badly for people when they get into discussions that are way over their head or beyond them. Teresa was one such person.

I spread out some books and articles on the table in front of the obstetricians. I pointed to one of the books and said, "Teresa, would you be so kind as to read that paragraph about Tetralogy of Fallot." Teresa read the paragraph, which said, "Corrected Tetralogy of Fallot does not present a significant risk to pregnancy. A corrected Tetralogy of Fallot requires no special prenatal care." I asked Teresa why she thought the patient would be better off delivered by one of them.

I then decided to have some fun with the obstetrics committee. I may as well hurt them all and put an end to their witch hunts forever. I said, "Are we all in agreement that your main concern about this patient is that she is a cardiac patient to your way of thinking?" They said that was their concern. I said, "From my office or hospital records do you see any prenatal problems that should have suggested a concern on my part or perhaps get a consultation from one of you?" The answer was no.

I then asked, "How many cardiac patients do you see in your practice?" The answer of course was none. They were a little irritated but they could now see the direction this conversation was going to take. Unfortunately, they now also saw it was too late for them. I feigned a little surprise. I said, "Not a day goes by that I do not deal with a cardiac patient."

I then asked, "How many of you have taken 'Advanced Cardiac Life Support'?" They all remained expressionless and quiet. "None!" I exclaimed. I said, "'I have taken Advanced Cardiac Life Support' many times. Why do you all think you are better trained to take care of this obstetric patient than I am?" None of them had an answer or any answer for me. They knew they were way in over their heads.

I then informed them, "I am an 'Advanced Cardiac Life Support' instructor. I think by now you all can surmise that of all of the people in this room, I am the one most qualified to take care of a patient with the cardiac history my patient has. Is there one of you that disagrees? Is there one of you who feels more qualified than me to deliver a patient with heart problems?" The room was silent. I said, "You sent a certified letter to me saying all my obstetrical privileges had been revoked. I want you to send me a letter of apology. I also want the letter to say Dr. Redalen has been completely restored and granted full privileges from the Department of Obstetrics and has all the rights in accordance with these privileges."

A little later that day, Mel Graves, the CEO and Head of Administration of Finley Hospital called me and said the obstetricians were having a hard time writing a letter of apology. They evidently said it would mean they had made an error in judgment when they revoked my privileges. I said, "You're damn right, they were in error. And they can even use that vernacular if they choose to." He said they were concerned about the liability incurred by writing such a letter. They were concerned it could be used in a court of law against them. I said, "Tell them not to worry. I am not going to sue them."

Mel said, "Dr. Redalen, the rumor is going around the hospital you are going to stop delivering babies soon anyway. What difference does it matter if you have a letter from the Obstetrics Committee?" I replied angrily, "I want a letter! You tell them if I do not get one, they can answer in court and then decide if they should have written a letter." He said he would pass it on. I told him to also pass on they should not delay in getting it to me and it should also be sent registered since that is the way they liked to send things.

Two days later I received a registered letter from the Committee of Obstetrics of Finley Hospital. It was short and succinct. It said, "Dr. Redalen, in review of your obstetrical privileges the Obstetric Committee feels no restrictions are warranted regarding your obstetrical privileges and you have all privileges requested to practice obstetrics." It didn't say, "We're sorry" but I guess it was okay. It satisfied my requirements of them and made them eat crow. I hope it tasted good.

I sent a registered letter to the Obstetrics Committee two days later. The letter said, "I have decided to terminate my privileges for obstetrics in Dubuque and I have terminated my malpractice insurance for doing same." I am sure nothing made them more pissed. They had probably hemmed and hawed and pissed and moaned and finally gotten up the gumption to grant all my privileges to deliver babies.

Now they were slapped in the face with my letter that basically stated 'I quit'. They realized the letter they wrote to restore my privileges had been for nothing. I thought my dealing with The Department of Obstetrics was finally at an end.

The one thing I did not do was to stop seeing obstetric patients in my practice. They could hardly be expected to run back and forth to Iowa City simply because the obstetricians in the town of Dubuque would not see them. I let all of my patients know I would no longer be able to deliver their babies but I would continue on with their prenatal care. They were unhappy I would not be there for their delivery but on the other hand were very happy they would not have to start running to Iowa City on a regular basis for their prenatal care.

A couple of months went by. Finley Administration called me, "Dr. Redalen, are you still seeing OB patients in your practice?" I said, "Yes I am." He said, "It came up in our obstetrics meeting today that you were still seeing OB patients. I thought you said you were not going to be delivering babies anymore." I replied, "That is true." He asked, "Then why is it you are still seeing them prenatally?" I said, "Someone has to see them. It is a long way to Iowa City once a month and then every week at the end of their pregnancy. They will still have to go to Iowa City when they go into labor. I am sure all of you know many of our indigent and Medicaid patients do not have reliable transportation. I am simply trying to help them out."

"I have asked them to stop in at the emergency room before they go to make sure they are not too far along in their labor for them to safely make the trip. Luckily your obstetricians are still delivering babies and surely they won't mind a few Medicaid patients to fill up their evenings." I think I could hear blood boiling.

It was no skin off the hospital administrator's hide, but he was going to have to put up with the ire of the obstetricians when he explained to them what was going on. There was nothing they could do about it however and I am sure they were now wishing they had not given me such a hard time. Now they were the ones delivering Medicaid patients.

They would have been even more unhappy if they could have heard some of the prenatal instructions I gave my pregnant patients as they were getting closer to delivery. Of course they were all worried about going to Iowa City when they went into labor. I asked them to time their contractions and when the contractions had gone on long enough so that they were a couple minutes apart and lasting for a good minute to continue to watch them and time them. I gave them instructions so most of the time when they went into the emergency department to be checked, the emergency department physicians were not going to want to send them off for a two hour trip and have the responsibility of having that patient deliver during transit. It was great. Our obstetricians were now in involuntary servitude. They were the new Medicaid Masters.

The nice thing about all this was all my patients, once they were delivered, came back to me for their six week post-partum check along with the new baby. How great was that. I got to take care of everything for the family except for the delivery itself. Dang. I should have thought of this sooner. I got to take care of the new carbon copies and the copy machines. Not only that, I no longer ran to the hospital in the middle of the night to deliver babies. Now the Dubuque obstetricians did this out of the goodness of their hearts. What kind souls.

Not delivering babies any more made life easier for me. Babies were the one thing I could not plan for and I still practiced medicine the way I did in my early days in Princeton. When a patient was getting close to delivering, I would hang around home most of the time to make sure I would not miss it. The newfound freedom was really exhilarating. I can write about this as I am now and make like this is all good, but in reality, not getting to bring a new baby into the world was definitely a loss for me and I did indeed miss delivering babies.

Chapter Twenty-six

Renee

One day a little gal came into my office who was obviously having an asthmatic attack. Jan put her in a room, I went in to examine her and rapidly confirmed what I thought when seeing her in the waiting room. I had Jan draw up the usual medication regimen I used. After about twenty minutes the little gal had calmed down a lot and her wheezing was pretty much gone. I listened to her chest and she had a few wheezes left but was markedly better.

We started talking and really hit it off. Her name was Renee Lewis. She was a little bit of a thing. Renee weighed all of ninety pounds dripping wet and she was not skinny. She was just a beautiful extremely petite dark haired brunette with big brown eyes. Renee told me she was married and had two children.

Renee's children were Russel and Tammy. Russel's father was Renee's current husband, Mark. Renee had Tammy by a previous marriage to John F. Tammy was now living with foster parents Louise and Jim F. in Los Angeles. Jim had previously been a patient of mine so I knew a little bit about him, but very little. Jim F. was related to Renee, I believe, through her mother.

Renee had grown up in the home of a career Army Major. She said she always answered the phone, Major Gaulke's residence. She said her dad was a strict taskmaster who made the kids toe the line. Renee had two brothers older than her. Her oldest brother was a cop in Galena, Illinois. Her mother Emma was a home maker. Renee did not elaborate but I think there were things that went on at home she did not much approve of. She didn't seem to have a real soft spot in her heart for her mother. It seemed as if she worshiped her dad however.

Over a period of several months, I would see Renee intermittently for asthma attacks. She would break through her medications. She said the worst problems were always at bedtime and she would often sit up to breathe at night. The medications did not seem to help much. I also got to meet Russel. He was a great little guy and bright as a whip. He was also a little person made much like his mother and had a ready smile when I would tease or kid him. At the time, Renee was working in a nursing home northeast of town called the Heritage Manor Nursing Home.

There was one thing I learned in a hurry from Renee. She said she was never going to live to be an old lady. She said it bothered her immensely to see the elderly sit looking out the windows of their rooms day after day. Renee knew they were hoping to see a car drive up they would recognize, a sign that a loved one was coming. Renee said that was never going to happen to her. She was not going to sit alone in a room on Christmas day hoping someone would come to visit. I could tell in spite of the misgivings Renee had about growing old, she loved the elderly and doted on them. Whatever their children were not bringing them, she was helping to edge out that loneliness.

Renee said she did not like how the elderly were treated all of the time either. She said you should treat these people the way you want your parents treated or yourself when you are that age. She saw one of the aides hit a patient one day and she reported it immediately. The person was dismissed the same day.

Renee said they had one patient with Alzheimer's disease. She said the patient could not really remember and her mind seemed to be completely gone. She then started laughing. She explained that about once a week someone comes to the nurses' station and says their car has been stolen. It seems the lady who can't remember anything remembers perfectly where she lived prior to coming to the nursing home. She wanders away from the facility and looks until she finds a car someone has left their keys in. Evidently, she jumps inside, starts the car and travels to her old home. She always managed to find that home several miles from where she was living now. The police had gotten used to this and they always return the car thief to the nursing home and the car to its rightful owner.

One other thing I found out about Renee was she loved horses. She said every Christmas when she was growing up in East Dubuque, she would run to the window in her bedroom that looked out on the back lawn to see if her dad had bought her a pony. Evidently every Christmas she had come up empty.

Now that I was living in Dubuque full time, Jan was also living with me full time. Our relationship was great but I was also seeing Kim when she came home and now JP was coming to visit when she could. One day when JP and I were talking, I asked how her divorce was coming along. It was a subject we did not talk about much. It had gotten to be a little bit of an uncomfortable subject to me so I never brought it up. When we were seeing each other regularly in Manitowoc and it got late at night JP would tell me she had to go home. Usually it was that she had to tuck Matt in for the night. There was one excuse or another.

I knew the relationships I had with Jan and Kim were not going to go on forever. As much as I cared for both of them and loved them, we could really never get beyond where we were right now. They both wanted families and it was a subject neither one of them was willing to give up on. I always said I would never have another family. I would never have had a family in the first place if I had known it was going to come to a tragic end. As much as I loved my children, I would have never chosen to have them if I had a crystal ball looking into the future to allow me to feel the pain that was going to come with their loss. I would never go through that again.

This was not a subject I had been unfair about. I think it was a subject about which both Jan and Kim thought someday, one way or another, I would change my mind. I did not want to feel loss again in my life but I knew the loss of a girlfriend would be a walk in the park compared to the loss of my children. I felt regardless of how much I cared for both Jan and Kim I simply could not have another family. People wanting to spend a lifetime together cannot do so when on opposite sides of a page, one person wanting children and the other with their child raising days at an end. I was not too old to have another family. I was just not going to do so. I guess in my mind, I thought someday I would be lucky enough that one of them would care enough for me to forego having a family.

Kim and I were gradually seeing less of each other. She had her hands full with nursing school. Also running back and forth between Freeport and Dubuque was not much of an option for Kim any more. She had a schedule just like all student nurses that was much too busy. I was not running back and forth between Madison and Freeport any more to visit her either. I was another person short on time. We finally came to the realization neither of us was able to change the course we were on and we terminated our relationship. We did not end our friendship and we parted as friends. I knew I would always love Kim.

A year or two later I would run into Kim during one of her summer breaks and she asked, "You know what the hardest thing about breaking up with you has been, Rick?" I replied, "No." She said, "It is really hard to go out with people my age again. It is like being around children. I am in a relationship with a guy my age now and it is going pretty well. We live in an apartment just a little way from here. Would you like to come over and meet my boyfriend?" I said, "Sure."

Kim and her beau lived within walking distance. I sat down, we talked a bit and I had a beer with them. A few minutes went by and what I remembered most about the meeting was Kim sitting with her back against the couch next to her boyfriend's legs. He set his beer can on her head and said, "Go get me another beer." Kim dutifully got up and went and got him his beer. I read it as a childish way of saying 'this is my property and she waits on me'. I felt embarrassed for Kim. I made an excuse and took my leave. I never saw Kim again. I heard years later she was working as a nurse in Dubuque. I knew whatever Kim chose to do with her life, she would be successful.

Suddenly out of the blue one day I got a huge surprise. Stacey Gilmore called. I was blown away and so happy to hear her voice again. I asked, "Stacy, what on earth are you doing? Where are you living?" Stacey replied, "Rick, after we split up I was so lonesome, I met a guy and we got married right away. My name is Stacey Cooper now. I really didn't even know him very well and he had five children." I asked, "Stacey what on earth were you thinking, barely knowing someone and getting married?" Stacey said, "God Rick, I'm too young to be the mother of five children. I've never even been around children and now I'm living in a house full of them. Do you care if I come and stay with you for a while?" I said, "No Stacey that would be great and I would love to see you." It was a wonderful day and shortly I was going to be seeing one of the loves of my life again.

It was a strange place in life. I was surrounded by beautiful girls and I think I really loved all of them. I would sometimes wonder how you can love more than one woman at the same time. Each person I was with was fun to be around and had something about them that was lovable. I guess if you had a computer and could put all of these characteristics together in one woman you would have the perfect lifetime companion. A few years later a movie came out called "Weird Science" about a couple of high school computer nerds who decided to create the perfect girl in the computer. When the girl suddenly came to life, they had created the ideal babe of any high school kid's dreams. Kelly LeBrock was the dynamite chic.

Is it any different with parents when they have five or six children? I mean, do parents only pick out one child to love and the others go without? Hardly. I knew from watching what happened in my family that my two younger sisters, Sally and Susie, surely seemed to get preferential treatment from my parents and Susie, the youngest, could do no wrong. Also in families each child requires different care and different handling. I knew if my parents ever gave Susie a cross look, she would start crying. She had the most tender feelings of anyone in our family. They were the kind of feelings that would lead her to become a caregiver. And what a caregiver she was and is. If anyone in life deserved or was looking for a great nurse and plugged this into Google, I am sure they would come up with the name of my sister Susie.

I continued to meet a lot of people in Dubuque I would stay connected to for the rest of my life. There are also people you meet you will remember for the rest of your life that you would be more blessed to forget. One such patient of mine was a little wrinkled old shrew by the name of Gretta M. who was married to Bill, a kindly soft spoken old gentleman. Some way or another they managed to stay married. The only thing Gretta didn't have was the stolen "Ruby Red Slippers."

One sunny afternoon day I got a call from Gretta who wanted me to come to see her. I was not doing anything else so decided to save Gretta a trip to the Xavier Emergency Department by ambulance. Gretta and Bill lived in a trailer house up on a bluff in East Dubuque that overlooked Dubuque and the Mississippi. I would often go to visit this couple as it was becoming progressively more difficult for Gretta to make it to my office. This was one of the problems I thought about while practicing medicine. Why should a person struggle and use every last ounce of strength they have to make it to a young healthy doctor's office, who in a few minutes time can jump into their car and make it to their patient's home? I continued to be one of those doctors they shot long ago. I still made house calls.

Golly, Gretta was obstinate and difficult to take care of and while I was talking to them Gretta and I would often get into it and end up having course words with each other. The main problem Gretta had was heart failure and she would intermittently get into problems with it and always call when she got short of breath. The calls were never frivolous calls. She really needed help but did not want to go to the hospital. Usually I just had to fine tune her medications.

This is a point all of you young people need to learn. In the late Seventies elderly people usually went to the hospital to die. This is what people like Gretta had observed during her life growing up.

This particular day was no different and Gretta really should have been in the hospital but that was going to be a no. Once again we got into it and to make a long story sort, Gretta told me I was a good for nothing SOB and only came to take care of her to make money. It didn't seem to matter to her that I had never charged for coming to the other side of the river to visit her. I called Gretta a mean spirited old bitch. I had found out from experience that unless you talk to people in their own vernacular they often don't hear you.

We parted company again and although we had said a lot of things that would have ended a relationship between any two other people, I knew I would be hearing again from Gretta.

I learned early in my formative years your time is precious. When you take the better part of your day to go sit with one of your patients with cancer or in Gretta's case shortness of breath, you can never possibly charge enough to come out okay monetarily for the time you have spent getting there and being with them.

The only way you can give away this time is to do so with your heart. When you do, you will always feel as though your heart is filled with such abundance, as though it is dancing out of your chest. I do not ever recall that feeling from sitting on a thicker billfold. We are here to serve our fellow man and if we approach every day thinking 'what can I do to make this world a better place' we will always be looking through rose colored glasses and sometimes, or I guess all the time, God is even smiling down on us working in our childlike ways.

One weekend JP came down from Manitowoc for the weekend. She left Matt with her husband. I still did not know what was going on between the two of them. I thought this was the longest divorce process I had ever seen. It was a subject that never came up. I did not care to hear about it and I assumed everything was progressing normally, whatever normal is in a divorce. I knew I could not let my divorce from Bette be used as a gold standard. I had finally let JP know I was not happy continuing a long distance relationship and I could feel no definite direction our relationship was heading.

When I asked JP what the holdup was, she landed a bombshell on me. She had not yet filed for divorce. It was inconceivable to me. What was even stranger, JP had been looking for jobs and it seemed Xavier Hospital wanted her to begin working immediately in the ICU.

I was completely distraught with JP. She had not really lied to me but she had not been totally truthful with me either. It was completely understandable I guess. JP probably wondered how you can be in a long distance relationship with someone who seems to have relationships with everyone. JP became angry one day and told me when she goes home it is not like she is going home to a boyfriend. My retort was, "You are going home to a husband with whom you have a committed legal relationship and a child. What would be the reason for us to continue a relationship?" I told JP I really did not want to continue our relationship any longer. JP said she wanted to continue with our relationship and she was going back to Manitowoc to take care of some things. She said she had also accepted a job in ICU at Xavier.

A couple of days later Stacey Cooper suddenly showed up at my door. She certainly had not had the time to get a divorce since we talked. I wondered if she had even let the guy know she was leaving. It really didn't matter to me and I think at the time, I would just as soon have found out she was still single. We were probably still married by common law in Colorado but we did not talk about any of this. Stacey was as slim, trim, fit and beautiful as she ever was. I was overjoyed to see her again. It made me wonder why we had ever broken up. It was not for lack of love, for sure.

Jan was still staying at my home all the time so Stacey took the spare bedroom. We spent a lot of time catching up and Stacey was still unhappy she had gotten connected to a guy with five kids. She said she was never going back to Wyoming. I suggested perhaps she should at least get legally divorced but Stacy was of the mind her husband was going to arrange for an annulment. Stacey did not talk to him again, nor about him, while she was living with me.

My troubles with the obstetrics committee seemed to come in a slow trickle. Mel Graves called one day and said a number of the prenatals I was taking care of were coming into the hospital to have their babies. I replied, "I am sure they are happy to be able to stay in town. With the transportation problems many of them have, I am sure they are pleased their family is close and can visit them." Mel did not mention any of the obstetricians by name but I am sure I could probably guess a couple of them. They evidently were wishing my patients would try to make it to Iowa City. Of course I told him I would encourage them to do so. I probably was a little weak in my encouragement.

It was about one week later that JP returned to Dubuque and moved in with me. This time she had come to stay. She had her belongings, at least what fit in her car, and she started work immediately at Xavier. In spite of four people living together in a relatively small condo, we all got along fine. I guess it was times like these it probably would have been good to be living in Utah. Polygamy sounded pretty good some days. I told our office girls one day how Brigham Young had gotten his name. He said, "Bring 'em young and bring 'em often." One of my Mormon friends told me that joke. I doubt the The Church of Jesus Christ of Latter-day Saints Elders would have approved.

One morning as I was walking out with the garbage, one of my male neighbors asked me how I did it. I asked, "What do you mean?" He said, "It is a great trick to have three beautiful girls living with you." I said, "We are all just really good friends." "I wish I had your success," my neighbor added. "If you ever get tired of one of your friends, please introduce me."

It was wonderful. I really appreciated their being around and they seemed to share in the enjoyment. Jan, Stacey and JP all got along excellently. I suggested one day if they didn't mind, to go out and get a barbecue grill. If they wanted to take a stab at it before I got home, they could try putting it together. I believe they decided they could put a grill together at least as well as I could and probably faster.

When I came home later that afternoon, Jan, Stacey and JP were all sitting on the deck with some of my tools working away at putting together what looked to be a nice grill from the picture on the box. They were laughing and having a good time. It was far from evident that all three of these girls were or had been involved with me. It seemed our friendship overcame any possible problems of living and working together.

Life went on in a usually uneventful way. We did a lot of barbecuing and I continued to play tennis. I was doing most of my hospital practice out of Xavier. Living just down the hill from Xavier made life really easy and the emergency department had coverage 24/7 so my evenings were free for us to do as we wanted.

Stacey came to talk with me one day. She said she thought it would be better if she moved on. I was not happy to hear that and not happy to see her go. I think the only thing I could have done to hold on to Stacey would have been to marry her but I was still not in the mind frame to go through that again with Bette still on my brain. Stacey and I hugged and kissed goodbye and reluctantly parted. In spite of doing what was right, it was hard on both of us. Several months later, I wished I could have gotten in touch with Stacey because I would have married her, if she would have had me.

One day the parents of a bright eyed little girl by the name of Sarah B. brought her in. The parents who I will leave un-named were teachers who were new to my practice. I examined Sarah who had a benign looking otitis media or routine middle ear infection. Sarah was three years old and she was started on an appropriate dose of Ceclor Suspension, 125 mg, or one teaspoon three times per day for a duration of ten days which was one of the standard treatments at the time. I gave the B. family my usual instructions. Make sure your child is taking in fluids and eating well every day. Make sure she gets her medications three times per day as ordered. If you have any changes in behavior, eating, stools, or development of any problems you think are abnormal, call me or see me immediately. They were good instructions and more than adequate for two college graduates.

In this situation a physician is always at a disadvantage. We have to believe our patient's parents are bright enough to follow our instructions. When you have two college graduates, as the B.s were, I assumed they could do so.

Three days later, I got an early morning call at home. It was the B. family. They said their little girl Sarah was not taking in fluids and was not responding. They could not get her to wake up. I said, "Get her to the hospital immediately. I will be at Xavier emergency room waiting for you." I shot out of the door and headed for the ED.

The B. family got to the ED about ten minutes later. I grabbed Sarah out of their arms and was shocked as I laid her on the table. Sarah was ashen gray and cool. What was absolutely terrifying was her pupils were dilated. I did not take the time to see if they reacted to light. We put tourniquets on all four extremities. I was desperate to find just one vein I could start an IV in. There were none. I asked for a cut down kit. I ran scalpels around both of Sarah's ankles hoping desperately to find something I could use. I could not. Little Sarah did not even move as the scalpels cut into both ankles.

Not only could I not find a vein, neither of Sarah's ankles bled one single solitary drop of blood. Sarah's heart rate was over two hundred. I was going to lose her. I asked my nurse for two large peritoneal trocars and rammed two of them into Sarah's abdomen, one on each side. Little Sarah still did not move as I shoved in the trocars, a sign she was near death. We immediately began to run in two liters of normal saline as fast as we could. There was still no movement by Sarah. Little Sarah's abdomen began to be distended but I still wanted the pressure in her little belly to be high enough to get fluids into her vascular compartment. It sounds as if we had done a lot, but all of these efforts transpired over only a couple of minutes. These are times when seconds stand between life and death, not minutes.

It is during these times you appreciate nurses such as we had at Xavier who did not wait to be asked for anything; they were ready. After three to four minutes went by, Sarah started to ooze blood from both ankles. They were tiny pinpoints of red in the lacerations I had created around her ankles. My heart just leapt. Sarah's heart was pumping blood to her lungs and she was oxygenating her blood. We reapplied the tourniquets to both ankles and gradually we began to see very tiny veins appearing. It would still be several more minutes before we would get a vein large enough to start an IV.

I managed to get an IV started in both of Sarah's ankles and they managed to accept the fluids we were giving them. Now it was a waiting game to see if Sarah was going to wake up and how severe an insult she had received to her little brain. I sewed up Sarah's ankles while we watched and waited. In spite of the painful stimuli of sewing Sarah up, she still did not respond to the repair. We watched and waited and finally were able to get a pulse-ox on Sarah. She was oxygenating well. The brightest sign I saw was Sarah's pupils had come down. At least that primitive brain stem reflex was still there. What I wanted more than anything right now was simple movement of any kind.

Physicians reading this are going to ask, what is wrong with this guy? He should have made sure the pupils reacted before doing resuscitation. Non-reactive pupils mean brain stem death and all you are going to get out of that resuscitation is a little girl in a vegetative state. All true my well-meaning colleagues. I did not have the time with this little patient to talk to the parents and make sure they had not given her a medication which dilated the pupils, therefore my logical progression.

We continued to watch Sarah and give her fluids and oxygen. The trocars remained in her abdomen but we had slowed the fluids way down, although with what we had to work with for a few minutes I was truly estimating fluids required by the seat of my pants. We put a Foley catheter in and got absolutely no urine back. We had to hope her kidneys along with the rest of her organs would recover. In the meantime, we waited for Sarah's lab to come back so we could get a firmer grip on what our fluid replacement had done and where we stood.

The minutes went painfully by. We had done everything humanly possible to give this little soul the opportunity to grow up and have children of her own. We waited and we waited. Sarah was still not responsive to painful stimuli, ascertained by gently moving the trocars. We didn't traumatize her little body any more than we absolutely had to. Finally, it seemed to be a miracle but little Sarah began moving her arms and then moved her lower extremities. We moved Sarah up into the ICU. We didn't have a NICU (neonatal intensive care unit) at Xavier.

I accompanied Sarah's gurney up to the ICU. I finally had the opportunity to talk to the B. family. I asked them what had happened at home that their daughter arrived today nearly dead. I asked, "Do you know that if you had arrived even ten minutes later, you would have handed me a dead daughter?"

The B.s explained Sarah had been having twenty to thirty small loose stools per day. Today when they called, Sarah had stopped taking fluids. Well why not! She was comatose. I was more than furious, but controlled my rage. "I asked, "What did I tell you before you left the office the other day?" The B's replied in unison, "You said for us to call you immediately if we had problems." I replied, "Well why the hell didn't you? This is nothing short of child abuse. Were it not for the tragedy of this situation I would have Sarah and your little boy removed from your home and your care immediately and put in the care of the state. How you have cared for Sarah is unconscionable, indefensible and wrong." I knew they had a little boy as I had seen him the day they brought Sarah in.

I said to S. B., "Here is what is going to happen over the next week. Over the next several days, we are going to see if Sarah is neurologically intact. That means we are going to see if her little brain still works. We have to make sure her kidneys still work. She still has not put out any urine which means her kidneys were badly deprived of blood and oxygen. I am going to assume the rest of the organs of her body have also been badly insulted. I am keeping her under 24 hour surveillance by one of our nurses and we will see what of this little soul we have saved. One more thought, are you able to care for your little boy?" They answered me affirmatively. I really had misgivings about whether I should allow that continued care to happen. Sarah was an avoidable tragedy brought about by parental negligence.

I walked back into the ICU and one of my nurses was smiling a little. She said, "Guess what? Sarah put out a couple drops of pale urine." One more bright sign for us and our little patient. Over the next several hours Sarah lay there mentally obtunded and unresponsive to our verbal commands. Nor did she cry. I was still pained and concerned. I went home and prayed to God that this little creation of His would be all right.

I wanted to be by myself that evening. I was mentally drained and felt as though I had been beaten. I broke down and cried and prayed God had given me the skills to save this little girl and thanked Him for staying by my side making sure I did everything right. Saves as miraculous as this are no credit to me, but to Him.

I stayed in close touch with ICU and went back a few hours later to see Sarah. She had now put out a couple hundred ccs of urine and her little body was now trying to straighten out the little missteps in fluid balance created by me.

The following morning Sarah finally opened her eyes and cried when she realized her parents were not there and she was in strange surroundings. One more bright ray of hope. I think we all breathed a sigh of relief. God came through again just as He always does for me. She reacted to her parents when they arrived a little later. Over the next couple of days Sarah began to have a little diarrhea again. She was no longer on a broad spectrum antibiotic and she was afebrile. It appeared Sarah was going to survive without sequelae. I was still concerned by the diarrhea. I realized as large a shock as all her tissues had taken, it was very possible she had also badly injured her bowels.

After about a week Sarah was back to the little girl I had seen in the clinic several days earlier, which now seemed like years. I talked with the B.s, "I think you should pray about this and hope God can give us back a whole little girl. I want to see her tomorrow and here is my deal, if you are even late for an appointment without letting me know, I am going to have social services at your door and they are going to remove both of your children from your home. Do you understand how firm and unwavering and unforgiving I am going to be about this? If you do not understand I will call social services right now. If Sarah even looks at you cross eyed I want her in my office. Do you understand?"

The B's were understandably terrified by me and they had good right to be. I was angry. These parents continued to bring their children to me for the next year and gradually I stretched out the time between appointments and the children seemed well cared for. Sometime later I did not see the B. family any more. I continued to hope their children were well cared for.

Let me fast forward this scenario two years. Remember I first saw Sarah when she was three years old so she would now be five. I was in one of the examining rooms seeing a patient. Sheila knocked at my door. That was strange. Sheila never interrupted me while I was seeing a patient. Sheila said, "Rick, there is a federal marshal at the door who wants to see you." I asked, "What about?" Sheila didn't know. I went out and indeed there was a federal marshal standing at the front desk in the waiting room. He said, "Dr. Redalen I have been retained and sent here by the Law Firm of Tom Riley in Cedar Rapids to give you these papers." As he was leaving he told me to have a good day. Generally, that is not the kind of day you have when a federal marshal serves you papers.

To break this all down to a brief synopsis of what the papers said: Dr. Rick Redalen you are hereby ordered to appear at the courthouse in Cedar Rapids in order to respond to a malpractice law suit filed by the Tom Riley Law Firm on behalf of the Sarah B. family.

I was probably more dumbfounded than anything. My only thoughts were, S. B. what an unappreciative dumb shit you are. I really couldn't have cared less about the malpractice suit. To me it was a nuisance. Nothing more, nothing less. I don't malpractice so I knew the minute I read the papers the suit had no merit. I called the St. Paul Company in Minneapolis to notify them of the claim. The St. Paul Company was the insurance company which carried my malpractice insurance. They thanked me for calling and said they would begin work to take care of it.

I had heard of the Tom Riley Law Firm. Tom Riley, the eldest in the firm, was well known for his legal prowess. They were supposedly one of the best law firms in the State of Iowa and Tom had a reputation which was also well known nationally. Knowing their reputation, it surprised me they would bring a frivolous law suit. The only thing I could figure out was one of his lackeys must have read the complaint by the B.s and filed the suit without doing their homework or consulting with their senior partner. It was indeed a little perplexing.

I had always been interested in malpractice and why cases of it occurred. I constantly advised my colleagues in medicine to always be involved. Physicians worry that if they get involved in a malpractice case as an expert witness, their fellow colleagues will look down on them as a 'hired gun'. I had always taken the opposite approach toward malpractice. It was my feeling, for example, if a potential plaintiff brings a complaint to an attorney of their choice, the attorney has to determine if there was malpractice. The attorney can only do so by looking at the case and hopefully asking an expert in medicine to evaluate the patient's claim and explain to the attorney his opinion of what has happened.

An unfortunate result happening to a patient is not bona fide evidence of malpractice. What may appear to the patient and attorney can often be explained away by a medical expert and that little added bit of insight can prevent a meritless lawsuit against an excellent well-meaning physician.

If an attorney is presented with a set of circumstances that have returned an unfortunate result for a patient and the attorney cannot find a physician to help him decipher the medical jargon, a lawsuit may be filed. Now the attorney is going to get expert medical advice from the defendant, the physician who is accused of doing malpractice. What must happen then, during depositions the doctor who is accused will be asked questions about why treatment or procedures led to the result obtained. It may be at that time the attorney who has filed the lawsuit on behalf of the plaintiff finds out that in actuality no malpractice was committed, and the suit may be dismissed.

Such was the case of Sarah B. I could not imagine in any state of mind how an attorney could file such a meaningless lawsuit as this and especially a law firm with the reputation of the Tom Riley Law Firm.

The other way to look at this, all attorneys know if they file a medical malpractice lawsuit, they are going to walk away with a check for $50,000 to $100,000 simply for filing the suit. Malpractice insurers cannot defend most suits for less than this and are willing to settle out of court. All of this creates an environment which is ultimately bad for the legal and medical professions and ultimately hurts and hinders patient care. These practices all present perverse incentives to make bad situations worse.

St. Paul Company filed a deposition time for the B. family. The lawsuit was brought because Sarah B. had a learning disorder. In other words, she was slow in school. The deposition was one in which you would actually feel sorry for the parents of Sarah B. "How is your daughter slow in school?" S. B. replied "Well she is not as smart as the other kids in her class." "What problems does she exhibit at home that tell you she is slow?" S. B. said, "Well she seems to do okay at home." This painstaking process dragged on and it appeared the Tom Riley Law Firm had not bothered to prep this family on how to answer questions in a deposition. It did not appear to me they had even talked to them.

I guess all of that may have been understandable. Prior to this deposition, no doubt the Tom Riley Law Firm had read the opinion and statement made by a well-known pediatrician from the Department of Pediatrics from the University of Minnesota.

The statement read that the patient in question, Sarah B. was seen by Doctor Rick R. Redalen on such and such a date. The statement basically reiterated the information obtained from the hospital chart about the patient's presentation to Xavier hospital at her time of admission. It said the patient had been presumably neglected prior to admission and entered Xavier Emergency Department in a moribund condition and near death.

After describing the treatment and ultimate disposition of Sarah B., the pediatrician went on to say, "This patient was the incredulous victim of gross parental stupidity and neglect." He then went on to further say, "This patient was the fortuitous recipient of heroic medical care by Dr. Rick Redalen who performed far beyond any foreseeable expectations to save the life of this patient."

The deposition went on and I could not possibly see how or why the Riley Law Firm would want to waste any more time on this. My attorney was now summing up the deposition in one easy statement. "Now let me make sure I understand you completely Mr. B. You are suing Dr. Redalen because your daughter is slow in school." I tugged on my attorney's sleeve. He bent over to hear what I had to say. I said, "These people are really dumb. Ask them if their son has a learning disability the same as Sarah's and then ask them if he has ever gone through medical problems like Sarah's." The questions were asked and the answers were, "Yes, my son has the same learning disability as Sarah's." My attorney said, "We have no further questions." Obviously the Riley Law Firm would have done better if they had shown up with a talking dog.

The St. Paul Company contacted me the following week via telephone and said the malpractice suit had been settled out of court with the Riley Law Firm agreeing to a settlement amount of $40,000. What a slap in the face to the Riley Law Firm. I knew anecdotally Tom Riley could not be hired for that small amount, so perhaps they were trying to at least pay for postage and their mileage. Oh well. One nuisance gone and one more debit in my column of thoughts about malpractice.

Later I would have the chance to talk to Tom Riley about this lawsuit and he said they perhaps made a mistake in filing it. On the other hand, how large a mistake can it be if one of your lackeys does no research, spends an hour filing a lawsuit, wastes a day on a deposition and collects a check for $40,000 which no doubt pays that person's salary for a year.

Probably not much of a mistake after all.

One afternoon while I was working in the clinic on my day off, I received a call from the Law Office of White and Warbasse which was also located in Cedar Rapids. Tim White was on the phone and asked, "Rick, can you run over to Cedar Rapids in the next couple of days. We have a probable malpractice suit and we would like you to evaluate it and see what you think." I replied, "I am off for the afternoon so how would it be if I headed over right now?" They were pleased. I had just bought a new corvette so I was anxious to take it for a spin on the highway. It was a bright warm sunny day.

When I arrived at Tim and Steve's office I was welcomed. They had to examine all of the papers on the possible malpractice case on their desk along with the patient's x-rays. They began to tell me their story. A middle aged, "grandmotherly" type had come to their office a few days ago. Her gallbladder had been removed several weeks earlier by a local reputable Cedar Rapids surgeon in Mercy Medical Center.

A few days following surgery the patient began having abdominal pain. They said the patient had developed a temperature and the surgeon had ordered repeat flat plates, or in other words plain x-rays, of her abdomen. The x-rays revealed she had several long needles in her abdomen. Both Tim White and Steve Warbasse asked me, "How do you suppose the surgeon left those in the patient?" I looked at the rest of the x-rays of the patient's abdomen, a couple of which had been taken immediately following surgery before leaving the operating room. Many hospitals now do this as a routine precaution to make sure a foreign body has not been left in the patient following surgery. The foreign body could be one of the sponges we dab and mop up blood with during a procedure or one of the instruments used during the procedure.

The x-rays taken immediately following surgery showed no evidence of a foreign body in the abdomen. I knew immediately something was not right. I also knew the problem was not one of the surgeon or hospital. I read through the hospital notes and the surgeon had done everything to evaluate the problem and of course the only action was to open up the patient again and remove the needles. That was accomplished by the surgeon without incident, the patient was closed and an uneventful post-operative course followed the second surgery.

Tim and Steve were still curious and wanted to know what I thought.

I said I was going to run over to the hospital to look at the needles that had been found in her abdomen. They had been kept in the pathologist's lockup to maintain the chain of evidence. They were in a sealed bottle with the date and time the needles were placed inside. The pathologist unsealed the bottle for me and I asked him if he could set up a binocular microscope with low resolution. I looked at the needles under the scope. What was readily apparent was the needles were made of aluminum. They were the length of the standard needle we use to do lumbar punctures or spinal taps. Not only was that abnormal and not something that was used in a hospital but the bevel was cut in the shape of a V, something I had never seen before.

The pathologist wanted to know what I thought. I just said it was strange and could not really comment in case I was later called as an expert medical witness. The curiosity of the pathologist had probably been raised so he would look at the needles as soon as I left and form his own conclusion. I headed back to Steve and Tim's office. They were waiting anxiously to see what I thought. They asked, "Can you imagine a good surgeon making a mistake like that?" I replied, "No, I really can't imagine that."

"Can you tell me a little more about this client of yours? Do you think she is reliable and accurate in the story she told you?" I asked. Tim said, "Well she seemed to be reliable but she had a boyfriend with her who was about thirty years younger and he was pretty strange." I said, "Strange like how?" They said, "He was just different and you could say he was a little 'squirrely'. Why are you asking?"

I said, "I am going to give you my best guess as to what happened and I can pretty much guarantee you I am 99.99% sure I am right. In the first place the surgeon did not leave any needles in the abdomen. Secondly, the needles are not stainless steel. They are made of aluminum and have a strange bevel at the pointed end. They would not be something used in a hospital. Before I left the hospital, I talked to a surgical nurse and asked if aluminum needles were ever used in the hospital and she replied they were not. I asked her if she had ever seen aluminum needles used during her entire nursing career to which she replied she had not.

I continued to explain, "There is no place in the body needles of that size could be left where they would end up in the peritoneal cavity. It is simply not possible. No foreign bodies were detected on x-rays taken when surgery was complete. Our patient in question did just fine for a couple days after surgery following which time she developed abdominal pain. The pain continued for the next twenty-four hours when repeat evaluation and x-rays revealed the needles in the belly."

"The only way those needles could have gotten into the peritoneal cavity was for her 'squirrely' boyfriend to have shoved those needles into her abdomen through her freshly stitched up surgical incision following her first set of x-rays. This is not a case of malpractice. It is a case of extortion. If I were you, I would get rid of this case as rapidly as possible. I would not file a lawsuit. If you were to do so and this went to court, I am afraid you could be counter sued by the defendants when all of this would come to light in the courtroom."

The dollar signs in my attorney friend's eyes disappeared. This case fully illustrates the reasons physicians have to do their duty and help attorneys sort out cases such as this. What Steve and Tim thought was obvious malpractice could not have been further from the truth.

I jumped back in the car and drove slowly back to Dubuque enjoying the bright sunny afternoon. I never called Steve and Tim back to ask them if they had filed a suit. I would have disappointed them if I had called and it would have disappointed me if they had filed the suit. I never saw anything in the paper so I guess they did the right thing.

Chapter Twenty-seven

JP

One day when I was seeing patients in the office, Renee came in wheezing badly. I asked Jan to put her right into a room. Jan asked, "Do you want me to draw up her usual medications?" I said, "No, I will go into the examining room and talk to her first." I went into the examining room and she was in rather severe respiratory distress. I asked, "Renee, do you mind if I treat your attack differently today?" Renee looked at me apprehensively but nodded her head and said that would be all right.

It was then I began talking slowly and softly, telling Renee I was going to teach her how to relax. "Renee, I want you to relax completely. I want you to listen to the soft sound of my voice and as you do and you become more relaxed, your breathing is going to become easier and easier. As you relax more you will gradually feel your body becoming very relaxed and as it relaxes, you will begin to feel sleepy. Now Renee, I want you to relax your eyelids and the muscles of your face. Relax your neck and you will begin to feel your head getting very heavy. Feel how much better you are breathing now. That is because the little passageways in your lungs are now relaxing and letting air in and gently letting it out.

"You can now feel your entire body getting very tired Renee and you are going to fall into a warm wonderful sleep. Every muscle in your body is now completely relaxed Renee and now you are in a deep wonderful sleep. Your breathing is now completely normal and you have never felt better in your life."

Renee was a wonderful subject and was capable of going into the deepest stages of hypnosis within a few minutes. I would now give Renee her posthypnotic suggestions. "Renee, whenever you hear me say, 'Go to sleep' once, you will become very tired. When you hear me say, 'Go to sleep' the second time, you are going to become more and more tired and all you will want to do is to lie down and fall asleep. When I say, 'Go to sleep' the third time you will fall into a deep, deep warm, wonderful sleep.

"Now Renee, I am going to wake you up. You will wake up at the count of three and when you wake up it will be the most pleasurable feeling and wonderful sleep you have ever had. One, Renee you are starting to wake up and you feel very good. At this point Renee began to move a little. She was still sitting on the table. Two, now Renee you are beginning to feel more and more awake and you feel wonderful. Three, you are wide awake and this is the most pleasant feeling you have ever had in your entire life."

Renee woke up with a big smile on her face and said, "Boy do I ever feel good. What did you do to me?" I said, "Renee, I just talked to you and helped you relax." All most asthmatics have to do when they feel an attack of asthma coming on is to relax. The problem of course is that when any person becomes short of breath, they become more anxious and the anxiety makes the breathing problems worse.

Renee walked out of the room with a smile on her face, said goodbye to the girls at the front desk and walked out. Jan looked at Renee with a perplexed look on her face and asked me, "What on earth did you do to her?" I replied, "I just talked to her a little." Jan said, "Wow! That must have been some talk." I laughed and then told Jan I had simply used hypnosis.

Somehow word would get around that 'Redalen' was doing hypnosis in his clinic. I guess one of the local doctors had asked, "What on earth does Redalen think he is doing anyway?" I guess the reply had been, "Oh, he doesn't think he is doing hypnosis, he is." I guess I must have seemed stranger by the day to the physicians of Dubuque.

I think this exchange happened one day when a little fifteen year old gal came into the office with some minor complaint and I asked her what her sleeping habits were like. Theresa replied, "Oh, I don't sleep." I asked, "What do you mean you don't sleep?" She again responded, "I don't sleep. Sometimes I lie down to take a nap, but that is probably once every six months or maybe a year. I just do not need sleep and I don't get tired."

Theresa's mom was outside in the waiting room so I asked Theresa if it was okay if I had her mom come in. I asked her to explain what Theresa's sleeping habits were like. Her mom proceeded to tell me Theresa did not sleep. I asked about taking naps during the day but her mom said there were no naps. A physician had once asked them to document Theresa's sleeping habits because evidently he did not believe them.

Mrs. O. said they had twelve children in their family. She said they assigned one member of the family to stay up with Theresa every night and they alternated turns. During school hours, Theresa's teachers took turns watching her. Mrs. O. said they had never managed to catch Theresa napping or sleeping. At the end of a several month time period which had been an ordeal for the entire family Theresa was bright eyed, wide awake and alert and the only one in the family not suffering from lack of sleep.

I asked Mrs. O. if she would like me to fix Theresa. She replied, "Don't bother. We have had her to at least half a dozen doctors from pediatricians to psychologists to psychiatrists and nobody can fix her so don't bother trying." I replied, "Well, I am not nobody, but I can fix her. Has hypnosis ever been tried?" "No," Mrs. O. replied. I asked Theresa if she wanted to sleep like other people and she said she thought it would be great to get a rest from the day sometimes. I did not want Theresa to be distracted during the session so I asked Mrs. O. to please excuse us. She returned to the waiting room.

I said, "Okay, let's go. Theresa, I am going to talk to you and while I am doing this you are going to become very tired. This talking is called hypnosis and I have been doing this for many years and what I use is called the 'sleep method'. I do not use swinging balls and things you may have seen on television. I just talk. All you have to do is listen and try to follow what I am saying."

Theresa sat on the table and I began my usual 'sleep talk'. I was in luck. Theresa was an excellent subject the same as Renee had been. Teresa went into the deepest sleep in hypnosis. This time I had to do something different. I had to provide Theresa's subconscious a reason for why she did not sleep at night. I thought I could come up with something appealing to a fifteen year old girl.

"Theresa, you are now in a deep warm wonderful sleep. I am going to get you to go back in time a little bit to the last time you were going to a dance with a boy you liked. I want you to remember how important that dance was and how much it meant to you. You were looking forward to meeting your friend at the school dance. You had your pretty dress ready to go and you thought you would take a nap just to rest up a little bit before the dance.

"Remember how you set your alarm for the time you wanted to wake up? Can you remember how disappointed you were when your alarm did not go off and you missed the dance. It was a huge disappointment. Now Theresa, you never go to sleep anymore because you do not want to miss something as important as that dance again. It is for this reason you no longer sleep at night.

"What I am going to do is set a little alarm clock in your head and it will always go off when you want it to. From now on you will always be able to sleep at night because you never have to worry about missing a dance or any important event again. You will now always sleep well at night when you want and you never need to be concerned about waking up on time again. Your little clock will keep you on time."

I gave Theresa a posthypnotic suggestion she would remember nothing of her time asleep. She would only remember it was the most pleasant sleep she had ever had. When I woke Theresa up in my usual manner, she said she felt wonderful. I asked Theresa to come back in two weeks and I asked Mrs. O. if she would come along. She said she would, but I am sure she was more than a little skeptical.

It was two weeks later when Theresa and her mom returned. I was anxious to see if the mind game I had created worked as I thought it would. I asked, "Well how did everything go?" Theresa immediately replied with a smile, "I slept every night and did not have one night without sleep. It was wonderful." I asked, "Mrs. O., what did you observe?" Mrs. O. had a smile on her face as she said, "Theresa now sleeps normally just like everyone else in the family. I can hardly believe this after all the doctors we have seen over the past two years and now you come along and fix this in one office visit. I just don't understand what you did or how you did it but we are eternally grateful. Thank you so very much." I continued to see Theresa over the years and her sleeping problems never returned.

I did not let her know about the little alarm clock in her head. I thought if she knew about that, when she was in college later and wanted to stay up all night to study she would probably seek me out to break the little clock.

Hypnosis is a wonderful tool and to the master of this tool the prospects for its use are almost endless. It sometimes feels like a key to the universe. For those of you who want to know, it is possible for a person to be hypnotized and not even realize they are under 'the spell'.

I continued to use hypnosis throughout all my practice years, if I had the time. Time was always the only detractor for hypnosis. This was not true with the good subjects but only about one in ten people are able to go into deepest stages of somnambulism the very first time. Almost all people can be hypnotized to some degree, but the ones entering the deepest stages during the very first exposure are probably less than 10 to 20% of the population.

It was a great night for a walk in the country and when JP and I got back from our walk we decided we would drive into town and see if we could find a movie that sounded entertaining. Just as we walked in the door the phone rang.

JP answered the phone. She said, "Finley is on phone." I asked what the problem was. The nurse identified herself and said, "We have one of your patients here. Renee Lewis is in the ER. She had an altercation with her husband and sustained a laceration to her back." I said, "I will be right there."

JP asked, "Rick, why don't you just have the ER see her?" JP had met Renee one day while working at the clinic. JP did not want Renee interfering with our plans to see a movie in about an hour. I said I would rather see Renee myself which did not sit well with JP. Renee and I had talked enough that I knew what was going on at home had probably taken its toll for the night. Renee had confided in me that often when she and Mark got into disagreements they escalated into physical confrontations with Renee on the receiving end.

Renee and Mark had gotten into an altercation which had once again ended up becoming physical. Mark had shoved Renee into a nail protruding from the wall in their home and Renee had sustained about a one-inch laceration to her right shoulder. I was relatively sure Mark had not meant to cause Renee this kind of damage but he had no right using any type of physical force on this tiny being.

Renee did not have much to say. She was upset but not crying. I prepped and draped her wound, repaired the laceration and my nurse put on a dressing. We gave Renee wound care instruction and I asked her to see me in a couple of days for a recheck. I was not as interested in the wound as I was interested in how Renee was doing and what was happening at home.

Many times it is important to know how your patient's psyche is. It is far more important than simply saying, "What is the problem today and how can I help you?" Unless you are tuned into your patient's state of mind, you are not going to do a good job of caring for them. I am embarrassed by using the word 'job'. This is not a job to me. It is my profession. How do I care for my patients? How do I show them my caring and love? I know how important love is. Jesus said in the NIV Bible, this is the greatest of his Commandments: "A new command I give you: Love one another as I have loved you."

I saw Renee in the clinic a couple of weeks later. She was doing well and her laceration had healed up nicely. When I asked how everything was going at home she said everything was about as good as it ever was. It seemed as if Mark and Renee got along just fine most of the time and it was only when Mark started drinking that problems arose and he would become abusive.

During all the counseling I did I could truthfully say the most troublesome problems I ran into almost always involved alcohol. I really thought most marital problems could be solved if you could do away with mind altering chemicals. Whenever I was counseling, one of the first questions I always asked was about drug or chemical use in the home and if there was, did it have a place in the current altercation.

It is impossible to deal with relationship problems if one or both of the people involved cannot get off their chemical use regardless of which chemical is being used or abused. I cannot emphasize enough how harmful alcohol was and is in relationships.

I continued to see Renee intermittently for her asthma problems. She said she still had problems at home and Mark would sometimes be abusive. She came in one day and said that in spite of medications I had given her she was still having frequent asthmatic attacks, most of them at night or when she was getting ready for bed. Renee asked, "Isn't there any kind of treatment that could get rid of this for good?" I said, "Yes there is one thing you can do to get rid of the attacks." Renee asked, "What is that?" I replied, "Get a divorce."

Renee had a hard time believing Mark was the reason for her asthma. I said, "Let me show you something Renee. I am going to put you to sleep and then very shortly I am going to put you in your bedroom and pretty soon you will feel as though you want to go to sleep." I put Renee into a deep hypnotic sleep, which now happened in less than thirty seconds because of the post-hypnotic suggestions I had left with her. Now in her mind, Renee was in her bedroom getting ready for bed. I let Renee know Mark was entering the bedroom. As he did, Renee's breathing became more labored. When Mark started talking to her, Renee went into a full blown asthmatic attack. Of course this was an imaginary talk. Mark did not really enter the room as I told Renee he had, and imaginary Mark did not talk as I suggested to Renee he was doing.

I left Renee with her breathing problems and said, "Now Renee I am going to wake you up and you are back in the examining room with me. You are not afraid." I woke Renee and said, "You are having breathing difficulties because you were just in the bedroom with your husband." Renee was apprehensive. I asked her, "Do you want me to put you to sleep to get rid of your attack?" Renee nodded her head. I rapidly induced a deep sleep and removed the breathing problem. This time Renee was awake the entire time and I had her remember the time only minutes ago she was in her bedroom with Mark.

I said, "Renee, do you understand now why you are having asthmatic attacks at night?" Renee nodded. I had suggested she would remember our entire session.

Renee filed for divorce from Mark only one or two weeks later. She had let Mark know why she was getting divorced and Mark realized how bad Renee's asthma had gotten at night. Renee and Russel had moved out of the house immediately and it was not long before their divorce was final. I am sure Mark loved Renee enough that he was willing to do anything to help her with her breathing problems. I do not think I can emphasize enough how helpful Mark was to Renee during their divorce and the process went completely uncontested. Since Renee did not have a place to go immediately other than with some girlfriends, Renee and Mark decided together it would be best for Russel in the short run if he stayed with his father. Mark was agreeable and he was a great father to Russel.

A few months later, Mark ran into Renee on the street and they talked. Mark asked Renee how her asthma was doing now that they had gotten divorced. Renee told Mark that since moving out of the house she had never had another attack. Mark said that was good and he was happy for her. I saw Mark periodically and he never seemed to bear me any ill will, although he knew I was the one who suggested the divorce to help Renee with her asthma.

I was at a time and place in my life in which everything seemed to be going well. I had a very busy practice which grew by the day. If you want to be considered great in medicine by your patients all you need do is follow a few simple rules. Take care of your patients the way you want your own family cared for. Return calls when your patients call you. If you cannot do that, never go home in the evening with unanswered calls sitting on your desk. What may seem unimportant to you may be immensely important to your patient. Also, you never know when that one answer you provide to a seemingly small question may be the information needed to save a life.

JP and I got along very well and occasionally we would go back to Manitowoc to see friends and family and walk along Lake Michigan. I really missed the lake but Eagle Point Park and the Mississippi had taken her place rather nicely.

JP got along well with her family but they took such a harsh view of life I really did not feel I could relate well with them. In fact, I did not like them very much. I told this to JP one day when we were driving back from Manitowoc. To my surprise, JP agreed with me, but added she was not like that. It made me think of the book written by Tom Sonnito on voir dire. The one thing I remembered distinctly was if you want to get a conviction on a defendant, you pick out a jury of German females during your jury selection process. After getting to know the family of JP better, I could see how true that statement was.

This type of information is obtained by going through thousands of trials and ascertaining how people voted. It was discovered that in all trials whether defendants were innocent or guilty, German females voted for a guilty verdict over 90% of the time. I think the females in JP's family would have voted guilty 100% of the time. I sensed in all my observations of them they probably felt they were right all the time. They reminded me a little of what Bette's dad Adrian said to me one day in good humor, "I can remember when I was wrong once Rick and that was when I thought I was wrong, but I was really right." Thinking of my dear friend Adrian made me smile.

Gradually the relationship between JP and me grew but one trait of hers continually bothered me. She always seemed to pick out someone's worst qualities or features and point them out rather than pointing out the good things in people. When I mentioned the trait was very much like her mother and her sister, she of course denied it and said she was nothing like them.

I thought I could help my relationship with JP by taking her to Maui for a couple of weeks. We bummed around the island and had a great time. As many times as I had been to Maui, it was a little like a second home to me. We stayed in a condominium complex where I had stayed numerous times, Honokowai Palms, about seven miles north of Lahaina on Honoapiiliani Highway. Right across the street from our condo toward the Lahaina was a quaint little green church where I had previously gone to Sunday services. Another hop, skip and a jump to the south was a small Hawaiian style super market.

This was not the plush Royal Hawaiian where Kim and I had stayed. What I loved about it was they were small light housekeeping apartments. Neither JP nor I liked to eat out constantly so it was great to have the luxury of a place to make our meals. Across the street heading west from our apartment was Honokowai Beach Park with the Pacific Ocean as the front door. The beach for the park was mostly made up of lava flow so it was not really suitable for running around in bare feet.

Occasionally JP and I would walk into Lahaina. It was a seven mile hike but one which was beautiful. We could walk on the sandy beach for several miles and when we came to the Royal Ka'anapali Golf Course we would take off our tennis shoes and walk on the grass. Sometimes we would stop at the Chart House to get a bite to eat. The Chart House was located on the island side of the highway across from the ocean at the north end of Front Street. They had great Caesar salads and escargot. JP had never eaten snails before but she liked the delicacy as much as I did.

It was fun for us to run around Lahaina. JP and I became regulars every night at happy hour at a bar and eatery called the Rusty Harpoon in Whalers Village. They had an African Grey by the name of Doc who was not that friendly and you certainly did not put your fingers in the cage. One day they put a broom stick in the cage to show Doc's biting prowess. He snapped that thick broom stick in two like it was a toothpick.

JP and I became friends with a guy by the name of Terry Andrews who sang during happy hour every night. Terry was a great singer who sang a lot of Jimmy Buffet and other island music. One night he introduced us to one of his friends, Greg L., who hung out at the Rusty Harpoon. Greg was a tall, slender, brown skinned hippy type of islander. We shared a number of happy hours together and did the evenings up right while drinking Mai Tais and watching the sun go down.

One night Greg asked JP and me to come up to his condo for exotic drinks. Greg ran the local camera shop near the Rusty Harpoon. His dad was a physician in Oregon who owned twenty-some hospitals in Washington and Oregon.

We were impressed with Greg's condo which was on the top floor of an impressive high-rise with an equally impressive view. The entire back of Greg's condo was made up of a balcony that ran the full length of his condo and looked out on the ocean for as far as you could see. The sun was gradually going down and we sat and drank some exotic layered drinks that Greg poured together like a mad chemist. They were great. The sunset was beautiful. What more could you ask for in paradise?

The phone rang. JP and I were seated on a couple of bar stools by the kitchen nook and bar. Greg held up his forefinger and said, "Just one minute, I have to take this." I could not help but hear what Greg was saying to the person on the other end of the line. When he ended the call, I asked, "Greg did I just hear you accept a shipment of cocaine here tonight and that you have one half million cash ready for when it gets here?" Greg smiled and said yes. I said, "Greg, JP and I have to get out of here."

Greg said, "You don't have to leave. Everything is cool. There aren't going to be any problems." I replied, "Greg half a million dollars is the kind of money people will kill for." He said, "No problems. You're safe." I said, "I don't think I want to expose JP or myself to this and I won't. I'll see you tomorrow at the Harpoon."

JP and I left Greg's place. It had been a great evening up until then. What had happened surely made it a memorable evening.

JP and I ran into Greg again the following day at the Harpoon. We had a few drinks and started talking. I asked, "Greg why on earth is a young handsome guy like you who is living in a penthouse condo in paradise taking a chance on throwing it all away by selling drugs? Here we were last night watching the sunset and having a great evening. Why do you take these chances and what will you do with that load of cocaine you accepted?"

Greg responded, "My dad is wealthy but do you know I make more in a year than he has probably made in his lifetime?" I asked, "What difference does it make Greg if you get caught?" Greg responded, "It doesn't matter if I get caught. We own every customs agent on the west coast. It is not possible for me to be detained by one of them. There is no risk for me."

JP and I continued to have a good time in Maui. We headed to Hana one day and visited the little four bed hospital I worked at while my family and I lived there. We visited the Seven Sacred Pools and got something to eat at the Hana Ranch. We saw Greg and Terry several more times prior to leaving the island. As much as we enjoyed our time away it was great to get back home.

Once we were home and settled back into the grind, JP started talking about moving to another home in Dubuque. She thought the home we were living in had too many memories. Of course I thought, what the heck, they were all good memories for me. I did not really care and I wished we could live out in the country where I could perhaps have horses again.

We drove around a lot looking at possible places to live. One day we wandered by an appealing place a short distance out in the country and about six to seven miles west of my office. The home was located in a beautiful wooded area with a modern home on the lot. I placed a call to the Realtor listed on the sign. JP and I set up a time to look at the home and we fell in love with it. The home had been built by an architect and was an energy efficient home so the natural gas usage per year was extremely low to the point of almost unbelievable. The entire home had medium brown carpeting and everything in the home was done in earth tones. There was a large master bedroom with a master bath upstairs and two bedrooms each with their own bathrooms and an entertainment room downstairs. All in all it was the location I was interested in and the home had all the qualities you could ask for.

I hated moving and decided not to sell my condo at Stonehill simply to avoid moving. It was great leaving all my furniture there and it was a great little home away from home. I don't know why I thought that as it was never used as such. Eventually I rented it out to friends so it was used as a rental property up until the time I sold it a couple of years later.

We moved into our new home and loved living out in the country. We got a striking large typical Collie by the name of Laddie, beautiful and affectionate. As usual, my love of animals was written all over me and I did not admit it to JP, but I loved Laddie more than I did her. It was pretty much where my heart always was in life. I liked people but I loved animals. God gave me such beautiful connections with animals and I got to have their support throughout my entire life. It is a wondrous gift, one of God's greatest blessings to me.

When we moved in during the summer and all the foliage was out you could not see another house from our place. The superintendent of schools lived just to the north of us. Our home was on a seven acre plot completely surrounded by trees.

It was great living out in the country. It was only a 10 minute scenic drive to work in the Dubuque Building and now I was doing more work in Finley Hospital which was a short jaunt up the hill from my office. I also did all of my stress testing at Finley. The respiratory therapy staff would get my patients set up and they would always be ready to go when I got there.

My attitude about stress testing was this. I did not feel it was necessary for people to die of heart attacks if they would simply keep up to date with their stress testing. I recommended stress tests to anyone I thought was at an increased risk for having a coronary. That included people with symptoms suggesting coronary artery insufficiency such as angina. I told all young men with a male dominant pattern of hair loss and build to get stress tests. A male dominant pattern of hair loss suggests early elevated male sex hormone or testosterone which was also associated with early coronary artery disease. A family history suggestive of heart problems also put someone on my list for intervention. In all my years in Dubuque I never lost a person to a myocardial infarction (heart attack) who had kept up with their stress tests. During my years at Finley Hospital, I performed more stress tests than all of the other doctors combined. Of course, that did not mean they were not as important to those physicians as to me. They probably did their tests in another location.

Other groups of people I always did stress tests on were those with occupational risks. Every year when truck drivers came in for their DOT physicals they always knew enough to come to me a month to six weeks in advance of their test so I could get their blood pressure in check in order for them to pass their physical. I am sure many of my patients put it off for as long as possible so they would not have to endure my yearly sermons on taking care of themselves.

Following my sermon, one truck driver asked me how he could live to be one hundred. I told him to quit smoking, quit drinking, exercise, avoid illicit love affairs and get as much rest as possible. He said, "Will that really help me live to be one hundred?" I said, "Hell no, but it will surely seem like you did."

Some occupations have occupational vulnerabilities. With truck drivers, the majority of them smoked and drank too much. Most of them were overweight because of sitting all day long and not having the opportunity to exercise. I could always get them in good enough shape to pass their physicals but it was almost a given that as soon as the physical was over the honeymoon with good blood pressure was gone too. Bad behavior returns unless you make a gallant effort to curb or eliminate it. God bless the truck drivers. They try to make the roads safer for all of us and most of them do a dang good job of doing so.

JP and I got into it one day after I brought home a nice letter from a songwriter and singer I had just met in the clinic a couple weeks earlier. I was interested in his profession and had asked him questions about song writing, how he went about publishing his work and what all went into making an album. He was great to talk to and I really appreciated his time and all the pointers he had in his letter about how I could go about accomplishing some of what he had done if I decided to proceed along those lines. This was something I had thought about for a long time. I felt deep gratitude for this songwriter to take the time to sit down and write out directions to help me accomplish some of the same things.

I showed the letter to JP and she slowly read it. It was astounding to me that JP commented about the stupid waste of time that person spent writing me the long letter. I said I thought the letter was beautiful and it was wonderful that someone who had met me in the clinic only once had taken his precious time to put down on paper what it would take for me to have some of my lyrics published and copyrighted and put to music. JP said, "I think it is just foolishness." I didn't ask if it was foolish for me to contemplate writing a song or foolish of him to let me know how to do it. I could only think of the harshness of a German female at that point. I was angry and she knew it.

About one week later, JP said she was going to Manitowoc to take care of some attorney problems and to see Matt. I had a dog sitter for Laddie and I decided to take off on the spur of the moment for Phoenix. My parents were wintering north of Phoenix in a motor home I had purchased for them. My parents did not know JP and they had never visited me in Dubuque. Things were still a little cool between us. JP's harshness still bothered me and I could see no way forward for us. JP and I both took off. Fortunately, we took off in separate directions.

I called a friend of mine by the name of Rita K., a cute little blonde cosmetologist I had met in one of the local barber shops. On the spur of the moment I decided to pay Rita a visit and ask her if she could take a couple of days off and go with me to Phoenix to visit my parents and just play a while. I was more interested in playing than visiting my parents. That was probably not a great decision but I thought my time with JP was probably coming to an end although I was not sure when.

It was fun seeing my parents and my aunt and uncle, Hazel and Marvin who lived in Paradise Valley not too many miles from the campground where Mom and Dad stayed. From listening to Mom and Dad I did not think they would stay many more winters, if any, at this campground.

Dad said, "Who wants to stay in a place where every day the ambulance shows up with its sirens wailing to drag some old person off to the hospital. Not only that, they rarely come back to live here again. I don't need to be reminded on a daily basis that it is going to be your mom or me riding in that damn cart one of these days and not coming back." I think Dad had already decided this was the last winter they would spend in Phoenix. He never told me if he had already decided not to take a ride in 'that damn cart'.

Rita and I had a great time in Phoenix. I did not talk to JP the entire time I was gone and had not decided if I would say anything when I got back. So many things continued to bother me about our relationship. The dishonesty about what was going on between JP and her husband while she was going through her supposed divorce that had not been filed was still troubling to me. It just did not make sense. However, if you have two hands of cards to choose from I would guess you can pick the best hand when you have everything sorted out. I didn't know if this was the game JP was playing.

I did not have to wait a long time before I would find out how life without JP would be. JP was doing some cleaning in the garage one day and she ran across the ticket stubs to Phoenix for Rita and me. That night when I got home JP announced she was leaving and going back to Manitowoc in a day or two when she had packed up some of her belongings.

The following day when I got home from work, my place was extremely quiet. I wondered where my furry companion was that greeted me every night. I called and called for Laddie but he did not come running. I thought JP must have accidentally locked Laddie inside the house. I looked in every room and called Laddie over and over. Laddie was not to be found.

I suddenly had a terrible thought about what she told me Mike had done to her dog when he left and wanted to hurt her. He had put the dog to sleep. My heart sank to the bottoms of my feet. I then thought about Tom Sonnito's book and how German females will vote for a guilty verdict 90% of the time. I knew in my heart JP was just as harsh.

I hurriedly rushed back toward town to Laddie's veterinarian. A friend and patient of mine was the first person I saw when I went in. Carol Petrick and I had been friends for several years and knew each other well. I blurted out, "Carol, have you seen Laddie?" Carol said, "He is okay, Rick. Judy brought him in a couple of hours ago and said she wanted him put to sleep immediately. I knew you would never allow such a thing to be done so we just told JP we would and waited for you to show up as we knew you would." She opened a door and Laddie came bounding out. My heart was back in its proper place as I knelt down on the floor and hugged my furry companion.

Laddie and I went on about life as we always did and Laddie was now my sleeping companion every night. I think it was probably a welcome reprieve. Laddie would never let me down. That is one trait pets have that many humans such as JP just do not have and can never develop. I was blessed.

I was not entirely happy about JP leaving but did know it was for the best and was probably going to happen in the long run. I went to Manitowoc about one week later to see if JP wanted to come back and that was a definite no. I don't know what the hell she was so upset about. I had continual relationships going on with Jan and Kim almost the entire time we were together. I guess the thought of one more girl was the final straw.

Chapter Twenty-eight

Renee Moves In

A couple of months later a certified letter was hand delivered by a court appointed courier. It was a letter from an attorney representing JP. She was suing me for palimony. She actually wanted me to reimburse her for the time she had been off nursing to be with me.

The trips all over I guess counted for nothing as she did not bother to subtract those monies I had spent on her. She also wanted all her jewelry back and an expensive coat I had purchased for her. I had purchased a lot of jewelry for JP which she had told me to keep when she left but I guess she had reconsidered when she realized I had spent over $50,000 on her for trinkets.

The unfortunate part of this was the jewelry was purchased from a Greek friend in Galena, Illinois. Dino had friends in Chicago and he was always able to get expensive jewelry at a great price. I could not in any way let Dino's name come up regarding the purchase of jewelry. I called JP and told her to get rid of the idea she was getting jewelry back. I didn't care about the jewelry but I was concerned Dino's name could come up. I informed her that should not happen.

I made a trip over to Galena and informed Dino what JP was doing. He repeated what I had already said to JP, that it would be unfortunate if his name came up. I did not have to be reminded. Dino and I would exchange $25,000 on a simple handshake with complete trust in each other. That was all that was required. I assured Dino JP had been warned by me and she would not bring up his name. Dino then asked me the name of JP's attorney and JP's address. I said, "Dino, I am not telling you that and I will take care of everything."

On the day of court, I had told my attorney Bill Blum about the jewelry issue. Bill was also the city attorney in addition to being a great friend of mine. His dad, Bill Blum Senior, a patient of mine, was one of the wealthiest men in Dubuque. A wonderful Jewish family that made good. How unlikely is that? I don't know what I thought Bill could do about it unless he was to warn the other attorney not to bring it up.

Almost the first thing out of this attorney's mouth was, "I understand you have a Greek friend in Galena you buy jewelry from. Is your friend a jeweler? Does he own a jewelry store?" I replied, "No, he is not a jeweler and he does not own a jewelry store." He then asked, "What is your friend's name?" I was under oath and could not lie in court. I replied, "My friend's name is Dino M." The questioning went on for too long about Dino and I knew I had to do something right away for JP's safety and that of her attorney.

The courtroom adjourned for lunch. I ran out into the hallway and got on the phone to Dino and said, "Dino you better come over here right away. Your name came up in court." Dino replied, "I'll be right there." In about twenty minutes Dino showed up in the courtroom and you could immediately sense the fear and panic on JP's face. JP had returned to the court room early and her attorney was not yet present. That was lucky for him and JP.

Dino was in a long black overcoat and truly looked ominous with his head newly bald from chemotherapy he had recently started. Dino's face was grim without a hint of pleasantness. Without looking at me, he spotted JP sitting at the table in the front of the courtroom. Dino walked up to JP and laid his hand on her shoulder and said, "How ya doing baby? How's your family baby? That cute little boy of yours doing okay?" JP was trembling and could hardly speak. Dino's voice was soft and ominous, reminiscent of the voice of Marlon Brando in "The Godfather." Her voice was tremulous when she said, "My family and Matt are doing fine Dino." It looked almost as if JP might cry. Dino had taken his hand off JP's shoulder and then he put it back on and said, "It's good to see you baby. I'm glad your little boy and family are okay." To my way of thinking that was probably about the last thing on Dino's mind. Dino then turned and walked out. He did not acknowledge me once or say hi.

Just a moment later JP's attorney walked back into the courtroom and he and JP had a very hurried conversation. The judge walked back into the room and the hearing reconvened. JP's attorney said almost immediately he had consulted with his client and she had forgotten she had told Dr. Redalen he was supposed to keep the jewelry he had purchased for her. His client had no claim on any jewelry owned by Dr. Redalen. Dino had the desired effect on JP. She realized she was walking on thin, slippery ice.

I did not like doing what I had done but I had just accompanied Dino out to Huntington Neurological Research Institute and he had a glioblastoma multiformes located in his right occipital lobe. I was not really sure what all the implications were but I knew if that line of questioning had continued in the courtroom I could not guarantee the safety of JP and her attorney. I was unsure what changes were taking place in my friend but occasionally they were not pleasing to me. Also, even during good times I do not think you want to conduct handshake business with Chicago businessmen and let them down.

I had no qualms about doing what I had done and had done so knowing full well intimidation of a witness was a federal crime. Unfortunately, at that point in time in those circumstances, I knew of no better way to protect JP and her attorney. Bill later let me know JP's attorney was really quite angry with me. I thought, so what, at least he is alive as is his client.

JP was awarded $18,000 plus I had to reimburse her $1,500 for a coat which I had given her. The coat was somewhere in our house and was not to be found in spite of JP searching through the entire house. I helped her search for the coat. After all I had no use for it. I later found out her attorney had thought of bringing charges against me for tampering with a witness. He had absolutely no idea the grief I had saved him by bringing Dino into the courtroom that day. I would think the last thing in life they would want is someone with a possible life ending brain tumor angry with them and not thinking correctly.

I rationalized I had not actually influenced JP at all. I had just asked a friend of ours to come over and say hi. It was not my fault JP had taken it more personally. I was however pleased the Dino eventuality had been taken care of. Life without JP continued on much the same although I missed parts of our relationship.

The time interval for me to be alone when JP left was very short.

After telling Mary and Renee they could move into the bottom of my house, it did not take them long to do so. Mary only stayed in my home for about one to two weeks. Her jealous married boyfriend did not like our living arrangement.

It was great having Renee live with me after Mary moved out to keep her married boyfriend happy. I never did understand that completely. Mary's boyfriend was married and went home to his family every night. In spite of his marriage, he did not want Mary living in the basement of my home even though Renee would have been her roommate.

Renee and I ran around and did things together and became fast friends. Now that Renee was no longer a patient of mine the idea of going out with her was no longer a question of medical ethics. I really didn't think anyone could criticize me for dating a former patient and actually I didn't care.

Renee had a dynamite smile which lit up the room. She had a ready little giggle at everything she found funny. She was just a treat to be around. Mark and Renee got along well now that they were no longer married. Renee could pretty much have Russel with her whenever she wanted him.

Russel was a small person just like his mother and he was smart like Renee. I asked one day, "Russel, where do you think a chicken comes from, the white part of the egg or the yolk?" Without hesitating one second, Russell replied, "The white part of course." I was surprised he was right. I said "How did you know that?" Russel replied, "You've never seen a yellow chicken, have you?"

Russel also ate like his mother. Renee always stopped eating when she was satisfied. Russel was the same way. Not at all like other little boys I had been exposed to. If you offered a candy bar to Russel and he was not hungry, he always said 'No thank you'. It was no wonder he was petite like his mother.

I thought there were a lot of reasons Renee was so petite. She was on the run and busy 24 hours per day. Renee was compulsive about having a clean house, almost to the point of obsessive-compulsive. She simply could not stand to have a speck of dust which could be seen any place in the house. As I was getting out of the shower, Renee was stepping in behind me to wipe it down.

One thing slightly different about Russel and Renee was Renee liked sweets. I was a diabetic and Renee always took that into account but some nights she would bake a huge cake and put a thick layer of frosting on it. She would always ask me if I would like a piece knowing I would always refuse. She would then proceed to eat the entire cake. My goodness, some evenings I am sure she put away 15,000 to 20,000 calories. In spite of this she remained the size of Tinker Bell and never ever put on a pound of weight.

I simply could not believe a person could eat like that and not gain a pound. Renee confided in me that she gained weight during her pregnancies. She said with both pregnancies she went up to 150 pounds. I could not imagine this perfect tiny person almost doubling her 85 pound weight during the length of a pregnancy. I asked her how long it took for her to get back to her pre-pregnancy weight and she said usually one to two weeks. I could not imagine how someone could change from a bowling ball to a bowling pin in only a couple of weeks.

Our life out in the country was about as good as life can get. We got along wonderfully well and I couldn't imagine a life more idyllic. Renee would set out a schedule on the kitchen counter every day and when I got up in the morning or came home during the day all it took was a glance and I knew exactly where she was. She kept her schedule down to the minute. I guess that is what comes of being raised in an army major's home. A typical schedule would look like the following:

8 to 9 ride Dan
9:30 to 10 brush Dan
10 to 10:30 bring Dan back to the pasture
10:30 to 11:30 mow the lawn, etc.

Every minute of Renee's day was accounted for on her list every day and dang, she did not vary from the list in the least. It was almost incomprehensible to me. I had never been able to keep to a schedule my entire life and always lived on the fly with impromptu sidebars. Now I lived with the most organized person I had ever met.

About the only thing Renee didn't like about living out in the country was the occasional garter snake she would see. I always kidded her about wearing her snake boots. She had tall cowgirl boots she thought gave her all the protection she needed against snakes. It looked strange some days if I came home unexpectedly to see Renee out mowing the lawn in a small bikini and her boots.

Renee had a great way of showing me how much she cared for me. She did so many little things to make my life wonderful. One thing I always loved, when I would come home and open the door in the evening I would find Renee standing there, golden brown in one of her skimpy bikinis. Wow, it would take my breath away. Not only that, she was always had a flute of champagne in each hand, one for her and one for me. I really loved this little gal. She was my entire life and I was finally all in and fully dedicated to the one I loved.

One thing little Renee never tired of was for us to stop along any field that had a horse in it and sit and watch for sometimes an hour. It was impossible not to see the love in Renee's eyes for horses. It was a joy for me because having grown up with these large furry friends, I had the same love for them as did she. I longed to be able to put my arms around my horse's neck again and whisper in their big ears how much I loved him or her.

One day as we were driving across the countryside only about a mile or so from our home, Renee said, "Rick, Rick, stop. Look at those little colts out in the field. Can we stop and watch them run around?" I said, "Of course." As we were sitting in the tall grass in the ditch watching the nearly new-born foals run around and kick up their heels, Renee asked, "Rick, do you think God made unicorns?" I put my arms around Renee's shoulders and replied, "Look around you honey. As far as we can see, we cannot see anything he has not made. I am sure he made some unicorns." Renee smiled at my answer. The more I thought about it, I was sure God had made unicorns. How blessed was I to have this little person in my life who loved everything about life the same as me.

I absolutely loved the touches Renee had put on her new home. There were soon very few walls in the house without a picture of a horse. I loved it. In addition to this Renee had soon made Laddie one of her best friends. I could not have a life any better.

Renee was telling me about a big golden retriever she had when she was a little girl. Renee would often say, "When I was little." I wouldn't let her get any farther without interrupting her saying, "Renee, you are still little." To this Renee replied, "Well, when I was little'er my dad would always tell me not to take the dog for a walk on his leash by myself. One day I thought, I should be able to take my own dog for a walk. I put his leash on and tied the other end around my wrist so he could not get away. We only walked for a little ways and he saw a cat. He took off and dragged me for a couple blocks before he stopped. I was covered with scratches and scrapes and blood." I could just picture this in my mind. I couldn't imagine how small Renee must have been when she was little'er but she really wasn't big enough to control a large dog right now. A slender 85 pound female is no match for a 100 pound dog after a cat.

At times, Renee could be a stern disciplinarian who did not tolerate nonsense. One day when Russel was visiting, he was behaving as all little boys do. I don't know what he was doing that was irritating Renee, but suddenly she said, "Russel, you better be good, or I'm taking you home." Russel looked at her and nodded his head yes. I asked for a minute of Renee's time. I said, "Honey, Russel is just being a little boy. You don't want to take him home or threaten him with that. We don't want him to think he is disposable just because he gets a little out of line. He has to feel he has a home with us regardless of what he does." Renee said, "Well he can behave." He always did from what I could tell.

I was seeing patients in the office, as always, when a blonde slightly built girl I had seen a couple months previously came in. The girl's name was Debbie B. I had seen her for a problem with enuresis. Debbie was in her early thirties and had never told me much about where she grew up. I did know one thing about her; as a child, she had been raped repeatedly starting at about the age of five by her father. That was also the time bed-wetting started. As you can imagine about the only defense against sexual abuse for a five year old would be wetting the bed. What adult wants to consummate a sexual assault in a wet bed?

I had given Debbie medications which she said had helped her problems but today she was in the office to talk with me. She said, "I am not here to talk about myself." Debbie asked me if I knew she was related to Jim F., her uncle who had previously been a patient of mine. Debbie then proceeded to ask me, "Do you know Tammy F.?" I replied slowly, "Isn't that the name of my wife Renee's daughter?" Debbie said, "Yes, Tammy is your stepdaughter. Do you know anything about her?" I said, "No, I only know she is living with Jim F. and his wife Louise in Los Angeles." I would not even know if I saw her on the street. I had never seen a picture of Tammy.

Debbie told me what she wanted me to know. She asked, "Do you know anything about Tammy's situation?" To which I replied, "What situation?" Debbie said, "I have been writing and in touch with Tammy since she was nine years old. Since then Tammy has been raped almost daily by her stepfather and his brothers." I was horrified. I asked, "Do you know this for a fact?" She replied that she did. Jim F. had also raped her when she was a child. I asked, 'Does Tammy's stepmother Louise know?" Debbie said, "No, I am almost sure she doesn't." Debbie gave me a contact number for Louise.

That night, I went home and discussed this with Renee and we were both very concerned. When I related the story Debbie told me, Renee said Jim F. had also tried to rape her when she was a young girl. Evidently he gave her a motorcycle ride and ended up in a secluded area of the country. Jim attacked Renee and tried to rip her clothes off. She ran from the assault and back to the city. Jim had never tried again. I said, "I think we have to call Louise and at least let her know what is going on." Renee was horrified by the story as much as I was and we were in agreement, we had to do something.

I called the F. residence that evening when I surmised it would be at an hour when Louise would be at home. Luckily I got Louise on the phone the very first ring. I introduced myself. I said I was Dr. Redalen and practiced medicine in Dubuque, Iowa. I explained I have a patient by the name of Debbie B. who I understand is related to you through your husband. I told her Debbie had come into my office. I related the story Debbie had told me about Louise's stepdaughter. At the time I really was not sure of the convoluted relationships by which everyone seemed to be bound.

Louise became furious with me when she heard the story. She slammed down the phone on me and that seemed to be the end of the conversation. I tried calling her back but she would hear nothing of what I had to say. The phone was again slammed down terminating the conversation.

Renee and I spent a couple hours talking that evening trying to decide what to do. Renee said that by now Tammy was thirteen years old so this continual assault had gone on for nearly four years according to the history I got from Debbie B. None of that was comforting but the fact Tammy was still alive and able to correspond regularly gave a very tiny amount of relief. What we were unsure of was what would happen to

Tammy if suddenly she was the only witness who could now verify the continual rapes had taken place. Were we putting her life in danger?

By now I had a long history of dealing with social services over the years. They are a bunch of people who for the most part are very dedicated and badly want to take care of all the children of the world. Sometimes they do a fantastic job. Other times they have failures not only due to the vagaries of their work but also through failures of our system. It seemed to me it was almost always a system failure and not due to the tough job our social workers do.

Out of concern for Tammy's welfare, we decided to wait to see how Louise would process the information I had given her. We knew from talking to other people Louise was not a person who would allow something such as this to happen in her home to the child for which she was a guardian.

Debbie B. stayed in touch with me and one day she said Louise was moving back to Dubuque with Tammy. Renee and I were both extremely happy. We did not know any details but thought this could only be good news. All we knew was Louise and Tammy were coming by themselves. This was also a good sign to us as now the rapist had supposedly been left behind. We found out later Tammy was going to a school in Dubuque and Debbie B. said she was doing well. I cannot imagine what resilience that must take. A life of being raped and now you are a regular school student. God bless you my child.

Dubuque was a different life for me. It was one where there was more of a drinking crowd. It was seldom you would go out that everyone did not have a cocktail. Since I was a solo practitioner I was not usually able to partake in the festivities unless I could get someone to cover for me for the night.

When summer rolled around, it seemed like the pig roasts would get started up. They were fun, usually rather huge gatherings of friends and neighbors to eat roasted pig and drink beer. One day after being at a hog roast at Dave and Karen Nebel's home I thought it would be good for Renee and me to put one on for our patients and friends. I talked to my friend Dave who regularly put on pig roasts and asked him if he would put one on at our house.

I explained to Dave it would have to be a large hog as I would anticipate hundreds of my patients would show up once the word got around.

Dave explained how that would work.

He said typically the pig would be started on the roaster about two to three in the morning. The roasting would go on until around noon or early afternoon the next day. Dave had a huge pig roaster which he had made himself. He said he would bring a 270 pound hog or thereabouts after being dressed and we would start getting everything together.

A couple days prior to the pig roast I asked Dave if he knew anyone who had quarter horses for sale. I said I planned to buy Renee a horse but it was supposed to be a surprise. Dave said, "I have a friend only about a mile or two just up the road from you who has a bunch of horses. His name is Bill Boge and he is a deputy sheriff. Shortly after that Dave took me up to Bill's place and introduced us. I asked Bill what he had for a gentle quarter horse a small woman could handle and be completely safe on its back. Bill said, "I have the perfect horse for you. He is a registered quarter horse gelding who is as gentle as a child."

Bill led me to the corral behind his house that held probably about twenty some horses. He went out and put a bridle on a beautiful chestnut gelding he led easily back to me. I stroked the horse's nose and looked into his big brown eyes. He had me immediately and I thought the same would be true of Renee. Bill said this horse's registered name was Scat Away Dan. I asked Bill how much he was and wrote out a check.

I said, "Bill, I am getting this horse for my wife, Renee, who has loved horses since the time she was a little girl. I want this to be a surprise for her." Pam Boge, Bill's wife came outside and Bill introduced me to her. Pam was a pretty redhead and also a horse person. I asked Pam if she and Bill would come to a pig roast at our home on Saturday. I said, "I am sure you will recognize hundreds of people."

Pam said that sounded great. I said, "Bill will you ride Dan over to our house that day? I know as soon as Renee sees you she is going to run up to you and say, 'Say mister, say mister, can I ride your horse?'" Why wouldn't she? That is what she always said when someone rode by on their horse. Sometimes riders were a little reserved and skeptical because of Renee's diminutive size. I do not recall Renee had ever been turned down after she told them she was a good rider. Big brown pleading eyes probably helped. Bill said he would be there.

On the day of the pig roast Dave and I had already been up for almost half a day. Dave surely knew how to add the trimmings to a hog roast.

He was a hunter and in addition to roasting this gigantic hog, he had stuffed the entire inside with wild game. I can't begin to tell you how good this already smelled by early morning. My mouth was watering and I was anxious to taste our work. Dave and his help had lined up another friend to deliver eight kegs of beer. It seemed like a lot to me but I thought better to be safe as the day was slated to be hot and sunny. Cold beer would probably go down pretty well.

By one or two in the afternoon, cars were parked down both sides of the quarter mile lane from our house to the highway and lined up for at least a quarter to one half mile on both sides of the highway both east and west from our lane. If we went by numbers the party was already a huge success.

Chapter Twenty-nine

Dreams

I could hear Renee saying, "I'm all right Rick, I'm all right." Renee was shaking me and trying to wake me from the recurrent dream that seemed to plague way too many nights of sleep. The dream was always the same. Renee was floating in a brightly colored hot air balloon of red, yellow, white and blue. The season was winter and the balloons looked much like all the hot air balloons we had seen in Steam Boat Springs when we had been there skiing with Jed and Marla Brickley.

Renee was waving at me on the ground and laughing. I was waving back. I suddenly realized the balloon Renee was in was drifting toward some high power lines. I started screaming, "Renee, look out, Renee, look out!" It was no use and I watched hopelessly as the balloon hit the wires, burst into flames and went crashing to the ground. I could see Renee lying on the ground with the power lines across her chest, her little body convulsing from the electric shocks.

When Renee finally got me awake, I was crying and the tears flowed heavily down my face as I had just watched the love of my life die before my eyes. The dream was so very realistic and I relived Renee's death over and over and the crying became an almost nightly terror. Dreams in the Redalen family always mean something. I could not figure out what this recurring dream meant though.

Did it mean Renee was going to die? I could only think my dream was a predictor of death and of course from my past experiences, I knew I could not change what would eventually happen. God, why do you let me see the future if I cannot change it? What I knew seemed strange when compared to the blessings of prophesy I associated with the prophets of biblical times. However, I guess they did not get to change what was going to happen either. They only knew what was going to happen.

It was not long after starting to have the dreams about Renee I began having another recurring dream. In the dream I was running in a race and I was the lead runner. Suddenly I began to get weaker and then I fell down and try as hard as I could, I could not get up. I was too weak to get to my knees and then I tried to crawl toward the finish line. I thought perhaps the dream meant I was powerless to do anything about the dreams I was having about Renee and the hot air balloon.

The only other interpretation of the dream I could come up with was I was going to develop a disease I could not control and the disease would be one which would control me. I viewed falling and being unable to get up as a complete failure of my body. I would not have to wait awfully long before I would learn what the dream meant.

This was long after the time I had dreamed of winning the gold medal in the Olympics in the mile run. I knew the dream did not have anything to do with that failure. I knew my mom had been having problems with her heart lately and she had gone into atrial fibrillation. That is a condition when the top part of our heart just quivers instead of beating regularly to fill the bottom part of your heart, the ventricles.

When atrial fibrillation is present the ventricles do not get filled as well and the cardiac output drops. A fib, as it is called, is a common heart condition in the elderly and can usually be handled with medications. The patient continues on with little change in life except perhaps a little less exercise tolerance.

Mom had recently had a workup and had an angiography done on her coronaries. The cardiologist said Mom's coronary arteries were like those of a teenager. She had absolutely no vascular disease. They decided that since there was no sign of disease in her coronary vessels they would have to look for other causes.

Mom was referred by her cardiologist to Dr. Smith in Minneapolis. Dr. Smith, a graying middle aged man of medium build and pleasant demeanor, was a specialist in mitochondrial and neuromuscular diseases. These specialists are very difficult to find. One reason is mitochondrial disease is not very common. There are only about 1,000 people born with this disease every year in the U.S.

After taking a very detailed medical history and doing an examination he decided to do a skeletal muscle biopsy on Mom. Skeletal muscle is just one of our regular muscles and not part of the heart. He thought that might give us an answer as to what was causing Mom's heart problem. When Mom returned to Dr. Smith about a week later she was given the results of her biopsy. What ended up being the cause of Mom's atrial failure was a genetic mutation. She had what was termed mitochondrial myopathy or mitochondrial muscular dystrophy. It was a condition in which mitochondria would gradually disappear from the body. Mitochondria are in every living cell and provide the power to all the cells of the body.

What had caused this mutation? With some research, my sisters started to piece together some plausible theories as to the cause. Fortunately, my sisters could have been younger sisters of Einstein. Mom and Dad had lived in Spokane, Washington during the Second World War when Dad was working on radar for our government. We were to find out later that our government in all of its thoughtfulness during the war had dumped the radiation of the Hanford, Washington nuclear plant into the Columbia River which at the time was one of the water supply sources for Spokane. Not only that, at night radioactive waste was released into the air. Our government probably thought, why not find out what this radiation will do to our citizens? After all, it will not last forever. Only twenty million years.

This would later come to be known as the 'Hanford Experiment' which would affect hundreds of thousands of people for which our government claimed and still claims no responsibility. However, the U.S. government settled many lawsuits for which they were not responsible. This hush, hush affair was not brought to the attention of most American people. In spite of all of this, the records of many people remain sealed to this day. The Hanford Experiment information is sealed and work with these records has been discontinued. Sweeping things under the rug seems to be our government's favorite way of handling things. Why should it be any different than the way they handled Agent Orange from the Vietnam era?

I know this is getting off on a side bar but it is important. The Hanford, Washington site is still extremely dangerous. It stores millions of gallons of radioactive waste and does so inadequately with leaky storage tanks. It is thought to be the most radioactively contaminated site in the United States and possibly the world.

It is still being cleaned up and the people of Hanford are so happy the government is giving them all these good jobs. Obama proposed cutting off millions of dollars in cleanup funding to this site. There was a $289 million dollar cut in 2016 with a proposed $800 million dollar budget for 2017. No worries that this site is on the Columbia River which remains a major water supply throughout the state. Do we worry the Columbia could at any time become contaminated and unusable and we would virtually lose a state?

Amazing isn't it? We worry about Chernobyl and Three Mile Island and the worst disaster in our country is hidden from the American people. At least the Russians had the sense to cap Chernobyl and we pretend that our disaster is nothing. Should cement be poured over the Hanford site?

I went with mom for one of her appointments. Dr. Smith informed her she would pass this down to all her children. He also explained the disease would gradually rob all of us of our strength. The mitochondria are the little power cells of our body and they would gradually become fewer in number and affect all the children to various degrees. It was an X-linked recessive gene so only the female children would continue to pass the disease on down to their offspring. After I learned this information, my recurring dream ended. I now knew what it meant. I would become weak and the little power cells in my body would gradually disappear. A few days later I left Minneapolis and headed back down to Dubuque.

Renee and I quietly married in a Lutheran church in Dubuque. How blessed I am the love of my life is now my wife.

Everything was going routinely at the office on a Friday when a good friend Jimmy Klauer called. He said he and Debbie were having a few drinks at the Dubuque Inn tonight and would Renee and I care to join them for happy hour? Jimmy said it was a goodbye party for Debbie. I told Jimmy I would have to check with Renee but thought it would probably work for us.

Renee and I decided to meet Jimmy Klauer and his girlfriend at the Dubuque Inn. They had been together for years and they were now saying goodbye. They had been going together for ages but Jimmy could never bring himself to ask Debbie to get married and that is what she wanted. She wanted the same thing as every girl nearing the beginning of the end of their reproductive years.

Now she was making a complete break by moving to Los Angeles to a new job and a new life. They really loved each other and it was inconceivable to Renee and me that this great relationship was coming to an end simply because Jimmy could not bring himself to make their relationship legal. To me it seemed more symbolic than anything else. They were together in every other way except marriage.

We were talking in between the sets sung by a group from Chicago. Both Jim and Debbie were kind to each other and it was obvious Jimmy did not want to see her go. I talked to Jimmy when the girls got up to go to the bathroom. I asked, "Why don't you just get married if that is all it takes to keep her in town? You love her so that is not the problem." Jimmy agreed with everything I was saying but said he just could not bring himself to tie the knot. When the girls came back, I think it was bothering Renee more than it was bothering Debbie.

We had a few cocktails and sat and talked some more and then Renee got up and I thought she was running back to the bathroom. After about twenty minutes Renee had not returned so I asked someone if they would check in the bathroom to see if she was there. The girl I asked returned and said she wasn't. I then went out to the car to see if I could find her there. She was in the car crying. I asked her what was wrong and she replied, "See, even great couples break up. Jimmy and Debbie have one of the strongest relationships we know. If they can break up, any couple can break up." I did not know how Renee extrapolated that the breakup of friends was portent of the breakup of our relationship.

I said, "Renee that is just foolishness. You and I are not going to break up. Their breakup is no indication the same will happen to us. You and I will be together forever. Our marriage will never go away. I love you so much. I would never allow that to happen. Let's go back inside and finish saying our goodbyes." Renee said, "I do not want to go back inside, Rick. Please just take me home and come back out here by yourself. I am just sad. You can still have fun and Debbie and Jimmy are good friends of yours." I begged Renee to stay but she would not hear of it.

I jumped into the driver's seat and we headed for home. The Dubuque Inn was only a few miles from Watters Forest Drive where we lived.

When I brought Renee inside she said she was going to lie down in a little bit and encouraged me to go back to the Dubuque Inn and finish saying goodbye to our friends. She said, "This may be the last time you get to see Debbie in your life." I told her I really did not want to go back alone. Again she said, "At least go back to say goodbye and then come home."

I went out, jumped into the car and then decided I had already said enough goodbyes. I was already backing out of the driveway so I put the car in forward and drove back in. Renee was already lying down in bed and had turned the TV on. We talked for a little bit and I tried to console her about Jimmy and Debbie's breakup.

As we were talking I noticed Renee started talking a little more slowly and I asked her if she was all right. She said, "I am just fine Rick, just tired." Renee's speech rapidly deteriorated. I said, "Renee, Renee, what have you taken. Did you have a drink?" It seemed impossible. I was only out of the house for sixty seconds at the most. Suddenly Renee could not talk. I literally screamed at her. "Renee what have you done?" She tried to gesture toward the kitchen.

I grabbed Renee by the waist and rushed with her under my arm to the kitchen. There was a brown pill bottle on the kitchen counter. I read the label and became immediately horrified. Renee had taken an entire bottle of amitriptyline. I had seen that bottle around one day and asked why she still had it. I had prescribed that medication to her a couple of years prior when she was going through a depression. It was during a time when Renee and Mark were not getting along. I knew this tricyclic anti-depressant even in small overdoses was deadly. I screamed again and said, "Renee, now I cannot even save your life." I was frantic. I ran out to the car and almost threw her into the passenger seat. I did not even take the time to put on her seat belt.

I threw the car into reverse and floored the Subaru heading toward Finley Hospital hoping against all hopes I could make it before Renee's first cardiac arrest. I drove as fast as the little car could go and almost did not keep it on the road. I kept one set of fingers on Renee's carotid pulse. It was remaining regular until we were almost at the hospital. It then began to start throwing PVCs. The extra beats were the first signs of the amitriptyline overdose. I knew Renee was getting ready to arrest. I almost drove through the front doors of the hospital which were next to the entrance doors of the emergency room.

I scooped Renee up and ran through the doors shouting, "Tricyclic overdose. She is getting ready to arrest." I ran into an empty room and threw Renee down on the table and as I did she had her first cardiac arrest. Dr. Mac was on call. I explained what had happened as the code had already gone into full alert. An IV was now going and one person was doing chest compressions.

Now Mac was intubating Renee and ambu respirations were going on. The electrodes had been attached and confirmed ventricular fibrillation. It was at this point in time the first cardioversion was attempted. The paramedic yelled clear and Renee was shocked the first time. Her little body leapt off the table as the current flowed through her. No result. She was still in fibrillation. They shocked her again and again but her heart remained in fibrillation.

As I watched the paddles delivering the electric shocks to Renee's chest, I finally understood what my recurring dreams were about. I knew in that very instant those dreams would now leave me forever. Why did God give me this warning and why was it given so far in advance of the actual happening? I was right about the dreams. I never had another dream about Renee in the hot air balloon. I was finally done with my middle of the night sobbing, aching and crying in my heart. I would never again in a dream see little Renee with the power lines laying across her chest shocking her to death. I was now watching the shocks in real life.

I was upset with the person doing inadequate chest compressions. As an advanced cardiac life instructor I ran very tight codes. Small things were often the difference between life and death. I screamed at the person doing the chest compressions and said, "Get the fuck out of there and let someone work who knows what they are doing." A nurse took her place who did them adequately.

Mac grabbed my arm and said, "Rick, please wait outside and let us do our work." I waited right outside the door for what seemed to me like an eternity and then Mac came out with a look on his face that said everything. He said, "Rick, I am sorry we lost Renee. She didn't make it." Mac was leading me toward the nursing station. Within thirty seconds a paramedic came running out and yelled, "Mac, we have a pulse."

Dr. McDermott ran back inside the room and again it seemed as though an eternity was passing. In actuality it was about ten minutes when Mac came back out and said, "Rick we have Renee in a regular rhythm right now but with very frequent PVCs we are doing our best to control. We are going to move her up to the ICU. I think we have a chance Rick, but Renee is completely unresponsive to any stimuli. I do not know what has happened to her brain through all of this." Mac apologized saying, "I am sorry Rick; we did the best we could."

By now they were taking Renee out of the room and she was hooked up to a couple IVs and some monitoring equipment. The little light of my life was clinging onto life. Now I could only pray continually and hope she would make it. I sat by Renee's bed in the darkened ICU room. The nurses had Renee hooked up to the cardiac monitor and I could see she was maintaining RSR (regular sinus rhythm), but was still throwing frequent PVCs. She was still completely unresponsive. One positive sign was her pupils still responded to light when the nurses checked them. They were not fixed and dilated which would have most likely been a sign of brain death.

We finally had some lab work back on Renee. The tricyclic dosage she had taken was five times the lethal dosage. No one had ever survived that level of an overdose. I guess when our hospital called out to numerous toxicology centers and poison control labs they had let the doctors know it was one of their own doctors' wives that had overdosed. Calls began coming in from around the United States. Evidently various poison control centers were now collaborating on trying to find a solution for one of their own and hoping to provide answers, any answers that might swing the pendulum in our favor. Some of them asked to talk to me in person to explain their thinking.

One doctor told me to have the attending physician give Renee charcoal. This was something done immediately after an overdose to absorb the medication or chemical in question so it would not have its full effect. His thinking was even though Renee had absorbed everything by now some of it would pass through the liver in her enterohepatic circulation in its original form and the charcoal would at least capture that small amount. We did so. We had to try everything. No one was likely to survive this level of tricyclics.

The calls continued to pour in during these first eight hours Renee remained critical. During this time she had a couple more cardiac arrests and each one had been successfully cardioverted. The Finley nurses were golden. I could not have asked for better, more attentive care of Renee. It was as if they were caring for their own child. Mac stopped by several times to see how she was doing. A couple of other physicians stopped by to give encouragement but the caring of the Finley nurses was unsurpassed and I was blessed to have them in my corner. If Renee did not survive it definitely was not going to be on the backs of my nurses.

Dr. Reddy, the anesthesiologist in charge of her airway said that part of her care was doing well. There were no airway difficulties. A portable chest x-ray had been taken and I walked down to the radiology department to see how it looked. I asked the radiologist who had just looked at Renee's x-ray to put it up for me. When it came to looking at patient x-rays, I was the gold standard, not some radiologist who did not even know the history. The radiologist put up the x-ray and asked, "Why do you care Rick? Is she a patient of yours? I heard she was brain dead anyway." It was an inappropriate and careless remark by a physician who momentarily was not thinking. I guess I forgave him.

I replied, "The patient you are referring to is my wife." The radiologist looked horrified and said, "My God, Rick. I am so very sorry. I am so very, very sorry." I turned around and left.

In the very early hours there was nothing but prayers to cling to. With Renee just lying there entirely motionless, all I could do was hold her hand and talk to her pleading with her not to leave me. The bottomless pit of emptiness was almost more than I could stand. At times I began sobbing uncontrollably and my tears sank into her bedding where I buried my face. Thoughts and emotions literally flooded my senses. Hundreds of thoughts ran through my mind. What could I have done differently to help this person I loved so much want to live?

I had the two pieces of medallion Renee and I always carried. The medallion was Mizpah from Genesis. Renee had one half and I had the other. The medallion said, 'The Lord watch between thee and me while we are absent one from the other'. I pinned Renee's half of the medal to her hospital gown and I pinned the other half to my shirt. Now indeed, the Lord had to watch between us even though we were only absent from one another by Renee's sleep. Sleep sounded better than coma.

I sat beside Renee's bed and prayed for three days without ceasing.

Renee was still completely unresponsive. I guess a few pastors from our church came to the hospital along with several of our friends but I cannot tell you who they were. I sat with my head on Renee's bed.

The nurses came and talked to me continually and asked me to go home or go get something to eat. I said I could not. They would bring me water and food which remained untouched but I did not leave Renee's side for five days. Then one day as I was sitting at Renee's bedside she opened her eyes and I could see she recognized me. It was my first glimmer of hope. God had answered my prayers. I now knew Renee was going to be with me. I do not think there had ever been a more joyous moment in my life.

On day five, Jim Muntz came and asked me to leave the hospital. I think some of the nurses had talked to Jim and asked him if he could get me away from the hospital for a while. I vaguely knew through my haze that Jim and Char had been regular visitors. I had not shaved, showered or eaten in five days. During my fast, God had answered my prayers. I had not seen the sunshine in five days. Jim took me to a sub shop and all at once I felt as though I could eat again. I ordered a foot long sub and asked them to put as many jalapeno peppers on as they could. Jim asked, "Are you sure you should be eating something like that after nothing for five days?" I could not imagine it but the food tasted great and it was if I had not eaten for five years.

I asked the hospital where they had put my car. I had not seen my car for five days since driving it up on the hospital sidewalk and almost into the emergency room. I drove home and once more felt as though we would survive. My clothes were falling off me and when I looked in the mirror I hardly recognized my own face. I weighed myself and had lost 30 pounds in only five days. I looked as though I was the one who belonged in the hospital.

Renee was still on the ventilator. Dr. Reddy visited in the afternoon and had decided she could come off and do so safely. Dr. Reddy removed the endotracheal tube and Renee seemed to do well at first but a couple of hours later in the early evening she developed some respiratory stridor. Shortly after this Renee's pulse ox began falling, she began throwing PVCs again and once more it looked as if she would arrest. Renee's pulse ox continued to go down. I asked the nurses to call Dr. Reddy to come back and intubate her again but they told me he was going to have supper first.

I told the nurses to tell Dr. Reddy if he did not get his ass back here immediately, I was going to shove his supper up his ass and then he could meet with an attorney to protect him through the malpractice suit I was filing. I could not imagine supper being more important to a physician than his patient but my Finley nurses said they had never known that not to be the case.

I would get a chance to talk to my nurses later and found they did not speak kindly about the doctor's responses to frantic calls from nurses in their own ICU. Dr. Reddy's unresponsiveness was not isolated, it was the norm. It makes some sense if you stop to think about it. Cardiologists are lost when it comes to codes. Why wouldn't they be? They never run them. They are a shadow of what a nurse is when it comes to handling a cardiac code. The only difference beyond the abilities are the letters behind a physician's name. Who really cares about that when it is the RN keeping you alive and not the MD?

What the general public does not know is our nurses and paramedics in an ICU are far superior in their care of cardiac arrests than the cardiologists they take orders from. They handle codes on a daily basis for a living. Often cardiologists just get in the way. That is why they are slow to respond. It's called inadequacy. At least we have to give them credit. They are aware of their inadequacies and fortunately it keeps many of them from intervening in a code better cared for by others.

Dr. Reddy was there immediately and I thanked him for leaving his meal. I am sure my anger was not lost on him. Renee's monitor went back to normal as soon as the hypoxia cleared. During this intubation when Renee could not talk, I told her that her bunny had brand new baby bunnies.

Renee did not know that one day I had put our little buck bunny in with our little doe for the day. I knew our little doe was soon going to have babies when I saw her start building the nest for the new arrivals. A female rabbit or doe begins pulling out the fur on the front of her chest to help make her nest prior to having her kittens or kits as a baby rabbit is called. Having the babies is called kindling.

Renee's eyes were smiling and laughing and she was smiling around her endotracheal tube. Only twenty-four hours later, Renee was once more weaned off the ventilator. This time she did well. The day following she was moved to a private room.

When I came in the following morning to visit, Renee was doing sit-ups in her bed. I asked, "Renee, what on earth are you doing?" She replied, "Well I have not gotten to work out in the past week and I have a lot of making up to do." I could hardly believe it. Here only a couple of days ago this little angel was battling to stay alive and now the little imp was working out to get back in shape.

When I began questioning her about little things I did not know if she could recall, she did not miss a beat. It was hard to believe that only several days ago, she had been in a coma and not expected to live, let alone ever be completely neurologically intact again. She was back to normal and God had returned her to me whole.

I left that afternoon and told Renee I would be back in the evening. When I returned the nurses were looking at me quizzically as I was carrying a brown paper bag and had a big smile on my face. I put my index finger over my pursed lips as if to tell them to not say anything. Several of them could not help but follow me into Renee's room. I gently laid the brown paper bag out sideways on the bed and out came hopping seven of the cutest little baby bunnies of all colors you can imagine. The smile on Renee's face lit up the room. Her recovery was now complete. Thank you so much God for your miracles. Without You in my life, I am nothing. Now You have also given Renee seven more little miracle reasons to want to leave the hospital.

When Renee was being rolled out in the wheelchair people in the hospital were gathered and lined up on both sides of her path. They were all saying the same thing as Renee rolled past, "Miracle Child." "Miracle Child." The name resonated strongly in my heart and indeed she was a Miracle Child. God had performed the miracle I had asked for.

That was a given. God had showed me and all of us what happens when He goes to work with his blessings. Renee, who had taken five times the lethal dose of a tricyclic anti-depressant and could not possibly survive, had just left the hospital, a testimonial to God's work.

A few days later it was as if nothing in Renee's life had even happened. She was back to the smiling happy person she was before the Dubuque Inn. Thunder and Ace greeted her as if she had been gone forever licking her face and almost knocking her down with happiness. I do not know if they knew how close they had come to losing her. The other thing Renee did immediately was to go see Dan. She was hugging him and loving on him and Dan was happy to see his friend. He and Renee were like conjoined twins when it came to their relationship. The next thing Renee did was to take Dan for a ride out in the pasture. She was whole again. Oh my God, how we were blessed.

It seemed as if life was completely beautiful again. It was hard for me to even conceive of what had happened and how close we had come to losing our idyllic life. But then I guess I was not thinking the same as Renee was.

One day she said to me, "Rick, you have given me everything I have ever wanted in life. This is the way I want to die. I know if I die now, I will have all of this beauty in heaven. I love my life with you Rick and I do not want it to end. It will never end if I die now." I could not imagine after surviving a threatening, near life ending ordeal, that Renee was once more talking about death and how dying now would preserve the way she was now living.

That kind of reasoning was very difficult for me to deal with. In spite of my constant reassurance that nothing was ever going to change between us, it did not seem to inspire Renee to the same level of confidence I had. I decided to take Renee to see Tom Sonnito again. Right after Renee left the hospital we had scheduled several sessions with him and now we were back again. After another number of sessions, I knew Tom was a little exasperated with Renee. It is hard to deal with someone who always says, "I do not have to be here" meaning Renee could leave this life at any time. I knew for a fact she felt this to the depth of her soul.

It is very difficult knowing the person you love is always hanging on to life by a thread or even a strand of spider web. How can our connection to something this beautiful be so infinitely small that we balance on the point of a pin? Such was life with Renee. We were so happy all the time and always living with death a few seconds away.

It was very hard for me to imagine someone taking their life when it was exactly what they had dreamed of. One thing I felt was certain; Renee could never leave someone else to care for Dan, Angel, Thunder and Ace. They were the loves of her life and as long as they were around I felt her life would be in an iron vice. Something she could not let go.

Life was idyllic following our return to a semblance of normality.

One problem I had was continual worry about Renee staying with me. One day when I called home and could not reach her, I made an excuse to Sheila and said I had to run home to see if she was all right. I asked her to tell my waiting room full of patients I would be right back.

I tore out of there in the Corvette I was driving that day and set new speed records. When I got there, Renee with her perfect little body was out mowing the lawn in one of her bikinis and her snake boots. I was so relieved.

When I got back to the office, Sheila said, "Rick, I have never known anybody like you who feels that every time they see a little bird with a broken wing they are going to fix it." I just said, "That is the way God made me, Sheila. It is unlikely in this life that anything is ever going to change. I have always been this way and guess I always will." I don't think Sheila knew how close she had come to describing the person she worked with. In life, every injury I had ever seen, I tried to make it right again and prior to medical school it was almost always the furry and feathered ones of the animal kingdom.

I thought back to the time when I told Mom and Dad I was going to medical school. They said it was great but they did not know how I could ever make it through the dog labs in school. Although Dad and Mom did not know much about medical school, they had heard of the dog labs where furry children were sacrificed following procedures and operations medical students performed on them.

It was part of the learning process. I had tried not to think about it and did not know how I could survive that part of school. Without seeing this part of school, on the face of things it seemed cruel and barbaric to me. How can you sacrifice a living animal just so you can learn something? Those memories now were in the distant past and I had made it through the dog labs. At this point in life I had tried to forget about them.

I knew Sheila was right about one thing. She said, "You know Rick, one of these days it is going to be you dying. It is not going to be Renee. She is dragging you down, Rick. You can't worry about someone 24 hours per day and survive yourself."

When I slept with Renee at night I always wrapped my arms so tightly around her I thought I might break her. I thought if I just held her tightly enough she would know how much I cared for her. I could not imagine someone held this closely in the arms of love would still want to leave in order to capture it forever. How could this be? That is simply not reasonable. If I love life this much why do I end it now in order to keep it forever? It does not make sense. Renee made me feel as though it was me clutching to the thread of life.

Renee and I went to see Tom Sonnito again and Renee would always say, "I do not have to be here." But I asked, "Renee, how can you continually think of ending your life when we have so much to live for? You are not being fair to me to continually think about death. It is hard on me. Look at how many times I run home during the day checking on you to make sure you are all right. Renee, Sheila said to me the other day she thought I was going to die before you did. You don't want to hear that do you?" Renee then said she would not kill herself but was not very convincing.

Tom interrupted at that point, "Renee, you are going to kill yourself one of these days and there is not a dang thing Rick or I can do about it. Do you have any idea how profoundly it will affect Rick for the rest of his life?" Renee replied, "Oh, I would never do anything to hurt Rick. I could never do that. He is the love of my life and has given me everything I could ever want. I would never hurt Rick." When we left Tom's office, I asked Renee, "Do you absolutely promise you will never hurt yourself, Renee? Please promise me again."

I was at the Dubuque Inn one night meeting some friends and a beautiful girl came up to me as the night was coming to a close. She asked me if I could give her a ride home. Her name was Tina Roussel. Tina looked as though she had stepped off the front page of Vogue. She was gorgeous and a target for all the men of Dubuque. I knew very little about her other than I thought she was beautiful, the same as every other eligible and ineligible male in the City of Dubuque. I took Tina out to my car, opened the door for her, walked to the other side and got in. Tina then leaned toward me, put her hands and arms around my neck, pulled me toward her and gave me a long soft sensuous kiss. It was completely unexpected but certainly hard not to want.

I leaned back into my seat and looked into the beautiful eyes of Tina Roussel and said, "Here comes trouble." And that was trouble with a capital 'T'. After that night, Tina and I started having lunch fairly often and for the very first time I was unfaithful to Renee. The first night Tina and I stayed together she brought out a bottle of Dom Pérignon to share.

We slept the night away in Tina's bedroom and I was oblivious to all of the troubles in my life. It felt good to hold Tina in my arms and it was a welcome reprieve knowing when I woke with this beautiful woman in the morning she would still be alive. The constant fear of what continually went on with Renee was taking its toll on me.

One day my friend Dick Schlindwein came in wondering if I would be interested in looking at a fingerprint identification system that was new on the market. I agreed. The name of the company was Finger Matrix. A fingerprint could be identified within approximately two seconds.

At the time I was working on building a company that would distribute pharmaceuticals for cost to the entire United States. I could not see how the giant pharmaceutical companies could continue to break the backs of the American people selling their medications at markedly higher prices than they did to the rest of the world. America was the wealthiest county in the world and I was sure giant pharmaceutical companies would eventually break the pocketbooks of Americans while their CEOs walked home with millions of dollars taken from the very clients who had made them rich. I really hated the fact that medicine had become a capitalistic enterprise and since it was a commodity almost every living person requires, why shouldn't everyone charge as much as possible? No point in conscience getting in the way of capitalism and making money.

When I explained to Dick what I was trying to do he was very interested in my project. I suggested we work on both fingerprint identification and the pharmaceutical part of things. I could foresee a time when fingerprint identification would be a very important part of patient identification. At a hospital in Cedar Rapids one of the neurosurgeons had operated on the wrong side of the brain four times. Guess he did not know right from left. I did not know how his operating room crew could have let him make those mistakes. It seemed impossible and even more impossible he still had his operating room privileges. This is one area where the medical profession is sadly lacking. They are not good at policing their own colleagues. What is their thinking? I have no idea. Perhaps, since it is the other doctor's patient being killed or dying they feel it is no skin off their hide, but I think the main reason is they do not want to call attention to themselves.

We are supposed to keep things like this from happening but it is always easier to turn a blind eye and go on about your work as if all is well in your world. After all, it is not your patients who are being harmed. It is your honesty and integrity which has seemingly gone down the toilet. About the only time you see doctors bitching about what another doctor is doing is when their turf is being invaded. We can't let that happen can we? That could actually affect a paycheck. When the wrong side of someone's brain is worked on, well golly gee, that didn't hurt at all did it?

I had gathered the drug laws from all fifty states and had them filed in our break room file cabinet in alphabetical order. Dick Schlindwein was working with a person in construction who had ties to Saudi Arabia, Kathy Anderson. I only knew of her through Dick. I had never met her. Dick had several pictures of her sitting around a circle of Saudis next to one of the kings. Evidently Mrs. Anderson had the ties to get us money for fingerprint identification and pharmaceutical distribution.

The State of California at the time was looking for a means of identifying fingerprints instantly and on the spot. They were only looking to match the prints of drivers who were pulled over to the prints on their driver's licenses. Tina was also interested in working with me on the project and the California DOT asked us if we would come out and do a demonstration for them. Previously they had wanted to use retinal scans but found they could not be done because it was considered a body cavity search. What we need in America are a few more laws. What is great about laws is you can hire more bureaucrats to make sure everyone keeps the laws. Not only that, we can hire more bureaucrats to watch the bureaucrats.

I asked Renee if she would go to California with me but she declined. She said she would rather stay at home with our furry children. That was understandable. It was hard to pry Renee away from Dan and our puppies. I had a hard time leaving them myself. Renee had met Tina and knew we were good friends. She suggested I take Tina with me.

Tina and I had worked together on the presentation and we were a great team for the California DOT presentation. I looked forward to the trip and a couple days away from worrying about Renee. Sometimes I felt as though my heart had already been crushed. Seldom a day went by that I was not concerned and overly so to the point where it was having devastating effects on my psyche. I was nearing the point Sheila had made, that I would die before Renee.

Tina and I went to California with Renee's blessings. This worried me. How can your wife let you go on a trip with a very beautiful woman and not be concerned? It bothered me, but when Tina and I were on the plane and on our way the world seemed sort of right again. We spent most of our time deciding how we were going to present our project. We thought we had an excellent shot at getting the DOT's business. Our fingerprint identification was the only one like it in existence, at least that we were aware of.

The Brainiac behind this project had come up with a brilliant idea. Our machine had an oscillating mirror inside that compared anything at millions of times per second. The mirror oscillated so fast it appeared it was not moving. The reason California needed this was they felt they had at least ten million drivers using false driver's licenses. That was only a guess. Their licenses each had a fingerprint so a machine that could instantly match the driver's print to their license would be invaluable.

Our travel to Fresno was uneventful and it was not long before Tina and I were at the California DOT which was several stories high and covered a good part of a block. We were led to the office where the presentation was to be held by a beautiful statuesque blonde. I thought she was in the wrong city and should be in Hollywood but as beautiful as she was, she did not hold a candle to Tina.

Tina and I were greeted warmly and we immediately began our presentation. The DOT board could not fool the machine. They put pieces of tape across part of their print. They had our machine identify a stamp and then tore it in half and the machine could still identify the remaining half. The DOT board was very impressed to say the least.

Tina and I had a great time and on the way back we stopped in Las Vegas. The highlight of our time there was going to a David Copperfield Show, which we really enjoyed. When David asked for volunteers, Tina was the first to raise her hand. Fortunately for me, he selected someone in the front row. That would not have happened if he had cast his eyes on Tina. I think I was probably worried when Tina raised her hand that she would stay behind and be a permanent part of Copperfield's show.

It was not long before we were back in Dubuque. Renee seemed to be doing well and there were no more threats of suicide. I was really happy to be back with Renee and our furry children. Getting away with Tina had been a welcome reprieve but now it was time to get on with life again. Renee said she was happy to have me at home and it seemed as if she was doing well. I could see no indications of an inclination by Renee to harm herself. I continually worried but hoped Renee's threats were behind us.

We started having problems with Dan who had developed a huge growth behind his ear. We had a vet out to look at the huge wart like growth. The vet gave us medication to put on it. Dan's ear had grown so sore it was becoming dangerous for Renee to put a bridle on him as it hurt him too much. It was hard on both Renee and Dan. Dan loved having his little rider on his back and his little rider missed being there immensely.

Renee still spent every day with Dan and I always felt warm at heart when I saw her kissing him on the nose and hugging his neck. Horse and rider were truly one. It made my heart swell. The vet came out several times to look at Dan and said we did not seem to be making any headway. I finally took some Xylocaine one day, anesthetized Dan's ear and cut the growth away in hopes we could get ahead of the problem. The vet was not encouraged and said he expected it to return. He thought my effort was good but did not expect me to be successful.

Renee still spent almost every waking minute with Dan. She was right to be concerned. She could no longer ride Dan and he was her greatest companion in life.

Chapter Thirty

Tammy

One day a car pulled up in our driveway and a young gal got out of the car. I walked up to her and said, "You must be Tammy F." Tammy said, "Yes, I am." Tammy was a tall beautiful woman who did not appear to be the 14 year old child I had been informed she was. When I asked her what she was doing, she explained she had gotten into an argument with Louise and in a moment of anger, Louise said, "You can go live with your mother." Louise evidently knew where Renee lived because she had found our driveway.

Renee and I had just loaded the car to go to Minneapolis. I asked Tammy where her clothes were and she replied she had not had time to gather them. I said, "That is not a problem. Do you want to come with us to Minneapolis?" She said she did. In only a couple of minutes we were on our way to Minneapolis. Renee said we could buy Tammy a wardrobe when we got to the city.

Our first stop was Dayton's Department Store, one of the largest department stores in Minneapolis owned by the well-known and wealthy Dayton Family. Tammy began picking out clothes. When she came to a beautiful leather jacket she liked, she just admired it. We said, "If you like it, go ahead and try it on." It fit Tammy beautifully. Renee asked, "Do you want it?" Tammy looking at the price tag of $300 said it was too expensive. Renee laughed and told Tammy to go ahead and get it. The surprised look on Tammy's face was priceless. She had never been able to spend that amount of money on a jacket in her life. It looked as though she was in dreamland or at least close to heaven.

We shopped for Tammy for hours until she had a large wardrobe she just loved. She thanked both of us profusely. We were happy for her. We did not know how long she would be staying with us but it was nice to have her around. The newly outfitted clothes she liked made Tammy immensely happy. Renee was finally getting to know the daughter she had never known. It seemed to me as if it would be a good fit for both of them. Renee was hopeful Tammy would be staying with us for good.

When we got home from Minneapolis we went back to life as usual. Renee set Tammy up in one of the downstairs bedrooms and she was very shortly enjoying her new bedroom and new home. She was attending one of the junior high schools in Dubuque so I often drove her to school. Tammy seemed to love this as we drove one of the Corvettes and put the top down. She felt special and Renee and I felt special having her.

After Tammy had been staying with us for less than a week, Renee said, "You should see Tammy dance. It is really something." I asked, "What is so special about it?" Renee replied, "She is very sensuous and incredibly sexy." Renee asked me to come down and watch Tammy dance. Renee's description of Tammy as sexy and sensuous was a marked understatement. She was all that and more in addition to being athletic and muscular.

I asked Tammy how she had become such a good dancer at such a young age. It turned out that when Tammy was growing up in California, she had the Phoenix family as her closest friends. Rivers Phoenix, one of Tammy's friends, was an actor as were a number of the Phoenix girls. Because of Tammy's natural abilities, one of the professional dance instructors had offered Tammy free dance lessons and she had begun taking them as a child. She had received a number of other benefits which came naturally as part of the movie set crowd even if you were very young.

Tammy was a wonderful addition to our household. She seemed to adopt me almost immediately and asked if she could call me Dad. I was blessed. Tammy calling me Dad reminded me of how much I had missed out on in my life, not hearing that from my daughters. Now I had a daughter to care for and it gave me a warm feeling. Renee seemed to really like having Tammy living in our home and she enjoyed being a mother to Tammy. I got to enjoy having the daughter I had missed.

I hoped my own daughters had a father as good as the kind of father I thought I was to Tammy.

Tammy started to tell me about her life in California. It was a startling story of abuse. The sexual molestation started when she was nine years old. She said she thought it was Jim F. and his brothers. The reason she was a little unsure was during these periods of molestation the men raping her would wear ski masks and tell her Jim was tied up in the back room. This became a fairly regular occurrence. Tammy went to her grandmother and told her what was happening and her grandmother got mad at her and said, "My sons would never do something like that." This is the way a lot of molestation cases go. There is often a refusal to even consider something this wrong is taking place in your own family. Regardless of everything Tammy had gone through, it seemed she was a well-balanced young girl who, as far as I could tell, was not carrying a lot of resentment or animosity.

Renee unloaded some disturbing information on me one day following an intrusion into Tammy's room. She said, "Rick, I want you to look at some notes I found in one of Tammy's drawers." I said, "Renee, you have no business going into Tammy's room and violating her privacy." Renee said, "Tammy is my daughter and I feel there is a lot going on with Tammy we are not aware of." There had been a disturbing phone call one night that precipitated Renee's search which led to all this distrust and suspicion.

The disturbing phone call was a source of great concern. I could tell Tammy was upset and she had answered the phone right next to me. I took the phone from her hand and a kid was going on about the fact Tammy should have already been out on the streets by now. She wasn't doing her job. I could only surmise what kind of job a 14 year old girl is supposed to be doing on the streets at this time of night. I asked, "Who is this?" The young man on the other end of the phone said, "This is Clarence G. Who are you?" he asked. I said, "I am Tammy's stepfather and I do not want you to ever call here again. If you do, there will be consequences."

I confronted Tammy. I asked her what she was supposed to be doing out on the streets at this time of night. Tammy was evasive. I asked her who Clarence G. was and she said he was a friend from school. I asked her what color he was. I asked Tammy that question because I took care of many different people in Dubuque and one of the groups of people I took care of were hookers. Almost all of them were white girls with black pimps.

Tammy said he was black. I would have known if she was lying. I suspected from Clarence's manner of speech he was black. The following day I called an acquaintance of mine, Joe Honey. Joe was a great black guy that ran a couple of strip clubs on the main street of East Dubuque. It seemed everyone knew Joe. I knew Joe because whenever one of his girls got into trouble, be it from a beating or picking up a dose, I would be there to take care of them. A dose is street slang for an STD or sexually transmitted disease.

I once asked Joe why he brought his girls all the way over to our 'side of town' to get them treated, not that it was that far, but it could have been done in East Dubuque. Joe said, "I bring my girls to you Rick because you treat them as though they are human beings the same as everyone else. You give them dignity and respect and I respect you immensely for that." I replied, "We are all the same in God's eyes, Joe. We all deserve to be treated with dignity and respect."

My conversation today with Joe was about Tammy. When I had asked Joe if I could meet with him, he said he was not doing anything and could come to my office if I wanted him to. It was not long before he showed up and I hit him with a litany of questions. I said, "My concern is Joe that my stepdaughter is hanging around with a young black man. I am not entirely sure but think he has had her working nights on the streets. I have no proof but have my suspicions. What do you think?" Joe said, "Rick, a young white girl going with a black man is on a dead end street to nowhere." He added, "Unless he is a professional athlete. Young black men knock up young white girls all the time and that is often the last time they see them. I do not like any of my girls out hooking but many of them do and none of them are ever run by a white man. As far as I am concerned, I have never known a white pimp. Get your stepdaughter out of that young man's life. Do it as soon as possible and make any contact with him impossible." I thanked Joe.

All of this is what prompted Renee to search Tammy's room. Renee gave me a box full of papers with notes on them. The notes were disturbing to say the least. They were all along these lines: "Sweets, you were neat between the sheets." Another note said, "Let's get it on in the boiler room between classes Sweets." Another note said, "A night on the sheets is best with Sweets." The notes went on and on and all of them strongly suggested sexual liaisons Tammy was having with fellow classmates.

Renee and I confronted Tammy the following day and of course Tammy was upset about the invasion of her privacy. But when we presented her with her box of notes she became defensive. I asked, "Tammy, what on earth is going on? You have a box full of notes suggesting all the guys at school know you as nothing but an easy piece of ass." I didn't know how else to put it. Tammy's response was, "Dad, they are just high school children. The notes do not mean anything." I said, "Are these notes written to you?" Tammy replied, "Yes, they were written to me." I asked, "Tammy, what is your nick name around the school?" Tammy replied, "The boys call me Sweets."

I replied, "Tammy the notes mean a lot and even if they are from high school 'children' as you put it, you are also a high school 'child' who appears to be satisfying all of the sexual needs of an awful lot of young boys. There is nothing for me to read between the lines here, Tammy. These notes say it all." Renee just stood and watched the discourse between us. She added nothing. There was nothing more to be said. I had no idea how she had not ended up pregnant or worse over the past five years of sexual promiscuity.

It all added up. I think because Tammy had regular sexual intercourse since the age of nine she had come to the conclusion she could probably gain a lot in life by plying her wares. It was an unhappy situation and there were no easy answers. In my professional life, girls that went down this path did not seem to change course through professional counseling. How do you reset someone's moral compass?

Days and weeks and months went by. Renee and I tried to keep our household routine the same. In spite of our conversations with Tammy about unsettling information, it seemed as if nothing had ever happened. The subject never came up again and I sincerely doubt Tammy was ever going to leave incriminating information in her room again.

The calls from Clarence G. stopped although Tammy was now on alert that Renee and I knew what kind of life she had been living. Tammy did not seem to have a lot of spare cash so at least it did not appear she was paid for her services. I didn't know whether to take solace from that or just assume she was a poor business woman. That may seem hard but how do you handle situations such as this in your own family. Despite all my medical knowledge and expertise, when things hit close to home a lot of professional wisdom seems to fly out the window.

I talked to a couple of my racquetball buddies from Hempstead High School. Jerry Abing and Phil Sanguideuci (Sorry if I misspelled your name Phil but really, couldn't you have a name like Nelson or Johnson) were counselors for the school. I presented my problem to each of them independently. I did not want one of my friends being influenced by the other when they started answering my questions.

They were both very helpful to me. Both Jerry and Phil said the number one problem they dealt with as counselors in their high school was incest. I had a hard time imagining this. They both were on the same page with everything they told me. They said the situation is so very difficult. Some of the cases come to them during routine questioning of students. The reason the problems are so difficult is that if a girl comes to you as a victim of incest from a well-known Dubuque family, what happens when the problem is confronted.?

Often the family is functioning well in every other way. If charges such as these become public, they must be dealt with in a public manner. Suppose the father goes to prison, the family is broken up and without a source of income, has no home. What have you really accomplished? Have you made things better or made them worse? I guess the answer is not so easy to see.

Jerry and Phil sympathized with the difficult problems in our home but in all honesty, Tammy's behavior did not seem to have any obvious effect on our home life. It did not change our opinion of her. We still loved her the same. The tragic circumstances in her life that determined her path rather than her choosing it were not her fault. She was the victim. We went on with life just like all the rest of the families on this planet do when they fall in a puddle. You jump up, wash off, learn from it and do your best with it to make yourself a better person.

It was not long before Tammy had learned to ride and she seemed to love our horses as much as Renee. She could not have had a better teacher than Renee. Watching Tammy and Renee on the horses was a blessing. Mother and daughter appeared to be one. I think it was a testimonial to how strong our family unit had become. We were not about to let a small inconvenience in life change anything for us.

Often the two of us would go for a ride on a couple of other riding horses Bill had. Living in the country made going out for short rides very easy and the country atmosphere was something we all took full advantage of.

One thing often seemed strange to me. When the three of us were out together, people often thought Tammy was my wife and Renee was our child. I guess it was fully understandable. Tammy was tall and statuesque and Renee small and more childlike in size. One would never mistake her for a child though with her perfect adult figure. I thought the role reversals were based on size and nothing else.

One day when I came home, Renee asked if she could talk to me. She asked, "Rick, if something ever happened to me would you take care of Tammy?" I replied, "Nothing is ever going to happen to you Renee. Everything is going along fine and why do you ask me something like this?" Renee answered, "I just want to feel good in my mind that if something ever did happen to me, Tammy would be okay." Now Renee was starting to worry me again.

Renee said, "If something ever happened to me would you love Tammy the way you love me?" I said, "Renee, I love you as my wife and I love Tammy as my daughter. Of course I would not love Tammy the way I love you. Stop saying things like this. Nothing is going to happen to you. No one could ever replace you. Not Tammy, not my friend Tina, not my office girls, not anybody. I am in love with you Renee. That love cannot be replaced. Don't you realize how deeply in love I am with you? What on earth do you keep thinking about? Tammy will be fine. She is a great young lady and she is lucky to have you in her life." I realized everything I said was completely true but probably to no avail.

None of these conversations ever seemed to leave my mind. They were a constant source of pain for me. I could not help but think about losing the love of my life. I did not know if all the love Renee knew I had for her was hurting her or helping her. We were standing in the living room by the fireplace having one of our rather heated discussions one night. When we got on the subject, 'I don't have to be here', I gesticulated with my arm when making a point and Renee jumped back from me.

I knew it was a reflex, but I said, "Renee, what on earth are you doing? I have never laid a hand on you and yet you jump back as if I am going to hit you." Renee replied, "I'm sorry Rick. It was a reflex." What kind of life can it be when a person is always looking to defend oneself? I cannot imagine. Renee's two abusive relationships had taught her well. It is the fight or flight phenomenon, the rules of engagement and survival. I could only un-teach this with love.

This discussion led to another. "Renee, did you ever threaten to take your life to your other two husbands?" Renee replied, "No." I asked, "Why not? If these two people were beating you up all the time why would you not want to leave them just as you always threaten to leave me?" Renee replied, "Because I did not love them Rick. I love you. My life with you is perfect. If I leave when my life is perfect, it will always be perfect. Don't you see?"

I really did not see. I said, "If I beat you every day, then will you stay with me?" At this Renee giggled a little bit which lightened my anger. Looking at this elfin bronze goddess that was my life and my wife, I could not possibly stay mad at her. No one could.

Renee and I thought it was a good time to light a fire in the fireplace, one thing that always made us relax and feel warm. It did not matter the time of year. If it was too hot out, we just turned the air-conditioning on low and fired it up anyway. This night was no different. The fire was the only light in the room and the snap, crackling and pop of the oak logs put us into a relaxed mood. We sat and cuddled on the couch until we fell asleep. After a couple of hours we got up and went to bed. With Renee snuggled in my arms, once again the cares of the world were gone or at least far away.

I thought if Renee, Tammy and I took off for a while perhaps Renee would see some light at the end of her tunnel. We headed west and really didn't have a plan as to where we would go but we enjoyed ourselves. We stopped in Albuquerque, New Mexico to look at some of the local artists' work. We headed down the road with no schedule to keep. It was not long before we were in Phoenix where we had been only a short time ago.

We had taken a trip to Phoenix and while there visiting my cousin Darrell and his wife Sandra Harmon, Tammy and Renee were both standing alongside the pool at the Desert's Edge Campground in their bikinis. Darrell and his wife Sandra were the managers of this campground which was owned by Sandra's father and mother. Both Renee and Tammy were in enviable shape with figures most girls would die for. The only difference in them was their skin color. Renee was a beautiful golden bronze. Tammy was far lighter than her mother, more of a fine porcelain color.

Darrell was standing at the fence around the pool talking to them and staring into their eyes and he said, "I can't even begin to tell which one of you has the most beautiful eyes." They were truly beautiful in every way, shape and form. I was blessed to have the most beautiful wife in the world and now I had a daughter to match.

We stayed for several days in Phoenix and went out to eat once in a while. One night Tammy asked us if we would take her to the movie "Dirty Dancing," a movie starring Patrick Swayze and Jennifer Grey. There had been a lot of hoopla about the movie and it was one I had wanted to see. Renee did not want to go and said, "Why don't the two of you go and have a good time." I took Tammy to the movie and we thought it was sensational. We thoroughly enjoyed it. We told Renee when we got home but she reaffirmed it was not her kind of movie and she was glad we had a good time.

It was not long before we were back in Dubuque and our usual activities. Renee was back spending long hours with Dan. I don't know if I ever met anyone as loving as Renee was toward horses. We looked at some more horses so I didn't have to borrow one of Bill's. Bill introduced me to an American Saddlebred by the name of Bourbon, a beautiful chestnut with white forefeet and a star on his forehead. Bourbon was a huge gelding about a half size larger than the rest of the horses in the pasture.

Bourbon was of the size that when he wanted to graze on the greener grass on the other side of the fence, he would just step over the fence. When he was done he would just step back over. To give you an idea of his size, one day when another large horse was bugging him, he turned in an instant and planted a kick into the horse's side that knocked the wind out of him and lifted him a foot off the ground before landing on his side. That horse had nothing to do with Bourbon from that time forward.

Renee got into some rodeos with one of her girlfriends by the name of Yvonne Nebel. Her husband Dave was the one who put on the pig roast at our place earlier and he was also the one who introduced me to Bill Boge. Both Dave and Yvonne were horse people and Renee and I often went riding with them. It was kind of sad the way some of our friends' marriages had worked out. Dave and Karen had gotten a divorce and Bill had gotten a divorce from Pam. Karen and Bill ended up married to each other later and Dave had ended up married to Renee's friend Yvonne. It's strange sometimes how life works out. About the only way you can keep things straight is with a scorecard.

It was fun watching them participate and it was obvious the rodeo was one of their first loves. They ran one race where one of the riders would sit on a scoop shovel pulled by a rope around a track. The rope was tied to the saddle horn of their partner's horse. Yvonne and Renee had quite the advantage since Renee was the smallest rider in the race and Bourbon was the largest horse and probably one of the fastest. They won the event. It was a fun day and at the end of the day it appeared Yvonne and Renee had been drug around the track without riding so much as a scoop shovel. But they were laughing and had on smiles a mile wide. I was really happy for Renee and it seemed as though she could not possibly love life more.

Our work with Finger Matrix had progressed well. We were fairly confident some of the hospitals were going to start fingerprint identification so as not to have patient identification errors. Tina set up a bunch of appointments for us one day in Chicago. Once again, Renee did not want to go along. She encouraged Tina and me to go and have a good time.

I had worked with Carol Koltes in my office to produce a brochure we were proud of. We had taken a good picture of Carol with her finger on the Finger Matrix and it became part of our brochure. It was hard for me to imagine a business not producing written materials detailing how their fingerprint identification worked and the accuracy, which was nothing short of amazing. If you did more than two million identifications, it would not be wrong once. That would be assuming the electricity did not go off. Who knows, it may even keep a neurosurgeon operating on the correct side of the brain.

Tina and I had a good time in Chicago. It was a hurried trip and we talked to numerous people in Chicago hospitals. On the way home we stopped in at a restaurant owned by Tina's sister and her husband. It was a large upper class restaurant with a great menu and we finished the day with a great meal and a couple of drinks. I was anxious to get home to Renee. It never seemed to matter how good a time I was having if I was away from Renee. There was always a deep empty feeling in my gut that did not allow me much if any pleasure.

I had tried calling but she did not answer. This was always a worry for me. Renee always, in the back of my mind, was thinking of doing away with herself. Why would it not be so? She felt the happier she was when she died, the happier she would be in heaven with me and Dan. How do you use logic against thinking like that? To me it seemed impossible just as it did with Dr. Sonnito.

I dropped Tina off at her house and hurried home. I was anxious to talk to Renee and tell her about our day. As I drove into our driveway, I opened the garage door. My heart leapt to my throat as exhaust was coming from the pipes of the little yellow Subaru. I jumped out of the car and ran to the Subaru. I was so happy to see the driver's seat empty but my relief turned to despair when I looked across the garage and saw Renee sitting in her big green Lincoln Continental looking as if she was sleeping. I ran over and sat on the ledge of the driver's door. I felt Renee's carotids and could feel no pulse. And then I realized early rigor mortis had already set it. I hugged my lovely little wife to me crying and said, "Now God, you finally have your tiniest angel."

I sobbed and sobbed. I did not know how Renee could do this to me. In the center of her steering wheel she had taped a great big red heart. In her clenched right hand, she clutched her half of our Mizpah medals, which said, 'The Lord Watch Between Thee and Me While We Are Absent, One From The Other'. Renee's left hand had clenched in it a medallion I had given to her with a horse head at the top and 'I Love Horses' beneath. Love was not spelled out but depicted with a pretty red heart. Renee had died having everything she had ever wanted in life. She had said, "I love you so much Rick. You have given me everything I have ever wanted in life and this is how I want to die."

I can understand some of this. I think if people were absolutely sure about life and death and heaven wouldn't we all commit suicide so we could get to the other side faster? Don't you suppose that is why God put this single solitary minuscule doubt in our mind so everyone would not go around committing suicide? After all Renee thought she had heaven on Earth and that if she died right here and now she would experience her earthly bliss forever. If everyone felt as strongly as Renee, wouldn't we all just go around killing ourselves? Doesn't seem too bad does it? Life down here is pretty tough sometimes.

Really, just think, if everyone thought all you had to do was push a button and suddenly you were in Disneyland or Walt Disney World for the rest of our lives who wouldn't do it? Or for that matter, your own version of what heaven is.

I called the operator and said, "This is Doctor Rick Redalen. There has been an accident out at our address on Watters Forest Drive. My wife Renee Redalen is dead. Would you please send out an ambulance and a coroner?" It was only minutes and one of our coroners was at my place. I informed him how I had found Renee when I had returned from Chicago where I had been all day visiting hospitals. The Dubuque Police Department was also at our home and they also took statements from me.

When I got home, Tammy was downstairs sleeping. I woke her and asked her what had happened. Tammy said Renee had been crying and burning all our albums in the fireplace. She then went out into the garage. Tammy said she had gone downstairs and gone to bed. I asked somewhat incredulously, "Did you not even go out and check to see what your mom was doing in the garage?" I guess I really did not know what all was going on between Renee and her daughter that evening but Tammy did not seem to exhibit the concern I thought she should. I was uncontrollably upset. Tammy did not seem to have the same emotional response I had to Renee's death.

Changes started to happen following Renee's death. Tammy began hanging on to me a little more. I did not think it completely appropriate. One thing that bothered me was Tammy always called me Dad and suddenly she started calling me Rick. I was concerned about what had suddenly changed between us that was caused by her mother's death. Why do you go from being someone's Dad to a close friend called by their first name? I did not have time to think much about this.

I could not dissuade Tammy from wanting to be near me at a time such as this. All in all, I guess I was not really that concerned with appearances at the time. I had too much grief in my heart to worry about what other people thought and I loved having Tammy near me.

They took Renee away from our home and the following day Tammy was removed from our home by Social Services, for what reason I could not imagine. The next days were absolutely nothing more than a blur for me. I had no idea where Tammy was. I found out later Tammy was appointed a guardian ad litum who would be handling the legal issues of where she would be located and cared for by whom. Tammy at age 14 was a minor but was considered to be of an age to make her own decisions about where and with whom she wanted to live. This was just one more instance of people taking law into their own hands regardless of the constitutional rights of the individual.

Chapter Thirty-one

Legalities

I was asked to come down to the police station the following day and I brought my attorney friend Bob Klauer with me. The Iowa Bureau of Criminal Investigation said they had questions they wanted to ask me. They wanted to know my whereabouts the night of Renee's death. They obviously were not calling this a suicide at this point in time which seemed odd to me.

Bob interjected at this point, "Why are you asking Doctor Redalen these questions when you already obviously know where he was, what he was doing and who he was with." They said, "Mr. Klauer, we are still trying to ascertain whether Renee Redalen's death was a suicide or a homicide. We just want to ask a few questions and it will not take long to clear things up in our minds. Then we will be done and Doctor Redalen can be on his way."

Their questioning was bizarre but what do you expect from a couple morons. They started asking questions about my hypnosis abilities. They asked me if I could make people do things they did not want to do. I thought I would play with these mental incompetents for a little bit. I told them I cannot make people do things they do not want to do but I can trick them into doing things they would not ordinarily do. I am sure this answer was not something Bob Klauer wanted to hear from me. I really did not care what they thought of me; however, if I had been thinking a little more clearly I would have guessed that this was not it.

Bob Klauer explained it was only a few months ago Renee had tried to take her own life by taking an overdose. He also said, "I had Renee for a client several times and she was always talking about taking her own life. It was always on her mind to the best of my knowledge. The other thing is Doctor Redalen was not even in the state the day this happened. What are all these questions about? You already know all these answers." Bob Klauer did not go gently on these interrogators.

The interrogator then asked me point blank, "Doctor Redalen, did you hypnotize your wife and ask her to kill herself?" This was ludicrous but I had to get serious now. These people did not want me in the City of Dubuque and they would do everything in their power to get rid of me one way or another. After all I was a physician in a city of about two hundred physicians and was of such popularity that I took care of roughly 10% of the population.

When you have the largest practice in town, often the rest of your profession becomes quite jealous. I do not know why, but that seems to be the way our profession runs. It is incredible if you think of it but the more specialists we have, the more laws we have to govern what everyone is able to do. The specialists of course make the governing laws. Also, there is an inverse correlation about doctors and the care we get. Have you noticed the more specialists we have practicing, the poorer our care becomes?

Bob Klauer interrupted again and asked, "Where is this going? You know Doctor Redalen was in Chicago with Tina Roussel. Have you questioned her?" The interrogator immediately replied, "Yes we have. She had her attorney with her and was told by her attorney to plead the Fifth." At this I was the one who was rather dumbfounded. I could not believe Tina would not tell them she was with me in Chicago. I was somewhat incredulous. I guess from that point on I knew Tina was not the right kind of friend in my time of need.

Bob asked, "Why don't you just check with the Roussel relatives they had supper with prior to returning to Dubuque?" Following this question and answer session, the first thing I did was to try to reach Tina. I was upset and confused as to why she would plead the Fifth when asked a simple question about where she was the night Renee died. It turned out Tina had immediately left town and was visiting the home of her mother.

What bizarre behavior. I have just lost my wife who I considered my best friend and the person I consider my other best friend has fled town.

Rather than support me in my time of need she had chosen to run away.

Tammy had been put in lockup. She had gone through juvenile court so her records were locked but the city for whatever reason decided she was going to remain in lockup. No reasons for any of this were given by anyone. It was as if I had suddenly awakened in Communist Russia, but come to think of it, they probably have far better things to do.

The day after Renee's death Tammy and I were standing in the pastor's office of the Lutheran Church making funeral arrangements. With the guidance of our minister and some of the church staff we were picking out the hymns and discussing what we wanted the service to be about, a celebration of Renee's life. We said Renee would have wanted this to be a joyous affair.

As we were about midway through the arrangements, two deputies from the Dubuque Sheriff's Department entered the room quite unceremoniously without a knock or anything. They said, "Doctor Redalen, you are under arrest. You are to be transported in handcuffs to a lockup facility in Des Moines." I asked what for and they said they did not know. I asked, "How can you come and arrest someone and not know why you are doing it?" They said they were just following orders. I said, "If you want to lock me up let's just go downtown and you can put me in lockup there. They have grown to like my face." They did not appreciate my humor and kept their stoic demeanor.

They reiterated what they had just said. All they knew was I was to be placed in handcuffs and taken to a lock up facility in Des Moines. I again asked, "What on earth for? I want to call my attorney first." They said they were informed I was to have no phone calls. They said I would be allowed one phone call when I arrived in Des Moines. I asked, "Can't I at least let people know where I am being taken?" They replied, "We are not allowed to do that." I told Tammy, "Get on the phone and call Bob Klauer, Bill Blum and Bill Olinger. Ask what any of them can find out and do about this. See if they can stop this trip to Des Moines before I even get there."

I asked the deputies to let me finish making funeral arrangements for my wife. I then asked my pastor, "Who from the church let the Sheriff's Office know I would be at the church at this hour so I could be arrested?" My pastor had a horrified look on his face and said, "Rick, we would never do such a thing." I was probably off base asking the question and said, "I am sorry."

Evidently the person in charge had thought of everything. I could only assume that he too was in on some of the homosexual activity in our law enforcement agency or agencies.

When I got into the car I unloaded on the two deputies, "Is it because you law officers like to take prisoners out in the country and have them perform oral sex on you? Is it because Kenny R. and Chuck Y. like to go out and smoke each other's pipe once in a while?" I was referring to some of the homosexual practices taking place within the Dubuque Police Force or Sheriff's Office. A few of their officers seemed to think it was okay to take advantage of their position in life to satisfy some of their primal urges.

I asked the deputies if they could at least put my handcuffs in front so I could be in a little comfort on our afternoon drive. They said they were instructed by their commanders I was to have my hands cuffed behind my back for their safety for the duration of the trip. Unbelievable. About one hour into our trip the officers stopped at a McDonald's to get a bite to eat. They asked me if I wanted to eat anything and I asked for a hamburger and a coke. I said, "You are either going to have to feed me or at least cuff my hands in front." They laughed and said they could accommodate me.

I was put into a lockup in Des Moines and did not know where I was other than what city I was in. I was a long way from friends and family and no one knew where I was. The one thing I was thankful for was the fact the Sheriff's Department or the Dubuque Police Department did not take me out in the country and dispose of me. I certainly did not think it beyond their purview. I now knew one thing. Dubuque law enforcement was going to get me far enough away from Dubuque that I could not cause them problems and when you are locked up over 100 miles away from where you live and no one knows where you are, your options are nonexistent.

I asked to be let go immediately. They said I had to have a psychiatric consult but they did not have a reason. They did not seem to know why I was transported to Des Moines. How strange is that? Isn't it like a patient being transferred to me? They just show up at your door and do not know why they are there.

It was not long before a psychiatrist showed up to see me who said,

"What seems to be the problem?" I said, "The problem appears to me I am being incarcerated against my will and would like to know what you are going to do about it." The psychiatrist was a little taken aback. I explained to him my wife had just died, I was taken away, incarcerated and no one knows why. I said, "You do not even know why you are here seeing me.

"Why don't you read between the lines. Dubuque law enforcement wants me out of their city because they have committed a bunch of indiscretions they do not want made public. I am the one who can do so and right now I am angry enough to bring full powers to bear on our law enforcement agency in Dubuque.

"This is what is going to happen. You have been brought into a process that you do not want to become involved in. You are a prisoner of politics the same as I am. You are going to give me a clear bill of health immediately and tell all authorities you see no reason for me to be in lockup.

"You will say in your report I am as sane as the day is long and I am not a danger to myself or anyone else. You will also say I should be freed and allowed to attend my wife's funeral later today. The reason you are going to do this is because if you do not I am going to do my best to have your licensed surgically excised from the frame on your wall and I have enough powerful friends to do so. I would like you to write your note immediately and within one to two days would like your dictation of a much more in depth note to be available for one of my attorneys to pick up.

"In your more in depth note, I want you to write an in-depth analysis of my psychiatric being and I hope you can put in enough descriptive superlatives that we do not have to have you elucidate further on the defense stand if one is forthcoming in a lawsuit."

The psychiatrist said he could find no psychiatric grounds based on his expertise to keep me for any medical reasons. I think he was probably unhappy putting up with my tirade but when a citizen of the United States is taken into custody and put into lockup with no reason being given, I do not think anyone wants to be a part of that.

Of course, I guess if you are on the police department and getting regular free blow jobs from your prisoners, perhaps the more prisoners to be brought in the better.

I was now allowed a phone call which I placed to Bill Olinger, a prestigious attorney from Cedar Rapids. I informed him I was in a Des Moines lock up facility and did not know why. I explained I did not have time to talk as Renee's funeral was being held that afternoon and it was going to take an act of God to get me there in time.

Bill said to give him a few minutes and he would see what he could do. I provided him with the phone number to the people in charge. Bill called me a short while later and said I was being released immediately. I asked for a phone book and found the number for a private flying service. I needed a plane immediately for the airport in Dubuque. They said we could take off as soon as I arrived at our FBO (fixed base of operation in pilot jargon).

Within minutes I was in a twin engine Bonanza on my way to Dubuque and I would be there in plenty of time for Renee's funeral. I had an airport car take me home and within a few minutes I was at the Lutheran Church where the ceremony was taking place. I was there in time to greet people when they started arriving. Tammy came to the funeral dressed in an elegant black sheath. She came up to me and gave me a hug. I asked how she was holding up and she said everything was okay.

I thought the main problem was I had become aware a couple of Dubuque deputies by the names of Chuck Y. and Kenny R. apparently got involved with a prisoner one night and evidently had that prisoner perform oral sex on them. I had also called when a Dubuque police car parked out in a yard about one mile from my home one night and asked who was in the squad car out at an intersection on the highway. It was rather cool outside. I did not tell them the car windows were steamed up. That would have been me implying something based entirely on guesstimation and supposition. That was not the night in question for that prisoner but it certainly raised questions about some of Dubuque's finest. Oh well, I guess if you are close enough, it is okay to smoke each other's pipe once in a while.

Gary Lippe from social services talked to me one day in the outer chambers of the courtroom. He said, "That stepdaughter of yours is really hot. I am going to apply to see if we can be her step parents. We have room in our house." All of what seemed to be happening was something out of "Alice in Wonderland" and I thought I had fallen down the 'rabbit hole'. I talked with the Juvenile Court Judge. Judge Jacobs said, "Doctor Redalen, it generally does not take very long to sort out these problems." I asked him what problems he was sorting out and he replied he really did not know. I could not believe what I was hearing. The Juvenile Court Judge did not know why they had Tammy in lockup or how long she would be there.

Nothing was making sense to me. The court had allowed Tammy and me to talk to each other several times, always under supervision. To me this was because someone thought I was a threat to Tammy. I do not know how they could have ever come up with that. The thing I was holding over their heads was hearsay knowledge about an indiscretion of local law enforcement and the liberties they had supposedly taken with one of their prisoners. Oh for gosh sakes, law enforcement should be able to have a little entertainment, shouldn't they? After all, the prisoners should be good for something.

The problem with me having this knowledge was I had friends on the police force who confirmed what I had heard. One of my friends, Larry H. said, "Sheriff Kennedy said 'Redalen' should be put in lock up forever." They actually did put me in lock up several times and never seemed to have a reason for it. Dubuque Law enforcement broke their laws over and over again without consequences. I could do nothing about this since I was now in survival mode.

The time Tammy was in detention grew into weeks and began to look as though it would be permanent. She was growing desperate to get out of juvenile detention. Tammy passed on some of the comments made by some of the supervisors at the detention center. They were definitely not very professional. Evidently a number of the guys wanted a little bit more of a relationship than our courts would have liked but they were not going to let her out.

Tammy ran away one day and said the guys that brought her back had managed to let their hands roam continually over her. They said, "Tammy you are really fun to play ping pong with. You make all us guys hot." When I mentioned some of the inappropriateness taking place where Tammy was locked up, Judge Jacobs said it should not be much longer, as if it didn't matter what was happening. Judge Jacobs did say the longest anyone had ever been in that lockup was about two to three days. This was now stretching into months. In actuality, I was not sure how many of the stories were instigated by Tammy. After all, I had to look at this the same way as when I did marriage counseling. I was only hearing one side. I had to wonder if Tammy's side of the story was embellished to make me more concerned about her and get her out of confinement. I did not know the answers but Tammy was traumatized by all of this. She had lost the only father she had ever known and lost her mother early in the re-establishment of their relationship.

One day I got a chance to talk to Tammy and she told me they were going to be allowed out of lockup to go to a movie downtown. I asked, "Are you ready to get out of there?" She replied, "In a second." I said, "When you see me coming in the Corvette, be ready to run and jump in the car. I will have the top down and as I drive by, you come running and jump in over the side."

I was waiting by the movie theater they were going to that night and within seconds as I drove by, Tammy was in the car and we were speeding to the home of one of my friends who had previously been on the Dubuque Police Force. I asked Larry if I could put my car in his garage. He opened the doors, drove his van out to the curb and I promptly drove in and closed the garage door. I knew Tammy and I could never make it out of town driving a 68 Indy Pace Car Corvette with RRR on the license plate. What a dumb shit I was to get vanity plates for a car that already said how vain I was. Nutso was all I could think.

Tammy and I told Larry what our plans were. I asked if he would let us use his van for a while and we did not know how long. I said he could use the Corvette for the duration. We were not going to tell him where we were going because he would be questioned and this way he did not have to lie to his friends in the police department.

Larry said, "Before you take off Rick, I have to talk to Tammy alone." I said that was fine and to take his time talking to her. I knew what he was talking to her about. I knew he was making sure she was not being taken or abducted against her will. After about fifteen to twenty minutes they came out of Larry's office and he told me he was satisfied and we could take off. He handed me the keys to the van and away we went in less conspicuous transportation, no longer a corvette with RRR license plates. No one would be looking for us in Larry's van. With the entire police force of Dubuque searching for us, there would have been no way we could have made it out of the city.

Larry did not drive the Corvette for a couple of days. He was being very thoughtful of Tammy and me. When he finally thought it was okay to drive it, he was immediately picked up by the Dubuque police. Much to the embarrassment of the local police they let him go but Larry was picked up several more times over the next week and finally told the police if they did so again he was filing harassment charges against them. They asked him why he was driving my car and he said because I had let him.

Once we were in another state, I called the Tom Riley Law Firm. I told Tom what I had done and he said, "My, you're rather impulsive aren't you?" Tom's next words were, "You're staying in separate rooms, aren't you?" I replied, "No, we are staying in the same room with separate beds. We are trying to save money." Tom said, "This is no time for you to be a cheapskate, Rick. I want you staying in separate rooms." I replied, "We are trying to save money in case that becomes an issue a little later." Tom said, "Right now what you have to worry about is staying out of jail. It will appear to everyone that you have abducted a minor and not only that, you have violated the Mann Act. You have taken a minor across a state line. This could mean serious trouble, Rick. I will have to think this through."

Tammy and I ended up staying the first night out of the state in separate rooms in the White Bear Inn in White Bear Lake, Minnesota. It was a stormy night with a lot of lightning and thunder and a couple hours into the night there was a knock on the door. I opened it to find Tammy standing at the door trembling. She was frightened by the thunder and lightning and wanted to know if she could sleep in my room. I replied she could.

It did not seem strange at all as often when Renee and I were lying in bed at night watching TV, Tammy would come to our room and ask if she could lie down with us and watch TV. Renee always said it would be fine. So here we were once again watching TV and listening to the thunder and watching the lightning flashes light up our room. It felt like a beautiful reprieve from all the nonsense and craziness in our Dubuque lives lately. It was hard to imagine what pleasure the elected officials in the City of Dubuque were getting out of this other than holding someone I loved over my head to prevent me from making some of the city dirt public.

I was talking to Tom Riley rather frequently while we were in Minnesota and I was going to start running out of money if we did not work something out. Tom finally sprung on me what he had been thinking about. He asked, "Would you and Tammy consider getting married?" I replied, "I am trying to help Tammy, Tom, not hurt her. She is 14 and she should not be married to someone twice her age."

Tom said, "This is what I am thinking, Rick. I do not know what kind of anger the Dubuque Police Department is holding against you, but they are anxious to get you in their custody. Of course that does not matter, but they will try to make your life miserable. They can do this by bringing 'statutory rape charges' against you. They cannot make this stick without Tammy's testimony, but they can try to carry this on long enough to break you. I am advising you to head down to Louisiana and get married there. I have talked to an attorney friend of mine and he says he can take care of it once you get there."

Tom said, "That City District Attorney of Dubuque's must not have a life. I cannot imagine a city DA wanting to pursue a well-known Dubuque physician for something like this when everyone seems to know what happened. She must be trying to make some headlines." I said to Tom, "As far as I am concerned Chris Corkin is a bitch. I personally could not imagine anyone porkin' Corkin."

I did not confide to Tom Riley I had heard rumors of the Dubuque police department taking prisoners out of their jail and making them perform oral sex on them. It was my fault that much of this harassment from the Dubuque police department was happening. I had repeated this information on several of my calls while I was vacationing in their jail compliments of the Dubuque tax payer. I knew the calls were all monitored so I managed to rub in this hearsay.

I asked Tammy what she thought and she wanted to get married. I said, "We are just doing this to get us out of this predicament you know, don't you?" Tammy said, "Yes, I understand." I said, "You realize when we finally have this behind us, we will have to get divorced," and again Tammy said she realized we would.

When we got down to Louisiana, we went to an attorney friend of Tom's. Tammy was of legal age to get married in Louisiana. But now we had another problem. Tammy had to have the signature of her guardians. At that time I did not even know Tammy had guardians but with some digging we found out they were Louise and Jack Lorenz. What was even more enlightening and astonishing was now we knew Tammy was illegally incarcerated. She had guardians that were not even consulted and she had just been put in a lockup facility for wayward troubled children.

Tammy and I were now heading back to Iowa. I had some spare cash stuck away in my bedroom. I called Larry, asked if he would go to our home, get some money and bring it to Freeport. We would meet him at the McDonald's on the main highway as you come into town from the west on Hwy I-20. I explained the money was in a cigar box on the top shelf in our closet. Larry agreed. I forgot to tell Larry there were two huge Dobermans in our home. Small point.

We called Larry when we were getting close to Freeport. When Larry met us, the first words out of his mouth were, "Why didn't you tell me there were going to be giant dogs in your home?" I said, "Oops. Oh well, you are here so I guess everything went okay." Larry said it went fine. He said, "That scared the shit out of me Rick. I was standing there looking at your closet and suddenly something is licking my hand and here it is that giant Doberman of yours." I guess Thunder just licked his hand and gave him a free pass. Great watchdogs. Big Thunder and slightly smaller Ace. Larry handed me the money so now we had an additional $15,000 in cash I kept for rainy days. We were good to go for a little bit.

We called Jack and Louise who were aware of our problems from the local papers and knew we were crossing the country evading the law. Well of course they knew. Everyone in the State of Iowa knew. Why would they not know? Tammy and I were in most of the papers in our part of the country and everyone seemed to know of our plight. We were a big story with a lot of interest. Of course there would be a lot of interest. A 14 year old girl takes off with a physician stepfather after his wife has committed suicide and now they are fugitives from the law. I think people can spin this any way they want to in their minds to make the story more entertaining. Of course, a 14 year old child whose mother had just killed herself could be part of the reason if she was involved with her stepfather. It is not very exciting reading to know a juvenile had been illegally incarcerated, immediately taken away from family and friends and not allowed visitors following her mother's death. Not only that, no reason was given and the city had violated all legalities entitled to this minor. When you are trying to control the busiest and perhaps well known physician in the city of Dubuque who has promised his deceased wife to care for her daughter, perhaps that makes sense to someone. I'm sure the Dubuque police department was happy, although most of my gay patients seemed to want their life a little less conspicuous.

Tammy and I made our way back to Dubuque. Jack and Louise made us welcome at a home across the street from where they lived in the country; it was owned by Louise's mother who was now living in California. Tammy and I had the home to ourselves.

Jack was kind of a renegade in Dubuque and did not take shit from anyone. He was a Vietnam veteran and had flown during the war. Following Nam, Jack had taken a job flying for McDonnell Douglas as a test pilot. During this time McDonnell Douglas sold some F16s to Saudi Arabia and Jack became a jet fighter instructor for them. He would fly 90 days on and 90 days off. During his off time he would head for Paris and go to the opera and travel around the world in his Saudi fighter.

It was not long after that Jack became a mercenary. He lived in Paris but had homes all over the world. He later worked for a secret force in the United States called AS&E (assassination, sabotage, and espionage). The name pretty much says it all; Jack was a paid assassin for a secret branch of our government.

Jack was very supportive of us. It would not be long before Dubuque law enforcement started hanging around Jack and Louise's property probably looking for Tammy or me. We stayed hidden. Louise and Jack got the necessary papers for them to sign giving permission for Tammy and me to get married. Once the papers were signed, all we had to do was execute them.

I went to Bedford, Texas to seek out the help of Kenny Pounds and Ted Tateravitch. They knew what had been going on with us and Ted made some crude unappreciated jokes about Tammy and me messing around. I had the appropriate papers with me, but Tammy was back in lockup. Social Services did not know what we were now doing. They were also oblivious to the law.

What we were doing was carrying out the advice from our legal counsel, Tom Riley. When you hire the most well known and powerful attorney in the entire Midwestern United States, you take his advice. We were, at the advice of our attorney, going to get married with the blessing of Tammy's legal guardians, Jack and Louise. Now we had all the paperwork out of the way from Tammy's guardians and there were no roadblocks to completing a marriage. Married, Tammy would now be an emancipated minor and the court could no longer legally keep her in lockup. I did not see how that was possible in the first place. It was of course illegal but what the heck, with a police department like Dubuque's, who cares about illegalities, especially when you have a juvenile judge who does not know why the person is in lockup. Desperate officials do desperate things. Tammy and I could, by Texas laws, get married with the permission of Tammy's legal guardians, Jack and Louise. Since Tammy was in lockup we were advised to get married by proxy. Our Texan attorney friends Kenny Pounds and Ted Tateravich were going to help us.

Kenny and I went to the Tarrant County Court Room one day with the papers. Ted came along with us to be a witness. Initially there was a lot of nervous joking in spite of the seriousness of the marriage Tammy and I were set to go through. Kenny joked just because he was marrying me I was not to expect a big honeymoon. Kenny was going to say the vows for Tammy by proxy. Ted and Kenny gave me a hard time but when we got into the courtroom we knew it was time to be serious. And extremely serious we were knowing the gravity of the situation.

The judge said all the usual things and asked if I Richard Redalen would take the hand of Tammy F. in marriage. I answered affirmatively. The Judge then asked Kenny Pounds, "Do you Kenny Pounds as proxy for Tammy F. take the hand of Richard Redalen in marriage?" Kenny said 'I do' and the judge pronounced us man and wife. Tammy's lockup was suddenly not a good thing for Dubuque. They knew this within minutes following the legalities. They had incarcerated a man's wife and it was against the law, disregarding the facts they had already broken several.

Tammy was now an emancipated minor in the eyes of the law. She had all the rights of an adult. Suddenly it was a whole new ballgame. Tammy was immediately released on her own recognizance and was once again a free person. I promptly drove back to Iowa and Tammy and I headed back to Bedford and the Crescent Tree Apartments.

We had only been back in Bedford a couple days when an administrator from Rhinelander, Wisconsin called me and asked if I would consider working there. The administrator was the CEO of the Rhinelander Clinic. He said he had heard from one of their doctors I might be available to work. He said their doctor had worked with me in one of the emergency rooms in Wisconsin and had spoken very highly of me. I thought, why not. I asked Tammy what she thought about the offer and she was excited.

Tammy and I packed some clothes and we were on the road again. This time I was introducing Tammy to some of my old stomping grounds. It was exciting for me, but I was still wondering how I was going to present the now 15 year old Tammy as my wife to a professional group. It was exciting and a great opportunity for both of us, but I already knew the opportunities were also going to present with some complexities.

We were greeted warmly at the Rhinelander Clinic. They showed us around the hospital and clinic. They also took us to a small clinic several miles away and asked if I would be interested in running it. They really liked all my qualifications. They wanted me to do stress testing, surgery and general family practice in a little town just north of Rhinelander. It was an ideal situation for me and the clinic did not present any challenges I could not easily handle. They also said I was the only physician they would have with all the capabilities in one physician who could handle all of this. For me, it was actually ideal.

Following our tour of the city we sat down with some of the doctors. They explained a little about the town of Rhinelander, located in the northern part of Wisconsin and on the Wisconsin Chain of Lakes. It was a beautiful area, very much like all the rest of northern Minnesota and Wisconsin.

Rhinelander was a city of 6,900 people in the wintertime and in the summer it swelled to 150,000. People came in from all over the country to spend the summer because it was so beautiful. Many of the summer residents were Chicago transplants. There were nearly thirty flights per day between Chicago and Rhinelander airports. In many ways it was almost a bedroom community for Chicago. Some of the physicians introduced us to a Realtor in the hope we would be residing in Rhinelander in the very near future.

The Realtor showed us some nice homes and we found one we really liked on the water front of the Chain of Lakes. The Realtor had just gotten the listing. It was an eight thousand square foot log cabin and when you walked in the front door you could see three gigantic stone fireplaces from the landing. The bed in the master bedroom was made of huge logs. It was obviously built in place as I did not think anyone could have possibly moved it upstairs. There was another huge stone fireplace in the master bedroom.

The property had over 5,000 linear feet of water frontage. Three more log cabins were included, each with large stone fireplaces. The main home had a large boat house with two iron railroad railings hanging from the ceiling so you could hoist a massive boat out of the water. It was a beautiful site and the person was asking only $360,000 for the entire setup. I asked the Realtor what the catch was. An old lady, nearly ninety, owned all of this and she had property just as spectacular all over the world. She wanted to find all her properties good homes. The Realtor thought Tammy and I would fit the bill. It was magnificent and well worth ten times the asking price.

At the end of the day we were shown to the room the hospital and clinic had provided for us. We had been asked to the home of the clinic administrator for the evening so we freshened up and changed for dinner. The doctors who were available were going to be present along with their wives and they thought it would give us a chance to meet everyone. Both Tammy and I were excited for the opportunity.

The evening was wonderful and Tammy stole the show as I knew she would. Her California upbringing would have allowed her to hobnob with almost any group of people. She wore a black form fitting dress which showed off her perfect athletic figure. She was a hit with the doctors and their wives. As I watched Tammy maneuver the social circumstances all night I became even more aware of her beauty and sophistication with a good sized group of physician's wives that were mostly more than 10 to 15 years her senior. We both had a good time and when we got back to our room, I asked Tammy what she thought. She thought we should move immediately. She loved the people, the area and the city.

Tammy and I started talking about how we were going to do this. We first thought Tammy could finish school in a nearby town, but eventually everyone would find out the new doctor's wife was only fifteen. We discussed Tammy getting her GED. She could then go to college and nobody would know anything. We talked about this, we talked about that and it was difficult to come up with a plan that would not make it seem as if we were being disingenuous.

We had told everyone as we were leaving we would really like to come to Rhinelander and work in the clinic. We decided the best thing to do was tell the doctors and their wives Tammy was 15. In retrospect, we should have probably have decided this prior to the Rhinelander visit.

The next day early in the morning, I requested a meeting with the clinic administrator and three of the doctors including the one who had recommended me for the job. When everyone was settled down at a desk with their cup of coffee, I told all of them we had really enjoyed meeting them.

They all volunteered immediately that we were a hit with everyone. They said their wives loved Tammy and she was immediately welcome into their family. I then asked them if they knew Tammy's age. They said they realized Tammy was a bit younger than me but they did not think anything more than that. That of course is a lot easier when you look several years younger than you are and your wife looks like the mid-twenties belle of the ball. They said, "Really, your wife Tammy was the hit of the party last night. She is a very pleasurable and entertaining young lady. We are anxious to have both of you join us. You have all the qualifications and perfectly fill the bill. Of all our doctors, you are the most qualified to run the clinic we showed you single-handedly and will take care of a huge need for us."

It was then I unloaded my bombshell. I said, "My wife Tammy is 15 years old." Initially they were too shocked to reply. I explained about the nightmare we had been through in Dubuque and Texas and they were dumbfounded. They said, "It is hard for us to believe this, but it is not something anyone could make up. This story you are telling us is bizarre." They began questioning me about Tammy going to school out of town. I said, "We think we have talked about nearly everything. We really want to come here but think scandal may follow us here. We do not want that for you."

The doctors all started offering suggestions and came up with dozens of possibilities but I told them in the long run regardless how careful we were, something, sometime would slip out, maybe even innocently, an accident of conversation. The Rhinelander doctors came up with more suggestions, even more than we had. They offered every possible scenario to help us stay. They finally agreed I was most likely right.

They did not want to see us go but understood their and our conundrum. Only a few short hours later, Tammy and I started our long drive back to Bedford.

It was a slow and unhappy trip for us. Tammy was very unhappy about our decision to leave and not come back, but we now realized we were going to keep running into the same problem if I wanted to continue practicing family medicine using the talents God had given me. I had come to the conclusion quite some months earlier the best thing I could do for Tammy was to divorce her as we had discussed when we first got married. This was all meant to be temporary. When you do something temporarily and it becomes comfortable, it is easy to continue on the same. There was no lack of love for Tammy on my part and Tammy did not want to get divorced. Other than the situation, we were the perfect couple and we were now truly in love.

I went up to Trinity High School one day when Tammy did not come home for the night. I was ushered into the principal's office. I explained I was the husband of Tammy Redalen. He immediately said, "I do not know what to think about you." I said, "How could you, you don't even know me. If you have an opinion about me without knowing me you would make one hell of a doctor with your diagnostic skills." Sometimes I just get pissed off with people and know I should refrain from putting them in their place, but on the other hand it may be a gift to some people to know their place. What a small minded judgmental asshole.

They got Tammy out of class and I got the chance to talk to her. She was really defiant. I realized I was making Tammy feel unwanted and unloved, but that could not have been further from the truth. I said, "Tammy we really have to meet with an attorney and get our paperwork done so we both can get on with life."

I thought what I was doing for Tammy was the kind and right thing to do, but I certainly could not say it was something I wanted to do. I really did not want this at all but I do not think I could have lived with my own conscience if I had not followed through with the divorce. Today, I would have said to hell with everyone, stayed married and had a family. I do not know where this sudden burst of ethics, morality or whatever you want to call it came from, but I hope in my heart it was my love of Tammy. There was no one in my life I loved more.

Tammy did not meet me after school to go to an attorney's office as she said she would. She did not return home either. I had no other choice. I had Tammy served divorce papers while she was in class one day. I did not want to do things this way but really had no other choice since Tammy refused to come to terms with me. I was uncertain there were not deeper issues with me. I really had a hard time coming to terms with Tammy's failure to rescue her mom in Renee's time of need. I could only look at it as mistaken judgment. Most of the time I repressed these unpleasant thoughts. I just did not want to think Tammy had any thoughts about her mom possibly thinking of suicide. Maybe she thought her mom was going out for a drive to settle down or relax. Tammy would not have known that from her downstairs bedroom.

A couple of days later when my credit card did not work I found Tammy had gone with a boyfriend and drained all our checking and savings accounts. I really did not see this coming but this beautiful girl I thought I knew had left me penniless. I guess this was payback for abandoning her. Perhaps it was something I deserved.

Some months later I learned Tammy had run off and married a classmate. The last I heard she was living in Iceland married to a serviceman and raising three boys. I was happy Tammy had managed to get on with her life. Guess I'll never know if our situation was handled correctly but it seemed to be the right thing to do at the time. It will remain an unanswered question for me in this game of life.

Epilogue
God's Gift of a Tiny Lori Angel

After I lost Renee it took me what seemed like forever to even begin wondering if I could have a relationship with anyone ever again. It was incomprehensible to me that I would someday get over the suicide of the person who was the light of my life. Renee wasn't just the light of my life, she *was* my life. It made me think of a verse by an unknown author I remembered from long ago: *Her candle burned at both ends, it glowed throughout the night, it lasted but a short while, but it gave a lovely light.*

How does a person get over losing someone you love to suicide and want to go on living? It is very difficult. What I finally realized is you never get over a suicide of a loved one. I want all of you who have been the victim of a suicide to pay close attention to what I am going to say. Do notice I called us victims. We are the victims. It is not the person who killed themselves. It is us who have had our love trampled on by the person committing this atrocity against us. Atrocity seems like such a harsh word, however for the brutality of that act, can you think of a better one?

The emotions I had following Renee's death waxed and waned from the very depths of despair to the heights of good memories flooding my heart. How does someone take themselves out of your life when life is at its best? Do our loved ones know how badly this will affect us for the rest of our lives? Did they care or was their grief and depression so blinding they could not see? Or did they see exactly what was going to happen to the people they left behind? Was this punishment intentional? Was it accidental and they thought they would be miraculously saved?

When do you get over a suicide? The answer is never. Take heart though, you do get so you are able to handle it better.

You keep a lot of emotions going through all this recovery. With me it ranged as far sometimes to wishing Renee was back here so I could whack her for doing something so foolish. Other times I wished she was back so I could hug her again and tell her how much I loved her.

The first several years after Renee's suicide are pretty much a blur. I never felt the urge to go out with someone and it looked as if my life's end would be one of solitary loneliness. I never heard from Tammy again and hope she is doing well in her life. I'm sure she has had to overcome enormous oceans of regret for lying in bed 50 feet away while her mother took her life.

Life was not much fun when I had no one to share it with. When you are with someone you love, enjoyment of happy times doubles. When you are alone the good times are just not that happy and you feel a sense of emptiness.

One night I decided to go to a cowboy bar in Dallas. I put some quarters down on a pool table, the accepted way of challenging the winner to a game of pool, with the winner keeping the table. I was still a pretty good shot and kept the table for several games. Playing next to me was a small pretty gal with a great smile who appeared to be a bit younger than me. She was playing with a tall lanky dude in a cowboy hat I just assumed was her boyfriend.

A little later I sat down at a table to have a cocktail and had barely taken a couple sips when the little gal that had been playing pool next to me came over, grabbed my hand, pulled me to my feet and said, "Let's dance." That was my introduction to Lorraine (Lori) O'Neal. Lori and I danced several dances and I asked her if she would like to sit down at my table. When I asked her about her boyfriend, she said Doug was one of several co-workers who were there.

Lori said she was an A and P mechanic. I asked her what that was and she said it stood for airframe and power plant. Lori was a jet engine mechanic. Really? At first glance that seemed incomprehensible to me. This little gal probably weighed at the most 100 pounds dripping wet. From my earlier days of being a parts picker for Boeing Aircraft in Minot, North Dakota, I knew some of the wrenches used on jet engines were as big as Lori.

Lori and I started comparing notes. It was a coincidence she was from

Minnesota and had pretty much grown up on Mille Lacs Lake, about 30 miles north of Princeton where I had first practiced medicine. Lori's parents had owned a resort on Mille Lacs and Lori had grown up fishing, searching for large night crawlers (worms) and renting out boats to people staying or camping at their resort. Lori told me one of the most favorite things she liked to do was fish. She said, "All you have to do is put a fishing pole in my hands and stand me alongside a lake with fish and I am happy."

Lori said, "My parents live in Cambridge, Minnesota now," and wow, another coincidence. Cambridge was the small town where I was presently directing the emergency department. I would work in Cambridge a few days and then drive back down to my apartment in Bedford. And now here I was sitting with this great little gal and the more we talked the more we had in common. Even our ages were a pretty good match. Lori was 10 years younger than me but was still the oldest woman I had ever been interested in. My parents would have been happy. Amazing isn't it? We are still trying to please our parents when they are dead and gone.

Lori and I talked for almost two hours that night at the cowboy bar. It was the first time in years I was interested in talking to someone of the gentle persuasion again. It was a good feeling for me and I really liked this little Lori gal in spite of only knowing her for a couple of hours. Lori and I mutually agreed we would like to see each other again so we exchanged phone numbers. We talked on the phone regularly until one day Lori and I decided to meet for dinner after she had finished work for the day. I volunteered to pick her up at her home but she said it would be easier for her to come to Bedford.

So Bedford it was and that evening we hit it off really well again. I definitely knew I seriously liked Lori and it seemed to me the feeling was mutual. After spending some more time together with Lori always wanting to come to Bedford, I asked her why she didn't want me to come to Dallas but she just said it was easier this way. I didn't argue. I got plenty of driving in every week and for Lori to volunteer to save me some time in the car was a welcome reprieve. I may have wondered whether or not she was truly single.

After meeting for dinner a couple more times, I asked Lori if she would like to stay with me for the night rather than driving back to Dallas so late and then having to get up early to make it to work on time.

Lori and I slept together in the same bed and it was a good feeling to have someone beside me after all those years. I had not really anticipated this would ever happen again. It was wonderful and we slept with our arms around each other. I really liked this wonderful little gal.

Do you ever wonder how sometimes the right people show up in your life at the right time? Lori was definitely the right person and it was definitely the right time. Luckily it was the right time for both of us. This was no coincidence.

It was a God event. We both needed each other at this particular time in our life. Thank you, God.

I am in my last season and pray to see all my friends when we reach heaven. God bless all of you.   rick r redalen

P.S. I am not much on titles. God made us all the same and some of us just chose different professions. You will understand completely if you read what Solomon says in Ecclesiastes.

Dr. Rick is on a mission to improve healthcare for Americans. Please stay in touch with his ongoing efforts on his Maverick Doctor website (www.MaverickDoctor.com) and on Facebook (Facebook.com/TheMaverickDoctor).

Dr. Rick is now working on his next book about founding and growing ExitCare, LLC, a provider of patient education solutions, with his wife Lori. We invite you to check back with him for the release of the second book. The working title is God's Gift of a Tiny Lori Angel.